Time and the Verb

Time and the Verb

A Guide to Tense and Aspect

ROBERT I. BINNICK

New York   Oxford
OXFORD UNIVERSITY PRESS
1991

4 1 5
B 6 1 4 t

Oxford University Press

Oxford   New York   Toronto
Delhi   Bombay   Calcutta   Madras   Karachi
Petaling Jaya   Singapore   Hong Kong   Tokyo
Nairobi   Dar es Salaam   Cape Town
Melbourne   Auckland

and associated companies in
Berlin   Ibadan

Library of Congress Cataloging-in-Publication Data
Binnick, Robert I.
Time and the verb : a guide to tense and aspect / Robert I. Binnick.
p.   cm.   Includes bibliographical references.
ISBN 0-19-506206-X
1. Grammar, Comparative and general—Tense.
2. Grammar, Comparative and general—Aspect.
3. Semantics.   4. Pragmatics.   I. Title.
P281.B56   1990
415—dc20   89-71032

Page 364. Reprinted with permission of the Linguistic Society of America and *Language*.

Pages 291, 292, 294, 369. Reprinted with permission of Kluwer Academic Publishers.

Page 196. From *Tense and Aspect in Modern Colloquial Japanese* by Matsuo Soga. Copyright © 1983 by The University of British Columbia Press. Reprinted by permission of the publisher.

Page 116. From William E. Bull, *Time, Tense, and the Verb*, 1960, University of California Publications in Linguistics, The University of California Press. Reprinted with permission of the publisher.

Page 341. From Arthur Prior, *Past Present and Future*, 1967, Oxford University Press. Reprinted with permission of the publisher.

Pages 111, 112. From Hans Reichenbach, *Elements of Symbolic Logic*, 1947, Dover Publications. Reprinted with permission of the publisher.

Page 181. From Alexander P. D. Mourelatos, "Events, Processes, and States," *Linguistics and Philosophy* 2, 1978, D. Reidel Publishing Company. Reprinted with permission of the publisher.

Page 181. From Dov Gabbay's and Julius Moravcsik's "Verbs, Events, and the Flow of Time" in Christian Rohrer, ed., *Time, Tense, and Quantifiers*, 1980, Max Niemeyer Verlag. Reprinted with permission of the publisher.

Pages 210, 298. From Marion R. Johnson, *A Semantic Analysis of Kikuyu Tense and Aspect*, 1977. Reprinted with permission of the author.

Pages 115, 209, 297. From Marion R. Johnson, "A Unified Temporal Theory of Tense and Aspect," *Syntax and Semantics* 14, 1981, Academic Press. Reprinted with permission of the publisher.

1 3 5 7 9 8 6 4 2

Printed in the United States of America
on acid-free paper

Cui dono lepidum novum libellum . . . tibi. . . .
                                        Catullus

To Wendy, with much love,
this little book is dedicated.

PREFACE

Whoever has read in one book that English has three tenses, in another that it has two, and in yet a third that it has sixteen; or has been told by one authority that the French *imparfait* represents an incomplete or habitual action in the past, by a second that it is used of an action simultaneous with another action, and by a third that it is used for circumstances and background description; or has read in one text that the perfective tenses of Russian are just like the perfect tenses of English, but in another that they are totally different; or has read here that Biblical Hebrew has tenses and there that it does not, may be pardoned for some confusion and some skepticism as to the claim of linguistic scholars to know a great deal about tense.

The reader may be surprised to learn that tense has been studied for almost twenty-five hundred years, since at least the time of the ancient Greeks, and that hundreds of books and articles have been devoted to it in general, and thousands more to the tenses of particular languages. It is no contradiction to say that we know a very great deal about tense, but understand it little. In the two decades since Robin Lakoff wrote that we "cannot account for many ways in which tenses are used in English and other languages," our knowledge of tense has increased greatly, but our understanding of it has deepened less.

It has been difficult even to know how much we do understand it, for confusing as discussions of the tenses of various languages may be, the scholarly literature concerning tense in general is, if anything, even more confusing. Philosophers, logicians, grammarians, general linguistic scholars, and scholars of particular languages approach tense in very different ways, with differing goals, and with assumptions drawn from sundry scholarly traditions, often employing confusing terminology and arcane symbolism inaccessible to outsiders, and applying special methods grounded in some particular school of linguistics or logic.

For example, an understanding of how distinctions of time are made in Arabic can be extremely important to many who do not know Arabic and have no interest in learning it but wish to understand what tense, in general, is all about. But Semiticists writing about Arabic often do not transliterate examples given in Arabic script, provide no detailed translation (or no translation at all), and use a special terminology unknown outside of Semitic studies.

The present work attempts to provide a complete guide to grammatical tense and the kindred phenomenon of grammatical aspect, both to characterize what we have learned about the expression of time in the verb and to render accessible to the interested reader as much of the relevant literature as possible.

Though it uses the methods and findings of linguistic science, this book is designed to be useful to anyone, scholar or layperson, who wishes to understand tense and aspect. Assuming on the part of the reader minimal background in grammar and linguistics, it presents the facts and theories which have been brought forward in the ongoing investigation of tense and aspect, explains in as nontechnical language as possible the terminology and symbolism used in the scholarly literature, and builds from the simplest concepts and approaches to the most complex.

This book does not pretend to present a coherent general theory, which scholars remain far from achieving, though at the end of the 1980s the outlines of one have perhaps begun to emerge. Nonetheless, it should contain as good an account as any available of the meanings and uses of the various tenses found in the languages most familiar to speakers of European languages, based on what is known about tense in general.

Comrie's *Tense* (1985) and *Aspect* (1976) have been criticized for excessive concentration on certain familiar languages. I would offer criticisms of both books, fine though they may be—obviously the present work was written because I believe they left a serious need unfilled—but I think this particular criticism invalid. The mere recitation of curious facts about a large number of "exotic" languages is in itself neither useful nor revealing. The languages discussed here are cited because facts about them illustrate points of theory or have been used to argue for or against certain hypotheses.

Emphasis has been placed on familiar languages not only because the discussion is more likely to be accessible to the reader but also because, for the most part, only the more familiar languages have been well-explored and entered crucially into theory-formation (with the noteworthy exception of the Bantu language Kikuyu). If the present work discusses mainly Greek, Latin, Romance, Germanic, Russian, and—yes—Kukuyu, it is not accidental.

My purpose has been to provide the sort of book James Pickbourn would have liked to have had, just two hundred years ago, when he was mortified to discover that neither he nor anyone else could adequately explain the uses of the tenses of the English verb. After much reading, he "began to suspect the subject [of tense] had never been minutely discussed by any of our grammarians," adding, "the result of these researches I confess much surprised me; for I had read all these authors without ever remarking the deficiency."

The present volume is designed to serve as three guidebooks in one. First, it encompasses a short history of the study of tense (part I) and of aspect (part II). Second, it provides a commentary on and guide to the scholarly literature, especially aiming to aid the reader in approaching the extraordinarily technical work of the last two decades. In chapters 7 and 8, in particular, recent developments are investigated in great detail. Assuming that few readers will have much background in formal semantics, I have included a lengthy introduction. A list is provided of all symbols and abbreviations used, which includes virtually all symbols found in the literature.

Third and last, the book constitutes a guide to the meanings and uses of the various tenses and aspects of the more familiar languages. The summary section points the reader interested in this or that question (e.g., the difference between the *imparfait* and the simple past tense of the Romance languages) to discussions of the various theories offered and of the best current thinking.

An historical approach allows movement from the presentation of the simplest ideas and phenomena to the most sophisticated. Part I begins with the earliest theories of tense, formulated by the ancient Greeks, and ends with the most recent theories of modern grammarians, formulated in the 1950s and 1960s. Since that time, theories of tense which do not take aspect into consideration, or which are based on traditional methods of grammar, have largely been supplanted, and the study of tense revolutionized, by new goals and methods.

Throughout this period, spanning some twenty-five hundred years, not only did theories of tense become ever more complex as simpler accounts provided inadequate, but the data utilized grew broader and more interesting as well. In chapter 1 we will see that the ancient Greeks largely confined themselves to the question of how many tenses there are. Not recognizing that tense and time are different, they had some difficulty in reconciling the three times—past, present, and future—with the half-dozen tenses of their own language.

Chapter 2 brings us up to the Renaissance, when the study of modern languages began. Though the goal remained one of accounting for the tenses by labeling them, the European languages had developed a much more complex system of tenses than had existed in Greek or Latin, requiring a considerable revision of ancient theories. What emerged were two streams of thought, aspectual theory and the theory of relative tense, which continue to influence research today.

The vast expansion of European exploration brought Westerners into contact with languages manifestly different from the familiar European ones. Starting in the eighteenth century, attempts to apply European grammatical concepts to these "new" languages revealed the inadequacies of the grammatical tradition and led ultimately to a radical break with the past. Nonetheless, the investigation of tense remained hampered by the false assumptions that to describe the meaning of a verb form is to explicate its use, and that contextually defined meanings of a tense are either insignificant or purely derivative of one basic meaning.

It was only in this century (chapter 3) that grammarians began to look at the full range of problems concerning the expression of time in the verb. Whereas formerly very little attention was paid to how tenses were actually used, as opposed to what they ideally meant, the focus on use now revealed a wide range of phenomena previously unconsidered. In particular, the relationship of tense to grammatical constructions and to syntax was specifically examined for the first time. The range of data considered by Hans Reichenbach (1947), William Bull (1960), and Robert Allen (1966) was far greater than that utilized by earlier scholars.

In part II the historical approach must be partly abandoned, since most important work on aspect is relatively recent. Although Aristotle discussed it some twenty-four hundred years ago, and aspect entered the Western grammatical tradition through Slavic studies not long after 1800, the modern concept of aspect was established only as recently as the 1930s. In our century tense and aspect have increasingly been viewed as two complementary facets of one set of phenomena (work on languages has revealed yet a third, called "status").

Part II first examines the traditional theory of the type of aspect found in Slavic languages (chapter 5), then shows how that theory was applied to Greek aspect, and finally (especially in chapter 6) illustrates how contemporary approaches developed largely in response to the failure of that enterprise.

Contemporary research on tense and aspect consists of two broad streams very much in opposition. The first, heavily influenced by philosophical logic, emphasizes explicitness and formal rigor, placing great emphasis on technical details. These theories (chapter 7) emphasize semantics in the narrow sense of a referential theory of how language is linked to the external world, and assume that the uses of an expression in some way follow its meaning or meanings, or at least that meaning is independent of use.

But scholars who have had to deal with real language as it occurs in literary texts or records of actual conversation are aware that the uses of tenses and aspects often do not accord with their nominal meanings. This second, informalist, stream (chapter 8) contains work by scholars who have emphasized use rather than meaning and have expressed some skepticism in regard to the notion of ''the'' meaning of a form or expression; some have gone so far as to propose that meaning follows use rather than the reverse. The methods of such scholars owe more to literary than to logical analysis. The two streams appear to be uniting in the work of those formal semanticists who apply to research on tense and aspect in discourse and text both the results of the informalist school and the methods of formal semantics.

The purpose of part II is, to a great extent, to explicate the various contentious issues in current research, to characterize what each of the schools of thought has achieved, and to point out problems remaining to be solved. As it happens, there are many such issues which either fall beyond the scope of tense and aspect proper (though they are related to them) or have not been treated by either of the current methodologies. Such borderline issues are not discussed at length, but some are described at the conclusion of part II.

The most important omission here is that of mood. While mood does not bear directly on temporal distinctions, it is so closely related to tense and aspect that originally this book was conceived of as a guide to tense, aspect, *and* mood. The reader interested in mood can refer to Palmer's *Mood and Modality* (1986); in the present work mood and modality are discussed only as they relate to tense and aspect.

Of necessity, emphasis has been placed on materials written in English and readily available to the average reader. Nonetheless, many obscure works in a number of languages have had to be utilized. Frequent quotation from these and other sources has been necessary because much of this material has never been translated or even, in some cases, edited or reprinted. It seemed worthwhile to let Priscian and Scaliger speak in their own (albeit translated!) words, as well as some contemporary writers (in and out of English) who are unusually articulate (or, occasionally, arcane). My own in-text translations of a source are indicated by ''(tr)'' following the entry in the References.

For a number of reasons, scholars writing in and about English are overrepresented here. While there is a very large and interesting body of literature—much of it untranslated—on the languages of the Soviet Union, practically none of this material is readily available, nor has it significantly affected Western scholarship. This is regrettable, as aspectological studies in eastern Europe and the Soviet Union have advanced further than most scholars in the West realize.

Despite the length of the present book, a great deal of material has unavoidably been omitted, and many scholars have perhaps been slighted. The tradition of tense logical studies represented by the work of Åqvist, Bäuerle, Guenther, Hoepelman, and Rohrer, while extraordinarily interesting, ultimately seems foreign to the concerns of the traditions discussed here.

I would have liked to say more as well about the ideas of Bartsch, Coseriu, Cresswell, Givón, Guillaume (and his followers), and Joos, and to have explained at greater length the foundations of Situation Semantics. More use could perhaps have been made of the work of Imbs (1960), Schogt (1968), Martin (1981), and Vet (1980, 1981, 1983) on French; of Hackman (1976) and others on Hindi and other Indian languages; of the extensive literatures on Japanese, German, Turkish (e.g., Johanson, 1971), and Slavic aspect aside from Russian; of Bertinetto (1986a) on Italian; of Holisky (1978, 1980, 1981) on aspect in Georgian; and of Fischer (1973), Cogen (1977), Fischer and Gough (1978), and Frishberg and Gough (n.d.) on American Sign Language; as well as S.-G. Andersson (1972) on telicness. I might have delved as deeply into the other "tenseless" languages, especially the creoles and sign languages, as I did into Biblical Hebrew. Since completing the manuscript, a number of interesting works have appeared which I have unfortunately not been able to utilize.

If I have insisted on a historical approach, it is partly because I do not share the prevailing prejudice that linguistic scholars need not concern themselves much with the works of the past. The consequence of this attitude is constant reinvention of the wheel and repeated announcement of the imminent appearance of the squared circle. In research for this book I have come across more than one publication which presents as novelties proposals already put forward—or rejected—by Aristotle, Jespersen (1924), Reichenbach (1947), and others in between.

Already in 1751 James Harris complained of writers' ignorance of older or foreign writings. What he says of his *Hermes* might equally be said of the present work:

[It aims] to pass, as far as possible, from small matters to the greatest. Nor is it formed upon sentiments that are now in fashion, or supported only by such authorities as are modern. Many Authors are quoted, that now a-days are but little studied; and some perhaps, whose very names are hardly known.

Nothing can more tend to enlarge the Mind, than . . . extensive views of Men, and human Knowledge; nothing can more effectually take us off from the foolish admiration of what is immediately before our eyes, and help us to a juster estimate both of present Men, and present Literature.

A like evil to that of admiring only the authors of our own age [and our own country], is that of admiring only the authors of one particular Science.

Such then is the Apology made by the Author of this Treatise, for the multiplicity of antient quotations, with which he has filled his Book. If he can excite in his readers a proper spirit of curiosity; if he can help in the least degree to enlarge the bounds of Science; to revive the decaying taste of antient Literature; to lessen the bigotted contempt of every thing not modern; and to assert to Authors of every age their just portion of esteem; if he can in the least degree contribute to these ends, he hopes it may be allowed, that he has done a service to mankind.

If the present book proves interesting or useful and contributes to future research, all the great effort of writing it will have proven worthwhile. The five years spent on the project came to seem interminable, and only the encouragement of wife and friends sustained me in this demanding task.

I gratefully acknowledge here the assistance variously provided by Keith Percival, Peter Salus, Harald Ohlendorf, Ian McDonald, Leslie Kobayashi, Barbara Jacennik, William Ladusaw, and others I may have unfortunately forgotten over the years. I am equally thankful to all those who granted permission to reproduce diagrams. I especially wish to thank my publisher's anonymous reader for useful comments, which I have sometimes ignored (to my peril) but more often profited from. Above all, thanks are due to Robin Lakoff, who with extraordinary kindness provided me with detailed commentary concerning almost every page of part I. The editorial team at Oxford University Press has done an extraordinary job in editing a demanding manuscript. In particular, I wish to thank my copy editor, Clifford Browder, and my associate editor, Henry Krawitz.

Work on this book was begun in two singular buildings—the Dwinelle Library of the University of California at Berkeley, and Frank Lloyd Wright's Marin County Civic Building, which houses the Marin County Library—while I was at Berkeley on a sabbatical research leave from the University of Toronto, which was partly funded by a grant from the Social Sciences and Humanities Research Council of Canada. Without the robber barons of the last century and the taxpayers of the present one, this work might never have been started.

The book may be regarded as an appendix either to Comrie's *Tense* and *Aspect* or to the section on tense in McCawley's *Everything That Linguists Have Always Wanted to Know about Logic*. But perhaps it is best considered an homage to two brilliant works, Pickbourn's *Dissertation on the English Verb* (1789) and Harris's *Hermes* (1751). I can only hope that my book belongs in such illustrious company.

Toronto   R.I.B.
March 1991

CONTENTS

ABBREVIATIONS AND SYMBOLS

The alphabetical order used for the entries is A, B, C, D, . . . , Z for Latin, and A, B, Γ, Δ, . . . , Ω for Greek. Keyboard symbols follow the order !1@2#3$4%5 ↑ 6&7*8(9)0__– + = {[}]|\:;''⟨≤,⟩≥.?/~'. The other symbols that follow are listed alphabetically by their glosses; thus "⇒" follows ~ and is alphabetized under *e* for *entails*. The difference between upper and lower case is ignored, and variants are "alphabetized" immediately following their prototype; ∀ follows A, and slashed epsilon (ɇ) follows episilon (ε). Subscripted and superscripted letters follow all letters in the text line; T_E follows TE. < is treated as ⟨, > as ⟩, and — as –.

	Explanation or Gloss	*Page*
A	model	238, 269
ABL	ablative case	59
ACC	accomplishment	402
ACC	accusative (object) case	59
ACH	achievement	402
ACT	active voice	19
ACT	activity	402
All x	universal quantifier	229
AOR	aorist tense	35
AP	Anticipated Point axis	116
ARP	Anticipated Retrospective Point axis	118
ASL	American Sign Language	444
$A_{s,e,r} \vDash p$	p is true in model A relative to times s, e, r	277
AT	occurrence operator	312
Aux	auxiliary verb, auxiliary component	357
∀	universal quantifier	235
B_A	set of all basic expressions belonging to category A	235
BECOME	operator for becoming	291
BSL	British Sign Language	444
c	connection	334
c	context	227
C	set of syntactic categories	232
CN	category of common nouns	232
ComesAbout	operator for becoming	330
COMP	completive aspect operator	296
COND	conditional	416
CR	current relevance	100
CRS	Current Relevant State	338
C_S	characteristic function for the set S	221
c_s	concept of situation s	337
C_α	set of all constants of type α	234
D	discourse	394
d	discourse situation	334
DAT	dative case	94
dom	domain	336
DRS	discourse representation structure	394

I	set of possible worlds (Montague)	238
IAV	category of adverbs modifying intransitive verbs	232
ID	indefinite past	100
iff	if and only if	218
IL	intensional logic	231
IMM	operator for imminent status	263
imparf, IMPARF	imperfect tense	405
IMPERF	operator for imperfect tense	296
IMPF	imperfect	21
IMPF	operator for "imperfect" aspect (Johnson)	296
IMPVE	operator for imperfective aspect	296
in$_a$	intension of a	236
INDIC	indicative mood	19
INF, INFIN	infinitive	21
-ing	present participial affix of English	356
Inr (I)	set of inertial histories of I	292
IV	category of intransitive verbs	232
j	instant of time (Johnson)	269
J	reference time (Johnson)	297
J	set of times (Montague)	238, 269
j	speech-act time (Dowty)	314
k	event time (Dowty)	319
l	location of a situation	331
L	necessity operator	335
LTL	logical translation language	230
l$_u$	universal location	336
M	model	229
M	possibility operator	235
MASC	masculine gender	33
ME$_\alpha$	set of all meaningful expressions of type α	234
MID	middle voice	19
MS, mS	main set, minor set	421
Mu, mu	main unit, minor unit	425
N	operator shifting reference to present time (Kamp)	314
N	the type of names	232
NEUT	neuter gender	84
NL	natural langauge	231
NOM	nominative (subject) case	35
Now, NOW	operator shifting reference to present time	329
NP	noun phrase	351
occ	occurrence operator (Cresswell)	322
OPT	optative (mood)	70
OT	orientation time	348
$^o\alpha$	operator o applied to α	240
O_i^+, O_i^-	overlap functions	404
P	predicate	221
P	Priorian past tense operator	243
P$_A$	set of all phrases (derived expressions) belonging to category A	232
PART	particle	164
PARTIC	participle	35
PASS	passive	21
passé, PASSÉ	simple past tense	405

PASSÉ COMPOSÉ	complex past tense	406
PASSÉ SIMPLE	simple past tense	406
PAST	past tense	471 (ch. 2, n. 60)
Past, PAST	past tense operator	244
PAST$_{def}$, PAST$_{indef}$	operators for definite and indefinite past tenses	246
Perf, PERF	operator for perfect aspect	244
PERF	(present) perfect tense	21
Pf	operator for indefinite past tense (Tichý)	246
PFVE	operator for perfective aspect	296
PL	plural	33
PLUPF	pluperfect	89
POSS	possibility operator	318
PP	past (or perfect) participle	33
PP	Present Point axis	116
Pres, PRES	operator for present tense	251
PRES	present tense	19
PROG	operator for progressive aspect	259
PROG	progressive (Hinrichs)	402
P(x)	x is a pause	322
QUEST	question marker	21
R	reference point (reference time)	111, 252
r	reference time	277
RAP	Retrospective Anticipated Point axis	116
R$_n$	n-place relation	336
RP	"Reichenbach's Pragmatics" (Nerbonne)	414
RP	Retrospective Point axis	116
RRP	Retrospective Retrospective Point axis	118
r$_s$	region of a situation s	337
R$_S$	syntactic rule	238
R$_{SI}$	rule of semantic interpretation	231
RT	reference time (Smith)	345
R$_T$	translation rule	231
S	the category of sentences	232, 351
s	forms intensional types	234
s	situation type	331
S, s	speech-act time	252
s	subject	221
SG	singular	35
Some x	existential quantifier	229
SOT	sequence of tense(s)	86
S$_\alpha^o$	set of situations open with respect to concept α	338
S$_p$(x)	x is a subevent of an event of type p	322
SS	Situation Semantics	330
ST	speech-act time (Smith)	345
ST	stative (Hinrichs)	402
ST$_s$	structure of a situation s	337
SUBJ	subjunctive mood	19; 471 (ch. 2, n. 60)
T	the category of terms	232
t	evaluation (speech-act) time	229
t	instant of time	253
T	model (Saurer)	227
T	set of times	238, 253

(x)	universal quantifier	312
. . . ,t$_i$)	interval ending at instant t$_{i-1}$	253
0	the null set	220
0	the truth-value false	217
0	unmarked value for features	159
0V	"zero" vector (prime point)	116
−	absolute complement of A: −A = everything which is not in set A	253
−	complement; A−B = complement of B relative to A: everything in A but not in B	253
−	negative value for features	159
−	separates morphemes; indicates affixes	13
−V	"minus" or retrospective vector	116
—	precedes: A—B = A precedes B	112
+	positive value for features	159
+V	"plus" or prospective vector	116
=	coincides with	111, 253
=	identity: A=B = A is identical with B	219
=$_{def}$	by definition: "A =$_{def}$ B" means A is defined as B	243
≠	A≠B = A is not identical with B	253
{. . .}	unordered set, e.g., {1, 2} is the set consisting of 1 and 2; {x:x is a cook} is the set of all cooks	219
[t$_i$, . . .	interval starting at instant t$_i$	253
[t]	moment of time	253
[T]	set of all intervals in T except the empty interval	253
[<]	wholly precedes	253
. . . ,t$_i$]	interval ending with the instant t$_i$	253
:	"such that": {x:x is a cook} is the set of all cooks	219
<	precedence relation	291
<	precedes: t<t′ = t precedes t′	253
⟨s,α⟩	intensional type corresponding to extensional type α	234
⟨α,β⟩	type of expression forming expressions of type β when applied to expressions of type α	234
<$_i^+$, <$_i^-$	precedence relations	402
<<	wholly precedes	327, 402
⟨. . .⟩	ordered set, e.g., ⟨1, 2, . . . , 9⟩ is the 9-membered set (9-tuple) consisting of the numbers 1 through 9 in order	220
≤	relation on T (ordering of time)	238, 253
≤	t$_i$≤t$_j$ = t$_i$ is earlier than, or coincides with, t$_j$	253
,	coincides: A,B = A coincides with B	112
>	t>t′ = t′ follows t (t precedes t′)	111, 253
.	separates morphemes	14
?	of questionable acceptability (grammaticality)	469 (ch. 1, n. 87)
?*	possibly unacceptable (ungrammatical)	469 (ch. 1, n. 87)
/	forms categories; A/B is the category of expressions forming expressions of category A when conjoined with an expression of category B	232
//	forms categories; A//B is the (second) cate-	232

PART ONE

TENSE

1

Ancient Theories
of the Simple Tenses

a. The Problem of Tense

As with so many other things, our most basic ideas about the verb go back to the ancient Greeks. Plato defines the verb as that word which denotes action, and it is still often called the "action word."[1] But for Aristotle, "a verb is a composite sound with a meaning, indicative of time"; it is tense which is its essential feature.[2] To this day the verb is thought of as a "time-word"—as in German, in which the usual term, alongside the learned *Verb*, is *Zeitwort*. It is that part of speech which is concerned with distinctions of time, that is, with tense.

Even after twenty-five hundred years of investigation by students of meaning, grammar, logic, and philosophy, tense is very poorly understood. "Tense is a mind boggling [*sic*] business," writes one scholar[3]; "we are very far from a general theory of time-related phenomena in natural language," write a couple of others.[4] Yet other scholars write of "getting lost in the subtleties of tense and aspect."[5] Despite the great amount of effort over the centuries toward understanding tense, it remains the case that of the many accounts which have been given of it, "none . . . is satisfactory, since they cannot account for many ways in which tenses are used in English and other languages."[6]

This appears puzzling to the speaker of a modern European language such as English, for it seems so natural to think simply in terms of three times—past, present, and future—and hence of three tenses corresponding to them. As the eighteenth-century grammarian James Harris put it, "The most obvious Division of TIME is into Present, Past, and Future, nor is any Language complete, whose Verbs have not TENSES to mark these Distinctions."[7]

This notion of three times was already old in the time of the ancient Greeks; it was part of their Indo-European heritage.[8] We find references to "the Three Times" in all periods and in nearly all the various branches of the Indo-European language

3

family.[9] In Homer's *Iliad* we find, for example, reference to "things that were, the things to come and the things past."[10]

Further evidence comes from the myth, preserved by a number of the ancient Indo-European–speaking peoples, of the three Fates or Weird Sisters, who foretell the destinies of the newly born.[11] These three are daughters of Necessity, on whose knees sits the turning spindle of fate; Clotho spins the thread of life, Lachesis allots it, and Atropos cuts it off. Naturally enough, Lachesis sings of the past, of what has been; Clotho of the present, of what is; and Atropos of the future, of what will be.

The identification of the Fates with the three times is quite explicit in the Germanic versions of the myth. The three Scandinavian *Norns* are called Urthr, Verthandi, and Skuld. The name Urthr is related to the past tense of the Old Norse verb 'to become'; Verthandi, to the present participle ('becoming') of the same word; and Skuld, to the English future-marking auxiliary verb *shall*. As Jacob Grimm observes, here "we have what was, what is, and what shall be, or the past, present and future, very aptly designated, and a Fate presiding over each."

Then and since, the Indo-European–speaking peoples have conceived of time in spatial terms, as shown by the terms used to speak about relations in time. Expressions borrowed from the language of location are used to situate events: we say *in 1990* as we say *in Toronto*; both *on December 4* and *on Fifth Avenue*; *at noon* and *at the corner of Fifth Avenue and Forty-second Street*; *before the party* and *before the judge*.

The three times are thought of as segments of an indefinitely long line passing through the point of the present. For Aristotle in the *Physics*, the present is merely the boundary between past and future.[12] However, there is some question as to what is meant by "point" in this connection, since we experience ourselves as being *in* the present. Accordingly Diogenes Laertius assigns the present duration, saying, "time past and time future are infinite, but time present is finite."[13]

Aristotle himself observes that, if the present is considered to be a point in time and without duration, this results in a paradox, for

> some of [time] is past and no longer exists, and the rest is future and does not yet exist; and all time . . . is entirely made up of the no-longer and not-yet; and how can we conceive of that which is composed of non-existents sharing in existence in any way?[14]

Nonetheless, Aristotle assumes that there are really only two times, the past and the future ("the present 'now' is not part of time at all"),[15] and rejects the idea that the present can be an interval,[16] though he contrasts the "proper 'now' " with a "derivative 'now'," noting that "now"

> is also used for 'not far off in time.' 'He will come now,' if he will come to-day; 'He has come but now,' if he came to-day. But we do not speak so of the Trojan war or Deucalion's flood; . . . these events . . . are not near.[17]

In English, in a similar way, we say *I did it just now* and *I will do it right now*, as well as *do it (right) now!*

Ordinarily, we think of humanly experienced time as actually containing three parts; the present is an interval of variable and indefinite duration, centered on the point of the true "now," and while the present is not infinite, as are past and future, it must, as Diogenes observes, have some, albeit finite, duration. In fact, languages treat it as having sometimes considerable duration, and it may even be used to express "eternal truths" (*two and two are four*).[18]

Harris points out that

> the *Present Century* is present in *the present Year*; that, in the present *Month*; that, in *the present Day*; that, in *the present Hour*; that, in *the present Minute*. 'Tis thus by circumscription within circumscription that we arrive at THAT REAL AND INDIVISIBLE INSTANT, which by being itself the *very Essence of the Present*, diffuses PRESENCE throughout all, even the largest of Times, which are found *to include it within their respective limits*.[19]

We can speak of it *now* being the twentieth century, even though "now" is, strictly speaking, a point in time.

It is no contradiction to say that it is now the twentieth century, but also that it is now a period of time which includes the nineteenth century (e.g., the second millennium A.D.), or that 1938 is in the twentieth century, which we are now in, though it is not now 1938.

Aristotle's "derivative" present we term the *extended now*, and this extended now can be indefinitely great in extent. It is true that we cannot say *Shakespeare has had children*, but we can certainly say *Shakespeare has become more and more popular*: in some respects Shakespeare belongs to our extended now.

Given that we think of time as a line, it is not surprising that there are rich systems of idiomatic expressions for temporal relations in many languages which make use of overtly (or etymologically) spatial terms.[20] We talk of *next year* and the *near future* (etymologically, *next* is related to *nearest*). They show further that we think of ourselves as oriented in time—sometimes we *face* the future, sometimes we *look back* to the past. The past is *behind* us, the future lies *ahead*.

In Dutch and German, present events may be marked by an expression with *aan/an* 'at, in': (Dutch) *ij is aan het tuinieren* 'he is at the gardening' = 'he is gardening'; (German) *Johann war am Schreiben eines Briefes, als Peter eintrat* 'Johann was at the writing of a letter (i.e., was writing a letter), when Peter entered'.[21] Compare the French *en passant*, the English *in passing*.

But time is of its nature dynamic, not static: we say that "time flies like an arrow," "time waits for no one," "time never stands still." Plato writes in the *Parmenides* of time "advancing," and similar statements could undoubtedly be drawn from almost any early philosopher writing in an Indo-European language.[22]

We may view time as a point moving inexorably *out of* the future past us *into* the past (the *past* being that which has *passed*), or, alternatively, we may see ourselves at a point, the "now," which is continuously moving along the line of time *out of* the past and *into* the future.

In French the recentness of past events is indicated by the expression *venir de* 'to come from': *je viens de manger* 'I have just eaten'. In both English and French, as well as many other languages, we are "going to" do things in the future. We *approach* the new year and then *enter* it, *leaving* the old one. We go *through*

experiences. In French and Italian the future is *l'avenir, avvenire*, that which is
to (*à*) come (*venir*); similar are the English phrase "things to come," and the
German *Zukunft* 'future, (what is) to come'. We are always "in the course of"
(French *en train de*) doing something.

Whether our "now" is moving along the line of time or time is moving through
a fixed "now," the relationship of the "now" to events strung along the time line
is constantly changing, so that the tense used to describe an event can never stay
the same. One moment we must say, "It *will be* noon (soon)"; the next, "It *is*
noon (now)"; and then, at yet a third moment, "It *was* noon (just now)." [23] In
an important sense, there is no such thing as *the* (unique) present time, any more
than there is a unique, unchanging future or past.

So we experience the world as having three times: the *present*, that which is
before our eyes, as it were (Latin *praesens* means 'being before'); the *past*, that
which has *passed* or gone by (from Latin *praeteritum* 'gone by' comes the name
of the *preterite* or simple past tense); and the *future* (*futurum*), 'that which is to
be'.[24]

The nature of these times—or of time in general—is not given by experience;
philosophers from before Aristotle and Augustine through Russell, McTaggart,
and Reichenbach in our century have debated the nature of time without reaching
any definitive conclusion. Be that as it may, we certainly talk and act as if these
times were real segments of the universe within which events and states of affairs
are situated.[25]

Therefore it seemed only natural to the Greeks that language should have signs
to express the concepts of past, present, and future time. "[T]here are three *Tenses*: Present, Past, Future," writes the grammarian Dionysius Thrax (second century B.C.).[26]

The notion that language necessarily reflects reality is in accord with the naive
perception that language, after all, is used to talk about the world and therefore
must in some way reflect it. This forms the basis of a theory of meaning developed by Greek philosophers, in which that reflection is indirect, mediated by concepts. Aristotle states in *On Interpretation* that

> words spoken are symbols or signs of affections or impressions of the soul; written
> words are the signs of words spoken. As writing, so also is speech not the same for
> all races of men. But the mental affections themselves, of which these words are
> primarily signs, are the same for the whole of mankind, as are also the objects of
> which those affections are representations or likenesses, images, copies.[27]

But for Aristotle (as for the structuralist linguist Ferdinand de Saussure in our
century), meaning is arbitrary: "a noun signifies this or that *by convention*. No
sound is by nature a noun: it becomes one, becoming a symbol. Inarticulate noises
mean something—for instance, those made by brute beasts. But no noises of that
kind are nouns."[28] The "impressions" or mental "affections" of necessity directly model the realities of the world, but the linguistic signs or expressions we
use to represent them need not.

That *dog*, for example, should mean anything at all, least of all 'canine', is a
historical accident which could have been otherwise. But once a word receives a

fixed meaning, the meanings of words and other expressions containing it are no longer arbitrary. Thus *dog food* can mean only 'sustenance for canines'; *he hates dogs* can mean only 'he has a strong dislike for canines'. (This would not be disputed by either Aristotle or Saussure.)

The relation of linguistic expression to mental impression is not one of reflection or modeling. Any mental "affection" regarding two individuals, for example, would necessarily have two parts, corresponding to the two individuals, but expressions such as *couple* or *pair* (unlike, say, *brother and sister*) do not, as each is a simple unit. Again, *heiress* is overtly marked as feminine in (natural) gender by the ending *-ess*, but there is no corresponding masculine marking in *heir*, though the two expressions denote the same kind of person, gender aside. Parallel concepts do not necessarily receive parallel expressions.

If the mental affections were impressions reflecting reality, and the simple signs (for example, words) signifying those affections were not purely conventional, then parallel ideas necessarily would receive parallel expressions, just as the reflections in mirrors of similar things look alike. But simple signs are conventional in meaning. What then guarantees that the form of a complex sign (for example, a phrase or sentence) expressing some idea should be predictable? Or that the meaning of a complex sign of a certain form should be so?

If complex signs such as phrases or sentences could relate in any conceivable way to their referents (what they refer to), then regularity would be the exception, not the rule. But then language could not systematically represent ideas. If *at* did not predictably mean in *at noon* what it means in *at midnight*, or if every past tense verb was as unrelated to its present tense as *went* is to *goes* or *was* to *is*, how could languages be learned or used?

That irregularity is not normal in language is confirmed by observations of the grammar of every language, and indeed it is hard to imagine how language could work in any other way. The Greeks observed that language can faithfully convey meanings only by virtue of *analogia* (English *analogy*). Most of the time languages are indeed quite "regular," in that analogous meanings are expressed by analogous expressions. But if the relationships of signs to their referents are purely conventional, how can this be?

If "dog" were naturally and inevitably expressed by the word *dog* and plurality by the ending *-s*, then "dogs" could not but be expressed by *dogs*, even in the absence of any grammar at all. But language is conventional, hence it requires a principle of analogy to function. This concept was central to Greek linguistic thought. The Greeks might never have discovered tenses (as opposed to times), and their theories of tense might have been quite different, if they had not developed the concept of analogy.

The theory of meaning of the Stoic philosophers is an elaboration of the Aristotelian theory. The meaningful linguistic expression or sign (*sēmaînon*) is used to express a signification (*sēmainómenon*). This latter is not, however, Aristotle's mental affect, which is presumably subjective (psychological); rather it is something objective.[29] One individual may have rather a different "impression" of what a dog, say, is, than another has, but for the two of them to meaningfully communicate, they must at least have a common *signification* for the word. For the Stoics, it is through these objective significations that signs are linked to the world, rather than through Aristotle's subjective "impressions" or "affections."

Because they inherited the notion of three times, their theory of meaning required the Greeks to view language as making reference to those times—as having three tenses, in effect. This three-time, three-tense view of the verb has since become an integral part of the Western grammatical tradition. It has long been customary in pedagogical grammars, for example, to consider the English verb to have three tenses:

past	*present*	*future*
loved	love(s)	will/shall love
went	go(es)	will/shall go
had	has/have	will/shall have
was/were	am/is/are	will/shall be

As with much of the grammatical tradition, this requires considerable qualification. The English verb in fact has no future tense form analogous to its past and present forms: the *go* of *will go* is simply the plain form of the verb (the "unmarked infinitive") with no tense marking; and *will* is a "modal" auxiliary ("helping") verb, much like *can, could, may, might, must, need,* and *ought*. On purely formal grounds English cannot (nor can German, Russian, or many other languages) be said to have a future tense of the kind found in Greek, Latin, and the Romance languages.[30]

If there are no formal grounds for three tenses in English, neither are there semantic grounds. The "future tense" of the verb can be used of present events (*that will be John coming up the stairs now*) and even of "timeless" truths (*boys will be boys*). The "present tense" can refer to future events (*the expedition leaves next Wednesday*), to "timeless" truths (*cows eat grass, time flies like an arrow*), and even, in the historical present, to past events (*Hannibal surprises his enemies by crossing the Alps*).

If we argue that *will* in the type of phrase *will go* serves to mark the future tense, then we must equally admit as future tense markers the *can* of *can go* and the *must* of *must go*, which also point to the future; as well, perhaps, as the *has* of *when John has gone, call me* and the *is* of *she is going to Rome next Tuesday*, or the combinations of auxiliary verbs in *will have gone* and *must be going*.[31]

Moreover, each such auxiliary verb or combination of auxiliaries which does not mark futurity might be considered a different tense, as for instance the past perfect (*had gone*) or the past perfect progressive (*had been going*). This would vastly increase the number of tenses in English, however, and while some grammarians have in fact assigned dozens of tenses to the English verb (and it has become standard to regard at least some of these phrasal combinations, e.g., the past perfect, as composite or "periphrastic" tenses), there appears to be something satisfying about the three-tense model that is lost in any such expanded list.

If we look beyond the Indo-European family, many languages have no tenses at all (in the sense of a change in, or marking on, the verb).[32] The verb of Chinese is invariable, and Chinese speakers consequently have considerable difficulty in learning to use the forms of verbs in languages which do have tense. Biblical Hebrew and Classical (Quranic) Arabic are also arguably languages in which verbs do not have different tense forms, though they do mark other distinctions such as aspect.[33] The American Sign Language of the deaf likewise has no tenses as such, nor do some creoles and pidgins. In all such "tenseless" languages, different relations in time can certainly be indicated, but not by using the forms of verbs to mark tense distinctions of the familiar kind.[34]

If English, German, Russian, and other languages have "too few" tenses, most of the other Indo-European languages have "too many" (as do even the afore-mentioned languages, if we admit complex, periphrastic tenses). French indeed has a future tense form (*sera* 'will be'), a present tense (*est* 'is'), and a past tense (*fut* 'was'), but it also has an "imperfect" tense (*était* 'was being, would be, used to be') and a "conditional" tense (*serait* 'would be').

While the ancient Greeks inherited the Indo-European conception of three times (and hence, by their theory of meaning, of three tenses), they had to confront the fact that Greek had "too many" tenses: present, aorist (a type of past), and future, but also imperfect, (present) perfect, and past perfect (pluperfect):

present	*lúomen*	'we free, are freeing'
aorist	*elúsamen*	'we freed'
future	*lúsomen*	'we shall free'
imperfect	*elúomen*	'we freed, were freeing'
perfect	*lelúkamen*	'we have freed'
pluperfect	*elelúkemen*	'we had freed'[35]

There is also a marginal future perfect tense (e.g., *lelūsómetha* 'we shall have been freed'), occurring only in certain dialects and with certain verbs, and re-stricted to certain voices and moods (e.g., the passive indicative).[36]

Even at the very beginning of grammatical study, the conflict between the no-tional three "times" (tenses) and the actual number of tenses marked in verbs proved to be a challenge.[37]

Since the Western grammatical tradition goes back to the work of the ancient Greeks, and in some ways has little changed in over two millennia, it is not surprising that this challenge has long persisted.[38] Grounded in naive conceptions of time and meaning, it is no wonder that the grammatical tradition is seemingly so at odds with the apparent reality of English and other modern European lan-guages, not to mention non-Indo-European languages like Chinese and Biblical Hebrew; or that, specifically, the expected close match between the times referred to and the tenses used to refer to them should be lacking in so many languages.

The challenge to grammatical theory is not only to reconcile the manifold forms of verbs with the expected three tenses, but to explicate the use of expressions in languages without tense to convey information about situations and events in time.

b. Tense in Greek

Diogenes Laertius tells us that it was the fifth-century B.C. philosopher Protagoras who first recognized tenses.[39] Although Plato implicitly suggests a tense distinc-tion in his discussions of the three times, his is usually interpreted as a purely logical categorization, not yet a grammatical one.[40]

In the beginning, the grammatical category of *tense* was not clearly distin-guished from the logical category of *time*. Time is of course not the same thing as tense, but because tenses were seen (in accord with the ancient theory of mean-ing) as reflecting times (albeit indirectly), this took a long time to be understood; in both Greek and Latin (and in the descendent Romance languages such as French), the same term makes do for both: Greek *khrónos*, Latin *tempus*, French *temps*, and so on; this usage obtains in German (*Zeit*) as well, and even occasionally in the case of English (*time*).[41]

It has been pointed out[42] that in earlier days "tense was customarily defined as 'distinctions of time', an expression which permitted . . . confusion between things and words," as exemplified by the eighteenth-century grammarian James Buch-anan, who answered the question "How many Tenses or Times are there?" by saying that "the most natural division" is into three, "but the common Number of Times are [*sic*] five."

Notionally, a past tense form refers to past time, but that a distinction must be drawn between past *tense* and past *time* is shown by two facts. On the one hand a language may have more than one past tense (as in Greek); and on the other, one can refer to past time without using any past tense (as in the historical pre-sent).

The Greeks not only used the same term, *khrónos*, for time and tense, but also used the same terms for times and their corresponding tenses ("past time" and "past tense"), and did not clearly comprehend the problems caused by doing so. When they came to examine the forms of verbs, they were unable to fully escape the misleading appeal of the model of three times, three tenses, though it was inadequate for accounting for the facts of their own language; their theories of meaning led them to conclude that, if there were three times, there must be three tenses.

Aristotle explicitly writes of tense, but in a confusing way. In *On Interpretation* he defines time distinctions as extrinsic to the verb: " 'He was healthy' [*hugíanen*] or 'he will be healthy' [*hugianeî*] I . . . should not call a verb. I should call it the tense of a verb. Verb and tenses in this respect differ: the verb indicates present time but the tenses all times save the present."[43]

There is a contradiction between what Aristotle says there and what he says in the *Poetics*: " 'walks' [*badízei*] and 'has walked' [*bebádiken*] connote present and past time respectively."[44] The contradictory statements reflect at least in part the differing contexts in which they are made by Aristotle.[45]

In *On Interpretation* Aristotle is concerned with the logical concept of the prop-osition: "a verb [is] an indication of something asserted *of* something." For Ar-istotle, the "verb," *rhêma*, is a logical category, not a grammatical one: in Greek *rhêma* means 'predicate' as well as 'verb'. As Robins, the historian of linguistics, observes, "the translation of [*rhêma*] by . . . verb at this stage in the develop-ment of Greek grammatical theory may be misleading."[46]

Taking *rhêma* in the sense of 'predicate' (an expression of a property asserted to hold of something), then obviously *hugíanen* 'he was healthy' is not only a *rhêma*, since it predicates of the subject being healthy, but not his or her having been so in the past (which is presupposed, though not asserted); the tense is outside the predication itself, and serves to tell of what time the predication is asserted to hold of the subject, of what time the asserted proposition is asserted to be true. Logically, *he was healthy* simply states that "he is healthy" is true in the past.

The distinction between "verb" and "tense" of a verb seen in Aristotle's treatment in *On Interpretation* may perhaps be similar to that which led the Stoics to "call only the infinitive 'verb,' but [to call] indicatives like *peripatei* ('he's walking') or *graphei* ('he's writing') [a] *katēgorēma* ('predicator') or *sumbama* ('event')."[47]

But in the *Poetics* Aristotle is concerned rather with diction or rhetoric; there he has nothing to say about propositions, predication, or assertion, but only about meaning. (In neither place, however, is he directly concerned with grammar, nor are grammatical categories distinguished by him from logical ones.)

Logically and experientially there are three times; hence, in accord with the Greek theory of meaning, there must be three tenses. If the Greek verb seemingly provides too many, then the extra tenses must be *varieties* of one (or more) of the three. For Dionysius Thrax, therefore, "the Past has four subspecies—Imperfect, Perfect, Pluperfect, and Aorist."[48]

These, though all are in some sense past tenses, cannot be used interchangeably. Although no account by Dionysius of how the past tenses differ from one another has survived, the terms he uses for them reflect a theory which is made explicit in the marginalia on Dionysius by the commentator Stephanos and in the work of the Latin grammarian Priscian (fifth century A.D.).

Dionysius calls the (present) perfect *parakeímenos* 'lying near' and the past perfect *hupersuntélikos*, which the Romans translated as *plusquamperfectus* 'more than perfect (i.e., completely done)'—our "pluperfect."[49] The present perfect represents a relatively recent past, near to the present, while the past perfect conveys a more distant past. Priscian says:

> it is easily distinguished whether deeds were done a very long time ago or just recently, or may have begun but are not yet completed. Thus . . . we name the tense [*tempus*] *praeteritum imperfectum* ["incomplete past"] in which something has begun to be done but is not yet finished, *praeteritum perfectum* ["complete past"] that in which the thing is shown as finished, *praeteritum plusquamperfectum* ["more-than-complete past"] that in which the thing is now shown as finished long ago.[50]

The third past tense is the "aorist," called *aóristos* 'indefinite, undefined' (from the verb *horízō* 'define, limit'), because it is indifferent to this distinction, and does not tell in itself whether the event happened just now or long ago:

> [the aorist is the tense] which can signify a recently completed thing as well as one completed long ago. But just as by [the Greeks] the aorist [*infinitum*] tense can signify the *parakeímenos*, that is, the 'lying nearby' [*adiacens*] tense, through the addition of the adverb *árti* ['just now'], and the pluperfect through addition of *pálai* ['long ago'], so by us can it (that is, the perfect [*praeteritum perfectum*]) be understood as completed either recently or a long time ago.[51]

The imperfect, Latin *imperfectus* or *infectus* 'incomplete, unfinished', was called by the Greeks *paratatikós* 'extended'.[52] Whereas the perfect and pluperfect represent events which are completely done, the imperfect is unfinished: it represents something ''partly done.''[53] *Élūon* 'I was freeing' does not tell us whether the act of freeing referred to was ever successfully completed: *léluka* 'I have freed' implies *élūon* 'I was freeing', but the reverse is not necessarily true.

From the point of view of completeness, too, the aorist is indefinite, for it is indifferent *in itself* to the distinction of complete and incomplete action; it says nothing about whether the action was finished, just as the English past tense does not (*I read that book for an hour*; *I read that book through*). And just as the English past tense *I freed* contrasts with both the past perfect *I had freed* and the past progressive *I was freeing*, so the aorist *élūsa* 'I freed' contrasts with the pluperfect *eléluke* 'I had freed' and the imperfect *élūon* 'I was freeing'.

The supernumerary past tenses could thus be explained by saying that each has its own sphere of meaning. The perfect and pluperfect differ from each other in relative recency; the imperfect differs from both in not representing a completed action; and the aorist is neutral in both regards. What then of the future perfect?[54]

If the perfect can be viewed as a variety of the past, then it is possible to treat the future perfect similarly as a variety of the future. We do find in the Greeks the notion that the future perfect represents ''in Attic'' a near future (*met' olígon méllōn* 'what is to be after a little [while]'—Latin *futurus* means 'what is to be')— just as the perfect represents a near past.[55]

Priscian once again reports the Greek theory: ''the Greeks divided the future . . . into the indefinite [*infinitum*] future, as *túpsomai*, and the near future [*paulo post futurum* 'what is to be after a little while'], which they also call 'Attic', as *tetúpsomai*.''[56] That is, the future tense is ''aorist'' in the same way as the aorist past tense: it is indifferent to distinctions of nearness or completion, whereas the future perfect (like the perfect past) is both near to the present and represents something completed.[57]

In Latin the future perfect is not a marginal usage as in Greek, but a commonly used feature of the language fully equal to the other tenses. Even so, Priscian goes on to reject such a division of the future into near and distant futures on the grounds that, since the future is uncertain, it is not possible to divide it up, as can be done with the past.[58]

Consequently, although Priscian was able to properly identify the future perfect in Greek, he mistakenly interpreted the Latin future perfect as a subjunctive. Priscian's various discussions of the future and the subjunctive suggest that this error may have followed from his concept of both of them as reflecting uncertainty.[59] Following Priscian and the even more influential fourth-century Latin grammarian Donatus, the subsequent Latin grammatical tradition generally treats the *futurum exactum* (future perfect) as a subjunctive form.

The division of the past into four tenses seems now to be arbitrary and unsystematic. Why should there be near and distant pasts (present perfect and pluperfect), especially as the imperfect and aorist are indifferent to any such distinction? Why distinguish perfect (complete) and imperfect (incomplete), when the aorist marks no such distinction, and there is no imperfect counterpart of the pluperfect? Why should there be four different past tenses at all?

While the ''four pasts'' theory serves to reconcile the three divisions of time with the half dozen tenses of most Greek dialects, it fails to explain why there are precisely the tenses that there are. The Greek verb seems not to have so much a system of tenses as a mere collection of them.

It is true that in language much is not systematic, but the result of historical accident. Of all the personal endings which the English verb once had, only the third person singular *-(e)s* has survived (except for the verb *be*), and that only in the present tense.

The Greeks could not but notice and make use of the formal structure, the *morphology*, of the Greek verb, noting how meaning distinctions are marked by changes of form in the verb. By a process of analogical analysis not dissimilar to that used by linguistic scholars today, they were able to construct the typical pattern (paradigm) of the forms of their verb. The methodology of modern, as of ancient, linguistics depends greatly on analogy.

The relationship between meaning and formal differentiation in the Greek verb played a great role in the Greeks' theories of tense. Indeed, had the Greek verb had a different structure, the entire history of Western grammar might very well have been quite different.

From this point of view, the "four pasts" theory was less than satisfactory. It is not surprising then that in their search for a rational reconciliation of the times with the tenses, it was not the only theory of the tenses developed by the Greeks. Even in Dionysius there is a suggestion of the quite different theory which we associate with the Stoic school of philosophers (founded at the end of the fourth century B.C.) and the Roman grammarian Varro (first century A.D.), for Dionysius writes that "[the tenses] stand in three respective relations: the Present is related to the Imperfect, the Perfect to the Pluperfect, and the Aorist to the Future."[60]

It is possible to interpret this remark as follows: the present, like the imperfect, represents an incomplete action, whereas both the perfect and the pluperfect represent completed ones; the future, like the aorist, is indefinite and can represent either complete or incomplete action.

This alternative theory is even more strongly grounded in the morphology and syntax of the Greek verb than the "four pasts" theory, for this interpretation of the tenses certainly does not follow from the theory of three times, as there is no constant temporal relationship holding between the members of the three pairs: the present and imperfect differ in time, but not in the way the future and aorist do, and the perfect and pluperfect are both past.

We are told by an ancient commentator that the tenses paired by Dionysius are related "both by sound and meaning."[61] Today we can see that the tenses grouped by Dionysius are those which are morphologically, that is, formally, similar.[62]

To understand how and why the Greeks developed the Stoic-Varronian theory of the tenses, it is necessary to appreciate the character of the Greek language and particularly the verb.

c. The Greek Verb

The verb in ancient Greek presents an extraordinarily complicated picture. In modern English, verbs usually have only four simple forms: the plain form and the forms in *-(e)s, -(e)d, -ing*:

love	push	paint
loves	pushes	paints
loved	pushed	painted
loving	pushing	painting

Yet some have a fifth form in *-en* distinct from that in *-(e)d*[63]:

go	fly	run
goes	flies	runs
went	flew	ran
going	flying	running
gone	flown	run

No verb has more than the eight of *be*: *be, am, are, is, was, were, being, been*.

In ancient Greek, on the contrary, each verb can have hundreds of forms as distinct as *lúō* 'I am freeing', *elúsamen* 'we freed', and *lelúsomai* 'I shall have been freed'; or *érkhomai* 'I go', *elélutha* 'I have gone', and *êlthon* 'I went'.

Unlike modern English, which is very nearly an *analytic* language—one in which each word contains only one (meaningful or functional) part, one "morpheme," and which marks grammatical distinctions by using separate, auxiliary words—a *synthetic* language like Greek generally marks such distinctions by modifying the form of the word itself.

Consequently, the Greek word tends to be quite long and complex and to contain many separate components. A word like *lelúsontai* 'they will have been freed', which contains six components (*le.lú.s.o.nt.ai*), is every bit as good Greek as *lú.ō* 'I free'. (We use dots here to separate the *formatives*—the components forming the words.) In contrast, in the equivalent English expression *they will have been freed*, each meaning or function is assigned to a separate word.

An important difference between the languages is that in the Greek verb the same meaning or grammatical function is often expressed in different verbs by different forms: *lú.ō* 'I free' but *phē.mí* 'I say'. It is also often the case in Greek that the same forms may express different meanings in different contexts: *-s* sometimes marks the future tense, sometimes the aorist. And, as is the case with *érkhomai, êlthen* 'I come, I came', different forms of the same verb may originate in forms of different verbs which are quite dissimilar.

These same phenomena are found in English, to be sure, as for instance the past participles *painted* and *broken*, with different endings, or the suppletion found in English *go, went*; *be, was*. But what is characteristic of the Greek verb is only sporadic in the English one.

That the Greeks saw regularity and system underlying the complexity and diversity of their verbal paradigms (patterned sets of forms of verbs) is due to their awareness of the grammatical categories expressed by the verb and the ways in which the verb can be modified to express them, as well as to the fact that the meaningful elements (or *morphemes*) of the Greek verb occur in a fixed order, which also helped the Greeks to observe the regularity underlying the confusing and complex facts of their verbs.[64]

The Greeks never developed the concept of the morpheme, however. To them, words were indivisible atoms. Aristotle even asserts that "the 'vessel' [in 'pirate-vessel'] has no sense whatever, except as a part of the whole.''[65] They operated instead in terms of a model we call ''word-and-paradigm.''

Instead of saying, for example, that *lúō* consists of *lū-* 'free' and an ending *-ō*, they would have said simply that *lúō* is that form of the verb 'free' which represents present tense, active voice, indicative mood, and first person singular subject ('I'). There is a pattern (''paradigm'') to the forms of verbs, with each form fitting into a precise position in that pattern.

Such paradigmatic patterns are defined by analogy, and it was analogy which enabled the Greeks to analyze their verbs. If we observe that *be* is in meaning to *is* (and to *been*) as the parallel form *go* is to *goes* (and to *gone*), we can ignore the pecularities of these verbs and fit these forms into parallel paradigms:

	plain form	-(e)s form	-en form
'be'	be	is	been
'go'	go	goes	gone

If *goes* may be said to be the (third person singular) present tense of *go*, then the same must be true of *is* and *be*, despite the dissimilarity between the two forms. By utilizing such systematic patterns of relationships between ''sound and meaning,'' the Greeks were able to develop the set of forms, the ''paradigm'' of each verb, and, through a process of abstraction, the ''typical'' paradigm of the Greek verb. This entailed some considerable abstraction, for few Greek verbs, prominent among them *lū-* 'free' (and its derivatives, for example, *sullū-* 'help to free'), are fully ''regular,'' that is, completely in accord with the ''typical'' pattern.

Further abstraction was then possible. The forms *lúō* and *phēmí* differ in their lexical meaning, but both are first singular present active indicatives. Despite the difference in their meaning, we can say they both represent the ''same'' form of the verb. Further, *lúō* 'I free', *élūsa* 'I freed', and *léluka* 'I have freed' all represent the first person singular. *Lúō* and *lúomen* differ only in number ('I free': 'we free'): they are both first person forms.

Lúō and *lúomen* differ, as do *lúeis* 'you (sing.) free' and *lúete* 'you (pl.) free', but also *élipon* 'I left' and *elípomen* 'we left'. We can speak of the abstract concept of ''number'' apart from either singular or plural, just as we can speak of the abstract concept of ''person'' apart from first, second, or third person.

While English normally marks in the verb itself only tense (*loves:loved*) and person-number (*s/he loves:they love*), ancient Greek also marked mood,[66] which is marked in English with modal verbs, and voice,[67] which is marked in English by the verb *be* with the passive participle. The Greeks were aware of these various ''accidents'' (*parepómena*)—the categories which are marked in the verb—at least as early as Dionysius Thrax.[68]

The Greek personal endings (''desinences'') serve, like the subject pronouns of English, to indicate the agent—the ''doer''—(''*it* ate'') or the patient—the undergoer—(''*it* was eaten'') of an action. The Greek desinences mark three *persons* (first—'I' and 'we'; second—'you'; and third—'he/she/it/they') and three *numbers*: singular ('I', 'she') and plural ('we', 'they'), but also duals of the second and third persons ('we two', 'those two').[69]

What form a particular desinence has depends on the context—the tense, mood, and voice, as well as the individual verb. For example, there is no one constant marker meaning 'I', but several: *-ō* in *lǘ.ō* 'I free'; *-mai* in the passive *lǘ.o.mai* 'I am freed'; *-mēn* in the aorist optative *lū.s.a.í.mēn* 'would that I had freed'.

Greek generally marks grammatical distinctions through inflectional affixation (the addition to the meaningful part of the word, "root" or "base", of morphemes having grammatical functions). In English, most verbs have their inflectional affixes added directly to the base: *loves, loved, loving; softens, softened, softening.* Even in English, however, the past participial endings (*-en* forms) of many verbs are added to a special form different from the base: thus *write, writes* but *written; weave, weaves* but *woven.*

A particular form to which affixes are added is called a "stem." In Greek the desinences are added not to the base directly, but to special stems which contain the indicators of tense, mood, and voice. In Greek there are quite a number of such different stems to which personal endings may be added. The stem *lū.o-,* seen in *lǘ.o.men* 'we are freeing', is of present tense, active voice, and indicative mood, whereas *lū.s.a.i-* (*lū.s.a.í.men* 'would that we had freed') is aorist tense, passive voice, and optative mood. As noted earlier, Greek stems combine indicators of voice, mood, and tense. The order in which these occur can be seen in this comparison:

e.lǘ.s.a.men	aorist indicative active first plural
e.lū.s.á.metha	aorist indicative middle first plural
e.lú.thē.men	aorist indicative passive first plural
lǘ.s.ō.men	aorist subjunctive active first plural
lǘ.s.a.i.men	aorist optative active first plural
lǘ.s.a.i.mi	aorist optative active first singular

Here, *-s* marks aorist tense; *-a* is a linking vowel used generally with aorists in the indicative and optative active and middle; *-o* is a linking vowel used with the aorist in the subjunctive active and middle; *-i* marks the optative mood; and the passive replaces *-s.a* with *-thē.* The general order of the markers is tense, voice, and mood, though one or more of these may be fused together or missing (as in the aorist passive *-thē*).

The Greeks were apparently aware not only of the specific categories of the verb (e.g., first person, 'I'), but also of the various "accidents" of the verb (e.g., person). In the same way, they abstracted from the specific stems: for example, from the "future active indicative" stem they abstracted away activity and indicativity, and arrived thereby at the more general notion of future stem.

Future stems are generally formed with an *-s* (the Greek letter sigma). But stems marking the aorist generally are formed with *-s* as well, the difference between the two being indicated by elements in the context (*lǘ.s.ō* 'I shall free' but *é.lū.s.a* 'I freed'). Moreover, both the future and aorist passives contain *-thē*: *lǘ.s.ō* 'I shall free' but *lu.thḗ.s.o.m.ai* 'I shall be freed'; *é.lū.s.a* 'I freed' but *e.lú.thē.n* 'I was freed'. Consequently the aorist and future stems are both considered "sigmatic," though not all such stems literally contain sigma.[70]

One difference between the aorist and the future is that Greek verbs referring to past time (that is, in the tenses) begin (in the indicative) with an *e-* (Greek *epsilon*) called the "augment": imperfect *é.lū.on* 'I was freeing'; pluperfect *e.le.lú.k.e* 'I had freed'; and aorist *é.lū.s.a* 'I freed'. Non-past tenses such as the future do not add the augment: *lǘ.s.ō* 'I shall free'.

The distinction of past and present is marked, apart from the augment (and the markers of the various specific tenses themselves), by the difference between "primary" and "secondary" personal endings. For example, the present tense 'I am being freed' is *lǘ.o.mai*, but the imperfect tense 'I was being freed' is *e.lū.ó.men*. Here the pastness is not marked by the stem, which is the so-called "present" stem in both cases, but rather by the augment *e-* and the fact that 'I' is the "secondary" *-mēn* in the imperfect, but the "primary," non-past *-mai* in the present. Similarly, the (present) perfect 'I have been freed' is *lé.lu.mai*, with primary *-mai*, while the past perfect (pluperfect) 'I had been freed' is *e.le.lú.mēn* with secondary *-mēn*.

The perfect tenses form stems with the Greek letter kappa (*-k*) and a partial reduplication of the root syllable (often its initial consonant plus *e*): thus 'I have freed', *lé.lu.k.a*. The forms of stems thus neatly divide the tenses (ignoring the future perfect) into those with sigmatic stems (the future and aorist), those with a kappa/reduplicative stem (the perfect and pluperfect), and those which use a stem with no consonant at all (present and imperfect). This trichotomy crosscuts that of primary and secondary tenses:

	primary (no augment, primary endings)	*secondary* (augment, secondary endings)
no consonant	present	imperfect
sigmatic	future	aorist
kappa	perfect	pluperfect

By abstracting away all the irregularities of form and complexities of meaning, we arrive at a system of tenses which is based purely on the forms of the desinences and the stems they are added to. Some such analysis as this (though probably not couched in these terms, which belong to modern theories of language) was known to the ancient Greeks and played an important role in their understanding of the tenses of the verb.

d. The Relations of the Tenses

It is possible now to interpret Thrax's comment that the tenses "stand in three respective relations: the Present is related to the Imperfect, the Perfect to the Pluperfect, and the Aorist to the Future."

Although the members of the first two pairs at least are obviously related in meaning,[71] these pairings are clearly based on "sound," that is, on form. The present and imperfect tenses are both built on the "present" stem—namely, the bare base plus a "linking vowel," *e* or *o*: 'we are freeing' *lǘ.o.men*, 'you (pl.) were freeing' *e.lǘ.e.te*. On the other hand, the perfect and pluperfect are both built on the "perfect" stem, which is formed by reduplication and/or by adding kappa: 'we have freed' *le.lú.k.a.men*; 'you (pl.) had been freed' *e.lé.lu.sthe*.

The aorist and future are paired because both stems are "sigmatic": 'we freed' *e.lú.s.a.men*, 'we shall free' *lú.s.o.men*. But they do not relate as do the first two pairs: the aorist is in no sense the past tense equivalent of the future, as the imperfect is of the present. But there is a sense in which the two may appropriately be paired on the basis of meaning. To understand the relationship of the aorist and future, we must first look at the members of the first two pairs.

The first member of each of the first two pairs is a "primary" or "present" tense, while the second member is a "secondary" or "past" tense.[72] Semantically, primary tenses differ from secondary tenses in that the latter refer to past time, whereas the former do not.

The first two pairs relate as follows:

	Primary	Secondary
Present stem	present	imperfect
Perfect stem	perfect	pluperfect

In the case of the perfect tense, its correlation with the pluperfect would seem to contradict the assertion of Dionysius that it is a variety of the past. Whatever its semantics, as regards its syntax and morphology it is certainly a primary tense, as the following facts demonstrate.

Apollonius points out that verbs "take the . . . augment in past tenses," and he contrasts *sémeron gráphō* 'today I'm writing' with *sémeron egráphon* 'today I was writing'.[73] Morphologically the imperfect tense is simply the secondary tense equivalent to the present. The pluperfect tense is formally related to the perfect in precisely the same way that the imperfect is to the present: *lelúkamen* 'we have freed', *elelúkamen* 'we had freed'. None of the primary tenses—present, perfect, future, future perfect—takes the augment.

The Greeks were also well aware of the differences between the primary and secondary desinences. In the middle and passive voices, the forms of the singular and the third plural personal endings as used with primary tenses (including the future perfect) are distinct from those used with seconary tenses[74]:

	primary	secondary
1 singular	-mai	-mēn
2 singular	-sai	-so
3 singular	-tai	-to
3 plural	-ntai	-nto

There are syntactic differences between the two types of tenses as well. Primary tenses in certain constructions may be followed by the indicative or the subjunctive, but in the same construction the secondary tenses require the optative mood.

In indirect discourse, when the complementizer (subordinating conjunction) *hóti* 'that' is used, after primary tenses (such as the present) the verb of the *hóti*-clause is normally indicative: *légei hóti gráphei* 'he says that he is writing' is a report of *gráphō* 'I am writing'. But with a secondary tense (such as the aorist), the following verb may be optative in form: *éleksen hóti gráphoi* 'he said that he was writing' is, again, a report of *gráphō*; he said, "I am writing."[75]

In purpose ("final") constructions with *hína* 'in order that', the subjunctive occurs in the purpose clause if the verb of the main clause is in a primary tense, but the optative occurs in the purpose clause if the main verb is secondary. 'He is coming that he may see this' is *érkhetai hína toûto ídēi* with subjunctive *ídēi* 'may see' after present *érkhetai* 'he is coming'; but 'he came that he might see this' is *êlthen hína toûto ídoi* with optative *ídoi* 'might see' after aorist *êlthen* 'he came'.[76]

Cautionary clauses with *mē* 'lest' are similar:

phoboûmai   mề toûto páthōsin
fear (PRES MID INDIC 1SG) not this   suffer (PRES ACT SUBJ 3PL)

'I fear lest they may suffer this'[77]

Here, subjunctive *páthōsin* follows present *phoboûmai*. But in *ephobéthēn mề toûto páthoien* 'I feared lest they should suffer this', optative *páthoien* follows aorist *ephobéthēn*.[78]

Apollonius Dyscolus has an ingenious argument to the effect that the perfect tense of Greek is a primary (and hence a kind of present) tense, not a secondary (past) tense. He observes that

> the conjunction *an* . . . has been said to combine with past tenses, but excluding the perfect . . . if anyone should ask what is the grammatical error in *grapsō an [a future], it is impossible to say what is wrong except on the basis of intuition . . . For there is no substitution . . . of a form in the wrong number or any other category in respect to which one could test the verb for agreement in number or tense or mood.
>
> The explanation is as follows: the conjunction *an* has a tendency to cancel the factuality of things . . . , changing them around to potentiality—whence it is also called "a potential conjunction." For *egrapsa* ("I wrote"), *egraphon* ("I was writing"), or *egegraphein* ("I had written"), represent acts that were either [done], or partly done or done long ago . . . Then *an* may be added to those tenses which are able to accept its force . . . , *egraphon an* ("I would be writing, I would write"); *egrapsa an* ("I would have written"), but not to *graphō* ("I am writing") or *grapsō* ("I will write"). For these [refer to events that] have not passed, so cannot accept the force of the conjunction. . . .
>
> From this we may be convinced that the perfect does not signify completion in the past, but rather in the present, so that it is incapable of accepting any future potentiality and consequently has become incompatible with the conjunction *an*.[79]

On the basis of these various criteria, then, the perfect is without question not a secondary tense: it does not take the augment; it takes primary, not secondary, endings; it requires ("governs") the subjunctive; and it cannot be used with *án*.

On the other hand, the aorist *is* just as surely secondary, showing the augment, taking secondary endings, governing the optative, and being unsable with *án*. And if the aorist is secondary, then by symmetry the future, if it is to pair with the aorist on the basis of the shared, sigmatic stem, ought to be primary. And it is. It shows no augment, takes primary endings, governs the subjunctive, and cannot be used with *án*.

But how can the future be a "present" tense? Here a clue is provided by Apollonius, who observes that most adverbs of time are "subdivided into different time-classes" and "do not [freely] combine with . . . all tenses."[80] A past adverb such as *ekhthés* 'yesterday' can be combined with the imperfect or aorist, but not with the present or future. A future adverb such as *aúrion* 'tomorrow' can be combined with the future tense but not with, say, the imperfect.

Interestingly enough, Apollonius observes as well that *aúrion* goes with the present: *aúrion grápho* 'tomorrow I write'.[81] If "tomorrow" can co-occur with both present and future tenses, then the present cannot refer distinctly to present, as opposed to future, time. Indeed, in many languages—English, German, Japanese—the present tense is essentially a non-past rather than, properly speaking, a present, as it readily combines with "future" adverbials (*I leave tomorrow*). Consequently the primary tenses (including the future and the future perfect) are not "present" tenses but rather non-past tenses.

We learn from the commentator Stephanos that the future, like the aorist, is *aóristos*.[82] This means, as we have seen, 'unbounded', 'indefinite'; these two tenses are not, somehow, as well defined as the four in the first two pairs, though it is not certainly known in what way the Greeks meant this. Possibly it was simply that the two are indifferent to the opposition of near and distant time.[83]

e. The Stoic-Varronian Theory of Tense and Aspect

It is possible, however, that in Dionysius we have a reflection of the Stoic-Varronian theory of tense, in which the perfect and pluperfect apparently share the meaning of completed action, and the present and imperfect that of incomplete, ongoing action. It is to this distinction of completion that the aorist and future are indifferent.

This is difficult to judge, however. Although the Stoics constituted one of the most important schools of Greek philosophy, only fragments of their writings have survived, and virtually nothing of those on theories of grammar. Our only sources are brief remarks by commentators such as Stephanos, and in the works of Priscian, Diogenes Laertius, and Sextus Empiricus (ca. A.D. 300). The works of Apollonius and Varro provide insights as well, but these too are fragmentary and require some interpretation.

It appears that Varro essentially adapted the Stoic theory to Latin. Unfortunately Varro's surviving writings do not clearly set forth a theory, though a theory can be inferred from them. He talks of

> the tenses of non-completion, like [imperfect] *discebam* 'I was learning,' [present] *disco* 'I learn,' [future] *discam* 'I shall learn,' and [those] of completion, thus [pluperfect] *didiceram* 'I had learned,' [perfect] *didici* 'I have learned,' [future perfect] *didicero* 'I shall have learned'.[84]

Later, in the course of a discussion of analogy ("regularity"), he says:

> The Regularities are . . . three-fold in the three tenses of verbs, such as [imperfect] *legebam* 'I was reading,' present *lego*, future *legam*, because the relation which *legebam* has to *lego*, this same relation *lego* has to *legam*.[85]

He says further that

some verbs denote incomplete action, like *lego* 'I read' and *legis* 'thou readest,' and others denote completed action, like *legi* 'I have read' and *legisti* 'thou hast read'. . . . [Verbs] ought to be connected with others of their own kind and by this principle *lego* is rightly related to *legebam*—[but] *lego* is not rightly related to *legi*, because *legi* denotes something completed.

We know that Greek influence on the Roman grammarians was pervasive; in methods, concepts, and terminology the Romans innovated little, and Latin grammar followed that of Greek closely. To some considerable extent this is appropriate, for Latin, being an Indo-European language like Greek, has much in common with it.

In Latin, as in Greek, a pairing of aspectually opposed—complete and incomplete—tenses is supported by the facts of morphology and syntax. The Latin imperfect, present, and future tenses all employ the "present" stem (e.g., *disc-* 'learn'):

'I was learning'	*disc-ebam*
'I learn, am learning'	*disc-o*
'I shall learn'	*disc-am*

But the pluperfect, perfect, and future perfect all employ the "perfect" stem (*didic-*):

'I had learned'	*didic-eram*
'I have learned'	*didic-i*
'I shall have learned'	*didic-ero*

The pairing of tenses is supported as well, as in Greek, by the facts of syntax. For example, Latin may use special epistolary tenses.[86] Where we write "while I write this," operating from the point of view of the writer and therefore using the present tense, the Romans might write from that of the reader and say "while I was writing this," using the imperfect of 'write' (*scribebam*). Similarly, the perfect of our letters, "I have answered," could be the pluperfect in theirs: "I had answered" (*rescripseram*) could mean 'I have answered'. The writer's present matches the reader's imperfect; perfect matches pluperfect.[87]

In the "indirect question" construction the indicative (*sentio* 'I think') becomes a subjunctive (*quid sentiam* 'what I think').[88] After a secondary tense in the main clause, the tense of the indirect question is shifted; present becomes imperfect:

id posset.ne   fieri
it be possible (IMPF SUBJ 3SG)-QUEST do (PRES PASS INF)
consuluit
consult (PERF ACT INDIC 3SG)

'he consulted whether it could be done'

Here the imperfect subjunctive (*possetne*) reflects a present indicative *potestne* 'can it be done?'.

Perfect (indicative) becomes pluperfect (subjunctive): *dixi quid fecissem* 'I said (*dixi*) what (*quid*) I had done'. This reflects *quid feci* 'what I have done'.

The facts of Latin syntax amply support a distinction of primary and secondary tenses, though there is no systematic distinction of primary and secondary desinences as in Greek.[89] But the future and future perfect do not enter into this system and in general present problems for the adaptation of Greek grammar to Latin.

Either because of the attractiveness of the notion of the three times, or because in Latin the present-stemmed future tense is opposed to a perfect-stemmed future perfect tense (there is no unique future stem), Varro used not the pairings of the Greeks but sets of three tenses. His system may be set forth as follows, using the first person singular active indicative forms of the verb 'learn'[90]:

	TIME		
	past	present	future
ASPECT			
incomplete	*discebam*	*disco*	*discam*
	'I was learning'	'I learn, am learning'	'I shall learn, shall be learning'
complete	*didiceram*	*didici*	*didicero*
	'I had learned'	'I have learned'	'I shall have learned'

Had the future perfect not been dismissed as marginal, the Greeks might well have utilized the Varronian model of three tenses and two aspects. But the future perfect in Greek is a "marked" or special kind of tense in two senses. First, it is limited (except for a very few verbs) to the passive voice, and even then to the indicative and optative moods.

Second, while the future perfect can express the perfect in the future tense, it is not needed to do so; the future can do this itself. The distinction of future and future perfect is in fact like the difference of aorist and pluperfect, not that of present and perfect.

The Stoics are generally considered (e.g., by Robins)[91] to have essentially originated the Varronian theory, and to have observed an aspectual distinction (complete vs. incomplete action) crosscutting the purely temporal one of past and present. (The interpretation of the Stoic treatment of the aorist and future is especially difficult.) Yet scholars have viewed the distinction of "completed" and "uncompleted" in many different ways:

	TENSE	
	present	*past*
ASPECT		
incomplete	present	imperfect
complete	perfect	pluperfect

Pinborg, one of the leading students of the Stoics, says that they called the present *enestós paratatikós* ("present extended") because it "stretches into the future (*parateínetai*)," and the imperfect *parōkhemenos paratatikós* ("past extended") because

> he who uses the imperfect states that he has performed most of the action, but not completed it. Present and imperfect thus have a 'kinship' (*syngeneia*) because both are incomplete (*atelés*) or durative (*paratatikós*). The perfect was called *enestós syntelikós* ["present perfect"], the pluperfect *téleios parōchēménos* ["perfect past"].

The distinction between *paratatikós* and *syntelikós/téleios* he sees as interpretable as one "between action in progress and result."[92]

Priscian notes that the Latin perfect is equivalent in meaning to both the Greek aorist and the (present) perfect, "which the Stoics call *téleios enestôs* ["perfect present"]."[93]

Assuming the Stoic scheme does differentiate aspects, some considerable controversy surrounds how the aorist and future fit into that scheme. For Jens Holt, aspect is irrelevant to these forms—the term *aóristoi*, applied to future as to aorist, he sees as meaning undetermined (indefinite) with regard to aspect.[94] Accordingly Holt interprets the Stoic system as follows[95]:

	definite tenses		indefinite tenses
	extended	complete	
present/future	present	perfect	future
past	imperfect	pluperfect	aorist

Another way of viewing this situation is that aspect is relevant to all the tense forms, but the aorist and future neutralize the aspectual opposition in the same way that the plural pronoun *they* neutralizes the gender distinction found in the singular (*he, she, it*). Accordingly Pinborg offers this scheme[96]:

	Past	Present	Future
Complete	Pluperfect	Perfect	
Neutral	Aorist		Future
Incomplete	Imperfect	Present	

The grammarian Goodwin in his study of Greek tenses categorizes them as follows. He is influenced by Varro or perhaps by a later grammatical tradition distinguishing the simple tenses (past, present, and future) of the European languages, which mark no aspectual distinctions, from their complex, periphrastic tenses, which do (e.g., *I have run* vs. *I am running*).

	Present Time	Past Time	Future Time
Action going on	Present	Imperfect	Future
Action simply taking place		Aorist	Future
Action finished	Perfect	Pluperfect	Future Perfect

In regard to the Greek tenses, Goodwin says that "they may designate the time of an action as *present, past, or future*; and also its character as *going on, finished*, or simply *taking place*."[97]

There is some support for Goodwin's action "simply taking place" over Pinborg's "neutral," especially when we consider use rather than meaning. For the aorist is not simply an optional variant of imperfect or pluperfect, not even in cases where aspect is not being stressed. Rather, the aorist is used in a *positive* way to indicate the occurrence of an event or change of state precisely *without* regard to completion as such.

Strictly from the point of view of *meaning*, we may surmise that Pinborg is more likely correct than Holt or Goodwin, but Goodwin probably captures better the facts of *use*, while Holt is perhaps closest in spirit to the intentions of the Stoics.

The distinction of "extended" versus "complete" can, however, be interpreted in quite another way, which does not involve aspect. The perfect (e.g., *I have eaten*) is complete at the present time; the action does not extend into the non-past.[98] Similarly the pluperfect is complete at some past time, the action not extending beyond that point. The imperfect, not being expressly completed in the past, may extend into the present and even the future.

This provides a slightly different theory from the one usually ascribed to Dionysius, but is not incompatible with it; the pluperfect, by this account, is further away from the present than the perfect, because it precedes a point already in the past. In any case, in this theory the distinction of extended and completed is purely one of tense and does not involve aspect.

Apollonius was aware of the distinction of extension (*parátasis*) and completion (*suntéleia*), but apparently interpreted it in terms of tense, so that completion refers to completion at the time of speech or writing, rather than a purely aspectual notion depending only on the nature of the act.[99]

Holt characterizes the ancient distinction as

> a distinction of time[100] only. . . . Despite the linguistic genius which the theory of tenses attests to, the Greek grammarians are not aware of the most important notion for the interpretation of the temporal system of the verb in ancient Greek.[101] This notion appears only in a sporadic fashion. Thus a scholiast (commentator) uses the term "achieved" (*suntelikós*)[102] to express the essential trait of the aorist, and in another scholiast we find the important distinction between time[103] (*khrónos*) and action (*érgon*): the imperfect indicates according to him past time, 'but the *action* happens by extension.'[104]

Heymann Steinthal in his history of Greek and Roman grammar expresses doubts that the Stoics, any more than the other Greeks, had a conception of aspect, and interprets their theory as follows:

> The *khrónoi* are in part *ateleîs* [imperfect], in part *suntelikoí* [perfect], corresponding to the *infectum* and *perfectum* of Varro. These two kinds[105] of verb, however, are not at all parallel, but rather all the tenses lie on the one line of time, and correspond to both kinds (*genera*) or modes of time (*modi temporum*) (not of action—*actionum*—or deeds, *gestorum*) of Varro, namely the imperfects and perfects, through the division of this line. On the one half lay the *khrónoi ateleîs* or *paratatikoí*, on the other the *téleioi* or *suntelikoí*.[106]

The *imperfectum* then involves time extended out of the past into the future; the difference of present (*praesens imperfectum*) and imperfect (*praeteritum imperfectum*) would simply be that in the former case most of the action falls in the future, while in the latter most falls in the past.[107]

Steinthal argues that the Stoic system is not an aspectual one.[108] If it were, they would divide the future into perfect and imperfect, but they do not, nor do they term it imperfect. Their names for the tenses are similar to those of grammarians who clearly make no aspectual distinctions. He points out, for example, that Apollonius observes that "the perfect [signifies] completion in the present," even though he uses for it the term "past perfect" (*parōkhēménos suntéleias*).[109] If the Stoics had had an aspectual distinction, he argues, surely later writers such as Priscian would have recognized it.

It is impossible now to determine precisely what the Stoic theory was, or what their terms meant. While it is most likely that the later Varronian aspect-based theory follows a Stoic scheme, and some such distinction as completive versus non-completive aspect is intended, the lack of any explicit account and the nature of the evidence preclude any certain conclusions on this point.

However we are to interpret the Stoic scheme, it is clear that the ancients had at least two theories of the tenses. All grammarians assumed three tenses corresponding to the three times, and accounted for the supernumerary tenses by making them species of the past or the future (since the present was not seen as divisible).

Some saw these species as differing in relative position in time: the perfect, for example, was a relatively recent past, and the pluperfect a relatively distant one, while the imperfect extended into the present. Others distinguished the tenses in terms of their stem morphology and associated (something like) incompleteness of action (Greek *érgon*, Latin *actio*) with the present stem, and (a corresponding) completeness with the perfect stem.

The two theories necessarily define the tenses rather differently. In the "four pasts" theory the perfect is a past tense; in the "aspect theory," a present. In the former theory, but not in the latter, the pluperfect and perfect refer to different periods of time into which the past is divided (as the future and future perfect divide the future). But it is in the application of the theories to Latin that their most significant consequences for tense can be seen.

The search for a neat schematization of tenses conspired with the lack of an aorist or preterite tense in Latin to lead to two undesirable consequences. Since there was no neutral, aorist past tense, and the future was in opposition to the future perfect, there was no recognition of the neutralization of aspect in Latin.

The Latin future is ambiguous. In contrast to the future perfect, it is formally imperfect in aspect, and semantically it often is used in that way. However, it also is often as neutral as the Greek future, being the mirror image of the aorist.

This occasions some confusion, as when Allen's Latin grammar correctly distinguishes the English future *I shall write* as an "indefinite" tense from both the "incomplete" *I shall be writing* and the "complete" *I shall have written*, but then goes on in its discussion of the Latin tenses to consider the future only under the rubric of "incomplete action," though the Latin future could as readily neutralize the aspectual opposition as the English and Greek futures. In what way is *rogabo* 'I shall ask' incomplete?[110]

Similarly, we find the Latin grammar of Andrews and Stoddard identifying the future as referring to "action not completed," but then stating that the "*future tense* denotes that an action will be going on hereafter, without reference to its completion; *amabo*, 'I shall love or be loving'."[111]

More disastrously, Varro had no way in his theory for dealing with the ambiguity of the (present) perfect. As Priscian notes, *scripsit* is at once a primary, perfect verb, 'he has written', and a secondary, neutral one, 'he wrote'. (Cf.

modern colloquial French *ils ont écrit* 'they have written, they wrote'.) Some modern Latin grammars distinguish the two uses as perfect definite and perfect historical respectively, noting that the latter use corresponds to the Greek aorist.

But while Varro could treat the perfect definite, he had no place in his scheme for the perfect historical. In the Varronian scheme the perfect represents complete action, and as a past tense would contrast with the pluperfect, which also represents completion. In Priscian's theory, on the contrary, it is possible to have two tenses which are both past and both complete, since the past is divided into near (perfect) and distant (pluperfect) segments.

But then Priscian can distinguish the future and future perfect only in terms of nearness in time, which he is unwilling to do on the grounds that the future is not yet known and hence cannot be divided up.

After Varro there were no major innovations in Latin (or Greek) grammar, and the most influential grammarians, Donatus and Priscian, are not original in thought. Donatus[112] ignores the future perfect and the ambiguity of the perfect and follows Dionysius in treating imperfect, perfect, and pluperfect alike as varieties of the preterite (e.g., the perfect is called the "preterite perfect").

It was Donatus and Priscian together who formed the foundations of Latin grammar in the Middle Ages and well into, and even beyond, the Renaissance. In the speculative grammar of the Middle Ages no effort was made to go beyond the Priscianic formulation or to take the Stoic-Varronian theory into account, although in the context of Scholasticism, "the view was now expressed that Priscian . . . should have investigated the underlying theory and justification for the elements and categories that he employed."[113]

The failure of both Varronian and Priscianic traditions lay in their ultimate inability to cope with the apparent incompatibility of the three tenses with the morphology and syntax of the classical verb. When, a thousand years later in the Renaissance, these traditions were applied to the grammars of the modern languages of Western Europe, they were to prove even less adequate.

2

Traditional Theories
of the Complex Tenses

a. General and Rational Grammar

Graeco-Roman grammars attempted to categorize verbal forms in terms of their meanings. Expressions such as verbs were viewed as signs expressing mental "affections." As the mind presumably apprehended in reality three segments of time (past, present, and future), so language, as a reflection of ideas in the mind, must have three tenses to convey this distinction.

But this required a reconciliation of the expected three tenses with the half dozen or so grammatical tenses actually found in the classical languages. Varro apparently drew on the notion of aspect (completion vs. incompletion) to accomplish this; there were indeed three times, but for each two aspects (perfect and imperfect), the combinations of tenses and aspects yielding the observed tense forms.

The alternative to the Varronian theory introduced the subsidiary notions of relative distance in time (the perfect a near, the pluperfect a distant, past), and a distinction of definite and indefinite. The perfect is definite, fixed relatively near the present, but the imperfect and aorist are indefinite, since they can refer to events anywhere in the past.

To the theory of tense the Middle Ages seem to have made no significant additions, so that when grammars of the modern European languages came to be written at the time of the Renaissance, all that was available was the ancient Latinate model, one not entirely suited to the new grammatical systems. Such a judgment must be qualified, however, for grammatical theory in the Middle Ages is a sea of obscurity surrounding only a few islands here and there.

In this "period of intense intellectual and scholarly ferment," as G. L. Bursill-Hall calls it, a great number of grammatical treatises were written.[1] But, as he points out, "[the grammatical literature of the Middle Ages] has often been considered a closed book to historians of . . . grammar," owing to its obscure terminology and special technical presuppositions. Relatively little of the extant literature has been edited, translated, or studied. When grammatical theory "resurfaced" in the Renaissance, it differed little from the inherited Latin grammar. But to discount the medieval grammarians as making no lasting contribution to the theory of tense would require a far better knowledge of their thought than we possess today.

Medieval grammar was philosophical, not empirical. Although such thinkers as Roger Bacon were aware of the importance of the study of languages (Bacon himself knew Greek and Arabic and wrote a grammar of Hebrew),[2] medieval grammar made no attempt to generalize over the grammars of diverse languages, nor did it seek to improve on the ancients' grammars as descriptions of the classical tongues.[3]

Rather the goal was a strictly logical science based on scholastic logic and viewing Latin as the ideal expression of an underlying reality mediated through human reason.[4] If Latin made a distinction of past, present, and future, it was presumably because the human intellect apprehended the corresponding division of time in reality. The major interest of grammarians was in stating the principles underlying grammatical systems in logical terms.

Consequently the methodology of the medieval grammarian was an aprioristic, semantic one, explaining the observed facts of language by deriving them from principles of meaning and logic, rather than an empirical, morphological, and syntactic one, generalizing from the observed facts of particular languages.[5]

The goals and methods of medieval grammar represented a divergence from ancient grammar and a presagement of the later, "rational" grammar of the sixteenth through eighteenth centuries. What had been an implicit appeal in the ancients to rational principles of grammar by way of analogy was made explicit, as was an implicit explanatory goal.[6] Rather than simply labeling forms or relating them unsystematically to this or that feature of reality, the aim was an entire deductive system of logic which could serve as the underpinning of the grammatical system.

Medieval grammar was more aprioristic than either ancient grammar, which utilized morphology and syntax, or the later rationalist grammar, which claimed to base at least some of its universals on the observation of languages. The vernacular grammarians of the Renaissance likewise avoided empirical universals, but if they drew on Latin, it was less in the name of logic than of necessity, Latinate grammar being all that was available to them.

Grammars of particular nonclassical languages are rare before the Renaissance. Vernacular, as opposed to Latin, grammar was undoubtedly connected with the rise of the modern languages to a higher political, scientific, and literary status. It was only when French replaced Latin as the language of diplomacy, when literature in modern European languages such as English, French, and German began to supplement literature in Latin, and when printing and the secularization of education promoted writing in the modern languages, that grammars of these vernaculars were produced.

The application of Graeco-Roman grammar to the Romance languages presented almost as little problem as the adaptation of Greek grammar to Latin, as the Latinists believed; "only a slight adjustment was necessary in order to make Latin the type and model of all languages."[7]

The Renaissance grammars of the European languages could simply translate Latin terms into the vernacular, freely employing Procrustean principles where necessary to fit the traditional categories to the modern languages. In the case of the Romance languages, at least, this was facilitated by the matching of the Romance tenses to those of Latin, though the corresponding tense forms are not always etymologically related, and a number of simple tenses of Latin have structurally dissimilar counterparts in Romance. So long as the grammarians' goal was simply to label forms, however, these differences could be ignored, as could any inconvenient forms without classical precedents.

Nebrija's Spanish grammar of 1492, for example, assigns to Spanish five tenses[8]:

present	*io amo*	'I love'
past imperfect	*io amava*	'I loved'
(passado no acabado)		
past perfect	*io ame*	'I loved'
(passado acabado)		
pluperfect	*io avia amado*	'I had loved'
(passado mas que acabado)		
future	*io amare*	'I shall love'
(venidero)		

His terminology reflects a close hewing to the Latinate model, as a result of which he is led to ignore the "conditional" tense (modern *yo amaría* 'I would love'), which is similar in form to the future (*yo amaré*), and to treat the complex pluperfect while neglecting all other periphrastic tenses,[9] including the present perfect (*yo he amado* 'I have loved') and the future perfect (*yo haré amado* 'I shall have loved').

In the case of the Germanic languages, too, the early grammars closely follow precisely the same model. Claius's German grammar of 1578, for example, states: "The tenses (*tempora*) in verbs are five: present, imperfect, perfect, pluperfect, and future."[10] The "imperfect" is the simple past tense (*ich schrieb* 'I wrote'), while both perfect and pluperfect are complex (*ich habe gelesen* 'I have read'; *ich hatte gelesen* 'I had read'). The future as well is periphrastic: *ich werde* (in this period also *ich will*) *lesen* 'I shall read'. The treatment of German by Claius differs in no essential way from that of Spanish by Nebrija.

It was not long, however, before the inadequacies of the Latinate model for describing the modern languages were noted. However logical the Latin system might have appeared, the grammars of other languages obviously deviated from it in diverse ways. Formally, Greek has at least six tenses, Latin six, Lithuanian three, English two. The earliest vernacular grammarians had purely descriptive or pedagogical purposes and could largely ignore such divergences. But in the sixteenth century an increasing number of grammarians once again sought a logical basis for grammar, which entailed a critical reevaluation of the Latinate model.

If grammar is to be a science, it must transcend the particulars of individual languages and seek to generalize over languages as a whole. In the seventeenth century the philosopher Tommaso Campanella distinguished language-particular grammar based on the usage of the "best" writers, *grammatica civilis*, from a universal, "general," "rational" grammar (*grammatica philosophica*); a similar distinction was made by Francis Bacon.[11]

At a time when such thinkers as Descartes, Spinoza, and Leibniz were developing philosophies based on reason, in which experience was seen as a less important guide to truth than logical deduction, a revival of philosophical grammar was inevitable.[12] The new movement claimed, however, to utilize not only aprioristic methods but also data from many different languages, to break with a purely Latin-based grammar. The masterpiece of rationalist grammar is the *Grammaire générale et raisonnée* (1660)[13] of the logicians of the Cistercian abbey at Port-Royal near Paris, an important seventeenth-century center of rationalist thought in France.

It "was based on a thorough knowledge of Hebrew, Greek, Latin, Romance languages, and German,"[14] and its authors "envisaged general grammar as underlying the actual make-up of all languages, rather than as particulars exemplified in any one,"[15] though the grammar tended to replace Latin with French as the model "logical language" so that, to some extent, "the Port-Royal grammar . . . is only the traditional grammar of Latin generalized enough to accommodate French, with some reference to other modern languages."[16] It is its tying of language to logic that gives its grammar universality, not its use of data.

The spirit of the universalist enterprise is exhibited in Harris's appeal to "natural signification," when he points out in the *Hermes* that "the *Latins* used their *Praeteritum Perfectum* in some instances after a very peculiar manner, so as to imply the very reverse of the Verb in its natural signification."[17]

The critique here of Latin is typical of the rationalist movement, but the tendency persisted to view Latin as superior to the vernaculars. If Latin is (generally) the "logical language," then any deviation from Latin is "illogical"; to this day normative, prescriptive grammar contrasts the rational and logical Latin with the "illogicalities" of particular vernacular languages. As vernaculars took on some of the prestige of Latin and Greek, however, this exalted "logicality" was transferred from Latin to other languages; Latin was relegated to the status of first among peers, no longer uniquely "logical."

Naturally the *Grammaire générale* often employs French as a benchmark, for example when it says, in regard to the difference between the uses of the preterite and the perfect, that "[our language] is so exact in the propriety of its expressions, that it admits of no exception to this rule, tho' the Spaniards and Italians sometimes confound these two preterits, using them indiscriminately."[18] This assumes natural, "logical" values for these tenses, values supposedly represented in French. (Ironically enough, colloquial French would soon replace the simple preterite with the periphrastic perfect, the *passé composé*.)

On the whole, though philosophical grammar was universalist, and the claims of particular languages, or even of languages in general, had to be secondary to those of logic, its theories could not be merely a priori; for if empirical observations were not generalizable, then the theory of rationalistic grammar would be contradicted, since language would then presumably not reflect human reason.

But neither was the major method of investigation in "general grammar," rationalism notwithstanding, the development of a logical theory from which grammar could be deduced. Despite the close relationship of the *Grammaire générale* to the Port-Royal *Logique* (Arnauld, 1964) much depended on observations of special distinctions in particular sets of languages. For there is no significant logic of tenses in the *Logique* or any other rationalist work, certainly none from which the elaboration of tenses found in rationalist grammars can be logically deduced. The philosophical grammars observe the facts of particular languages, albeit selectively.

The lack of a logic of tense meant that the traditional theory of tenses was all that a rationalist grammar could draw on. As there are three times in reality, so must there be three tenses in language "to signify these diverse times."[19] The past is subdivided into the three traditional tenses of imperfect, perfect, and pluperfect, providing five simple tenses. Thus far the *Grammaire générale* goes no further than Priscian or the early vernacular grammarians such as Robert Estienne.

Estienne's French grammar of 1557 defines the imperfect as denoting "neither an accomplishment nor completion (*perfection*) of a past action or passion,[20] but only its having been begun, as *l'aimoye*."[21] (Cf. Nebrija's "unfinished past.") And Castelvetro says of Italian, "as someone can 'have loved' and 'not have finished loving', or 'have loved' and 'love no more',"[22] our language possesses two separate tenses susceptible of designating these two actions, one partly passed, and the other entirely passed, *amava* and *amai*."[23]

But the rationalists had to confront the fact that the Romance languages had split the Latin perfect into a simple preterite (e.g., 'I loved') and a periphrastic perfect ('I have loved'):

	preterite	perfect
French	*j'amai*	*j'ai aimé*
Spanish	*amé*	*he amado*
Italian	*amai*	*ho amato*

The traditional distinction of a definite (i.e., recent) past, "precisely done" (*j'ai écrit* 'I have written'), and an indefinite past or aorist (*j'écrivis* 'I wrote'), is repeated in the *Grammaire générale* but presented as an empirical fact about "most vulgar languages" (vernaculars), though dependent on the logical possibility of such a distinction in past tenses.

The rationalist concern with logic and naturalness meant, however, that the traditional approach could not be maintained. If tenses categorized time, and the system of times was logical, then that of tenses must be, too. With the simple tense systems of the classical languages this presented no difficulties. But in the case of the Romance languages (and many other European languages such as English and German), by the time of the Renaissance there had developed a lack of parallelism between form and content in the systems of tenses. In each of the three times a simple tense contrasts with a periphrastic perfect.

Presumably, then, whatever the difference of past and perfect is, that of present and present perfect, future and future perfect must be the same by analogy. But the Priscianic model does not allow for this analogy, because there can be no division of the future into segments, and because the perfect is not a present but a past tense.

At the same time, the three-way contrast of a complex perfect, a simplex imperfect, and a simplex preterite precluded adoption of a Varronian model. The problem of the ambiguity of the Latin perfect, never solved by Varro or his followers, continued to haunt grammatical theory. Although Romance now had explicit markers for each of the two sides of the Latin perfect, the Varronian model still had no place for at least one of them.

b. The Problem of Complex Tenses

The system of tenses found in the modern Romance languages differs radically from that in Greek and Latin, in that most of the manifold synthetic forms of the classical languages, marking distinctions of voice, mood, and tense in the verb itself, have been replaced or supplemented by analytic constructions—complex forms—in which auxiliary words are used as markers instead. It is even the case that some of the new synthetic forms which supplanted the Latin ones (e.g., the Romance future in *-r-*) had their origins in periphrastic tenses.

Not only was the number of tenses in the subjunctive reduced (modern French has only the present and fragments of the imperfect, though formal Spanish at least has retained a full complement of subjunctive tenses), but distinct passive stems disappeared, and the marking of voice was assigned either to auxiliary verbs or to the reflexive construction.

The classical languages had complex forms, but the use of complex forms was sporadic and played no essential role in the grammatical systems, so that the periphrastics of the classical languages parallel those of the modern languages little in regard either to form or to content. The Latin perfect tenses, for example, are complex in form in the passive voice (*amatus eram* 'I had been loved'), but simplex in the active (*amaveram* 'I had loved').

The Greek verb shows periphrastic forms only in the middle voice, in the perfect subjunctive and optative. The subjunctive active of the perfect is simple (*lelúkō*, roughly 'that I may have freed'), as is the optative (*lelúkoimi*, 'that I might have freed'). But the corresponding middle perfects of these moods are periphrastic complexes formed with the subjunctive and optative present of the auxiliary verb *eimí* 'be' plus a middle perfect participle. 'That I may have been freed' is *leluménos ō*, while 'that I might have been freed' is *leluménos eíēn*.

In Latin, too, the passive voice is periphrastic in the perfect tenses (in both indicative and subjunctive moods, as well as the perfect infinitive *amatus esse* 'to have been loved'):

INDICATIVE		
present	*amor*	'I am loved'
imperfect	*amabar*	'I was loved'
future	*amabor*	'I shall be loved'
perfect	*amatus sum*	'I have been loved'
pluperfect	*amatus eram*	'I had been loved'

SUBJUNCTIVE

present	*amer*	'that I (may) be loved'
imperfect	*amarer*	
perfect	*amatus sim*	'that I (should) have been loved'
pluperfect	*amatus essem*	

The periphrastic passive was extended to all tenses in Romance. It is perfectly possible to say, for example, in Spanish:

los ladrones son ·   perseguidos   por el   alguacil
the thieves   be (PRES INDIC 3PL) pursue (PP MASC PL) by the sheriff
'the thieves are pursued by the sheriff'[24]

But in all the Romance languages this usage is limited, and in general is much less common in the colloquial language than in the formal, written one. To a great extent it is replaced by a construction using reflexive pronouns, especially when no agent is indicated:

eso se   hará   fácilmente
that self do (FUT INDIC 3SG) easily
'that will be done easily' (literally 'that will do itself easily')[25]

Often too an indefinite pronoun is used: (French) *on le bat* 'one beats him', 'he is being beaten'.[26]

The Latin verb relied almost entirely on simple forms in the active voice, where the only periphrastic is the future infinitive (*amaturus esse* 'to be about to love'). But Latin also possessed a full set of periphrastic relatively future forms in the active and passive indicative, subjunctive, and infinitive:

ACTIVE

Indicative (all tenses)

present	*amaturus sum*	'I am about to love'
imperfect	*amaturus eram*	'I was about to love'
(etc.)		

Subjunctive (except future and future perfect)

present	*amaturus sim*	'that I may be about to love'
imperfect	*amaturus essem*	'that I might have been about to love'
(etc.)		

Infinitive

present	*amaturus esse*	'to be about to love'
perfect	*amaturus fuisse*	'to have been about to love'

PASSIVE

Indicative (all tenses)

present	*amandus sum*	'I have to be loved'
imperfect	*amandus eram*	'I had to be loved'
(etc.)		

Subjunctive (except future and future perfect)

present	*amandus sim*	'that I may have to be loved'
imperfect	*amandus essem*	'that I might have had to be loved'
(etc.)		

Infinitive

present	*amandus esse*	'to have to be loved'
perfect	*amandus fuisse*	'to have had to be loved'

These have quite special functions and are not comparable to the periphrastic future tenses of the Germanic languages. A major use, in indirect quotation and elsewhere, is to supply the missing future subjunctive.

Both Greek and Latin show a number of other periphrastic constructions which resemble tense forms but which differ from true tenses in not being fully grammaticized, partaking as much of the nature of idiomatic constructions as of grammatical markers.

There are two distinctions between grammaticized and ungrammaticized categories. First, grammaticized categories are systematic, whereas ungrammaticized ones are not. English distinguishes its *used to*-plus-infinitive construction from both the simple past and the *would*-plus-infinitive construction: *John used to like cake, John liked cake*, and *John would like cake* (from time to time). There are a number of semantic differences between the three forms, and they are not freely interchangeable. But this three-way distinction forms no part of the English tense *system*: it is limited to the past only, there are no present or future forms of *used to*, and no future corresponding to *would* (though *will* arguably provides its present).

Second, grammaticized distinctions are obligatory, whereas ungrammaticized ones are optional. For example, Turkish has two different past tense forms, the evidential and the inferential, and the distinction between them is obligatorily indicated in Turkish. The inferential in Turkish is a regular verb form basically used to indicate that the statement is inferred or based on hearsay, but not personally vouched for by the speaker: "if you say *kar yağmış* 'snow has fallen', it means either that someone has told you so or that you have seen the ground covered with snow, but not that you actually saw the snow falling."[27]

On the other hand, the evidential is a verb form used when the speaker actually witnessed the event or can vouch for it: "if one has witnessed the arrival of a tourist-ship, one may report the event in the words *bir turist vapuru geldi*" ['a tourist-ship has come'].[28]

It is possible in English to convey something of the same difference by using various devices. The modal auxiliary verbs *will* (e.g., in *that will be John coming in now*) and *must* (*it must be noon*) are often inferential, for example. But whereas the distinction between past and non-past is obligatory in English, that of evidential and inferential is not. *It snowed last night* says nothing about whether the speaker witnessed the snowfall, inferred it from snow on the ground, or read about it in the newspaper. To English speakers, there is no vagueness or ambiguity here.[29]

Many of the periphrastic constructions of the classical languages are not part of their grammatical systems and do not mark grammaticized distinctions. Greek, for example, may form periphrastic perfects with either the verb *eimí* 'be' plus perfect participle or *ékhō* 'have' plus aorist or perfect participle.

The construction with 'be' indicates the continuance of a state resultant from prior action. Goodwin contrasts this sentence:

oúte   gàr ên   presbeía pròs oudéna
and not for be (IMPF ACT INDIC 3SG) embassy to   any

apestalménē   tóte tôn   Hellénōn
send off (PERF MID PARTIC FEM NOM SG) then the (GEN PL) Greek (GEN PL)

'for there was no embassy then out on a mission to any of the Greeks'

with the same sentence using *apéstalto* (pluperfect middle indicative): "this would have given the meaning 'for no embassy had ever been sent out'."[30]

The construction with *ékhō* stands somewhere between that with *eimí* and the regular perfect. While strictly speaking a resultative construction (cf. 'I have the job finished'), it often conveys a perfect sense ('I have finished the job'), as in

epitrépsantes   hēméas autoùs ékhomen
give over (AOR ACT PARTIC MASC   us   selves have (PRES ACT
NOM PL)   INDIC 1PL)

'we have entrusted ourselves'[31]

These constructions are neither systematic nor obligatory, but merely supplement the regular temporal devices of the language. Similarly, the periphrastic future of Greek with the auxiliary verb *méllō* 'be about to, likely to' and the indicatives of the Latin periphrastic future are not fully part of the grammatical systems.

Consequently, the periphrastics found in the classical languages do not on the whole challenge the traditional grammatical theories. Had the classical languages had the same system of periphrastics found in modern European languages, presumably a rather different theory of tenses would have emerged.

Where the indicative active tenses are concerned, the new system which emerged was radically different from the Latin one and extended it in three ways. The present and imperfect were retained unchanged, but all the other tense forms except the perfect were replaced. The perfect form was retained, but it became a preterite—a simple past tense.

In the new system the two sides of the Latin perfect are marked in different ways and the ambiguity eliminated. Latin now had in the preterite a counterpart of the Greek aorist, while the present perfect was a periphrastic tense like the English *I have gone*.

The future was at first an idiomatic construction, *amare habeo* 'I have to love', that is, 'I am going to love', 'I shall love'. But it was also possible to say *amare habebam* 'I had to love'. Thus not only was *amabo* 'I shall love' eventually replaced by the infinite plus a reduced form of the present tense of the auxiliary 'have' (Spanish *amaré*, French *j'aimerai*, Italian *amerò*, 'I shall love'), but a new tense, the future-in-the-past or "conditional," was born, based on the imperfect (in Italian, the old perfect) of the auxiliary (*amaría, j'aimerais, amerei*).

The verb 'have' (Latin *habere*, except in Portuguese, which used Latin *tenere* 'hold', later 'have') became the main auxiliary marking the perfect aspect. In some languages, under certain circumstances 'be' is used instead, as in French *je suis venu* 'I have come', but this does not affect the system as such.

In each tense the simple form, marking an imperfect aspect, corresponds to a complex form—that tense of 'have' plus a perfect participle—marking the perfect. Thus the combination with present tense 'have' marked the present-perfect side of the Latin perfect tense, while the old perfect, now called the "preterite," marked its past-tense, aorist-like side.

But the Romance languages now had a distinction of imperfect and preterite. This meant that in the new system there could be both an imperfect perfect and a preterite perfect (e.g., Spanish *había amado* and *hubo amado*).

In modern terminology, the complex with auxiliary in the imperfect is called the pluperfect or sometimes the "past imperfect," while that with preterite auxiliary is called the *passé antérieur*, "preterite perfect," or "past perfect." In Italian these two tenses are, respectively, the *trapassato prossimo* ('near trans-past') and the *trapassato remoto* ('remote trans-past').[32]

Furthermore, because there was now a conditional alongside the future, not only was a periphrastic future perfect available, but likewise an entirely new tense, the conditional perfect or past conditional, based on the conditional of the auxiliary. Thus whereas Latin has a six-tense system of three times crosscut by the two aspects, the Romance languages have a system, in morphological terms, of ten tenses—five simple ones and five periphrastic perfects corresponding to them. For example, in Italian:

	SIMPLE	COMPLEX
present	*amo* 'I love'	*ho amato* 'I have loved'
imperfect	*amavo* 'I loved'	*avevo amato* 'I had loved'
preterite	*amai* 'I loved'	*ebbi amato* 'I had loved'
future	*amerò* 'I shall love'	*avrò amato* 'I shall have loved'
conditional	*amerei* 'I should love'	*avrei amato* 'I should have loved'

Possibly under Romance influence, a very similar system evolved in Germanic languages. Germanic had originally made do with two simple tenses, past and present (present-future or non-past). But a periphrastic future developed, though in every regard its development has been utterly unlike the Romance one. It has never developed into a synthetic tense, and the auxiliary retains to a greater or lesser extent its base meaning of a modal verb.

Indeed, Germanic cannot even decide on what auxiliary to choose. Standard German has settled on *werden* 'become', but uses *wollen* 'will' and *sollen* 'ought' for some special purposes. Standard British English splits the paradigm between the cognate verbs *will* and *shall*, while American English has largely reduced both to the clitic *'ll*.

The possibility of a periphrasis leaves open use of the past tense of the auxiliary, and Germanic has followed Romance in developing a conditional tense (*I should go, he would go*), though German uses the past subjunctive of *werden* (*ich würde gehen* 'I would go').

The development of periphrastic perfects with *be* and *have* (standard English once had, but has lost, this use of *be*), based on this system of four tenses (Germanic has no imperfect tense distinct from the preterite), yielded an eight-tense system not dissimilar from the ten-tense system of Romance.

But English extended this system yet further, in a way unknown to either German or most of Romance, by developing the periphrastic progressives and thereby allowing a three-way distinction of aspect in each of the four tenses. While the Romance languages have a progressive or continuative construction of the type of

(Spanish) *ella está tocando el piano* 'she is playing the piano',[33] this is different in some respects from the corresponding English form.[34]

In English the progressive has become the regular expression of actually present time. The "present tense" of the verb expresses actual present time only with certain verbs: auxiliary verbs such as *am, have, may, will, need*; a few "stative" verbs referring to states rather than actions (*love, feel, think, believe, continue,* etc.); and "performative" verbs (*agree, estimate, sentence, challenge,* etc.), the mere utterance of which constitutes the act they name—merely saying "I deny that" constitutes denying that.[35] With other verbs, the present tense has many uses:

future	I leave on Friday.
frequentative	I eat lunch at noon.
general	Beggars can't be choosers.

But it does not express what is going on or what is true right now.

In the past and other tenses, the progressive contrasts with neutral simple tenses which can convey what the progressives do. Depending on the context, *he read* can mean 'he was reading' (*he read all night*) as well as 'he read through' (*he read* Hamlet *in half an hour*). But these neutral simple tenses do not in themselves indicate aspect.

This gives English a twelve-tense system even richer than the Romance one. With the periphrastic passives, this means that the indicative in English has at least twenty-four different forms, all but two of them complex.[36]

For the most part, the new Romance tenses simply replaced the Latin forms without any break in the syntactic or semantic traditions. Where this was not the case, as for example where the conditional and conditional perfect tenses were concerned, the earliest vernacular grammarians were generally constrained to ignore the new tenses (as we have seen in the case of Nebrija), as they did not fit into the Latinate scheme.

But the later general grammarians claimed to seek a rational, universal grammar, though they could hardly achieve it. The challenge was to find a systematic categorization of the complex tense forms of the vernaculars which was at once reconcilable with their a priori notions of tense and the observed morphological and syntactic systems of the languages in question.

c. Theories of Relative Tense

Grammarians of the vernacular languages had to confront systems with forms that did not correspond to simple tenses of the classical languages. The Romance languages have at least one simple tense—the conditional—unknown to Latin and Greek. Both Romance and Germanic have complex tense forms lacking counterparts in one or another of those tongues. The progressive of English introduced supercomplex forms such as *(she) will have been running*.

The new theories which developed out of the old Latinate grammar all made a fundamental distinction between simple and complex tenses. Priscian and all other ancient writers knew no such dichotomy; periphrastics were simply variants of the simple forms or represented at best semigrammaticized categories. Further, the various distinctions of time applied equally to all tenses except where their sense precluded such an application (as when Priscian rejects the division of the future).

The "compound" or complex tenses of the vernacular grammarians were, however, not our complex tenses, defined as such by their analytic, periphrastic structure, but rather tenses which could be simple, synthetic forms, defined as complex in purely notional terms. Perhaps because periphrastic forms had occured in the classical tongues but had not differed essentially from the simple ones, the problem with the new tenses was seen as one not of form but of meaning. The theories devised to account for them long made no distinction between simplexes like the Romance imperfect and complexes such as the various perfect tenses.

Until the late eighteenth century, meaning served as the sole criterion for classifying tenses. Few grammarians before the time of White (1761) and Lowth (1762) seem to have paid much attention, while classifying tenses, to the forms which marked them. Today we observe a systematic difference in meaning (and use) between the complex, periphrastic, perfect tenses and the corresponding simplex tenses:

> *goes* and *has gone*
> *went* and *had gone*
> *va* and *est allé(e)*
> *allait* and *était allé(e)*
> *alla* and *fut allé(e)*
> *ira* and *sera allé(e)*
> *irait* and *serait allé(e)*

But this was only recognized almost at the end of the development of the grammatical tradition, and but sporadically then.

At the end of the fifteenth century, scholars were just beginning to modify the ancient theories of Dionysius, Priscian, Varro, and others in order to cope with these new systems. Over the next three hundred years change would be very slow, but real. Although Madvig's Latin grammar of 1887 is visibly in the tradition of Nebrija and the *Grammaire générale*, it presents a theory unlike anything the ancients had known. By the late eighteenth century quite modern and untraditional theories of tense and aspect had developed, though the revolutionary break with Priscian was not to come until our century, with Otto Jespersen's critique of Madvig.[37]

In modern as in ancient times, the goal of the grammatical tradition remained the classification of the tenses and their distinction by various criteria. By the seventeenth century it was generally accepted that there are two fundamental differences between tenses of the vernaculars. One difference, agreed upon by theorists of all schools, was a distinction of definiteness and indefiniteness—the preterite was indefinite, the perfect definite—a distinction which grew out of one found in the ancients.

Today we call the preterite (simple past tense) "definite" because it fixes the event at some definite time in the past: *he went home* presupposes a definite time at which he went home, so that *he did not go home* does not mean 'he never went home', but rather denies that he went home at some given time. We call the perfect, on the other hand, "indefinite," because it does not assume a particular time: *he has gone home* states that there is some time in the past at which he went home; there need not be a definite point assumed by the speaker (who indeed may well have forgotten when the subject had gone home).[38] Consequently, *he has not gone home* may imply "he has never gone home."

In the early centuries of vernacular grammar just the reverse holds true: the preterite is called the indefinite past (*passé indéfini*) and the perfect the definite past (*passé défini*), because the former requires some accompanying indication of the time of the action, whereas the latter does not.[39]

The first to define this difference in French grammar was apparently Jean Pillot, who writes in 1550 that

> the perfect preterite in the indicative is two-fold,[40] the first of which [*sic*] can be called 'Indefinite': for it signifies a time assuredly preterite, but not determined, and a thing long past. The second of these in truth denotes a more determinate perfect time, and but a little past, as when we say: *I'ay lu auiourd'hui l'Evangile.*[41]

His contemporary Robert Estienne says similarly that the "perfect preterite" is

> of two sorts: one is simple, which denotes the perfect action or passion: of which nonetheless the time is not well determined, in that it depends on something else, as, *Ie uei le Roy lors qu'il fut corrone. . . .*[42] The other is composed of the verb *avoir*[43] and a participle of past time: and it signifies time which is completely past, not requiring anything following which may be necessary to give completion to the sense: as, *I'ay veu le Roy.*[44]

The periphrastic perfect is "determined" by the fact that the time of the action is immediately prior to, or continues into, the present (as in "I have been here an hour"). As in the ancient theory, the present perfect is a recent past and the preterite a relatively more distant one.[45]

The difference of preterite and pluperfect could not be accounted for in terms of definiteness, however. Nebrija's Spanish grammar of 1492 presents an instructive innovation in this regard. He defines the pluperfect as "that [tense] in which something had been done, when something was done, as 'io te avia amado, cuando tu me amaste'."[46] This is essentially the view that the pluperfect refers to a time earlier than some given time in the past.

Nebrija's understanding of the tense is essentially that of Scaliger, who criticizes the term *plusquamperfectum*, saying that "one time cannot be more perfect than another."[47] He argues that the imperfect and perfect may refer to the very same time, and that all that is implied by the Greek term *hupersuntelikón* is that the pluperfect refers to something "beyond" the perfect from the present, so that *transperfectum* would have been a better translation for the term.

Richard Johnson, following Scaliger, is very critical of the concept of a "perfectly past time" found in Lily's English grammar.[48] The ancient definition of the pluperfect as representing "an action long past," found in Lily's Latin grammar,[49] is attacked by Johnson, who notes "that the Preterpluperfect Tense may be us'd of a Time lately Past, nay even but just Past," as in Scaliger's example *I had read the verse yesterday before I drank.*[50] (On the other hand, the perfect may be used of the distant past: *England has only once been ruled by an unmarried queen.*)

Johnson, like Nebrija (and Scaliger), treats the pluperfect as a past relative to some time itself past (''a thing perfected before some other''), a past-in-the-past. There are only hints of the relative tenses in such Renaissance writers as Nebrija, however, who, if he defines the pluperfect as a relative past, does not define the other tenses in relative terms.

The theory of relative tenses, if not originated by Scaliger, was certainly perfected by him. Scaliger, in *De causis linguae Latinae libri tredecim* (1540), is apparently the first to distinguish *absolute tenses,* which are regarded purely from the point of view of the present (the moment of speech or writing), from *relative tenses*, which are regarded from the point of view of another time.[51]

The perfect (presumably in its historical, preterite sense) for him simply ''shows a complete[52] action, of which no part remains [to be done].'' For him the pluperfect is, as we have seen, an action already past in relation to another time itself past. The imperfect is a present relative to the past. Of *legebam, quum venisti* 'I was reading when you came', he writes, ''nothing intervenes between the reading and the arrival.''[53]

In the *Grammaire générale* the influence of Scaliger is evident. Apart from the three ''simple'' tenses, ''considered simply in their nature,'' there are ''compound'' tenses, ''as it has been thought proper to mark also each of these tenses, with respect to another, by one word; other inflexions have been therefore invented in the verbs, which may be called compound tenses, and are three in number.''[54]

The *preterimperfect* ''marks the past in relation to the present'' and

> does not signify the thing simply and properly as done, but as imperfect, and present with respect to a thing which is nevertheless already past. Thus when I say, *cum intravit, caenabam, I was at supper when he came in*; the action of supping is indeed past with regard to the time, in which I speak; but I mark it as present, with respect to the thing of which I speak; which is the entrance of such a person.

Similarly the *preterpluperfect* is said to mark something as ''past not only in itself, but likewise with regard to some other thing, which is also past.'' The future perfect ''denotes the time to come, with relation to the past . . . as past with respect to another thing to come.'' They note the lack of a fourth, ''compound'' tense, ''future with relation to the present,'' which would bring the number of future tenses up to that of the compound preterites.

It is to be noticed, in this treatment by the *Grammaire générale*, that whether a tense is absolute or compound is determined solely by its meaning and has nothing to do with its form. It is true that the complex pluperfect and future perfect of the Romance languages are, in its view, compound, but so is the simplex imperfect. Its use of the term ''compound'' (tense) is different from our use of the term ''complex.''

Grammarians of English and German working within this tradition generally treat the periphrastic futures (and conditionals) of these languages as absolute and not compound tenses. Although couched in terms of his theory of aspect, Harris distinguishes aorist or ''indefinite'' tenses which ''mark Present, Past and Future Time . . . without reference to any Beginning, Middle, or End'' from ''definite'' tenses which do.[55] (The preterite is for him still indefinite, while the perfect is definite.) He calls the future, *I shall write*, the "Aorist of the Future" because it does not mark any aspectual distinctions, but merely (and "absolutely") refers to future action—this despite the fact that it is complex in form.

Similarly, Aichinger writes that the "tenses are mainly three, the *present, past, future*."[56] He goes on to say of the future that "besides the simple [future], it is mixed with the three kinds of past [the imperfect, *unvollkommene*; perfect, *vollkommene*; and more-than-perfect, *mehr als vollkommene*]." This "mixture" is defined in terms of meaning, not form, however. Aichinger says:

> The *futurum imperfecto mixtum*[57] . . . contrasts with the *futurum simplex*[58] just as the *imperfectum coniunctiui*[59] does with the *praesens*. It designates something that will happen, if a certain condition is already fulfilled: or it designates a negation of the *futurum*, which is prevented by a circumstance; or something, about which one is uncertain, whether it will follow or not. E.g., *Ich wuerde gehen, wenn mir der Gang bezahlet wuerde; Wir hofften, er wuerde Israel erloesen.*[60]

Another observation to be made in regard to the scheme in the *Grammaire générale* is that the relative tenses are only present and past, never future. This was originally because the conditional was understood by grammarians to be a subjunctive tense, so that no future-in-the-past was recognized. Nor did any of the familiar languages have tenses which were recognized as future-in-the-present, much less future-in-the-future.

Moreover, the relative tenses are related only to the past and future, because the present was considered indivisible. How could there be a "past-in-the-present"? The fundamental insight that the perfect often serves precisely as a past-in-relation-to-the-present could not be captured in the traditional theories, and as late as 1887 Madvig continues to refuse to use terms like *praeteritum in praesenti*, though he comes close to a fully relative system of tenses which loses the distinction of absolute and relative tenses, and in which the absolute tenses are past, present, and future "in relation to the present."

Madvig not only treated the Latin periphrastic futures (*scripturus eram* 'I was about to write' and *scripturus ero* 'I shall be about to write') as compound tenses in relation to the past and future respectively, but revised the very concept of relative tense. Where the *Grammaire générale* regards the imperfect, for example, as a past in relation to the present, because the action is absolutely past but at the same time is present relative to some past time, Madvig understands it to be a present-in-the-past (*praesens in praeterito*), because it requires an implicit past time at which the action is understood to have been happening.

Madvig's system is this[61]:

	PRAESENS	PRAETERITUM	FUTURUM
	Scribo	Scripsi	Scribam
In Praeterito.	Scribebam, I was writing (at that time).	Scripseram, I had written.	Scripturus eram (fui), I was (at that time) on the point of writing.
In Futuro.	Scribam, I shall (then) write.	Scripsero, I shall have written.	Scripturus ero, I shall (then) be on the point of writing.

He adds: "Besides these a future thing is designated as *now* at hand (and referred to the present) in a particular way, by the periphrasis *scripturus sum.*"

Following the tradition, Madvig does not label the first line "*in praesenti*," and says that "the thing asserted is either simply referred to one of the three leading tenses . . . or stated (mediately, relatively) with reference to a certain past or future point of time." [62] But for all that, his is very nearly a fully relative scheme; he admits future relative tenses, and in his remark on *scripturus sum* comes close to admitting a tense which is relative to the present.

I shall examine in the next chapter the criticisms Jespersen makes of Madvig's scheme; here I need only point out two peculiarities. First, Madvig has two different forms for the *futurum in praeterito*, formed respectively with the imperfect (*eram*) and perfect (*fui*) of 'be'. Second, the future (*scribam*, 'I shall write') occurs in two positions: as a "leading" tense in its own right, and as a *praesens in futuro*. This is the traditional distinction of indefinite (aoristic) and definite, but imperfect, future which is found both in the *Grammaire générale* and in Scaliger.

The future perfect Madvig calls a *praeteritum in futuro*—a past in the future. This seems not to have occurred to any ancient writer. The Greek future perfect was accounted a definite tense of the near future, as opposed to the indefinite future. Priscian rejects the division of the future and is constrained to regard the future perfect as a subjunctive. In the Varronian tradition the future perfect represents an action complete in the future.

The future perfect proved troublesome for the grammatical tradition, occasioning from the start considerable confusion. The earliest grammarian known to have distinguished two Latin futures is Asper (ca. 600 A.D.), who writes that "the grades of the future are two: perfect, as *legam* and pluperfect, as *legero.*" [63]

There is some controversy as to how William Grocyn treated the future perfect. It was Grocyn (ca. 1442–1519), godfather of Lily and friend of Erasmus and Colet (all of whom wrote important grammars), who first revived that rival of relative tense theory, the Varronian theory. [64] Grocyn published next to nothing, and in his lifetime his theory became known only by word of mouth. [65] Michael's presentation of Grocyn's scheme is this:

present imperfect	*scribo*	'I write'
present perfect	*scripsi*	'I wrote, have written'
future imperfect	*scribam*	'I shall write'
future *exactum*	*scripsero*	'I shall have written'
preter[ite] imperfect	*scribebam*	'I was writing'
preter[ite] perfect	*scripseram*	'I had written'

Scaliger writes that he prefers Grocyn's theory to those of the ancients; the future perfect does not predict the "celerity" of a happening—that it will occur soon—but rather "the completion of the deed." [66] Scaliger reports a contrast between the imperfect (*amabo*) and the perfect (*amavero*) futures, which he attributes to Grocyn.

But the grammarian Thomas Linacre attributes to Grocyn the term "*futurum exactum* or *absolutum.*" [67] This latter term is used by Scaliger; the former Linacre attributes to Julius Pomponius (d. 1498), the first editor of Varro.[68] Erasmus describes the future perfect as being "like a future mixed with the sense of the preterite."[69]

The *futurm exactum* was generally understood in the tradition to be a past-in-the-future. The question is what Grocyn meant by the term. If he did use *exactum,* it is likely that he (and Pomponius) would have meant nothing more than Scaliger did by *absolutum,* namely, perfect.

It is not entirely clear what is meant by "future perfect" as used by traditional grammarians. The term is found in Nebrija's Latin grammar of 1508, Dubois's French grammar of 1531, and Oliger's German one of 1573.[70] But is is not clear if they meant anything more than what Aichinger meant by *"futurum exactum* or *perfecto mixtum,"* 'exact future or future mixed with the perfect'.[71]

Theories of relative tense were one approach to solving the problem posed by the vernacular tense systems. But such theories were not completely successful in doing so, and had to compete with alternative accounts—many, but not all, crucially based on the theory of Varro.

d. Aspectual and Other Theories

Although the theory of relative tenses seems in some respects less insightful than the Varronian system, since it does not account in a systematic way for aspectual distinctions, it is not clear that it really differs from it in any substantive way. Nor is it entirely clear that the two types of theory are not simply terminology variants of each another. For one thing, just what the followers of Varro meant by "perfect" and "imperfect" is not known.

Varro distinguishes pairs of perfect and imperfect tenses on the basis of the two types of stem found in Latin. This is a great advance over the theory of Dionysius, in that it takes form into account, rather than relying solely on judgments of meaning, and in that it reconciles the three times with the six tenses of Latin without introducing any concepts extrinsic to the grammar of the language (like definiteness), that is, concepts which are not actually marked. But it has its costs: for example, it has no category for the aorist sides of the perfect and the future.

The perfect tenses designate actions which are complete at the time in question. The pluperfect, for example, represents an action complete by some time in the past and no longer ongoing at that time. The imperfect, on the contrary, represents an action incomplete at some point in the past. We find many authors therefore wrongly defining the imperfect as representing action extending into the present, which seemed to them to follow from the fact that the action was incomplete in the past.

Defined in this way, it is apparent that there is no very great difference between an action which was complete at a given point in the past and a (complete) action which had taken place prior to that point. Varronian aspect theory, as interpreted by the rationalist grammarians, and relative tense theory of the *Grammaire générale* kind, perhaps do not differ as much as they might seem to on the surface.

In Scaliger we find both the roots of the *Grammaire générale* theory and approval of Grocyn's theory.

It is plain that Scaliger's account of the tenses left ample scope for either kind of interpretation. Not only did relative tense theory descend from it, but Harris makes it plain that, in developing his aspectual theory of the tenses, he believes himself to be fully following in the footsteps not only of the *Grammaire générale* and Scaliger, but even Theodore Gaza (1398–1478), whose theory is essentially that of Dionysius and Apollonius with a touch of the Stoics'.[72]

Even in James Pickbourn's grammar of 1789, in which the terms "definite" and "indefinite" are used for the first time in their modern senses, there are resonances of both Harris and the relative tense tradition. The difference between aspect and relative tense in traditional grammar involves a question of emphasis and seemingly does not entail, as it would today, a real difference.

In practice the two concepts have given rise, and continue to this day to give rise, to considerable controversy in regard to the tense systems of various languages which lack absolute tense, for example Classical (Quranic) Arabic and Biblical Hebrew, and the sign languages of the deaf.[73] These languages are tenseless, in that they have no explicit markers of "time" (past, present, future) but do have markers of something like aspectual distinctions.

But many scholars have treated these languages as involving relative tense rather than aspect. We shall see in chapter 8 that what criteria would lead one to prefer one or the other treatment for the so-called "tenseless" languages depends on how aspect is defined. Comrie is led to argue, for example, for markers in Arabic which combine *both* aspectual and relative-temporal meaning.[74]

The Varronian theory differs from the relative tense tradition not only in basing itself on aspectual oppositions rather than relative tense, but also in rejecting the distinction of definite and indefinite in simple tenses, which the distinction of aspect renders superfluous. For Harris, the simple tenses are all "indefinite" or "aorist," marking action as past, present, or future, and the complex ones all "definite," distinguishing the beginning, middle, and end of actions.[75] This is different from the traditional scheme, in that earlier thinkers did not have an inceptive aspect marking beginning. Furthermore, Harris sees the imperfect as indicating not a lack of completion, but an ongoingness of action.

Harris's system is this[76]:

> Aorist of the Present
> gráphō. *Scribo*. I write.
> Aorist of the Past
> égrapsa. *Scripsi*. I wrote.
> Aorist of the Future
> grápsō. *Scribam*. I shall write.
>
> Inceptive Present
> méllō gráphein. *Scripturus sum*. I am going to write.
> Middle or extended Present
> tugkhánō gráphōn. *Scribo* or *Scribens sum*. I am writing.
> Completive Present
> gégrapha. *Scripsi*. I have written.

Inceptive Past
émellon gráphein. *Scripturus eram.* I was beginning to write.
Middle or extended Past
égraphon or etúgkhanon gráphōn. *Scribebam.* I was writing.
Completive Past
egegráphein. *Scripseram.* I had done writing.
Inceptive Future
mellḗsō gráphein. *Scripturus ero.* I shall be beginning to write.
Middle or extended Future
ésomai gráphōn. *Scribens ero.* I shall be writing.
Completive Future
ésomai gegraphṓs. *Scripsero.* I shall have done writing.

The virtue of Harris's scheme is that it can encompass a large number, if not all, of the many periphrastic tenses of English. Harris's system of tenses has a number of problems, however. It fails to systematically relate form to meaning. There is no way to extract from Harris's work, for example, what contributions each of the component forms makes to the meaning of the whole. Nothing in the theory suggests that the future participle of Latin (*scripturus*) has inceptive force, or the present participle of English ('writing') has that of extension.

There is no consideration of the principle of compositionality, which states that the meaning of a linguistic expression in part depends on the meanings of its constituent parts, nor is there concern for the systematicity of forms. Instead there is a grab bag of forms—*égraphon* is an extended past, as is *etugkhánon gráphein*; the completive present is exemplified by 'I have written', but the completive future by 'I shall have done writing', not 'I shall have written'.

By choosing to emphasize the beginning, middle, and end of a process, Harris moves away from the traditional Varronian distinction of completion. An event only begun is incomplete, to be sure, but the reverse is not necessarily true. Moreover, the theory fails to distinguish grammaticized distinctions from nongrammaticized ones; consequently many of the forms offered appear rather artificial (*etugkhánōn gráphein, scribens ero* 'I shall have done writing').

Harris's theory fails to deal with the reasons (if any) for the ambiguity of the Latin perfect; fails to distinguish *scribo* from *scribens sum*; and is rather awkward: Harris's inceptives were rejected as superfluous by most later writers.[77] There is a considerable sense of artificiality in the forms he cites, and the arrangement, while very "logical," fails to convincingly capture the facts of any of the languages. But Harris comes closer than Varro to an understanding of the semantics of aspect.

By deleting the inceptive and reverting to a more traditional terminology, Bishop Lowth achieves a sort of compromise between a purely Varronian system and Harris's[78]:

Indefinite or undetermined
present   love
past   loved
future   shall love

Definite or determined

present imperfect	am loving
present perfect	have loved
past imperfect	was loving
past perfect	had loved
future imperfect	shall be loving
future perfect	shall have loved

Lowth makes it clear that he means by "indefinite" what Harris means by "aorist"; the "definite" tenses are those which mark a distinction of perfect and imperfect.

The main advantage of Lowth's system is that it is possible to extract from it the generalization that the imperfect aspect is marked in English by some form of the auxiliary verb *be* plus the present participial ending (*-ing*) of the main verb, while the perfect is marked by a form of *have* plus the past participial ending (*-ed, -en*); Lowth speaks of "Imperfect and Perfect times."[79] This goes, potentially, a long way toward providing a systematic account of how distinctions of tense and aspect are marked in English, and toward reconciling a philosophical theory of tense of the Harris variety with the morphology and syntax of English.

Lowth's system solves many problems of earlier grammars. It provides a systematic theory of possible tenses (three times by two aspects, plus indefinite tenses neutral as to aspect), and accounts for the distinction of (present) perfect, pluperfect (past perfect), and (past) imperfect. It fails to say anything about relative tense, however, and its greatest shortcoming is its failure to distinguish definiteness of tense from that of aspect. The "indefinite" tenses are neutral as to aspect. But they are *not* indefinite as to tense, in either the Renaissance sense or the modern one.

Lowth's grammar is one of the first in modern times to take into account the forms of tense markers when classifying tenses. At about the same time (1761), James White published a grammar of English which also does so, albeit in a less enlightening way, as witness the treatment of the future perfect[80]:

present	love
1st past or historical tense	loved
2nd past	have loved
3rd past	had loved
1st future or prophetic tense	shall love
2nd future	will love
3rd future	will have loved

White's scheme is not untypical of traditional approaches. As late as 1898 we find a similarly unsystematic, form-based scheme of tenses in Sweet's *Syntax*, the second part of his *New English Grammar* (the passive forms are omitted here)[81]:

Indicative

present	I see
definite present	I am seeing
preterite	I saw
def. pret.	I was seeing
perfect	I have seen
def. perf.	I have been seeing
pluperfect	I had seen
def. plup.	I had been seeing

future	I shall see
def. fut.	I shall be seeing
future preterite	I should see
def. fut. pret.	I should be seeing
future perfect	I shall have seen
def. fut. perf.	I shall have been seeing
Conditional	
present	I should see
def. pres.	I should be seeing
preterite	I should have seen
def. pret.	I should have been seeing

The influence of systems such as those of Lowth and White, or of Priestley's (discussed below), is evident. Structurally parallel forms do not receive parallel treatment, however. *I should have* is not called the present perfect of the "conditional" mood, nor are the perfect and pluperfect called present and preterite perfects of the indicative.

But notional criteria are not consistent either, as is plain from a reading of Sweet's discussion of the tenses.[82] His system is largely an eclectic compromise between relative tense theory (*future preterite*), Varronian aspect theory (*future perfect*), and form-based grammar (the "definite" tenses).

Systems partly based on forms are in radical contrast to that of Pickbourn's *Dissertation on the English Verb* (1789), which, while introducing the modern distinction of definite tenses (which can presuppose given points in time) and indefinite tenses (which cannot), totally disregards form. Michael characterizes the book as "original, and deservedly described . . . as a 'truly great book.'" He sees Pickbourn's greatest contribution as the use of the terms *definite* and *indefinite* "to refer to the way in which any tense could be used." Pickbourn is "unusual, too, in recognizing the importance . . . of context . . . he was at times thinking of the function of the whole sentence and not only of the verb."[83]

Another noteworthy aspect of Pickbourn's work is his development of Harris's system of aspects. Whereas Lowth retreated to a strictly Varronian system of two aspects distinguished as to completion, Pickbourn extends Harris's scheme of aspects, arriving at a system in which there is a notion of the various phases of action—from being about to do something to having done it.[84]

Pickbourn's system is shown below.

TENSES BELONGING TO PRESENT TIME

———————	I have been { going / about } to write.	———————
Scripturus sum.	I am { going / about } to write.	{ Je vais / Je m'en vais } écrire.
Scribo.	{ I write, / I do write, / I am writing. }	J'écris.
———————	I have been writing.	———————
Scripsi.	I have written.	J'ai écrit.

TENSES BELONGING TO PAST TIME

Scripturus fueram.	I had been $\left\{\begin{array}{l}\text{going}\\\text{about}\end{array}\right\}$ to write. ———————	
Scripturus $\left\{\begin{array}{l}\text{eram}\\\quad\text{fui.}\end{array}\right\}$	I was $\left\{\begin{array}{l}\text{going}\\\text{about}\end{array}\right\}$ to write.	$\left\{\begin{array}{l}\text{J'allois}\\\text{Je m'en}\\\text{allois}\end{array}\right\}$ écrire.
Scribebam.	I was writing.	J'écrivois.
Scribebam.	$\left\{\begin{array}{l}\text{I wrote,}\\\text{I did write,}\end{array}\right.$ $\left\{\begin{array}{l}\text{when used inde-}\\\text{finitely, }i.e.\text{ to}\\\text{signify habits.}\end{array}\right\}$	J'écrivois.
Scripsi.	$\left\{\begin{array}{l}\text{I wrote,}\\\text{I did write,}\end{array}\right.$ $\left\{\begin{array}{l}\text{(when used defi-}\\\text{nitely)}\end{array}\right\}$	J'écrivis.
———————	I had been writing.	———————
Scripseram.	I had written.	$\left\{\begin{array}{l}\text{J'avois}\\\text{J'eus}\end{array}\right\}$ écrit.

TENSES BELONGING TO FUTURE TIME

Scripturus ero.	I shall or will be $\left\{\begin{array}{l}\text{going}\\\text{about}\end{array}\right\}$ to write. ———————	
Scribam.	I shall or will $\left\{\begin{array}{l}\text{write,}\\\text{be writing.}\end{array}\right\}$	J'écrirai.
———————	I shall or will have been writing. ———————	
Scripsero	I shall or will have written.	J'aurai écrit.

There are nonetheless suggestions of a Lowthian aspectual system in Pickbourn: "The [participle in -*ing*] denotes an imperfect or unfinished action; and [that in -*ed*] a perfect or finished one. . . . [The -*ing* form] represents an action as having already been begun, as being in progress, or going on, but as not yet finished. Thus, yesterday at ten o'clock, he was *writing* a letter."[85]

He uses "definite" and "indefinite" in the modern senses: "By an aoristical, or indefinite tense, is . . . meant a tense which cannot be used in ascertaining the precise time of an individual action; and by a definite tense, is meant one that is capable of being applied to that purpose."[86] These terms are applied equally by him to tense ("time") and aspect ("action"), but the two are distinguished, as shown by his examples:

indefinite with respect to:
   action and time
      wisdom EXCELLS folly
      sometimes he WORKS
   action only
      when she first appeared upon the stage she DANCED elegantly
   time only
      Mr. Horne Tooke PUBLISHED an excellent grammatical work, called The
      Diversion of Purley

According to him, the first two examples do not fix definite times, nor do they indicate whether the actions are complete or incomplete; the third example fixes the time precisely but is ambiguous as to aspect; and the last example is clear as to the perfect aspect but indefinite as to time.

Pickbourn also notes an aspectual distinction made in the "complex" future between continuance (*shall have been loving*) and completion (*shall have loved*).[87]

There are echoes of a relative tense system in his notion of "tenses belonging to" the three times. He calls the progressives "definite," the perfects "indefinite." The past progressive, accordingly, is definite and belongs to the past. But it is definite precisely because it fixes the time of the event absolutely, as present relative to the past, whereas the perfect fixes it only relatively, as past in relation to the past.

Pickbourn is not a system-builder; the greatest weakness of his approach is in its lack of an overarching system. Pickbourn's is very much a mixed, eclectic system, with elements of Varronian aspect theory, relative tense theory, Guillaume-like phases, and yet other categories. It was a brilliant work, but left behind no solid foundation for further research.

It is particularly weak in its lack of a definite methodology. The approaches of Lowth and White are equally based on usage, and though perhaps weaker in their abilities to elucidate forms, are sounder in their methodologies. They reflect to some extent a movement away from rationalism in grammar and a transition to a new conception of grammar.

A number of developments contributed at the end of the eighteenth century to an empiricist reaction to rationalist grammar, and the replacement of "logical," universal semantic grammar with one based more closely on the morphological and syntactic facts of particular languages.

Where languages were descended from Latin, as were French, Italian, Spanish, and Portuguese, and retained significant similarities to it, the adaptation of Latin grammar could be viewed as trivial. It was not so with the Germanic and other Indo-European languages, much less the non-Indo-European languages of Europe (e.g., Finnish, Hungarian, Turkish). Here the application of Latin grammar was not as easy a task.

The advancement of empiricism at the expense of rationalism was an aspect of a general cultural revolution in which the age of Romanticism succeeded that of Reason, and nationalism elevated the vernaculars to the status of bearers of national consciousnesses in opposition to the internationalism associated with the classical tongues. The more the modern languages were seen to merit serious study, the more they were seen to deserve a status coequal with Latin. There was little room for universalism or an appeal to the pristine logicality of Latin, nor did logicality as such appeal to the Romantic mentality.

It was also at this time that modern empirical science was evolving out of "natural philosophy," and it is no accident that the staunchest advocate of an empirical, non-a-priori approach to grammar should have been an important scientist, Joseph Priestley, the discoverer of oxygen, writing at about the same time (1762) as White and Lowth. Priestley argues that the

only natural rule for the use of technical terms to express time, &c. is to apply them
to distinguish the different modifications of words. . . . A little reflection may . . .
suffice to convince any person, that we have no more business with a *future tense* in
our language, than we have with the whole system of Latin moods and tenses; because we have no modifications of our verbs to correspond with it.[88]

Consequently he systematically assigns complex forms to different "orders,"
depending on the number and nature of the auxiliary verbs involved:

first order	present	shall love
	preterite	should love
second order	present	am loving
	preterite	was loving
first double compound	present	shall be loving
	preterite	should be loving
second double compound	present	have been loving
	preterite	had been loving
third double compound	present	shall have been loving
	preterite	should have been loving
third order	present	am loved
	preterite	was loved
first double compound (etc.)	present	shall be loved

This is very much in the same vein as White's grammar, but as befits the work of
a scientist, it is considerably more systematized.

Priestley admits that on this basis there can be no universal scheme of tenses,
and Michael characterizes his treatment as enabling him "to see the irrelevance,
for English, of many inherited grammatical categories," but also as leading "to
misleading oversimplifications." The difficulty with such an empirical method is
that it provides no guide to analysis, and once the analysis is completed, assigns
no meaning, or at least no language-independent meaning, to the sundry forms of
the verb. To say that *shall love* is a first-order compounded tense says nothing; to
say that it is a (periphrastic) future says a lot.

The rise of empiricist thought in philosophy progressed in tandem with the rise
of empirical science. Especially in the English-speaking world, rationalism as a
philosophical approach to psychology, logic, and semantics was fading away. The
new philosophy was one suited to the requirements of the new science. Although
theories of a quasi-rationalist tinge persisted well into the twentieth century and
served to inform idealist theories of mind and language, the empiricist viewpoint
interacted significantly with the new descriptive linguistics attempting to describe
the various "new" non-Indo-European languages which European exploration was
revealing to the world—languages for which the "logical" grammar based on
Latin and the European vernaculars was often radically unsuited.

e. Tense in Non-Indo-European Languages

The rise of empiricism resulted in a descriptive and structural approach in linguistics, but only after some time had passed. Many writers were ignorant of these
new developments. It remained as true after 1800 as before that non-Indo-

European languages were seen by authors of grammars to conform to the Latin model.

Often enough the first grammarians were missionaries, explorers, or traders with no special training in linguistics and only an elementary, schoolroom acquaintance with grammar; their intent was not a scientific one, but rather practical and pedagogic. Languages of distinct structural types tended to be treated as if synthetic, and the systems of meanings of the particular languages in question, as reflected in their morphosyntactic systems, were obscured if not completely ignored.

Today it is recognized, for example, that in Turkish sundry ''tense''-marking endings (past, conditional, evidential) are added to stems already formed with ''tense''-markers (present, future, aorist, inferential, necessitative, evidential, conditional, subjunctive); and further, that a conditional ending may be added atop the past (evidential) or inferential.[89]

The simple ''present'' form *gel.iyor.um* 'I am coming' (come-present-I) may be expanded by the addition of a past (evidential) marker (*-du*) to *gel.iyor.du.m* 'I was coming'; or by that of a conditional marker (*-(i)sa*) to *gel.iyor.sa.m* 'if I am coming'; or by that of inferential (past) marker (*-muş*) to *gel.iyor.muş.um* 'I was said to be coming, I gather that I was coming'. Or it may be further expanded to the past conditional *gel.iyor.du.ysa.m* 'if I was coming', or to the inferential conditional *gel.iyor.muş.sa.m* 'if I was, as they say, coming'.

This ability of an agglutinative language like Turkish to pile up endings is absent from Thomas Vaughan's *Grammar of the Turkish Language* of 1709. Vaughan finds in the language the familiar present, preterimperfect, preterperfect, and future tenses[90]:

present	*severem*	'I love'
preterimperfect	*severidum*	'I did love'
preterperfect	*sevdum*	'I have loved'
future	*sevaim*	'I shall/will love'

(An earlier 1670 grammar by William Seaman had also found a preterpluperfect, but Vaughan rejects this.) The subjunctive is said to have the same tenses.[91]

Vaughan recognizes the agglutinativity of Turkish verbs. For example, he notes that the preterimperfect ''is formed by adding [the] Terminations to . . . the third person Singular of the Present Tense Indicative.'' But the analysis is incorrect, does not recognize the significance of stems in Turkish, and fails completely to exhibit the systematic relationship of form to meaning.

Similarly, Manchu allows a sequence of endings, and can even incorporate into the verb the auxiliary *bi* 'be'. Manchu has, properly speaking, no finite, indicative verb forms at all. It does have two sets of non-finite forms, the participles (verbal adjectives) and converbs (verbal adverbs or gerunds)[92]:

	participle	converb
imperfect	*ara.ra*	*ara.me*
perfect	*ara.ha*	*ara.fi*

The participles may stand by themselves as predicates, in which case *araha* means 'wrote' and *arara* 'will write'.[93]

The plain forms of the auxiliary can be incorporated into a verb to form a "tense." Added to the imperfect converb (*-me* then becomes *-m*), it forms the present (non-past) tense: *ara.m.bi* 'writes, is writing, will write'.[94] Added to the perfect participle, it forms a perfect; *ara.ha.bi* means 'has written'. But the auxiliary *bi* may take all the forms other verbs do. Consequently forms such as *ara.m.bi.he, ara.m.bi.me, ara.m.bi.he.bi,* and so forth, are all possible, each conveying a different temporal-aspectual meaning.[95]

We see none of this in the 1892 grammar of P. G. von Möllendorff, who observes that to "express the moods and tenses the Manchu verb has 23 forms," of which "eight are the fundamental forms" upon which the additional ones are based.[96] The "fundamental forms" include:

present	*arambi*	'I write'
preterite	*araha*	'I wrote'
future	*arara*	'I shall write'
conditional	*araci*	'I should write, if I write, should I write'

The other forms add various affixes to these. For example:

imperfect	*arambihe*	'I was writing'
indefinite past	*arahabi*	'I have written'
pluperfect	*arahabihe*	'I had written'
past conditional	*arahabici*	'if I had written'

At the other extreme from agglutinative languages like these are isolating, analytic languages like Samoan, which marks distinctions of tense, aspect, and mood with separate particles and not in the verb itself.[97] Neffgen's (1902) grammar of Samoan lists present, imperfect, perfect (these last two with identical German glosses), and future tenses.[98] Of the conjunctive (subjunctive) mood he says only that "the so-called conjunctive is rare in Samoan; it is introduced by the particle 'ana' and the following verb has precisely the usual form."[99] Of the tenses he says that

> [the] Samoan verb differs considerably from other languages; there is no real conjugation such as in the European languages. The verb remains unchanged in all tenses in the singular and only in the plural does a change occur, which depends almost solely on euphony,[100] and for which up to now no fast rules have been found. There are no endings for the indication of person and tense. The tenses are expressed by putting adverbs before [the verb], if such is necessary.[101]

This account obviously imposes categories on the language which are not completely appropriate.

Fr. Minguella in his Tagalog grammar notes that "rigorously speaking, in Tagalog, there are only three tenses—past, present, and future. . . . Those [tenses] that correspond to the imperfect preterite, pluperfect preterite, and future perfect of the Spanish conjugation, are designated by context, or by means of determining adverbs."[102] He also finds a subjunctive in Tagalog, though this consists simply of the indicative verb accompanied by various "adverbs" (i.e., particles).[103]

It is interesting to observe that these grammars apply to languages of the most diverse types the system of tenses (and moods) developed for the classical languages, and do so without any regard to (1) the morphology and syntax of the languages in question, (2) the internal structure of the tense systems of these languages, or (3) the semantics of the tenses in question.

The number of tenses is rarely in accord with the number of morphological forms. Parallel endings which do not mark tense distinctions, and hence call into question the status of the "tense" endings, are ignored. The labels on the tenses may or may not depend on the semantic values of the affixes and/or auxiliary verbs used to mark them. The forms of verbs are not criterial for their semantic status.

Consequently quite parallel tenses will be marked by unparallel constructions, or parallel constructions will mark unparallel distinctions. In Manchu, for example, adding -he to the present yields the imperfect, but adding it to the indefinite past yields the pluperfect. It would have been much more revealing if these had been called "present imperfect," "past imperfect," "present perfect," and "past perfect" respectively.

The labels assigned to the tenses rarely are very informative as to how the forms are actually used. By implication they have roughly the same range as the corresponding tenses in European languages. But the European languages differ considerably in their use of the various tenses. Moreover, vital clues as to the meaning and use of the sundry tenses are often ignored in the grammars, partly as the result of misleading labeling. In von Möllendorff's Manchu grammar, the presence of -bi in the "simple" present form is ignored, and no conclusions regarding parallelism to the other forms containing it are drawn.

Tense distinctions marked in each language which have no place in the Latinate system are simply ignored or treated as non-tense phenomena. On the other hand, much that is not tense (or mood) is treated as such, by analogy with true tense forms, as when von Möllendorff sets up a category of indefinite verb in -le *(arale)*. This is simply the nominalized verb, 'writing'.[104]

Latinate, aprioristic grammar is not in itself misplaced in this context. To be sure, a proper regard for the facts of particular languages is necessary. But grammatical categories cannot be developed directly from the structures of individual languages—any more than they can be imposed on languages—if they are to be useful for understanding temporal semantics.

What is chiefly lacking in these grammars is a full appreciation, which was to come only in the twentieth century with Saussure, that form and meaning are separate, although linked. Each language has a system of forms that can be used to express meanings, which have their own system. The two systems need not be homologous, although there must be a systematic linkage between them (albeit partly interfered with by idiomaticity): language works because we can "read off" from the expressions of languages what they mean. That regularity, analogy, is tied exclusively to meaning (or exclusively to form) is a critically mistaken assumption of premodern grammatical theory.

f. Jespersen's Structuralist Approach to Tense

It is only in the first decades of the twentieth century, with the Danish grammarian Otto Jespersen, one of the greatest students of the English language, that the traditional treatments of tense are superseded and the (linguistic) scientific study of tense begins. Jespersen is a crux: at once the last of the traditional grammarians and the first modern linguist-grammarian.

Jespersen broke with the tradition of grammatical thought and initiated new and more fruitful lines of approach to the study of the verb which continue to shape research today. While little if any of his own thinking on tense has gone unchallenged, Jespersen's works remain a fruitful source of matters for investigation, and many of the issues he raised remain controversial and poorly understood to this day.

Though he was a descriptivist and an empiricist, seeking to ground his grammars in observed facts rather than a priori concepts, Jespersen was nonetheless a universalist. He believed that behind the myriad idiosyncrasies of particular languages there lay a set of universals, of generalizations holding true for all tongues, if only these could be abstracted from the various facts of individual languages, as he attempted to do in *The Philosophy of Grammar* (1924). For Jespersen, it is only by understanding the properties of language in general that we can provide an adequate understanding of those of individual languages.

Earlier writers had been hard put to reconcile the "rational" system of tenses their theories predicated with the various actual systems revealed by the investigation of languages. Some writers, such as Priestley, abandoned any universal system as illusory. Others saw in actual systems illogicality, or mere chance alteration of a historical or ideal underlying schematism. Some fit the morphological and syntactic facts into a rational Procrustean bed by neglecting ambiguities, ignoring inconvenient forms, or finding distinctions where there were none.

Jespersen was able for the first time to reconcile a universal, rational system with particular facts, without at the same time either distorting the facts or trivializing the relationship between them and the theoretical concepts. He achieved this because he was able to go a long way toward reconciling the seemingly contradictory theories of multiple past theory, Varronian tense-aspect theory, and relative tense theories, accommodating all three within a coherent, consistent theory of tenses.

Jespersen is able to resolve the paradoxical ill-matching of formal devices and semantic categories by explicitly distinguishing form, function, and notional meaning. He gives as an example the preterite or past tense. For Jespersen this is a "functional" category, mediating between the various forms used in English to express it—the ending *-ed* in the case of most verbs, and vowel change *(run, ran)*, replacement *(go, went)*, and so on in the case of others—and the various notions which it is used in English to convey: not only past time but unreality (*I wish we knew*), futurity (*it is time you went to bed*), and various others.[105]

As well as "pointing" to the forms, he sees the preterite as pointing to various "notions." Forms belong to "the world of sounds" (phonology), notions to "the world of ideas" (semantics). For Jespersen, meanings are ideas: one of the ideas expressed or conveyed by the preterite tense is that of past time.

But Jespersen does not regard the preterite as simply pointing to a notion of past time. Rather he gives five different notions corresponding to the preterite tense. For him, one functional category can correspond to different notions. The preterite in English (as above) may convey an unreal situation at the present time, a future event, or something true at all times, or it may represent a "shifted" present tense, as in indirect discourse.

The distinction of category (e.g., preterite) and notion (e.g., past time) is a major and significant advance. Earlier scholars were generally concerned with relating the forms of languages with meanings, ideas, or categories which were either subjective and psychological, or objective and logical. Although grammatical categories such as "preterite" were set up, this was really a shorthand for referring to the place that a particular form had in a paradigm of the word-and-paradigm type, as in "*went* is the past tense of *go*."

If a form is ambiguous, as the Latin perfect is, it can be dealt with in a traditional model only by assigning it different categories. Such an approach can lead to over- or underdifferentiation of grammatical categories, since it tends to obscure the difference between semantic and grammatical categories.

Varro was forced to ignore the ambiguity of the Latin perfect because he had no formal category for its second meaning. This does not imply, however, that it would not be a mistake to assign two different grammatical categories to the Latin future on the grounds that it is sometimes imperfect, but sometimes indifferent to the opposition of aspects, and thus to admit two different futures, as Madvig does.[106]

This sort of treatment also tends to obscure the difference between the meaning of a form and its various uses. The present perfect may well imply recency, whereas the pluperfect implies distance in time. But these implications are no part of the meanings of these forms. It is quite possible to use the perfect of a distant past (*England has only once been ruled by an unmarried woman*) or the pluperfect of a recent one (*I had barely gotten up this morning when she called*).

Similarly, in a great many languages the present tense may be used for the future, especially with verbs of motion (*Tom flies to Rome on Saturday, is flying to Rome on Saturday*); equally it may be used for the past (the historical present: *Napoleon stands before the Pyramids and addresses his troops*). But clearly the present tense does not mean what either the future or the past means, though it can sometimes be *used* in lieu of one or the other of them.

Earlier scholars were forced either to assume that each tense had only one label, roughly one meaning or use, thereby ignoring the many different uses of the tenses; or to recognize different uses, but to treat these as idiomatic and not truly grammatical; or to regard the tenses as ambiguous and place some tenses in more than one position each on their charts. Jespersen, on the other hand, can capture the many uses in the variety of notions attached to a tense, while capturing the essential unity of the grammatical category itself.

The fact that languages can differ in the uses they make of tenses does not affect the categories themselves, nor does a difference in use imply a difference in category. This enables Jespersen to define a universal set of functional categories, while recognizing the vast differences in use of tenses in various languages with identical labels.

The English perfect, for example, sometimes is equivalent to the present in Romance or in other Germanic languages: *I've been living here for ten years*,

German *ich wohne (schon) 10 Jahre hier* 'I live (already) 10 years here'.[107] There is no contradiction for Jespersen between the equation of the perfect with the German present and the fact that the English perfect is the ''same'' tense as the German one, while different from the German present.

Jespersen's ideas reflect the new structural linguistics which emerged at the beginning of the twentieth century from the descriptive linguistics of the previous one. In the course of the nineteenth century a de facto split had developed between a field which called itself comparative philology and which studied the historical development of languages, and an anthropological or descriptive linguistics which sought to find new means for the study of the grammars of the ''new'' languages discovered by European exploration. Comparative philology had its roots in classical studies and in Indo-European philology, while descriptive linguistics came out of grammar but also out of philosophy and anthropology.

The two fields were not incompatible and some scholars practiced both. But the Swiss linguist Ferdinand de Saussure established the distinction between a purely historical or *diachronic* linguistics and the purely *synchronic* one which sought to describe things as they were at one time, usually the present, and explicate them not in historical but in purely phenomenological terms.

For Saussure the failure to distinguish the two is a major methodological and theoretical weakness in earlier studies, for

> succession in time does not exist insofar as the speaker is concerned. He is confronted with a state. That is why the linguist who wishes to understand a state must discard all knowledge of everything that produced it and ignore diachrony. He can enter the minds of speakers only by completely suppressing the past. The intervention of history can only falsify his judgment.[108]

Saussure further objected to the atomistic approach which diachronic and synchronic scholarship alike had earlier taken. By structuralism Saussure and later structuralists do not mean merely the doctrine that linguistic forms and the structures they enter into are better studied than their functions or uses, and that linguistic statements are to be couched in terms of structures rather than functions. Rather they mean that definitions and categories are not to be taken as absolute, but rather always as relative to a system.

Each language has a system of signs, defined by its phonology, morphology, and syntax. The place of any sign in this system is solely defined by the rules of the language and is independent of meaning and use. *Roses* bears the same relation to *rose* as does *residuaries* to *residuary*, which any speaker of English can attest, without even knowing what *residuary* means. Yet at the same time every language has a system of meanings. The meaning of *duckling* bears the same relation to that of *duck* as the meaning of *cub* does to *bear*. This relationship is independent of the signs used to express these meanings.

This leaves open the question of whether languages can differ in their systems of meanings. If we understand ''meanings'' in a traditional, idealistic sense, then this is surely true; Greek opposes the aorist to both the imperfect and the past perfect (pluperfect), but English has only the past tense. Even if we admit the periphrastic past progressive and past perfect, the systems are still different, since

English has a past perfect progressive with a meaning not like anything in Greek.

The relation of signifier and signified, Saussure insists, is arbitrary. There is no *necessary* reason why *hound*, for example, means 'hound' and not 'cat' (or, as it formerly did, 'dog').

For an atomist, an element of a language is simply an element; the vowel sound spelled *a* in standard French *passé* is a sound essentially identical to the first *a* in standard English *father* as regards phonetics, just as Latin *pater* means essentially what English *father* does. But the fact is that the French and English sounds, as systematic units, phonemes, differ greatly, since the French sound is (in standard French) in opposition to the vowel sound of *ma*, whereas English has no such opposition. The vowel of *tent* is pronounced in some dialects similarly to that of French *tint*, but the two sounds represent phonemes which do not correspond (one is nonnasal, the other nasal). Similarly, *pater* contrasts with *genitor*, while *father* has no such contrastive term—it means both '(male) head of the family' and 'natural male parent'.

Thus it is possible to say that two sounds are (phonetically, phenomenologically) identical, but also, without contradiction, to say that structurally they are different. They are different, in the same way a word or other expression in one language may translate an expression in another, may correspond in "speech" (*parole*) with it, without structurally corresponding to it, in the system of language (*langue*). And two expressions may correspond structurally without necessarily corresponding in *parole*.

For example, Jespersen lines up the past tenses of Greek, Latin, French, English, and German in a table.[109] He assigns them four distinct functions—present perfect, aorist or preterite (simple past tense), habitual imperfect, and descriptive imperfect. The various languages divide up this spectrum of functions differently. Standard German has only two forms—for 'wrote', *schrieb* and *hat geschrieben*. It marks all the categories but the perfect (*hat geschrieben*) with the preterite (*schrieb*). English goes further and differentiates the descriptive imperfect—the past progressive (*was writing*)—from the simple past. Greek, Latin, and French combine the imperfects into their imperfect tenses. But whereas Latin has only the perfect to mark both perfect and past, Greek distinguishes these as perfect and aorist, and standard French distinguishes them as perfect (*ai écrit*) and simple past (*écrivit*).

For Jespersen this survey shows "how some languages confuse time distinctions which in others are kept strictly apart." He is able to line up the corresponding tenses in terms of their real-world denotations and their functions in *parole*. He has language-independent categories through which the forms of different languages may correspond.

But we can see that, in terms of the systems of these languages themselves, the forms on each line do not correspond at all. Greek, formal French, and English have three different past tenses, but Latin and formal German only two. Even if we treat the Latin perfect as ambiguous and differentiate its "true" perfect meaning from its purely aorist meaning, the Latin perfect does not correspond to the "perfect" tenses of these other languages.

As part of the Latin system of signs, its perfect stem contrasts with an imperfect stem form, but Greek has three, not two, sets of stems. The modern languages contrast complex to simple forms, a distinction unknown to the classical tongues, but lack the kind of stem they had. As part of the system of meanings, Latin has three perfect tenses—all perfects correspond to non-perfects (save in the case of the aorist)—but Greek has at best a marginal future perfect. The modern languages have perfects in all tenses.

Jespersen is the first important grammarian who is also a structural linguist. His distinction of the functional category of "preterite," for example, and the "notion" of "past time" neatly allows one to capture the fact that both the Latin perfect and the English past tense express past time without conceding the obvious false point that both belong to the same functional category (even in Jespersen's universalist terms). The English and German perfects belong to the same category, but whereas the German can express the notion of purely past time (*Goethe hat* Hermann und Dorothea *geschrieben* 'Goethe wrote *Hermann und Dorothea*'),[110] the English cannot (!*Goethe has written* Hermann und Dorothea: which can be used in certain contexts but is not "in the past tense").

Jespersen is not fully structuralist in his thought, however. Saussure had proposed that the meaning of a form is its place in a system. But though Jespersen defines each tense once and for all as representing the corresponding time (e.g., the present tense expressing the present time), he recognized that languages differ in their number of tenses without necessarily failing to express the same times. His functional categories are options languages can select from; the tense system of each language is a partial exemplification of one universal system. The notions are distributed among different categories.

This is an advance over traditional models, which made the differences in systems totally unprincipled. But it is not a structuralist scheme, for the categories of tense forms are independent of the system of the language itself. Consequently there is no direct way of capturing the notion of grammatical categories—that is, systematic, obligatory categories as opposed to nongrammaticized, nonsystematic, nonobligatory ones. In this, Jespersen the traditional grammarian takes precedence over Jespersen the structural linguist.

Of the infinite number of distinctions which human languages can convey, some are regularized, systematized, grammatically marked: grammaticized distinctions. English has ways of conveying what the Turkish inferential and evidential forms convey, though it has no such grammatical distinction. Modal verbs may be used:

> Snow *must* have fallen.
> That *will* be Tom coming in now.
> I *can* see people moving over there.[111]

Certain quasi-performative verbs may also be used.[112]

> I *suppose* snow fell.
> I *gather* you want a raise.
> I *hear* Tom is ill.
> I *believe* snow fell.

Certain adverbs and interjections can likewise be used:

> *So* Tom has been here after all.
> *Probably* Tom was never here.
> *Ah*, snow has fallen!
> *Then* Tom wasn't the killer?

Also various special constructions:

> *I see*, Tom was never here at all.
> *They say* Tom was never here.
> *I'm told* Tom was never here.

Another conveyable distinction not grammaticized in English is that of completive aspect. In many languages the definite completion of an action is regularly marked by a grammatical form. English has no such completive marking, since both its past and present perfect tenses are neutral in this regard (neither *Tom read the book* nor *Tom has read the book* carries any implications in itself as to whether he finished reading it). But the particles, especially *up*, may serve to mark (among other things) completion. *Ate* is neutral as to completion, but *ate up* is completive:

> Tom *ate* Sue's cake: Tom *ate up* Sue's cake.
> Tom *tore* the bill: Tom *tore up* the bill.
> Tom *drank* some wine: Tom *drank up* some wine.

Other particles may have the same effect on meaning:

> Tom *broke off, pulled off* the handle.
> Tom *tore off, ripped off* the tag.
> Tom *pulled away* the curtain.
> Tom *pulled out* the driver from the burning wreck.[113]

Jespersen captures systematic, obligatory categories in his functional categories, and unsystematic, optional ones in his notional uses. But he fails to show how functional categories relate to such uses. Clearly there is, in general, a system to the uses of tenses.

Some grammatical distinctions relate directly to differences of meaning. The past tense forms of the English verb refer to past time, denote pastness. The two tense forms of the English verb differ in regard to time (past vs. non-past). The periphrastic future construction (*shall, will go*) refers to the future.

But each of these categories is associated with other uses as well. Some of these are idiosyncratic to certain verbs or idiomatic in certain languages. As we have noted, in many languages the present may be used to narrate events in the past; it may also be used for the future. But in Greek the present and imperfect have a distinctive "conative" use, expressing the attempt to do something: *peíthousin humâs* 'they are trying to persuade you'; *Halónnēson edídou* 'he offered (tried to give) Halonnesus'.[114]

Similar usages occur in Latin:

iam   iam.que   manu   tenet
now   now-and   hand (ABL SG)   hold (PRES ACT INDIC 3SG)

'and now, even now, he attempts to grasp him'

in   exsilium   eiciebam   quem   iam
into   exile   send out (IMPF ACT INDIC 1SG)   who (MASC ACC SG)   already

ingressum	esse	in	bellum
enter (PERF PASS PARTIC MASC ACC SG)	be (PRES ACT INF)	into	war

videbam
see (IMPF ACT INDIC 1SG)

'was I trying to send into exile one who I saw had already gone into war?'[115]

Somewhat similar conative uses occur in English, especially with the progressives: *we're opening the box* can mean 'we're trying to open the box' (as well as 'we intend to open the box' and 'we're getting the box open').

In Greek the aorist of a verb denoting a state may express entrance into that state: *eploútoun* (imperfect) 'I was rich' but *eploútēsa* (aorist) 'I became rich'.[116] On the other hand, the perfects of some verbs denoting changes of state or causation may express present meaning: *thnḗiskein* (present) 'to die' but *tethnēkénai* (perfect) 'to be dead'; *mimnḗiskein* 'to remind', but *memnêsthai* 'to remember'. But the present tense of the Greek verbs *hḗkō* 'I am come' and *oíkhomai* 'I am gone' has perfect force, while that of *eîmi* 'I am going' has future force.[117]

In these uses the tenses do not refer to the times they normally do, and so may be considered idiomatic. Such uses do not show that the various tenses do not refer to specific times, or that they refer ambiguously to different times. The use of the past for the perfect or vice versa in various languages likewise should not lead us to assert that there is an overlap in the meaning of the two tenses.

There are, however, many usages which cannot be considered idiomatic, if only because they occur in so many languages. The historical present, the present tense for future events, the past tense for irrealities in the present, are common uses and function systematically in those languages they occur in.

This is quite different from, for example, the periphrastic past of Catalan, formed with the auxiliary verb 'go': *jo vaig anar*, literally 'I'm going to go', that is, 'I went'. While completely systematic within Catalan, this tense form is idiomatic from the point of view of tense periphrasis in general: it is unusual for the combination of a verb meaning 'go' with an infinitive to be anything but a future.

The question is how to develop a theory of universal categories in terms of which language-specific theories of systematic and nonidiomatic, but nonetheless nonliteral, uses can be stated. Jespersen was not completely successful in doing this, but he was the first to recognize the problem. His solution continues to this day to influence thinking about tense.

g. Retrospective and Prospective Tenses

To develop a neat and "consistent" yet universal scheme of functional tenses, Jespersen first sets out "the three main divisions of time" in a single line (using the "notional" terms past, present, and future), with grammatical tenses corresponding to each—preterite, present, and future. Then he inserts "intermediate 'times'" corresponding to additional tenses—the before-past corresponding to the ante-preterite tense, the after-past to the post-preterite, and similarly the before-future to the ante-future, and the after-future to the post-future.[118] (Here I will refer to anterior and posterior tenses of the past and future.)

In Jespersen's model there are only times; tenses represent these in a one-to-one fashion. He defines the principal tenses by relating them spatially to the "present-time" point, each tense occurring a number of units to the right or left of that point: for example, the past is one unit to the left. The intermediate times are oriented to the past or future in the same way: the anterior past is one unit to the left of the preterite (and hence two units to the left of the present). Each tense is thus fixed directly—or indirectly—in relation to the speaker's "now," that is, absolutely. This scheme draws on relative tense theory, for all Jespersen's critique of Madvig.

Jespersen can now associate the past tense forms of English with the preterite tense, the present tense forms with the present tense, and the periphrastic future with the future tense. The periphrastic tenses with *have* represent the ante-preterite (the traditional *passé antérieur*: e.g., *had gone*) and the ante-future (*will have gone*); the conditional (*would go*) is the post-preterite.

Jespersen was quite critical of any two-dimensional model, as witness his critique in the *Philosophy of Grammar* of Madvig's relative tense analysis of the Latin tenses.[119] We have seen (in section c) that Madvig called the perfect (*scripsi* 'I have written, I wrote') the *praeteritum*, the preterite or past tense; the pluperfect (*scripseram* 'I had written') he called the *praeteritum in praeterito*, the past-in-the-past; and the future perfect (*scripsero* 'I shall have written') is the *praeteritum in futuro*, the past-in-the-future. Furthermore, he has a three-by-three scheme.

Jespersen recognizes that, unlike some other writers who had a similar but a priori "logical" system of tenses, Madvig probably intended this as a purely descriptive, empirical scheme for Latin, since he does not employ it for his grammar of Greek. Nonetheless, Jespersen criticizes Madvig for the lack of a label for the forms on the first line of his table (given in section c); parallel to the others, they should be called *in praesenti*, "in the present." Jespersen notes the difficulty that *scribam* must appear in two different places, as future-in-the-present and as present-in-the-future.

Jespersen does accept the view that words and morphemes could have multiple meanings, could be ambiguous, polysemous. But he sees no real ambiguity here, merely an artifact of Madvig's scheme. Further, Jespersen observes that the future-in-the-present really ought to be *scripturus sum* 'I am (about) to write'. But Madvig has avoided this because it implies a near future, and he did not wish to concern himself with distance in time. (Yet he did something like this in treating semigrammaticized periphrastic futures in his Greek grammar.)

A further weakness of the scheme is that *scripturus eram* and *scripturus fui* are both in the same position. They are not synonymous, differing as do *scribebam* and *scripsi*. Neither the distinction, nor the parallelisms between the pairs, can be captured in Madvig's scheme, which ignores aspect.

It was Jespersen's rejection of relative tenses as such which prevented him from recognizing that the retrospective (perfect or ante-) tenses—including the present perfect—can be viewed simply as pasts relative to the main divisions of past, present, and future; and similarly that the prospective (post-) tenses—including the conditional—can be viewed as futures relative to those same main divisions. Many uses of such tenses in subordinate structures, which a relative tense theory can account for directly, are at best handled indirectly in Jespersen's theory.

Jespersen's scheme leaves no room for the present perfect (*has gone*), while leaving open a slot for the post-future which few, if any, languages fill (as he notes). But Jespersen has reasons for not recognizing an ante-present. First, he argues that as the present is really a point, it cannot be divided into ante-present, present, and post-present, as the past and future can be.[120]

This argument is weak on two grounds. As Jespersen himself recognizes, ''in practice 'now' means a time with an appreciable duration, the length of which varies greatly according to circumstances; cf. such sentences as 'he is hungry | he is ill | he is dead'.''[121] As well, English, like many other languages, has a number of constructions which can only be considered post-presents: *he is to go tomorrow, he is about to go, he is going to go*. The sentence *Susan predicted that Max was going to leave town* relates to *Susan predicted that Max would leave town* in the same way as *Max is going to leave town* relates to *Max will leave town*.

That these are not simply futures is shown by the difference in acceptability of sentences such as *hopefully tomorrow will be a better day* and *?hopefully tomorrow is going to be a better day; tomorrow he will kiss Sue, ?tomorrow he is (going) to kiss Sue, ?*tomorrow he is about to kiss Sue*.

By fitting all the tenses onto a single line, Jespersen turns relative tense into absolute tense. The pluperfect may well represent a past relative to the past, but if so, it must be the leftmost tense on his line. Similarly, a future relative to the future would be the rightmost tense. In these cases the difference of absolute and relative position does not affect position on the line.

But it is quite otherwise in the cases of a present prospective and present perfect. A present prospective does not fix the time referred to relative to the future, but only relative to the present. But the only position for it on the line is in an absolute position between present and future, hence it really cannot be fitted into the line without incorrectly assigning it a kind of future perfect meaning. Correspondingly, the present perfect would have to be assigned a kind of conditional (past prospective) meaning. The gratuitous assumption that, since time is linear, a diagram of time (and tense) must likewise be linear, prevents Jespersen from fitting the present perfect and prospective into his scheme.

Jespersen recognized that his scheme did not deal with the perfects, but offered a second reason for ignoring the present perfect:

> The system of tenses given above will probably have to meet the objection that it assigns no place to the perfect, *have written, habe geschrieben, ai écrit*, etc., one of the two sides of Lat[in] *scripsi*. . . . This, however, is really no defect in the system, for the perfect cannot be fitted into the simple series, because besides the purely temporal element it contains the element of result. It is a present, but a permansive present: it represents the present state as the outcome of past events, and may therefore be called a retrospective variety of the present.[122]

Perhaps the most obvious failing of Jespersen's theory is in its treatment of the perfects. Allen finds Jespersen's arguments for rejecting a nine-tense system in favor of a seven-tense one "not very convincing."[123] For Jespersen has no way of differentiating the preterite from the present perfect other than to give "a rather vague definition of the present perfect and call it a 'retrospective variety of the present,' " as Reichenbach puts it.[124]

The statement in *Essentials of English Grammar* (1933) that "the Preterit refers to some time in the past without telling anything about the connexion with the present moment, while the Perfect is a retrospective present, which connects a past occurrence with the present time," has been criticized by Diver among others.[125] Diver argues that, in both (i) and (ii) below, the first clause is unconnected with the present, yet in one case we use the preterite and in the other the present perfect:

(i) I lived in Chelsea until 1914, but since then I have lived in London.
(ii) I have lived in Chelsea, but since 1914 I have lived in London.

Another aspect of Jespersen's difficulties with the preterite and perfect is his inability to explain why the two tenses are united in the Latin perfect form (*amavi* 'I have loved, I loved') and the *passé composé* of colloquial French (and many German dialects) (*j'ai écrit, ich hab' geschrieben* 'I have written', 'I wrote'). Nor can he adequately account for the colloquial North American English use of the preterite for the perfect (*I never went to Europe* for *I have never gone to Europe*).

Although there is some close, principled, connection of the perfect to the preterite, for Jespersen the two are unrelated, for one is past time and the other is present. Jespersen points out that the perfect co-occurs with *now* (*now I have eaten enough*) and therefore is a present tense, so that *he has become mad* means that he is mad now, whereas *he became mad* has no implications for his present state.[126] Jespersen also cites the difference between *he has given orders that all spies* are *to be shot* and *he gave orders that all spies* were *to be shot* (my emphases). This suggests that the perfect is a primary tense (in the sense this term is used in Greek grammar), and the preterite secondary.

The third reason why Jespersen has no present perfect has to do with the phenomenon he labels "shifting" or "back-shifting," namely, the use of a tense normally linked notionally to a certain time for situations in another time. He observes that in wishes (*I wish I were rich*), hypotheses (*if I were rich, I would buy a huge yacht*), and contrary-to-fact conditions (*if I were rich, would I be working here?*), the tense of the verb is backshifted one step relative to the time the statement applies to.

A wish in regard to past time appears in the ante-preterite (pluperfect) tense: *I wish I had been rich as a child*. A wish in regard to the present, however, is not in an ante-present: **I wish I have been rich now* is not an English sentence. Rather, the backshifted version of the present is the preterite (past): *I wish I were* (colloquial *was*) *rich now*.

To maintain the generalization that in backshifting the displacement is always by one step, we must allow no post- or ante-present tenses. Problems are caused, however, by the future perfect. *John will have left by noon* is translated into the conditional perfect in a past context—*(they said that) John would have left by noon*—not into a present: **(they said that) John leaves by noon.*

Jespersen is able to accommodate the past perfect and future perfect forms, because he makes a distinction between the "ante-preterite" referring to events occurring before the past and "a retrospective past time, bearing the same relation to some period in the past as the perfect does to the present . . . : *had written.*" [127] He illustrates the difference with an example from an essay by R. B. McKerrow. In the sense of *Caesar had thrown a bridge across the Rhine in the previous season*, which implies that the bridge was still standing, we have his retrospective past, what we have been calling the past perfect. But McKerrow shows that this implication can be canceled by appending the tag *but it had been swept away by the winter floods*. This is then the ante-past, the event of Caesar's bridge-building preceding the past time presupposed by the statement.

The difficulty here is that in the familiar European languages, at least, the pluperfect (past perfect) and this ante-preterite always coincide in a pluperfect (past perfect) tense. Not only does Jespersen's scheme lack any place for the three (retrospective) perfects (past, present, and future), but it treats the coincidence of the ante-past with the pluperfect and the ante-future with the future perfect as coincidental, whereas it would seem somehow to be a systematic fact.

And indeed, while his distinction between, for example, the ante-preterite and the pluperfect is an important and interesting observation, until relatively recently few if any grammarians have followed him in treating the pluperfect tense as an ante-preterite, rather than a past perfect, tense. The question is how to capture Jespersen's distinction without losing sight of the unified pluperfect tense.

A pecularity of Jespersen's treatment, in light of the Varronian treatment of the perfect tenses, is that he clearly does not view the "permansive" quality of the perfects as having anything to do with aspect. Jespersen discusses aspect in *The Philosophy of Grammar*, but nowhere in this section does he mention perfect tenses. [128]

That the perfect is not an aspect has been argued by Comrie, among others, who points out that—unlike aspects, which represent "the internal temporal constitution of a situation"—the perfect "relates some situation to a preceding situation." [129] Comrie observes that *Bill had arrived at six o'clock* can mean either that at six o'clock there existed a state of affairs resulting from a previous arrival by Bill (Jespersen's "permansive" reading), or that Bill's arrival at six o'clock is viewed from some later perspective (the ante-past). [130]

Comrie interprets this as a difference in viewpoint. Jespersen views it as the difference between a relative tense, and an absolute tense combined with permansive meaning. In any case, Comrie goes on to note that the future perfect "can be either a perfect-in-the-future, or a past-in-the-future—*Bill will have arrived at six o'clock* has precisely the ambiguity of *Bill had arrived at six o'clock.*"

One would think that, at least in his treatment of the perfect infinitive and participle, Jespersen would be forced to recognize the aspectual character of the perfect, for there are no tense distinctions as such in these forms. He notes that "the infinitive . . . is an old verbal substantive, and it still has something of the old indifference to time-distinctions: *I am glad to see her* refers to present time, *I was glad to see her* to past, and *I am anxious to see her* to future time.''[131]

But he seems to view this indifference not in terms of aspect so much as a neutralization, or obliteration, of tense distinctions, for he says that ''the English perfect infinitive corresponds not only to the perfect ('Tis better to *have loved and lost* / Than never to *have loved* at all), but also to an ordinary preterit [*sic*] (You meant that? I suppose I must *have meant* that) and to an ante-future (future perfect: This day week I hope to *have finished* my work).''[132]

Similarly, in discussing the perfect imperative (*be gone!, have done!*), he says merely that it also refers to future time. Of the participle, he writes: ''The combination of *having* with the second participle [perfect or past participle] bears the same relation to the simple first [present] participle as the perfect does to the present tense; in some combinations there is hardly any difference: *The clock striking ten*—or, *the clock having struck ten*—we shook hands and left.''[133]

This theory of neutralization of tense has come in for much criticism. For example, McCoard records a number of counterexamples to Jespersen's generalization that the preterite appears as a perfect infinitive: *Jack was leaving the next day, Jill believed Jack to be leaving the next day*, not ! *Jill believed Jack to have been leaving the next day.*[134] *Maureen leaves tomorrow* and *Jack left the next day* do not readily embed within longer sentences of this type at all.[135]

McCoard notes that the preterite of *John was in Africa last month* can appear either as perfect or plain infinitive in *John was rumored to be/to have been in Africa last month.*[136] But Jespersen has no way of accounting for this: if it is due to ambiguity of the preterite, his scheme assigns the preterite just one place (functional category); if it is due to some unknown factors, his theory offers no insight into what these might be.

The same problems arise in regard to the ''futurates''—the present, present progressive, and present perfect used for future and future perfect. If the present and present perfect substitute for the future and future perfect when futurity is presupposed and requires no overt indication, as Jespersen claims, then why can the future reference not be omitted in an example such as *we will not eat until 8 o'clock tomorrow night because John will not be home until then*?[137]

The difficulties for Jespersen come about, first, because he does not characterize the difference between the present and the perfect as aspectual, and second, because he does not recognize a distinction of absolute and relative tense. In rejecting a two-dimensional tense scheme, he forces himself to treat subordinate tenses as special cases of the ''normal'' uses of tenses found in independent clauses.

His distinction of formal and notional category allows, and requires, no more than this. His recognition of shifting does not make good the lack, for the theory does not allow for explanation of why it is precisely by one step down that shifting takes place. What is required, and what scholars since Jespersen have sought to provide, is an account of the tenses which adequately recognizes the unique nature of tense in subordinate expressions.

3

Modern Theories of the Subordinate Tenses

a. Mood and Tense

As complicated as the meanings and uses of the tenses considered so far may seem, we have principally been examining only a narrow range of phenomena, namely those in which the tense forms have their "normal," nominal values. In the Indo-European languages this actually occurs only under certain special conditions—generally when the verb is the main verb of an independent clause and is in the indicative mood. Otherwise the tense forms exhibit other values, dependent to a large extent on mood.

The grammatical tradition never attempted to provide a *general* theory for tenses under *all* conditions, but merely related the various paradigmatic forms of verbs directly to notional times, and defined a set of "natural" uses (alongside idiomatic ones such as the historical present). It did not allow for *systematic* uses of verb forms which do not equate to the notionally defined tenses, though it was already known to the earliest Greek and Roman grammarians that under many conditions a verb may occur in some other tense (and/or mood) than that in accord with its "normal" meaning.

Such uses of the tenses were, however, relegated to syntax, since they depend on the syntax of constructions. The Greeks and Romans both wrote on syntax, and while syntax was seen as a distinct area, it was only one of several (accentology, metrics, declension, etymology, etc.) which might or might not be treated in a work claiming to be grammatical in nature. Later syntax and grammar came, perhaps as a result of their different roles in education, to be considered not only distinct but mutually exclusive, and it has only been in relatively modern times that syntax is considered once again an integral part of grammar.

The theory of tenses as it evolved within grammar was designed almost exclusively with the tenses of the indicative mood in mind, since it is largely in constructions in which the indicative mood is usual, and in which they exhibit "inherent'' values independent of particular syntactic constructions, that the tenses have the sorts of ''natural'' values we have mainly been discussing here.

Consequently it is only in the twentieth century that any attempt has been made to develop a theory of tenses in general, including the various syntax-dependent uses of the tenses. Earlier grammarians failed to see that such uses of the tenses require any explanation, since such values were thought to derive ''naturally'' from the inherent values of the tenses, given the nature of the constructions the verbs entered into.

While mood in itself is not concerned with temporal relations and hence falls outside the scope of the present work, it interacts with both tense and aspect in important ways and therefore is of considerable relevance to the study of both. To understand that interaction, it is necessary to know something of what mood is and how the moods function.

Mood, which has in part to do with (very roughly) the speaker's ''attitude'' toward what is said—it may be asserted, hypothesized, expressed as a wish, and so on—is usually marked in English by the use of ''modal'' auxiliary verbs such as *may, might, should.* But in Greek (and Latin) such distinctions of meaning are usually indicated by modifying the verb itself. *Mood* sometimes is used to refer to a formal category of the verb, and sometimes to a meaning category marked by such a form; here we will follow this ambiguous practice.

Formally, Greek has three moods, properly speaking: indicative, subjunctive, and optative. Etymologically, the indicative (Latin *indicativus*) is the ''indicating'' or ''pointing out'' mood; the subjunctive is the ''subordinating'' or ''subjoining'' (''conjoining'') mood; the optative (*optativus*) is the ''wishing'' or ''desiring'' mood.

The indicative (e.g., *lúsō* 'I shall free') is assertive (or in questions, interrogative); the optative (*lúsoimi* 'would that I freed') may express a wish. The subjunctive, however, as its name suggests, is primarily used in the classical languages to indicate the subordination of one verb to another, and has no such clearly defined ''attitudinal'' characterization as the indicative and optative. Take this Latin example:

ab   aratro abduxerunt
from plow take away (PERF ACT INDIC 3PL)
Cincinnatum, ut   dictator esset
Cincinnatus   so that dictator be (IMPF SUBJ 3SG)
'they brought Cincinnatus from the plow that he might be dictator'[1]

Here *esset* is in the subjunctive mood largely if not entirely because it is in a clause headed by the subordinating conjunction *ut* 'so that'. (Note the use of the modal auxiliary *might* in the translation.)

The Greek optative is often (and typically) used to express wishes or make exhortations. The Latin subjunctive can also be used thus, and in such a role has sometimes been termed the optative mood:

falsus utinam   vates sim
false   would that prophet be (PRES SUBJ 1SG)
'I wish I may be a false prophet'[2]

On the other hand, in Greek the optative is often used in precisely the same constructions and with essentially the same meaning (or lack thereof) as the subjunctive, differing only in that the optative depends on verbs referring to past time, whereas the subjunctive does not:

érkhetai   hína
come (PRES ACT INDIC 3SG) so that
ídēi
see (PRES ACT SUBJ 3SG)

'he comes that he may see'

But:

êlthen   hína
come (AOR ACT INDIC 3SG) so that
ídoi
see (PRES ACT OPT 3SG)

'he came that he might see'[3]

In general, the subjunctive and optative moods have these two roles: the syntactic, in which they merely mark the verb as subordinate to another; and the pragmatic, in which they actually mark some difference in function from that of the indicative. That these moods have both functional and syntactic reasons for being has led to some confusion, since many have sought to define unique and essential meanings for the optative and subjunctive *forms*, which in fact need not always represent special optative and subjunctive *meanings*.

The Greeks and the Romans were already aware of the "moods" (Latin *modi*, Greek *egklíseis*) among the various formal categories ("accidents"—Greek *parepómena*) of their verbs. Dionysius lists five moods: *horistikḗ*, 'defining'; *prostatikḗ*, 'suppliant'; *euktikḗ*, 'wishing'; *hupotatikḗ*, 'subjoining, subordinating'; *aparémphatos*, 'unassertive, unindicative, indefinite, infinitive'.[4]

The Romans fairly literally translated these (respectively) as *indicativus, imperativus, optativus, subjunctivus*, and *infinitivus*, from whence come our modern terms. The indicative they also called "declarative," "pronunciative," "finitive," and "definitive." (Donatus called the subjunctive "conjunctive," and others simply called it "junctive.") The infinitive was sometimes called *perpetuus* 'general, universal', from its not marking many of the distinctions (viz., person and number) marked by the other moods.

The root meanings of "imperative" (cf. *imperatus* 'commanded'), "optative" (*optatus* 'wished-for'), and "subjunctive" (*subjunctus* 'subjoined') are clear. Those of the "finitive" ("indicative") and "infinitive" are less so; their root sense is the vague "delimiting, demarcating, defining."

Most Roman grammarians accept Dionysius's five moods for Latin,[5] though Diomedes (like Charisius and Donatus, A.D. fourth century) notes that some grammarians list up to ten moods.[6] Donatus gives eight: indicative or *pronuntiativus*; promissive or the "future of the indicative"; imperative; infinitive or *perpetuus*; optative; conjunctive or junctive; impersonal; and the gerunds. The commentator on Donatus, however, omits the impersonal and the gerunds.[7]

There is a basic dichotomy between the moods listed. Only the indicative, sub-junctive, and (in Greek, though not in Latin) the optative may appear as the main verb of a full, independent clause, and these are the only moods which allow personal endings on the verb[8]; they have come to be known as "finite" moods. (To a limited extent the imperative also marks distinctions of person and number, and may appear as the main verb of something close to a full clause.) The infini-tive is a classical "non-finite" mood, since neither of these things is true of it.

The stems in the classical languages to which the personal endings, the desin-ences, are added, mix tense, aspect, voice, and mood. From this point of view the imperative and the non-finites alike are not true moods, since there are no distinct imperative or infinitive stems. The marking of these "moods" is entirely in the desinences, which occur where the finite moods have personal endings, as for instance in Greek: *lú.ō* 'I free', *lú.ein* 'to free', *lû.e* 'free!'. In this regard the imperative is a non-finite mood.

Because there were modal markers—*moods*—in their languages, it was as-sumed by the ancients that there was a coherent set of categories—*modes*—which those markers marked. Ever since, the search has been on for a characterization of the modes represented by the moods. In logic, modality early developed into a coherent field. The semantics of the modal markers is certainly closely tied to logical modality, but possibility and necessity, which largely constitute the subject matter of the *logical* study, far from exhaust that of *grammatical* modality.

From the beginning, grammarians have developed two different types of theo-ries as to the nature of the modes marked by the moods. The first is the attitudinal theory.[9] According to Apollonius, the moods reflect "mental attitudes" of speak-ers (the "soul's dispositions," *psūkhiké diátheseis*). Priscian calls the moods "the various inclinations of the spirit." For Lyons, mood expresses "the opinion or attitude of the speaker"; Jespersen says that the moods may express "certain attitudes of mind of the speaker towards the contents of the sentence."[10]

The second is the *functional theory.* Apollonius seems sometimes to support it, as when he speaks of moods

> which receive their names from their meanings. . . . The . . . *horistikē* ("deter-minative, i.e., indicative") . . . is also called *apophatikē* ("declarative"). . . . When we declare by means of this [mood], we also define or determine. This is why the so-called asseverative . . . and causal . . . conjunctions occur with this [mood]. We are 'determining' when we say *gegrapha* ("I have written") and 'asseverating' when we say *hoti gegrapha* ("that I have written").[11]

What Apollonius is claiming here is that the indicative mood is used to make assertions (statements of fact), but it is also used to ask questions: (Greek) *gráphei* 'he writes', (Latin) *scripsit* 'he has written', (German) *wer liebt ihm?* 'who loves him?' A clause which is used to assert or question is called an independent clause, because it is not grammatically dependent on any other expressions, and may serve either as the main clause of a sentence or as a simple, one-clause sentence in its own right:

Tom is tall.	Is Tom tall?
I'm so foolish.	Am I so foolish?
Tom will leave.	Will Tom leave?

It is in such an independent clause (the main verb of which is in the indicative mood) that tense forms most often exhibit their nominal, "inherent" values.

In certain contexts sentences may retain the characteristics of independent expressions, including the aforementioned nominal uses of the tenses, while "encapsulated" in a larger sentence:

> direct quotation:
> Max said, *"Tom is tall."*
> Max asked, *"Is Tom tall?"*
> parenthetical:
> I actually admitted (*I'm so foolish*) that I liked chewing gum.
> I really hated my vacation in (*are you ready?*) Bulgaria.
> conjoined structure:
> *The sun will rise in the east* and *Tom will leave.*
> *Where is Tom* and *why is he late?*

Apollonius notes that the subjunctive is so called because of its dependence on subordinators, and relates the optative to the noun *eukhḗ* 'prayer, wish'.[12] Elsewhere, however, he reverts to an attitudinal theory. To others who argue that the subjunctive is not properly called a "hypothetical" or "dubitative" mood (it is used in *if*-clauses in so-called "contrary-to-fact" conditions), he replies that the other moods "have inherent meanings of their own from which they have received their names."[13] Apollonius says that it is only because the subjunctive never occurs (in Greek) on its own that its inherent value is undetermined and we are forced to call it "subjunctive" from its syntactic function. The Greek subjunctive *does* occur on its own, as in *íōmen* 'let's go', but Apollonius denies that first person subjunctives are "imperative"; rather, he calls them "hortative" or "suggestive," and does not view this use as "inherent."[14]

It is in independent clauses that the moods are most distinct and most likely to seem to reflect the "attitude" of the speaker. The subjunctive and imperative moods (and the optative of Greek) can be used in independent clauses. In independent clauses these moods serve mainly to fulfill some nonconstative function, to perform some type of speech act other than declaration: the imperative is used to command or request, and the subjunctive and optative serve to express a wish (*God save the Queen!*), a prohibition (Spanish: *no cante* 'don't sing'), or the like, but they are not used to *assert that* or *inquire whether* something is the case, as is the indicative.

The independent optative in Greek is typically used for wishes or exhortations:

> ekselthṓn   tis   ídoi
> go out (PRES ACT PARTIC MASC NOM SG) someone see (AOR ACT OPT 3SG)
> 'may someone go out and see'[15]

The subjunctive may be used for exhortations as well; Goodwin cites *ekselthṓn tis idétō* 'let someone go out and see'.

As the subjunctive may be used for exhortations and prohibitions, it easily becomes a kind of imperative, especially in persons other than the second: (Greek) *íōmen* 'let's go', *mḕ thaumásēte* 'do not (*mḕ*) wonder'; (Latin) *veniant* 'let them come', *ne veniant* 'let them not (*ne*) come', *ne hoc feceris* 'do not do this'.[16] In the Romance languages the subjunctive may provide a regular "polite" or formal imperative, as in Spanish: *hable Vd. mas alto* 'speak (subjunctive, 'may you speak', *hable*) louder'.

no hagas   lo que te prohibo
not do (PRES SUBJ 2SG) the which you forbid (PRES INDIC SG)
'do not do what I forbid you' [17]

In the Germanic languages the use of the subjunctive in independent clauses is much more restricted. In German the present subjunctive form has largely fallen together in form with the indicative, so that the subjunctive as imperative is limited to the third person. Lockwood offers the example of a placard in a streetcar:

wer aussteigen   will   melde   sich bitte
who get off (INF) want (PRES INDIC 3SG) move (PRES SUBJ 3SG) self please
rechtzeitig
in time
'whoever wishes to get off should please move in plenty of time' [18]

The Latin subjunctive also has the range of the Greek optative; indeed, the Roman grammarians consider Latin to have an optative mood, even though it lacks a distinctive set of optative forms. [19] Apart from the fact that the optative use of the subjunctive, like the Greek optative, represents a wish (and the fact that it may occur with the distinctive conjunction *utinam* 'would that'), there were two reasons why they assumed a separate optative mood.

First, whereas the subjunctive is often negated with *non* (as in the first example below), the negation of the optative is *ne*:

certum affirmare   non ausim
sure   affirm (PRES ACT INF) not dare (PERF SUBJ 1SG)
'I should not dare to assert as sure'

utinam   ne vere scriberem
would that not truly write (IMPF SUBJ ACT 1SG)
'would that I were not writing the truth' [20]

(However, many other uses of the subjunctive also take *ne*.)

Second and more important, the tenses are used differently with the optative than with other uses of the subjunctive. [21] In the optative "the present tense denotes the wish as *possible*, the imperfect as *unaccomplished* in present time, the pluperfect as *unaccomplished* in past time." [22]

The present optative has future force and so was considered a future: *sint incolumes* 'may they be (*sint*) safe from harm'. The imperfect and pluperfect are respectively markers of "irreality" in the present and the past (note the "backshifted" tenses in the English glosses):

utinam Clodius viveret
'would that Clodius were now alive'
utinam me mortuum vidisses
'would that you had seen me dead'

Hence the imperfect and pluperfect were considered respectively present and past in tense. Here is a further example of the "future" optative:

O mihi praeteritos
oh to me go by (PERF ACT PARTIC MASC ACC PL)
referat   si Iuppiter annos!
bring back (PRES ACT SUBJ 3SG)if Jupiter years

'Oh if only Jupiter would bring back to me my past years!'

Another example of the "present" is: *utinam ita essem* 'would that I were [so now]'.[23] The perfect optative (archaic in classical Latin) refers to the future but conveys perfect aspect: *di faxint* 'may the gods (*di*) grant'. On the basis of the two moods' differential use of the tense forms, the Romans were not necessarily wrong in distinguishing between subjunctive and optative, despite their identity of form.

It probably reflects a functional theory of the moods when the Stoics (apparently) refer to the indicative as *orthós* 'direct' and the other moods as *plágiai* 'oblique'.[24] We may compare Lyons's view that the "declarative" or indicative mood is "unmarked" for mood, "strictly speaking, non-modal": "it is customary to refer to the 'unmarked' sentences also (by courtesy as it were) as being 'in a certain mood.' "[25]

Apollonius declares the indicative the "most transparent" and says that, in a now lost book, he had declared it to be the "primary verb form." But he also says that the infinitive is the most general mood, since it marks so few distinctions.[26] (It is unclear, however, whether by this he means formal or functional distinctions.)

The functional approach to the moods has led some writers—including Harris[27]— to interpret the moods as reflecting *any* distinct use of sentences, and hence to include among the moods the interrogative, and so forth. Like many of the traditional writers, Harris does not take care to distinguish the formal category of mood from the category of mode and uses the term "mode" for both.

The ancients generally recognized that the subordinate moods had, however, a dual nature. In independent clauses the subjunctive and optative may have "natural" values quite different from those of indicative clauses, whereas the moods found in dependent, subordinate structures do not show their "natural" values; there the subjunctive and the Greek optative lose their special values and serve merely to mark syntactic subordination.

The Latin term *subiunctivus* or *coniunctivus* (*conjunctive*), translating the Greek *upotáktikē*, 'subjoining, subordinating,' is quite appropriate in those cases in which this is precisely the function of the subjunctive (and the Greek optative)—namely, that of simply marking the verb as subordinate to the main verb.[28]

Even in independent clauses, however, it is plainly futile to seek an essential or prototypical meaning for each of the moods. Although Lyons writes that the "notion of subjectivity is of the greatest importance . . . for the understanding of . . . modality," Gonda criticizes the view that "in contradistinction to the indicative which enables the speaker to make objective statements, [the subjunctive and optative] are . . . subjective in character."[29]

Against the "objectivity" of the indicative and the "subjectivity" of the other finite moods, it has been argued[30] that the indicative is just as "subjective" as the other moods. After all, the "reality" of the proposition asserted is solely in the judgment of the speaker, and hence the indicative must always involve a more or less subjective judgment.

Against the "factuality" of the indicative it has been similarly argued that, though the speaker *represents* the statement as factual, of course it need not be; as Jespersen points out, *twice four is seven* is also indicative.[31] If it be argued that the indicative is simply used to claim factuality, Jespersen observes that this still does not account for subordinate uses of the indicative, as in *if*-clauses. Nor does it necessarily account for usages in the *then*-clauses either, since it is arguable that, if the proposition expressed by the *if*-clause is false, then that expressed in the consequent has no truth value at all. In contrary-to-fact hypotheticals, in fact, the consequent is presumed to be nonfactual. In point of fact, the speaker does not always present the proposition as factual; this is certainly not the case in questions.

The idea that the indicative is used to assert, and the subjunctive not to assert, has been criticized by Palmer, who points out, in regard to Spanish, that while in certain constructions it is true that the indicative and subjunctive differ in the degree of commitment of the speaker to what is being said, this differs from the contrast of assertion and nonassertion. Further, the distribution of the two is "fairly arbitrary": the subjunctive is not used in direct questions, though these are obviously nonassertive. He sees a degree of circularity or question-begging in the definition of the indicative in terms of assertion.[32]

Indeed, the correlation of moods as markers with meanings is very much called into question by the fact that choice of moods is often governed by the choice of verb or conjunction. In English the complementizer *that* takes the indicative with certain verbs, as for instance *he says that he* is *ill*, but takes the subjunctive with others: *he demands that he* be *released* (cf. German *dass* with subjunctive in *er sagt, dass er krank sei* 'he says that he is ill'). In Latin the verb *iubeo* 'command, order' takes the infinitive, but the synonymous *impero* 'command, order' takes the subjunctive:

Eum venire   iubet
him come (PRES INF) order (PRES INDIC 3SG)
Ei   ut   veniat   imperat
to him that come (PRES SUBJ 3SG) order (PRES INDIC 3SG)

'he orders him to come'[33]

In fact, mood (morphological marking) is independent of modality (meaning categorization). There are many devices for expressing modality other than mood. Palmer cites the modal verbs (*may, can, must, ought* [*to*], *will, shall*) and modal particles (German *ja, doch, denn, schon, wohl*). Though he expresses doubt concerning the modal status of these latter, there are particles in many languages which are appropriately deemed modal.[34]

On the other hand, it is plain that, as we have seen, there are diverse uses of the moods, not all of which fit into either the category of "attitudinal" modality or that of "functional" modality. The subjunctive sometimes does express doubtfulness or irreality: the difference between embedded indicatives and embedded subjunctives is indeed sometimes that the latter are used when the speaker qualifies the truth of the statement.

In *if Tom is tall, I'll eat my hat*, the clause *if Tom is tall* presupposes the possiblity of Tom's being tall, leaving open the question of whether in fact he is; but *if Tom were tall, I'd eat my hat*, his being tall is merely a hypothesis, possibly even contrary to fact. It would be odd to say, for example, "if New York City were in the U.S., it would be a great town," since this hypothesizes something well known to be true.

We are forced to conclude that, like so many other grammatical systems, that of mood is not pure—neither purely syntactic nor purely semantic nor purely pragmatic, but mixing all three types of categorization.

Here we are not directly concerned with mood. Its importance for us is solely in how it interacts with tense and aspect. It is impossible, however, to consider either of these without considering mood at the same time.

b. Mood in Subordinate Structures

Tensed verbs occur not only as the main verbs of independent clauses, but in subordinate structures embedded within larger structures. In such a case they are generally subordinated to another tensed verb; the subjunctive and optative often function precisely to mark such subordination.

The subordination of a verb in a finite mood to another generally has consequences for tense in both Latin and the modern European languages, if only because the subordinate moods lack the full complement of tenses found in the indicative mood. The Latin subjunctive lacks the future and future perfect and the "optative" has even fewer tenses. The Greek subjunctive has no imperfect, pluperfect, future, or future perfect forms. The Greek optative has no imperfect or pluperfect.

While in standard, written Spanish and Portuguese there are full complements of formal (if not always functional) tenses in the subjunctive, other Roman languages have reduced systems. French has only four tenses of the subjunctive— two morphological (present and imperfect: *aime, aimasse*), two periphrastic (past and pluperfect: *aime aimé, eusse aimé*). This last is used only in the standard language, however, and the imperfect is largely vestigial.[35]

The Germanic languages have impoverished sets of subjunctive tenses. German has only present and past (imperfect) in the simple tenses (*singe, sänge*), and perfect, pluperfect, and future periphrastics (*habe geliebt, hätte geliebt, werde lieben*). (The conditional is a subjunctive in form: *würde lieben*.)

The English present subjunctive is the plain form of the verb: *be, sing, love*. The past subjunctive has a distinct form only in the case of singular *were*, though even here the indicative *was* tends in colloquial speech to replace it. Thus *if I was rich* is rendered ambiguous: it is subjunctive in *If I was rich I'd buy a big house*, but indicative in *If I was rich, at least I wasn't a snob*.

In British English the subjunctive is largely a fossil, replaced by the modal verbs, whereas it has undergone something of a revival in North America. Wilson attributes this to German influence, citing the following equivalent forms:

AMERICAN

ENGLISH

It was imperative that he be present.

It was imperative for him to be present.

It was imperative that he should be present.

He requested that the officer go at once.

He requested that the officer should go at once.

She suggested that they stop at the hotel.

She suggested that they should stop at the hotel.

He ordered that the men remain there.

He ordered that the men should remain there.[36]

There are of course constructions in which both use the modals: *wherever he may go*, **wherever he go*. On the other hand, in some constructions neither uses the modals.

In *I wish that I were rich*, the past tense *were* is used for the present; if one were speaking of the past, the sentence would be instead *I wish that I had been rich*. The subjunctive *were* (the use of the form *were* for the singular shows this is not indicative) is used for what in the indicative would be *was*; if my wish were fulfilled, I could say, "I am rich" (or in the past, "I was rich").

The impoverishment of English subjunctive tenses means that in many embedded clauses in the subjunctive, the present subjunctive must occur for past time:[37]

he suggested that Lyman *be* put forward as the candidate[38]
the neatness with which he had arranged that she *go* with her brother[39]
Descartes had burned a book which he had written . . . lest he, too, *get* into trouble[40]
Madame Curie agreed to this, on condition that when she came for him again at six, she *stay* for half an hour[41]

The tenses of subordinate moods in Greek work rather differently than in Latin or the modern European languages. In Greek, the use of a verb in any of the various subordinate constructions (including indirect speech) depends principally on the underlying tense and mood of the verb—the tense and mood it would have in an independent clause.

As we have seen, after primary tenses, those referring to non-past time, there is no change in the tense of the subordinate verb, and the values of the various apparent tenses are precisely those they have in direct discourse.[42] Thus a report of *grápho* 'I am writing' in the present would use the present tense: *légei hóti gráphei* 'he says (*légei*) that (*hóti*) he is writing (*gráphei*)'; a report of *égraphon* 'I was writing' similarly uses the imperfect: *légei hóti égraphen* 'he says that he was writing'.[43] The same is true of "indirect questions": *erōtâi tí boúlontai* 'he asks (*erōtâi*) what (*tí*) they want' (*boúlontai*).

After a secondary verb, however, the verb may either change to the optative or be retained in its underlying mood, but in either case the underlying tense is retained. A report of *gráphō* 'I am writing' uses either the present indicative (*éleksen hóti gráphei* 'he said that he was [literally "is"] writing') or the present optative (*éleksen hóti gráphoi*).[44]

Although the imperfect and pluperfect lack optatives, this presents no problem, as they can retain the indicative; in some cases, however, the present optative may exceptionally be used for the imperfect, since both are imperfect in aspect.[45] The present infinitive and perfect infinitive may likewise be used for the imperfect and pluperfect respectively.[46]

In Greek, the use of the non-indicative moods (except in indirect discourse) is largely limited to the present, aorist, and perfect tenses, and these differ not in tense, that is, time reference, but solely in aspect.[47] The present subjunctive indicates ongoingness or repetition: *eàn poiêi toûto* 'if (*eàn*) he shall be doing (*poiêi*, present subjunctive) this (*toûto*)' or 'if he shall do this (habitually)'. The aorist indicates mere occurrence: *eàn poiḗsēi toûto* 'if he shall do this'.

The optative present and aorist are similar: *ei poioíē toûto* 'if he should be doing this' or 'if he should do this (habitually)', but *ei poiḗseie toûto* 'if he should do this'. The imperative likewise: *poíei toûto* 'do this (habitually)' but *poíēson toûto* 'do this'.

The relative tense of such non-indicatives depends on the construction and the governing verb, not on the tense of the verb itself, though these present and aorist non-indicatives are generally relatively future in meaning, as in the example above. The subjunctive is, however, relatively present in general conditions:

ḕn eggùs élthēi   thánatos, oudeìs boúletai
if near   come (AOR SUBJ 3SG) death   no one wish (PRES ACT INDIC 3SG)
thnḗiskein
die (PRES INF)

'if (or when) death comes near, no one is (ever) willing to die'[48]

The aorist subjunctive may also in certain constructions be relatively past to the main verb, so that *epeidàn toûto ídō, apérkhomai* means 'after (*epeidàn*) I have seen (subjunctive, *ídō*) this (*toûto*), I (always) depart (*apérkhomai*)'. The same is true of the aorist optative.[49]

When embedded within another clause, an independent indicative clause may be replaced not only by a dependent clause in a subordinate finite mood (such as the subjunctive), but also by a non-finite mood (for example, the infinitive):

Tom went to school ⎧ so that he *should be able* to read.
                    ⎩ in order *to be able* to read.

I wish ⎧ that I *weren't* so foolish.
       ⎪ not *to be* so foolish.
       ⎨ that I *hadn't been* so foolish.
       ⎩ not *to have been* so foolish.

It astounds me that you ⎧ *could ask* such a thing.
                        ⎩ *could have asked* such a thing.

I would hate ⎧ your *leaving*.
             ⎪ you *to leave*.
             ⎨ for you *to leave*.
             ⎩ it, if you ⎧ *left*.
                          ⎨ *should leave*.
                          ⎩ *were to leave*.

Your *asking* ⎫
That you *should* ask ⎪
Your *having asked* ⎬ a thing like that astounds me.
That you *should have asked* ⎭

For Tom *to leave* ⎫
Tom's *leaving* ⎪
If Tom *left*, it ⎬ would disturb me.
If Tom *should leave*, it ⎪
If Tom *were to leave*, it ⎭

In examples like these, many of the clauses embedded within the larger sentences would be ungrammatical (or at best of dubious grammaticality), if they stood alone as simple sentences:

> *I weren't so foolish.
> *Tom were to leave.
> ?*You could have asked such a thing.
> ?*You should ask a thing like that.

Others are grammatical, but only in a different meaning from the intended one:

!I hadn't been so foolish. (above: 'I wasn't foolish'; cf.: 'I hadn't been foolish')
!You should leave. (above: 'were you to leave'; cf.: 'you ought to leave')

This is part of what we mean by saying that such structures are dependent; they lack an independent existence and depend for their grammaticality on the structures which include them—the "matrix" they are embedded in. They are also dependent in that their particular forms are governed by the matrix structures. For example, the verb *believe* can be followed either by a subordinate finite clause or an infinitive phrase: by either (John believes) *that Sue is sweet* or (John believes) *Sue to be sweet.* But the semantically related verb *think* allows only *John thinks that Sue is sweet,* not **John thinks Sue to be sweet.*

Structures in which a clause is reduced to a phrase, that is, in which the main verb of the clause appears in infinitival or other non-finite form, generally exhibit very different kinds of temporal values from those found in the finite verbs. It is not even clear that such forms have tense in the sense that finite forms do, not only in the modern European languages, but even in Latin and Greek with their fairly full complements of "tenses" in non-finite forms (cf. Greek *lúein* 'to free'; *lúsein* 'to be going to free, be about to free'; *lûsai* 'to have freed'—aorist; *lelukénai* 'to have freed'—perfect; *lelúsesthai* 'to be going to have been freed').

The tenses of the subordinate finite moods—those which appear in dependent clauses, the subjunctive and optative—show similar *kinds* of values to those found in the indicative, though particular tenses may have "shifted" values, as when the present subjunctive refers to future, rather than present, time. In dependent clauses all three of the finite moods may show tense values defined relative to the tense of the matrix, rather than absolute tense values defined relative to the time of the speech act.

Non-finite forms such as the infinitives do not exhibit absolute tense, but are always relative to the tense of their matrix. In both *Tom wants to go* and *Tom wanted to go, to go* is relatively future. But infinitives may also be relatively present (*Tom likes to swim, Tom liked to swim*). And the "perfect" infinitive (*to have gone, to have swum*) seems ambiguously relatively past and relatively perfect: *Tom believes Sue to have swum* reports indifferently either (Tom believes) "Sue swam," (Tom believes) "Sue has swum," or (Tom believes) "Sue had swum." It appears simpler to say that the simple infinitive marks imperfect aspect and the perfect one perfect aspect—and neither marks tense at all.

In some languages, and under certain circumstances, the only change involved in a construction such as indirect discourse is in the deictics. (These are referential terms defined relative to the situation of the speech act; they include pronominal references—the speaker is *I*, the addressee *you*, a third party *he, she, they*; references to place—the speaker is *here*, others are *there*, things near the speaker are *this*, other things are *that;* and references to time—the time of the speech act is *now*, other times *then*; etc.) Thus "*they* say that *they* are happy in *that* place" is an indirect report of the direct statement "*we* are happy in *this* place," the only change being the shift of *we* and *this* to *they* and *that* with the change in speaker (and therefore in speaker's perspective). In the Slavic languages [50] as well as in Hebrew and many other such languages,[51] this is largely all there is to indirect discourse.

In some cases there may be a shift in mood, but no shift in tense. This happens in English when we use the infinitive or subjunctive to report an imperative: *leave!* (spoken to a woman) may be reported as *I told her to leave* or *I demanded that she leave.* Here we use the infinitive (*to leave*) or a subjunctive ([*that*] *she leave*) in indirect discourse.

In English, as in many other languages, however, there may be substantial consequences for the tense of the embedded verb. The use of tenses in the dependent clauses of indirect discourse (and certain other constructions) quite generally involves an apparent shifting of temporal values.

The tense of a verb depends in part on the construction that the verb (as the main verb of a clause) occurs in, but the construction itself depends on certain contextual and pragmatic factors. There are many ways in which a subordinate structure (whether a tensed clause or a non-finite phrase) may be dependent on another, and each determines in part the choice of construction. Syntactically, a subordinate structure centered on a verb can serve:

1. as subject of a verb: *running* is hard; *to err* is human; *that John was ill* perplexed Sue; *John's being ill* perplexed Sue; *whether the earth is flat or not* is an interesting question
2. as object of a verb: he wants *to go*; he prefers *walking*; she said *that John was ill*; you know *why Bill left*
3. as object of a preposition: he thought of *running away*; he is unhappy at *Sue's having cooked dinner*
4. as complement of a verb: she started *running;* she began *to run*; he encouraged Max *to cheat*; they appear *to have left*
5. as complement of an adjective: he is afraid *to swim in the ocean*; she is uncertain *whether to go or to stay*
6. as a subordinate clause (in adverbial position): *finding himself alone*, he let out a yell; *having left Canada as a child*, Bill had no desire to return; Max was quite unpopular, *being the tightwad he was*; *whenever she can*, Sue eats out; she ate caviar *when she could*; *if he falls*, catch him

7. as a modifier (in adjectival position): the woman *running past us*; this water *boiling in the kettle*; the suspect *sought by the police*; all those *having recently arrived in Cuba*; the man *who loves her*; the man *she loves*

The form of a clause or phrase is partly (but only partly) correlated with its syntactic function. When subject or object of a verb, a clause often is nominalized—that is, its main verb appears as an infinitive (Latin *errare*, English *to err*, German *das Irren*), gerund (English *erring*, German *die Irrung*), or some other deverbal noun (Latin *error*). The object of a preposition, however, cannot be an infinitive in English:

$$he \begin{Bmatrix} \text{believes in} \\ \text{is fond of} \\ \text{hears about} \end{Bmatrix} \begin{Bmatrix} \text{walking} \\ \text{a walk} \\ \text{*(to) walk} \end{Bmatrix} \text{to work every day.}$$

The subject or object of a verb may be marked by a complementizer such as *that* (French *que*, Greek *hóti*, etc.), in which case the verb is in a finite form; whether this is indicative or not may depend on the governing verb:

I know that I *am* poor.
I wish that I *were* rich.

In most languages there is a close relationship between the form of the clause and whether its subject is coreferential with that of the main clause: *I demand to go* but *I demand that Sam go* (compare **I demand Sam to go*, ?! *I demand that I go*). This correlation is not as strong in English as in many other languages, and both coreferential and non-coreferential subjects may occur for at least some speakers both in constructions with non-finites and in those with finites (depending on the governing verb):

I prefer not to be your delegate to the congress.
I prefer that I not be your delegate to the congress.
I prefer (for) Sam not to be your delegate to the congress.
I prefer that Sam not be your delegate to the congress.

A complement clause which is governed by a verb, adjective, and so on, is usually non-finite. Whether it is an infinitive (*[to] love*), participle (*loving*), or other form, depends on the governing expression:

complement of a verb:

$$he \begin{Bmatrix} \textit{began} \\ \textit{started} \end{Bmatrix} \begin{Bmatrix} \textit{to hate} \\ \textit{hating} \\ \textit{*hate} \end{Bmatrix} \text{television}$$

$$\text{they might} \begin{Bmatrix} \textit{*to hate} \\ \textit{*hating} \\ \textit{hate} \end{Bmatrix} \text{television}$$

complement of an adjective:

$$he\ is \begin{Bmatrix} \textit{likely} \\ \textit{afraid} \end{Bmatrix} \begin{Bmatrix} \textit{to leave} \\ \textit{! leaving} \\ \textit{*leave} \end{Bmatrix}$$

$$we\ are \begin{Bmatrix} \textit{certain} \\ \textit{*uncertain} \end{Bmatrix} \textit{to leave}$$

A clause marked as a complement by a complementizer again takes a finite verb of either mood, depending on the governing predicate (verb or adjective):

indicative: he is certain that Susan *is* gone
subjunctive: he is insistent that Susan *be* excluded

The choice of the form of the complement may also depend on the syntactic construction:

It seems that Tom *is* here.
Tom seems *to be* here.

Subordinating conjunctions and relative pronouns govern only finite verbs:

if he *is* rich, I'm not aware of it
if he *were* rich, I'd know it
after Rex *has eaten*, he's quiet
**if* his *being* rich, I'm not aware of it
**if* (for) him *to be* rich, I'm not aware of it
**after* Rex('s) *having eaten*, he's quiet

The choice of mood may depend on the governing conjunction or relative pronoun. Relative pronouns take only the indicative in English; *if* allows either indicative or subjunctive.

If-clauses ("protases") in conditionals choose the indicative in ordinary conditionals in which the protasis is presupposed, or in which there is no implication of reality or unreality:

if Tom *is* so poor, it's because he's honest
if you *are* truly happy together, it's OK with me

si Caesarem   *probatis,*
if Caesar (MASC ACC SG) favour (PRES ACT INDIC 2PL)
in me offenditis
in me find fault (PRES ACT INDIC 2PL)
'if you favour Caesar, you find fault with me'[52]

The subjunctive is chosen in "contrary-to-fact" conditionals:

if I *were* rich, I'd soon retire

si *viveret,*   verba eius audiretis
if live (IMPF SUBJ 3SG) words his   hear (IMPF ACT SUBJ 2PL)
'if he were living, you would hear his words'[53]

Grammars sometimes make a distinction of more or less vivid future conditions—"if he does this, if he will do this" versus "if he should do this." In Greek, this distinction can be marked by using the subjunctive with *eán* 'if' (or even the indicative with *ei* 'if') for the more vivid condition, and the optative with *ei* for the less:

eàn oûn   íeis   nûn, póte ései   oíkoi?
if   therefore go (PRES SUBJ 2SG) now when be (FUT INDIC 2SG) home-LOC
'if therefore you go now, when will you be at home?'

ei mè̃ kathékseis   glôssan, éstai   soi   kaká
if not restrain (FUT ACT INDIC 2SG) tongue   be (FUT INDIC 3SG) to you evils
'if you do not restrain your tongue, you will have [=there will be to you] trouble'

ou pollè àn   alogía   eíē,   ei phoboîto
not great PART absurdity be (PRES OPT 3SG) if fear (PRES MID OPT 3SG)
tòn thánaton ho toioûtos?
the death   the such

'would it not be a great absurdity, if such a man should fear death?'[54]

In the case of the "vivid" condition, the possibility of the fulfillment of the condition depends on the discoursal context—on *how things are*. The "less vivid" condition, however, concerns something which, while possible, lacks any immediate reason to lead one to believe that it is fulfillable, at least *as things stand*.

In English and many other languages an "imaginative" backshift is used to the same end as the Greek optative; *if it rains tomorrow* (as you say, as the forecast predicts), *if it rained tomorrow* (as is possible), *if it were to rain tomorrow* (as is possible).

No English conjunction requires the subjunctive alone. But in languages such as Latin some conjunctions require the subjunctive, others the indicative.

Subordinate (adverbial) clauses are headed by subordinating conjunctions such as *because*, *although*, and *since;* these conjunctions are related to the complementizers which head *that*-clauses. Both subordinating conjunctions and complementizers—along with the relative pronouns heading relative clauses—may govern mood, selecting either indicative or subjunctive.

The choice in many languages is determined for the most part by the pragmatics of the subordinator. (The choice of subordinator in turn may be determined by the pragmatics of the governing predicate.) If the clause is presupposed by the speaker, then the subordinator typically governs the indicative:

Aristotle knew *that* the earth *is* round.
I'm looking for *what* the man *stole*.
Although Tom *is* poor, he's honest.

quod   *rediit*   nobis mirabile   videtur
that   return (PERF ACT INDIC 3SG) to us wonderful see (PRES PASS INDIC 3SG)
'that he returned seems wonderful to us' (Latin)

légei   *hóti gráphei*
say (PRES ACT INDIC 3SG) that write (PRES ACT INDIC 3SG)
'he says that he's writing' (Greek)[55]

On the other hand, if the subordinator marks the clause as non-presupposed (or hypothetical, contrary-to-fact, etc.), then it tends to govern the subjunctive:

Aristotle wondered *if* the earth *were* flat after all.
We would prefer *that* the matter *be* kept quiet.

Although the subordination in the case of *were Tom even poorer than he is, he'd still contribute to charity* is indicated by syntactic inversion rather than by a marker, the inversion in effect governs the subjunctive; compare *be it ever so humble there's no place like home*.

Nonrestrictive relative clauses act essentially like "encapsulated" independent clauses. While they may not be used to assert propositions, they presuppose them. It is impossible to say *I saw Tom, who has a new car*, without implicitly claiming to believe, and hence implying, that Tom has a new car.

Restrictive relative clauses may (*I saw a man who has a huge nose*) or may not
(*I'm looking for anyone who can read Urdu*) presuppose their proposition. A
relative clause in the indicative generally does so. The speaker of (Spanish) *busco
a un hombre que* tiene *el dinero* 'I'm looking for a man who *has* the money'
presupposes that there is a definite individual who has the money in question. But
if the same clause is in the subjunctive, *busco un hombre que* tenga *el dinero* 'I'm
looking for a man who *has* (*may have*) the money', no such thing is presupposed;
for all the speaker knows, there may be no such person.

The choice of mood depends in part on the specific syntactic construction in
question. Since the value of a tense depends on mood, both directly and indirectly
it is partly dependent on the syntactic construction it occurs in.

c. Tense in Subordinate Structures

The problem of the interaction of mood and tense concerns the indicative as well
as the other moods. The indicative mood may occur (as well as in independent
clauses) in dependent clauses of various types—clauses which cannot exist on
their own, but depend on some other expression for their existence and their form:
relative clauses (*the man that Sue will marry*), subordinate (adverbial) clauses
(*although Tom is an honorable man*), "indirect questions" (*whether Tom is here*),
and clauses which are headed by a complementizer such as *that* (*that the earth is
actually pear-shaped*).

Dependent clauses in the indicative are not used to assert or question, but may
be presupposed. In *Tom found out that Sue is sweet*, the clause *Sue is sweet*,
although indicative, does not assert Sue's sweetness, though that is presupposed
by the speaker; *find out* normally requires that the speaker presuppose the truth of
the dependent clause governed by that expression.[56]

Intuitively we feel that *John wishes that he were handsome* is grammatical and
coherent, whereas there is something wrong with the verb of the second clause of
*John wishes that he is handsome. This difference has to do with the relationship
of the tense and mood of the verb in the dependent clause with those of the verb
in the main, independent clause, but also with their relationship to the tense
and mood the dependent verb would have had, if the clause had been independent.

In dependent clauses, even the indicative tenses may not exhibit their "normal"
values. For example, the pluperfect in independent clauses represents a past relative to some time itself in the past (*Max said that Susan* had gotten married *the
year before*). But in some contexts it refers rather to a past relative to some non-
past time (*if you overdo it at the party tonight, tomorrow morning you'll wish you*
hadn't drunk *so much*); or to a past relative to an already pluperfect time (*Susan
had previously claimed that she* had *already* eaten); or even to the absolute past
time (*the police wish that the suspect* hadn't been *as elusive as he was*).

As we have seen, in dependent clauses tenses may "backshift" (in Jespersen's
terms) to accommodate the matrix structure. In these examples, the embedded past

tenses represent not the past but the present (non-past), albeit a present relative to some point itself in the past:

> Tom thought that they weren't so bad.
> (Tom thought, ''They're not so bad.'')
> He knew he could depend on Bill.
> (He knew: ''I can depend on Bill.'')

The ancients were already aware that the correspondence of actual tenses and moods to underlying, notional ones is not random, though no very general account has survived from antiquity.

The choice of mood and tense in subordinate structures is complicated. The tense of the matrix, or governing, verb can determine not only the embedded tense, but its mood: in such cases in Greek, the difference between subjunctive and optative is determined purely by whether the tense of the matrix verb is primary (non-past) or secondary (past).

Indirect discourse—embedding a clause or sentence within the scope of a verb of saying, writing, thinking—and other constructions in which clauses (whether in the indicative or in some other mood) and clauselike structures (e.g., infinitival phrases) are included within other clauses, introduce many complications to tense.

Tense in dependent structures and the tenses of non-indicative (''subordinate'') moods are related problems. When a clause or sentence is embedded within a larger sentence, the embedded structure is generally not used to assert or question, therefore in many languages the indicative is relatively uncommon in such contexts.

Another set of constructions involve object clauses—indirect discourse and indirect questions. Indirect discourse (*oratio obliqua*) differs from direct discourse (*oratio recta*) in that statements and the like are put in the context of a governing verb, usually a verb of saying, thinking, wishing, rather than directly in the context of the act of speaking or writing:

> Tom *said* that he was happy.
> Aristotle *thought* that insects had eight legs.
> Bill *wished* that he weren't so clumsy.

Each sentence in indirect discourse represents a report of something said, thought, written.

The embedded statement, thought, or whatever is generally headed by a complementizer such as *that* (French *que*, Italian *che*), as in the examples above. It may also appear as a non-finite form such as an infinitive:

> I { thought / believed / knew / knew / considered / imagined / *called / ?declared } him to be an idiot.

Related to this accusative-plus-infinitive construction is another, the nominal complement construction:

$$I \left\{ \begin{array}{l} \text{thought} \\ \text{believed} \\ \text{*knew} \\ \text{considered} \\ \text{imagined} \\ \text{called} \\ \text{declared} \end{array} \right\} \text{him an idiot.}$$

Both of these are much more freely used in Latin than in the modern languages. In Latin, indeed, the accusative-plus-infinitive construction is the most common construction in "indirect discourse," not the construction with a *that*-clause, and it occurs with a wide range of verbs of saying, thinking, and writing:

scio   me paene incredibilem rem   polliceri
know (PRES ACT INDIC 1SG) me almost incredible   thing promise (PRES INF)
'I know that I am promising an almost incredible thing'

non arbitror   te   ita   sentire
not suppose (PRES INDIC 1SG) you thus feel (PRES ACT INF)
'I do not suppose that you feel thus'—literally, 'I do not suppose you (*te* = 'thee') to feel thus'[57]

Because the verb "to be" is so readily omitted, the two constructions are for all intents and purposes the same, except insofar as the predicate nominal construction, as in the modern European languages, is restricted to certain verbs which tie their objects closely to them in limited ways:

hominem   prae   se   neminem
man (MASC ACC SG) before self no one (MASC ACC SG)
'he thought nobody a man in comparison with himself'

rex   ab suis   appellatur
king (MASC NOM SG) by his own (MASC ABL PL) call (PRES PASS INDIC 3SG)
'he is called king by his subjects'[58]

The effects of omitting *esse* 'to be' resemble this construction so closely that some grammarians have proposed that the predicate nominal construction is a special case of the accusative-plus-infinitive construction. Whether it is or not, on the surface the structure is very similar:

negant   quidquam   bonum
deny (PRES ACT INDIC 3PL) anything (NEUT ACC SG) good (NEUT ACC SG)
nisi   quod   honestum   sit
except what (NEUT NOM SG) right (NEUT NOM SG) be (PRES SUBJ 3SG)
'they assert that nothing is good but what is right'[59]

This example points out something else about indirect discourse in Latin. An already subordinate clause, when embedded, generally appears in the subjunctive; the constructions we have been discussing are limited to the main clauses of embedded sentences.

Related to indirect discourse is the indirect question construction, in which the embedded clause is equivalent to an independent question, whether a "WH question" (*where is Jane?*) or a "yes-no question" (*is Jane here?*):

Sue asked, "Where did Max go?"
Sue asked where Max went.
Sue wondered, "Who is Batman?"
Sue wondered who Batman was.
Sue inquired, "Has Jane left?"
Sue inquired ⎰ if   ⎱ Jane had left.
              ⎱ whether ⎰

Except in the case with *if*, the embedded indirect question has the form of a relative clause. Although relative clauses are thought of as primarily modifiers (*the man* who wanted to marry Jane), they can occur in any position taken by nominals—as subject, object (of verb or preposition), or indirect object, and so forth:

subject:
    where Jane went is a mystery to me
    who steals my wallet steals trash
    whatever you do now is useless
object (of a verb):
    I wrote you *where Jane had gone*
    I know *who stole your wallet*
    I can do *whatever you can*
object (of a preposition):
    I wrote you about *where Jane had gone*
    I know all about *who stole your wallet*
    I'm not afraid of *whatever you can do*
indirect object:
    I gave the money to *whoever was here*
    I did *whoever was here* as many favors as I could

The indirect question construction (*I wondered where he had gone, I wondered whether he had gone*) resembles this construction, since the indirect question generally has the form of a relative clause and is syntactically an object. Functionally the two constructions differ, however, and in languages different from the familiar European languages they do not necessarily overlap.

As regards tense, the form of the subordinate verb in indirect discourse and indirect questions does not depend solely on the temporal relationship of the event or state to the time of the speech act (absolute time), but rather also on its relationship to the time of the governing verb (relative time). In a past context the statement "we're happy" is reported as *they were happy* (*they said they were happy*). The tense is brought into accord with the tense of the governing verb.

Aspect is not affected in indirect discourse; in ancient and modern languages alike, the aspect of a verb remains the same as in direct discourse. The mood of a verb in a subordinate structure depends, as we have noted, on the syntactic context, namely, on the nature of the construction in question. It also depends on that of the verb, preposition, or subordinating conjunction which governs the subordinate verb or the structure of which that subordinate verb is the main verb.

We have seen that indirect discourse in Latin typically utilizes the infinitive mood for the main clause of the sentence to be embedded, and the subjunctive for already subordinate clauses. Indirect questions go into the subjunctive: *nescio ubi sim* 'I don't know (*nescio*) where (*ubi*) I am (*sim*, 'may be')'.[60]

In Greek, both a finite clause headed by *hóti* 'that' and an infinitival construction are possible, depending on the governing verb:

légei	tis	hóti taûta	boúletai
say (PRES ACT INDIC 3SG)	someone	that these things	wish (PRES ACT INDIC 3SG)
phesí	tis	taûta	boúlesthai
say (PRES ACT INDIC 3SG)	someone	these things	wish (PRES MID INF)

'someone says that he wishes for this'[61]

The modern European languages in general use a finite clause, but the mood of
the clause—whether indicative or subjunctive—depends on several factors, vary-
ing from language to language (and from period to period or dialect to dialect
within one language). These factors include the mood governed by the complementizer (or, in the case of the indirect question, the interrogative pronoun heading the clause); the mood governed by the governing verb; and of course the
speaker's "attitude," as for instance whether the clause is presupposed (*je suppose qu'il est là* 'I take it that he's there') or not *(Je suppose qu'il soit là* 'I
postulate, for the purposes of argument, that he's there').[62]

The tense and mood of an embedded (dependent) verb depend, then, on several
factors which are of various kinds—syntactic, semantic, pragmatic (functional).
In the effort to find a simple account of the dependent tenses, the grammatical
tradition has, however, constantly sought to find a purely grammatical account. In
the case of Latin in particular there grew up the doctrine of the *consecutio temporum*, the "sequence of tenses," which has proven influential in the theory of
tense to this day, despite numerous problematic aspects.

d. Sequence of Tense Rules

Things are more complicated in Latin than in Greek. The Roman grammarians
recognized that the tense of a finite verb is governed by that of the verb of the
matrix or including clause, and defined rules for what was variously called the
"connection" (*coniectio*), 'conjunction' (*coniunctio*), 'coming together' (*conven-
tio*), or 'sequence' (*consecutio*) of tenses (*temporum*); today these rules are known
as "sequence-of-tense(s)" rules (henceforth SOT).

Charisius and Diomedes say[63]:

> tenses are conjoined in this way: the present indicative is joined with the present
> subjunctive, e.g., *dico quamvis intellegas*[64]; likewise this same present indicative
> tense is joined with the perfect subjunctive, e.g., *dico quamvis intellexeris*[65]; this
> same tense is joined also with the future optative, e.g., *dico ut intellegas.*[66]
>
> . . . the imperfect indicative is joined with the imperfect subjunctive, e.g., *dice-
> bam quamvis intellegeris*[67]; likewise this same tense is joined also with the pluper-
> fect subjunctive, e.g., *dicebam quamvis intellexeris.*[68]
>
> The perfect indicative[69] and the pluperfect are joined with the imperfect and plu-
> perfect subjunctive, e.g., *dixi quamvis intellegeres,*[70] *dixi quamvis intellexisses,*[71]
> *dixeram quamvis intellegeres,*[72] *dixeram quamvis intellexisses.*[73]

The future indicative is joined with the present, perfect, and future subjunctive [*sic*] and with the future optative, thus: *dicam quamvis intellegas*,[74] *dicam quamvis intellexeris*,[75] *dicam si intellexeris*,[76] *dicam ut intellegas.*[77]

The perfect indicative is sometimes joined with the future optative, as *dixi ut facias.*[78] This is different from its being joined with the imperfect subjunctive, mentioned above. In *dixi ut faceres*[79] both the time in which I speak and the time in which it may be done are past; in *dixi ut facias* the time of speaking is past, but the time of the deed is left to the future[80] . . . it is uncertain whether it will be done or not.

The subjunctives likewise are joined with each other, as follows: imperfect with imperfect, as *dicerem si scirem*,[81] pluperfect with pluperfect, as *dixissem si scissem*[82]; likewise the imperfect with the pluperfect, as *scriberem tibi si scissem*[83]; likewise pluperfect with imperfect, as *scripsissem tibi si scirem.*[84]

Essentially the same rules apply in Latin to the indicative as to the subjunctives.[85] Diomedes says:

The present indicative is joined with the present indicative, e.g., in Cicero 'de te autem, Catilina, cum quiescunt, probant, cum patiuntur, decernunt, cum tacent, clamant'. . . .[86]

The perfect of of the indicative mood is joined . . . with the imperfect indicative, e.g., *venit et ad ripas, ubi ludere saepe solebat*[87]; . . .

The pluperfect of the indicative mood is joined with the present indicative, e.g., *dixerat ille, et iam per moenia clarior ignis auditur*[88]; the present indicative is joined with the future indicative, as in Virgil: *quamquam animus meminisse horret luctuque refugit, incipiam.*[89]

In the grammatical tradition the Latin SOT rules are often summarized as follows[90]:

In complex sentences a Primary tense in the main clause is followed by the Present or Perfect in the dependent clause, and a Secondary tense by the Imperfect or Pluperfect:—

PRIMARY TENSES

rogo,	*I ask, am asking*	quid facias, *what you are doing.*
rogabo,	*I shall ask*	quid feceris, *what you did, were doing, have done, have been doing.*
rogavi (sometimes),	*I have asked*	quid facturus sis, *what you will do.*
rogavero,	*I shall have asked*	
scribit,	*he writes*	ut nos moneat, *to warn us.*
scribet,	*he will write*	
scribe (scribito),	*write*	ut nos moneas, *to warn us.*
scribit,	*he writes*	quasi oblitus sit, *as if he had forgotten.*

SECONDARY TENSES

rogabam,	*I asked, was asking*	quid faceres, *what you were doing.*
rogavi,	*I asked, have asked*	quid fecisses, what *you had done, had been doing.*
rogaveram,	*I had asked*	quid facturus esses, *what you would do.*
scripsit,	*he wrote*	ut nos moneret, *to warn us.*
scripsit,	*he wrote*	quasi oblitus esset, *as if he had forgotten.*

If the leading verb is *primary*, the dependent verb must be in the *Present* if it denotes *incomplete action*, in the *Perfect* if it denotes *completed action*.

If the leading verb is *secondary*, the dependent verb must be in the *Imperfect* if it denotes *incomplete action*, in the *Pluperfect* if it denotes *completed action*:—

(1) *He writes* [primary] *to warn* [incomplete action] *us*, scribit ut nos moneat. *I ask* [primary] *what you were doing* [now past], rogo quid feceris.

(2) *He wrote* [secondary] *to warn* [incomplete] *us*, scripsit ut nos moneret. *I asked* [secondary] *what you were doing* [incomplete], rogavi quid faceres.

A somewhat more explanatory presentation is that of Andrews and Stoddard, who capture another aspect of the traditional rule:

> Similar tenses [both primary or both secondary] only can, in general, be made to depend on each other, by means of those connectives [conjunctions] which are followed by the subjunctive mood.
>
> In clauses thus connected, the present, [the] perfect, and the periphrastic forms with *sim* and *fuerim*, may depend on [the present, the perfect definite, the futures].
>
> So the imperfect, pluperfect, and periphrastic forms with *essem* and *fuissem*, may depend on [the imperfect, the perfect indefinite, the pluperfect].
>
> Dissimilar tenses may be made to depend on each other, in order to express actions whose time is different. . . . So the perfect indefinite may be followed by the present, to express the present result of a past event.[91]

Considerable doubt has been expressed concerning the traditional SOT rule in Latin. Lakoff writes that "the whole question of sequence of tenses and the relationships among the tenses of verbs in complex sentences is one that has been studied too little and dismissed with overly simple answers too often."[92] In the same vein Ronconi is led "to doubt the existence of a *consecutio temporum*, at least such a rigid body as normative grammar presents. . . . We doubt if it is possible to speak of a 'sequence' of tenses, understood as dependence of a subordinate tense on the tense of a governing verb."[93]

Ernout and Thomas point out that "the concordance of tenses does not come down to a unique 'rule'; it is not an artificial procedure, but the expression of a natural tendency which favoured the morphological parallelism of the subjunctive and the indicative in conjugation."[94]

The rule as stated in the grammars is an artificial summation of the effects of sundry processes, both historical and synchronic, and is subject to numerous exceptions: "the forced simplicity of this rule has the consequence of rejecting numerous facts amongst its exceptions. One should consider, better than is done, conditions imposed by the particular values of the tenses themselves and by the nature of the various subordinate clauses."[95]

There are such a large number of exceptions as to call into question the value of the generalized rule. The spoken language was less strict than the written, and it was possible as well to follow the absolute tenses of direct discourse or to assimilate one tense to another, adjacent one without regard to meaning.[96]

For the most part, however, exceptions are due either to the particular character of each of the tenses or to that of each of the constructions. The historical present naturally acts as a secondary tense, but it may take a primary sequence; there is a famous example in which Cicero switches sequence in midsentence:

rogat		ut curet		quod

ask (PRES ACT INDIC 3SG) that take care of (PRES ACT SUBJ 3SG) what

dixisset
say (PLUPF ACT SUBJ 3SG)

'he asks him to attend to ('that he should take care of') the thing he had spoken of '[97]

The perfect of the governing verb naturally acts as a primary verb when used in a present perfect sense ("perfect indefinite," as in Allen and Stoddard), but as a secondary when a past tense ("perfect definite," like the Greek aorist). But in some cases there is confusion between the two:

te   huc   foras seduxi,   ut   tuam
you to here off   take (PERF ACT INDIC 1SG) that your (FEM ACC SG)

rem   ego te.cum   hic   loquerer
thing (FEM ACC SG) I   you-with here talk (IMPF SUBJ 1SG)

familiarem
familiar (FEM ACC SG)

'I have taken you off to here, in order that I should discuss with you this business of your family' ('this family thing')[98]

Here the primary-tense present perfect is treated like an aoristic, secondary-tense present perfect.

The perfect of the subordinate verb usually represents any past completed action. But it may represent everything from a pluperfect to a present perfect, and even non-completed action.[99]

The tenses in various constructions do not follow the SOT rules. Some constructions, such as parenthetical remarks, are outside the context of the main verb of the sentence or clause; in other cases a choice of relative or absolute tenses is optional.[100] In conditional constructions particularly, the tense and mood of a verb depends on a large number of independent factors and no simple, general rule is possible at all.[101]

The European languages inherited the Latin SOT rules, either directly or indirectly. The rule for Spanish is sufficiently similar to the Latin rule. The use of the tense forms of the subjunctive is conventional and little dependent on the notional time values implied by the names of the tenses; it is generally controlled by the tense of the main verb. An independent verb in a primary (non-past) tense governs the present subjunctive; one in the conditional[102] or a past tense governs the imperfect:

Le digo	I tell him	
Le diré	I shall tell him	que se marche
Le he dicho	I have told him	to go away
Le habré dicho	I shall have told him	
Le decía	I told him	
Le dije	I told him	que se marchara ([march]ase)
Le he dicho	I told him	
Le diría	I should tell him	to go away
Le había dicho	I had told him	
Le habría dicho	I should have told him	

When the perfect tense acts as a past tense, it may be followed by a past subjunctive:

Me ha pedido repetidas veces que registre [present] por todos los rincones. He has asked me repeatedly to look everywhere. . . .

Me ha quedado aquí para que Rosalia pudiera [imperfect] salir. I stayed here so that Rosalie might go out. . . .

Similarly, in French:

After verbs followed by *que* + [subjunctive], the rule governing the sequence of tenses is: the [present and perfect subjunctive] (*j'aie chanté*) are used in the dependent clause if the principal verb is in the present, future, or past indefinite; the [imperfect subjunctive] (*je chantasse*) and the [pluperfect subjunctive] (*j'eusse chanté*) are used in the dependent clause if the principal verb is in the imperfect, the past definite, the conditional, or the pluperfect.[103]

In German the rule once was this:

A present, present perfect, future or future perfect follows a present: Er sagt, er sei krank, er habe es schon getan, er werde morgen kommen, er werde es innerhalb einer Woche getan haben.

A simple past, past perfect, periphrastic past subjunctive, or periphrastic past perfect subjunctive follows a past or past perfect: Er sagte, er wäre krank, er hätte es schon getan, er würde (would) morgen kommen, er würde es innerhalb einer Woche getan haben.[104]

In English and other modern European languages various factors considerably complicate the sequence of tenses, and the operation of any SOT rule is far from the systematicity and regularity of the Latin rule—which, as we have seen, is itself far from uniform and exceptionless.

English, like many other languages, avoids the future and future perfect in subordinate clauses, substituting the present and present perfect respectively. A report of "I'm happy" in a future context (*he will say that . . .*) is not in the future (!*he will be happy*) but in the present tense (*he will say that he is happy*).[105] Likewise *he will say that he has eaten* (not !*he will say that he will have eaten*). Similarly, a pluperfect is represented as a past: *he had said that he was happy* reports "I am happy" in a pluperfect context.

In French the gradual disappearance of the imperfect and pluperfect subjunctive has necessarily disrupted the operation of the traditional rules as well. We are told that

the [imperfect subjunctive] (*je chantasse*) and the [pluperfect subjunctive] (*j'eusse chanté*) are used in the dependent clause if the principal verb is in the imperfect, the past definite, the conditional, or the pluperfect [i.e., the secondary, past tenses].

Otherwise, the present or perfect subjunctive is used.[106]

But the imperfect subjunctive is now replaced in the colloquial language by the present subjunctive, as in *il fallait qu'un jour le général de Gaulle revienne à la tête de l'état* 'it was necessary—IMPF SUBJ—that one day General de Gaulle should return—PRES SUBJ—to the head of the state'. Even in the literary language it is principally restricted to the third person singular.[107]

Brunot and Bruneau are as skeptical of the traditional rule in French as the scholars cited earlier are of that in Latin: "Some modern grammarians have imagined a so-called rule of the *concord* of tenses. This rule has never been observed by good writers."[108]

As we have noted, German once had a Latinate SOT rule. The tense of the main clause was the determinant: if this was in the present (or future), then the subjunctive of the dependent clause had equally to be in the present; if the main clause was in the past, then the subjunctive of the past was to be used in the dependent clause.[109]

But by 1922, when Curme offered the following examples, a "new" SOT system had developed:

DIRECT	INDIRECT
Ich bin krank	Er sagt or sagte, er sei krank
Ich tat es	
Ich habe es getan	Er sagt or sagte, er habe es getan
Ich hatte es getan	
Nachdem ich gelesen hatte, schrieb ich einen Brief	Er sagt or sagte, nachdem er gelesen [habe], habe er einen Brief geschrieben . . .
Ich werde kommen	Er sagt or sagte, er werde kommen
Ich werde es innerhalb einer Woche getan habe	Er sagt or sagte, er werde es innerhalb einer Woche getan haben.[110]

Curme says, however, that this "new" sequence is most often employed where the subjunctive forms are distinct from the indicative; the driving force is "a desire to secure a clear subjunctive form." While the indicative often replaces the subjunctive in a subordinate clause, the SOT rule used in such cases is the same as for the subjunctive: *ich dachte, er arbeitet immer* 'I thought he always worked' (literally, 'works').

German usage is obviously in transition. Jespersen refers to "various and often conflicting tendencies" governing tense sequencing, namely

> the tendency to harmonize the tense with that of the main verb . . . and on the other hand the tendency to keep the same tense as the original statement, further the tendency to use the subjunctive mood as an indication of doubt or uncertainty, the tendency to use the subjunctive simply as a mark of subordination even where no doubt is implied, and finally the general tendency to restrict the use of the subjunctive and to use the indicative instead.[111]

These tendencies are in conflict; different individuals, dialects, and periods resolve the conflict in different ways, yielding the range of possibilities cited by Jespersen:

> Er sagt, dass er krank ist.
> Er sagt, er ist krank.
> Er sagt, dass er krank sei.
> Er sagt, er sei krank.
> Er sagt, dass er krank wäre.
> Er sagt, er wäre krank.
> Er sagt, dass er krank war.
> Er sagt, er war krank.
> Er sagt, dass er krank sei.
> Er sagte, dass er krank wäre.
> Er sagte, er wäre krank.

"Of course," Jespersen says, "matters are not quite so chaotic as might be inferred from this list."

A half century later, the indicative has become customary when the main verb is in the present: *er ruft, damit jemand kommt*. But when the main verb is in the preterite, the subjunctive is often used, precisely because the preterite is largely a literary tense: *er rief, damit jemand käme*. In the colloquial spoken language, which generally replaces the preterite with the perfect (as in French), the present indicative is regularly used in the subordinate clause without regard to SOT rules: *er hat gerufen, damit jemand kommt*.[112] Nor do subjunctives in dependent clauses adjust their tenses any longer to those of the main clauses.

> Er *sagt,* dass er komme (dass sie kämen).
> Er *sagte,* dass er komme (dass sie kämen).
> Er *hat gesagt,* dass er komme (dass sie kämen).[113]

It would seem that, in English and German alike, the tense of an embedded subjunctive to a large extent no longer depends on that of the higher, matrix clause.

The same rules of tense shift that apply in indirect discourse apply as well to *discours indirect style libre* (free indirect discourse), in which the governing verb is not stated but merely implicit:

iam   enim agros   deploratos
already for   fields (MASC ACC) despair of (PERF ACT PARTIC MASC ACC PL)
esse
be (PRES INF)

'for the fields (they said) were (to be) already given up as lost'

Paetus omnes   libros   .   quos
Paetus all (MASC ACC PL) book (MASC ACC PL) which (MASC ACC PL)
frater   suus reliquisset   mihi   donavit
brother his   leave (PLUPF ACT SUBJ) to me give (PERF ACT INDIC 3SG)

'Paetus presented me with all the books which (he said) his brother had left'[114]

On the surface, at least, these constitute cases of tense shift in main clauses, but functionally speaking such clauses might as well be subordinate; their matrix is in the discourse structure rather than in a higher clause in the same sentence. These are essentially equivalent:

> Tom thought Sue a bad sort and predicted that she would meet a bad end some day.
> Tom thought Sue a bad sort. She would meet a bad end some day.

The conditional *would* normally cannot appear in an independent clause except as a case of "imaginative" backshift from the future (*would you please leave* roughly = *will you please leave*). Here, apparently in a main clause, it is a true future-in-the-past. The value of the tense derives from the temporal content and can be understood only in context.

Jespersen discusses what he calls "the imaginative use of tenses," of which the Latin optative would seem to be a special case, for in English also "verbal forms which are primarily used to indicate past time are often used without that temporal import to denote unreality, impossibility, improbability or non-fulfillment."[115]

The meaning of time is blotted out or indistinct in the preterit of imagination, which may refer to the present time (*if I had money enough now*) or the future (*if I had money enough tomorrow*); if some time in the past is referred to, the pluperfect is generally used, but that tense may in some cases refer to the present time, [e.g., *I wish I had been rich enough to give you the money*]. . . . It is worth noting that the preterit indicative is used in the same way and has . . . ousted the preterit subjunctive in modern Danish and in modern French (*si j'avais l'argent*, formerly *si j'eusse l'argent*).[116]

In the following examples, the past tense forms actually represent non-past time:

I wish I weren't so foolish.
    (Past: I wish I hadn't been so foolish.)
If you could spend one day in my shoes, you'd change your mind.
    (Past: If you could have spent one day in my shoes, you'd have changed your mind.)
What would you say if I ate your lunch?
    (Past: What would you have said if I had eaten your lunch?)

In Latin and other languages, the subjunctive often is used in this way.

Latin often utilized non-finite forms where the modern European languages use finite ones. Here too a deficiency of tenses led to shifts, and to the development of SOT rules. But tense in non-finites is not of the same kind as tense in finites; it presents unique problems.

e. Non-finites and Tense

In Greek, there were a fairly full complement of non-finite forms. The Greek infinitives and participles have five tenses—present, future, aorist, present perfect, and future perfect—thus, all but the imperfect and pluperfect:

GREEK INFINITIVES		
present	active	*lúein* 'to free'
	middle	*lúesthai* 'to free'
	passive	= middle 'to be freed'
future	active	*lúsein* 'to be going to free'
	middle	*lúsesthai* 'to be going to free'
	passive	*luthésesthai* 'to be going to be freed'
aorist	active	*lûsai* 'to free, to have freed'
	middle	*lúsasthai* 'to free, to have freed'
	passive	*luthênai* 'to be freed, to have been freed'
perfect	active	*lelukénai* 'to have freed'
	middle	*lelústhai* 'to have freed'
	passive	= middle 'to have been freed'
future perfect	passive (only)	*lelúsesthai* 'to be about to have been freed'
GREEK PARTICIPLES		
present	active	*lúōn* 'freeing'
	middle	*lūómenos* 'freeing'
	passive	= middle 'being freed'
future	active	*lúsōn* 'going to free'

	middle	*lūsómenos* 'going to free'
	passive	*luthēsómenos* 'going to be freed'
aorist	active	*lū́sās* 'freeing, having freed'
	middle	*lūsámenos* 'freeing, having freed'
	passive	*lutheís* 'being freed, 'having been freed'
perfect	active	*lelukṓs* 'having freed'
	middle	*leluménos* 'having freed'
	passive	= middle 'having been freed'
future perfect	passive (only)	*lelūsómenos* 'being about to have been freed'

The present and aorist infinitives differ mainly in aspect, as both are relatively future in certain constructions and relatively present in others:

relatively future
present:
   déomai humôn ménein 'I beg (*déomai*) you (*humôn*) to remain'
aorist:
   boúlomai nikêsai 'I wish (*boúlomai*) to be victorious'

relatively present
present:
   tò gàr gnônai epistḗmēn pou labeîn estin 'for to learn (*tò gnônai,* 'the learning')
     is (*estin*) to obtain (*labeîn*) knowledge'
aorist:
   tòn hupèr toû mḕ genésthai taût' agôna 'the contest (*agôna*) to prevent these from
     being done' ('the over the not to-be-done these contest')[117]

Note the contrast in Aristotle's *Ethics* (X.3,4) between the present *hēsthênai* '(to) become pleased' and aorist *hḗdesthai* '(to) be pleased'.[118]

The perfect tense in the subordinate moods contrasts with the present in representing an act as completed:

andreîón	ge	pánu nomízomen,		hòs àn
manly (ACC)	PART	very consider (PRES ACT INDIC 1PL)		who PART
peplḗgēi			patéra	
beat (PERF ACT SUBJ 3SG)			father	

'we always consider one very manly who has (may have) beaten (his) father'

édeisan	mḕ lússa	hēmîn empeptókoi	
fear (AOR ACT INDIC 3PL)	not madness	us	fall upon (PERF ACT OPT 3SG)

'they feared lest madness might (prove to) have fallen upon us'[119]

The perfect infinitive similarly marks completion. Note the contrast in Plato's *Crito* between *bouleúesthai* 'to be deliberating' and *bebouleûesthai* 'to have done deliberating'.[120]

The future in similar cases to these is used only in the optative and infinitive and even there relatively rarely, since it is effectively equivalent in tense to the other forms, relatively future rather than absolutely so:

edeḗthēsan		dè	kaì tôn
want (AOR INDIC 3PL)[121]		PART	and the (MASC GEN PL)
Megaréōn		nausì	sphâs ksumpropémpsein
Megarean (MASC GEN PL)		ship (DAT PL)	them send with (FUT ACT INFIN)

'they asked the Megareans also to escort them with ships'[122]

The participles are relative in time as well. The present represents ongoingness and relatively present time:

toûto poioûsin   nomízontes
this   do (PRES ACT INDIC 3PL) think (PRES ACT PARTIC MASC NOM PL)
díkaion   eînai
just (NEUT NOM SG) be (PRES INF)

'they do this thinking it is (to be) just'

toûto epoíoun nomízontes díkaion eînai
'they were doing this thinking it was just'

toûto epoíēsan nomízontes díkaion eînai
'they did this thinking it was just' [123]

The perfect is a relative present perfect:

epainoûsi   toùs
praise (PRES ACT INDIC 3PL) those (MASC ACC PL)
eirēkótas
speak (AOR ACT PARTIC MASC ACC PL)

'they praise those who have (having) spoken'

epḗinesan toùs eirēkótas
'they praised those who had spoken' [124]

The aorist is a relative past:

taûta   poiḗsantes   apeltheîn
these things do (AOR ACT PARTIC MASC NOM PL) go away (PRES INF)
boúlontai
wish (PRES ACT INDIC 3PL)

'having done this, they (now) wish to go away'

In a few constructions, however, it is a relative present. [125]

The future is a relative future: *toûto poiḗsōn érkhetai* 'he is coming (*érkhetai*) to do (*poiḗsōn*) this (*toûto*)'. [126]

On the whole, we can generalize that the non-finites of Greek do not mark even relative tense, but simply aspect; their effective relative tense derives only in part from the nominal tense.

The Latin infinitives are of three tenses, with the future periphrastic in both voices, and the perfect in the passive:

		Latin Infinitives
present	active	*amare* 'to love'
	passive	*amari* 'to be loved'
perfect	active	*amavisse* 'to have loved'
	passive	*amatus esse* 'to have been loved'
future	active	*amaturus esse* 'to be going to love'
	passive	*amatum iri* 'to be going to be loved'

The participles are present (*amans* 'loving') and future (*amaturus* 'being about to love') in the active, and perfect (*amatus* 'loved') and future (*amandus* 'having to be loved, about to be loved, yet to be loved') in the passive.

Except in indirect discourse, only the present and perfect infinitives are used. They differ only in aspect, the present indicating imperfection and the perfect perfection, while the present and perfect participles are similar in meaning, and the future participle indicates something "still to take place." [127]

In indirect discourse, however, the participles and infinitives represent tense relative to the governing verb: "the Present, the Perfect, or the Future Infinitive is used in Indirect Discourse, according as the time indicated is *present, past,* or *future* with reference to the verb of *saying* etc. by which the Indirect Discourse is introduced":

	cado, I am falling.
dicit se cadere,	'he says he is falling.'
dixit se cadere,	'he said he was falling.'

	cadebam, I was falling; *cecidi,* I fell, have fallen;
	cecideram, I had fallen.
dicit se cecidisse,	'he says he was falling.'
dixit se cecidisse,	'he said he had fallen.'

	cadam, I shall fall.
dicit se casurum [*esse*],	'he says he shall fall.'
dixit se casurum [*esse*],	'he said he should fall.' [128]

However, the present participle implies continuous action, whereas the perfect implies completed action, and the future is neutral in this regard.

present: *aut sedens aut ambulans disputabam* 'I conducted the discussion (*disputabam*) either sitting (*sedens*) or walking (*ambulans*).

perfect: *post natos homines* 'since the creation of men'; lit. 'after (*post*) men (*homines*) (were) born (*natos*)'

future: *rem ausus plus famae habituram* 'having dared (*ausus*) a thing (*rem*) which would have (*habituram*) more repute (*plus famae*)'; *si periturus abis* 'if (*si*) you are going away (*abis*) to perish (*periturus,* lit. 'about to perish'). [129]

The modern European languages have an even more reduced complement of non-finites—just one infinitive: French *aimer,* Italian *amare,* Spanish *amar,* German *lieben,* and English (*to*) *love,* though they form a periphrastic perfect infinitive: French *avoir aimé,* Italian *avere amato,* Spanish *haber amado,* German *geliebt haben,* English (*to*) *have loved.* Portuguese however has what are in effect personal endings on the infinitive, the so-called "personal infinitive." *Falarmos* is 'for us to speak, our speaking'; *falarem* 'for them to speak, their speaking'.

The participles (verbal adjectives) are two. One is used indifferently as past and/or perfect and/or passive: French *aimé,* Italian *amato,* Spanish *amado,* German *geliebt,* English *loved.* The other is non-past ("present")/imperfect/active: French *aimant,* Italian/Spanish *amando,* German *liebend,* English *loving.* In all these languages but English the participles are declined for number and gender; following traditional grammars, only the masculine singulars have been given as illustrations above. There is only a present active gerund (verbal adverb), though there is a periphrastic perfect or past gerund and periphrastic passives: *loving, having loved, being loved, having been loved.*

It is an old debate whether the non-finite moods of the modern European languages can be considered to have tense at all. English has a simple, morphological infinitive (*to love*) and a periphrastic perfect infinitive (*to have loved*), and pairs active participles and gerunds in the same way (*loving* and *having loved*). The "imperfect" forms (the simple infinitive and the -*ing* forms) represent relatively non-past time:

> He wanted to leave. (The time of leaving is future relative to some time in the past.)
> He continued to yell. (The time of yelling is present relative to some time in the past.)
> He continued yelling. (The time of yelling is present relative to sometime in the past.)
> He exited yelling. (The time of yelling is present relative to some time in the past.)

The perfects (perfect infinitive and the -*en* forms) represent relatively past time:

> He seemed to have left. (The time of leaving is past relative to some time in the past.)
> He was reported as having escaped. (The time of escaping is past relative to some time in the past.)
> Having escaped from jail, he had no wish to return. (The time of escaping is past relative to some time in the past.)

The perfects however may represent not only a relative past, but also merely perfect aspect, whether in the (relative) past, present, or future:

> The police hoped to have captured the escapee by noon. (*To have captured* is a future perfect relative to some point in the past; cf. *the police hoped they would have captured the escapee by noon.*)
> The police claim to have captured the escapee. (*To have captured* is a past or a present perfect relative to the present: *the police claim that they have captured/they captured the escapee.*)
> The police had already claimed three times to have captured the escapee. (*To have captured* is a past perfect relative to some time in the past: *the police three times claimed that they had captured the escapee.*)

But it is not clear whether the non-finite forms of the modern languages represent relative tense, with tense distinctions neutralized (some forms are ambiguous, that is), or represent simply the aspect, with tense being implied but not stated by the forms themselves. It is obvious that in practice there can be little difference between the two.

From the point of view of a general theory of tense and aspect, however, this is a very difficult question, essentially that of the difference between aspect and relative tense. We will return to this question in part II when we consider the so-called "tenseless" languages, for it is controversial whether such languages mark aspect but not tense, or possess markers of relative tense.

The various constraints and generalizations on sequence of tenses—involving both finite and non-finite tenses—leave open two questions. First, why do the dependent moods not have the same number and uses of tenses as the indicative? Second, is there any generalized, principled way of predicting how underlying tenses match the actual tenses?

Traditional grammar never achieved answers to these questions. Without an answer to the second of these, especially in the form of a unified theory of independent and dependent tensed verbs, no theory of tense can be considered adequate even in descriptive terms. Without an answer to the first, no such theory can be considered explanatory. Jespersen, who proposed the first unified, explanatory answer to such questions, was ultimately not successful, though he permanently altered the way in which these questions were (and are) approached.

Before considering the work of later scholars who sought to supersede Jespersen's theories, another aspect of his work should be examined. Jespersen's treatment of the perfect tenses, even in independent clauses, has numerous difficulties. Partly, we have seen, this results from his inadequate approach to aspect (and relative tense). But it also results from problems relating to *use,* for while Jespersen is the first scholar to distinguish meaning from use in a significant way, his approach to use ultimately fails. In this area too the issues raised by his work continue to affect contemporary approaches to sense.

f. The Uses of the Perfect Tenses

Jespersen's treatment of the perfect is manifestly inadequate, but the perfect is notoriously difficult for theorists in all periods. We have seen that, for the ancients, the central issue is how the perfect of Greek and the historic perfect of Latin differ from the imperfect, pluperfect, and (in Greek) aorist tenses. All ancient grammarians agree that the perfect differs from the imperfect in something like aspect, and from the pluperfect in tense (whether understood as a different time or a different segment of the same time).

But what of the aorist? For Dionysius, the aorist is neutral in regard to the opposition of recent and distant past. For the Stoics and presumably Varro, however, it would be aspectual distinctions to which the aorist is indifferent.

The grammatical tradition usually treats the present perfect tense of the modern languages as a recent or definite past in distinction to the indefinite preterite. Pickbourn, however, sees the perfect as indefinite, since it does not refer to any specific time in the past, whereas the preterite is incomplete without such a time reference. Hence the difference in meaning between *I haven't gone to Europe* and *I didn't go to Europe.*

The concern with labeling categories and the assumption that use follows meaning obscured for scholars prior to Jespersen the many different notions conveyed by the perfect. Even when indefinite, the perfect has a number of different uses. Those who commented on these issues at all tended to see only a very large number of different uses, but since McCawley (1971) grammarians have usually subsumed these under four broad categories, called by him the universal, existential, stative, and "hot news" perfects, and by Comrie (1976) respectively the perfect of persistent situation, the experiential perfect, the perfect of result, and the perfect of recent past.[130]

The universal perfect (perfect of persistent situation) is not considered by Jespersen to be a central use of the perfect. As Comrie notes, many languages use the present tense for this, as for example French: *j'attends depuis trois jours* 'I have been waiting for three days' ('I await since three days').[131]

Examples such as *I've known Max since 1960* are used to "indicate that a state of affairs prevailed throughout some interval stretching from the past to the present." [132] It is for this reason that McCawley has called this the "universal" perfect, since its logic involves the universal quantifier "all" ("throughout some interval" = "at *all* times during some interval").

The "indefinite" perfect principally consists of the existential and the stative perfect. Examples such as *I have read* Principia Mathematica *five times* are used to "indicate the existence of past events," to indicate "that a given situation has held at least once during some time in the past leading up to the present." [133] Examples such as *I can't come to your party—I've caught the flu* are used to "indicate that the direct effect of a past event still continues." Comrie relates this use in English to the so-called present use of perfects in ancient Greek: *memnês-thai* 'to remember' ('to have been reminded'). [134]

Comrie observes that whereas *Bill has gone to America* (the perfect of result) implies that Bill is now in America, *Bill has been to America* (the experiential perfect) has no such implication. [135] In North American English, at least, *Bill has gone to Europe* is ambiguously either existential or stative—as is even *Bill went to Europe*.

Totally new is McCawley's "hot news" perfect, identified by Comrie [136] with the recent past. McCawley (1971) says that examples such as *Malcolm X has just been assassinated* are used "to report hot news"; the sentence *Malcolm X has been assassinated* has presumably become less and less acceptable over time since then. There is some truth in both McCawley's and Comrie's positions, but essentially this use is neither a perfect of "hot news" nor a perfect of recent past.

Slobin and Aksu point out that the Turkish inferential can be used to convey surprise, and note (following Haarman) the occasional use of "indirect experience" forms in numerous languages, when the consequences of an event are represented as having been unexpected by the speaker. [137] There is no necessary implication of recency of the event in such cases. As it happens, the speaker is unlikely to be surprised by an event which is not recent; at the very least, recency is as shadowy and pragmatically dependent a concept as current relevance.

Accordingly, the perfect properly speaking may be ambiguous only between stative and existential perfect, though it also has the meaning of universal perfect and in certain contexts that of relative past. As well, it may *convey* surprise or *invite an inference of* recent past.

The Varronian tradition, as in Harris's *Hermes,* sees the perfect as the completive aspect of the present tense. Jespersen does not treat the perfect as completive in nature, but rather as permansive. He does recognize that it can be used for continuing states.

Jespersen is probably the first important figure to discuss the ambiguity of the modern perfects. While he admits no ante-present, he treats the past and future perfects as ambiguously ante- (relative) tenses and permansives. *Max had gone* can refer either to an act in the past of the past (*Max had gone to Europe only once before*), or to a previous act with permansive results in the past (*Max had gone to the store and was expected back shortly*).

In certain contexts the distinction of perfect and (relative) past is lost, and the perfects stand for both the ante-tenses and the relative pasts. Both *Sue believed Max to have gone* and *Sue believed that Max had gone* ambiguously report either of the beliefs "Max went" and "Max has gone." In many contexts a perfect will be multiply ambiguous, since "Max has gone" is itself ambiguous: it can imply either "Max (has gone and) continues to be gone" or "Max (has gone at some time in the past but) has subsequently returned."

But it is possible to use indirect discourse out of its embedding matrix—*discours indirect style libre*. If the ante-past represents a kind of free indirect discourse, then there is no need to postulate Jespersen's ambiguity of the perfect, although at least one other ambiguity remains, namely that of stative and existential perfect.

All earlier scholars had sought a general meaning (*Gesamtbedeutung*) or basic meaning (*Gemeinbedeutung*) for the perfect (and each of the other tenses). Jespersen neatly dealt with this by differentiating functional and notional categories. If he had admitted an ante-present, he might well have treated it as having the notion of permansive present among those which it expressed. But his system, strictly speaking, can assign no systematic ambiguity to the perfect, and in this he follows the tradition.

Today some scholars continue to seek the elusive *Gesamtbedeutung* of the perfect, while others accept that it is ambiguous. The latter treatment avoids the difficulties in its apparent ambiguity, but introduces the problem of explaining why precisely this miscellany of meanings should be attached in so many languages to the same linguistic category.

One approach to the resolution of this paradox is to deny that there is any paradox, indeed that precisely this miscellany *is* assigned to the same category of perfect. L. Anderson argues that a grammatical category such as "perfect" does not have precisely the same range of uses in different languages, and that the use of the same name for categories in different languages reflects rather similarity on a language-independent "map" of semantic space.[138] That is, it is precisely when certain concepts cluster and partially overlap, when categories in two languages cover largely the same portion of such a map, that we are justified in calling those categories by the same name. Not surprisingly, the concepts of current relevance, anteriority, stativity, result, and experientiality are central on Anderson's maps of the perfect.

While admitting that the perfect tenses of sundry languages may have various semirelated uses, semanticists have nonetheless generally assumed a central (or core) meaning (or use). McCoard (1978) identifies four main types of theory of the meaning of the perfect which occur in the literature, which he terms the ID ("indefinite past"), CR ("current relevance"), XN ("extended now"), and EB ("embedded past") theories, to which we may add the Harris-Varronian aspectual theory.

Indefinite past (ID) theory begins with Pickbourn, though the idea has its roots in the earlier tradition:

> By an aoristical, or indefinite tense, is . . . meant a tense which cannot be used in ascertaining the precise time of an individual action; and, by a definite tense, is

meant one that is capable of being applied to that purpose . . . indefinite with respect to . . . time only: *Mr. Horne Tooke HAS PUBLISHED an excellent grammatical work, called The Diversion of Purley.*[139]

Thus the five tenses of the past time—

> I wrote
> I did write
> I was writing
> I had been writing
> I had written

—"all relate to a certain time past, no part of which is now remaining."[140]

We do not say, *I have been* writing at ten o'clock . . . but . . . I *was* writing at
ten o'clock. . . . This tense therefore evidently belongs to present time; for though
it denotes something past, yet it implies that it passed in a period of time, some part
of which still remains unexpired.[141]

This contrasts with the "five present tenses":

> I write
> I do write
> I am writing
> I have been writing
> I have written[142]

The preterite tense . . . limits the sense of the verb to a certain time past, none of
which now remains; as the last hour, yesterday, . . . The present tense . . . confines the meaning of the verb to the present time. By present time, is meant any
portion of time which includes in it the now, or present instant; or a part of time
some of which still remains unexpired; as the present moment, the present
hour, . . .[143]

It is evident to what extent Pickbourn has drawn on the oldest grammatical tradition here.

However attractive the ID theory and however important its conclusions, McCoard
has argued that "definiteness is neither a sufficient nor a necessary condition for
the choice of tense-form."[144]

Although the indefinite past (ID) theory was for long highly influential, it has
tended to be eclipsed by the current relevance (CR) and extended-now (XN) theories. Since the appearance of McCoard's book, the issues involved in the case of
the perfect have been considerably clarified, and the various theories better known,
but even after 1978 this passage by Partee was considered sufficiently revolutionary to become one of the most quoted ones of recent years:

The deictic use of the past tense morpheme appears in a sentence like (3):

(3) I didn't turn off the stove

When uttered, for instance, halfway down the turnpike, such a sentence clearly does
not mean that there exists some time in the past at which I did not turn off the stove
or that there exists no time in the past at which I turned off the stove. The sentence
clearly refers to a particular time . . . whose identity is generally clear from the
extralinguistic context.[145]

Barwise and Perry point out that Reichenbach is unique among tense logicians in recognizing that the past tense "directly" refers "to a past time."[146] It is not clear whether the logical tradition has treated the past tense as if it were the existential perfect (i.e., as if *John ate* means "at some time *t* before now, 'John eats' is true") out of convenience or willful ignorance of the grammatical literature.

Current relevance (CR) theory has a very large number of subvarieties, depending on how "current relevance" is understood, and what are taken to be its criterial features. White writes, for example:

> We make use of the First Past Tense,[147] when we refer to actions long since past, and the performers of which have already left the present stage of life . . . it might be called the *Historical* Tense. We also make use of it, when we refer to actions of ourselves, or others now alive, when taken in a distant view, or unconnected with present proceedings.
>
> The Second Past Tense is seldom us'd [*sic*] with us but with respect to persons now existing, and with respect to such actions of theirs, as have either been but lately performed, or such at least as are taken into view as connected with their present proceedings.[148]

McCoard agrees with Bryan that "any idea there is of results or consequences is not implied in the present tense form but derives from the meaning or character of the verb, or from the context, or . . . the statement as a whole," and that consequently any notion of current relevance is likewise contextual and not essential.[149]

McCoard is further critical of CR theory because no one has been able to satisfactorily define "current relevance." He cites a number of suggested critical properties of "current relevance":

> recency
> present existence
>   of the surface-subject referent;
>   of the deep-subject referent;
>   of a certain state of the subject referent;
>   of a "posthumous" personage;
>   of a belief in the subject referent or in some kind of validity;
>   of the object referent
> unspecified "connection with the present"
> continuance of a state into the present
> iterativity
> experientiality
> present possibility[150]

He argues that the preterite is not consistently opposed to the perfect in any of the above regards. None of the specific versions of current relevance is applicable to more than a small range of examples. He concludes that CR is not a semantic value attached to a verb form, but only the "name of diverse implications that may attach to sentences."

As we have seen, Pickbourn at times comes close to espousing XN theory (a theory with a pedigree going back to Aristotle). This is in fact the preferred theory of McCoard, who cites in this regard the work of Bryan (1936). The following statement of Bryan's could easily have been made by Pickbourn (or McCoard):

> The preterite tense represents an action or state as having occurred or having existed at a past moment or during a past period of time that is definitely separated from the actual present moment . . . the perfect tense merely includes an action or state within certain limits of time.[151]

For example: "[the perfect] expresses . . . an action that has been completed or perfected in the present time, i.e. in the present year, the present aeon, etc."[152]

As against theories in which the perfect has different meanings, McCoard notes that "all that remains invariant in the meaning of the perfect is an identification of prior events with the 'extended' now which is continuous with the moment of coding."[153]

XN theory has proven greatly influential in recent years. For example, David Dowty states: "Following Bennett and Partee (1973) [and] Robert McCoard (1978) . . . I assumed that the appropriate way to treat the present perfect is as asserting that its sentence is true at (or perhaps within) . . . an 'extended now.' "[154]

XN theory implicitly contains some version of CR theory, however, since the dividing line between Aristotle's derivative present and the true past on the one hand, and the expanded present and the present proper on the other, depends solely on pragmatic, not semantic, factors. Many linguists have pointed out the difference in acceptability between *Shakespeare has written many plays* and *Shakespeare has won many plaudits,* between *Shakespeare has been born in Stratford-on-Avon* and *Shakespeare was born in Stratford-on-Avon.*

It is not that the nonpreferred versions of these sentences are worse in all contexts—in some they may even be better—but in null context, in the absence of any supporting matrix, they are certainly not as good. This is precisely what current relevance (CR) theory seeks to account for.

In any case, extended-now (XN) theory is a *semantic* solution to the problem of the perfect tenses, in that it characterizes them solely in terms of time *reference.* The Harris-Varronian aspectual theory is also semantic, but is based on aspect rather than tense. CR theory, however, is *pragmatic,* and defines pragmatic conditions on the *use* of the perfect tense which XN theory merely assumes. To a certain extent in theory, and to a greater extent in practice, the XN and CR approaches reflect different views as to the relationship of meaning and use, rather than different understandings of the perfect.

The embedded past (EB or EP) theory is a purely *syntactic* approach. It attempts to remove the issue of the perfect from the arena of tense semantics entirely. In EB theory the perfect is treated as a form which conveys the meaning of the past when that meaning is within the scope of another tense. The perfect introduces no new distinctions of meaning at all, beyond those pertaining to the other tenses.

In EB theory the perfect is a kind of past tense, but it is accounted for not in the theory of meaning (where the perfect might be assigned a different meaning from the preterite), but rather in the syntax (where the use of the perfect for a

relative past, rather than being seen as an aberration, is viewed as a special case
of the normal use of the perfect).

It is precisely cases of neutralization of the distinction between perfect and
relative past in indirect discourse and other embedded structures that EB was designed to handle and in which it is strongest.[155]

g. Context and Autonomy

There is a certain tension between the search for the *unique meaning* of a tense
such as the (present) perfect and the *multiplicity of uses* which all tenses show.
While the grammatical tradition offers a number of competing theories as to *the*
difference between the preterite and the perfect, it has become clear that the perfect and preterite alike have various uses, some of which they hold in common.

The search for the *Gesamtbedeutung* of each tense was the assumed task of the
traditional grammarian, but it has become controversial in the last few decades. If
the tenses (and aspects) have multiple uses, the effort to capture *all* the uses of a
category under the umbrella of one categorial label is a difficult and perhaps futile
one.

What Hermerén has pointed out in regard to the modal verbs of Germanic could
equally well be said in regard to any proposed *Gesamtbedeutung*: "the danger in
assigning a unitary meaning to each [one] seems to be that the definition . . . has
to be so vague and general that it becomes anything but informative."[156] Comrie
argues, for example, that the various uses of the progressive in English cannot be
accounted for by any general meaning assigned it.[157]

It may be that a form such as the perfect (with its supposed equivalents in other
languages) tends only to convey a certain cluster of meanings, and that there is
no one essential meaning to it (as has been argued, for example, by L. Anderson).
Alternatively, it may be that the form is systematically ambiguous. In either case,
whether it has no one central meaning or it has more than one, it would lack a
Gesamtbedeutung.

A radical empiricist such as Priestley would not be surprised by such a result:
why believe that the so-called "present perfect" of English has anything more to
do with the so-called "present perfect" of any other language than it does with
any other tense? Why believe that a grammatical category conveys one and only
one meaning?

Hockett has called the search for the *Gesamtbedeutung* "chimerical,"[158] and
Chatterjee is generally skeptical about it, characterizing the search for "essential,
ultimate categories" as a "philosophical illness" caused by the lack of a post-
structuralist viewpoint in linguistics.[159]

On the other hand, it has been argued that "a form must have a consistent
value or else communication is impossible; we cannot have linguistic forms which
derive all their meanings only from context"; that "it seems difficult to believe
that a native speaker could extend the restrictions applying to a given category of
words to a new word [without] some common core of meaning."[160]

The question is, how do we account for the sundry uses, the various implications, the apparent ambiguities of the tenses, especially in light of the traditional assumption that use follows meaning, that meaning consists of *the* idea which is "conveyed," "expressed," or "represented" by a grammatical category?

Every part of this view has come under scrutiny in recent years. Some scholars, we shall see in part II, even argue that meaning *follows* use, rather than vice versa; some doubt that there is a unique meaning to each category; and many have questioned how, or even if, meaning is "conveyed": "A sentence does not 'convey' meaning the way a truck conveys cargo, complete and packaged. It is more like a blueprint that allows the hearer to reconstruct the meaning from his own knowledge."[161]

These are all questions having to do with meaning, but meaning in a sense which was largely ignored in the tradition. Traditionally, to say that the present perfect is a recent past, a "definite" past, a "permansive" present, the "completive" aspect of the present, or the like, is to define the meaning of the tense, to put a semantic label on it.

But as the discussion in the previous section of the various theories of the perfect makes clear, this ignores two important aspects of the study of tense. The alleged ambiguity of the perfect is tied up with the pragmatics (use) of the perfect and with the logic of the perfect—its implications, entailments, and the like. It was assumed in traditional grammar that both use and logic follow directly from the meaning assigned the grammatical category. Apart from general principles of language, all that suffices, then, to understand the use of the perfect tense (and its logic) is a knowledge of its meaning.

The problem is that the present perfect, for example, is known to have, in some sense, at least four uses (or meanings). Is there an appropriately general level of analysis at which these various uses can be treated as consequences of one overarching meaning?

There is an apparent conflict between the assumption that use follows meaning and the identification of meaning with notion. For if use follows meaning, then a multiplicity of uses would seem to imply a multiplicity of meanings; but the search for the *Gesamtbedeutung* of each category is driven by the intuition that, if meanings are concepts, then it would be incoherent for each category to lack one core meaning.

Yet the tradition did not ascribe a multiplicity of use to ambiguity; it distinguished the case of the Latin perfect from that of the English perfect. The tradition recognized atypical uses such as the historical present, the futurate present perfect, and so on. But such uses depend on context.

Out of context, *Tom eats lunch* cannot be said to have past meaning, nor can *Tom has eaten lunch* refer to the future. *Hannibal crosses the Alps* is visibly historic-present in tense, but only because of the past reference inherent in *Hannibal*: if this sentence describes the actions of an actor in a scene (as in a screenplay), in which case the name lacks past reference, the pastness is lost.

It is only when a form can convey different meanings outside of context that the tradition ascribes ambiguity, as in the case of the Latin perfect: *scripserunt* can mean either 'they wrote' or 'they have written'. That this is true ambiguity and not vagueness is shown by the differing syntax of the "historic" perfect (a secondary tense) and the "definite" perfect (which is primary). From this point of view neither the present nor the (English) present perfect is ambiguous.

In this way the tradition could hold that, in the *ideal* system, each category is unambiguous and has a distinct "core" or "basic" meaning—a *Grund-* or *Gesamtbedeutung*—though in practice languages may conflate different such categories, as when Latin combines the aorist (preterite) and "definite" perfect in its present perfect tense. Even Latin does not represent the ideal system; but in theory at least, to define the meaning of a tense is to find its *Gesamtbedeutung*.

Jespersen's theory combines, as we have noted, elements of the tradition and of structuralist thought. This is not as difficult as it would appear, for there has always been a structuralist vein in traditional grammatical thought. The Priscianic tradition held that the Latin perfect combines aorist and definite perfect into one. This was not simply because the writers followed Dionysian grammatical theory or thought Latin should be like Greek. The meaning distinctions which they saw marked in the verb implied a richer system than Latin showed. As well, the two sides of the perfect have demonstrably different syntax.

The Varronian tradition seems not to have found the Latin perfect ambiguous, because there was no place in the system for the aorist. Here the essential categories seem to have been morphological rather than semantic. The imperfect or "present" stem is in opposition to the perfect stem; there is no third stem as in Greek. If there is no marker, then there is nothing to mark.

The failing of the tradition, then, is not essentially in utilizing notions as meanings or confusing grammatical with "logical" categories, nor is it necessarily in failing to recognize that meanings are places in systems and not directly the contents assigned to those places—both of these points being central issues for structuralist thought. Rather, the tradition fails to recognize that the relationship of marker (the form of the signifier) to meaning (the signified) is not a direct one, but rather one mediated through grammatical categories.

This is Jespersen's innovation. By distinguishing functional and notional categories, Jespersen is not forced to place form and meaning in a one-to-one relationship, though it is unfortunate that the ideal system which he develops, based on extralinguistic considerations, has so little predictive power as to the actual tense systems found in languages. As a result, in some respects it is less advanced than the Stoic-Varronian approach.

The fact that the sundry notions attached to one functional category are distinct from that category means that Jespersen can retain notions as meanings without ascribing ambiguity to every tense. But it has the unwelcome consequence that Jespersen can ignore the role of context; he treats every *meaning* (though not every *use*) as absolute, context-free, with the result that relative tenses are necessarily treated as essentially absolute.

While (if we disregard Jespersen's difficulties with aspect) every important point regarding tense can be extracted from his theory, virtually no important point follows as a consequence *of and within* his theory. Though Jespersen was a brilliant observer and analyst of language, his theory is quite as unexplanatory as the grammatical tradition.

"The primary concern of the analyst," says Allen, "should be with obligatory uses rather than optional or facultative ones." [162] But Jespersen does not, and on principled grounds cannot, distinguish the two. He fails also to distinguish language-specific, idiomatic uses (the fact that the perfect of persistent situation in English corresponds to the present of persistent situation in Romance and German) from language-independent, possibly universal uses (the fact that the perfects may be relative ante-tenses as well as absolute, retrospective ones). Likewise he cannot distinguish purely contextual uses, dependent on conditions of use (the futurate present perfect in subordinate clauses, for example), from independent, systematic uses.

There are other respects in which neither the tradition nor Jespersen's reworking of it provides a satisfactory account. If use follows meaning, how and why does it do so? In what way does the meaning of a form provide a key to its range of uses? In particular, how does context serve to disambiguate? Here the first requirement is an adequate semantic theory, which neither Jespersen nor the tradition supplies.

While Jespersen was primarily concerned with meaning, by which he meant notionality, from the viewpoint of modern semantics he had no semantic theory at all. Jespersen distinguished *form, function,* and *notion.* To any given functional category there could correspond more than one notion; we have seen that he gives five different notions corresponding to the preterite tense. But he does not seem to separate out what we would regard as purely syntactic relations (backshifting in indirect discourse, say) from truly semantic distinctions. He does not seem to distinguish cases of systematic phenomena such as shifting from the unsystematic ones like the "gnomic" (*men were deceivers ever*).

Moreover, he has no explicit, theoretical distinction between meaning (*semantics*) and use (*pragmatics*), though he distinguishes them in practice, in that he assigns only one location in the scheme of tenses to the preterite (past) tense, while recognizing that it has various uses. Or again, he talks of two different perfects, the retrospective present (*he has gone*) and the inclusive present (*he has been here a week*), apparently meaning that there are two different notions corresponding to the perfect even as a "present" tense.[163]

These other notions are, presumably, merely uses of the present perfect; he often says that such and such a tense in a particular use "corresponds to" such and such another tense, which in our terms must mean "has the same use as," although he clearly does not think in these terms.

Jespersen could not, and never attempted to, accommodate all uses of all tenses within his one notional scheme. Alongside the primary uses of the tenses and the systematic, shifted uses, he recognized a number of usages that are not part of the normal range of meanings of a form. For these he had no systematic description or explanation at all. The present can be used (in narration) of historical events: *Napoleon crosses/is crossing the Alps.* Almost any tense can be used in making general statements: *boys will be boys, men were deceivers ever, the earth is round.*

Most scholars would say that pastness is no part of the *meaning* of the present tense, though under certain exceptional circumstances the present can be *used* of past events. Very few would argue that the present tense is ambiguous in that it refers in various sentences to present, past, or general time, or, in *he leaves on Tuesday*, even to future time.

If under certain conditions a form such as the present can be used of, say, future time, and we assume that the present tense "really" refers to the present time, then in this case where do the futurity, pastness, "timelessness," and so forth come from but the context? For they are no part of the meaning of the form itself. But what does it mean to say that meaning "comes from" the context? Indeed, what does it mean to say that a form "conveys" meaning? What *is* a meaning, that it can be conveyed?

We must leave the further discussion of many of these questions to part II, but Jespersen's theory raises the question of the relationship of the meanings of categories and the contribution of context to meaning in a strong way. Traditionally there have been two positions to this question. The "monosemanticist" position holds that categories have one central or core meaning, one *Grund-* or *Gesamtbedeutung*, while the "polysemanticist" position holds that categories may have many meanings.[164] For the monosemanticist, if a category has different meanings or uses, these proceed from context; for the polysemanticist, the role of context is to select out one or more of the meanings adherent to the category. Many have taken the position that it is natural for one form to represent one meaning, and for one meaning to be represented by one form, while others have felt that every difference in a word's use represents a difference in meaning.[165]

These positions have different implications for the question of the role of context in disambiguation. The monosemanticist approach is essentially allied to the "autonomist" position discussed by Antal, while the polysemanticist approach is Antal's "contextualist" position.[166]

Autonomists are those who believe that "what seems to belong to the meaning of the word in a specific context is not, in fact, a part of the meaning of the word but only of its context." (Structuralism naturally leads to autonomism, and a radical structuralist would surely agree with Hjelmslev[167] that in absolute isolation no sign has any meaning.) Ehrman argues that each of the modal verbs, for example, has a "basic meaning" not dependent on context.[168]

Jespersen was a "contextualist." He believed that each functional category "pointed to" a number of different uses—primary, shifted, or nonsystematic. In any given context, of course, certain of these meanings are blocked. For example the French *passé composé*, like the Latin perfect, serves as both present perfect and past tense, but in any given context it serves only as one or the other. In general, the *passé composé* is ambiguous, but on any particular occasion of its use, it has one and only one of these uses.

For the "autonomist," on the other hand, each form or construction, except in cases of homonymy (such as *row* 'a noisy quarrel' and *row* 'a linear arrangement', or the *combing* of hair and the *combing* of waves), has precisely one meaning, which is perhaps vague in the sense that it has a different application in each context rather than a different meaning per se. A strict autonomist would hold that in colloquial French there is no distinction between perfect and past, that what we understand from the *passé composé* is given by the context, and by no part of the meaning of the form or construction itself. Colloquial French lacks the opposition in its system of meanings.

We might further explicate this distinction with an analogy. The word *today* sometimes refers to October 14, 1066, but most of the time does not. An extreme contextualist might go so far as to claim that the term is infinitely ambiguous in its reference, although the use of the word on any given day selects out one and only one possible referent for it (such as May 4, 1989).

On the other hand, an extreme autonomist must claim that *today* has precisely one meaning, something like "the day on which I am speaking or writing," though it is the context which identifies the application of the term, namely, in this case, May 4, 1989, but it is not, nor is it ever, part of the meaning of the term itself that it can or does refer to May 4, 1989, or October 14, 1066, or any other day.

This issue looms large in discussions of the English future tense and modals, since the English periphrastic future is formally a modal construction, and since modal verbs in general are further systematically ambiguous between "root" or *deontic* readings (*you must leave*) and *epistemic* readings (*that must be John now.*)

The facts of the futurate perfect might seem hopeless for a contextualist like Jespersen. However, here Jespersen makes a proposal ahead of its time which allowed him to maintain his contextualist position without at the same time admitting that the present perfect is also a future tense. He proposed that in a sequence-of-tense situation the future perfect is "replaced" by the present perfect. On the notional level it *represents*, in some way, the future perfect, although it *appears* literally as the present perfect. Transformationalists naturally interpreted this proposal in transformational terms, as a literal replacement. But it is possible to take it simply to mean that the present perfect form is *to be understood as* the future perfect in a future context. (This would come close to an autonomist position.)

The question comes back to whether futurity is part of the meaning of the futurate present perfect, whether permansiveness is part of that of the "regular" present perfect, or whether these meanings come from the context. Without an adequate semantic theory it is impossible to resolve these issues, for in strictly grammatical terms there is no difference between the positions.

For example, we have viewed the Dionysian-Priscianic approach to the past tenses as a theory stating that, since there are different tenses referring to the one segment of time which is past (passed), there must be subsidiary differences of meaning associated with the various forms. This is a contextualist position. But there is a way of viewing it as an autonomist position, namely, that past time is expressed by different tense forms in various contexts. Let the context be distant time and the pluperfect must be used (though the aorist may be).

It is obvious that the issue cannot be understood *within* grammar. But in the absence of any concept of meaning independent of language—of anything more helpful than the vague view of meanings as "notions" or "concepts" somehow "conveyed" or "expressed"—no progress can be made toward resolving the issue. We must leave further discussion to part II.

h. Multidimensional Theories: Reichenbach and Bull

Jespersen's treatment of the conditional (*would go, should go: Tom thought that Bill would go the next day*) and the conditional perfect (*would have gone, should have gone: Tom predicted that Bill would have gained several pounds within the week*) is clearly as much a problem as his treatment of the perfect tenses. Jespersen gives as post-preterite expressions those like *was to*, parallel to the missing prospective presents or post-presents (*is to*).[169] He ignores the construction in *would*. And there is no room in Jespersen's scheme for *would have*, which would have to be a retrospective (ante-) prospective (post-) preterite. Jespersen has no room for such a tertiary division of time.

It was partly to deal with the problems of Jespersen's treatment of the retrospective and prospective tenses that William Bull and Hans Reichenbach devised their systems." "[Jespersen] correctly sees the close connexion between the present tense and the present perfect, recognizable in such sentences as 'now I have eaten enough,' " comments Reichenbach, but there is no more principled reason for connecting, or contrasting, the perfect with the present than with the past, for Jespersen's tenses are primitives.[170] Since the perfect is not aspectual for Jespersen, it is not clear in what way, in semantic terms, it differs from the present, yet it is clearly not simply a present.

Jespersen did not fully appreciate the role of covert, inexplicit categories such as aspect in the grammar of the Indo-European verb, and had no clear or consistent concept of a grammatical or notional category not tied to an overt form or forms. In this he was very much within the tradition. He did recognize some degree of abstraction: he was willing to ascribe something like an aorist or preterite (i.e., a past) tense to Latin which just happens to always formally coincide with the perfect tense (*amavi* ambiguously meaning either 'I have loved' or 'I loved'). But while he understood aspect and discussed it at length in the *Philosophy of Grammar*, he never developed a model of aspect corresponding to his model of tense.[171] For him the perfect present, the pluperfect, and the present were all equally and simply tenses.

This is merely to point out that his theory treated the verb endings traditionally called "tense markers" as just that, essentially markers of tense. Aspect was not seen to have an equal status in relation to the Indo-European verb. Of course, in most European languages today the verb endings are overtly concerned with tense distinctions, whereas aspect is marked in other ways. But something like aspect plays a role in the semantics of the "tense markers" as well. The imperfect and the preterite of the Romance languages, for example, are different (morphological) tenses, but do not differ in time reference.

As Jespersen himself recognized, while his system "seems to be logically impregnable, . . . it does not claim to comprise all possible time-categories nor all those tenses that are actually found in languages."[172] Thus it fails in terms of both descriptive and explanatory adequacy. But it was precisely the inadequacies of his system which inspired later scholars to attempt to solve the problems Jespersen could not handle. It is through these later schemes that contemporary treatments of tense descend from that of Jespersen.

A scheme of relative tenses was introduced by the philosopher-logician Reichenbach (1947) to deal with the difficulties of Jespersen's system of absolute tenses. Unlike in Madvig and Jespersen, whose tenses are primitives—defined in Madvig's case only implicitly (although by Jespersen explicitly) in terms of points in time which they represent—Reichenbach's tenses are explicitly defined in terms of three independently defined points in time.

Reichenbach recognizes a line of time.[173] But for him tenses are not primitives and do not correspond to simple notions such as "past time." Where Jespersen allows the "now" to split time into three segments of past, present, and future, and relates each basic tense to one of these time segments, or at least to the notional concept of that segment (i.e., tenses depend on the "now"), Reichenbach defines tenses as relations holding between S ("now," the time of speech act), E (the time of the event or state of affairs), and a third, more abstract time R (the reference point, the temporal "point of view").

The same event may be viewed in various ways. Suppose that the speaker during the course of a day's events misses eating lunch. In a narration of the day's events, the speaker might say, "I didn't have lunch." Here the (non-) event is reported from the viewpoint of the past. But, if asked why he or she is wolfing down a sandwich at 3:00 P.M., someone might reply, speaking from the viewpoint of the present, "I haven't had lunch." Imagining how hungry he or she would feel when going home, the speaker might say, earlier in the day but taking a future viewpoint, "I won't have had lunch."

The reader may have noticed in the present book the alternations of perspective. Speaking from the viewpoint of the intentions or actions of some past writer, I say, "Aristotle already *knew* that the present tense could be used of recent events." But when writing from the present point of view in regard to extant works and their meaning today, I say, "Dionysius *distinguishes* the pluperfect and the perfect in terms of relative remoteness in time." Speaking *of* the Stoics, one might claim that they *had* an aspectual concept of the tenses; speaking *of* Varro, that they *had had* one.

The reference point R may precede, follow, or coincide with S, the time of the speech act, just as E, the time of the event or state of affairs, may precede, follow, or coincide with R. This approach enables Reichenbach to define the set of all possible tenses on principled grounds in terms of the primitives E, R, S, along with the relations "precedes," $<$; "follows," $>$; and "coincides-with," $=$.

The simple and retrospective (perfect) tenses are diagrammed by Reichenbach, using a comma to indicate coincidence and an arrow for the line of time.[174]

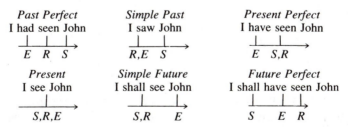

While Jespersen can define possible tense, he does so in terms of the time line and the single notion of precedence. In effect, the relationship of the simple past to the prospective past is no different from that of the prospective past to the present. Even if Jespersen admitted present retrospective and prospective tenses, it would remain the case that pairs of tenses can be related only in one way, by sheer precedence. For example, the past retrospective does not specifically relate to the future retrospective in any way. And although Jespersen acts as if the simple tenses have a special status apart from the semantically complex subordinate tenses, this is not built into the theory.

There are two consequences of this. First, apart from backshifting, no syntactic phenomena are predictable in terms of the theory itself; it is hard to see how Jespersen could explicate the neutralization of relative past and perfect, if both are primitives. And second, there is no possible distinction between systematic and unsystematic uses of the tenses, which are jumbled together as "notional" categories. The perfect can be used as a kind of present because it *is* a kind of present; but nothing *in* the theory predicts that "present" tenses will act alike, any more than it predicts that "perfect" tenses will do so.

Reichenbach, however, has a way of systematizing the tenses. Relative tense has to do with the relationship of R to S. The simple or absolute tenses (Harris's aorists) are those in which R coincides with S. In this case, if E precedes R it necessarily precedes S, and a past tense results; similarly, if E follows R, it follows S, and the result is the future. If all three coincide, the present results.

But the point of view may be that of the past (R precedes S) or future (R follows S), rather than the present. In this case, if E precedes R, a retrospective tense results; if E follows R, a prospective one. (The relative tenses may be prospective or retrospective.) The difference of absolute and relative tense has to do with whether R coincides with S or not.

Reichenbach presents "nine fundamental forms" which he labels "anterior" when E precedes S, "posterior" when E follows S, and "simple" when E coincides with S[175]:

STRUCTURE	NEW NAME	TRADITIONAL NAME
E—R—S	Anterior past	Past perfect
E,R—S	Simple past	Simple past
R—E—S		
R—S,E	Posterior past	—
R—S—E		
E—S,R	Anterior present	Present perfect
S,R,E	Simple present	Present
S,R—E	Posterior present	Simple future
S—E—R		
S,E—R	Anterior future	Future perfect
E—S—R		
S—R,E	Simple future	Simple future
S—R—E	Posterior future	—

He has no difficulty in accounting for the difference between the perfect and the preterite. In both cases the time of the event E precedes S. But the preterite is a tense in which the reference time R precedes S, and E coincides with R. On the other hand, the present perfect is a tense in which the reference point coincides with S, while E precedes R.

Reichenbach also makes good use of his notion of the R point in attempting to solve problems involving adverbials. For Reichenbach, the time of adverbials is the time of the reference point and not the time of the event. Consequently he can account for the co-occurrence not only of "present" adverbials such as *today* and *now* with the present perfect (*now we have seen everything*), but also of "past" adverbials with the conditional (*yesterday he would have left*), where a system of primitive tenses renders this inexplicable. The adverb *now* in *now we have seen everything* establishes a reference point R necessarily coincident with S. But our "seeing everything" is in the past—it precedes R. Hence the present perfect.

If the present perfect is a primitive of the system—and Jespersen treats it as such—its "presentness" is a special fact about the tense and does not follow from anything in the theory. But in Reichenbach this follows simply from the fact that the perfect has R coincident with S. It is no more than a special case of the general fact that the perfect or retrospective ("anterior") tenses involve the relationship E—R, while the "present" tenses involve R,S.

The fact that adverbials apply to R, not E, means that

in the sentence 'Now I shall go' the simple future has the meaning $S,R—E$; this follows from the principle of positional use of the reference point. However, in the sentence 'I shall go tomorrow' the same principle compels us to interpret the future tense in the form $S—R,E$. The simple future, then, is capable of two interpretations, and since there is no prevalent usage of the one or the other we cannot regard one interpretation as the correct one.[176]

He identifies the one interpretation with the French prospective *je vais voir* 'I'm going to see', the other with the French future *je verrai* 'I shall see'.

This result is an artifact of Reichenbach's failure to recognize that adverbials may relate to different times within the same sentence. He ignores cases such as *now I shall go tomorrow (whereas formerly I was going to go next week)*. In *I shall go tomorrow*, the future reference point is not indicated by the adverbial; compare *he knew that he was going to go tomorrow*, with past reference point. Rather, the future reference point is assumed; in discourse or text it would be gotten from the context. The future tense is not ambiguous as regards the relationship of R to S, although, as we have indicated, it *is* aspectually ambiguous.

But Reichenbach has little if anything to say about aspect, properly speaking, and his system is not designed to accommodate it. The prospective (posterior) and retrospective (anterior) tenses are relative tenses. While it is possible to interpret the pluperfect (anterior past), for example, as the perfect-in-the-past, because the event wholly precedes the past reference point, this is not even implied by Reichenbach's system.

The major advantage to Reichenbach's system is that a very simple account of sequence-of-tense rules can be given (although the account is not adequate). Reichenbach observed: "When several sentences are combined to form a compound[177] sentence, the tenses of the various clauses are adjusted to one another by certain rules which the grammarians call the rules for the *sequence of tenses*." Unlike Jespersen, however, he does not interpret his literally as a shift.[178] Rather, he says:

We can interpret these rules as the principle that, although the events referred to in the clauses may occupy different time points, the reference point should be the same for all clauses—a principle which, we shall say, demands *the permanence of the reference point*. Thus, the tenses of the sentence, 'I had mailed the letter when John came and told me the news', may be diagrammed as follows:

1st clause: E_1—R_1 —S
2nd clause: R_2,E_2—S
3rd clause: R_3,E_3—S

Here the three reference points coincide. It would be incorrect to say, 'I had mailed the letter when John has come'. . . .

For Reichenbach the general rule is that within a sentence or other coherent narration, the reference point is maintained. In the case of sequences of time in narration, however, "the rule of the permanence of the reference point can . . . no longer be maintained"[179]; in Reichenbach's example *if he telephoned before he came*, R_1 precedes R_2. Yet another type of example illustrates what he calls "the more general rule of the *positional use of the reference point*."[180] In the case of *he was healthier when I saw him than he is now*, the R point is not maintained:

1st clause: R_1,E_1—S
2nd clause: R_2,E_2—S
3rd clause: S,R_3,E_3

Reichenbach had no need of a theory of shifting because, given general properties of the R point and its use, the correct tense automatically falls out. In *John likes cheese*, some E_1 (John's liking cheese) coincides with some R_1 (the present time, the viewpoint generally adopted in making statements of fact), and this R_1 coincides with S (the time of the speech act).

In *Susan realized that (John likes cheese)*, E_2 (her realization) coincides with R_2 (this R_2 is the past time of narration), and R_2 precedes S (or else we would have *Susan has realized that John likes cheese*).

In *Susan realized that John liked cheese* we have this situation:

$$E_2,R_2\text{—}S$$
$$E_1,R_1,S$$

But since point R is maintained in indirect discourse (by the sequence of tense rules), R_1 must "shift" to R_2, and since this point precedes S, we now have E_1,R_1—S, which defines the past tense.

Reichenbach's theory requires no special apparatus for shifted, "adjusted" tenses, once we have ways of determining basic relations between S, R, and E, and general rules for sequences of R points. However, Reichenbach's treatment can be accused of begging the question, for his rather vague "general rule" presents precisely the challenge of defining principles covering the cases cited by Jespersen of the failure of shifting to occur.

A number of commentators have discussed the possibility under certain circumstances of not shifting the tense, as in: *Susan realized that John likes cheese*. At least Reichenbach's theory has to be considerably elaborated, if it is not to achieve generality in its explanatory adequacy by dint of failure to achieve descriptive adequacy at all.

Reichenbach's system has a number of other problems. The system is too rich.

The posterior past and the anterior future each has three different definitions. As Comrie points out, this is not totally inappropriate:

> If someone asks me: *Will John have finished his paper by tomorrow?* and I answer: *Yes*, then my reply will be judged truthful (i) if John finishes the paper between the time of my reply and tomorrow (*S—E—R*), (ii) if John in fact finishes the paper at the moment I reply (*S,E—R*), or (iii) if John has in fact already finished the paper (*E—S—R.*).[181]

However, Comrie denies that English or any other language provides evidence for Reichenbach's treatment of the future perfect as being three ways ambiguous, rather than merely vague.

As Comrie points out, the only things that matter in the case of the future perfect are that R follow S (future) and that E precede R (perfect): the future perfect does not *state* anything about the relationship of E to S. The problem comes from Reichenbach's use of one ordering of E, R, and S to define tenses; the proposal has often been made that we need not define each tense by a strict ordering of all three parameters, but rather by two pairwise orderings of E and R, and R and S.[182]

Such a proposal is much more revealing in that it separates tense from aspect (or relative tense). It may be observed that all the past tenses show the pattern R—S (R precedes S); all the present tenses, the pattern R,S (R at S); and all the future tenses, the pattern, S—R (R after S). Tense is a matter of how R relates to S. All of Reichenbach's anterior tenses show the pattern E—R (E before the R point); all the simple tenses E,R (E at the R point); and all the posterior tenses R—E (E after the R point). What the relationship of E and R has to do with is, roughly, aspect (and/or relative tense). For example, instead of E—R—S for the definition of the anterior past, we have E—R:R—S. Now we can define the posterior past strictly as R—E:R—S and the anterior future as E—R:S—R with only one set of relations each.

In recent theories there is yet a third kind of pairwise relation, termed status, alongside tense and aspect.[183]

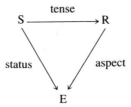

But this is not required for the semantics of the languages we have been discussing.[184]

The reason for the differentiation of tense and aspect relations is important in another respect as well. Reichenbach diagrams the future as S,R—E. This of course violates the generalization that in the future tenses R follows S. We expect a simple future, namely S—R,E. This is in fact what Reichenbach gives in his chart of the fundamental forms. The discrepancy comes from Reichenbach's claim

that the traditional simple future tense can be either S,R—E or S—R,E, while he
calls the former the posterior present.

But how the traditional tenses accord with Reichenbach's "new names" is merely
implicit in his theory. It is only by explicitly identifying the separate roles of R—
S and R—E relations that the theory can accommodate such identifications. This
is not simply a terminological issue, for while Reichenbach's theory supplies a
specification of possible tenses, *in itself* it provides none for the tense system of
English, let alone any other language.

A somewhat similar proposal to Reichenbach's is that of Bull, who distinguishes four "axes of orientation" which are roughly equivalent to points of reference in the Reichenbachian system.[185] Bull points out that "any act of observation, the actual experiencing of any event, automatically becomes an axis of
observation. This act is the objective referent of the term 'point present', which
. . . will be symbolized by PP."[186] Each axis is centered on a "prime point."

Bull allows three "vectors," saying that "any act of observation at an axis of
orientation . . . may be considered to have direction."[187] These are a zero vector, pointing to the prime point of each axis, a "minus" or retrospective vector,
and a "plus" or prospective vector. Accordingly, along the Present Point axis we
have an event $E(PP-V)$ (a retrospective), corresponding to the perfect (*has sung*);
$E(PP0V)$, corresponding to the present (*sings*); and $E(PP+V)$, corresponding to
the future (*will sing*).

But "it is self-evident that man can place himself in relation to the events in
just four fashions. He can experience an event at PP. He can recall at PP any
experienced event. He can . . . at PP, anticipate events which he has not experienced."[188] As times goes on, the experience (or recall or anticipation) at PP
recedes into the past and becomes an experience which can further be recalled.

Thus the PP axis, as an abstract object, points to the Anticipated Point (AP)
axis as well as the Retrospective Point (RP) axis. Bull, like Reichenbach, develops a two-dimensional model, as opposed to Jespersen's one-dimensional one.

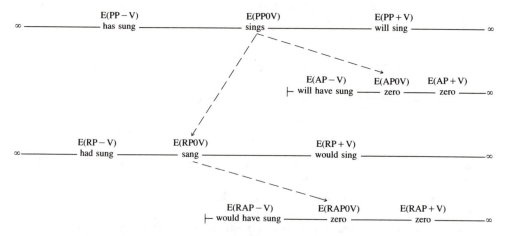

Bull's theory has one important feature which differentiates it from both Jespersen's and Reichenbach's: he "is the only person . . . to have analyzed the

tense system of English in such a way as to accommodate all eight of the different kinds of verb-clusters."[189] Specifically, unlike Reichenbach, Bull can accommodate the conditional perfect (*would have*).[190]

Bull does this by introducing a fourth axis, the Retrospective Anticipated Point (RAP) axis, which is pointed to not directly by the Point Present axis, as are the other two axes, but by the Retrospective Point axis. The conditional perfect refers to an event which, it is recalled, was once anticipated. Thus, *would have sung* is accessed from *sang* and not from, say, *has sung or will sing*. Bull's axes do *not* lie on the same line of time.

The difficulty presented by the conditional perfect form Jespersen does not consider, for he breaks it down into a future and a perfect infinitive. Jespersen has no concept of conditional tenses, much less the conditional perfect, since the prospective past is represented for him by expressions such as *was to*, *was going to* and not by the conditional *would*. Jespersen cannot treat *would* as a backshifted *will*, but this is in accord with his theory of shifting, since a future to conditional (past prospective) shift would entail a shift of two steps, not just one, as with the other shifts.

Reichenbach likewise has no mechanism for handling the conditional perfect, though he can handle the simple conditional. He cannot differentiate the former from the future retrospective *will have sung*, for in both cases E follows S, and his way of differentiating future perfect and simple future, the relationship between S and a point R, would likewise be the same for both (both would have R following S).

Many observers are unconvinced by Bull's discussion of the nature of time and the relationship of private, experiential and objective, public times. For them, the main problem is that he seems to be concerned exclusively with the subjective viewpoint of the speaker.[191] There is apparently no external, objective reality to the axes, and they do not represent either times or kinds of "action." We do not have any reason, other than the need to accommodate in a single scheme the eight forms of English in question, for setting up precisely four axes with precisely three points on each, though Bull sees the system as valid for other languages as well, and possibly universal.

While there obviously is a relationship between the axes of Bull's and Reichenbach's reference times, the latter's system is assertedly a referential one, grounded in a theory of times and points in time, whereas Bull's is ideational, grounded only in the rather subjective "point of view." Possibly this view of Bull's system represents a misunderstanding, but like the system of Gustave Guillaume (1929, 1965), Bull's has been the source of considerable controversy. Ardent supporters claim that their concepts are at least as clear and well grounded as those of Reichenbach, while many current scholars either ignore the theory or merely pay lip service to it.

Bull's system has been praised for avoiding the problems posed by Reichenbach's: "Bull is attempting to deal with the problem [that] we do not want our theoretical tense-system to imply that certain distinctions are available, but that they happen not to be used in languages."[192]

But Bull's system shares with Reichenbach's the failing of being overly rich.

Bull criticizes Reichenbach for allowing three "meanings" for *he will have sung*. Yet the selection of slots for the various tenses in Bull seems equally unrealistic, even arbitrary. The form *will sing* is identified as E(PP + V), though it could with equal justice, McCoard asserts, be put in the E(AP0V) slot, which is empty. *Would sing* similarly would go in both E(RP + V) and E(RAP0V). This would resolve the problem that two of the axes, AP and RAP, have no verb forms in two of their slots, including their prime points. "Despite Bull's attempt to avoid the consequences of Reichenbach's overrich symbolism, some of the same excess appears in Bull's unfilled slots," McCoard observes.

But Bull's scheme may also not be rich enough; parallel to the "compound" RAP axis, McCoard "can also imagine an axis defined as ARP, . . . a point that will be looked back on (viewed retrospectively) at some time in the future." He argues that this is one of the meanings of the future perfect, as in *he will have bought a new suit on Saturday, so he'll probably want to go out on Sunday.* This would be E(ARP0V). Notes McCoard: "Bull's system does not rule out an ARP axis; it merely does not happen to include it."

Similarly, *had sung* is only E(RP − V), but the past perfect also reflects back-shifting (or embedding) of preterites in the past: *Marsha graduated last Friday* becomes, in a report, *(I was told) Marsha had graduated the Friday before.* As McCoard notes, this would be E(RRP0V), the axis being a point viewed retrospectively from a point viewed retrospectively from the present.

Bull's system is in some respects better than Reichenbach's at capturing the facts of English, but it fails to adequately capture the notion of possible tense, because no distinction is built into the theory between slots which *happen not* to be filled and those which *in principle cannot* be. Moreover, Bull is no more able than Reichenbach to make explicit the relationships of tenses. While Jespersen can generalize that shifting involves one step back and Reichenbach's approach allows a theory of SOT as maintenance of the reference point, no constant relationship of "shifted" tenses proceeds from Bull's theory. And while Jespersen cannot generalize over types of tenses (e.g., future or perfect), Reichenbach can. But Bull's approach obscures the relationships of tenses, both within and across axes.

McCoard notes further that while *has sung* is on the same axis as *sings*, and *had sung* is in line with *sang*, *will have sung* is on a different axis from *will sing*, and *would have sung* is separated from *would sing*. "Bull's tactic of separating all the axes one from the other . . . brings with it a certain artificiality of its own. There is a complete blindness to certain connections that *do* hold between axes. This suggests indirectly that associating the preterit and present perfect with different axes may be, at least in part, a misrepresentation."

Bull's treatment of the conditional perfect (past conditional) is genuinely insightful, and the theory has proven influential. The notion of axis of orientation reflects the concept of viewpoint or perspective, which is important (as we shall see in chapter 8) for the understanding of the use of tense in discourse or text. But Bull, no more than Jespersen—or Reichenbach—presents an adequate, explanatory account of the tenses.

i. Allen on the Futurates

The expression of future time is not restricted to the future tense. Languages have idiomatic periphrases for (relative) future time, as for instance:

> be to:
>> Tom is to leave tomorrow.
>> Tom was to leave the next day.
>
> be about to:
>> You're about to do something silly.
>> You were about to do something silly.
>
> be going to:
>> She's going to thank me for this.
>> She was going to thank me for this.

The conditional and conditional perfect are in effect relative future and future perfect (relative to the past), respectively. There is the same relationship between *would*, *would have*, and *was (about) to, was going to* as there is between *will, will have*, and *is (about) to, is going to*.

It has long been known that the present tense can refer to future events and situations; we have seen that even Aristotle comments on the use of the present for the near future. The commentary on Donatus observes that since the present refers to what is happening now and the future to what is only imminent,

> those speak wrongly who say *expecta, modo egredior*,[193] for they join future meaning and present time. Also those who say *Cras tibi lego lectionem*[194] speak wrongly, for while *lego* is of present time, *cras* is a future adverb, so this locution is incoherent.[195]

The vernacular grammarians early on notice that in the familiar European languages the present is readily used for the future. Miege's English grammar of 1688 observes:

> The *Present* Tense [is sometimes used] for the 1. Future Tense. For Exemple, *What Day is to morrow? To morrow is a Holy Day; As long as I live; As long as the World indures.* Whereas we should properly say, *What Day shall be to morrow? To morrow will be a Holy Day; As long as I shall live; As long as the World shall indure.*[196]

At about the same time (1696), de la Touche's French grammar observes the same of that language: "One makes use of this Tense [the present] in place of the Future. Examples: *Je pars demain. Ils s'en vont la semaine prochaine. Elle donne lundi la colation* [sic] à ses amies, etc."[197]

It was also recognized that the present subjunctive made up for the lack of a future subjunctive. De la Touche writes: "One very often uses this tense [the present subjunctive] in place of the Future of the Indicative. Examples: Je doute que mon frére [sic] *vienne* aujourd'hui. . . . Dieu veuille que *vous gagniez* votre [sic] procès. . . . Avant *qu'il meure*. . . . Afin *qu'ils ne périssent* point, etc."[198]

The relative nature of this use of the present and its connection to conjunction is pointed out by Pickbourn:

> This tense [the present] preceded by the words *when, before, after, till, as soon as,*
> &c. is sometimes used to point out the relative time of a future action, *i.e.* to shew
> a relation, with respect to time, between two subsequent actions, one of which is
> always expressed in the future tense: as, when he *arrives*, he will hear the news; he
> will not hear the news, till he *arrives*; he will hear it before he *arrives*, or as soon
> as he *arrives*, or, at farthest, soon after he *arrives*. The verb *arrives* is here an aorist;
> for, though it is definite with respect to action, *i.e.* means an individual action; yet
> it is indefinite with respect to time, *i.e.* the absolute time of the arrival cannot be
> ascertained by it.[199]

This indicates already two important differences between the use of the present
for the future and the future itself. (Henceforth we shall slightly extend the term
futurate, introduced in section g of chapter 2, and refer to the use for the future
of *any* present tense expression as the futurate—i.e., the use for future time of the
present itself, the present perfect, the present progressive, the present perfect progressive, and any of the idiomatic expressions like *be going to*, as well as the use
of relatively present versions of these in any other tense. However, this use of the
term takes in more phenomena than some scholars mean to include by the use
of it.)

The future is definite—*he will die* implies a definite occasion—but the futurate
is indefinite, Pickbourn tells us. And while the future is absolute, the futurate is
relative. (A future relative to the present is of course similar to the absolute future
in time reference.) The same differences obtain with *would be gone* and futurate
was gone. Compare *they all knew he would be gone the next day; after he was
gone, who would they turn to?*

The present perfect may also serve in place of the future perfect. Pickbourn
comments:

> The compound tense, *I have written*, is so perfectly *aoristical* that, like the *Greek
> aorists*, it may be applied not only to *past*, but even to *future* actions: as, 'I shall
> send the letter as soon as *I have written* it.' 'When he *has acquired* a fortune by his
> industry, and *has purchased* a good estate, he will retire into the country, and build
> himself a house. But as soon as he *has built* it, and perhaps before he *has furnished*
> it, or, at farthest, soon after he *has arranged* his gardens in proper order, and *has*
> fully *completed* his plan, he will be weary of an inactive life.'[200]

The various futurate forms have occasioned considerable confusion. The major
issue which gradually emerged was in what way each of the idiomatic usages
differed in meaning from the simple future, since it was assumed that they were
not merely alternative ways of saying precisely the same thing.[201] Intuitively this
seems correct—each of the following differs from the others in shading of meaning, even if it is not easy to say what the differences are:

> I shall sign a lucrative contract (tomorrow).
> I am to sign a lucrative contract (tomorrow).
> I am about to sign a lucrative contract (??tomorrow).
> I am going to sign a lucrative contract (tomorrow).
> I am signing a lucrative contract (tomorrow).
> I sign a lucrative contract ?*(tomorrow).

But only relatively recently has it been recognized that meaning alone is insufficient to account for the use of the futurate, and in particular of the futurate present and present perfect. Reichenbach's account of these is typical of the general approach to the futurates in its unhelpfulness:

> Consider the sentence: 'I shall take your photograph when you come.' The form 'when you shall come' would be more correct; but we prefer to use here the present tense instead of the future. . . . The neglect [of the future] is possible because the word 'when' refers the reference point of the second clause clearly to a future event. A similar anomaly is found in the sentence, 'We shall hear the record when we have dined,' where the present perfect is used instead of the future perfect 'when we shall have dined.'[202]

Reichenbach is correct in that this usage is not merely idiomatic and has something to do with the fact that futurity is predictable. Jespersen points out that "many languages have no future tenses proper or have even . . . replaced them by circuitous substitutes"; where they do have them, the present may nonetheless be used, particularly "when the sentence contains a precise indication of time in the form of a subjunct and when the distance in time from the present moment is not very great: I dine with my uncle to-night. . . . The present tense is also extensively used in clauses beginning with *when* and *if*."[203] He says too that "the use of the perfect for before-future time in temporal [e.g., *when he has dined*] and conditional [e.g., *if he has dined*] clauses corresponds exactly with the use of the present tense for future time."[204]

But there is no question that meaning alone cannot explain why in certain cases the future and future perfect *cannot* be used. After certain subordinating conjunctions (e.g., *if, when, after*) the future (perfect) cannot be used[205]: *after John will come, we will see what is what; *after John will have arrived, we will greet him. (Cf. *after John comes, we will see what is what; after John has arrived, we will greet him.*)

Reichenbach refers to the "positional use of the reference point" to account for the futurate, but nothing in his theory truly deals with this "anomaly." Moreover, Reichenbach shares with Jespersen the problem that no systematic solution is possible to the problem of the futurate, since no generalization over all times is possible. In the case of Jespersen this is because his tenses are primitives. In the case of Reichenbach this is because his account does not explain why we cannot replace the past by the present in *I took your photograph when you came* (in which the *when* presumably refers the event to past time); and because in *I should take your photograph when you came*, it is impossible to explain the *past* tense of *came* by saying that *when* clearly refers the event to future time (relative to the past).

A solution in terms of something like Bull's theory is, however, possible, and is pointed out by Allen.[206] He says that the auxiliary *would*, used in a clause included in a sentence, or in another clause containing a preterite verb form, has been seen as signaling a "later time" time relationship. The treatments of both Jespersen and Reichenbach suggest this. But Allen denies it, saying that reference in an included clause to a time later than that of the main verb is signaled by a past verb form, not by *would*, as may be seen from these examples:

She *sewed* a whole dress for Alice before they *rowed* her across the river . . .
Things *were* so different when I was here . . . before I *married*.
Percy *got* there before I *did*.
They *were* considered unsafe for passenger use until Elisha Graves Otis *invented* a protective ratchet device which prevented falls.

Similarly, "later time" in the present is expressed in included clauses by means of a present verb form:

He *meant* to speak to you before he *left*. . . .
He *means* to speak to you before he *leaves*. . . .

Similarly:

[. . . she had promised me that she wouldn't eat it till we *got* home.]
. . . she has promised me that she won't eat it till we *get* home.

The question then is what it is that an embedded "verb-cluster introduced by *would*" indicates. The answer is suggested to Allen by the following sentence:

Percy said that he *would* come early, and he *did* (OR: he didn't).

He proposes that the "verb-cluster introduced by *would*" expresses, not an *action* later than that referred to by the matrix verb-cluster, but rather *anticipation* of that action. "When we wish to show the action really took place (or did not take place), we use a past verb-cluster, not one introduced by *would*." He accordingly distinguishes the " 'later' time-relationship" from the " 'anticipated' time-relationship."

Allen's observation is supported by an examination of indirect discourse and relative clauses. *The man who left the next day* differs from *the man who would leave the next day* in several respects. The former is in fact ambiguous, as is the parallel phrase with *leaves*. In one (albeit marginal) reading, *leaves/left*[207] means "is/was intended/scheduled/etc. to leave": *Tom is the one who leaves early tomorrow morning, so let him get the bed.*

In this reading, the speaker takes no responsibility for whether the (relatively) future event is actually fulfilled. But there is a reading in which the speaker presupposes such a fulfillment. The normal interpretation of *the man who left the next day was Bill* is that Bill did leave the next day—it would be odd to say *the man who left the next day was killed that very evening*.

No such ambiguity obtains with *the man who would leave*; this can only be the speaker's description and presupposes that the man did in fact leave. Unfortunately there *is* an ambiguity which affects such descriptions, because *will* has a modal reading. *The man who would be king* can be simply a present *or past* report of a desire.

Indirect discourse exhibits similar phenomena. *He said that he would help* merely reports the subject's intentions, but says nothing about whether he did in fact later help. But *he never guessed that he would become President one day* is the speaker's report of relatively future events. Compare *he said that he would help, but he never did*; *?!he never guessed that he would become President one day, and he never did.*[208]

A solution within the terms of Bull's theory presumably would involve treating "later" events as $+V$, while "anticipated" events would be placed on the AP or RAP axes.

Allen developed a theory in which the use of the present for the future is not an anomaly, but rather just what we would expect. His was probably the first systematic approach to "included" tenses, since neither Jespersen's nor Reichenbach's theory can accommodate both "ordinary" shifts (Jespersen's one-step backshifts, in which Reichenbach's reference point is preserved) and the "anomalous" cases.

Allen distinguishes a "point of orientation" (roughly, S) from a "point of reference" (very rough, R). This would allow him presumably to distinguish *who will be king* and *who would be king*, which present such a problem for Reichenbachian theories. More important, Allen stresses that he does not relate included tenses to a single point of orientation, but rather to the point of reference ("the time expressed by the verb-cluster on the next higher level"), which varies from example to example:

In each of the following sentences . . . the same included clause—*while he ate supper*—refers to a different time (with reference to the point of orientation—i.e., to the time of Percy's speaking):

Percy said that he *had listened* to the radio while he *ate* supper.
Percy said that he always *listened* to the radio while he *ate* supper.
Percy said that he *would listen* to the radio while he *ate* supper.[209]

In the following example, the included clause *after he had eaten supper* shows earlier time relationship with reference to Percy's going to bed, not to the time of his speaking:

Percy said that he *would* go to bed after he *had eaten* supper.

For Allen, the matching of tenses does not involve a global, established-once-and-for-all reference point, but rather pairwise matchings of tenses with greater or lesser scope of application:

In the following sentence . . . each included verb-cluster shows some kind of time-relationship (earlier, later or same) with reference to the preceding verb-cluster. Each cluster's clause is included in a larger construction—clause or sentence—with a main verb preceding the clause included in it. . . . In other words, the time indicated by each verb-cluster serves as the point of reference for the time-relationship signaled by the verb-cluster on the next lower level (in this sentence, by the next following verb-cluster in all cases). I *had* it wrapped in tissue paper [because she *had promised* me [that she *wouldn't eat* it [till we *got* home]]].

1st cluster:		R_1,E_1		$- S$
2nd cluster:	$E_2 -$		R_2	$- S$
3rd cluster:	R_3		$- E_3$	$- S$
4th cluster:			R_4,E_4	$- S$

It will be seen . . . that it is not true that the reference point remains permanent throughout; rather, each E . . . serves as the reference point for the E on the next lower level. This is probably a more generally followed principle than Reichenbach's principle of the permanence of the reference point.[210]

Compare the comment by the tense logician Prior that an example such as *I shall have been going to see John* in effect has *two* points of reference. But then, says Prior, it "becomes unnecessary and misleading to make such a sharp distinction between the point or points of reference and the point of speech; the point of speech is just the *first* point of reference. . . . This makes pastness and futurity *always* relative to *some* point of reference—maybe the first one . . . or maybe some other."[211]

Prior recognizes that a single reference point throughout a sentence is neither sufficient nor necessary to account for the tenses found, but he ascribes no special status to S: it is just, as he says, the *first* point of reference. In this his position contrasts with Reichenbach's but not necessarily with Allen's, though he differs from Allen in failing to recognize that *have been going to see* is *not* semantically a simple tense form, but rather is complex. While not syntactically the same as any of the cases Allen considers, it is related to them in that the time expressed by *be going to* is here related to the time of the perfect.

Allen's system differs from Bull's mainly in recognizing only present and past axes. The tense of an included verb depends on that of the next higher verb. If that higher verb belongs to the present system, the lower verb does, too, and if the higher is past, so is the lower:

> Tom *liked* Susan because she *was* rich.
> Tom *likes* susan because she *is* rich.

Within each system, Bull's vectors still apply. In *Tom liked Susan because she* had helped *him*, the pastness of *had helped* comes from that of *liked*; the perfectness reflects the fact that her helping him preceded his liking him.

Allen bases his rejection of the future on the fact that the future is essentially equivalent to the post-present (that is, it is equal to Bull's PP + V), while the future perfect is of vanishingly small occurrence in his corpus of data.[212] But he could equally have based that rejection on the fact that the future does not provide a point of reference in the way that the present and past do.

Consider ?!*Tom* will like *Susan because she* will be *rich*. The only reading for this is that his liking is associated with the fact that she is going to be rich, *not* with the fact she *is* rich at the time he likes her; compare *Tom* will like *Susan because she* is *rich*.

This latter example has two readings, one of which *does* mean that he will like her because she *is* rich at the time he likes her. (The other reading is the problematical one which takes the point of orientation as the point of reference: he will like her because she is rich *now*, or in general.)

McCoard has criticized Allen for treating embedded and unembedded preterites differently.[213] More important, he points out that Allen's system cannot account for the possibility of embedding a preterite within the scope of the present perfect, as in *I've often stayed up as late as I wanted.* Under the present reference point of *'ve stayed* we would expect the present *want* or present perfect *have wanted*, not the past *wanted*. Allen has no explanation for this, which seems to be the same sort of problem posed by the problematical *a child was born who will be king*, which involves reorientation to the point of orientation (R = S) from a past point of reference (R—S).[214]

But McCoard points out other fundamental difficulties with Allen's system than its inability to cope with reorientation. He cites several examples which are not predicted by Allen's theory.[215] For example, *Percy said that he* had listened *to the radio while he* had eaten *supper*, is normally interpreted as meaning that the eating was simultaneous with the listening, not prior to it. Again, *Percy has often* listened *to the radio while he* has eaten *supper* is simultaneous with the listening, not prior to it.

McCoard proposes that Allen puts too much onto mere sequence of tenses and ignores the vital role of the conjunctions themselves. He shows that replacing *while* by another conjunction with "simultaneous" time meaning, namely *even though*, has devastating effects:

> ?Percy said that he *had listened* to the radio even though he *ate* supper.
> ?Percy said that he always *listened* to the radio even though he *ate* supper.
> *Percy said that he *would listen* to the radio even though he *ate* supper.[216]

Likewise, Allen's theory can make no sense out of *Percy usually* listens *to the radio before he* has eaten *supper*. His theory predicts that we should have *eats* here.

In some respects, Allen's theory is a throwback to the traditional SOT rule, which is concerned solely with matching tenses to a past or present of the next highest verb. His strategy is a radically different one from Reichenbach's. Reichenbach does not take tenses as primitives and does not regard shifting as a matching of tenses but rather as reflecting a shared underlying reference point.

While Allen can explicate some of the anomalies pointed out by Pickbourn, Jespersen, Reichenbach, and others, there remains a residue of cases none of the theories we have discussed can handle. In part II we shall see what approaches current theories take to these problems.

4

Beyond Theories of Tense

Whether, as some grammarians in the tradition have done, we assume that there are three times and hence three tenses, or as others have done, we base ourselves on formal, morphological, or syntactic properties of particular languages such as English, we must at some point ask ourselves in what way tenses mean, have meaning.

It was assumed by the Greeks and all who followed them in the tradition of school grammar that tenses at least partially refer to times, and that the task of the grammarian is to label each tense in such a way that it becomes clear which time it refers to. Thus the present progressive of English (*he is running*) may make reference to progressive, continuing, ongoing action, but it also makes reference to the present time.

So we may think of events strung along a line, the relationship of which to the "now" is ever changing. At any given moment all of time is divided by that point into two times, the past before it and the future after. In practice the "now" is itself not merely a point, but an interval or expanse of time, since things that are now true or are happening now have been true and will be true, or have been occurring and will be occurring, for some time past and some time to come. Corresponding to these three regions are the three "natural" tenses.

As seemingly "natural" as this picture may be, it is so fraught with problems that no scholar of language today would take it very seriously. Lyons has observed that "it has often been supposed that the . . . three-way opposition of tense is a universal feature of language. This is not so. In fact tense itself is not found in all languages; and the opposition of 'past', 'present' and 'future' is not simply a matter of tense even in Greek and Latin."[1]

Gonda observes that "tense is far from being common to any form of human speech" and lists numerous languages which lack what we would strictly speaking call tense.[2] It is hard for the speaker of most modern European languages to imagine a language without tense. How can the necessary distinctions of time be expressed if not by tense? Isn't it the job of the verb to mark tense? And if there are three times, why are there not precisely three tenses?

But even in the so-called tensed languages, including the familiar European ones, a number of serious problems arise with regard to the concept of verb tenses reflecting three times given in nature. In few if any European languages do we find precisely three tenses. It may be that English, for example, has a present tense (*they sing*), a past tense (*they sang*), and a future tense (*they will sing*). But it also has at least a (present) perfect (*they have sung*), a pluperfect (*they had sung*), and a conditional (*they would sing*).

If it be argued that these are not, properly speaking, tenses, being formed with auxiliary ("helping") verbs, rather than by modifying the verb itself or replacing all (*go: went*) or part (*bring: brought*) of it, then of course we must deny that the future is a tense in this sense as well. And in fact it has often been claimed that English has but two tenses.

Similarly, the Romance languages all have more than three tenses formed by modifying the verb. Moreover, as we have seen in section f of chapter 2, Jespersen neatly showed in a diagram that there is no very good correspondence in (ancient) Greek, Latin, French, English, and German between tenses all of which purport to refer to past time.[3]

One could cite numerous other ways in which the closely related (Indo-)European languages differ in their ways of expressing tense distinctions. It is plain that, if time is naturally divided into three segments and language makes reference to those segments, it generally does not do so in any simple or universal fashion.

Yet we must not conclude that tense is random and chaotic. On the one hand, universal, general features of tense in languages can certainly be discerned, while on the other hand not every conceivable pattern of relationship is actually possible. The question is, wherein does this order lie? Clearly there is a problem here, and it is the attempt to solve it, to understand how languages can handle tense in such apparently different ways while nonetheless adequately signaling relationships in time, which constitutes the study of the temporal semantics of the verb.

Compounding the problem of time and tense is the fact that, even in so-called tenseless languages, there are ways of indicating when events take place and of marking other temporal distinctions; the question then is whether tense is indeed a necessary expression of time. The major difference between languages is not in whether they can make such distinctions, but in whether they require the speaker to do so.

Here we might recall the distinction between grammaticized and nongrammaticized categories. We have seen that in Turkish, speakers must indicate in certain cases whether the information they are conveying was observed or witnessed by them, or merely told them by someone else (or possibly surmised or inferred by them). This difference is as fully grammaticized in Turkish as is the difference in tenses in English. It is a required category in Turkish, just as tense is in English, and the verb is modified in form to mark this distinction, just as tense distinctions are marked in both Turkish and English. But just as it is possible to mark this distinction optionally in English, by other means than the form of the verb (e.g., *snow must have fallen*), so tenseless languages can mark temporal distinctions by other means than modifying the verb.

Tenselessness, as Gonda noted, is quite widespread, sufficiently so as to raise doubt concerning the naturalness of tense. The older Semitic languages, such as Biblical Hebrew and Classical Arabic, do not show anything quite like the absolute tense of the modern Indo-European languages. Many of the sign languages of the deaf are tenseless. Many tensed languages at earlier stages in their histories lacked tense markers.[4]

Although the tradition treats the tenses as referring to (expressing) times, tense in fact has to do with pairs of times and the relation between them, specifically between the times of events and the moment "now," defined as the time (or "moment") of speech or utterance (S). The same event must be described using different tenses at different times because *now* keeps referring to different times, just as *she* and *he* keep referring to different people.

This is what is meant by saying, as is sometimes done, that tense is deictic or a deictic category. Deictic categories (as noted in section b) are those which involve indicating something, usually from the perspective of the speaker (or writer or manual signer) who is "I" and "here" and "now," near "this" and "these."

The pair *now* and *then* is very similar to *here* and *there* (the *th* of *there* and *then* is a deictic marker), and tense is obviously a deictic category in this sense; events near in time to the time of the speech act are "now" (or "just now," "but now"), recounted in the present tense, whereas those away from it are "then," recounted in the past or future. (*Then* can be used of both past and future events, just as *there* can be used of places either before or behind the speaker.)

Because tense depends on the "now" of the speaker (the moment of speech), it has often been seen as subjective, as opposed to aspect, which is objective. Aspect has to do with unchanging relationships of events on the time line. In many languages the perfect aspect marks events completed prior to some other event, such as the speech act: *John has eaten; John had left by the time Sue arrived.* An imperfect aspect marks events not so completed: *John is eating; John was leaving when Sue arrived.*

We can see an aspectual distinction in the sentences *he hopes to leave at noon* and *he hopes to have left by noon.* In the first case, his desired leaving is simultaneous with noon, but in the latter it is prior to it. The choice of aspect (*to leave* vs. *to have left*) has nothing to do with when these sentences might be spoken or written, but only with how the two events (his leaving, its being noon) are related in time.

Such temporal relationships are matters of fact and hence objective. But choice of tense is not given in nature; rather, it depends on one's viewpoint, hence can be said to be subjective. In narration we may use the historical present, talking as if "now" were coincident with the events being described, so as to give the story greater liveliness. In some languages, French for example, the future tense may be used in a similar way. There are many usages in every language which seem to shift the point of view of the speaker away from the objective "now."

This can happen because the relation of events in time is not enough to determine tense. Suppose that I have eaten; if I view my eating from the perspective of the present, I would say that I *ate*, and it is often the case in colloquial language that the distinction in the formal, standard language between the present perfect tense (*have eaten, a mangé*) and the preterite or past tense (*ate, mangea*) is limited or lost.

Waugh writes: "We will define tense for French as characterizing the narrated situation with reference to the speech situation, and particularly with reference to the speaker's subjective attitude toward the relationship between the narrated situation and the speech situation."[5] The viewpoint adopted affects the tense used.

But in many cases tenses relate the time of events not to S itself but to some other time. It is possible to say both *someone came in who would be king someday*, in which the conditional tense ("would . . .") marks someone being king as an event future to the time of their coming in, and *someone came in who will be king someday*, in which the future tense marks their being king as an event future to the time of the speech act.

Moreover, a tense may not serve to relate definite times at all. In the case of so-called "gnomic" tenses which express "eternal" or "timeless" truths such as *two and two make four, men were deceivers ever, the poet will go to any end to make a rhyme*, tenses do not relate events or situations to any definite times at all. In many languages there seems to be great latitude in the use of tenses to make such statements.

Once again, if by "deixis" we mean indication of definite tenses, we must also recognize the use of tenses to refer to indefinite times. *I turned off the stove* points to a definite time at which I turned off the stove, and *I turned off the stove and left the house* constitutes a narration. But *I have turned off the stove* does not point to a definite time, and *I have turned off the stove and left the house* does not necessarily define a definite sequence of events and hence might not be a narration.

Whorf has criticized the "three-times, three-tenses" model from yet another point of view, arguing that, though the Hopi language (a native American language) "conceals a METAPHYSICS" different from that which our "so-called naive view of space and time" reflects, "the Hopi language is capable of accounting for and describing correctly, in a pragmatic or operational sense, all observable phenomena of the universe," while lacking all the time-line apparatus laid out above.[6] He argues, indeed, that

> the Hopi language is seen to contain no words, grammatical forms, constructions or expressions that refer directly to what we call "time," or to past, present, or future, or to enduring or lasting, or to motion as kinematic rather than dynamic . . . the Hopi language contains no reference to "time."[7]

In general, Whorf

> [finds] it gratuitous to assume that a Hopi who knows only the Hopi language and the cultural ideas of his own society has the same notions, often assumed to be intuitions, of time and space that we have, and that are generally assumed to be universal. In particular, he has no general notion or intuition of TIME as a smooth flowing continuum in which everything in the universe proceeds at an equal rate, out of a future, through a present, into a past.

Whether Whorf is correct about Hopi or not—his ideas are viewed very skepti-
cally today—the point is well taken that the aprioristic, three-times-on-a-line view
on which many scholars have based their conception of tense is largely culture-
and language-bound, and has little or nothing behind it beyond a naive intuition
that it is correct.

If the naive theory of tense which seemed so self-evident can be criticized from
so many points of view, what is it that we want to say about time and tense?
Given the diversity of tense systems and time expression in various languages, is
there anything general to say?

There evidently is. There are many interesting and important problems associated with tense. If there are not three tenses, then are there any limits at all on
the number of tenses? What distinctions of time are possible, and how do languages use tenses to mark them? If there are tenseless languages, how do they
express relations of time such as pastness or futurity? If tense is not always deictic, how can we specify when and under what conditions it is?

Clearly language use, however complex it may be, is not chaotic. If it were,
no one could learn languages or use them. Certainly languages have evolved to
be efficient tools of communication, and in our time-conscious world we seem to
have no difficulty in using them to communicate about time. Obviously there are
principles underlying tense and aspect, both in particular languages and in general.
Ultimately what we require is a general theory of tense.

It is plain, however, that the tradition inherited from the Greeks does not constitute a sound basis for elucidating questions such as these, much less for answering them. If that tradition could lead only to confusion where English and
other Indo-European languages are concerned, how much less satisfactory must it
be for non-Indo-European languages, not to mention languages like Biblical Hebrew apparently lacking tense or those, like Hopi, which (are claimed to) have no
direct reference to time at all.

We need not conjecture how unsatisfactory the tradition might be on these scores,
for the modern grammatical study of the non-Indo-European tongues has its roots
in the Graeco-Roman tradition, which the early European explorers of Africa,
Asia, Oceania, and the Americas naturally applied to the newly "discovered"
languages.

How problematical the extension of a Graeco-Roman grammar could be is exemplified by a statement of N. W. Schroeder's concerning Hebrew:

> . . . the Future has yet another [use]—unique and peculiar to the Hebrews, in that
> it receives the force of our Past, and designates a matter as truly past—not however
> by itself nor absolutely, but in relation to some preceding past event—for when
> different events are to be narrated, which follow the one from the other in some kind
> of continuous series, the Hebrews consider the first as past, the others, however,
> which follow—as future on account of the preceding [past].[8]

Such conceptual gymnastics could be avoided only by recognizing that the "future" and "past" *tenses* as such are alien to Biblical Hebrew, though of course
the writers of that language could perfectly well indicate which events were past
and which future.

It was only at the beginning of the twentieth century that linguists, in the course of describing the newly "discovered" non-Indo-European languages, and philologists, in the course of attempting to understand the use of grammatical tenses in the literatures of the various European tongues, began to rethink the tenets of the grammatical tradition and arrive at a new and sounder foundation for an understanding of the verb. In the work of such scholars as Jespersen, Reichenbach, and Bull we see an attempt to come to grips with these problems. But none of these efforts proved very successful.

This lack of success was partly due to the attempt to elaborate an autonomous theory of tense in isolation from aspect and mood. Wallace has even questioned whether what he calls the "trivium of tense, mood, and aspect, based on the inflectional categories of the older Indo-European languages," is not "an arbitrary division of verbal semantics into compartments which are not quite as easily separable as one is led to believe."[9] At the least, as Comrie points out, tense and aspect interrelate, and co-occur in typical patterns.[10] Traugott has argued as well that the temporal system is deeply interconnected with other categories of the language, future tense with modality, aspect with quantification, and so forth.[11] Without an understanding of aspect and mood, we can hardly feel confident that we adequately understand tense.

The ancient Greeks had already achieved a high degree of what contemporary linguists call "observational adequacy." They were largely able to accurately record the facts of their language. But they failed to a great extent to provide any "descriptively adequate" account, being unable to organize the facts of tense into a coherent, explicit system. And insofar as they made any attempt at an "explanatorily adequate" account, they were unsuccessful.

The modern theories of tense discussed here—from the Renaissance through the work of Bull and Allen—approach descriptive adequacy, although obviously even for the well-studied European languages many problems remain unresolved. But in explanatory adequacy these theories radically fail.

The greatest failing of all the theories we have considered, from the Greeks to Allen, is the lack of any external criterion of adequacy. It is impossible to tell which theory (if any) is the "correct" one, without any external means of comparison. Scholars such as Jespersen had only their intuitions to draw on, and no external, objective framework upon which to hang their categories. What is required is a way of objectifying the theories. Otherwise we cannot test theories, cannot judge them on other grounds than the unsatisfactory ones of simplicity and coherence.

Specifically, a *semantic* theory is required, one in which linguistic expressions can be systematically defined in terms of their relationships to aspects of reality. Part II will review the efforts that have been made in the last few decades to provide such a theory.

In the work reviewed in part I, aspect has largely been ignored, not considered an integral part of a theory of tense. While grammarians since the Greeks have been constrained to recognize aspectual distinctions, these are not systematically marked in many languages, and in any case seem to form a separate system from tense. But we shall see that any theory which purports to be a semantic theory for tense must at the same time be one for aspect as well. Thus we find in the work of the last few decades no sharp division between tense and aspect.

There are two reasons for this. First, the tense markers clearly mark aspectual distinctions. The Romance preterite and imperfect tenses, for example, differ only in aspect, and there is no possible account of them which is not couched in terms of aspectual distinctions. A second and more important reason is that a semantic theory for tense must essentially involve invariant relationships in time. In part II we shall see why this is so.

PART TWO

ASPECT

5

The Problem of Aspect

a. Slavic Aspect

The study of aspect has been likened to a dark and savage forest full of "obstacles, pitfalls, and mazes which have trapped most of those who have ventured into this much explored but poorly mapped territory."[1] Tense is perhaps equally confusing, but at least it is a well-known traditional area with concepts intuitively clear to speakers of the familiar Western European languages. Whatever tense, or the tenses, may be, speakers have some sort of notions about them: it is satisfying, for example, to consider the past tense to express past time. But aspect is not a traditional concept in the same way, and speakers of most European languages have no very clear notions concerning it. Nonetheless it is equal in importance to tense for the purpose of understanding how temporal relations are expressed in language.

As in the case of tense, aspect was first discussed by the Greeks. The earliest Greek grammarians seem to have been aware that alongside tense their language marked a second type of distinction, the one which we call aspect. This is not to say that they understood it in the way that we do or that they even necessarily distinguished aspectual phenomena as a distinct type apart from tense. But it was clear to the Greeks that whatever the difference between the imperfect and aorist tenses was, it was not the sort of difference—tense—which obtains between the imperfect and the present.

As we have seen, Varro is usually understood to have arrived at something like the modern conception of aspect: the Latin imperfect represents an action which is incomplete (*imperfectus*), while the perfect represents one which is complete (*perfectus*). It is possible that the Stoics had already arrived at the same theory for Greek.

Nonetheless, however ancient the concept, the term "aspect" is recent; according to the *Oxford English Dictionary*, it appeared in English for the first time in

135

1853. Imported early in the nineteenth century into the Western grammatical tradition from the study of Slavic grammar, it fully became part of that tradition only at the end of that century.

The term "aspect" is a loan translation from the Slavic (e.g., Russian *vid*). "Aspect" is a good choice of translation, for *vid* is etymologically cognate with the words *view* and *vision*, while the etymological root of *aspect* is *spect-*, which means 'see, look (at), view' (cf. *prospect, inspect, spectacle,* etc.).

The meaning of the term "aspect" (*vid*) in the grammar of the Slavic languages is relatively clear and precise, since aspect in Slavic is overtly and morphologically marked. With few exceptions, all verbs in Russian (to take one Slavic language as an example) have two complete sets of tense forms, called respectively *imperfective* and *perfective*. For example, 'she read' may be translated by either *čitala* (imperfective) or the nonsynonymous *pročitala* (perfective).

The difference in meaning is intuitively clear to Russian speakers, though the difference between the two aspects is difficult to state, and the treatment of Slavic aspect remains controversial. The perfective, as its name suggests, is felt to express a completed action, while the imperfective does not; *čitala* may translate roughly as 'she was reading', and *pročitala* as 'she had read'. While *pročitala knigu* 'she read the book' implies that she finished the book or read it all the way through, *čitala knigu* 'she read the book' does not.

The difference of meaning between the two aspects may be seen clearly in an example from Dostoevsky: "Oh, rest assured that Columbus was happy not when he discovered (*otkril,* perfective) America, but while he was discovering (*otkryval,* imperfective) it; rest assured that the greatest moment of his happiness was, perhaps, exactly three days before the discovery of the New World."[2]

The use of the term "aspect" (*vid*) proceeds from the fact that the very same situation (event or state of affairs) may be *viewed* either imperfectively or perfectively. In a given context one or the other aspect may be preferred or even obligatory, but often enough either could be used to describe precisely the same episode, just as in English we may say either *just the other day I* visited *Aunt Martha and saw your picture,* or *just the other day I* was visiting *Aunt Martha and saw your picture.* Both of these sentences describe the same event, although one views the visit as a completed whole, from the outside as it were, while the other views it as an ongoing, incomplete action, as if from the inside.

Because aspectual marking in Slavic is overt and fully grammaticized, and forms a relatively simple system (in Russian there is only an opposition of two aspects, as opposed to the three-way split exemplified by imperfect-pluperfect-aorist in Greek), Slavic aspect is often taken to be the prototypical exemplar of aspectual systems.

In outline, the morphology of Russian aspect is simple. Generally, as in the case of *čitat'* 'to read' (imperfective) : *pročitat'* (perfective), the perfective is formed from the imperfective stem, which may be the root itself. (Still, some primary perfective stems exist, such as *dat'* 'to give', from which may be derived the imperfective *davat'*.)

The perfective is usually formed through prefixation, though many other devices are used as well, such as vowel change and stem change (perfective *izučit'* 'to study' : imperfective *izučat'*), or even choice of another lexical item (imperfective *govorit'* 'to speak' : perfective *skazat'* 'to tell, say'). A large number of more or less unpredictable changes are also observed, as in the case of the perfective *načat'* 'to begin' : imperfective *načinat'*. Some verbs change aspect through stress shift alone, as in the case of the imperfective *srezat'* 'to cut', with stress on the second syllable; the corresponding perfective has stress on the first. These various devices are, however, the exception, and prefixation the rule.

Although there are a fairly large number of prefixes which may be used to form perfectives, the most common are:

na-:	*pisat'* 'to write' : *napisat'*
o-:	*slepnut'* 'to go blind' : *oslepnut'*
po-:	*stroit'* 'to build' : *postroit'*
pro-:	*čitat'* 'to read' : *pročitat'*
raz-:	*delit'* 'to divide' : *razdelit'*
s-:	*delat'* 'to do' : *sdelat'*

Although these commonly used perfectivizing prefixes originally were meaningful elements, most of them corresponding to prepositions or adverbs (e.g., *na* 'on', *s* 'with'), today generally they are semantically empty, serving merely to mark aspect. (However, some scholars argue that all perfectivizing prefixes retain some of their etymological value.)

Some of these common prefixes, however, at least with certain words, do yield additional temporal implications. *Po-*, for example, sometimes implies a limited amount of time: *počitala* means '(she) read for a little while'. *Po-* may in some cases have an inchoative sense: *letet'* 'to fly' : *poletet'* 'to start flying, take off'.

Moreover, most of the less common perfectivizing prefixes not only change the aspect of the verb, but act like the verbal prefixes of other Indo-European languages and the verbal particles of English in deriving verbs with a different lexical content. From *pisat'* 'to write' may be formed the derived perfective verb *perepisat'* 'to copy'. (Cf. *underwrite, write in, write down, write up, write out, inscribe, subscribe, transcribe*, etc.)

The imperfective of such derived verbs must be further derived by means of a suffix, usually one of *-va-, -iva-* and *-yva-*. The secondary imperfective verb *perepisyvat'*, for example, is formed from an already derived perfective.

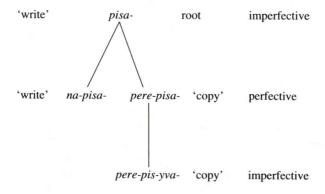

Most Indo-European languages have a rich array of such derivational prefixes, most of them closely related to, or derived from, prepositions or related adverbs. Compare the Latin *in-* 'in' (*include, intrude, infuse*); *pre-* '(be)fore' (*preclude, prevent, prepare*); *ob-* 'against' (*object, obtrude*); *con-* (*conclude, convene*); and so on.

Aspect is important to Slavic grammar not only because the distinction between imperfective and perfective is an obligatorily marked category of the verb, but also because aspect interacts in important ways with tense. Russian has, like English, only two morphologically marked tenses, traditionally called past and present. This latter we may term the "non-past" (or "present-future"). With an imperfective verb, the non-past tense markers indicate a present tense: *dumaem* means '(we) think, are thinking', and the past tense markers indicate past tense (which includes the range of the English perfect): *dumali* means '(we, you, they) thought, were thinking, have thought, have been thinking'.

But with perfective verbs it is quite otherwise. Here the past tense is an aorist (preterite, but including the range of the pluperfect): *podumali* means '(we, you, they) thought, had thought', and the non-past is a future tense: *podumaem* means 'we will think'. To express the future with an imperfective verb, a periphrasis using the verb 'to be' is required: *my budem dumat'* 'we will be thinking', literally 'we are to (be) think(ing)'.

The tense-aspect system of a typical Russian verb is this:

	TENSE/ASPECT	
	Perfective	Imperfective
Past	*podumali*	*dumali*
	'(we, you, they) thought, had thought'	'(we, you, they) thought, were thinking, have thought, have been thinking'
Non-past	*podumayut*	*dumayut*
	'(they) will think'	'(they) think, are thinking'
Future	—	*budut dumat'*
		'(they) will think, will be thinking'

The apparent simplicity of the Russian aspectual opposition of perfective and imperfective has often been taken as revealing a fundamental system underlying the apparent complexity of aspect in languages such as Greek and Latin. But when scholars working in the Western tradition attempted to analyze Greek aspect in terms of the Slavic system, a number of unexpected difficulties ensued.

For one thing, aspect is overtly marked in Slavic by the difference of stems. The prefix *po-* may render a verb perfective; the suffix *-yva* may render it imperfective. Aspect crosscuts tense, so that a form like *napisali* 'they wrote' can be analyzed unambiguously as perfective (*na-*) and past (*-li*).

But aspect in Greek requires some abstraction to see. While a form like *lé.lu.k.a* 'I have freed' does mark perfect aspect by the reduplication and the stem-formative kappa, and marks present tense by the desinence *-a* and the absence of the augment, it does not fully isolate tense from aspect, since most of these elements have implications for aspect and tense alike. The desinence *-a*, for example, occurs only with the aorist and perfect aspects, never with the imperfect. Most desinences are constrained in this way.

The same phenomena appear in the case of the stem-formatives; the sigmatic stems are only aorist in aspect, but also are never present tense. Nor is it possible to specify unique markers, or unique types of markers. Past tense is marked both by the augment (a prefix) and by special secondary-tense desinences (suffixes).

It is tempting to identify the Slavic system as well with the perfect and progressive constructions of the Western European languages, since the imperfective does roughly translate the progressive (*čitali* = 'they were reading') and the perfective the perfect (*pročitali* = 'they had read'). But the grammaticization of aspect is an important difference between the Slavic and most other European languages. In a language such as English it is possible to indicate whether an action is already completed, or is ongoing but not necessarily ever to be completed—*she had read the book* (*when John arrived*) versus *she was reading the book* (*when John arrived*). But this indication is optional, not obligatory; *she read the book* is neutral in this regard: *she read the book* (*in under an hour*) versus *she read the book* (*for a few minutes but soon tired of it*). But note: *She read the book when John arrived* is not ambiguous.

English has various devices for indicating aspectual distinctions of completion (e.g., the participles *up* and *through* as in *eat up, read through*), but their use is not obligatory, nor can such distinctions be marked simply by altering the form of the verb itself. It is quite otherwise in the Slavic languages, where aspectual distinctions are obligatorily marked, this being done by differences in the form of the verb.

Although there are superficial similarities between the Slavic aspects, the aspects of ancient Greek, and the expanded tenses of the modern Germanic and Romance languages, there are also important differences. When aspect entered into Western grammatical thought, there began a long debate concerning the universality of aspectual categories. In the absence of such well-defined intuitive notions as obtained in the case of tense, this debate was bound to be a confused one. It is no wonder that the study of aspect has proven to be such a "dark wood."

b. Aspect and *Aktionsarten*

Notwithstanding the antiquity of the recognition of aspect in the classical languages and the clear-cut nature of the phenomenon in the Slavic languages, aspect, once it entered into the Western grammatical tradition, was to occasion great confusion. Writing in 1940, Goedsche observes that "in spite of a great amount of research, a wide divergence of opinion prevails today regarding the character of aspect and regarding the fundamental principles to be pursued in that study."[3]

The source of this confusion is not only to be sought in the way in which the concept of aspect developed within the Western grammatical tradition. Although the term *vid* first appeared in an early seventeenth-century work by Meletiy Smetritskiy, the modern concept of Russian aspect as consisting in the opposition of

perfective and imperfective had to await the middle of the last century and Mik-
losisch's *Vergleichende Grammatik der slavischen Sprachen* (*Comparative Grammar of the Slavic Languages*) of 1868–74.[4] This concept, indeed, was not firmly
established until the work of Jakobson (1932), despite its present-day appearance
of great venerability.

At the time when Western scholars first had Slavic aspectology brought to their
attention, there reigned in it considerable controversy and confusion, which was
to be reflected in the ensuing Western studies. M. Lomonosov's Russian grammar
of 1757 ignored aspect altogether, and described the perfective past *glotnul* 'swallowed (once)', for example, as simply the "semelfactive past tense" of the verb
"swallow" in a language with eight "simple" and two "compound" tenses.

L. Boldyrev replied in *Rassuzdenie o glagolax* (*Reflection on Verbs*) in 1812
that semelfactives and the like are not simply tense forms, or indeed forms of one
verb; *glotat'* 'swallow' and *glotnut'* 'swallow (once)' are different verbs, he observed, while Russian has but two tenses, present and past. However, he started
a tradition by distinguishing five semantic classes of verbs:

inchoatives: *belet'* 'pale, blanche, whiten, fade'
indeterminate duratives: *delat'* 'do'
frequentatives: *delyvat'* 'do (repeatedly)'
semelfactives: *dernut'* 'pull (once)'
unitary completives: *srubit'* 'cut down (in one action)'

The term "aspect" (*vid*) was first applied in Russian grammar to a non-tense
distinction by N. Greč in his "practical" Russian grammar (1827, second ed.,
1834). But his use of the term is solely in the context of semantic classes of verb:

the times are limited in nature to three: the present, past, and future, but in grammatical tenses, that is in the forms of language by which times are expressed, there
can be expressed accessory circumstances by which are more closely defined the
signification and the extent of the action. . . . The forms serving to express these
circumstances of the action are called "aspects."

Throughout the nineteenth century various schemes of such aspects were proposed, based on such distinctions as accomplished-unaccomplished, durative-
nondurative, and semelfactive-frequentative. At the end of the century, Slavic
aspectology was strongly influenced by Western aspectology which, as part of
Indo-European philology, had undergone a long development of its own. For quite
some time no significant independent development took place in Slavic aspectology.

But Western and Slavic aspectology had in parallel sought to find the appropriate set of distinctions of *Aktionsarten, modes d'action*, "kinds of action" to
base their sets of aspects on. Brugmann had written in 1886 that "aspect indicates
. . . the way in which action takes place (marked in the verb)." G. Ul'yanov's
1895 observation that those meanings are aspectual which determine the *interior*
orientation of the verbal sign is prescient, but not typical of the Slavic aspectological tradition.

Even after the two Russian aspects were distinguished from the sundry *Aktionsarten*, there continued to be posited an essential link between aspect and *mode*

d'action (*Aktionsart*). As late as 1924 we find Meillet saying that "an imperfective verb expresses an action which lasts or develops, whether this development is continuous, or results from the repetition of the same process. . . . A perfective verb expresses the process pure and simple, abstracted from all notion of duration."[5]

Throughout the nineteenth century Slavic aspectologists could not decide how forms such as *delat'* and *sdelat'* related to each other, whether they were forms of one verb or two different, albeit related, verbs, nor whether they represented different aspects of the same action or different kinds of action (*Aktionsarten*). Nor was it generally agreed whether aspect was a grammatical or a lexical phenomenon. These confusions in Slavic aspectology were fully paralleled in Western aspectology.

Despite the formal, morphological and syntactic, differences between aspect in the classical and Slavic languages, it was assumed by 1846, with the publication of Georg Curtius's *Formation of the Tenses and Moods in Greek and Latin, Presented Comparatively*, that Greek and Slavic aspect represented the same phenomenon.[6]

It was Jacob Grimm who first extended the concept of aspect to non-Slavic languages, namely the Germanic: "It is not impossible to find in the Germanic languages also the traces of a distinction which so permeates the Slavic languages. Composites with *ver-*, *be-*, *hin-*, *durch-*, etc. (as in Slavic with *po-*, *do-*, *na-*, etc.) perhaps represent perfectives, uncomposed verbs on the contrary imperfectives."[7]

It was not merely a formal similarity Grimm saw between the prefixal verb stems of Slavic and the prefixal derived verbs of other Indo-European languages. It is well documented that such pairs of simple and composite (derived) verbs as Grimm commented on do differ in something like aspect. Many scholars have commented, for example, on the difference between (German) *jagen* 'chase, hunt' and *erjagen* 'catch'.[8]

Erjagen implies successful, completed action, whereas *jagen* does not; it is possible to say *sie jagten den Hirsch den ganzen Tag* 'they (*sie*) chased (hunted, *jagten*) the stag (*den Hirsch*) the whole day (*den ganzen Tag*) long' but not **sie erjagten den Hirsch den ganzen Tag*, which is quite as odd as **they caught the stag all day*.

In his studies of the Gothic prefix *ga-*, Streitberg explicitly identifies it as a marker of the perfective aspect, contrasting for example *slepan* (German *schlafen*) 'to sleep' with *gaslepan* (*entschlafen*) 'to fall asleep'.[9] It is certainly possible (if awkward) to say "he fell asleep all day" (i.e., he kept falling asleep, he would fall asleep now and then), just as it is to say "he slept all day."

But the difference is that, while the latter refers to a *single* occurrence which occurs *over* the whole day, the former refers to a *series* of occurrences occurring *during* the day. *Slepan* thus is "durative" or "continuative," referring to an action which endures through time, whereas *geslepan* refers to something instantaneous or momentaneous, taking place instantly and having no duration (you sleep *for* a certain *period* of time, but you fall asleep *at* a certain *point* in time), though such an action may be repeated or iterated over time (you may keep falling asleep).

Furthermore, the simple, non-composite member of such a pair refers no more than the Slavic imperfective to the completion of the action, while the composite member refers, as the perfective may do, to completion or to some result. Consequently Streitberg calls the perfective verbs "resultative" or "completive." *Steigen* 'climb' makes no reference to any consequence: you can ascend a mountain without ever reaching the top, but *ersteigen* 'ascend' refers specifically to consequence: it entails that the top or goal is reached. *Climb* is ambiguously equivalent either to *steigen* or *ersteigen*, but in *he was the first man to climb Mt. Everest*, *climb* is normally understood in the sense of *ersteigen*, not *steigen*. While *ascend* is accounted a synonym of *climb*, for some English speakers it necessarily implies completion and hence is equivalent to *ersteigen*, not *steigen*.

On formal, morphological and syntactic, as well as semantic grounds, Streitberg distinguishes Germanic non-composites, which are durative (that is, imperfective), from composites, which are non-durative, momentaneous, completive (perfective). He identifies the Germanic categories with those of Slavic (e.g., the non-composite, durative *čitat'*, 'read', *lesen*, as opposed to the composite, non-durative *pročitat'*, 'read through', *durchlesen*.

Streitberg, however, further divides the perfectives into two subclasses: *momentaneous* verbs like *erschlagen* 'kill' and durative-perfectives like *durchlesen* 'read through'. Perfectives

> are momentaneous, if they lay emphasis simply and solely on the moment of completion, the moment of the result, and leave everything else unconsidered, e.g., *erschlagen*, i.e., to achieve a result through the act of hitting (*schlagen*). Here there can be no talk of durative, continuative character of the action. The entire conceptual complex on the contrary concentrates itself simply on the point in time which brings the completion, the result.

The durative-perfectives are in contrast to this:

> They too lay stress on the moment of completion, but set it however in explicit opposition to the preceding duration of the action. The meaning of the verb is thus a combination of a durative and a perfective element. Compare Slovene *preberem* 'ich lese durch, I am reading through', i.e. I am engaged in the durative action of reading, however, I carry it on until a conclusion.[10]

Streitberg recognizes here that there are two aspectual distinctions, not just that of perfective (completive, resultative) and imperfective (non-completive), since some, though not all, perfectives can be durative. (All imperfectives are durative.) This latter distinction is (formally, structurally) more like Greek aspect than like Slavic, since it is linked to tense and not to a systematic stem distinction.

Semantically, the distinction Streitberg is making is rather like a distinction which may have been implicitly recognized by Plato and was first explicitly made by Aristotle in *On Metaphysics* IX.6 and elsewhere.[11] Here we accordingly refer henceforth to "Aristotelian aspect."

Plato in the *Ion* (530A) has Socrates ask, "And did you compete [*ēgōnízou*, imperfect]? And how did you succeed [*ēgōnísō*, perfect]?"[12] The aspectual distinction of imperfect and perfect is not merely one of completion and non-completion, but also one of action enduring over a period of time (here, competition) and "action" which has to do only with a culminating moment of time (here, success or failure).

The passage in Aristotle's *Metaphysics* has often been cited. There he says:

> Since no action which has a limit is an end, but only a means to the end, as, *e.g.* the process of thinning [removing of fat], and since the parts of the body themselves, when one is thinning them, are in motion in the sense that they are not already that which it is the object of the motion to make them, this process is not an action, or at least not a complete one, since it is not an end; it is the process which includes the end that is an action. *E.g.* at the same time we see and have seen, understand and have understood, think and have thought; but we cannot at the same time learn and have learnt, or become healthy and have become healthy. We are living well and have lived well, we are happy and have been happy, at the same time; otherwise, the process would have had to cease at some time, like the thinning-process; but it has not ceased at the present moment: we both are living and have lived.
>
> Now of these processes we should call the one type motions, and the other actualizations.[13] Every motion is incomplete—the processes of thinning, learning, walking, building—these are motions, and incomplete at that. For it is not the same thing which at the same time is walking and has walked, or is building and has built, or is becoming and has become, or is being moved and has been moved, but two different things; and that which is causing motion is different from that which has caused motion. But the same thing at the same time is seeing and has seen, is thinking and has thought. The latter kind of process, then, is what I mean by actualization, and the former what I mean by motion.[14]

He is saying that the act of losing weight through exercise includes the resultant loss of weight, whereas the mere losing of weight through exercise is not an *act*, or at least not a complete one, though of course it is an *activity*. In activities like thinking, at any given moment in which we are in that activity, we are not only engaged in that activity (thinking), but we have been thinking, we have thought. But an action like learning differs from thinking in that it culminates in having learned; at any moment in which we are engaged in learning, we certainly have been learning, but we have not yet learned. Only at the moment at which we have finally learned can we truly say that we have learned as well as that we have been learning.

The normal meaning of *kínēsis* is 'movement, motion', whereas that of *enérgeia* is 'action, operation, energy'. This distinction has had to be rediscovered several times (or at least reinterpreted)—by such philosophers as Ryle, who distinguished (1949) culminative *achievements* such as learning something from non-culminative *activities* like thinking; Kenny, who introduced (1963) a further distinction between *states* like knowing and activities like thinking (you can be engaged in thinking something, but you can't be engaged in knowing something); and Vendler, who distinguished (1957) *achievements*, which happen at a particular moment (such as dying or finding something), from *accomplishments* like losing five pounds, thinking up an advertising slogan, or learning Spanish well enough to speak it, all of which take time.[15]

It is not clear to what extent, and in precisely what sense, Aristotle may himself have distinguished these various categories. Kenny identifies Aristotle's *kínēseis* with his own "performances" and the *enérgeiai* with both "states" and "activities." [16] But in the *De Animo* (*On the Soul*) 417a.30–b.2, Aristotle distinguishes *ékhein* 'having' from *energeîn* 'being active', which Kenny equates respectively to his own "states" and "activities." [17] Elsewhere (*Nicomachean Ethics* 1140a.1–24), Aristotle distinguishes *poíēsis* 'making' from *prâksis* 'doing', which seem to accord respectively with Kenny's "performance" and "activity." [18]

The relationship of these distinctions to Streitberg's subcategories of the perfective is vague but nonetheless apparent. Reading through something is an "accomplishment"; it takes time but also in a sense is completed in an instant, that of (finally) having read that thing through. On the other hand, an achievement like finding something on the street merely happens at a point in time. Thus Streitberg assumes not merely the well-known Slavic aspectual distinction, but something like Aristotelian aspect as well.

Streitberg goes on to introduce a third fundamental aspect, namely the iterative, with durative and perfective subcategories. [19] The Old Bulgarian verb *bivati* (*widerholt schlagen*, 'repeatedly hit') is imperfective but iterative, while *ubivati* (*widerholt erschlagen*, 'repeatedly kill') is perfective but iterative. Thus Streitberg is operating with a semantics in which there are three fundamental dichotomies: perfective versus imperfective, iterative versus non-iterative (semelfactive, occurring once), and durative versus momentaneous (instantaneous).

In Streitberg's system morphological markers represent aspectual distinctions. Consequently those distinctions can be defined in either morphological or semantic terms. For a universal theory obviously the latter is crucial, for otherwise it would be impossible to compare aspects across languages or to define aspects other than in a language-specific way. Indeed, it is clear that Streitberg was primarily interested neither in classes of derived verbs (or forms of verbs) nor in universal semantic categories.

Rather, we can view him as primarily interested in the meanings which derive from verbs in particular contexts; that is, we can interpret his aspectual subcategories as contextual meanings. A verb in an iterative form carries with it the (im)perfectivity of its base verb, but adds to it the meaning of repetition. In languages lacking explicitly iterative forms, verbs may either be inherently iterative (*chatter*) or may be given iterativity by a tense form (*be hitting*) or some contextual feature (*all day he fell asleep*).

When Streitberg used the term *Aktionsart* ('kind of action', *mode d'action*) he was simply creating a technical term for aspect, so it does no harm to replace his *Aktionsarten* with "aspects" (*Aspekte* in German). But what Streitberg meant was not rendered explicit by this terminology.

Some scholars who followed Streitberg understood *Aktionsarten* to be defined, or primarily definable, in formal, that is, morphological and syntactic terms, while others understood them to be definable in purely semantic terms. As a result *Aktionsart* came to be understood in two different ways, neither of which accords with the modern concept of aspect. The central point of the paper by Goedsche (1940)—and incidentally that of Garey (1957)—is that *Aktionsart*, as it has come to be used, is *not* the same thing as aspect.

The *Duden Grammatik* defines *Aktionsart* thus: "The Aktionsarten . . . say something about the way the state [*Sein*] or occurrence develops [*sich vollzieht*]. It is in particular a question especially of the temporal manner of the process of a state or occurrence, of the degree, the intensity of an occurrence."[20]

Consequently the *Aktionsarten* include the perfective, with two subspecies: (1) inchoative or ingressive verbs having to do with the moment of entering into a state (*erblassen* 'turn pale'), and (2) resultative verbs (*erschlagen* 'kill'), the imperfective or durative, and iteratives, but also intensive verbs indicating the intensity of the action (*schnitzen* 'carve' is glossed as *kräftig schneiden* 'to cut strongly').

It is apparent that the category of intensive has little if anything to do with aspect, but it is not clear that the semantics of intensity is completely divorced from that of the various other *Aktionsarten*, and in any case in many languages distinctions such as that of intensity do not differ in their morphology and syntax from categories like perfectivity.

Indeed, the main motivation for including intensity under the heading of *Aktionsarten* would seem to be the lexical relationship exhibited by members of such pairs as *lieben* 'love' and *liebeln* (the latter glossed *oberflächlich lieben*, 'love superficially'), and *lachen* 'laugh' and *lächeln* (*verhalten lachen*, 'laugh restrainedly'). This is not very different, if at all, from the kind of relationship exhibited by truly "aspectual" pairs (involving differences in *Aktionsart*) in German and other languages, for example the English pairs involving iterative *-le* (*spark, sparkle; suck, suckle; wag, waggle*).

Aktionsarten have often been defined in terms of specific morphological markers. Thus Forsyth links the various *Aktionsarten* or what he calls the "procedurals" with specific Russian prefixes. Here are sample verbs for various procedural prefixes:

inceptive	*za*plakat', 'to burst into tears' (cf. English inchoative *-en*, as in *soften*)
absorptive	*za*govorilis', 'became absorbed in conversation'
attenuative	*po*yest', 'to have something to eat'
terminative	*do*goreli, 'have burned out'
totalizing	*pro*delali, 'have done' (seen as a single juncture)
resultative	*do*budils'a, 'succeeded in waking'
durative	*po*spal, 'had a (little) sleep'
	*pro*stoyal, 'stood (for quite a while)'
comitative	*pod*svistyval, 'whistled (at the same time)'
intermittent action	*po*kašlival 'kept on coughing'
semelfactive	stuk*nut*', 'to knock once'[21]

Once again, as in the case of the intensive mentioned by the *Duden Grammatik*, it is not clear that the formal similarity of all these categories implies a semantic or functional similarity. In particular, such categories as the absorptive, comitative, attenuative, and perhaps the totalizing, while telling us in some sense how something happened, do not quite tell us how they happened, *aspectually* speaking.

Up to now we have been concerned with types of derived verbs, but it is also possible to define *Aktionsarten* in semantic terms, in which case we would be concerned with verbs that may or may not be derived. This is clearly the case with the list of *Aktionsarten* (*modes d'action*) in Maurice Grevisse's *Bon Usage*. Grevisse's definition of aspect is somewhat similar to that of the *Duden*, but introduces the important notion of "phase" or "stage":

> the aspect of the verb is the character of the action considered in its development, the particular angle under which the progress (the "process") of that action is viewed, the indication of the stage at which this "process" is in its progress; it is, then, in sum, the way in which the action is situated in the duration or the parts of the duration.[22]

But a consideration of the actual aspects and typical examples shows that again there is no consistency in what sort of meaning counts as aspectual in these terms. However, form at least is no longer criterial, and there is movement beyond the verb itself to syntactic collocations—a very important difference from the *Duden*, which sees the *Aktionsarten* as a way of classifying verbs and not expressions as a whole (note that swimming is an "activity," but swimming across the pool is an "accomplishment").

momentaneous aspect:	*la bombe éclate* 'the bomb explodes'
durative aspect:	*je suis en train de lire* 'I am reading, engaged in reading'
inchoative, ingressive aspect:	*il se met à rire* 'he starts laughing'
iterative [frequentative] aspect:	*je relis la lettre* 'I reread the letter'
progressive aspect:	*il ne fait que rire* 'he doesn't do anything but laugh'
perfective aspect:	*j'ai trouvé* 'I have found'
imperfective aspect:	*je cherche une solution* 'I'm looking for a solution'
the aspect which expresses proximity in the future:	*il va lire* 'he's going to read'
the aspect which expresses proximity in the past:	*je viens de le voir* 'I just saw him'

To these Golian adds the terminative (or effective) aspect, citing as example *discréditer* 'discredit' (terminative, as opposed to the inchoative *accréditer* 'accredit').[23]

What these sundry categories have in common is neither a formal similarity, which they lack, nor a categorial similarity. Some have to do with lexical categories (*relire* 'reread' vs. *lire* 'read'), some with syntactic collocations or tense forms (*je suis en train de lire* 'I'm reading' vs. *je vais lire* 'I'm going to read'), while yet others concern neither (*il ne fait que lire* 'he doesn't do anything but read'). Rather, they share the property of having something vaguely to do with a temporal (time) distinction which is not primarily grammatically "temporal"— that is, which does not have mainly to with tense as such.

This distinction specifically has to do with the stages in which action progresses. The proximal future concerns an event about to happen, the inchoative an event starting to happen, the continuative an event continuing to happen, the terminative an event concluding, and the proximal past an event which has just happened.[24]

It is apparent that Grevisse's *modes d'action*, Forsyth's procedurals, and (to some extent) Streitberg's *Aktionsarten* are quite different from Slavic and Greek aspects, and differ among themselves to a great extent as well. It is precisely the vastly different ways in which Streitberg's concept of aspect or *Aktionsart* was developed by those after him that led to negative considerations of aspectual theory by such scholars as Jespersen. Jespersen noted that when scholars began to find in other language families something similar to the kind of aspectual distinction found in Slavic, "where it is fundamental and comparatively clear and clean-cut, . . . each of them as a rule partially or wholly rejected the systems of his predecessors . . . so that nowadays it would be possible . . . to give a long list of terms . . . some of which are not at all easy to understand."[25]

He points out that each of the following distinctions has been called aspectual by some scholar or other:

(1) The tempo-distinction between the aorist and the imperfect. . . .
(2) The distinction between conclusive and non-conclusive verbs.
(3) The distinction between durative or permanent and punctual or transitory.
(4) The distinction between finished and unfinished.
(5) The distinction between what has taken place only once, and repeated or habitual action or happening.
(6) The distinction between stability [*have*] and change [*get*].
(7) The distinction according to the implication or non-implication of a result. The G[erman] compounds with *er-* frequently are resultative. . . .

He ends by suggesting that such terms as perfective and imperfective be restricted to the Slavic verb, "where they have a definite sense and have long been in universal use." He is especially critical of Streitberg's treatment of the Gothic prefix *ga-* as a marker of perfectivity, seeing it as denoting completion in the case of *gaswalt* 'was dead' (versus *swalt* 'lay dying'), change of state in that of *gaslepan* 'fall asleep' (*slepan* 'sleep, be asleep'), and obtainment in that of *gafraihnan* 'learn by asking' (*fraihnan* 'ask').

Similarly, Verkuyl sees the literature on aspect, from Streitberg's work (e.g., the 1891 book) through about 1935, as "characterized by terminological confusion and vague definition, which reveals the inadequacy of the semantic theory implicit in the relevant studies."[26] Most scholars have seen the cause of this confusion as the application of the term "aspect" (or *Aktionsart*) to "egregiously diverse phenomena"; "the meaning of the word ASPECT as far as French is concerned varies considerably from author to author."[27]

One central dilemma is that, given the diversity of languages, it is not clear whether there is any one set of universal concepts that are equally applicable to all. Inappropriate application of concepts from one language to another may render them contentless, while an insufficient application of universal categories renders language-specific categories meaningless.

But are formal, functional, or semantic categories the ones that link language-specific phenomena to universal categories? And can specific categories be linked without concern for the overall systems of languages? Is the Greek imperfect aspect, for example, the same as the Slavic imperfective? How do we know, and what do we mean by saying this?

Here there are widely differing opinions. Zandvoort is skeptical: "The fact that aspect is not systematically marked in English grammar or lexicon can be taken as an argument for the exclusion of 'aspect' from the categories of English grammar.'' Yet he adds: ''so long as we allow for . . . formal disparity . . . and concern ourselves mainly with functional oppositions, we can retain the terminology of aspect in English.''[28]

The issue is how to achieve universality, and what the appropriate level of comparison is. Holt for one, as a structuralist, opts for a comparison of systems as a whole, rather than of particular elements:

> the notion of aspect is not at all defined in a generally adopted fashion, and as a consequence it is impossible to define the differences . . . within languages as differences of aspect . . . linguistic notions have been confused with logical notions or general psychological concepts. . . . [Linguistic forms] relate first of all to the interior of the linguistic system itself, and it is only as a set that the system of linguistic notions corresponds to a system of logical notions. . . . the first task . . . will be to study the forms of aspect in the languages; . . . it will be necessary . . . to study [the different systems] successively [to] avoid premature comparisons.[29]

The difficulty here is that neither the semantics nor the morphology and syntax of aspect seem to transport well from one language to another. To discount formal similarities and base comparison purely on meaning requires some theory of the semantics of aspect, but up to the point where many of these criticisms were being made, there was no idea even of what the relevant meaning categories were, given the diversity of concepts which had been assigned the rubric of ''aspect.''

At the very least, it should be apparent that aspect of the Slavic type is not the same thing as Aristotelian aspect, and that Streitberg was in error in attempting to combine the two within one scheme of aspects. But it is also clear that the concept of *Aktionsarten* or *modes d'action*, as this has developed on either a formal or a semantic basis, is distinct from either. Aspect, Aristotelian aspect, and *Aktionsarten* are distinct (albeit interactive) phenomena.

Aspect is grammatical. Virtually any Slavic verb may have either perfective or imperfective stems. It is an obligatory category of the Slavic verb and pervades the system of tense and aspect. But Aristotelian aspect and *Aktionsarten* are lexical, pertaining to classes of verbs or larger expressions. The difference between durative and perfective-durative, to use Streitberg's terminology, is not a grammatical, obligatory one; it is simply the case that a verb or collocation fits into the one or the other category.

If aspect is taken as a ''subjective'' choice on the part of the speaker, neither Aristotelian aspect nor *Aktionsarten* are subjective. *Čital* and *pročital* may describe precisely the same situation, but surely there is a vast difference between reading and reading through: not all cases of the former are cases of the latter; and it is equally well the case that *je viens de lire* 'I have just read' and *je suis en train de lire* 'I am in the course of reading' do not describe the same situation any more than *jagen* and *erjagen* do.

Such a discrimination leaves a number of questions unanswered, however. In particular, how do the particular meanings expressed (or implied) by the markers of the *Aktionsarten*, those expressed (or implied) by the aspectual forms of verbs, and the meanings expressed (or implied) by expressions belonging to the various

Aristotelian categories, relate to one another? What is the appropriate level of generalization in each case? And how universal are the various categories?

c. Opposition and Markedness

In retrospect, the study of aspect was doomed to failure so long as scholars failed to recognize that the aspects, like the tenses, form a system. Only in the twentieth century, with the advent of structuralism, was this recognized. The theory of oppositions which came out of the work of the early structuralists, especially Saussure and the Prague School linguists and above all Jakobson, provided a great advance in understanding aspect.

Structuralism holds that linguistics must study the structures of languages and analyze language in terms of structures, rather than functions. Saussure made for the first time the crucial distinction between the *signifier*, the marker or indicator, and the *signified*, that which is marked or indicated: form and content. But more important, he emphasized that the structures of languages participate in systems, and that the meanings of particular units depend on their places in systems of signs; this was completely opposed to the earlier atomistic approach which looked at items in isolation.

For Saussure, language as a system consists of "form, not substance."[30] The value of a linguistic sign (expression) is not independent of its place in the system as a whole. A singular noun does not have the same meaning in Chinese as in English, because the latter language obligatorily opposes plural nouns to singular ones, whereas the former does not. On the level of contents, or uses, a particular occurrence of a noun in Chinese may convey precisely the same information as, and hence be perfectly equivalent to, the corresponding English singular noun, but on the level of meanings the two differ.

Russian *podumali* may legitimately translate English *they have thought* in certain contexts, but Russian has no perfect tense distinct from the preterite (past tense). Nor does the ability of the perfective non-past to convey futurity indicate that such a form constitutes a future tense, since no perfective present exists.

Holt writes: "The Greek Aorist has often been compared with the perfective verbs in Slavic. This is not good methodology. . . . what ought to be compared is the system as a whole."[31] Ruipérez similarly criticizes the speculations of such earlier scholars as Curtius on the relationship of the Greek aorist with the Slavic perfective.[32] Ruipérez likewise insists on a systematic structuralist approach. The value of the aorist is determinable for him only in terms of the system of Greek as a whole, as that of the Slavic perfective depends on that system as a whole. Thus it only makes sense to compare the two systems, and not isolated elements of each.

Saussure did not precisely define what he meant by meanings, other than, perhaps, the relationship holding between signs and their contents, though what this could be other than their place in the system was not clarified. As Holt says, "only the boundaries between terms are marked by linguistic oppositions, the content not being considered."[33]

For the Prague School linguists and those following them, the structure of linguistic systems is built out of the primitive opposition of two elements, that is, *binary* oppositions: "Meaning categories are defined in terms of semantic binary distinctive features."[34] From a set of such primitive oppositions more complex structures can be built, and in general, a system of 2^n elements can be built out of n such binary oppositions. Thus to structure the English words *man*, *woman*, *boy*, *girl* (4 and hence 2^2 terms) we require only two features, those which distinguish male/female and non-young/young.[35]

The opposition male/female is systematic in the English language. It is represented in the difference between the pronouns *he* and *she*, and in the constant difference in meaning between such pairs as

man	woman
boy	girl
son	daughter
brother	sister
uncle	aunt
father	mother

Furthermore, it is captured formally by such affixal markers as *-ess*, *-ix*, and the like:

host	hostess
lion	lioness
sculptor	sculptress
aviator	aviatrix
executor	executrix

Similarly, the young of a species are systematically differentiated from the species in general:

man	boy
woman	girl
bear	cub
dog	pup(py)
cat	kitten

Only sporadically, though, are they marked by such affixes as *-ling* and *-let*:

duck	duckling
goose	gosling
pig	piglet
goose	goslet

Boy can be defined within the subsystem of terms referring to human beings by the characteristics (features) of maleness and youngness. Yet other features would be necessary to uniquely characterize it within the system of all terms. It is important to emphasize that the system of oppositions does not deal with contents as such. It obviously does not exhaust the meaning of *boy*, even within the system of terms pertaining to human beings, to assign it the features "male" and "young."

The opposition of young and species-in-general is not like that of male and female. The latter is a contradictory opposition: to be the one is automatically not to be the other. But to be a girl is precisely to be a woman, that is, a female human being, except in those contexts in which "woman" is being used in the narrower sense of *adult* female human being. In general, a girl *is* a woman. Gustave Klimt's painting of *The Three Ages of Woman* is not incorrectly titled because it includes a child.

The male-female opposition is "equipollent," with two coequal and exclusive values, whereas that of young and species in general is "privative"; we cannot define *woman* or *duck* as adult, since girls are women and ducklings are ducks. Whereas *girl* specifies "young," *woman* does not (in its more general meaning) specify age at all. The young/species-in-general opposition is privative in that one term does not exclude the other, but the more general term must be defined by taking away the defining feature of the more specific term.

In many languages singular and plural number are in opposition: in Latin all nouns are either singular, like *globus* 'ball', or plural, like *globi* 'balls'. Each number has its own marker: -*us* and -*i* differ only in number, the former marking certain nouns as singular, the latter marking them as plural.

This is rather different from the case of the endings in English which form nouns expressing the young of animal species. Here there is a marker indicating the young, but there is none for the adult of the species; indeed, there is no term for the adult alone, since a duckling is a duck. While *duckling* can be defined positively as a 'young duck', the best we can do with *duck* itself, in regard to its opposition in meaning to *duckling*, is 'a duck (but not specifically a young one)'. That is, *duck* no more tells us anything about age than *they* tells us about gender or *you* about number.

Usually this is interpreted not as an antonymous relationship but as a privative one, with "non-" interpreted not as 'the opposition of' but as 'the absence of'. That is, the non-youngness of *duck* is not the opposite of the youngness of *duckling* but simply represents the lack of any indication of age; the general term is used except where the youngness is being asserted. The reason for this interpretation is that the general term can be used to refer to the young (*young duck*), but the reverse is not true: **mature duckling* cannot be used to refer to adult ducks.

In his analysis of Greek Ruipérez follows Jakobson, who postulated that all grammatical oppositions are privative and denied the need for equipollent ones in grammar.[36] In his *Struktur* paper (1932) Jakobson attempts to construct a system of tenses and aspects for the Russian verb on such privative oppositions with no residue.

In a privative opposition, one of the members, the one positively defined, is explicitly marked, either by a morphological marker or a syntactic one. Hence it is called the "marked" member of the opposition; the member not so marked is called "unmarked." The assumption is that explicit markers generally reflect oppositions in meaning, and that oppositions in meaning are generally reflected in explicit markers. However, a semantic opposition is not of necessity always explicitly marked, though the semantic relationship remains the same whether an explicit marker is present or not.

By extension, then, "marked" is used for the member of an opposition which is semantically more specific, and "unmarked" for the one which is nonspecific, even where there is no explicit marker. *Puppy* is the marked member of the opposition *puppy/dog*, even though it contains no explicit marker and is morphologically unrelated to the more general term. Semantically, however, the relationship is precisely parallel to that of *duckling* and *duck*.

In privative oppositions

> the general meaning of a marked category states the presence of a certain (whether positive or negative) property A; the general meaning of the corresponding unmarked category states nothing about the presence of A, and is used chiefly, but not exclusively, to indicate the absence of A. . . . on the level of general meaning the opposition of the two contradictories may be interpreted as "statement of A *versus* no statement of A", whereas on the level of "narrowed", nuclear meanings, we encounter the opposition "statement of A" versus "statement of non-A".[37]

Holt points out that the Stoic terms *"syntelikos—ateles* resemble greatly the terminology of our time, indicating purely an opposition between a positive term (*syntelikos*) and a negative one (*ateles*)."[38]

The meaning of the marked member of an opposition is more specific, more easily characterized with precision. As the more specific term, it will necessarily occur in a narrower range of contexts than the unmarked member and hence it is less usual, and its frequency should be lower; it should be statistically less common.[39]

The referential range of the marked term is included in that of the unmarked one: a duckling is a duck. The unmarked member may "compete" with the marked member, but the reverse is not true: a duckling is a duck, but a duck is not (in general) a duckling. Except where the differentiating feature of the marked term is stressed, as in contrast with the absence of that quality in the unmarked term (*all ducks were once ducklings*), the unmarked member may be freely substituted for the marked one.

The imperfective is clearly the unmarked term of the aspectual opposition in Russian, not only because it lacks a specific positively defined meaning (as we shall see), but because it freely competes with the perfective. While it is possible to use *čital knigu* to mean 'I read the book (through)', it is not possible to use *pročital knigu* to mean 'I was reading the book'.

Because the marked member may be explicitly marked, it generally contains more morphological material than the unmarked: *duckling* adds to *duck* the morpheme *-ling*. While primary perfectives do exist in Russian, and affixation is used to form the imperfectives of secondary perfectives, most primary verbs are imperfective, and hence most perfectives are morphologically more complex than their corresponding imperfectives.[40]

As the more common term, the unmarked member often exhibits greater morphological irregularity than the marked one. Many names of animal species in English have irregular plurals, but the corresponding plural terms for young are almost invariably regular: *goose/geese* but *gosling/goslings*. Perfectivizing a Russian verb generally introduces no morphological irregularity, though many of the imperfectives are irregular.

The paradigms of marked forms often lack categories or exhibit a falling together (syncretism) of categories kept distinct in the paradigms of unmarked forms.

The English past tense, for instance, has but one form and lacks any distinction of person or number, except for the irregular verb *be*, which has singular (*was*) and plural (*were*) past tense forms. But the present tense of all verbs has a special third person singular form, *-(e)s*. In the present, *be* distinguishes not only singular and plural but also, in the singular, the three persons as well: I *am*, you *are*, and the third person *is*. It is not surprising then that the Russian imperfective has three tenses (past, present, and future) while the perfective has only two: past and future.

In contexts in which the distinctive characteristic of the marked term is neutralized, the unmarked member of the opposition may occur but not the marked, and this is as true diachronically as it is synchronically; when a distinction is lost, it is the unmarked member which tends to survive. Many of the terms for the young of animals are obsolescent or obsolete, replaced by some such circumlocution as "young . . ." or occasionally ". . . cub," ". . . pup." While this distinction has no specific application to the system of Russian aspects, it is criterial for other systems, as for instance that of Greek.

These various properties serve as criteria for markedness. It would appear, based on these considerations, that the imperfective is the unmarked member of the aspectual opposition. This is in accord with naive intuitions, for the perfective is defined by some such characteristic as completeness, whereas the imperfective is not positively characterized, but rather negatively and in relation to perfectivity.

While the difference in meaning of the two aspects is intuitively clear and to the native speaker in some general way quite obvious, the precise definition of the difference in meaning of the two aspects is a controversial topic which has led to much discussion.[41] There is likewise something intuitively obvious about the interaction of aspect and tense, but it requires more than a vague intuitive understanding of the two to explain precisely why, for example, the perfective non-past can and must have only future meaning.

As in the case of the Greek and Latin perfect and imperfect, traditionally the perfective aspect has been identified with completion, the imperfective with non-completion. There are two great difficulties with this approach where Russian aspect is concerned, however. First, as every author points out, the imperfective verb does not exclude completion:

—Vy čitali ⟨⟨Annu Kareninu⟩⟩?
—Čital.
"Have you read *Anna Karenina*?"
"I have." (literally, '(I) read')

Vy budete pokupat' etu šl'apu?
"Will you buy (are you going to buy) this hat?"

Nor does the perfective always imply it: *zasmeyals'a* '(he) laughed' can also mean '(he) began to laugh'.[42]

Some scholars have sought consequently to make duration the central factor in differentiating the two, for typically the perfective represents the action as punctual (occurring at a point in time) or momentary (*stuknul* '[he] knocked'), whereas the imperfective represents it as enduring, occurring over a period of time (*stučal* '[he] was knocking'). Once again, however, examples can be found in which the perfective represents action taking place over time—*zvuk postepenno zatix* 'the sound gradually abated'[43]—or in which the imperfective represents relatively instantaneous action: *zakryvajte dver'* 'shut the door'.[44]

There are a number of other values which are characteristic of the perfectives in various languages, and which have been suggested as typical or definitional for the perfective, though Comrie[45] points out that there are counterexamples to all these, and none of them can be its *essential* characteristic:

1. Short duration. The perfective may imply a shorter period of time than the corresponding imperfective; however, as the examples above show, the perfective may refer to a relatively long period of time and the imperfective to a short one.
2. Limited duration. This is what many mean when they term the perfective "bounded" (*telic*, having a natural end) as opposed to the "unbounded" (*atelic*) imperfective. But the perfective may not presuppose a limit or bound on the action (*started to laugh*), while the imperfective may do so (*shut the door*).
3. Ingressive (inchoative) meaning. Often the perfective refers to the commencement of an action or state, while the imperfective views it as in progress; but it is perfectly possible to use verbs such as *begin* and *start* in the imperfective, and generally a perfective verb makes no reference to the commencement of an action.
4. Resultative meaning: often the perfective refers to, or implies, the result of an action. But there need in fact be no result of a perfective, while an imperfective may imply a result, as in *shut the door*.

There are many sets of terminology in the literature which reflect yet other oppositional values of the two aspects:

Perfective	*Imperfective*
non-progressive	progressive
semelfactive	iterative
punctuative	habitual
dynamic	static
transitory	permanent

Once again, however, none of these distinctions captures the essence of the opposition.

Aside from the counterexamples to any of these distinctions, that no distinction captures the essence of the opposition is shown by the fact that pairs of these distinctions may co-occur in various languages, marked in different ways. In English, for example, the progressive/non-progressive distinction is marked by the progressive construction (*be-ing*) as opposed to the simple verb (*we were eating the cake/we ate the cake*), while that of completion/non-completion is (sometimes) marked by the particles (e.g., *up*) versus the bare verb (*we ate up the cake/we ate the cake*).

Since the two may co-occur and are independent of each other (*we were eating up the cake* is distinct in meaning from both *we were eating the cake* and *we ate up the cake*), they must represent different distinctions. Moreover, insofar as both distinctions go into the making of the meaning difference between the aspects, neither can represent their essential difference.

On the whole there are a number of different *contextual* meanings which the aspects seem to bear in particular contexts, though they may not bear each of these meanings in *all* contexts. A short list, based on the work of J. S. Maslov, is provided by Rassudova[46]; her terminology is in double quotation marks:

IMPERFECTIVE ASPECT:

(1) "concrete-processural" (roughly the traditional 'durational,' 'continuative'—a single specific episode viewed in its extension): "The young woman was sitting (*sidela*) by the window of the railroad car and was reading (*čitala*)."

(2) "indefinite-iterative" ('habitual'—repetitive episodes somewhat distantly spaced in time and viewed as distinct): "Sometimes I would reread (*perečityval*) writers whom I especially liked."

(3) "general-factual" ('indefinite'—a nonspecific episode): "Have you read (*čitali*) this story? In what journal did you read (*čitali*) it?"

PERFECTIVE ASPECT:

(1) "concrete-factual" ('definite'—a specific episode viewed strictly as an occurrence): "He repeated (*povtoril*) his question to me."

(2) "aggregate meaning" ('iterative'—repetitive episodes rather closely spaced in time and viewed as a unit): "He repeated (*povtoril*) his question several times."

(3) "graphic-exemplary" (without reference to any real episode): "If you don't understand (*poymete*) my explanation, I can always repeat it for you. I'll repeat (*povtor'u*) it for you any time."

Some scholars have attempted to capture the various uses of the aspects in one overarching definition. The *Academy Grammar* defines the aspects thus:

> The category of aspect indicates that the action expressed by the verb is presented: (*a*) in its course, in process of its performance, *consequently* in its duration or repetition, e,g., *žit'* 'to live', *pet'* 'to sing', *rabotat'* 'to work', *xodit'* 'to go', *čitat'* 'to read' (imperfective); (*b*) as something restricted, concentrated at some limit of its performance, be it the moment of origin or beginning of the action or the moment of its completion or result, e.g., *zapet'* 'to start singing', *končit'* 'to finish', *pobežat'* 'to break into a run', *propet'* 'to sing', *priyti* 'to come', *uznat'* 'to recognize', *uyti* 'to go away' (perfective).[47]

Forsyth is critical of this type of definition, commenting that it does not provide "any simple opposition between these characteristics—'duration-or-repetition' cannot be meaningfully opposed to 'limited-at-beginning-or-end.' " There are too many alternative criteria—duration *or* repetition, completion *or* result. He adds that it does not suffice to list the meanings which the forms may convey at various times, since what is desired is some account of the essential difference between the aspects, from which their various uses follow. We seek a system, not merely a collection of uses replete with exceptions and anomalies.

The question is what, if anything, those essential differences are. Although there is some intuitively felt essential difference between the aspects, each has a multiplicity of uses which do not seem to share any essential feature. The perfective, like the perfect in Greek, seems to have something to do with completion, while the Greek imperfect and the Slavic imperfective have to do with incompletion. But often enough the perfective has no implication of completion, while the imperfective is not incompatible with it.

That the opposition of perfective and imperfective is not merely an accident of morphology but captures some truth about the semantics of aspect is shown by the fact that the same, or a very similar, bundle of uses for each of the aspects is found in each of those languages which share this opposition. The imperfect(ive) has continual, habitual, and generic uses in many languages, while the perfect(ive) has punctual, iterative, and resultative uses.

One way out of the dilemma would be to recognize different *uses* of grammatical categories which have only one *meaning* each. As we have seen, this is the approach taken by Jespersen (1924), who distinguishes the grammatical category of preterite, for example, from the various notions, such as pastness or irreality in the present, which it can be used to express.

Several difficulties arise in regard to such an approach, however, the most significant of which has to do with the relationship of the *use* of a marker to express a certain notion and the *meaning* of the marker itself. Is the ability to express past time a necessary condition and/or a sufficient condition for a marker to be a past tense (preterite) marker?

Jespersen does not deal with this question, though it would seem that such is indeed a necessary, though apparently not a sufficient, condition. Further, in Jespersen's theory "preterite" is simply a label for the set of forms most often used to convey past time—a set of forms that has no independent status in the theory. Consequently the labeling of a particular form is arbitrary and unprincipled in terms of the theory itself.

A theory of aspect must account for aspect choice in general, and many scholars have held that such an account can be provided only in terms of a basic (*Grund-*) or common (*Gesamt-*) meaning (*Bedeutung*),[48] as we have seen in part I. Allen argues that it is "difficult to believe that a native speaker could extend the restrictions applying to a given category of words to a new word [without] some common core of meaning." Hopper similarly argues that a "form must have a consistent value or else communication is impossible; we cannot have linguistic forms which derive all their meanings only from context."[49] These various authors all differentiate the contextually determined uses (such as iterativity) from the invariant meaning (*Gesamtbedeutung*) which attaches to each invariant formal distinction. Waugh is highly critical of studies which "have not extracted an invariant of meaning from each tense in all its uses, but have treated certain uses as essentially different."[50]

Most contemporary scholars of Russian reject the view that the sundry values borne, or implied, by the aspects are their meanings as such, but consider them merely meanings which are entirely dependent on context—i.e. contextual meanings.[51] They seek basic meanings in opposition, and view that opposition as purely privative, in that, while the perfective is "marked," or explicitly defined, the imperfective is "unmarked," being defined negatively in terms of it: the imperfective lacks the criterial feature of the perfective.[52] This treatment of the Russian aspectual opposition as privative was first offered by Jakobson in his 1932 paper "Zum Struktur des russischen Verbums" ("On the Structure of the Russian Verb").

The major question then is what the *positive* definition of the perfective is. While there are competing formulations, the basic idea most widely accepted today is that of what Rassudova calls "integral action." Forsyth[53] refers to Maslov's concept of the perfective as representing the action as "an indivisible whole," while the imperfective presents it "without reference to the totality of the action," which forms the basis of Forsyth's own definition of the perfective as involving "the presentation of the action as a total event related to a specific single juncture."[54] Similar definitions are offered by others such as Comrie.[55]

For Forsyth, "the [essential and only *inherent*] function of the imperfective . . . is simply to name the type of action . . . without reference to perfectivity."[56] The imperfective "as the unmarked member of the opposition does not oppose any positive or negative meaning to that of the perfective, but is simply devoid of any inherent indication of the kind of meaning which is inherent in the perfective." And its "basic function . . . is to denote the type of action without reference to totality, frequency, mode of procedure etc."[57]

A similar idea is expressed by Rassudova:

> The [imperfective] conveys action without any special limitation; for this reason its semantic sphere is wider than and not so clearly defined as that of the [perfective]. Theoretically, the [imperfective] could be used very freely, but this does not happen because the [imperfective] is associated with the [perfective] by opposition. . . . The [imperfective] "possesses no positive semantic mark". . . . The relationship of the [imperfective] to the mark of integrality . . . varies depending on its use in different situations.
>
> The [imperfective] can neutralize the mark of integrality; it can implicitly express this mark or leave it indefinite. Thus, out of context or situation . . . *Turisty podnimalis'* [imperfective] *na goru* can be understood in two ways: (1) as conveying action in progress; i.e., not yet having attained its boundary and, consequently, nonintegral (The hikers *were climbing* the mountain); (2) as conveying the fact of an action which has taken place and, consequently, [is] implicitly integral (The hikers *had climbed* the mountain).[58]

This neutralization is linked precisely with the possibility of using the unmarked member of an opposition in the sense of the marked member, negating thereby the distinctive feature. For example, nouns of English unmarked for gender such as *actor, aviator*, and *sculptor* may be used freely to refer to females, whereas the corresponding marked female terms *actress, aviatrix*, and *sculptress* may not be used for males.

In the structuralist view the perfective essentially presents the action as a whole, while the imperfective essentially indicates only the lack of any such presentation. This may be interpreted either as indifference to wholeness or as a positive lack of it, as when the imperfective indicates incompletion; but this is dependent on context. The sundry uses of the aspects are seen as following from this fundamental dichotomy.

d. The Analysis of Greek

We saw in part I that the Stoics may already have had an analysis of Greek which tacitly recognized a category of aspect. If so, their system necessarily involved a good deal of abstraction. In Slavic, aspect is explicitly marked in the stems of verbs and exists quite apart from the tense modifications, which are common to both aspects. But there is no distinct marking of aspect in Greek.

Instead, aspect is mixed in with the other "accidents" (verbal categories). While Greek has distinctive stems, these combine aspect with tense and, arguably, voice and mood as well. If Greek morphology is so analyzed as to abstract away these last two categories, there are traditionally these thematic stem forms: present, future (sigmatic), aorist (sigmatic), and perfect (reduplicated).

Holt[59] presents the following scheme, noting that it "presents a chaotic enough picture":

	present stem	*future stem*	*aorist stem*	*perfect stem*[60]
past	imperfect		aorist	pluperfect
present	present			perfect
future		future		

In the Stoic analysis (as interpreted by Holt and others), the present and imperfect constitute *paratatikoí*, tenses "of extension," while the perfect and pluperfect are *syntelikoí*, "completed" tenses. These are the "determined" (*horísmenoi*) tenses, as opposed to the aorist and future, which are "undefined" (*aóristoi*)[61]:

	definite tenses		*indefinite tenses*
	extension	completed	
present-future	present	perfect	future
past	imperfect	pluperfect	aorist

Assuming that it is correct to abstract a distinction of imperfect aspect (represented by the "present" stem) and perfect aspect (represented by the "perfect" stem) out of the Greek thematic system, and assuming that the two form an aspectual opposition (however we wish ultimately to treat the aorist and future stems), two questions arise in regard to the Greek system: is this opposition of imperfect and perfect the same as that of imperfective and perfective in Slavic, and if so, is the imperfect the unmarked member of the opposition, as is the imperfective?

Some scholars have identified the Greek system with the Slavic, assuming a common perfect(ive)-imperfect(ive) aspectual opposition, which has even been postulated to exist in other branches of the Indo-European family, such as Germanic.[62] But even if the categories of one language could so straightforwardly be applied to another, a difficulty remains: the Greek system does not just comprise a pair—the imperfect and the perfect—but has a third component, the undefined or aorist, consisting of the sigmatic stems. A priori, this raises significant questions concerning the applicability of the Slavic system to Greek.

The aorist is in some sense "doubly unmarked" for aspect, as it is neutral in regard to the aspectual distinction of perfect and imperfect: there is no "aorist perfect" tense. Even the future may be doubly unmarked in this sense. Ranged against the future perfect, it is obviously the unmarked member of an aspectual opposition. But the future is also indifferent to aspect, in the same way that the English past tense is. Certainly in the active voice (even in those dialects which have the future perfect), the Greek future is neutral as to aspect.[63] *Gegrápsontai* 'they will have been written' indicates completion, but *grápsō* 'I shall write' in and of itself does not, and can translate 'I shall be writing'.

Accordingly Holt, distinguishing the opposite of the marked member of an opposition from a category that is neutral and unmarked in regard to the criterial feature of that opposition, sets up for the Greek aspects a system of three terms: the perfect as the positive, "plus" ($+$) term; the imperfect as the negative, "minus" ($-$) one; and the aorist as the a neutral, "zero" term (0).[64]

In this he parts company from the Prague School tradition of markedness theory. Jakobson, as we have seen, draws a distinction between the occasional *use* of a marker to *express* the negation (complement) of a marked feature and its *meaning in general* as unmarked for that feature.[65] For him, the "general meaning" of the unmarked category is the absence of the criterial feature: "The unmarked term is always the negative of the marked term, but on the level of general meaning the opposition of the two contradictories may be interpreted as 'statement of [the criterial feature] A' *versus* 'no statement of A', whereas on the level of 'narrowed', nuclear meanings, we encounter the opposition 'statement of A' *versus* 'statement of non-A'."[66]

Meaning must be independent of context. Waugh identifies "marked" (i.e., [+feature X]) as "the necessary presence of that feature in all the contexts, in all the uses, of a particular form. . . . Unmarked [0feature X] means that the information given by the feature X is not necessarily present in all the contexts where the unmarked form occurs." Yet "in some contexts the unmarked form may have the same connotation as the marked form."[67]

Ruipérez emphasizes the criterial value of the dual nature of the unmarked term:

> The unmarked term [of an opposition] possesses a double function. Insofar as it is unmarked, . . . it is indifferent to the indication of the distinctive notion (neutral value). But also insofar as it is a term opposed [to the marked term], the [unmarked] term signifies the absence or negation of the notion expressed by [the marked term] (negative value). . . . In the unmarked term of a privative morphological opposition, together with the neutral value or that of indifference to the distinctive notion, the sign possesses the negative value, consisting in the indication of the absence or negation of the basic notion. . . . the double function of the unmarked term constitutes a sure criterion for the identification of the terms of a morphological opposition.[68]

In the mainstream of structuralist thought, the Greek imperfect, if this is the unmarked member of an opposition similar to the Slavic one, would lack perfectivity, be non-perfective in a privative sense, which in many contexts will be actualized as the opposite of perfectivity ([−perfective]); in others, however, it will be actualized as perfective ([+perfective]), while in yet others it will be neutral as to perfectivity. In this view Holt ignores the difference between specific, contextual values and meaning as such.

In the Prague School tradition, whenever more than two terms are apparently in opposition, it is assumed that two or more features are involved. A set of 2^n elements can be uniquely characterized by n features. The three tenses of English can be analyzed in terms of the features of pastness and futurity: the past tense is [+past] in opposition to the present and future tenses; the future is [+future] in opposition to the present tense.

As the unmarked term, the non-past can stand for the past, as in historical narration, but not vice versa. As unmarked in the present-future opposition, the (futurate) present can stand for the future, but again, the reverse is not true.[69]

Such pairs or sets of features are not independent of one another. The opposition of future and non-future does not apply to the past tense, but only to the non-past. This opposition is subordinate to that of past and non-past. Hence the past is automatically unmarked for futurity. This situation is diagramed in the accompanying illustration.

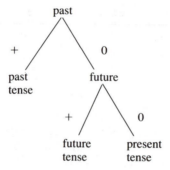

Accordingly there is no need to set up a three-way opposition of perfect-imperfect-aorist, since two features can uniquely capture the Greek system. The question is what the second feature F is and whether it is empirically justified.

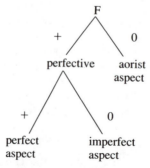

Holt has two arguments against this standard binary approach and in support of his tripartite one.[70] First, given four terms, A, B, C, and D, it is necessary using binary features to split these into two pairs, say A-B and C-D. But this "creates thus sub-categories inside ordinary categories, which would lead to the establishment of units not existent in language, because they do not possess any corresponding expression." Thus Holt denies that such supplementary features have anything more than an artefactual existence, since they lack any marker. He would deny F above any empirical status.

Second, the analysis using binary features requires an arbitrary grouping of the terms. But, using number as an example, "how can one demonstrate, concerning the category of number, that the dual is nearer to the plural than to the singular?" He is dubious of any principled, nonarbitrary way of providing such a grouping for the Greek aspects.

Ruipérez rejects Holt's approach, arguing that the distinction of aorist and imperfect is not like that of perfect and imperfect or aorist and perfect: the former distinction is indeed separate from the latter.[71] Ruipérez's work provides, he believes, a demonstration that two features for the Greek system *are* empirically justified, and that the grouping of the aorist with the imperfect is logically necessary, not arbitrary.

The main thrust of his argument is theoretical. The Stoics seem to have held that there is a distinctive opposition between the perfect and the imperfect which is neutralized in the cases of the future and aorist tenses. That is, aspect is a matter of completed or noncompleted action (or alternatively, or resultant state vs. no resultant state), but this opposition is not relevant to the aorist and the future. From the structuralist point of view it is wrong to put the aorist and the imperfect on the same plane (as opposed to the perfect), because absence of a value for perfectness removes the aorist from the plane of the opposition altogether.

If two features are needed, then the analysis of the Greek system becomes considerably more complicated. What are the criterial features? Which is subordinate to which? And which of the markers represent the unmarked terms?

Although some scholars[72] apply terms such as "perfective" and "imperfective" to the Greek system, and identify the imperfect with the imperfective, since Curtius's work it has been usual to identify the Slavic perfective not with the Greek *perfect* but rather with the *aorist*, and accordingly to distinguish perfect from perfective. Consequently, some scholars distinguish the future from the aorist, since the future is not clearly perfective. Holt, for example, treats the future tense forms as of the same aspect as the present and the imperfect, while the future perfect has perfect aspect.[73] This is essentially the Varronian analysis of Latin.

So long as the perfect and perfective were both seen as presenting a completive aspect, the aorist fell outside the oppositional system of the Slavic type. But it is questionable whether completion is the criterial feature of either the Greek perfect or the Slavic perfective. Most scholars today see the perfect as resultative or stative, referring to the enduring resultant state subsequent to a completed action, while the perfective is viewed by most as, like the Greek aorist, representing an action as a whole, without regard for the progress or development of the action— that is, as "complexive" or "totalizing."

To some extent the identification of the aorist with the perfective is misleading, in a way which Holt points out. For it is clear that the Slavic perfective is the *marked* member of the perfectivity opposition, whereas the aorist is considered by most scholars to be *unmarked* relative to the other Greek aspects, whether it is equivalent in meaning (that is, in content) to the perfective or not. There are compelling reasons, in any case, for not identifying the perfect with the perfective.[74] The perfect has something to do with resultant state, but the perfective does not necessarily imply results, nor does it presuppose any state.

There have been a number of competing analyses of the Greek aspects and tenses in terms of the components of oppositions and markedness theory (componential analysis).[75] Early scholars such as the Neogrammarians or Junggrammatiker tended to split up the verb into present/aorist/perfect in a tripartite system; the earliest scholar cited by Friedrich who developed a markedness theory for Greek is Delbrück, who in the 1897 *Comparative Syntax of the Indo-European Languages* analyzed the three aspects (aorist, present-imperfect, perfect) by means of two features.[76] The perfect is most marked, as an "achieved state"; the others represent actions, the aorist ($+$)punctual, the present-imperfect non- (or $-$)punctual.

A similar, albeit fully binary, analysis is that of Lyons.[77] Here the "perfective" (perfect) is again split off as [+completive], the others being [−completive]. Now, however, the "imperfective" is treated as marked, being the [+durative] term, the aorist being the unmarked, [−durative] term.

For most scholars, the aorist and imperfect are both in opposition to the perfect, as the most marked of the aspects. For Goodwin the perfect "represents an action as already finished at the *present* time; as gégrapha, *I have written* (that is, *my writing is now finished*). The pluperfect represents an action as already finished at a given past time; as egegráphein, *I had written.*"[78] The perfect, "although it implies the perfection of the action in past time, yet states only that it *stands completed* at the present time. This explains why the perfect is classed with the present as a primary tense, that is, as a tense of *present* time." The perfect *indicates* a current state but *implies* an anterior action completed in the past.

Ruipérez says similarly that the perfect theme (stem) alone has a generally agreed-upon meaning: "the perfect would express the state resulting from a previous [anterior] action. Thus *téthnēke* 'is dead', *héstēka* 'I am on foot', *pepoíēka* 'I have made/done' (and it is made/done), *kéktēmai* 'I have acquired' (i.e., 'I possess')."[79] There is no opposition of momentary and durational meaning, only a resultant state which may or may not endure: "the perfect is indifferent to the expression of duration."[80]

Holt also criticizes any view that the duration of the state is in question: "the use of the perfect stem ascribes to the verbal stem the signification of a state; . . . whether this state continues or does not concern us. The difference between the perfect stem and the present one stands out in examples like *oudè bouleúesthai éti hóra, allà bebouleûsthai* 'it is no longer the moment for deliberating but for having deliberated' (Plato, *Crito*, 46a)."[81]

Holt agrees that the perfect "indicates the state obtained by an earlier process: *téthnēke* 'he is dead', *lélogxa* 'I have received this share', ..." He asserts that "the notion of aspect is the indication of the termination and of the non-termination of a process." On such grounds he argues that "the significance of the perfect stem is . . . the most delimited. . . . It is also much less frequent than the other stems, which leads one to suppose that it designates a more specific notion. The aspect of the perfect stem is purely the positive term of the category of aspects.''

In Holt's view, ''the negative term ought to indicate the process without termination . . . the negative term can designate a process with its termination . . . the true opposition is found between the aspect of the present and that of the perfect . . . [the aspect] of the present [designates the process] without its termination . . . [the] present is the negative term.''

This picture of the perfect depends on accounting for the so-called ''anomalous'' perfects. These are perfect verbs the meaning of which is essentially that of a present (or imperfect in the case of the pluperfect), that is, where there is no anterior action and the verb does not necessarily refer to any state. Ruipérez offers the examples *dédorka = dérkomai* 'I see' and *gégētha = gēthéō* 'I am happy'.[82] The anomalous perfect is ''irreducible'' to the ''normal'' perfect.[83] Rather, the two perfects ''constitute a significative unit in the system of 'la langue' '', so that ''the 'normal' perfect and the 'anomalous' perfect have to be two distinct realizations of the same aspectual value of perfect with two distinct types of semantemes.''

The same aspectual *meaning* has different specific *values* in the differing contexts of the two types of meaningful units (semantemes): ''In a transformative verbal semanteme, the perfect indicates the state resulting from the action (*téthnēke*, . . .): it is the so-called 'normal' perfect. In a non-transformative verbal semanteme, the perfect indicates the 'action' itself (*dédorka*, . . .): it is that which we call the 'anomalous' perfect.''[84]

That is, ''in a transformative semanteme, the notion of termination operates with the final termination of the verbal content,'' but ''in a non-transformative semanteme, it operates with the initial termination of the verbal content. The value of the perfect theme (stem) is to express the verbal content after its termination.''[85]

By transformative verbal semantemes, Ruipérez means ''those which express a transformation, a modification of the state'' such as *thnéskein* 'to die' or certain *verbi sentendiendi* (verbs of sensation) such as *ideîn* 'to see'.[86] By nontransformative verbal semantemes, Ruipérez means ''those whose signification excludes any idea of modification as much in the subject as in the object,'' as for example *basileúein* 'to be king'.

By reducing the problem of anomalous perfects to that of contextually defined meaning, he can say that, on the level of *la langue*, the systematic in language, ''the theme of the perfect possesses a single value. . . , defined as consideration of the verbal content after its termination, besides which all the types and uses of the perfect are explained as realizations of 'la parole','' this being the level of specific actualization in speech or writing.[87] Here he is referring to ''the iterative sense of some anomalous perfects,'' which ''is a product of the realization of the perfect in momentary non-transformative semantemes,'' and ''the intensive sense of the 'anomalous' perfects,'' which ''is a realization of the aspectual value of the perfect as expression of the verbal content after its termination.''[88]

Further arguments come from the competition of terms. The unmarked member may in certain contexts replace the marked member, but the reverse is not true. Both the present and the aorist may compete with the perfect.[89] Ruipérez offers as an example (among others) of the present-for-perfect:

Héktor, pêi dé   toi ménos oíkhetai,
Hektor where PART then strength have gone (PRES MID INDIC 3SG)
hò   prìn   ékheskes
which formerly have (IMPF ACT INDIC 2SG)
'Hektor, where now then has gone the strength which you had?' (*Iliad*, book E).[90]

Of the aortist-as-perfect he offers an example from Thucydides (V.5.1):

egéneto   Messénē Lokrôn   tina   khrónon
become (AOR INDIC 3 SG) Messene of Locrians some time
'Messene was (away) from the Locrians during some time.'

Assuming that the perfect does indeed represent the marked member of an opposition, what now of the imperfect (present stem) and the aorist (sigmatic stem)?

According to Goodwin the present tense of Greek represents the "action as *going on* at the time of speaking . . . gráphō, *I write*, or *I am writing*," although it may also refer to the future, "to express *likelihood, intention* or *danger*"; or may be "used . . . in the sense of a perfect and a present combined" as in *keînon ikhneúō pálai, I have been tracking him a long time* (and still continue it).[91] Similarly, the imperfect "represents an action as *going on* in the past time; as égraphon, *I was writing*."[92] He notes that "in narration it dwells on the course of an event instead of merely stating its occurrence." It may refer to attempted action (conation) or likelihood of action.

The imperfect may also

[represent] an action or state as . . . repeated. The aorist is therefore more common in rapid narration, the imperfect in detailed description. It must be remembered that the same event may be looked upon from different points of view by the same person; thus in Dem[osthenes] xviii. 71 and 73 (quoted in [section] 35), élue tèn eirénēn and tèn eirénēn éluse refer to the same thing, once as an act in progress, and once as a fact accomplished.[93]

Ruipérez reports that traditionally the present is considered to possess "a great complexity of values."[94] The major one given to it, however, is that of duration or nonpunctuality. He points out that, "in order to establish the aspectual value of the theme of the present, the present of the indicative is unusable, because of its being neutral as regards the distinction between present [that is, imperfect aspect—RB] and aorist," and argues that here the notion of "with its (final) termination" plays no basic role in the opposition of present and aorist, nor does punctuality.[95] Rather, "we can consider that the theme of the present, defined as durative, constitutes the marked term of the aspectual opposition present:aorist."[96] The aorist, as unmarked term, "expresses punctuality (negative value) and the indifference to the notions of duration and of punctuality (neutral value)."[97]

For Goodwin the aorist of Greek "expresses the simple *occurrence* of an action in past time; as égrapsa, *I wrote*."[98] This is the fundamental characteristic of the aorist even in dependent moods: "the aorist takes its name (aóristos, *unlimited*, *unqualified*) from its . . . denoting merely the occurrence of an action, without any of the limitations (hóroi) as to *completion, continuance, repetition,* etc., which belong to other tenses.'' He notes, however, that ''the aorist of verbs which denote a *state* or *condition* generally expresses the entrance into that state of condition. *E.g.*, basileúō *I am king*, ebasíleusa *I became king*.'' Here, as we have seen above, it contrasts with the imperfect tense.

Ruipérez presents a number of traditional views of the aorist. It has been considered ''punctual,'' sometimes ''inceptive/perfective,'' marking momentary action (*bênai* 'to go'—AOR INFIN), initial point (*dakrûsai* 'to commence to cry'—AOR INFIN), or final point (*peîsai* 'to succeed in persuading'—AOR INFIN). This view, however, is countered by the ''complexive'' example *ebasíleuse* (AOR ACT INDIC 3SG) *triákonta étē:* 'he reigned thirty years'.[99] Delbrück, Brugmann, and others subsume these uses under ''action in its totality is as if concentrated in a point,''[100] which is similar to Forsyth's treatment of the Slavic perfective.

Others have seen the aorist as ''confective''—''the realization or effectuation of the action''—or as ''completely happened, as having occurred'' (*schlechthin geschehen, vollendet*).

Meillet writes of the aorist as denoting ''the process without indicating its development.''

Ruipérez observes that ''in a transformative verbal semanteme seen from the point of view of duration, the punctual aorist is realized as finitive,'' whereas ''in a non-transformative verbal semanteme, from the point of view of duration, the punctual aorist is realized as initive.''[101] He states that ''in the stem of the aorist the punctual value ('momentary, initive, finitive') and the neutral value are values belonging to this form in the system of 'la langue'.''[102] We have seen above that the aorist, as unmarked term, ''expresses punctuality (negative value) and the indifference to the notions of duration and of punctuality (neutral value).''[103]

Ruipérez notes that ''the neutralization of the aspectual opposition present:aorist in the position of present time is conditioned by the impossibility of the aorist being realized in the present time.'' Thus ''the present of the indicative is a unity of neutral value, indifferent as regards the aspectual opposition present/aorist.''[104] He says that ''the general aorist is fundamentally neutral as regards aspect. In the position of neutral time there is neutralization of the aspectual opposition present:aorist.''[105]

Holt is against the aorist representing a total act, including its achievement, and offers the familiar example of *ebasíleuse* 'he became king (*il devint roi*)'; he rejects any interpretation in terms of terminations:

> the aorist indicates a process that is not considered either before or after the termination. That is because this value can be employed as much with a ''terminative'' sense . . . as with an ''ingressive'' sense . . . [or] a ''complexive'' sense. . . . A. Meillet has advanced the idea most near to the truth, in defining the aorist as indicating ''the process pure and simple without consideration of duration.''

He rejects any temporal definition of the aspect:

> As with all the aspects of ancient Greek [the aorist] is non-temporal outside of the indicative, and it is only in the indicative that it becomes temporal; and when the aorist receives a temporal determination by the very fact of being used in the indic-

ative, it ought necessarily to come closer to the introspective, for its value is neutral in regard to the place of the process before or after the termination.[106]

It is curious that Friedrich argues for the unmarked character of the aorist from the fact that it has no equivalent of the tense distinction he sees in the perfect and imperfect systems:

Anterior	Primary stem	Posterior
imperfect	"present" [sic]	("future") [sic]
pluperfect	perfect	future perfect
	aorist	

"The aorist has no overtly marked anterior or posterior theme, and hence has more tense functions, as is natural for the less marked term."[107]

Golian similarly argues from the fact that "the perfective theme (aorist) . . . does not enter into the temporal opposition past/not past. From the formal point of view, it does not possess, as do the imperfect and perfect aspects, two series of desinences, primary and secondary desinences."[108]

This is a curious argument: as we have seen, it is usually assumed that it is the marked member of the opposition, for example the Slavic perfective, which is characterized by syncretism of categories. The aorist has only one tense as opposed to the two (or three) of the other Greek aspects, just as the perfective in Russian has but two tenses, as opposed to the three of the imperfective. That the aorist is unmarked for *tense* does not touch directly on its markedness for *aspect*.

The difficulties of determining the markedness of the Greek aspects may be further illustrated by considering the analysis given by Friedrich (1974). Friedrich opts for a model in which the most marked term is the present, as [+durative]; then the [−durative] (perfect and aorist) are split off into the [+realized] (perfect) and the [−realized] (aorist).

He offers two arguments for grouping the aorist with the perfect.[109] First, he groups the perfect and aorist together ("as against the durative [present-future]"), not only on "internal, semantic grounds, but also because of typological considerations," citing in comparison Yokuts, Chinook, and Hittite. Further, "and even more compellingly," he argues from the falling together of the aorist and perfect in medieval Greek.[110]

Typological and diachronic arguments also are used to argue for treating the present as the most marked aspect, as well as considerations of frequency and neutralized context.[111] To support the claim that the durative is the marked term of the opposition, he draws support first from the fact that the durative is the marked term in many other languages (e.g., English). Furthermore, the Homeric "durative themes" (i.e., present and imperfect) are of lower frequency than the aorist in non-indicative moods. This relates to Greenberg's quantitative criterion that the marked term tends to be the less frequent one. Too, the semantic facts are seen to "support Chantraine's claim that the durative theme, and especially the imperfect, were 'used to insist on the duration of a process.' " Confirmation of this comes from the fact that in the later Attic Greek the aorist became the more general form for narrative; presumably the unmarked term can displace the marked term diachronically as well as synchronically.

Yet another view is that of Kahane, who argues that the present-imperfect is the least marked aspect; further, the perfect and aorist are equally marked in opposition to the present-imperfect, but do not relate to each other at all:

in aspectual contrasts . . . the present is unmarked as to perfectivity,[112] the perfect is marked; again, the present is unmarked as to punctuality, the aorist is marked. Perfect and aorist are never contrasted, only perfect and present, or only aorist and present.[113]

It is apparent that Kahane's system is equivalent to a Holtian system, but with two features:

	present-imperfect	aorist	perfect
"perfective"	−	0	+
punctual	−	+	0

That the present-imperfect is the most unmarked aspect is justified by Kahane on developmental grounds. Jakobson (1941) and his followers have argued that the most unmarked terms are learned earliest and the most marked last; the acquisition of language by the child involves the acquisition of the marked members of oppositions. Kahane writes of a study of child language by Renee Kahane, Sol Saporta, and himself which "shows that, in the first stage of child language in which verbs appear, the only verb form is the present: it expresses all tenses and all aspects. In the second stage the other forms develop, each marked for only one of the meanings that had been expressed in the first stage by the present."[114] The competition of the historical present with the past is adduced as further evidence for its unmarked character.

Most writers on aspect have commented on methodological difficulties in regard to determining the grouping and hierarchization of terms in opposition, and the determination of markedness.[115] The most objective method of determining markedness involves frequency, but this method is beset with indeterminacies. Even assuming the availability of adequate statistics, it is not clear how to interpret them. Many other factors besides markedness enter into sheer frequency, and it is dubious that unmarked terms are invariably more frequent overall than marked ones. It is unclear whether all contexts are equally relevant. Doubt has been expressed that markedness is constant over all contexts; if not, overall frequencies are clearly irrelevant if not downright misleading.[116]

Competition and the appearance of unmarked terms in neutral contexts involve similar indeterminancies. The nature of each context needs to be taken into consideration and the use of each term in those contexts evaluated. Both criteria are beset with subjectivity and especially in the case of dead languages are highly problematical.

The argument from diachrony is perhaps sounder, but even here one problem is the assumption that a form in one period constitutes the *same* category as the same form in another period. It is not clear that either formal or semantic criteria serve to confer such identity. Where the system as a whole changes, it cannot be assumed that any individual element retains its value. For the purpose of markedness theory it cannot be assumed that a formally identical theme such as the aorist in two periods constitutes the same structural unit; hence the diachronic argument would seem to beg the question.

Typological considerations and developmental ones, too, given the present state of our knowledge, or rather of our ignorance, present the danger of circular reasoning. And the remaining "semantic" criteria invite subjectivity. Often enough it is only the epiphenomena of markedness which provide objective evidence for markedness. Furthermore, rather than the criterial feature determining markedness, often enough in practice it is the markedness which determines the feature. If the present is more marked than the perfect, then there must presumably be some feature, say durativity, for which it is positive; if it is less marked, then there must be some feature, say perfectness, for which it is negative.

What often gets lost in the debate over Greek aspect is the fact that the question of the criterial feature is different from the question of markedness, since componential analysis is not concerned with contents. To label *woman* "female" is simply to place it in opposition to all such terms as *father, uncle, boy, bull.* It can be *inferred* from the set of features which structure the domain in question that "female" must have femaleness as its content, but the label itself has no status in structuralist theory and might equally be replaced with an arbitrary symbol such as "$" or "1."

In phonology, similarly, the symbol /s/ for the first sound in the word *say* is arbitrary and could be replaced by /$/ or /1/. It is not the fact that the systematic, distinctive sound (phoneme) represented by /s/ generally is realized as the phonetic sound (phone) symbolized by [s] that gives it its meaningfulness, but the fact that the phoneme /s/ is distinguished from all others by a set of phonetic features such as [+continuous] and [−voiced], which have straightforward articulatory and/or acoustic definitions in phonetic theory.

But in the absence of a parallel semantic theory which would define a feature such as "female" in semantic terms, that is, in terms external to the system of language, the fact that all terms which are "female" refer to females is considerably less salient, if salient at all, than the fact that all terms which are "female" are in one regard mutually contradictory with all terms which are "male."

Thus the question of whether the present is [+durative] or [−punctual], for example, really constitutes two separate questions, one of which cannot be answered in the absence of a semantic theory, a theory which relates linguistic expressions to the "real world." The most we can decide is whether there is or is not a single feature distinguishing, say, the present and the aorist, and if there is, which is the marked term. What that feature can be called on objective, principled grounds does not lie in the province of structuralist componential analysis, nor is it possible to decide, given the tools which that realm provides.

Another problem with the application of markedness theory to the debate over Greek aspect is the lack of explanatory power inherent in the enterprise. To know, for example, that the perfect is the marked member of an opposition of perfectness with the imperfect and perfective (aorist), and that the imperfect is the marked member of an opposition of durativeness with the aorist, neither explicates how the relevant forms are actually used in the language (e.g., when can, or must, the aorist be used?), nor does it raise, much less answer, questions regarding the learning and use of the system as a whole, or its relation to the systems of other languages.

Even if Greek lacked the aorist and had only the opposition of perfect and imperfect, and even if the perfect were the marked member of that opposition, nothing within the theory of componential analysis would justify equating the two systems, and the choice of the terminology "perfective" and "imperfective" for the Greek aspects would be arbitrary *within* the theory. That the sundry contextual meanings of the Greek perfective would under these circumstances more or less match those of the Slavic perfective might justify (in a different component of the theory) the use of the same labels, but it would still not truly explicate the nature of the perfective:imperfective opposition.

We intuit that there are substantive universals of aspect, even if weak, implicational ones, and that the systems of various languages are not merely contingent, historical accidents, but rather reflect deep principles of meaning and use of language. The theory does not address such issues, not does it provide adequate tools for their investigation. A search for a deeper understanding requires substantially more sophisticated tools than structuralism can provide.

6

Explanation in Aspectology

a. Aristotelian Aspect

We have seen in the previous chapter how two different categorizations were long confused which Goedsche (1940) and Garey (1957) were to distinguish as "aspect" and "*Aktionsarten,*" though these occasionally are still confounded. Both may be marked by differences in verb stems, and both have to do with the internal structures of events or situations, rather than with the sort of temporal relations involved in tense. Aspect is a fully grammaticized, obligatory, systematic category of languages, operating with general oppositions such as that of perfective and non-perfective, while *Aktionsarten* are purely lexical categories, nongrammatical, optional, and unsystematic, defined in very specific terms such as inceptive or resumptive.

We saw too that both differ from a third categorization which is not morphologically marked, but which also has to do with the structure of events, namely that which we have called "Aristotelian aspect." Mourelatos relates this to the *Aktionsarten,* saying the "neither Vendler nor Kenny realized that the distinctions they sought to articulate had long been studied by linguists under the heading of 'verb aspect'. This . . . phenomenon . . . was first correctly understood by the grammarians of Slavic languages."[1]

This is not quite right, insofar as the Aristotelian categorization is not identical either with aspect or the *Aktionsarten,* and hence the distinctions brought forward by Ryle, Kenny, and Vendler are not identical with those which had already become part and parcel of the linguistic treatment of aspect.

There is no great harm in the use of the term *verb aspect* for Aristotelian aspect, although its ultimate utility is not clear (and is brought into question by Verkuyl's 1972 observation that more than the verb alone must be taken into consideration).[2] For Dowty, who used the term "verb aspect" to refer to what we call here the Aristotelian classification, aspect markers serve to distinguish such things as whether the beginning, middle or end of an event is being referred to, whether the event is a single one or a repeated one, and whether the event is completed or possibly left incomplete.[3] . . . in all languages, semantic differences inherent in the meanings of verbs [interact with aspect markers and adverbials]. It is because of this intimate interaction . . . that the term *aspect* is justified in a wider sense . . . we can . . . distinguish the *aspectual class* of a verb . . . from the *aspectual form*.[4]

The Aristotelian categories are like the *Aktionsarten* in that they are purely lexical and nongrammatical, and also unsystematic. But the categorization is obligatory, in the sense that all verbs are classified by it. It is broader than the *Aktionsarten* (though narrower than the aspects). Many scholars have, however, considered it too to be "aspect" or at least "aspectual."

The question is how the aspects, *Aktionsarten*, and Aristotelian classes interrelate. At the very least, they clearly are closely related, since each category restricts choice of the others. Are they three facets of one phenomenon, three linguistic means for expressing the *same* sort of thing? Or do they represent three *different* phenomena which nonetheless somehow interrelate? And what are the semantic natures of the distinctions that the various linguistic devices mark? What, apart from the linguistic manifestations (markers) themselves, are we talking about, when we talk about "aspect" in any of these three senses?

One of the difficulties in answering these questions is that there are a myriad devices which mark these distinctions, and further, as Freed[5] observes,

> the interplay of linguistic items that carry different aspectual meanings is not straightforward. . . . we restrict ourselves to considering the interrelations of the aspectual operator verbs[6] and their complements[7] . . . this means taking into consideration (1) the inherent lexical (or literal) meaning of the aspectual and complement verbs along with their aspectual interpretation, (2) the different aspectual types of verbal expressions found in complements (accomplishments, achievements, activities, etc.), (3) the syntactic form of the complement and (4) the *be*-prog operator[8] as it is related to the *V-ing* complement form.[9]

Given the complexity of the structures and semantic oppositions involved, we must first look at isolated elements of the problem before attempting an overall synthesis. Let us start by looking at Aristotelian aspect.

Aristotle is generally credited with discovering the distinctions that we are calling here "Aristotelian." Somewhat similar distinctions seem to have appeared at about the same time in Indian thought. The Sanskrit grammarian Yāska (fifth century B.C.) distinguished the state (*bhava*) as a condition brought about by an action from the action (*kriyā*, in later writers *karma*) itself, and stated that "a verb is chiefly concerned with the manner of expression," by which he may have meant aspect.[10]

The thought of Pāṇini (fourth century B.C.) on verbal aspect is too rich for us to discuss here. He and such successors of his as Bhartṛhari (A.D. seventh century) elaborated a system which could have made a signal contribution to Western grammatical thought, but such concepts in the Indian tradition as *kriyā-prabandha* 'performing an action with continuity', *kriyā-samabhihāra* 'repetition of action',

and *kriyātipatti* 'non-completion of an action' had to be independently rediscovered. It is only because Indian logical and grammatical thought has not helped to
inform non-Indian scholarship that this important chapter of the history of grammar is ignored here.

Indeed, even Aristotle's ideas, while never completely forgotten, had no direct
influence on grammatical thought where aspect is concerned; many who have utilized the ''Vendlerian'' categories were completely unaware of Aristotle's observations. One reason for this is that Aristotle's concerns were not specifically linguistic.

The various distinctions had probably been dimly felt even before Aristotle's
time, if only because they interact with the concept of completion. (As we have
seen, Plato implicitly observes such an opposition in the *Crito*.) But once again,
these were observations in regard to logic, not grammar.

The Aristotelian distinctions have considerable import for the philosophy of
action and intention. For this reason, to this day philosophers have had much to
say about the linguistics of the Aristotelian categorization, which indeed was largely
introduced into the modern linguistic literature by the philosophers Vendler (1957)
and Kenny (1963), although a related discussion had earlier been published by
Ryle (1949).

Of the attempts at a definitive Aristotelian classification, the Vendlerian system
is the most familiar. Vendler distinguishes four categories:

Activities	*Accomplishments*
run	run a mile
walk	walk to school
swim	paint a picture
push a cart	grow up
drive a car	deliver a sermon
	recover from illness

Achievements	*States*
recognize	desire
find	want
win the race	love
stop/start/resume	hate
be born/die	know/believe[11]

A distinction of inconclusive *enérgiai* and conclusive *kínēsis* was made by Aristotle in the *Metaphysics* (1048b.18–36).[12] The *enérgeiai* accord both with
states and activities, which Aristotle however distinguished in *De Animo* (*On the
Soul* 417a.30–b.2) as *ékhein* 'having' (state) and *energeîn* 'acting' (activity).[13]
The *prâksis* 'doing' of the *Nicomachean Ethics* (1140a.1–24) seems to equate
with ''activity'' as well, as contrasted with *poíēsis* 'making', which seems to
equate with the *kínēsis* of the *Metaphysics*, that is, to both achievements and
accomplishments.[14]

Something like three of the four Vendlerian categories are thus already to be
found in Aristotle, though taken as categories of states of affairs, processes, and
the like, not directly as categories of verbal expressions denoting these. (Admit-

tedly it is hard to distinguish statements of the Greek philosophers about things from statements about expressions.)

Ryle distinguishes activities from achievements, "try" verbs from "got it" verbs, as he puts it.[15] The latter, unlike the former, result in a state. While he does not explicitly distinguish a category of achievements in the narrower Vendlerian sense (e.g., winning an Oscar or noticing lint on one's sleeve) from accomplishments (e.g., running a mile or recovering from illness), he does distinguish "achievements" which involve the performance of a task, that is, an activity, from those which do not, pointing out that in the former case a person can be said to have done two things (having been running and having run a mile), but in the latter case only one (having won an Oscar but not having been winning an Oscar).[16]

Further, he notes that adverbials appropriate for tasks are also appropriate for accomplishments, but not for other achievements: *she ran attentively, she ran a mile attentively,* but **she noticed lint on her sleeve attentively*. The essence of the Vendlerian classification is already present in Ryle.

Kenny (1963) does not distinguish achievements from accomplishments, calling both "performances." But like Vendler he notes a number of logical and linguistic distinctions between the various categories which serve as criteria for membership in each. The characterization of the various Aristotelian categories, however done, calls for such a set of criteria, not only to justify the classification, but to assign particular verbs to categories.

Prior to a deep theoretical understanding of the categorization, scholars have made use of rough-and-ready empirical criteria, specifically a number of facts about co-occurrence and semantic relations. Furthermore, all the scholars who have discussed the Aristotelian classification present various tests to distinguish members of the categories. A list of many such tests in three categories follows, based on the list given by Dowty (itself mainly culled from the work of Ryle; Vendler; Kenny; G. Lakoff, 1965; and others) and on the work of Freed.[17]

States versus Non-States

1. Only non-statives (expressions other than those of states) occur in the progressive:

> *John is knowing the answer.
> John is running.
> John is building a house.

There are, however, idiomatic uses of "static" verbs with the progressive form, as for instance *I am hoping, intending*.[18] It is also true that a progressive use of statives is possible, especially with, but not restricted to, a series of occurrences: *John is knowing all the answers to test questions more and more often, Sue is believing in God ever more strongly*.

2. When an activity or accomplishment occurs in the simple present tense (or any non-progressive tense), it has a frequentative (or habitual) interpretation in normal contexts (while in null context a stative is a true present):

> John knows the answer. (right now)
> John runs. (habitual)
> John recites a poem. (habitual)

3. Only non-statives occur as complements of verbs like *force* and *persuade*:

> *John forced Henry to know the answer.
> John persuaded Henry to run.
> John forced Henry to build a house.

4. Only non-statives occur as imperatives:

> *Know the answer!
> Run!
> Build a house!

5. Only non-statives co-occur with the adverbs *deliberately, carefully*:

> *John deliberately knew the answer.
> John ran carefully.
> John carefully built a house.

Notice that while there is a considerable difference between *John carefully built a house* and *John built a house carefully*, this difference in kind of meaning, and associated scope of modification, apparently plays no role here: *John knew the answer deliberately* seems no better than *John deliberately knew the answer*.

6. Only non-statives appear in pseudo-cleft constructions:

> *What John did was know the answer.
> What John did was run.
> What John did was build a house.

These facts (in no. 3–6 above) follow from the nonvolitional nature of states, but there are some volitional uses of stative verbs which do act as complements of these verbs: *John forced Sue to be* (i.e., pretend to be, act, play) *as dumb as Max thought she was*; *Igor persuaded us to know the answer* (e.g., not to pretend, or to stop pretending, not to know the answer); *know the answer to every question—just read my book,* The Guide to All Knowledge, *on sale everywhere*.

7. The Aristotelian classes act differently as complements of the aspectual auxiliary verbs.[19] Statives do not normally occur with aspectual auxiliary verbs such as *start, stop, finish*, though they do so occur in a habitual or frequentative sense (but only in the complement in *-ing*):

> Joan started being ill (all the time).
>   stopped being ill (all the time).
> *finished being ill.

However, some statives do occur with some aspectual auxiliary verbs when in the infinitival complement form: *Joan started to be ill, she began to understand it*.[20] An activity or accomplishment verb such as *run* or *paint a picture* readily occurs with such auxiliaries in both complement forms: *Joan started running (to run), she started painting (to paint) a picture*.

The behavior of achievements with respect to the stativity tests is complicated.[21] This is because achievements have various quasi-accomplishment senses—conative, progressive, and the like. Sentences such as *Susan was winning the Oscar (noticing some lint on her dress, being reborn as a worm); Susan was successful in winning the Oscar (noticing some lint on her dress, being reborn as a worm);* and *Susan succeeded in winning the Oscar (noticing some lint on her dress, being reborn as a worm)* are all acceptable in certain specific contexts. (Susan carefully won the Oscar by keeping her nose clean and advertising daily in *Variety.*)

Activities versus Accomplishments

1. Whereas accomplishment verbs take adverbial preposition phrases with *in* but only very marginally with *for*, activity verbs allow only the phrases with *for*:

> ?John painted a picture for an hour.
> John painted a picture in an hour.

> John walked for an hour.
> *John walked in an hour.

2. *For*-phrases such as *for four years* have ambiguous scope with some accomplishment verbs, but not with activities.[22] *The sheriff of Nottingham jailed Robin Hood for four years* can mean either that the sheriff jailed Robin Hood in four years, or that Robin Hood was sentenced to four years in jail. *The sheriff of Nottingham rode a white horse for four years* can mean only that he rode the horse in four years.

Dahl points out the ambiguity of *for*-adverbials in English:

Some languages are more systematic than English in distinguishing indicators of actual and potential terminal points. Thus, Swedish uses different prepositions . . . :

> Jeg reser till Frankrike *på* två månader.
> 'I am going to France for two months.'
> Jeg reste i Frankrike *i* två månader.
> 'I traveled in France for two months.'

It is even possible to construct a sentence that contains both kinds of terminal point indicators. . . .

> Han har suttit inne på två år i sex veckor.
> 'He has been serving a two-year sentence for six weeks.'[23]

3. Semantically related to the *for-an-hour* and *in-an-hour* sentences above are these:

> John spent an hour painting a picture.
> It took John an hour to paint a picture.
> John spent an hour walking.
> *It took John an hour to walk.

With achievements there are special senses in which John can take an hour to notice lint on his suit or Susan can spend an hour noticing lint on her suit. With *take* the meaning is 'it was . . . (amount of time) before (the achievement occurred)'; with *spend* the sense is that of passing time while a series of achievements occurred.

4. For activity verbs, *x VERBed for y time* entails that at any time during *y*, *x VERBed* was true. For accomplishment verbs, *x VERBed for y time* does not entail that *x VERBed* was true during any time within *y* at all. *John walked for an hour* entails that during that hour it was true that *John walked*. *John painted a picture for an hour* does not entail that during that hour it was true that *John painted a picture*.

5. For activity verbs, *x is (now) VERBing* (or *x VERBs*, this latter too with statives) entails that *x has VERBed*. For accomplishment verbs, *x is (now) VERBing* entails that *x has not yet VERBed*. *John is painting* entails that *John has painted*. *John is ill* entails that *John has been ill*. *John is painting a picture* entails that *John has not yet painted a picture*.

This is not entirely correct, however, as shown by the case of John's painting a series of pictures. When he is engaged in painting the second picture, it would be false to say that he has not yet painted a picture: rather he has not yet painted *this* (or *the*) picture, as Dowty points out.

6. Activities have the so-called "subinterval" property. This means that if John ran from noon till 3:00 p.m., then at any time, or over any subinterval during that interval of time, *John was running* is true. Further, as Kenny points out, with activities, *A was VERBing* if and only if *A Verbed*, but this is not true of accomplishments.[24] However, with accomplishments, *A Verbed* if and only if *A was VERBing*.

7. For activity verbs, *x stopped VERBing* entails that *x did VERB*, but for accomplishments, *x stopped VERBing* does not entail *x VERBed* but only *x was VERBing*. *John stopped walking* implies *John did walk*. *John stopped painting a picture* does not imply *John did paint a picture*, but only *John was painting a picture*.

8. Only accomplishment verbs can normally occur as the complement of the verb *finish*:

> John finished painting a picture.
> *John finished walking.

There is a quasi-accomplishment sense of activities, however, which is acceptable here.[25] John can be said to have finished walking, if it constitutes or is part of a prescribed task or definite habit: if it is his regularly scheduled job or his custom, for example. Compare: ?*John finished working (for the day);* ?*John finished swimming early (today)*. *Finish* with an accomplishment (e.g., *John finished painting the picture*) entails that he painted the picture, whereas *John stopped painting the picture* does not entail that he painted the picture.[26] On the other hand, the marginal *John finished running*, like *John stopped running*, entails that he ran.

9. As Morgan pointed out (1969), *almost* is ambiguous with accomplishments in a way that it is not with activities.[27]

> *John almost walked* entails that he did not walk. *John almost walked to Rome* means either that John did walk but did not reach his goal, or that he did not (on this occasion) walk—at least toward Rome.

Achievements versus Accomplishments

1. Although accomplishments allow both *for*-phrase and *in*-phrase time adverbials with equal success, achievements are generally quite strange with a *for*-phrase.

> John noticed the painting in a few minutes.
> ??John noticed the painting for a few minutes.

2. The same goes for the *spend-an-hour/take-an-hour* distinction:

> It took John a few minutes to notice the painting.
> ??John spent a few minutes noticing the painting.

3. Accomplishments like *paint a picture* have an entailment that achievements like *notice a picture* lack. *John painted a picture in an hour* entails *John was painting a picture* during that hour. But *John noticed a picture in a few minutes* does not entail *John was noticing a picture* during those minutes.

4. Unlike accomplishment verbs, achievements are generally unacceptable as complements of *finish*:

> *John finished noticing the picture.
> John finished painting the picture.

5. *Stop* occurs with achievements only in a habitual sense: *John stopped noticing the picture* can only mean that he was broken of the habit of noticing the picture, not that he "finished" noticing the picture on a certain occasion.

The same is true of *start: Joan started noticing the lint on her suit* can only have a progressive or frequentative/habitual sense: over a period of time she noticed more and more lint, or she over and over again had occasion to notice lint, on her suit.[28]

With achievements, but not accomplishments, *start VERBing* entails *VERBed*: if Joan started winning the race at 12:01, she must have won the race. But if she started painting a picture at 12:01, she didn't necessarily ever paint a picture.

6. *Almost* does not produce the ambiguity with achievements that it does with accomplishments. *John almost noticed the painting* entails that he did not notice the painting. *John almost painted the picture* can mean either that he was not painting the picture, or that he was but did not finish it.

7. As Ryle observed, there is a class of adverbs which are semantically anomalous with achievement verbs:

> ??John { attentively / studiously / vigilantly / conscientiously / obediently / carefully } { discovered the solution / detected an error / found a penny / reached Boston / noticed the painting }

As Dowty says, this test also distinguishes states from the other categories. (See stativity test 5, above.)

On the basis of the behavior of verbs with the aspectual verbs, Freed is led to conclude that there is a fifth Aristotelian category, which she calls the "series" and identifies as a "special type of state." Series, unlike states, allow *keep VERB-ing*:

> series: John kept being ill.
> state: John was ill.
>
> John understood French.
> ?John kept understanding French.
>
> John loved Mary.
> ?John kept loving Mary.[29]

The sentences marked with "?" above have marginal serial readings: *Susan doubted John really understood French, and kept having people speak to him in French, but each time he replied appropriately. John tried hard not to feel anything for Mary, but each time he saw her, he felt his affection for her anew.*

Series differ from non-statives in that *stopped VERBing* presupposes *used to VERB* (and not *was VERBing earlier/before*) and entails *is/does not VERB now* (and *is not VERBing now*):

Series: *John stopped driving to work* presupposes *John used to drive to work* and entails that *John does not (is not) drive (driving) to work now.*

Activity: *John stopped running* (on one occasion) does not presuppose that *John used to run*, nor does it entail that *John does not run (is not running) now.*

Achievement: *John stopped noticing the lint on his suit* (on one occasion) does not presuppose that *John used to notice the lint on his suit*, nor does it entail that *John does not notice (is not noticing) the lint on his suit now.*

She presents various other tests for series built on achievements or accomplishments as well.[30] The fact is, each constituent of a series can be of any of the four other types.

The question is how and why these various tests work. Obviously there are deep relationships which these tests are reflecting. The co-occurence restrictions follow from the meanings of the verbs (or the expressions containing them) and those of the associated adverbials. For example, we sense that what is odd about *John obediently noticed the painting* (in its usual reading) is that *obediently* presupposes intentional behavior, whereas noticing a painting is not normally intentional. Similarly, *John finished walking* in its normal, activity sense is odd, because *finish* presupposes a delimited goal, whereas walking is normally an activity without a delimited goal.

The question is what the essential properties are which underlie the categories. We need such properties to explain how the various tests work, how compositionality works (e.g., why the various adjuncts of the verb affect the categorization as they do), and most important, why there are only (if indeed there are only) four Aristotelian categories (or five, if we include Freed's "series"). In general, from what specific semantic facts do these various linguistic and logical facts follow? To satisfactorily answer these questions requires an understanding of the nature of the various kinds of occurrences which the various Aristotelian categories of expressions represent.

b. The Ontology of Situations

To understand the Aristotelian categories, why there are precisely the categories there are, and why the members of particular categories have the properties which they do, requires an understanding of the entities which the expressions thus categorized represent, namely activities, states, and the like. To understand the semantic properties of expressions such as *swims*, *swims to Rome*, *swims every day*, we require an ontology, a set of models of situations, states of affairs, events, courses of events.

To this end a number of scholars have attempted a classificatory taxonomy of situations. Sometimes this is based on the categories and relationships needed to account for the syntax and semantics of expressions such as verbs and collocations containing them, and there is only a limited attempt at an independent justification of the taxonomies, so that their explicatory value for the deeper analysis of Aristotelian categories is questionable. In recent years, however, a deeper understanding has begun to develop.

One difficulty with writings in this area is that there is a manifest terminological confusion. The same term, for instance *process* or *event*, may be used in different ways by various authors, or the same thing called by different terms (e.g., what most authors call an "occurrence" seems to be what Rescher and Urquhart mean by a "process").

Most authors are agreed in calling the most general type of "instantiation of temporal properties" a *situation*,[31] though Pinkster (1984) calls it a *state of affairs*. "Situation" is a concept which is difficult to define, though intuitively clear enough. Barwise and Perry say that "reality consists of situations—individuals having properties and standing in relations at various spatiotemporal locations."[32] This is ultimately not much more helpful than the ordinary dictionary's question-begging "state of affairs; combination of circumstances." We very likely must take "situation" (or "state-of-affairs") as an undefined primitive.

At any given point in time and space certain situations "are the case," while others are not. At any given moment it is either raining where I am or it is not. Many situations persist and hold over an entire interval of time. Thus it might be raining where I am from noon on a certain day till 3:13 that afternoon. At any given moment during that interval "it is raining here" would be true. On the other hand, some "situations" are momentaneous, in that they do not persist and do not hold true over an interval. There is an interval over which a car is stopping, and an interval over which it is stopped, but there can be only one instant at which "the car stops" is literally true.

There are a number of philosophical problems connected with the notion of instant (point, moment) of time. For example, given any two successive points in time, t_n and t_{n+j}, is it the case that there must (cannot) be a third point $t_{n+m<j}$ between the two?

This problem concerns boundary instants. At some instant t_n a car is stopping, but has not yet stopped. Let t_n be the last instant of which this is true. Now at some later instant, t_{n+j}, the car has already stopped and is no longer stopping.

Let t_{n+j} be the first such instant. Now what is the relationship of t_n to t_{n+j}? For many speakers, the intuition is that the two instants are simply successive—there is no instant between them; the last instant at which the car is stopping simply *is* the instant at which it stops. At one instant the car is stopping, at the very next it is already stopped.

But some speakers intuit that there is a transient, a boundary instant t_{n+m} *at which* the car literally stops: so long as it is stopping, it cannot be said to stop. If we assume that time is *discrete*, that there can be two successive instants with no instant between them, then the last instant at which the car is stopping, the transient at which it stops, and the first instant at which it is stopped form a series of three instants. But if we assume that time is *dense*—that between any given points t_n and t_{n+j} there is at least one point t_{n+m} (and hence an infinite number of points) distinct from both—then it is not clear that it makes any sense to speak of such a transient. However, neither is it clear that there is any difference between the semantics of the language of speakers who accept the reality of the boundary instant and that of those who do not.

We shall see in chapter 7 that some semanticists assume that time is discrete and others that it is dense. There seems at present no very good reason to assume either position, and here we will be agnostic on the issue.[33]

In modeling situations, whether instantaneous or enduring over an interval of time, we need to pay careful attention to the notions of *phase* and *occasion*. The time interval of an occurrence—a temporal instantiation—is a single occasion. However, a series of such occasions can fall within a certain time interval; in this case we may represent the occurrence as a single situation (cf. *I ran off and on for an hour, I ran and ran for an hour, I would run and then run some more*).

Every occasion contains within it subintervals of time which may or may not correspond to stages or phases of the situation. To a certain extent, whether something is viewed as a phase of an occurrence or an occasion in a series of occurrences is purely a question of viewpoint: *he bobbed for apples twice* is ambiguous, depending on whether a single rapid vertical motion occurred twice or a rapid series of vertical motions. We shall see too that the phases of occurrences themselves may have subphases; the termination of an action, for example, has a beginning (*she started to cease running*). Here we may refer to Rescher and Urquhart's notion of the "generic realization-history of any proposition" as a sequence of phases (stages).[34]

There have been two approaches to the semantics of expressions for situations. One, which we will principally follow here, falls within the tradition of formal semantics, namely model theory. For a number of technical reasons, however, it has been argued by advocates of what is called *situation semantics* that it, rather than the traditional model-theoretic semantics, provides the most adequate approach to natural language.[35]

There are a number of different taxonomies, but most scholars would agree with that, based on the one which Mourelatos presents,[36] closely following the usual Vendlerian categorization.

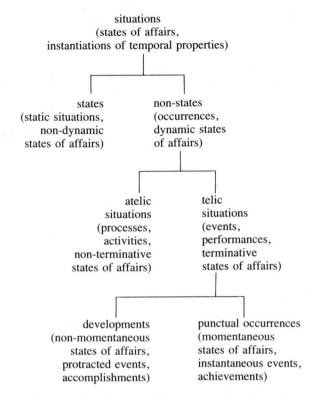

situations
(states of affairs,
instantiations of temporal properties)

states
(static situations,
non-dynamic
states of affairs)

non-states
(occurrences,
dynamic states
of affairs)

atelic
situations
(processes,
activities,
non-terminative
states of affairs)

telic
situations
(events,
performances,
terminative
states of affairs)

developments
(non-momentaneous
states of affairs,
protracted events,
accomplishments)

punctual occurrences
(momentaneous
states of affairs,
instantaneous events,
achievements)

Gabbay and Moravcsik[37] follow Mourelatos, but their model is more precisely founded on the notions of *duration* (occurrence over time), *repetition*, and quantification.

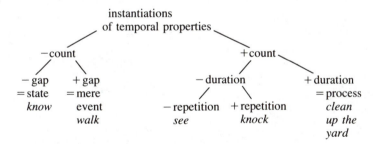

instantiations
of temporal properties

−count

+count

− gap
= state
know

+ gap
= mere
event
walk

− duration

+ duration
= process
*clean
up the
yard*

− repetition
see

+ repetition
knock

It is not at all clear what is meant here by the feature "count." Gabbay and Moravcsik say that "state and non-process durational V[erb] P[hrase]s are count-terms. . . . For given a state *S* many subparts of it are also S; furthermore, many states that are S when taken together add up to an S."[38]

States are often said (e.g., by Vendler) to be unbroken and without gaps: if someone is ill from noon to 3:00 p.m., then at any time t during that interval it is true that they are ill; but Gabbay and Moravcsik allow states to be "gappy," noting that "not all parts of a state are necessarily also the instantiation of the same property as the state itself." Thus, "if someone is sick over a period of

time, then he is in that state also over most if not all of the parts of that state.''
(We will return to this point in the next section.)

Gabbay and Moravcsik's hierarchization of the features of duration and repetition is not entirely felicitous. A single knock has no substantial duration, but the act of knocking (especially several times) does—and without duration we cannot speak of repetition.

Freed[39] extensively discusses repetition, presenting a taxonomy of events containing a basic distinction of *series*, which she identifies as represented by a fifth Aristotelian category, and single occurrences.

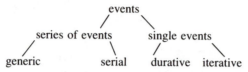

Series are repetitions of situations each of which may be viewed as a single situation in its own right. As opposed to single events, occurring over a unique interval of time on one occasion, a series of events may occur on several occasions (albeit within a given interval): *she slept from noon to 3:00 p.m.* is a single event, but *she slept in hotel rooms from May to August* is a series of events, each of which is an event in its own right. Consequently, if John knocks on Susan's door every Tuesday, the question "at what time does John knock on Susan's door?" cannot be answered, except by characterizing each occurrence individually, unless they always occur at the "same" (corresponding) time.

For Freed, series can comprise repeated or habitual recurrences of any of the Vendlerian types—state, activity, accomplishment, or achievement.[40] Single events are either "durative," temporally extended—*she is sleeping*; or "iterative," uninterrupted but not "even," a set of subevents viewed as a single event during a particular interval—*she is sneezing*. As we have noted, iteration is to be distinguished from serial repetition. An iteration is a single situation, although one involving repeated phases. It makes sense to ask at what time John knocked on Susan's door or Bill rocked back and forth, even if these were iterative and not strictly semelfactive (unless we take this to refer to any occurrence on one occasion).

Repetitions are relatively widely spaced in time and viewed as more distinct than are iterations: *Fido growls at strangers*. Iterative acts are relatively close together in time and may be viewed as constituting phases of one act: *Fido growled and growled at Bill*. A frequentative, strictly speaking, is a type of process where the phases or acts occur not only most of the time, but regularly and frequently—a large number of short bursts rather than a few long ones, as it were: (when John came in) *they wagged their tails*, as opposed to (every now and then) *they would wag their tails*.

Freed divides series into "serial" series, which involve reference to specific individual events, and "generics," which do not.[41] Generics may involve regular repetition (like traditional "frequentatives") or uniformity (in the case of general states). Generics include expressions for general states (*they own a house*), occupations (*she teaches college*), and habitual occurrences (*he smokes a lot*).

To say "she teaches college" involves no reference to any specific act. Teaching college is more a status than an activity or series of activities; someone can be said to teach college even when they are only nominally college teachers. But teaching classes does involve a series of activities. Similarly, *he smokes a lot* refers to a set of events, while *he smokes* may mean no more than *he is a smoker*. *When did he last smoke?* normally inquires after the time of an event, but *when did she last teach college?* inquires about a state of affairs (her being a college teacher).

Soga[42] distinguishes repetitive from successive processes, a distinction he finds significant for Japanese, but which may be of universal application.

Examples from English might be:

uninterrupted:	He left the office.
repetitive:	People left the office all morning.
successive:	People left the office one after the other.

Compare *they sang and sang* (no indication of how frequently or often, may even be uninterrupted; cf. *they kept on singing*); *they kept singing* (if interrupted, successive or nearly so); and *they would sing* (repetitive, certainly not uninterrupted, and not necessarily successive).[43] Successive occurrences are interesting in that they provide an example of a type of series which is not in general gappy (except perhaps trivially: if John left immediately after Susan, that does not literally mean that *no* time intervened between Susan's leaving and John's).

As regards the tests for the various Aristotelian categories, series are unlike any other category, and series built out of a certain Vendlerian category generally do not act like that category. Series are most like activities, but act like states in a number of respects (e.g., the present tense is a "true present": *I eat lunch at home, ?*/!I am eating lunch at home*).

c. States

The most fundamental distinction among types of single situations is between *states* (represented by *stative* predicates) and non-states (represented by *non-stative* ones). States have also been called *static*[44] or *non-dynamic*[45] situations (states of affairs). Non-states (Mourelatos's "occurrences") are correspondingly *dynamic* ones (Bergman, Pinkster).

States are naturally static, that is, unchanging throughout their duration, while activities and the like are dynamic. One way of characterizing the difference is to say that while all phases or stages of a state are the same, those of dynamic situations are not. But non-states are dynamic—if Tom paints a picture from Tuesday through Friday, more and more of the picture gets done. On Tuesday he is only beginning to paint the picture, whereas on Friday he is finishing it, and at some point on Friday he literally does finish it. Against this view it cannot be argued that Tom can be falling ill on Tuesday and getting better on Thursday and finally well at some point on Friday, for being ill is itself potentially just a phase in a process of falling ill and getting well, and this process taken as a whole is not stative in character.[46]

We are not concerned here with reality, which is non-discrete: there are no spatial or temporal boundaries in nature, no lines demarcating here from there, now from then; nor do states in the real world neatly begin or end at points. It is language which represents the world as consisting of discrete blobs called situations, and these are arbitrary in the sense that subsituations may be situations, too. The very same instant (say, during a temporary relapse) can even be viewed alternatively as belonging to Tom's getting ill or to Tom's getting well, depending on how *we* choose to describe the situation.

The non-dynamicity of states is not to be confused with the *subinterval property*. An expression has the latter if, and only if, when it is true over an interval $t_i, \ldots, t_n$, then it is true over any subinterval $t_j, \ldots, t_m$ within $t_i, \ldots, t_n$. States share the subinterval property with (dynamic) activities. If Tom is ill from Tuesday through Friday, then at any time during that interval *Tom is ill* is true, and likewise over any subinterval during that interval. For example, on Thursday *Tom has been ill since Tuesday* is true. Performances lack this property: if Tom paints a picture from Monday through Saturday, it is not true on Tuesday that Tom *has painted* a picture, though it is true that he *has been painting* a picture.

Another way of viewing the difference of state and non-state is that states are persistent.[47] In this regard they differ from processes or actions, which, even if they occur over intervals of time, are not inherently persistent and tend to stop unless actively continued. You can continue to be ill, but you can't continue being ill (unless you actively thwart your recovery), though you can continue running.

Related to persistence is the property of volitionality or agency, which states normally lack, while non-states often involve acts of will. You don't under usual circumstances choose to be tall (or short): being tall isn't something you *do*, and it requires no effort to continue being tall (or short). But to be running requires an effort, so that if you don't continue running, you automatically cease running. The distinction between *action* and *occurrence* (*activity* and *process*, *act* and *event*), which distinguishes agentive from non-agentive happenings, has often been seen as fundamental.

It is possible to regard what the progressive expresses in English as characterizing a volitional state. In the same way that someone *is* tall, they might *be* running. Once again there is a period of time during which the individual is in the state of being running. The only real difference between this and the state of being tall is that the individual is free to stop—or continue—being running, whereas one is not free (in the same way) to stop—or continue—being tall.

Being on the phone, being a patriot, and being a believer (in God, say) could also be considered volitional states. Volitional states, like activities, allow at least trivial gaps, while non-volitional ones for the most part do not. Given the close relationship of volitional states to activities, this is not surprising, since activities are (at least trivially) gappy. To some extent the difference between, for example, *be a patriot* and *be being a patriot* resembles the temporary/permanent difference reflected in Russian adjectival short versus long forms or the difference of temporary, inessential versus permanent and essential reflected in Spanish constructions with *estar* and *ser*.[48]

An agentive activity must be maintained. It can be halted at any moment, and it involves trivial or casual gaps: one can be said to have worked all day, although obviously one need not have literally been at work all during that day. On the other hand, processes, while they may stop, are not maintained from moment to moment, and while they can temporarily be in abeyance, it is not clear they have gaps in the same way that activities do. If both activities and states may be agentive and both may be persistent, these distinctions are not criterial for the Aristotelian classification.

The prototypical state is non-volitional and persistent, but more important, it is without gaps, whereas other types of situations are gap-ridden.[49] We have noted that if Sue is ill from Monday through Friday, then at any instant t during that interval, say at 3:00 p.m. on Wednesday, *Sue is ill* is true. As we have also seen, some states do allow for a kind of gap. In the present instance, if Sue is in pain from Monday through Friday, this does not preclude there being moments when she is not in pain (periodically she might have a few minutes of relief).

Activities and accomplishments readily allow gaps, as do even achievements in their conative, tentative sense (as in *it took a while for her to notice the vase was missing*). But normally achievements, being punctual and accordingly non-phasic, do not refer to intervals and hence allow no gaps (**Sue noticed a dollar, except for a tenth of a second when her attention wandered*).

In their pioneering attempt at a classification of "processes,"[50] Rescher and Urquhart distinguish four types of processes on the basis of what portion of an interval the process literally is true of.[51]

1. A *homogeneous process* or *activity* "can go on at *all* times throughout the interval" of time over which the process takes place. To engage in these activities (e.g., bathing or flying a plane) during a certain interval of time is to "engage in them during all sub-periods [sub-intervals]": that is, an activity (homogeneous process) obtaining over an interval *I* also holds true of all times *t* in *I* (this is the so-called subinterval property). Thus *bathe* (*oneself*): if John bathed from noon to 3:00 p.m., then it is true that he bathed from 2:00 to 2:30 p.m.

2. A *majoritative process* is one that "can go on at *most* times throughout the interval (but not invariably at all such times)." Thus writing a letter or doing a crossword puzzle are activities such that "one can be said correctly to have spent a certain hour at these activities without having spent every second of that hour at them." A majoritative process is one obtaining at most times during the interval *I* (and presumably including the first and last times *t* in *I*). Thus *write a letter*: if John wrote a letter from noon to 3:00 p.m. it is not necessarily the case that he literally wrote a letter from 2:00 to 2:30 p.m. But he must have started the letter at noon and finished at 3:00 p.m.

3. An *occasional process* "can go on at *some* times throughout the interval [in

question] (but not necessarily at most times)." An occasional process is one obtaining at some times during the interval *I* (and presumably including the first and last times *t* in *I*). Thus, *drink wine*: if John drank wine from noon to 3:00 p.m., it might very well be the case that most of the time in that interval he did not literally drink wine. But he must have started drinking at noon and stopped at 3:00 p.m.

4. A *wholistic process* relates "to the structure of the interval as a whole, with the result that if the process consumes a certain period it *cannot possibly* transpire during any subinterval thereof. Examples are reciting [all of] *Hiawatha* . . . or baking a cake or flying from New York to Los Angeles." A wholistic process is one which can hold true at no time *in I*, but holds true only *of I* as a whole. Thus, *bake a cake, fly from New York to L.A.*: if John baked a cake from noon to 3:00 p.m., it cannot be true that he baked a cake from 2:00 to 2:30 p.m., though he must have finished baking a cake at 3:00 p.m.

Rescher and Urquhart discuss what they call a "quasi-process."[52] This term comprises processes like starting and stopping, birth and death, beginning and ending, which "are oriented towards the anterior or posterior nonexistence of the item at issue." To characterize these as processes requires that nonexistence be treated as "a state of a system."

There has been some confusion in regard to the "gappiness" of processes. From the point of view of the Aristotelian categorization, the Rescher-Urquhart distinctions are not really significant. Walking is an activity regardless whether a particular act of walking, or walking as a type of activity for that matter, is homogeneous or not, as long as it is not wholistic. Sometimes an act of walking is continuous, sometimes gappy.

Series are like activities in being gap-ridden. They are not just trivially non-gappy, of course, but inherently involve real gaps. Eating cheese now and then is not the same as continuously eating cheese. Suppose someone becomes a vegetarian at the age of twenty but resumes eating meat at the age of eighty. It is true that they sometimes (during their lifetime) eat meat, but it is certainly not true of most of the intervals in their lifetime that they (sometimes) eat meat.

This is not to say that it is possible absolutely to distinguish trivial from non-trivial gaps. If a runner stops in midrace, announces his intention to not finish the race, but is talked out of it and starts running again, do we say that the runner is continuing to run the race, resuming running the race, or again running the race?

When cars in a race stop under a warning flag, we do not say that they have stopped *running the race*, only that they have stopped *running*. A car may be running the race although it is not in motion, and presumably the same is true of humans or animals running. What is clear is that the triviality of gaps has nothing to do with continuance or cessation of activity per se, but rather with possible outcomes, and in the case of volitional activities, with intention.

Gappiness is much less satisfactory as a criterion than its prominence in the literature would suggest, because it is so unclear what difference, if any, there is between trivial and non-trivial gaps, and what role the kind of distinction Rescher and Urquhart make may play in semantics. Once again, whether a gap counts as part of a situation or not is a question of viewpoint; a worker on a lunch break may be said to be working—or not—depending on the context and the speaker's intentions.

A more important difference between states and non-states is that states have no phasic structure. By this we do not mean that they are non-dynamic. We must distinguish *stage* from *phase* in order to capture this distinction. Any time in the occurrence of a situation may be termed a stage. The stages of an accomplishment successively approach the goal; however, two such stages of an accomplishment may be alike in constituting part of the activity leading to the culmination, the completion of the accomplishment.

All such stages are part of the activity *phase* of the accomplishment. The stage at which the accomplishment itself is achieved is unlike such stages, not only in being as close as possible to the goal or the last stage, but also in representing a boundary beyond which the activity qua accomplishment cannot continue (though when, following a race, a runner cools down by running, the activity itself can continue). The last interval in a particular activity token is always its terminal stage, but only the culmination of an accomplishment is its last phase.

The variation in the phasic structures of various types of non-states serves to distinguish them, and underlies many of the linguistic tests for the Aristotelian classification. States are all a uniform "main part" (nucleus); as a state, a situation has no natural boundaries, no inherent structure of onset and culmination.

It is possible to *stop* or *cease* being ill, but not possible to *finish* being ill. Of course, in an extended sense, a stative expression may be accepted as activity or performance expression, at least by some speakers. A con man, to fool his victim, may pretend to be ill. As soon as he has fleeced the mark, he might be said to have "finished being ill."

Similarly, *he's ill* cannot mean *he's starting to be ill* or *he's about to be ill*. Other types of situations, activities, and performances do have inchoative, prospective, or conative senses. *He's running (the race)* can be said as the runner approaches the blocks, leaps off the blocks, or even enters the stadium.

Any two subintervals not containing the inception or the termination will be identical (except possibly for trivial gaps). The same is essentially true of activities, though we must again allow for trivial gaps: there may be subintervals over which activity is not literally going on.

The syntactic properties differentiating linguistic expressions for states from other types are explicable in terms of either volitionality or homogeneity. States are largely involitional, involuntary. Therefore they cannot be agentive, and consequently any structure presupposing agency, for example the pseudo-cleft construction (*what he did was be tall*) and the imperative (*be tall!*) are excluded.

Homogeneity accounts for other properties, for example the interaction of aspectualizers (aspectual auxiliary verbs) and stative expressions. Freed offers a number of criterial tests for the Aristotelian classes involving the aspectualizers *stop*, *start*, *finish*, and so on, and the logical consequences of expression conjoining these aspectualizers and verbs of the various types.[53] All of the aspectual verbs discussed by Freed[54] (with the possible exception of *keep*) occur with accomplishments, but with the other four types, certain ones cannot occur.

Aspectualizers referring to phases other than the nucleus itself are not appropriate with the *-ing* complement, except in a special sense:

> !John started being ill.
> !Susan ceased being tall.
> ?!Max finished being rich
> ?!Igor continued being patriotic.

Compare:

> John started running the race. (accomplishment)
> Susan ceased running. (activity)
> Max finished running the mile. (accomplishment)
> Igor continued running in the morning. (series)

Other of the facts about the aspectualizers, however, have nothing to do with temporal properties. Some aspectualizers, for example, presuppose volition and may be incompatible with those states which are nonvolitional: **John quit being tall*, **John kept on being tall*. (Cf. *John quit being bigotted*, *John kept on being foolish*.)

The only property of the stative which does not obviously flow from either non-agency or homogeneity is the "realness" of the present tense. We intuit that this follows from a state's possibly obtaining *at* an instant. Achievements, the culminations of accomplishments, and "instantaneous" activities (*he shoots, he scores!*) also allow "real" presents. We shall see in chapters 7 and 8 that this particular test has more to do with the present tense than with the phasic structure of states.

d. Activities and Events

"Occurrences," "processes," or "events" differ from states in developing from an initial state to a terminal state.[55] An *event* is bounded by states, and Von Wright, Davidson, and Dowty characterize an event as necessarily involving a change of state. As Dowty puts it, *events* are properties of intervals of time, but only those at which something enters into a new state.[56] Thus the event of Susan's returning home is bounded by her not being home and her subsequent being home.

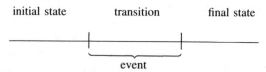

initial state   transition   final state

event

However, since an event is dynamic, there are intermediary states during its course. Consider Susan's walking across the street. It is bounded by her being motionless on one side of the street and by her being motionless on the other.

(These states may obtain only momentarily.) But during the course of her walking across the street, many different states obtain. She may be in the middle of the street, just going up on the sidewalk, and so forth. Thus an event potentially contains within it an infinite number of subevents. If Susan knocks (repeatedly) on a door, for example, each separate knock is a subevent, yet each of these itself contains subevents, for example striking the door with her hand or withdrawing her hand from the door. Each subevent involves a change of state.[57]

Woisetschlaeger[58] defines a *subevent* as what happens between two states, at least one of which is an intermediate state.

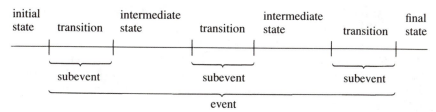

If activities as non-states contrast with states, they also contrast with performances. Performances, unlike activities, have a culminative phase, and can *finish* as well as merely *stop* or *cease*.

Aristotle is generally credited with first observing that the meanings of some verbs necessarily involve an "end" or "result," while those of other verbs do not.[59] From Garey (1957) comes the term *telic* for expressions which have natural culminations, and *atelic,* for those "which do not have to wait for a goal for their realization."[60] *Writing* represents an activity and hence constitutes an atelic expression; *Tom was writing* has the subinterval property and entails that Tom wrote. *Write a novel* is however an accomplishment; *Tom was writing a novel* does not entail that Tom wrote a novel.

The distinction of telic and atelic had actually been made by Jespersen, prior to Garey, using the terminology *conclusive/nonconclusive.* Dahl, following Allen, calls it a distinction of *bounded* and *nonbounded.*[61] Other terms have been used, reflecting different definitions of the distinction:

resultative/irresultative
nondurative/durative
transformative/nontransformative
(Russian) *predel'nyj* 'bounding'/*nepredel'nyj* 'non-bounding'
(German) *grenzbezogen* 'related to a boundary'/*nicht-grenzbezogen* 'not related to a boundary'[62]

The crucial distinctive property of telicness has been viewed at various times as fundamentally one of terminativity, durationness or momentaneousness, or potential termination.[63]

Telicness serves to distinguish "performances" (achievements in the wider sense, including accomplishments) from states and activities. Performances—achievements and accomplishments—involve a product, upshot, or outcome, something resultant. This is not necessarily the case with an activity (Mourelatos's "process"), which "just happens," nor with a state, which "just is."

Hence it is attractive to identify telicness with the possibility of a resultant state, or with potential achievement of a goal. Pinkster calls atelic situations "nonterminative states of affairs" and telic ones "terminative" ("events" in Mourelatos's terminology and that of Bach, 1980). The problem with this terminology is that perfectivity and telicness both involve terminativity (cf. *I am reading through,* which shows the crosscutting of the two categories).

The nature of telicness and its relationship to perfectivity have been the occasion of some controversy, precisely because both seem to crucially involve termination or terminal boundedness. Thus some scholars have defined telicness in ways which are remarkably close to definitions of perfectivity, and some have even identified the two.[64]

While the perfective verb in Slavic may indeed tend to represent completion or boundedness (as opposed to the tendency of the imperfective to represent noncompletion or unboundedness), and performances also represent completion or boundedness (while nonperformances represent noncompletion or unboundedness), the two categorizations are nonetheless independent.

The activity of running may be perfective or imperfective (*he ran, he was running*), but so may the performance of painting a picture (*he painted a picture, he was painting a picture*). This was already observed by Garey, who exhibited the independence of the telic/atelic and perfective/imperfective oppositions in a table:

	Imperfective	Perfective
Telic	Pierre arrivait	Pierre est arrivé
Atelic	Pierre jouait	Pierre a joué[65]

Telic expressions may be used with imperfective aspect to indicate noncompletion of a situation which is naturally bounded: *I am writing the letter.* Declerck points out that while durational adverbials (*for how long*) typically occur with atelics, and "containers" (*within what time*) with telics, either type can occur with certain expressions:

> The insect crawled through the tube for hours.
> The insect crawled through the tube in two hours' time.[66]

The past tense of English is neutral as to perfectivity, so these results are not unexpected. In fact, any telic expression in the English past tense is ambiguous in this way, so long as it denotes a situation having an activity phase:

> John earned the gold medal for the first ten seconds of the sprint and then coasted.
> John earned the gold medal in the first ten seconds of the sprint and then coasted.
> Max wrote his speech all afternoon but finally gave up in disgust.
> Max wrote his speech within ten minutes of learning the proposed topic.
> *John noticed the dollar lying on the sidewalk for five minutes before picking it up.
> John noticed the dollar lying on the sidewalk within five minutes of arriving there.

The relationship of telicness to perfectivity raises a number of problems. We have been assuming that telicness is a property of situations and (secondarily) of the linguistic expressions referring to those situations. This follows from the observations of Verkuyl, who first made linguists aware of their importance, although they had been pointed out earlier by a number of others,[67] and have since become a commonplace of the study of aspect. For example, Comrie has stated that "situations are not described by verbs alone, but rather by the verb together with its arguments (subjects and objects)."[68] He offers the examples:

John is singing	atelic
John is singing a song	telic
John is singing songs	atelic
John is singing five songs	telic

The property of telicness is not just a property of verbs or verb phrases; we need at least to refer to telic and atelic expressions in general, since a telic verb may enter into a larger atelic expression and vice versa. But it is only at the level of the sentence that telicness can truly be defined,[69] since the telicness of an expression in isolation is inconsequential for its telicness in any larger expression, up to the level of sentence.

The difficulty is that if telicness is a property of sentences (describing situations), then it makes no sense to talk of the perfective or imperfective of a telic (or non-telic) expression, since perfectivity is a verbal category, and hence of smaller scope than telicness. Furthermore, telicness and perfectivity are not properties of the same sort and hence are not applicable to the same sort of entity. Telicness has to do with *types* of situations (and secondarily is applicable to expressions for them). It is not overtly marked, but is merely implicit in the meanings of expressions. But perfectivity has to do with the representation of *individual* events. It is a category overtly marked in the verb or by an auxiliary verb.

Some scholars (e.g., Declerck) avoid these problems, because for them the progressive of a telic expression is simply atelic,[70] just as the progressive of an accomplishment is simply an activity. This raises other problems, however.

Dahl argues that "the [telic] property cannot be a property of a situation or process per se: It comes only as the result of describing the situation."[71] Writing a letter (telic) can also be described as writing (atelic). At any given moment, what is happening at a certain place to certain entities, or being done by them, or the state they are in, may be described in an indefinitely large number of ways. But within the terms of *each* of those descriptions, a particular type of situation is involved, and it is either telic or non-telic. This categorization is secondarily applicable to linguistic expressions for those various situations, as Dahl notes. It should occasion no confusion, if here we use the same terminology indifferently for both situations and the linguistic expressions referring to them.

But this observation can also be misleading. For example, Dahl cites sentences with well-defined potential terminations which nonetheless do not seem to have the property of telicness:

John is studying for a bachelor's degree.
The submarine moved towards the North Pole.[72]

This shows a confusion between what we might term effective (coincidental) and inherent boundedness. If a submarine is moving toward the North Pole, there is an effective bound for that process, since as things stand in the real world the sub can go only as far as the North Pole before achieving the goal of the action. This *seems* to be what we mean by the telic property. But in fact, moving toward the North Pole is not like flying to Rome—rather, it is like flying. While the act of moving *toward* the North Pole can terminate only in success upon moving *to* the North Pole or in failure to move *to* the North Pole, moving *toward* the North Pole is *not* the same situation as moving *to* it, though a certain type of situation-in-the-world could be described either way.

Movement toward something is determinate movement, with no inherent culmination in its phasic structure; movement to something does have within its phasic structure a culmination. It is coincidental that every point on the earth is on a line of finite length with the North Pole. Compare *the value of* x *approaches (tends toward) infinity*, where there is no effective bound.

The definition of telicness must take into account that what is crucial is not that there be a potential culmination of the *actual* process described, but rather that the phasic structure of the situation include a culminatory phase distinct from mere termination. And it must be emphasized that "situation" does not mean situation-in-the-world but, as Dahl says, how that situation is described, that is, its characterization.

To say that a sub is sailing *to* the North Pole is to assign an inherent culmination to the event, to explicitly render it a potential accomplishment; the point of saying that it is sailing *toward* the Pole is expressly to avoid any such claim, to assert motion which is at best temporally determinate, to render the event merely an activity. The sub can *cease* sailing toward the North Pole, but it cannot ordinarily *finish* doing so.

The appropriate definition of telicness involves neither the achievement of a goal, nor the potentiality of such an achievement, but the inference of such a potentiality in the characterization of the situation. But if telicness is a property of expressions for situations and not of any smaller expressions, and the imperfective renders a situation atelic, how do we capture the distinction between the natural but merely effective boundedness of sailing *toward* the North Pole, and the equally natural but inherent boundedness of sailing *to* the North Pole?

The way to resolve the dilemma is to recognize that every type of *verb-centered* linguistic expression assigns a phasic structure. Then there is no contradiction in saying that *write* is atelic (and an activity), but *write a novel* telic (and an accomplishment). What we mean by *activity*, for example, is a structural type which is uniform, if gappy, and lacks any culminative phase. The verb *sail* refers to such a type; sailing is an activity. But sailing around the world is not an activity, it is an accomplishment, since it denotes a phasic structure containing a culmination.

In the imperfective, the actualization of a culmination is not asserted. To say that someone is sailing around the world is to say that they are engaged in an activity which potentially leads to an accomplishment (i.e., they are in the activity phase of an accomplishment). *They were sailing around the world* is the imperfective of a telic. A solution for the problems of telicness along such lines—in terms of phasic structure—depends of course on achieving an adequate semantic theory of phase.

A difference in phasic structure accounts for the syntactic properties which distinguish activities from accomplishments (and to some extent from achievements). *In an hour* sets a bound; as activities have no natural bound, it is odd to say **she* *walked in an hour* but natural to say *she walked around the town in a hour. Within an hour, she was walking* refers to the initiation of walking, not the walking itself.

Expressions are sometimes ambiguously activities or accomplishments. There is a difference between *she walked across the frozen lake in an hour* and *she walked across the frozen lake for an hour*. It is possible to walk across the lake in an hour, but not to just walk in an hour (except in the sense of starting to walk within an hour). It is possible to say she walked across the frozen lake for an hour, because this reports the activity phases of the accomplishment of crossing the lake, not the accomplishment itself.

As an accomplishment it has a definite bound defined by the diameter of the lake. Walking in a straight line at a mile an hour and without stopping, if the lake is a mile across, she must finish walking across it in an hour. But this does not mean that in *she walked across the frozen lake for an hour* an accomplishment is reported, or that *for* is compatible with accomplishments as such. The failure to recognize this distinction of bounded accomplishment and activity phase (with only an implied, natural bound) has led to much confusion, as we have seen.

Similar to the *in/for* facts are those involving *spend* and *take*. You can spend an hour jumping up and down, and you can in some sense (or senses) spend it jumping over a wall; but while you can take an hour to jump over a wall, you cannot really take an hour to jump up and down, except in the conative sense (of taking an hour to get to jumping up and down just as you can take an hour to notice a vase missing).

Russian makes a distinction in verbs of motion between indeterminate action, *walk around for an hour*, and determinate action, *walk around in an hour*. To some extent this parallels the distinction of activity and accomplishment, but it also crosscuts it. It is possible to say both *itti v gorod* 'to go (determinate) to town' and *xodit' v gorod* 'to go (indeterminate) to town'; while the latter is an accomplishment, either semelfactive or iterative, the former is an activity.

But the difference is not simply one of boundedness or culminativity; it is entirely possible to say *poyezd šёl bystro* 'the train was going fast' (*itti*) or *Val'gan xodil iz ugla v ugol v svoyey komnate* 'Val'gan paced his room from corner to corner'. Nor does the difference correlate with aspect, as both types can be found in either aspect. While the intuitive difference is clear for Russian speakers, and a number of rough oppositions have been stated (''definite'' vs. ''indefinite''; ''actual, concrete'' vs. ''abstract''; ''durative, non-frequentative'' vs. ''frequentive, iterative''; etc.), the treatment of the Russian verbs of motion remains controversial.[73]

She almost walked to the store and *she walked to the store* are ambiguous, since the focus can be either on the accomplishment as a whole or merely on the activity phase. But an activity is all activity phase and hence no such ambiguity is possible. Similarly, *finish* is possible with some activities, but only because they are conceived of as bounded: if you intend to run, but only for an hour, you can be said to have *finished* running when finally you *stop*.

You can, however, always *stop* doing an activity. But *he stopped walking*, like *he was walking*, entails that *he walks* was true at some point during the interval over which the walking took place—activities have the subinterval property because of their relative phasic homogeneity. This is rather different from the case of accomplishments. *She stopped drawing the picture* entails (as we infer from *she was drawing the picture*) that at that moment she had not yet drawn (if she ever would have drawn) the picture.

e. Telicness and Performances

"Performances" are divided up into accomplishments and achievements on the basis of whether they contain an activity phase or not. Another way of characterizing them, however, is as either durative—taking place over an interval—or punctural—occurring at a point in time. Bergman and Comrie call durative performances "processes," while Mourelatos calls them "developments." Bergman and Comrie call punctual performances "events," while Mourelatos calls them "punctual occurrences". Similarly, Pinkster distinguishes "momentaneous" from "non-momentaneous" terminative states of affairs, while Bach distinguishes "instantaneous" from "protracted events".

Accomplishments have what we may call the "counter-subinterval-property." If Mr. Blandings builds his dream house from June 1 to September 9, then it must be the case at any time during that interval, or over any subinterval, that "Mr. Blandings is building his dream house" is true, but also that "Mr. Blandings builds his dream house" is false; there is *no* proper subinterval (that is, any subinterval other than itself as a whole) over which "Mr. Blandings builds his dream house" is true. The same fact is trivially true of achievements: since an achievement takes place at a single point in time, the only subinterval is the interval, the point, itself.

Although achievements are classically characterized as instantaneous, some authors have distinguished "gradual achievements."[74] Freed observes that, contrary to what Dowty, Vendler, and others have stated, some achievements—the "gradual" ones—do occur in the progressive.[75] She offers as examples *he is dying, the colors are fading, I am falling asleep.* These are either all gradual achievements, or the verbs in such examples "are functioning as activities and are improperly classified as achievements."

Dowty distinguishes "single change of state" predicates—non-agentive *notice, realize, ignite*, and agentive *kill, point out (something to someone)*—from "complex change of state" predicates like *flow from x to y, dissolve, build (a house), walk a mile.*[76] We might view this distinction as one of achievement versus accomplishment, but for the fact that Freed's gradual achievements are complex. Dowty's test is the verb *finish*: you can finish building a house, but cannot be said to finish pointing out something. But you can be said to finish dying or finish falling asleep, if these are protracted, and possibly finish voluntarily.

It may be that gradual achievements are actually a type of accomplishment; winning a race is the possible culmination of running in it; coming to be asleep is that of falling asleep. *I am falling asleep, I am winning the race, I am painting the house* report activity phases; where gradual achievements differ from accomplishments, however, is that *he painted the house from noon to 3:00 p.m.* refers (ambiguously) to the activity (with or without a culmination), whereas *he fell asleep from noon to 3:00 p.m.* presupposes the resultant state. *?He painted the house from noon to 3:00 p.m., but didn't finish it* is acceptable for many speakers in the sense of *he was painting. . . ,* but **he fell asleep from noon to 3:00 p.m., but was never asleep* is contradictory.

Accomplishments add to their activity phase an achievement phase, which is a point. They naturally terminate at this point.

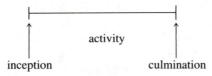

An achievement is all culmination; though the achievement is possibly preceded by some activity (spotting something is preceded by looking for it), the verb refers only to the achievement phase, not to the preceding activity. While achievements have a conative or tentative sense (*it took an hour for her to find the book*), this is rather different from a similar accomplishment (*it took an hour for her to draw the picture*). The act which results in finding is searching, not finding, but that which results in having drawn a picture *is* drawing a picture.

An achievement such as finding a dollar on the pavement or noticing a vase missing is actually the culminative phase of an accomplishment, and trying (but failing) to find a vase missing or a dollar on the pavement is really no different from trying (but failing) to (successfully) draw a picture. It is just that we do not call the activity phases "finding" a dollar or "noticing" a vase missing, as we call it "drawing a picture": *she tried to draw a picture* is ambiguous, as is *she almost drew a picture*; but *she tried to find a dollar on the pavement* is not, nor is *she almost found a dollar on the pavement.*

There is, however, one problem with treating accomplishments as a combination of activity and achievement: this approach fails to distinguish two things, namely the telic property and the perfective property. If John ran from noon till 3:00 p.m., and decided at 2:50 to quit running, we can identify the running from 2:50 to 3:00 as the terminative phase of his running. But so can we identify the last phase of his painting a picture as terminative, whether he finished the picture or not. The fact is that *John was ceasing/stopping/quitting painting the picture* refers to a point within the terminative phase of his painting the picture, but it differs from *John was finishing painting the picture.*

Accordingly we must distinguish the *potential* or *nominal* phases of an event from the *actual* phases. Eating a three-course dinner has a beginning, middle, and end, but not every act of eating a three-course dinner is successfully brought to a conclusion; the existence or nonexistence of a natural culmination is entirely independent of whether the event has a termination. You can *stop* running at any time, but there is only one time you can *finish* running at.

We can resolve this problem by distinguishing the culminative phase from the terminal (final) phase of the action itself, the nucleus, the central phase of the event, when it can be said to be ongoing.[77] If an accomplishment is halted before its culmination, there is still a terminal phase, the final subinterval in which the accomplishment occurs. It might be true that *John is ceasing to run around the block* or that *John ceases to run*, without it necessarily being true that *John is finishing running around the block* or *John finishes running around the block*.

In addition to the three subphases of the nucleus (initial, medial, and final), Freed introduces a further *onset* of an event between initiation and the initial phase of the nucleus, as well as a *coda* between the terminal phase of the nucleus and the culmination. The onset is a phase during which it is true that the event or action is starting, but not yet in progress. The futurate provides good reason for assuming such a preinceptive phase, as does the conative (e.g., *opening the box* = 'trying to open the box') and other expressions which refer not to events themselves but to the stages leading up to those events.

Freed defines the coda as the phase between the termination and culmination; it is what we call here the culminative phase.

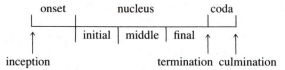

It seems useful as well to recognize some kind of post-culminative phase, because of the perfect. Soga presents a diagram capturing these various phases.[78]

Pre-Inceptive   Inceptive   On-Going   Terminative   Post-Terminative

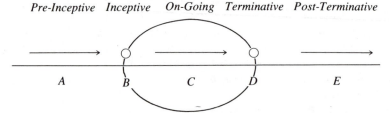

The event proper is contained within B–D, while E represents the perfect phase and A its mirror image. If Guillaume's terminology (see below) were not confusing, we might have termed E, the post-terminative, the "extension" of the event, and we might correspondingly have termed A its "intension."

Although we can view the difference between accomplishment and achievement as one of having or not having an activity phase, or of being durative or instantaneous[79]—Mourelatos writes of the "development" involved in the accomplishment as opposed to the punctualness of the achievement.[80] It has also been viewed as involving repetition or its lack: you can keep on drawing a picture but you can't keep on noticing the same vase missing.[81] (At least not as part of the same act. Because you *can* keep on finding the same dollar bill on the pavement, if you keep dropping and losing it, some writers have stressed the notion of occasion. Here we must be careful to indicate that an achievement cannot be continued or repeated on the *same* occasion. An accomplishment qua activity can be continued or iterated over short, trivial gaps.) Non-repetition seems however purely derivative of the punctual, non-durational character of the achievement.

The properties of the achievement differentiating it from the accomplishment follow from this lack of an activity phase (and hence its punctuality). You can draw a picture for an hour as you can draw for an hour, but you cannot notice a vase missing except at an instant. You can draw a picture in an hour *and* notice a vase missing in an hour, because here the bounded activity is what leads to noticing, and not the noticing itself. The facts about *spend* and *take* are parallel.

Once again, you cannot finish noticing something, because there is no activity phase as such to noticing. Noticing as a durative situation is serial: you can spend your whole life noticing new *things*. But noticing things has no natural bound; you cannot spend your life noticing *five* new things. You can, consequently, *stop* noticing new things, but not *finish* doing it.

Again, if you draw a picture in an hour, you are drawing it all during that hour; but if you notice something in an hour, you do not notice it all during that hour. For the same reason, adverbials which involve continued effort, such as *attentively*, are excluded by achievements but not by accomplishments.

End, resume and other verbs presuppose medial, activity phases and hence are likewise incompatible with achievements, though acceptable with accomplishments: you can resume finding your way out of an unfamiliar room in the dark (or finding the solution to a puzzle), but not finding that you hate cheese or finding a fly in your soup.

f. Phase

So far we have been looking at how phasic structure serves to distinguish and characterize the temporal entities represented by expressions belonging to the various Aristotelian categories. But phase had played an equally central role in the study both of aspect proper and of the *Aktionsarten*.[82] The study of phase was in fact first undertaken not in connection with the Aristotelian classification, but as part of the study of the *Aktionsarten*, and in recent times it has become closely associated with the study of aspectual auxiliary verbs, as in the work of Freed and Woisetschlaeger. The concept of phase itself was developed, however, in the context of theories of aspect.

A number of writers have incorporated phase into their theories of aspect: Guillaume (1929), Keniston (1936), Holt (1943), Trager and Smith (1951), Bull (1960), Joos (1964), Coseriu (1976). One of these deserves special notice, namely Guillaume, the earliest theorist to have made a deep study of phase, introducing some of the central concepts associated with it, albeit within the context of a rather idiosyncratic theory.

Guillaume's work is inherently of interest, but further deserves a brief excursus here because it has led to much work by later followers, and continues to have a considerable influence in the French-speaking world,[83] though little known outside it.

There are two reasons for this relative neglect. First, Guillaume is a radical idealist. The time Guillaume concerns himself with is not an objective, external time but a subjective, internal one. And the flow of time which he considers relevant to language is not the "arrow of time," but the direction of the mind as *it* creates time by conceiving an image of it.

Guillaume furthermore thinks of the tenses, aspects, and moods as facets of *one and the same* process of "chronogenesis." He therefore rejects the commonplace notion that mood is different in kind from tense and aspect, and each of these from the other. Furthermore, he makes no distinction of reference time and event time. He would not accept Bull's different axes: the mind has but *one* point of view. This is not to say that Guillaume does not accept many of the findings of modern linguistics—in many respects he is fully a structuralist in the tradition of Saussure—nor that he could not capture them in this theory.

A second reason why many students of tense and aspect find Guillaume difficult is the peculiarity of his terminology and the near-mysticism of his thought. Terms such as "bi-transcendent aspect," "merotropy," and "chronothesis" are unfamiliar, and the theory employs ideationalist concepts of great abstractness. Consider the following passage from one of his followers:

> Thus one sees the system first of all provide the mind, in the immanent aspect, with the event. Then with the transcendent and bi-transcendent aspects, it is seen to propose [*sic*] successively to this *matter* a first *form*, then a second—this second form of the memory being no longer a simple memory of the first degree, but a memory of the second degree, a memory of the memory, that is to say, a memory able to register in itself the recollection of a first memory.[84]

The following brief and partial summary of Guillaume's theory is based on Guillaume (1965), Hirtle (1967, 1975), and Valin (1975). The central idea is that of *chronogenesis*, the mental operation of forming an image of time. This operation may be intercepted at any point, producing as a kind of cross-section the image produced up to that point. This image is called a *chronothesis*.

For Guillaume, mood marks where in the operation of chronogenesis the chronothesis is. English has three moods—if the chronothesis is near the beginning of chronogenesis, when the process has barely begun, the *quasi-nominal* mood (marked by non-finite forms) results. If it is at the end, the indicative results; and if in the middle, the subjunctive.

There is a fundamental distinction between *ascending time*, in which the event is unfolding, developing toward completion and a resultant state of affairs, and *descending time*, in which it is not. At the beginning of chronogenesis, universe time (the abstract totality of time, which contains events, as opposed to event time, the time which is contained within an event) is descending. In the quasi-nominal mood, since chronogenesis has barely begun, time is descending, and there is no development: the French infinitive *marcher* 'to go' represents an event without any regard for its development in time at all.

The subjunctive mood allows for either descending time, as in the case of counter-to-fact conditionals, which are unlikely and not getting any more likely, or as-cending time, as in the case of those subjunctives which do allow for development in time. The indicative mood allows only for ascending time, for development, as chronogenesis is complete.[85] This is diagramed in the accompanying illustration.

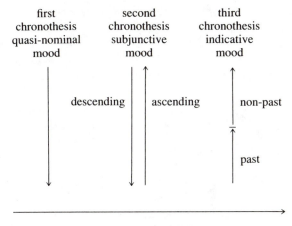

CHRONOGENESIS

In effect, we have in chronogenesis a passage from the abstract to the actual, successively passing from the possibility of an event to its reality via its probability, increasing probability, certainty, and increasing reality. Guillaume distinguishes the abstract possibility marked by non-finite forms such as the infinitive and participle as *temps in posse* ('time in possibility', where the event is only beginning, is at the initial point, I) from the incomplete chronogenesis, *temps in fieri* ('time in being-done') of the subjunctive (where the event is at a medial point M of coming into actuality), and from the completed *temps in esse* ('time in being'), the indicative, in which the event has fully emerged in the mind as an actuality (and is at the final point, F, of the process).[86]

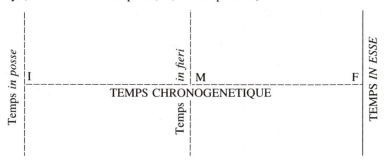

An event which is not actual is said to be in *tension*, to be *tensive*. When it is completed and fully actualized, it is *detensive*. Thus the infinitive (*marcher* 'to go, going'), representing an act without development, is fully tensive, whereas the past participle (*marché*, '[having] gone'), representing the complete detension of the event, is fully detensive.

The present participle (*marchant* 'going') represents a movement from complete tension to complete detension—from *marcher* to *marché*. This development is the *immanent* aspect. Having fully entered the realm of the actual, the event subsists in its consequences, in the resultant state; it is now in the *extensive* or *transcendent* aspect, captured by the perfect forms—*ayant marché* 'having marched'. Here too, however, there is a development: from the complete tension of *avoir marché* 'to have marched' to the complete detension of *eu marché* 'had marched'.

At this point, in colloquial French at least, the event transcends the transcendent and enters the bi-extensive or *bi-transcendent* aspect. Guillaumists see as fundamental the parallelism of the simple, perfect (*composés*) and supercomposite (*surcomposés*) tenses.[87]

j'écris	*j'ai écrit*	*j'ai eu écrit*
'I write'	'I have written'	'I had written'
j'écrivis	*j'eus écrit*	(not used)
'I wrote'	'I had written	
j'écrivais	*j'avais écrit*	*j'aurais eu écrit*
'I wrote'	'I had written'	'I would have written'
que j'écrive	*que j'aie écrit*	*j'aie eu écrit*
'that I write'	'that I have written'	'that I had written'

In more conventional terms, the immanent aspect is the imperfective, in which the event is in the process of occurring but may or may not be completed, and the transcendent is the perfect, in which the event is implicit in its results but is not asserted. However, the bi-transcendent does not correspond to anything in other theories. One reason for this is that few apart from the Guillaumists have made serious studies of the *surcomposés* of colloquial French and German.

In Guillaumist theory, as in more conventional ones, aspect represents how events are viewed. However, the distinctions of point of view are different. In this theory, if our view is from within the event, we have an *endotropic* view; if from without, an *exotropic* one. The former provides the becoming phase, the later the result phase—respectively, the immanent and transcendent aspects. When the event is viewed in its entirety, from beginning to end, we essentially have the perfective aspect, whereas a partial view provides the imperfective. In this regard, the perfect is radically disjoint from both, representing as it does a totally different phase.[88]

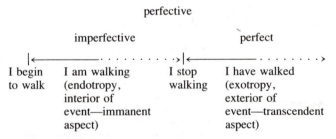

For present purposes, the significance of Guillaume's work is that it was the first fully elaborated account of events in terms of phase. He recognizes that aspect has to do with the phasic structure of events, and essentially equates the perfect with the resultant state consequent to an event. In effect, he distinguishes aspect, as the way an event is viewed (the imperfective being an interior view of the event as it develops in time, and the perfective an exterior view, the event given as already fully developed), from tense, the position of the event in time, but also from the *Aktionsarten*, which he does not discuss.

A system somewhat like Guillaume's but with less exotic foundations, and in various respects like those of both Bull and Keniston (below), is that of Coseriu (1976).[89] He distinguishes the plane of the actual (present) from that of the inactual (past).[90] Within each plane there are three perspectives—retrospective (action anterior to the speech act), parallel (concurrent with the speech act), and prospective (posterior to the speech act). This gives six simple tenses in Portuguese[91]:

	retrospective	parallel	prospective
actual	*fiz*	*faço*	*farei*
	'I did'	'I do'	'I shall do'
inactual	*fizera*[92]	*fazia*	*faria*
	'I had done'	'I did'	'I should do'

Within each of these there is a secondary perspective, also divisible into retrospective, parallel, and prospective. The retrospective constitutes the perfects, the prospective the periphrastic futures. The Portuguese system (the actual plane only is given here) is as follows[93]:

	retrospective	parallel	prospective
present	*tenho feito*	*faço*	*vou fazer*
	'I have done'	'I do'	'I am going to do'
past	*tive feito*	*fiz*	*fui fazer*
	'I had done'	'I did'	'I was going to do'
future	*terei feito*	*farei*	*irei fazer*
	'I shall have done'	'I shall do'	'I shall be going to do'

For Coseriu, the *surcomposé* tenses constitute a tertiary perspective, though he says little on this.

The theories presented in Trager and Smith (1951) and, following this work, in Joos (1964), although conventional, partly resemble that of Guillaume as regards the treatment of the perfect—and the futurate. Trager and Smith refer to the perfect *(has gone, had gone)* and resultative *(is gone, was gone)* as "phases," with no further comment.[94]

Joos sees a fundamental distinction of *current* and *perfect* phase—the one, expressed by simple verbs, concerning the action in itself, the other, expressed by the perfect, concerning the resultant state, the effects of the action.[95] In current phase, "the principal effects are in phase with the specified event, their cause." Of the passage below, he says that it "is not simply a narration of events in sequence; instead, certain of them *(is seated, rustle and subside)* are presented as *effects* (or at least the possibility of their occurrence is an effect) of the earlier-in-time events stated in the perfect phase." They themselves are not marked as effects, but rather the perfect marking of the verbs for the precedent events so indicates: "The perfect-marked verbs are there specifically *for* the sake of the effects of the events they designate, and that is the essential meaning."

> The high-backed chair *has been pulled,* helped forward, the figure is SEATED, *has bowed* and the hundred or so people who *had gathered* themselves at split notice to their feet RUSTLE AND SUBSIDE into apportioned place.

Joos views the futurate as the mirror image of the perfect: "The meaning of BE GOING TO . . . turns out to be the exact reversal . . . of the meaning of perfect phase: it simply exchanges 'previous' and 'subsequent' ''[96] The eventual occurrences are "out of phase" with the preparatory conditions.

The notion of *phase* remained a rather vague one until it was applied to the definition of the *Aktionsarten,* especially in the context of a semantic theory, as exemplified in the next section.

g. Phase and the *Aktionsarten*

The earliest work on the *Aktionsarten,* Streitberg's, makes no explicit reference to phase. Since Streitberg there has been a great proliferation of schemes of *Aktionsarten* and of *Aktionsarten* themselves, too many to review here.[97] Each scholar attempted to establish a logical taxonomy, a principled organization of the sundry *Aktionsarten* such that their various differences in meaning could be revealed and the set of all possible *Aktionsarten* be logically defined and organized. In the absence of a clearly defined concept of phase, these efforts were doomed to futility.

One such attempt was that of Noreen in his *Vårt Språk* of 1911–12.[98] The *Aktionsarten,* we have seen, are miscellaneous. The same types of markers seem to mark a grab bag of different types of categories, as for instance intensive, inceptive, of-short-duration, iterative, and others even less homogeneous. In many languages such distinctions are marked by affixes (e.g., the inchoative verbs of Indo-European such as Latin *cale.sc.o* 'grow warm'; the iterative verbs of Turkish such as *serp.iş.tir–*'scatter about' and *sor.uş.tur–*'make inquiries'[99]). But they may also be marked by auxiliary verbs such as the aspectual verbs ("aspectualizers")—*start, stop, cease, continue, resume,* and the like.

An excessive regard for traditional grammatical categories led to too broad a definition of "kinds of action." Though by Noreen's time it was starting to be recognized that *Aktionsarten* properly have to do with the way actions proceed—with their "stages" or phases: how they begin, stop, proceed, continue, resume—Noreen's taxonomy still reflects an older conception.

Noreen first distinguishes "continuous" and "discontinuous" happenings, and thus the uniform *Aktionsarten* from the intermittent. From there he taxonomizes as follows in the accompanying illustration.

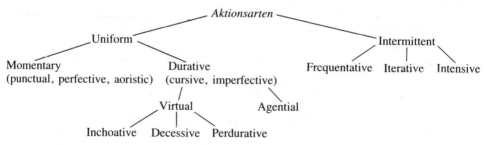

While Noreen defines the various categories in terms of the nature of the events or actions in question, this is of course a classification of verbs or expressions built on verbs, and the examples he offers are verbs or verb-based expressions.

Uniform refers to a homogeneous and unbroken course of events, while *intermittent* refers to one which is broken. Here are contrasted *nodding* (once) from *nodding and nodding*. The "uniform" *Aktionsarten* split into the *momentary*, in which the unity of the action is stressed and that action is viewed as compressed into a moment, and the *durative*, in which the action is not bounded, or is represented independently of any fixed duration.

Thus *er kommt gewiss* 'he is certainly coming' is momentary, while *der Komet kommt uns immer näher* 'the comet is coming ever (*immer*) nearer (*näher*) to us (*uns*)' is durative. Momentary *Aktionsarten* differ from durative ones in having no temporal extension, in occurring at a point in time. Noreen's examples here are not entirely felicitous, but the distinction is a familiar one.

The category of durative splits into the *agential* and the *virtual*, in which some phase of the action is in question—its beginning (*inchoative*, i.e., "inceptive," "ingressive," or "initive"), its ending (*decessive*, i.e., "egressive," "terminative," or "finitive"), or its duration (*perdurative*).

The "inchoative" refers to processes which are beginning and are leading to a state which is increasingly the case—paling and getting tired are examples. "Decessive" refers to processes which are coming to an end, which represent states that are diminishingly true: for example, fading (away) and dying (away). "Perdurative" refers to processes which simply go on, like hating.

The agential is defined as the category of "the performance of an intention," whereas the virtual is that of "the result, maintenance, or disappearance of a property or characteristic." There are two ways of looking at this: the virtual are non-agentive and the agential are agentive, or alternatively, the virtual refer to the phases of events or actions (beginning, middle, or end), while the agential refers to actions as wholes.

The agentials do not have to do with how the action or occurrence proceeds, but with such categories as the factitive (or causative: *kill*), effective (*build*), affective (*wound*), privative (*degrade*), and the like, which have principally to do with the nature of the consequent state, and not with the nature of the causative process itself. It is plain from the above-mentioned subdivisions of the agential that it really has nothing to do with temporal relationships; it is therefore not clear that it has much of anything to do with kinds of actions (*Aktionsarten*) or aspect at all.

The *intermittent Aktionsarten* have to do with noncontinuous action. The *frequentative* is said to concern an irregularly (*unregelmässig*) repeated action like *zappeln* 'wriggle, fidget', while the *iterative* concerns regularly repeated actions like *es tropft und tropft* 'it drips and drips'. If a durative is repeated, however, it is an "intensive": *he studies and studies*.

Noreen adds other types of intermittents like diminutives, cooperatives (which include reciprocals), and so on. These types of verbs are related to the *Aktionsarten* and have temporal consequences: *they lifted the piano* is uniform if cooperative, that is, if they did it together, but intermittent if noncooperative, if it was done individually and on separate occasions. But such verbs do not taxonomize with the iterative and frequentative.

While Noreen offers some kind of conceptual criteria differentiating and hierarchizing the various *Aktionsarten*, his scheme is not very sound from the methodological point of view, since it is consistently founded neither on the formal marking of categories (morphology and syntax) nor on the semantics. Ultimately it is not very satisfactory in terms of explicating why there are precisely the *Aktionsarten* there are, whether yet others are possible, or how the semantics of these categories affects both the taxonomy itself and the relationships of the *Aktionsarten* to the Aristotelian categorization, to aspect, and to the logic of aspect.

One scheme which is based in part on markers, specifically the auxiliary verbs of Spanish, is that of Keniston (1936).[100] He distinguishes "aspects conditioned by the attitude of the speaker," "subjective" aspect,[101] from "aspects which are phases of the action or state itself," "objective" aspect, more akin to Pollak's *Aktionsarten*.

For Keniston there are two attitudes: the action may be viewed as a whole ("integrative") or as a series of acts ("fractionative"). The fractionative "attitude" may be "particularizing" in "phase," referring to a specific situation, or "generalizing." In the former case, he distinguishes the progressive (uninterrupted series), iterative (intermittent), and continuative. Here are some examples (with very rough glosses):

> subjective aspect:
>   integrative attitude: *tomo y hago* 'I have done'
>   fractionative attitude:
>   particularizing phase:
>   progressive aspect: *estar haciendo* 'to be doing'
>   iterative aspect: *andar haciendo* 'to go on doing'
>   continuative aspect: *seguir haciendo* 'to go on doing'
>   generalizing phase: *soler hacer* 'to be used to doing'

He distinguishes the "phases" of beginning and ending and the "aspect" of repetition. Within the first, he distinguishes *effective* aspect from mere *inceptive* aspect. In the same way he distinguishes *perfective* aspect from *terminative* aspect. Both distinctions have to do with the structure of the events in question. Some examples:

> objective aspect:
>   phases of beginning:
>   effective aspect: *llegó a ser* 'he managed to be'
>   inceptive aspect: *comenzó lavar* 'he started washing'
>   phases of ending:
>   perfective aspect: *concluir de vestirse* 'to finish getting dressed'
>   terminative aspect: *cesar de dar* 'to cease giving'
>   aspect of single repetition: *volver a hacer* 'to do again'

Clearly an adequate approach to the *Aktionsarten* requires some consideration of the phases of events and actions, since the *Aktionsarten* seem, like the Aristotelian categories of verbs, to be definable in terms of phase. Noreen's division of the virtual *Aktionsarten* into inchoative, decessive, and perdurative, for example, reflects the fact that the nuclei of events have beginnings, middles, and ends. But the lack of a semantic theory of phase renders Keniston's marker-based approach no more sound than Noreen's notion-based one.

Woisetschlaeger's is one of the first models, if not the very first, to attempt an explicit definition of the possible *Aktionsarten* in terms of logical temporal structures. Woisetschlaeger defines aspect as quantifying "over the subevents of an event" and offers a taxonomy as "the structure of aspect." [102] We may represent this taxonomy in the following chart:

I. existential quantification over subevents
  1. independence from sequential information
    A. no references to pauses
      imperfective: *Walter was filing the day's mail*
    B. references to pauses
      interruptive (no expression in English?)
  2. dependence on sequential information
    A. no references to pauses
      i. first subevent
        inceptive: *Walter began filing the day's mail*
      ii. last subevent
        completive: *Walter finished filing the day's mail*
    B. references to pauses
      i. subevent before pause
        a. pause asserted
          cessative: *Walter stopped filing the day's mail*
        b. pause negated
          continuative: *Walter kept* [103] *filing the day's mail*
      ii. subevent after pause
        resumptive: *Walter resumed filing the day's mail*
II. universal quantification over subevents
  1. references to pauses
    determinate (no expression in English?)
  2. no references to pauses
    perfective: *Walter filed the day's mail*

Woisetschlaeger notes "that this entire structure is built out of only three nonlogical concepts: that of subevent, that of pause, and that of temporal precedence." [104] Herein lies its superiority over such notional schemes as Noreen's—it is based on the possible logical relations of a small number of objectively definable entities.

A *pause* is an interval which does not contain an occurrence or state but is bounded by intervals which do. Thus if Walter pauses in filing the day's mail, it must be the case that he has just been engaged in filing the day's mail, and will immediately be so engaged again.

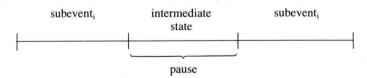

Here the repetition of the subscript identifies the subevents not as identical (the same token) but as similar (the same type). Walter's filing the mail from noon to 2:00 p.m. is in some important sense the same activity as his filing the mail from

3:00 to 5:00 p.m., though it is not *literally* the *same* activity, since it took place at a different time.[105]

We can see then how Woisetschlaeger's criteria are built out of these notions. In describing an occurrence, we can choose to refer to *all* phases of an occurrence, as in *Walter filed the day's mail*, or only *some*, as in *Walter began filing the day's mail*. If we refer to all, we can refer to pauses or not (*Walter filed the day's mail*). If we refer to some, we can describe occurrences without regard to information about sequencing, as in *Walter was filing the day's mail*, or with regard to it, as in *Walter resumed filing the day's mail*. In the latter case we can refer to pauses, as in *Walter resumed filing the day's mail*, or not, as in *Walter began filing the day's mail*, and so on.

Woisetschlaeger's proposal is not without problems, but it shows the lines along which an adequate account of the *Aktionsarten*, and the use of aspectual auxiliaries to express them, might run. We will postpone any discussion of the logical relationships Woisetschlaeger bases his system on till the next chapter, but a few comments are in order in regard to the nonlogical problems of this system.

There are some problems with Woisetschlaeger's treatment of *Walter filed the day's mail*. His analysis says that every portion of Walter's filing the day's mail took place during a certain interval. Yet as it stands, this precludes Walter's having done any filing of the mail on any other day. What is meant, of course, is the event of filing on one day, on one occasion. (*Walter often files the day's mail* refers to a series of events, in which case *the day* is variable; in *Walter filed the day's mail, the day* is undefined but constant.)

Another problem with the approach is that it does not distinguish the terminal from the culminative phase. Woisetschlaeger says, "completion is only entailed if the LAST subinterval is asserted."[106] But the last subinterval which *actually* occurs need not be a culmination; Woisetschlaeger cannot distinguish the case of *Walter stopped filing the day's mail*, which does not entail that Walter completed filing the day's mail, from *Walter finished filing the day's mail*, which does.

Also, the interpretation of *stop* as pre-gap is too narrow; *stop* does not presuppose or entail resumption. This cannot be saved by defining a "pause" as *any* interval in which the process does not proceed, since then *Walter started filing the day's mail* would be essentially indistinguishable from *Walter resumed filing the day's mail*. A pause is a non-trivial gap between phases of the same process.[107]

Woisetschlaeger makes no systematic distinction between types of gaps—trivial gaps such as occur in a majoritative process, deliberate gaps (pauses), and the types of gaps which characterize both iteration and frequentatives. Freed's study of series partly makes up for this lack.

Another important failing of the system is that it is not compositional, and hence not explanatory. *Stop V-ing* is analyzed as a unit, but *stop* and *V-ing* as such have no analyses. The meaning of *stop V-ing* is not analyzed further and is not seen as depending on the meanings of its individual parts.

Aspectual devices, in the broadest sense, are reiterable, and their semantics is compositional in the sense, first, that they have greater or lesser scope, and further that their interpretation depends on that of their constituent arts. At the heart of a clause such as *they have been beginning to fade*, is a verbal expression, an intransitive verb, *fade*. This expression denotes a type of occurrence, which in turn has an ideal phasic structure.

The phases of an occurrence may be denoted, as when *begin to fade* denotes the initial phase of fading. But the phases may themselves be divided into subphases: *start to finish eating dinner* denotes the initial subphase of the culminative phase of an accomplishment. An adequate semantics would have to account for such expressions as well as expressions for events and phases. Freed (1979) attempts, like Dowty (1979), to characterize *V-ing* independently and thus allow for a compositional treatment of expressions containing aspectualizers.

A further problem is that Woisetschlaeger's system does not distinguish *Aktionsarten* from aspects, although it shares this with that of Freed. This returns us to the question of how the various facets of ''aspect'' interrelate—what the aspects, *Aktionsarten*, and Aristotelian classes are and how they differ if they do.

h. Defining Aspect

The *Aktionsarten*, whether morphological (as in the case of Latin *calesco* 'grow warm') or periphrastic (using aspectual auxiliary verbs, e.g., *resume*), denote phases or phase sequences, and may be iterated to denote subphases or subphase sequences. If *run home* denotes an accomplishment with a full complement of phases, *finish running home* denotes only the culminative phase. *Begin to finish running home* denotes the initial subphase of the culminative phase.

Some expressions refer to whole events from inception to culmination: *Mr. Blandings builds his dream house*. Others refer to activities having no culmination and hence no coda: *Lilian is sneezing*.[108] Some events have a culmination, but no onset: *Pat is writing a letter*. Others, ''uniform'' events or states, lack both onset and coda (*the painting is peeling, David owns a painting*).

Each of the various phases—prospective, onset, inceptive (initial), durative (medial), terminative (final), coda (culminative), and retrospective—is itself a subevent with its own phases. We can in theory endlessly recursively pile modifier upon modifier to indicate ever subtler shadings of meaning:

> She ran.
> She continued to run.
> She ceased to continue to run.
> She started to cease to continue to run.
> She resumed starting to cease to continue to run.
> She was about to continue to run.
> She was continuing to run.
> She had been about to continue to run.
> She had been continuing to run.
> She had continued to run.

Verbs (and expressions containing them) can refer to events as wholes or to phases (or sets of phases) within them. *He painted the picture* refers to an entire accomplishment, from beginning to end. *He was painting the picture*, however, refers only to the activity phase. He had already begun painting the picture, and any termination was yet to be (if at all). Compare *he painted the picture from noon to 3:00 p.m.* with *he finished at 3:00 p.m.* and *he was painting the picture from noon to 3:00 p.m.*; he may never have finished it at all. For states and activities, the onset and coda may be nonexistent.

The distinction of finishing and stopping shows that it is aspectual auxiliary verbs which allow one to refer most explicitly to phases or subphases of events. And it is by considering the various ways such auxiliaries can modify expressions containing verbs that Freed and especially Woisetschlaeger are able to build up a characterization of events in terms of their possible phasic structure.

As we have noted, it is reference to different phases or sets of phases which distinguish the *Aktionsarten*, properly speaking. For both Freed and Woisetschlaeger, however, the imperfective and the perfective are merely two among the various *Aktionsarten*. The question then is whether aspect and *Aktionsarten* represent the same kind of phenomenon.

The classic definition of aspect, often quoted in the literature, is that of Comrie: "aspects are different ways of viewing the internal temporal constituency of a situation." This, Comrie tells us, is based on the definition by Holt: "les manières diverses de concevoir l'écoulement du procès même," which Comrie translates as "different ways of conceiving the flow of the process itself." Friedrich's translation makes aspect "a way of conceiving the passage of action." [109]

It is plain from Comrie's context that aspectual markers mean something much more precise than these definitions suggest. He is talking about the contrast between reference to the internal constituency (e.g., in the Russian imperfective or the French *imparfait*) versus references to the totality of the event, without such reference (the perfective, the *parfait*). Holt too makes reference to the Slavic system.

But as they stand, Holt's and Comrie's definitions allow the "relatively broad conception of aspect" which Lyons "tacitly adopted," namely one in which aspect "is extended to cover a variety of other oppositions, in so far as they are grammaticalized in the structure of particular languages—oppositions based upon the notions of duration, instantaneity, frequency, initiation, completion, etc." [110] A very similar treatment could be read into Freed's statement that aspect "deals with the internal temporal structuring, e.g., the relative duration, inception, and completion of verbal activities." [111]

The grammatical tradition has generally operated with a rather broad treatment of aspect of just this kind, making minimal assumptions about the nature of aspectual phenomena: aspectual oppositions have to do with the nature of temporal objects (situations, events, episodes, etc.), without deictic considerations, without reference to the speech-act time. The consequence of such broad latitude is considerable confusion.

For example, Bybee says that "aspect . . . refers exclusively to the action or state described by the verb," identifying *Aktionsarten* as "aspectual distinctions expressed lexically." [112] Nonetheless she states, "*Aspect* refers to the way the internal temporal constituency of the situation is viewed." [113] She lists as aspectual categories *perfective, imperfective, habitual, continuous, iterative, incep-*

tive.[114] It is evident that for Bybee "aspect" includes both what we have been calling Aristotelian aspect and the *Aktionsarten*.

Freed assimilates the two for other reasons, characterizing aspect as a "time-ordering distinct from tense which deals with the internal temporal structuring, e.g. the relative duration, inception, and completion of verbal activities" and parts of those activities.[115] We view the *Aktionsarten* indeed as involving reference to parts of events—to phases or strings of phases.

Lyons is expressly critical of the usual distinction between "aspect" and "*Aktionsart*," because it is based sometimes on the distinction of grammatical and lexical, but sometimes on that of inflectional and derivational, neither of which is clear-cut.[116] Further, he objects to the narrowness of the term "action" in this context, and to the fact that the categorization properly pertains to the temporal entities denoted by the linguistic expressions, rather than to those expressions themselves.

To *Aktionsart* he prefers the term "aspectual character." But it is plain from his discussion that he means by this what we have been calling Aristotelian aspect, "verb aspect," and not *Aktionsart* in the traditional sense. A stative expression belongs to an Aristotelian category, an inchoative to a type of *Aktionsart*.

The broad definition of aspect not only allows both Aristotelian aspect and the *Aktionsarten* to be subsumed under aspect, but is also not incompatible with something like the Guillaumian treatment. The term "view" is sufficiently neutral to allow both objective and subjective interpretations. Further it can refer either to the point of view—from outside or from within—or to a specific characterization (e.g., dynamic, inceptive, of long duration).

There is nothing ipso facto wrong with allowing the term "aspect" the widest possible scope; the problem comes when we try to understand what it is that the speaker of a language with aspectual oppositions knows which a nonspeaker does not know, and consider how to model this knowledge in the grammar. Clearly, something more precise by way of definition of aspect is required, if the various confusions and contradictions to be found in the literature are to be avoided. A radically different approach to aspect is one taken, for example, by Johnson.[117] She gives a rather different treatment from the usual one in which "aspect . . . characterize[s] the narrated event itself . . . without reference to the speech event."[118] Calling an occurrence over a period of time an "episode," she states that aspectual distinctions "involve relations between episode-time[119] and reference-time"; that is, aspect involves E-R relations.[120] Her diagram may be repeated at this point.

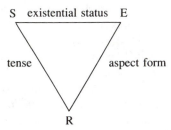

In Kikuyu there are three aspects, and these in fact accord closely with the three traditionally discussed: the progressive (similar to the imperfective), the completive (similar to the perfective), and the perfect.[121]

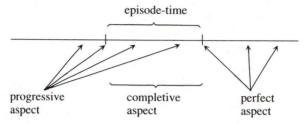

In the case of the Kikuyu progressive aspect, reference time may be included within episode time or may just precede it; in that of the completive aspect, reference time and episode time coincide; and in the case of the perfect, reference time can be any time later than the episode time.

According to the Johnsonian understanding of aspect, the aspects relate the actual occurrences (as a sequence of phases) to the reference time. Are the perfect and progressive to be considered aspects, then? They are, so long as we take non-overlap to be a relation. The perfect aspect designates the case in which the action is immediately prior to, but does not overlap with, the event frame. The progressive designates the case in which the action partly overlaps with the frame.

This returns us to the problem of adverbials. The Johnsonian definition does not quite work as it stands. "John was running" is normally interpreted as meaning that John's running fills the event frame. But of course that holds only for certain frames; for others like *during the party, sometime yesterday, ever in the past*, it means that the frame includes the event. It is not possible, therefore, to interpret the E-R relation in terms of a purely temporal sequence, as Reichenbach does with the relationships $E<R$, $R>E$, $E=R$, since for non-subinterval adverbials each of the first two of these relationships can be fulfilled in two ways:

$E<R$: (1) E terminates within R:
         That week, Tom had sailed into Rome.
     (2) E has no overlap with R:
         The previous week, Tom had sailed to Rome.
$R<E$: (1) E commences within R:
         That week, Tom was to sail for Rome.
     (2) E has no overlap with R:
         The next week, Tom was to sail to Rome.

We can rescue a more strictly Reichenbachian interpretation only by saying that in these cases the adverbial does not designate the event frame itself but rather a period of time *containing* the event frame. In that case, there can be only three relationships between E and R, namely $E<R$, $R<E$, and $R=E$ (though as Johnson's work shows, aspect is not so simple as that).

It is not necessarily incorrect to subsume the *Aktionsarten* as subcases of the Aristotelian categorization, as the latter denotes the phasic structure of whole events and the former, subsequences within them; we can trivially let the whole event count as the maximal sequence of phases.

But what about Freed's and Woisetschlaeger's subsuming aspect in the *Aktionsarten*? Potentially one could do so, in that the relation of the event to the reference time defines aspect; *Aktionsarten* can be viewed as the equivalent partial relation—the inceptive *Aktionsart* means that only the inceptive phase occurs in the reference frame. This treatment, however, confuses the ideal, potential structure of events with the actual. The *Aktionsarten*, like the Aristotelian categories, concern ideal (sub)sequences. *Finishing building a house*, like *building a house*, specifies a type of episode. Aspect, however, has to do with actual sequences. *Mr. Blandings was building his dream house* neither asserts nor implies, neither presupposes nor entails, that he built his dream house.

When we relate events to event frames we are relating event tokens, not event types, to frame tokens, not frame types. Thus from this point of view it makes no sense to say that imperfective aspect and inceptive *Aktionsart* are the same sort of thing, though the durative *Aktionsart is* the same sort of thing as the inceptive.

The traditional treatments of aspect as having to do with how the action or event is *viewed*, or how it *develops in time*, are apparently completely in opposition to Johnson's, in which aspect has to do solely with the relationship of reference time to event time. The latter is objective; the first, potentially subjective. The latter says nothing about the action itself, whereas the former may be based on the nature of the action.

The key to reconciling the Johnsonian and the traditional treatments is provided by the treatment of aspect by Chung and Timberlake, who define it as characterizing "the relationship of a predicate to the time interval over which it occurs." [122] This somewhat confused statement (*predicates* are not the sort of things which can *occur*) which is vague as well (what time interval? what sort of time interval?), nonetheless serves to reconcile Johnson's approach with that of Comrie and others as follows.

For Chung and Timberlake, "an event is simply whatever occurs (or could occur) at some time period under some set of conditions." [123] The time period in question during which the event occurs is called the "event frame." There is one privileged time, the "tense locus"; tense concerns "the nature of the relationship between the tense locus and the event frame." It is possible to equate the event frame with the reference time of Reichenbach, and the tense locus with speech-act time.

However, Chung and Timberlake explicitly refer to "the selection of the tense locus." Although many tense systems "give priority to the tense locus defined by the moment of speech," not all do.

> Typically no further context or adverbial specification is required to use the speech moment as tense locus, but some contextual specification—for example, deictic adverbial phrases of the type 'then', 'at that time', 'when'—is required to establish some other point as the tense locus. Tense systems (or subsystems) in which the speech moment serves as the tense locus are traditionally called absolute tense; systems (or subsystems) in which some other point is the tense locus are called relative tense.

True as far as it goes, this statement is misleading to the extent that it implies that relative tense is fundamentally different from absolute tense. The fact is, as

Prior points out and Allen assumes, the speech-act time is simply the *first* reference point. Even in absolute tense systems (e.g., those of the familiar Indo-European languages), the speech-act time is not as privileged as is usually thought. It plays a definitely subsidiary role under syntactic subordination, and phenomena such as historical tenses and free indirect discourse are sufficiently prominent as to call into question its uniqueness even in independent structures.

The important question is not whether the language assigns an assumed default value to the "tense locus," but how aspectual and temporal (tense) distinctions are marked. It is merely an assumption, which must ultimately receive confirmation, that events, reference times, and speech-act times are (linguistically) different kinds of times.

"Aspect characterizes the different relationships of a predicate to the event frame." Here Chung and Timberlake understand four parameters of characterization: dynamicity—whether there is change; closure—whether the event is bounded; iterativity—whether there is repetition; and durativity—whether the event is instantaneous or occurs over an interval of time. This has much in common with Bybee's treatment of aspect and accords with that side of the traditional treatment of aspect which subsumes the *Aktionsarten* under it.

But there is another way of interpreting the relation of event and frame. If in reference to the event frame "all during the party" (or "from 8:00 p.m. to midnight") we say *John was reading the book, Jean lisait le livre*, or *Ivan čital knigu*, we mean that "over a certain interval of time *I*—that designated by the adverbial—*John is reading* the book is true," we mean that the event (activity) of John's reading *fills* the event frame. If, in reference to the event frame "during the party" (or "last night"), we say *John had read the book, Jean avait lu le livre*, or *Ivan pročital knigu*,[124] we mean that "within a certain interval of time *I*—that designated by the adverbial—*John reads the book* is true." We mean that the event (activity) of John's reading *occurs within* the event frame.

In traditional terms, we can understand the past imperfective here as giving a view of the action as ongoing *over* the frame, while the perfective indicates that the action occurs *within* the frame. This seems a possible translation into the terms of Chung and Timberlake of the traditional notion of the imperfective as looking at the action from within, as a development *over* time, and of the perfective as an external view, as a single locus *in* time. But it is possible to understand this in Johnsonian terms as the topological relationship of event time to reference time (event frame). There thus need be no profound contradiction between Comrie's definition of aspect and Johnson's.

One point in regard to the above needs to be made. It is at best misleading and confusing to say (a) *all during the party John read the book*, if we mean (b) *all during the party, John was reading the book*. Contrast: (c) *during the party, John read the book*; (d) *during the party John was reading the book*. (This last, [d], has a reading like [b], but let us ignore it here.) Now the adverbial *all during* . . . requires that the event fill the event frame, and that the subinterval property hold, and thus (b) is acceptable. But while (a) fills the frame, in the accomplishment reading the subinterval property does not hold: (a) is acceptable only in an activity sense.

But the adverbial *during* . . . not only does not require the event to fill the frame (but merely to be contained within it), but also does not require the subinterval property, so that both achievements and accomplishments are allowed. Thus (c) can mean that sometime at or after the commencement of the party John began to read the book and finished at or before the termination of the party, and (d) can mean that John was engaged in reading over some time within that occupied by the party, though he may or may not have started or stopped reading during the frame time.

Thus the interpretation of the relationship of the event to the event frame depends not only on the nature of the situations denoted by the event and frame verbal expressions, but on the nature of the adverbial as well. Or to put it another way, more than strict relationships of temporal precedence are involved in determining how a situation (such as John's having read a book during the party) are to be expressed. This is a facet of aspect which we have neglected up to now, but which has loomed large in recent literature on aspect; it will be discussed in chapter 8.

In summary, the Aristotelian categorization represents a classification of situations (and the linguistic expressions denoting these) in terms of abstract phasic structures. The *Aktionsarten* represent rather a classification of (expressions for) phases of situations and subsituations. But aspect proper is a distinction having to do with the relationship of a situation to the temporal frame against which it is set; it does not classify types of occurrences.

The principal task of the student of aspect is to create a general theory which makes predictions as to possible aspects, *Aktionsarten*, and Aristotelian types, as well as possible combinations of these. Johnson attempts to provide a theory of possible aspect within the Reichenbachian tradition, and Woisetschlaeger a theory of possible *Aktionsarten* essentially in terms of phasic structures; the Aristotelian classes can be defined in terms of phase as well. But we are far from a fully explanatory account of why just those categories are utilized in languages which actually exist, and the interactions of the three systems have yet to be systematically explored.

Within the grammar (special theory) of each language there must be a statement of the distinctions of aspect, *Aktionsart*, and Aristotelian aspect actually made by the language, and how these are marked. This task too is just beginning to be fulfilled. No complete aspectual description of any language exists. Nor does current aspectological theory provide an adequate theoretical base for such description.

As regards the universality of aspectual systems, there are initially several possibilities. There may be a universal set of possible categories from which languages pick and choose. There may be implicational universals—in effect, tendencies: if a language does such and such, then it is likely to act thus. Or it may be that there are a small, discrete set of categories, so that aspect may be "parameterized": there may be only a small number of ways in which aspectual systems may differ, and in general they might be essentially the same.

One of the difficulties with discussing these issues as we have been is the lack of a sound foundation in an objective semantic theory. Just as an understanding of tense requires the more sophisticated structural and semantic tools of modern linguistics, and could not adequately be undertaken before the present century, given the naive view of language held, it is plain that informal consideration of aspect can only delineate the problems. To solve them, more powerful tools are needed. These tools students of aspect have found only in the realm of formal logic. The formal semantics of tense and aspect is discussed in the next chapter.

7

Formal Semantics
of Tense and Aspect

a. Theories of Semantics

The problem with much earlier research into tense and aspect is the lack of any objective theory against which the ideas of individual theorists can be judged. What König has to say regarding the literature on the English progressive can well be extended to all the earlier discussion on tense and aspect: "The most serious shortcoming of the older analyses is that they have not been made precise to such a degree that they are falsifiable."[1] An adequate semantic theory of tense and aspect must be an objective and explicit semantics.

Semantics starts with the natural assumption that, as language can be used to communicate about the world, it must somehow be grounded in the world. It is the goal of a general theory of meaning to tell us how that is, and to answer such fundamental questions as: what is meaning? what are meanings? how do linguistic expressions (such as words, phrases, sentences) mean?

Most recent scholarship on the semantics of natural languages has been conducted within the framework of a *referential* semantics—one in which meaning is principally identified with referring, and the meaning of a linguistic expression with its relationship to the thing it refers to, its "referent." In this view, language is grounded in the world through its referring to the world; linguistic expressions have meaning insofar as they "stand for" aspects of the world: *Henry VII* stands for Henry VII, *John loves Mary* stands for John's loving Mary. Meanings are referential relationships holding between linguistic expressions and parts of the world.

This is not the only possible framework for semantics. Other frameworks which have been developed include *ideational* and *functional* semantics, both of which are, on the whole, considerably more intuitively satisfying than the referential type of theories, though all three frameworks have particular advantages and disadvantages.[2]

215

For a certain class of linguistic expressions, the characterization of meaning as reference (referring) is quite straightforward. Names are entirely arbitrary and have no "meaning" beyond the fact that they refer to, "stand for," things: *New York* quite simply stands for New York, as *Einstein* stands for Einstein. Descriptive phrases, especially definite ones (*the man I met last week in Rome*) likewise are naturally taken to refer to individual entities, or sets of such entities (e.g., *the citizens of Ontario*), in the world.

But many types of expressions lack any referent. For example, *nobody* does not name "nobody," and when Ulysses tells the Cyclops that his name is Nobody (Latin *Nemo*), he is simply playing on the giant's stupidity.[3] Nor do expressions such as verbs, adverbs, and conjunctions seem to refer to anything.

Ideational theories of meaning proceed from the intuition, already set forth in Aristotle's *On Interpretation*, that our ideas mirror the world and our words express those ideas.[4] *Nobody* expresses the idea of nobody-ness or the lack of any-body; a verb like *go* expresses the idea of going; and the sentence *John loves Mary* expresses the idea of John's loving Mary.

There are two principal problems with ideational theories. First, the concept of "idea" is as vague and mysterious as the idea of "meaning," so that it is difficult to see how an explanatory theory of meaning can be based upon it. Second, it is unclear what it means for an expression to "express" an idea, and likewise what it means for an idea to "mirror" reality. (It is, however, relatively clear what it means for *New York* to "stand for" New York.) An ideational theory of meaning has struck many observers as begging the question of how expressions mean.

Furthermore, while the meanings of expressions seem impersonal and public and in some sense objective, ideas are highly personal and private, very subjective. My idea of a dog may considerably differ from yours, yet most speakers of English would generally agree on the meaning of the word *dog*. It does not seem to differ from person to person in the way that ideas of doghood do.

Functional theories are quite diverse in character, and varieties of them have been called "behavioral," "operational," "use," and "speech-act" theories of meaning. What they have in common is an attempt to explicate the meanings of linguistic expressions in terms of their uses, especially in the case of expressions, such as imperative sentences (*go!*), which seem not to be used to refer to things or to express ideas, but rather to get things done—as the philosopher J. L. Austin put it, "to do things with words." Whereas referential and ideational theories of semantics view the uses of expressions as depending on their meanings, functional theories either identify meanings with uses or view meanings as depending on uses.

There is no doubt that the uses to which an expression can be put are closely related to its meaning. A definite descriptive expression of the form "the *x*," for example, can be used to refer to an individual: *the paternal grandfather of Queen Elizabeth I* refers to King Henry VII of England. A verb cannot be used in that way. On the other hand a verb, or a verb phrase (like *rode horses*), can be used as a predicate (*the grandfather of Queen Elizabeth I rode horses*), whereas a definite expression can be so used only with a copular verb (*Henry VII was the paternal grandfather of Queen Elizabeth I*), and an adverbial expression (e.g., *into the house*) cannot be so used at all.

Declarative sentences (e.g., *New York is large*) are typically true or false and function to assert things. In an ideational theory, a declarative sentence can be taken as expressing the idea of a situation: *New York is large* expresses the idea of New York's being large. But interrogative sentences (*is New York large?*) and imperative ones (*be quiet!*) are not used to convey information and do not, except coincidentally, express ideas. Rather, an interrogative sentence is used to elicit information, and an imperative to elicit an action. In functional theories of meaning the meaning of a sentence is either taken to be its set of possible uses, or is directly related to its uses, as for instance the set of contexts in which it could appropriately be used.

Referential theories obviously make considerable sense for referential expressions such as names; ideational ones seem appropriate for declarative sentences and other apparently non-referential expressions which nonetheless are meaningful by dint of expressing ideas; and functional theories seem valid for expressions which are useful rather than meaningful per se.

Is there no way of capturing all three kinds of meaning in one type of theory? As it happens, to date no one has been entirely successful in doing so. Nonetheless, many scholars believe that an adequate theory is not only possible within a referential framework, but possible *only* within that type of framework.

Whether ultimately this is correct remains to be seen, but we will assume such a framework here, because the vast preponderance of serious work on the semantics of tense and aspect has been done from a referential point of view. In recent years the leading theory in this area (and the one which in consequence we will most refer to here) is that known as *Montague semantics*, after the logician Richard Montague.[5]

b. Referential Semantics

The initial problem with referential semantics is that, apart from names (*New York, Einstein*) and descriptive terms (*the largest city in the United States*), linguistic expressions do not obviously "stand for" things. Even if sentences such as *John loves Jane* were taken to refer to things such as John's loving Jane, it would be unclear what sorts of "thing" these are. Is John's loving Jane an idea? a fact? a proposition? a situation? Furthermore, it still would be unclear what kind of meanings should be assigned to other types of expressions, such as verb phrases and adverbs.

A widely accepted solution to this problem is to regard sentences as having as referents *truth values*—either "true" (usually symbolized T or 1) or "false"(F or 0). This rather strange result, first proposed by the philosopher Gottlob Frege in the late nineteenth century, is a consequence of *Leibniz's Law*, or the *Substitutivity of Identicals*, discovered by the seventeenth-century philosopher G. W. Leibniz.[6]

Leibniz's Law says that expressions referring to the same individual object can be substituted for each other *salva veritate*, that is, without affecting the truth value of sentences containing them. This follows from the way in which expressions contribute to the truth values of sentences. It should be obvious that substituting the description *the first President of the United States* for the coreferential name *George Washington* generally has no affect on the truth value of a sentence containing the latter expression: if *George Washington was a Virginian* is true, then *the first president of the United States was a Virginian* must be true as well.

This principle allows us to assign a referent to declarative sentences. If for a given expression S_1, which is a sentence (say, *Tom is tall*) within a larger sentence S (*it's not true that Tom is tall*), we substitute another expression S_2 which is a sentence and which is coreferential to (refers to the same thing as) S_1, then by Leibniz's Law the truth of the larger sentence S is preserved: it has the same truth value with S_2 as with S_1.

But under what conditions, in general, is the truth value preserved, when we replace one declarative sentence by another? Obviously only when the two sentences have the same truth value. If we substitute *New York is large* for *Tom is tall* in *it is not true that Tom is tall*, the truth value of the containing (*matrix*) sentence will be preserved if, and only if, *New York is large* has the same truth value as the included (*constituent*) sentence *Tom is tall*. By Leibniz's Law, the referent of a sentence can only be a truth value.[7]

If naming expressions have as referents individuals (or, in the case of plural and certain other nouns, sets of individuals), and declarative sentences have truth values, what can the referents of other types of expressions such as verb phrases and adverbs be, and how is the meaning of an expression dependent on those of its constituent parts, given that the different kinds of expressions have different kinds of meanings?

This latter problem arises from the generally accepted principle (the *Principle of Compositionality*) which states that the meaning of an expression is a function of (is dependent on) the meanings of its constituent parts, along with their mode of composition—how they are put together to form the matrix expression (i.e., it depends on the internal syntax of the matrix expression). It is clear that language could hardly be used to communicate with, if this were not the case. This principle is usually attributed to Frege as *Frege's Principle*, though it is not entirely clear if he actually stated it: several authors have reported being unable to find any statement of precisely this principle in Frege's writings.[8]

If the meaning (*semantic value*) of a simple sentence such as *John loves Jane* is a truth value (T or F), and that of the subject phrase *John* is the individual, John, who is referred to, then how can the predicate phrase *loves Jane* contribute to the meaning of the sentence? Here we must consider under what conditions *John loves Jane* is true. It is true if John does indeed love Jane, of course. Another way of putting this is that John belongs to the set of those who love Jane. From this point of view, *loves Jane* designates a set of individuals—all those who love Jane; then *John loves Jane* is true if, and only if (this cumbersome phrase is normally abbreviated as ''iff''), John belongs to that set.

More generally, a simple sentence of subject-predicate form is true iff the individual (or individuals) designated by the subject phrase belongs (belong) to the set designated by the predicate phrase. But this still does not tell us how the predicate phrase can contribute to the semantic value—the truth value—of the sentence, if it refers to a set. The assignment of a set of entities as the referent of a predicate phrase satisfies Frege's understanding that meanings, and hence referents, are objective—things—and not subjective—ideas or concepts. But it fails to explicate semantic compositionality, since sets and individual entities are radically different things from truth values. Yet adding a predicate phrase such as *loves Jane* to a referring expression such as *John* results in a linguistic expression—a sentence such as *John loves Jane*—which has a truth value as its referent.

There is a kind of thing which can act as intermediary, transforming individuals into truth values, a thing which can take something in—its *argument*—and put something out—its *value* for that argument. This thing is a *function*. Functions are consequently the obvious candidates for the referents of predicate phrases. In this case, we would be taking the term "function" in Frege's Principle literally.

Admittedly, functions are "things" only in an abstract sense, but then so are truth values (and indeed sets, since the set of all people who love Jane is obviously something apart from, and different in kind from, each of the individuals in that set). The only requirement for referents in semantic theory is that they be fully and objectively specifiable, not that they "exist" in the common-sense understanding of existence. A function can be thought of as an abstract machine taking in arguments and putting out values, or as a table which contains a list of arguments with a corresponding value opposite each argument.

In fact, the function is technically defined as a set of ordered pairs. A very brief excursus on sets for those unfamiliar with set theory might be useful here. A *set* is any arbitrary collection of things—we can speak, for example, of the set consisting of George Washington, the number 4, and the Empire State Building. Sets are often given arbitrary capital letters as names, and the membership of the set in question is specified by listing its members within curved brackets; for example, let us call the set mentioned above A, and say that A = {George Washington, 4, the Empire State Building}. A set is fully specified by such a listing. The order of the list does not matter; A = {George Washington, 4, the Empire State Building} = {4, George Washington, the Empire State Building}, and so forth.

Usually, however, sets are coherent, and membership in a set is definable other than by listing. In this case we specify membership as follows: W = {x:x>1}. This says that the set W has as members those things (i.e., numbers) which are greater than 1; its members could *not* in fact be listed. A set whose members would be difficult though possible to list is C = {x:x is a Chinese waiter}.

When all the members of one set A are also members of a second set B, we say that A is a *subset* of B, which is symbolized thus: A⊆B or B⊇A. If A⊆B and A⊇B, then clearly A=B, that is, they are identical (the same set, with two different names). If A⊆B, but B⊄A (A is a subset of B, but B is *not* a subset of A, that is, B is not identical to A), then we call A a *proper subset* of B. (Clearly A⊆B means "A is a proper subset of, or is identical with, B.") The set of things which belong to both A and B is called the *intersection* of A and B and is written: A ∩ B; the set of things which belong either to A or to B is called the *union* of A and B and is written A ∪ B. Clearly (A ∩ B) ⊆ (A ∪ B).

A special set which is a subset of all other sets is the *null* set, symbolized by zero (0) or the upper-case Greek letter lambda: Λ. This set has no members. Since sets are defined by membership, there can be only *one* null set. It is easy to show that the null set is a subset of all other sets—the union of any set S and some subset of S is clearly S. But S ∪ 0 = S; therefore 0⊆S, for any S whatever.

We indicate membership with the lower-case Greek letter epsilon: if N is the set of counting numbers, 4 ε N. But the set {4} consisting just of 4 is not a counting number and hence not a member of N: {4} ɇ N. There are some paradoxes connected with the notion of sets being members of other sets (is the set of all sets not members of themselves a member of itself?), but for present purposes we can ignore these and allow sets unrestrictedly to be members of other sets. For example, let F be the set {4} and L be the set of all sets whose members are counting numbers; clearly F ε L.

Sometimes it does matter what order the members of a set occur in. In this case we speak of an *ordered* set; the member are listed in angle (or round) brackets. Thus ⟨Oregon, Alaska⟩ is *not* the same set as ⟨Alaska, Oregon⟩. An ordered set with *n* members is normally called an *n*-tuple, though there are special names for some *n*-tuples; for example, a 2-tuple is known as a *pair*, a 3-tuple a *triple*, a 4-tuple a *quadruple*, and so on.

A set of pairs is called a *relation*; we can use relations to model relationships. For example, the relationship of fatherhood pairs individuals. If Joe is Sheila's father, ⟨Sheila, Joe⟩ (read "Joe is paired with Sheila") will be a member of the relation "is the father of"; ⟨Sheila, Joe⟩ means then that "Joe is Sheila's father."

Notice that not everything in the world will be on the left-hand side of one of these pairs. It makes no sense to ask who is the father of the number 4. Nor will everything in the world be on the right-hand side—4 is nobody's father either. The set of possible right-hand members is called the *range* of the relation (the set of things which the right-hand members of the pairs in the relation can "range" over), and the set of possible left-hand members is called its *domain* (the set of things the left-hand members of the pairs in the relation can range over). These terms are more intuitively obvious in connection, however, with the special kind of relation known as the *function*.

Functions are relations in which no item appears more than once as the left-hand member of a pair. Genetic fatherhood is a function, because each child will appear only once—Sheila has only one genetic father, after all. But fatherhood in a broad sense as ordinarily understood is a relation, though not a function; if Joe is Sheila's natural father but she has been adopted by Carl, then both ⟨Sheila, Joe⟩ and ⟨Sheila, Carl⟩ appear in the "is the father of" relation—she has no one, unique father. (Note that functions, like relations, are sets: "is the father of" = {⟨x,y⟩:y is the father of x}.)

In the case of functions, the domain comprises the set of possible arguments the functions takes, and the range comprises its set of possible values. We say that a function is a function *from* members of its domain *to* members of its range. "Is the genetic father of" is a function from people (or animals) to people (or animals). We say that a function *maps* its domain *into* its range. Thus the "is the capital of" function maps countries into cities. If, in addition, every member of the range is on the right-hand side of some pair which is a member of the function, we say it is a function *from* the domain *onto* the range—it *maps* the domain onto the *range*. Thus the function "is identical with" maps the universal set having as members everything (symbolized 1 or U) onto itself.

A function like the identity function which maps a set A into A (the domain and the range are the same set) is called an *operation*. Many mathematical functions are obviously operations (e.g., "is twice"), but so are others (e.g., "is the coworker of"). The marker or name of a function is called a *functor*, and that of an operation an *operator*. The square root sign is a familiar operator, as are the negators in natural languages, as for instance *not*.

Functions are most familiar in mathematics: *x is the immediate successor of y* is a function. We can think of this function as a list of all the ordinary counting numbers, with the number immediately following it paired with each. One entry might read: $\langle 2, 3 \rangle$, read "3 is the immediate successor of 2." Here the function is "applied to" the *argument* 2 and "returns" the *value* 3 for that argument. Similarly, the squaring function, x^2, contains the entry $\langle 4, 16 \rangle$—applied to the argument 4, it returns the value 16: 16 *is the square of* 4.

Functions need not be mathematical in this sense, of course. For example, *x is the head of state of y* is a function whose domain consists of countries and whose range consists of humans. One member of this function might be $\langle$Canada, Queen Elizabeth II$\rangle$, read: "Queen Elizabeth II is the head of state of Canada." It may be helpful to conceptualize functions in this way as tables of correspondences, or machines which transform arguments into, or exchange them for, values—although, as we have noted, technically functions are simply sets of pairs.

But, getting back to predicates, how can a predicate phrase refer to a function—a set of pairs—when it refers to a set of individuals? We want the semantic value of a predicate phrase to be a function from individuals (or sets of individuals, in the case of plural nouns) to truth values. But the contributions that predicate phrases make to the meanings of their simple sentences seem related to the fact that they refer to sets of individuals, so that a simple sentence of subject-predicate form *s P* will be true if and only if the referent of *s* is a member of that of *P*. Here there is a neat little trick we use to reconcile these different interpretations of the predicate phrase—we interpret the set as its *characteristic function*.

The characteristic function of some set S is that function C_S which has as its domain the members of S and as its range the truth values. It is precisely a function from individuals to truth values, and just what we need in order to mediate between the referents of subject phrases and those of simple (subject-predicate) declarative sentences.

If the referent (semantic value) of a sentence is a truth value; if that of a name or definite descriptive phrase is an individual; and if that of a predicate phrase is a characteristic function from individuals to truth values, then we can easily see how the meaning of a simple sentence depends on (is literally a function of) that

of its constituent parts. For example, let *loves Jane* denote the characteristic function of the set of all persons who love Jane, and let *John* denote John. The semantic value of the sentence *John loves Jane* will be T (true) just in case ⟨John,T⟩
is a member of the function denoted by *loves Jane*, that is, iff *loves Jane*(John) = T
(applied to the argument John, *loves Jane* returns the value T).

In the case of negation, however, we have a different type of function, known
as a *truth table*. (Negation is in fact an operation, since it is a function from truth
values to truth values. A negator like *not*, as we have noted, is an operator.) If
the semantic value of a sentence (say *John loves Jane*) is T, then that of its
negation (*John does not love Jane*) is F, and vice versa. The function denoted by
the negator thus has only two members, ⟨T,F⟩ and ⟨F,T⟩—the negation of a true
sentence is false and that of a false sentence true.

The appropriate referent for a coordinating conjunction such as *and* or *or* (when
these are used with sentences), or *but*, is a function from a *pair* of truth values to
a truth value. These *connectives* are said to be *truth-functional* because the semantic value—the truth value—of a compound sentence built with their help depends
solely on the truth values of the constituent sentences. A sentence of the form X
and Y is true iff X and Y are both true, and is false otherwise; one of the form X
or Y is true iff at least one of X and Y is true, and false otherwise. (Some
linguists treat *or* as ambiguous: either *inclusive or*, true iff at least one of the
conjunct constituent sentences is true, or *exclusive or*, true iff precisely one of
the conjuncts is true.)

The subordinating conjunctions are, however, not truth-functional: neither sentences of the form X *because* Y nor X *before* Y can be assigned truth values
simply on the basis of the truth of X or Y. Nonetheless, a subordinating conjunction can also be regarded as denoting a function, although one with an infinite
number of members: added to a pair of expressions having truth values as referents (e.g., *Napoleon was sent into exile* and *all Europe was in fear of him*), it
forms an expression which has a truth value as its referent (e.g., *Napoleon was
sent into exile because all Europe was in fear of him*).

In fact, functions of one kind or another provide precisely the kind of object
which seems to fill the bill for referents of *all* kinds of expressions other than
ordinary referring expressions (names and definite descriptions) and sentences.
One tack taken in contemporary referential theories of meaning is to treat essentially all meanings, that is, referents (with the possible exceptions of the truth
values of sentences and the referents of ordinary referring expressions), as functions. The literal interpretation of "function" in Frege's Principle allows us to
construct referents for every kind of apparently non-referring expressions, while
explicating the role of such expressions in Fregean compositionality.

All this, while initially strange, is in fact ultimately satisfying. If a linguistic
expression (say a declarative sentence) "refers" to a semantic value (say a truth
value), and that linguistic expression consists of a set of constituent linguistic
expressions (say a subject phrase and a predicate phrase), then the semantic values
of those constituent expressions (say, respectively, an individual and a characteristic function from individuals to truth values) must, by Fregean compositionality,

be such as to yield the value of the matrix expression (as these assignments of referents do).

Intransitive verbs are like predicate phrases (e.g., *loves Jane*) in designating characteristic functions. For example, *runs* is the functor of the characteristic function of the set of all those who run. *John runs* will be true iff ⟨John, T⟩ is a member of the function *runs*, that is, if John belongs to the set of those who run.

But what about the predicate phrase *runs quickly*? How does the meaning of the adverb *quickly* contribute to the meaning of the phrase *runs quickly*? Adding adverbials—*runs quickly, runs all day, runs just for fun*—to a verb (or verb phrase, built on a verb) alters the set referred to and hence the characteristic function in question—the set of those who run quickly is a subset of all those who run—but the resultant expressions are still verb phrases (predicate phrases) and continue to designate characteristic functions. Clearly then, adverbials must denote something which takes expressions (*runs*) designating functions and creates expressions (*runs quickly*) also designating functions—they must denote functions from (characteristic) functions to (characteristic) functions!

Let R be the function denoted by *runs*. Now, let *quickly* be a function Q such as we have described. Suppose ⟨R,R$_Q$⟩ is a member of the function *quickly* (Q). Now, R$_Q$ is the function *runs quickly*. We don't know what function that really is, but then we don't care. All we care about is, for example, that *John runs quickly* will be true iff ⟨John,T⟩ is a member of this R$_Q$.

Similarly, transitive verbs like *loves* must denote functions from individuals to characteristic functions, since when added to noun phrases—at least to names and descriptive phrases—they yield expressions which denote characteristic functions of sets (e.g., *loves Jane*).

Treating the meaning of all expressions—except ones naming individuals (*Henry VII*), and sentences—as functions allows us not only to assign referents as meanings to expressions which are apparently non-referential, but incidentally to explicate Fregean compositionality, to show precisely how the meanings of expressions can depend on those of their immediate constituent expressions.

The function is a logical object and is in theory constructible from the world. The question is, where precisely do the functions come from? How do we construct them? In ideational terms, we have a very good idea about what *rode horses* means, but where does the function to which (in Fregean theory) *rode horses* refers come from? Obviously it comes from the fact that some individuals rode horses and others did not; it is constructible, at least in theory, from the facts of the world.

This seems to create, however, the difficulty that our semantic theory must concern itself with the facts of the world. But we really do not need to know whether John loves Jane to know that *John loves Jane* is meaningful, and indeed *what* it means. Nor do we need to know whether John runs quickly or Joe is Sheila's father in order to understand the sentence *John runs quickly*, the phrase *is Sheila's father*, or the words *quickly, runs,* and *father*. This seems to be an important difficulty with the kind of referential semantics we have been developing here.

c. Formal, Truth-Conditional Semantics

To know that the sentence *Henry VII rode horses* is meaningful, and to know what it means, obviously do not require that we know *whether* it is true. Yet we have assigned as the semantic value—the meaning, and in a referential theory of meaning, the referent—of the sentence a truth value: T or F.

Further, we have assigned as the semantic value of the predicate expression *rode horses* the set R of all those who rode horses, or alternatively the characteristic function, C_R, of that set. But to know that the verb phrase *rode horses* is meaningful, that it can serve as a predicate phrase, and what it means, obviously does not require that we know for any particular entity, such as Henry VII, what value this function C_R would return when applied to it, nor does it require that we know the membership of R.

In fact we do not state any such absurd requirements as these on semantic theories. It is not for linguistics to tell us whether it is true that Henry VII rode horses. But it *is* for linguistics to predict, given the lexicon, the grammar, and the semantics of English, that the sentence *Henry VII rode horses* will be true iff in fact Henry VII *did* ride horses—or more generally, that a simple declarative sentence of subject-predicate form is true iff the referent of the subject phrase is a member of the referent of the predicate phrase, or alternatively, that $\langle s,T \rangle$ is a member of the characteristic function C_P for the set denoted by the predicate phrase, where *s* denotes the entity denoted by the subject phrase.

In fact, the familiar referential semantic theories belong to *truth-conditional semantics*. We identify the meaning of a linguistic expression either with the conditions under which it would be true (as in the case of sentences), or with its contribution to those conditions for the sentence containing it. Since the pioneering work of the logician Alfred Tarski, it has been the goal of truth-conditional semantics to predict for any given (declarative) sentence under what conditions it would be true—its *truth conditions*.[9]

The semantic interpretation of sentences—the provision of truth conditions for them—is *recursive* and *formal*. It is recursive in that the semantic interpretation of a sentence depends on those of its constituent parts. To know under what conditions *Henry VII rode horses* would be true, we must first know to whom or what *Henry VII* refers and to what set (function) *rode horses* refers, and so on down to the level of words. The process of semantic interpretation then must start with the words and build outward until the sentence as a whole is reached; the rules of semantic interpretation must be applied over and over again (they are *recursive*), starting with applications on the level of the word and ending with an application on the level of the sentence as a whole.

The process is *formal*, and hence our semantics is formal. Ultimately we are not interested in having an infinite number of particular semantic rules such as "*Henry VII rode horses* is true iff Henry VII rode horses"; rather, we want rules that are concerned solely with the *form* of expressions, as for instance, *a sentence of subject-predicate form is true iff the entity denoted by the subject belongs to the set denoted by the predicate.*

This rule is formal in the sense that it says nothing about the meaning or content of the sentence in question, but only about its form. We do not need to know what "mome raths" are or what "outgrabe" means to know under what conditions the sentence *mome raths outgrabe* would be true; assuming the sentence is a well-formed English sentence with the same subject-predicate form as *Henry VII rode horses* or *New York is the largest city in the United States*, we automatically know that it is true iff the property expressed by "outgrabe" is true of the individuals called "mome raths." A semantic theory must be formal in just this sense: it must disregard the actual contents of expressions and regard only their forms.[10]

We cannot know what function—what set of pairs—*rode horses* denotes, nor do we need to know it in order to know that *rode* is meaningful, and what it means. But in this case we cannot simply assert conditions under which an expression is true—truth conditions—as we did in the case of sentences. All we can say is that the function denoted by this verb contributes in a particular way to the meaning of larger phrases such as *rode horses*, and hence to the truth values of sentences containing the function in question.

This is a perfectly sensible, albeit rather structuralist, way of viewing the meaning of expressions. But it is not very satisfying, for we intuit that in knowing *what* a word means, we know more than just what entity or set of entities it denotes, or how it contributes to indicating the membership in a set denoted by a matrix expression containing it. It would seem that nothing less is required than the idea or concept. For in order, in the end, to know whether John does love Jane, or Henry VII did ride horses, we cannot escape circularity unless we have some idea, prior to any notion of set membership, of what sort of thing loving or riding horses is. Then and only then can we see if in fact John loves Jane or Henry VII rode horses. How then can we escape ideational semantics or retain Frege's dictum that meanings are objective and public?

That sentences have truth values as their referents is a counterintuitive result; truth values don't normally seem like the sorts of things that could be referents or meanings, and more important, according to this theory all true sentences *mean* the same thing (as do all false ones)! Frege certainly recognized that there was another way in which sentences could "mean," and indeed mean different things from other sentences with the same truth value—that they each have a distinct *sense*.

The difference between sense (German *Sinn*) and reference (*Bedeutung* in Frege's terminology) was noted long before Frege. Some such distinction was called that of *comprehension* and *extension* by the seventeenth-century Port Royal philosopher-logician Antoine Arnauld; *intension* and *extension* by the nineteenth-century Scottish logician William Hamilton; *connotation* and *denotation* by J. S. Mill; and *depth* and *breadth* by C. S. Peirce.[11]

When we say that we know what the sentence *Henry VII rode horses* means, we ordinarily mean that we know under what conditions it is true. Under certain conditions it is true, under others false. Let us suppose that, as things are, it is true. But had things been different (Henry VII could have lost both legs in an accident at age four), it might have been false. The referent—the extension—of the sentence changes from one set of conditions to another, but the sense, the intension, remains the same.

We often talk about the real world, but we also speculate about how things might have been or might yet be. If Elizabeth I had married and had children, the sentence *James I was Elizabeth I's successor* might now be false. Truth values then depend on how things are—in the real world this sentence is true, but there is at least some set of circumstances under which it would be false. The term we use for a set of circumstances is *world*, and sentences are always evaluated against some particular world. (In the world of comic books, mice and ducks speak, wear clothing, etc. That doesn't happen in the real world.)

All kinds of expressions, not just sentences, will have both extensions and intensions. Consider the sentence *the paternal grandfather of Elizabeth I rode horses*. The fact is that this sentence depends for its truth value on more than we have said; it depends, for example, on who the paternal grandfather of Elizabeth I was. As it happens, that was Henry VII. But the sense of the sentence does not depend on the contingencies of real world history; nor does the sense of the expression *the paternal grandfather of Elizabeth I*. This expression would still have precisely the same meaning—same intension—even if it turned out tomorrow that the paternal grandfather of Elizabeth I had been someone other than Henry VII. But in that case the extension of the expression would have changed.

We have been interpreting the name Henry VII as referring to the grandfather of Queen Elizabeth I of England, but there have been other Henry VIIs, for example a fourteenth-century German king. (The plot of Pirandello's play *Henry IV* turns on the confusion between two kings of that name.) The one Henry VII may well have ridden horses while the other did not. The truth of the sentence *Henry VII rode horses* depends on who "Henry VII" was. But the sense of the sentence does not. This is perhaps more clearly seen in the case of descriptive terms: we can apprehend the sense of *the twelfth president of the United States*, even if we do not know to whom this description refers.

The truth values of sentences containing ordinary referring expressions depend on the interpretations we place on those expressions. The truth of a sentence then is *relative to an interpretation*, that is, an assignment of extensions to expressions. Under some assignment of referents to terms (referring expressions), a sentence will be true: if "Henry VII" refers to Elizabeth's grandfather, *Henry VII was the father of Elizabeth I's father* is true; if it refers to that fourteenth-century king, it is false.

The assignment of referents to expressions may also vary over time. The set of people who have ever ridden horses is changing all the time. Consequently, the truth values of sentences containing expressions referring to horse riding are constantly changing. For example, suppose that Henry VII never rode a horse till he was ten years old. Uttered when Henry was nine, the sentence *Henry VII has ridden horses* would be false, but uttered when he was eleven, it would be true. At the time Henry VII is nine, the referent of the sentence is F; at the time he is ten, it is T.

Even names may have different referents at different times. Traditional logic recognizes that definite expressions like *the president of the United States* and *the king of England* have different referents at different times. Thus *George Bush is the president of the United States* is true only during that period of time during which George Bush is president of the United States, and is false either before or after it. There are names that work the same way. *Miss Canada* denotes a different individual each year.

There are, however, sentences that seemingly are indifferent to the extension of such expressions. *Miss Canada gets to wear a crown* is true no matter who Miss Canada happens to be, and *the president of the United States is the commander-in-chief of the American armed forces* is likewise true whether George Bush is the American president or not. Expressions of this type are said to have *de re* readings when they are used referentially (*de re* means 'of a thing'), and the truth of sentences containing them depends on their referent. They are said to have *de dicto* readings (*de dicto* means 'of something said') when they are used to say something about whoever or whatever happens to be referred to by them—when their "sense," not their reference, is in question.

Thus *John wants to marry a Swede* is ambiguous. If *a Swede* has its *de re* reading, John has a specific person in mind who just happens to be Swedish; he might not even know that person's nationality. If it has its *de dicto* reading, he has no specific person in mind but intends that whoever he marries be Swedish.

Thus every kind of expression will receive a referent depending on three things— the time of evaluation, the world relative to which the expression is evaluated, and a presupposed assignment of interpretations. To know whether the sentence *Ronald Reagan is president of the United States* is true, we must know three things: (1) whether "Ronald Reagan" refers to the ex-actor husband of Nancy Reagan or some other person of the same name, and whether "United States" refers to the USA and not, say, some other country calling itself "the United States" (e.g., Mexico, officially Los Estados Unidos Mexicanos, 'the United States of Mexico'); (2) when the sentence is evaluated (in 1975? 1990? 2001?); and (3) what world we are talking about—the real world, the world of a comic book in which Donald Duck was elected president in 1984, or some other.

But the expressions *president of the United States* and *is president of the United States* likewise require to be evaluated relative to these things—time, reference, and assignment of interpretations. What about names? There is a philosophical controversy about whether names are constant or likewise require these three terms of reference (a set of such parameters is called an *index*). To simplify matters here we will assume that *all* linguistic expressions are evaluated in the same way.

So far, Fregean compositionality concerns only the referents of expressions. We have seen that the contribution which a sentence makes to the truth of compound sentences containing it sometimes depends solely on its truth value. "A and B" will be true iff A is true and B is true. But there are contexts in which the truth of the larger sentence does not depend on the referent (the truth value) of the sentence but rather on its sense.

In such contexts, Leibniz's Law fails. Consider *John believes that Jane loves Bill*. From the fact that Jane loves Bill we cannot draw any conclusions as to whether it is true that John believes this; he may or may not. Moreover, even if it were true that John believes that Jane loves Bill, substitution of a coreferential sentence (one having the same truth value) does not guarantee preservation of the truth value of the larger sentence: John might very well believe that Jane loves

Bill, but might not happen to believe that Henry VII was the grandfather of Queen Elizabeth I of England, even though the referent of both constituent sentences is T.

Such contexts are called *intensional* because within them the contributions of constituent expressions to the meaning of the matrix expressions containing them do not seem to depend on their referents—their extensions—but rather on their senses, their intensions. Only intensionally equivalent expressions—not merely things that happen to share the same referent, but things that *necessarily* share the same referent—are substitutible in such contexts, so as to preserve the truth of the matrix sentence. If it is true that John believes that Jane loves Bill, then it is necessarily true that John believes that Bill is loved by Jane, since *Jane loves Bill* and *Bill is loved by Jane* have the same sense, the same intension.

To preserve Leibniz's Law, Frege went so far as to claim that in intensional contexts the extension of an expression *is in fact its intension*! This result has not satisfied everyone. It seems, intuitively, that the problem in intensional contexts is that we are concerned not with the referent of an expression but with the idea which it conveys. This however would let in ideational semantics with all its subjectivity. Frege always insisted that senses were entities quite as objective as extensions.

But what are intensions, if not ideas? To avoid letting in ideas by the back door, intensions must be some kind of abstract, logical entities. But what kind of entities? It was the logician-philosopher Rudolf Carnap who proposed that intensions too be functions: they are treated today as functions from indices to extensions.[12] In this way we recognize that the referent (extension) which an expression happens to have is different from its sense (intension), without admitting ideas to our theory.

Consider the expression *the president of the United States in 1987*. This refers to Ronald Reagan. But had the previous election turned out differently, it would have had a different referent. We cannot now know who will be president of the United States in 2001. Yet we can say many things about whoever will then be president. Some, which depend on a *de dicto* reading of "president of the United States," can be evaluated today: it is true that the president in 2001 will be an official of the U.S. government, and false that the president will not be.

Other things, which depend on a *de re* reading, cannot yet be evaluated. If the individual who happens to be president in 2001 is in the set of individuals who by 2001 will have ever ridden horses, then *the president of the United States in 2001 has ridden a horse* will be true, but we of course cannot know now if it will be.

The intension of an expression is treated as a function from an index to an extension. To evaluate the expression *president of the United States*, that is, to determine its referent, we need to know a time, a world, and a set of referents assigned to its terms, as for instance nouns (a *model*).

We have assumed an assignment of referents to constants (e.g., names and definite descriptions), but in fact we must also concern ourselves with variables which cannot be assigned definite references. This will happen, for example, in the case of quantification. A sentence like *everyone loves Bill* has the logical form (*All* x) x loves Bill, read "for all x, x loves Bill."

The "logical form" of a sentence is the form of its translation into an unambiguous language in which the semantic relationships holding between parts of sentences are rendered explicit. There is nothing *in* the sentence *you can fool some of the people all of the time* that tells us the sentence is ambiguous, depending on which of the quantifiers *All* or *Some* takes in more of the sentence, has wider *scope*. But the two logical translations below mark scope explicitly:

> (*All* x) (*Some* y) you can fool x at y
> (*Some* y) (*All* x) you can fool x at y

The first is the translation of the reading which means that for any given person, there is some time at which you can fool them. You can fool Tom on Holloween, Sue next Tuesday at noon, and so on. The second reading is that which means that there is some time—say, April Fool's Day—at which you can fool everybody.

But since expressions are evaluated compositionally, that is, from the smallest constituents out to the largest (ultimately the expression as a whole), we cannot know, when evaluating a constituent (e.g., "x loves Bill" or "you can fool x at y"), how the expression containing it will be evaluated, so that any variable bound by a quantifier (as *x* is bound by *All* in the former case) will be indistinguishable from a free variable at the time of evaluation. But free variables (such as relative pronouns) have no referents. (In *who loves Sue*, to whom does *who* refer?)

Therefore, for a compositional semantic interpretation to operate, we must assign to variables what are essentially dummy referents. Let us symbolize an assignment of dummy values by "g." There are then four parameters in the index relative to which an expression is evaluated—a model M, an assignment g, a world w, and an evaluation time t: $\langle M,g,w,t \rangle$. We accordingly treat senses (intensions) as functions from 4-tuples (quadruples) to extensions.[13]

In one notational system, that used in Montague semantics, the semantic value (extension) of an expression is symbolized by placing it between doubled square brackets and placing the index as a superscript to its right. We write, for example: $[\![$*the morning star*$]\!]^{M,g,w,t}$ = Venus, where w is some world (say, the real world of the speaker/writer); t is the time of evaluation (say, the speech-act time); and M is some assignment of interpretations (say, those that the speaker/writer normally presupposes for real-world entities usually referred to by them).

The intension of a sentence, called a *proposition*, is a function. Given as argument a quadruple of world, time, model, and the assignment of values g, it yields as a value the extension of that sentence at that index. "Ronald Reagan is president of the United States" ($\langle M,g,w,t \rangle$) = $[\![$*Ronald Reagan is president of the United States*$]\!]^{M,g,w,t}$ = T, for example. Relative to the triple $\langle M,g,t \rangle$, a proposition may be interpreted as the set of worlds in which it is true. (A *tautology* or necessarily true sentence, such as *two and two are four*, is true, relative to $\langle M,g \rangle$, in all worlds and at all times, while a *contradiction*, or necessarily false sentence, is false under the same conditions.)

Likewise, the intension of a predicate phrase, called a *property*, is a function. For example, "is president of the United States" denotes a set with only one member at any given time (relative to $\langle M,g,w \rangle$). Thus "is president of the United States" ($\langle M,g,w,t \rangle$) = $[\![$*is president of the United States*$]\!]^{M,g,w,t}$ = P, where P is the characteristic function containing one member with T on the right-hand side (namely, in mid-1989, $\langle$George Bush,T$\rangle$) and an indefinitely large number of entries with F (e.g., $\langle$Jimmy Carter,F$\rangle$, $\langle$George McGovern,F$\rangle$, $\langle$Ronald Reagan,F$\rangle$, etc.). The *value* of the intension varies from index to index. (Notice, by the way, that it is George Bush who is paired with truth in this intension, *not* the name *George Bush*.)

The intension of an ordinary referring expression, called an *individual concept*, is likewise a function from an index to an extension. As we have noted, some philosophers believe the individual concept is a constant function for names—the right-hand side of each member is always the same. Certainly there are names (or quasi-names), namely titles and the like, that are not constant (e.g., *Miss Canada*).

Intensions are always functions, and extensions are functions except in the case of sentences, which have truth values as their semantic values (referents), and expressions referring to individuals (or sets of individuals). It is important to note that, just as the set of individuals who have ever ridden a horse changes from time to time, from world to world, and so on, so must the characteristic function of that set change. So the extension of the expression *has ever ridden a horse* is not constant. The intension of this expression is a function with different right-hand sides to its members, each of which is itself a function.

In referential, truth-conditional semantics, semantic interpretation consists of the recursive prediction for linguistic expressions of referents, or alternatively, of the prediction of truth conditions for sentences along with the contribution each component of the sentence makes to those truth conditions. The question is what a formal semantic theory which makes such predictions is like.

We have alluded to the fact that natural language sentences may be ambiguous and may not reveal explicitly the semantic relationships holding between their constituent parts. This would tend to render rules for formal semantic interpretation extremely complicated, since the rules cannot be stated in a very simple way. Rather than saying, for example, "an expression of form f receives the interpretation i," a rule would probably have to say something like "under condition c, an expression of form f, and under condition c_1, an expression of form f_1, receives the interpretation i," and/or "under condition c an expression of form f receives the interpretation i, and under condition c_1, it receives the interpretation j."

For this reason, to simplify semantic interpretation, Montague proposed that the expressions of natural languages first be translated into a logical translation language (LTL), and that it be the expressions of this LTL and not those of the natural language itself which are directly semantically interpreted. Since the LTL expression in question translates that of the natural language, we say that semantic interpretation of the LTL expression *induces* one for the natural language expression.

But assuming that an appropriate LTL for which simple, formal, recursive rules of semantic interpretation can be found is possible, what guarantees either that there will always be an accurate and unambiguous LTL translation for each reading of a natural language expression, or that semantic interpretation of any given LTL expression will in fact induce an interpretation, and the correct interpretation, of the natural language expression?

Montague assures this as follows. He recursively defines the syntax of the set of grammatical sentences of the natural language (NL) in question. He then provides a syntax for the LTL. Montague did not require that the syntaxes be homologous. But he did require that they match to the extent that there would always be enough expressions of the LTL to match those of the NL, and that the translation rules would always properly match sentences of the LTL to those of the NL. We shall see how the syntax of NL, the syntax of LTL, and the translation rules do this.

To assure that the semantic interpretation of an LTL expression does indeed properly induce that of its corresponding NL expression, Montague treats the rules of semantic interpretation as homologous to those of translation. For each translation rule R_T there will be a corresponding rule of semantic interpretation R_{SI}.

Montague's theory is highly technical. But to discuss work on the semantics of tense and aspect conducted within referential semantics, it is necessary here to review some of its technicalities.

d. Montague Semantics

The most thoroughly worked-out semantic theory to date is that incorporated in *Montague grammar*. It was developed in the 1960s by the logician Richard Montague (1974) to solve certain problems in natural language semantics, coincidentally demonstrating the feasibility of a model-theoretic, truth-conditional semantics which adequately takes into account what has been learned about natural language syntax. It has since been further elaborated and revised by a number of scholars.[14]

The Montague grammar theory for some natural language NL contains a syntax for NL, a syntax for the logical translation language (the one Montague used is the language of intensional logic, called *IL*), a set R_T of translation rules, and a set R_{SI} of semantic interpretation rules for the translation language. For purposes of demonstration, we will here take English as the NL, though many other languages have by now received treatments within this paradigm, and Montague grammar is not designed to be more adequate for one type of language than another. Indeed, Montague intended what he called *universal grammar* to be adequate for any language whatever, even artificial ones. He was uninterested in such issues as the psychological reality of grammars and regarded linguistics as a branch not of psychology (as Noam Chomsky does, for example), nor of cognitive science, but of mathematics.

The syntax is similar to familiar systems of syntax, but is based on Fregean compositionality. Each expression is built out of smaller, constituent expressions down to the level of the word. Montague grammar utilizes *categorial grammar*, principally developed by the logician Kazimierz Ajdukiewicz.[15]

Intuitively, a categorial grammar defines a set of *categories* of expressions. A "pure" categorical grammar is in fact equivalent to the familiar context-free phrase-structure grammar of linguistics, but is simple to define recursively. Let C be the smallest set of syntactic categories of English expressions, and let N and S be two categories in C (intuitively, the categories of names and sentences, respectively—in Montague, e and t). Then for any two syntactic categories A and B, A/B and $A//B$ are categories in C. Nothing else is a category in C.

Thus N, S/N, and $S/(S/N)$ are all categories. There are in fact an infinite number of categories—more, obviously, than the small finite number that are needed. But this is no problem; most are simply empty and have no members.

In a categorial grammar, an expression of category A/B or $A//B$ combines with one of type B to yield an expression of type A. For example, N denotes the class of expressions (names) referring to individual entities, as for instance *Napoleon*, while S denotes that of expressions (namely sentences) referring to truth values: *Napoleon swims*. The category S/N will denote the class of expressions referring to functions from (having as domain) the kind of entity named by expressions of type N to (having as range) the kind of entity named by expressions of type S; obviously the category S/N is that of verb phrases and intransitive verbs: *swims*. Since *Napoleon* is of type N and *swims* is of type S/N, we may combine the two to yield an expression of type S, namely, *Napoleon swims*.

$$
\begin{array}{c}
S \\
\diagup\diagdown \\
N \quad\quad S/N \\
| \quad\quad\quad | \\
\textit{Napoleon} \quad \textit{swims}
\end{array}
$$

Certain categories correspond closely to traditional ones and may be abbreviated as follows (from here on we will use Montague's system):

t/e is the category *IV* of intransitive verb phrases (e.g., *swim well*).
t/IV is the category *T* of terms (roughly noun phrases, e.g., *many people, the man I met last year in Chicago*).
IV/T is the category *TV* of transitive verbs (e.g., *like, see*)
IV/IV is the category *IAV* of IV-modifying adverbs (e.g., *rapidly, well*)

There is a second category e to t, designated $t//e$. This is the category *CN* of common nouns (e.g., *dog*). (We will discuss below the reasons for this seemingly odd assignment of category.)

For each category of expression A, there is a set B_A of *basic expressions* of that category. For example, *Napoleon* ϵ B_e. Each such set B_A is listed in the lexicon (vocabulary) of the language. There is also a set P_A of expressions of each type A, which includes B_A ($B_A \subseteq P_A$) as well as members of A derived syntactically. For example, *Napoleon swims* ϵ P_t. Some of these sets of expressions are empty. There are no basic expressions of type B_t, for example, so $B_t = \Lambda$; on the other hand, there are probably no derived names: if so, $P_e = B_e$. There are an infinite number of categories A for which both P_A and B_A are empty, because English does not utilize those categories.

The advantage of this treatment of the phrase structure grammar of English is not merely that it provides a simple mechanism for generating the expressions of English. Because it is functional in nature and definable by recursive rules, it makes it simple to provide the translation rules and rules of semantic interpretation which we require—each of which is likewise functional in nature and defined by recursive rules.

Though we can state, in general, that the result of combining an expression of category A/B with an expression of category B is one of category A, we still have said nothing about *how* they are combined. Lewis (1969) ignores this problem, but others have offered various solutions. Lyons,[16] for example, proposes that left-to-right order be indicated as follows:

$$(1) \quad \begin{array}{c} A \\ \rightarrow \\ B \end{array} \qquad (2) \quad \begin{array}{c} A \\ \leftarrow \\ B \end{array}$$

(1) designates the category of expression which results in an expression of category A when an expression of category B is added to its *left*, and (2) designates the category of expression which results in an expression of category A when an expression of category B is added to its *right*; t/e would in this system be

$$\begin{array}{c} t \\ \rightarrow \\ e \end{array}$$

Another problem ignored in many versions of categorical grammar is that of morphology. Although *swim* is of category t/e and *Napoleon* is of category e, **Napoleon swim* is not a grammatical expression of category t.

To deal with both of these problems, Montague utilized special syntactic rules which increase the power of categorial grammars to that of transformational grammars. These rules state the order of combination of constituent expressions, along with any morphological adjustments (such as number and person agreement between subject and verb) which may be required. These are stated in terms of functions, so it is necessary to state rules of functional application for the syntax of the NL.

For example, the rule for forming simple subject-predicate sentences reads:

S1. If $\alpha \in P_T$ and $\delta \in P_{IV}$, then $F_1(\alpha, \delta) \in P_t$, where $F_1(\alpha, \delta) = \alpha \delta'$, and δ' is the result of replacing the first *verb* (i.e., member of B_{IV}, B_{TV}, $B_{IV/t}$, or $B_{IV//IV}$) in δ by its third person singular present form.

This forbidding formalism actually says something quite simple. For example, let α be *everybody in Chicago* (a member of P_T) and δ be *love bananas* (a member of P_{IV}). Then, the value of the function F_1 applied to the pair $\langle \alpha, \delta \rangle$ is an expression of category t, namely $\alpha \delta'$, where this is the left-to-right concatenation of α and δ, with the first verb in δ (here *love*) replaced by its *-s* form ($\delta' = $ *loves bananas*); that is, F_1(*everybody in Chicago, love bananas*) = *everybody in Chicago loves bananas*.

The fragments of English syntax given in the various works within the Montague paradigm remain inadequate for English as a whole, but for present purposes let us assume that a version adequate for English is possible in theory, and that one adequate for present purposes is available.[17]

Corresponding to each category A of expressions of English are the *meaningful expressions of type* α (ME_α) of the translation language, *IL*. Let Y be the smallest set of types for *IL*. For any two members α and β of Y, $\langle\alpha,\beta\rangle$ is a member of Y.

Confusingly, Montague designates by this not a function from the kind of entity named by β to that named by α, but rather one from that named by α to one named by β, just the reverse of his practice with NL (English), where A/B is the category of an expression yielding an expression of category A when combined with an expression of category B. ($A/B + B = A$ but $\langle\alpha/\beta\rangle + \alpha = \beta$!) Unfortunately, the tradition within Montague grammar has hallowed this confusing usage. If category A corresponds to type α and B to β, then an English expression of category A/B is translated as an *IL* meaningful expression of type $\langle\beta,\alpha\rangle$ (i.e., a member *of* $ME_{\langle\beta,\alpha\rangle}$).

Because *IL* is an intensional logic, it will also have to have expressions naming functions whose domains include world-time pairs. Whenever α is a member of Y, $\langle s,\alpha\rangle$ is a member of Y as well, where s represents an indexical pair (though s itself is not a type).

The type of a sentence, an expression denoting a truth value, is t; $\langle s,t\rangle$ is the type of a *proposition*, an expression denoting a function from an index (of world and time) to a truth value. $\langle e/t\rangle$ is the type of an intransitive verb or verb phrase, denoting a function from entities to truth values; $\langle s,\langle e,t\rangle\rangle$ is the type of a *property*, denoting a function from indices to the characteristic functions of sets. e is the type of an individual entity; $\langle s,e\rangle$ denotes an *individual concept*, a function from indices to entities.

IL has, for each type α, an infinite set V_α of variables, and an infinite set of C_α of constants. The latter correspond to the names (*Napoleon*), common nouns (*dog*), predicates (*swim, tall*), and so on, of natural languages, while the former correspond to the pronouns (*he, who, someone*) and other pro-terms (*thus, so*) of these.

The remainder of the meaningful expressions of type α (ME_α) are defined recursively as follows:

   (1) If a is a member of ME_α and u is a variable of type β, then λua is a member of $ME_{\langle\beta,\alpha\rangle}$.

We introduced earlier a notation for defining sets: $W = \{x{:}x$ is a waiter$\} =$ the set of all those who are waiters. We saw that this can be characterized as the characteristic function C_W of the set in question (W); if C_W is applied to an entity like Ronald Reagan, it returns as a value a truth value. In a sense, then, to say: "Ronald Reagan $\notin W$" is equivalent to saying "C_W(Ronald Reagan)$=0$."

Here a propositional function such as x *is a waiter* is used to define membership in the set; the variable x is "bound," in that we understand it to pertain to *all those x* who meet that definition. A method of formalizing (and generalizing) this was found by Alonzo Church (1940) with his *lambda-calculus*, which utilizes the *set abstractor* or *functional abstractor* denoted by the lower-case Greek letter lambda

(λ). $\lambda x \, [W(x)]$ has the same meaning as $\{x:x$ is a waiter$\}$, if W translates *is a waiter*, though taken as the expression of a function, rather than a set directly.

$\lambda x \, [W(x)]$ is in fact an *abstraction* from an infinitely large number of expressions of the form $W(c)$—for example $W(a)$, where c is a constant of the same type as x, obtained by replacing any c (of type e) by a variable u (here x) of the same type e and prefacing λ plus u. It may be understood informally as equivalent to $\{x:x$ is a $W\}$.

We can get back to the original expressions by a process of *lambda-conversion*. For example, $(\lambda x \, [W(x)])(c) = W(c)$; that is, lambda-conversion provides a "disabstraction" from the abstract, lambda expression to a specific, concrete expression of the appropriate kind.

So far we have simply complicated the system. The payoff comes when we generalize to *any* function. Lambda-abstraction allows us to create expressions for functions of *any* type whatsoever. Given any variable u of type α and any expression v of type β containing u, we can prefix to it λu, thereby denoting a function of type $\langle \alpha, \beta \rangle$. For example, we translate *John loves Sue* as $(L(s))(j)$, and *John loves Mary as* $(L(m))(j)$. Now we can abstract out the expression $\lambda x \, [(L(x))(j)]$, which is in fact a function of type $\langle e,t \rangle$, since it takes in entities and puts out truth values; it is the characteristic function for the set of those whom John loves. But we could also abstract out $\lambda x \, [(L(m))(x)]$, the characteristic function for the set of those who love Mary—or even $\lambda P \, [(P(m))(j)]$, the characteristic function for *the set of relations holding between John and Mary!* This function is obviously of type $\langle \langle e,t \rangle,t \rangle$.

We shall see that the payoff of the Lambda-abstractor comes when we assign *IL* translations to certain NL expressions, for example quantifiers like *every* and noun phrases like *every dog*. The value of this type of function lies particularly in the translation (and interpretation) of noun phrases.

(2) If a is a member of $ME_{\langle \alpha,\beta \rangle}$, and b is a member of ME_α, then $a(b)$ is a member of ME_β.

Rule (2) matches the corresponding rule for subject-predicate sentences in English.

(3) If a,b are members of ME_α, then $a = b$ is a member of ME_t.

Rule (3) allows for the identity operator.

(4) If v,y are members of ME_t and u is a variable, then the following are members of ME_t: $\sim v$, $v \vee y$, $v \wedge y$, $v \rightarrow y$, $v \leftrightarrow y$, $\exists u \, v$, $\forall u \, v$, Lv, Mv.

Rule (4) allows for complex sentences with operators denoting truth functions (those translating, respectively, *not, or, and/but, if . . . then, if and only if*), quantifiers ($\exists u$, translating *some, a*; $\forall u$, translating *all, every*), and the modal operators for necessity ("it is necessarily true that p," Lp) and possibility ("it is possibly true that p," Mp).

(5) If a is a member of ME_α, then $[{}^\wedge a]$ is a member of $ME_{\langle s,\alpha \rangle}$.
(6) If a is a member of $ME_{\langle s,\alpha \rangle}$, then $[{}^\vee a]$ is a member of ME_α.

Rules (5) and (6) allow the formation of, respectively, expressions for the intension of any expression a (^{in}a or $^{\wedge}a$) and the extension of any expression a (^{ex}a or
$^{\vee}a$).[18] $^{ex}(^{in}a)$ is simply a.[19]

(7) Nothing else is in any set ME_α except as required by these rules.

e. Semantic Interpretation

We require a function f which states the correspondences of the categories of
English and the types of *IL*. We can say:

$f(t)=t$
$f(e)=e$
For all categories A and B, $f(A/B)=f(A//B)=\langle\langle s,f(B)\rangle,f(A)\rangle$.

This says that the *IL* types t and e correspond respectively to the English categories t and e, and for any other category involving A and B, the corresponding type
involves $\langle s,(\text{the correspondent of})\ B\rangle$ and A. For example, an intransitive verb of
English (of category t/e) corresponds to an *IL* expression of type $\langle\langle s,\ e\rangle,\ t\rangle$.
This denotes a function from an individual concept to a truth value.

The reason for the role here of s is that our logic is intensional. We have seen
that in intensional contexts, an expression has as its semantic value not its extension, but its intension. Montague decided to generalize the replacement of extensions by intensions, and say that in *all* contexts functional application involves
treating the argument as the intension, not the extension, of the expression. Therefore the category A/B or $A//B$ is not matched to the type $\langle f(B),\ f(A)\rangle$, which
would represent a function from the type translating B to that translating A. This
introduces a certain problem, however, because s is not itself a type. Consider
how we interpret *John swims*. It is true if John has the property of swimming.
But we cannot directly assert this, since properties are functions from indices to
characteristic functions. But an individual may be in the extension of a property
(i.e., a set). That is, given a property ζ and an individual α, it is possible that
$^{\vee}\zeta(\alpha)$ is true. Montague introduced the abbreviation $\zeta\{\alpha\}$ for this, as a "natural"
expression of "α has the property ζ."

Let us look at the interpretation of simple sentences some more. Intuitively,
simple sentences are uniformly interpreted; that is, application of the function
denoted by *loves Jane* to *my neighbor* should be the same as its application to
Napoleon. But so far we have different categories for these expressions—names,
of category e, and common nouns, which are of category $t//e$.

But whereas linguists accept that *Napoleon, my neighbor, the man I met last
year in Chicago,* and *someone* are all noun phrases and can equally well serve as
subject (or object) of a verb, there is no category of noun phrase as such in
Montague grammar. Other than names, the category which comes closest to the
traditional noun phrase in Montague grammar is the *term*, whose category is abbreviated T and is defined as t/IV, that is, adding something like *loves bananas* to
something like *everybody in Chicago* yields a sentence, *everybody in Chicago
loves bananas.*

If common nouns are of category *t//e*, and terms are of category *t/IV*, then clearly an expression like *every*, which can transform a common noun like *dog* into a term like *every dog*, must be of category *(t/IV)/(t//e)*, that is, *(t/(t/e))/(t//e)*.

Consider the normal translation in logic of *every dog swims*, $\forall x\ [D(x){\mapsto}S(x)]$, that is, *for all x, if x is a dog, then x swims.* By lambda-abstraction, we arrive at the function $\lambda P\ [\forall x\ [D(x){\mapsto}P(x)]]$, which is the set of properties dogs have, but we can further abstract to $\lambda Q\ [\lambda P\ [\forall x\ Q(x){\mapsto}P(x)]]$. This now is the translation in the LTL *IL* of *every*.

Applied to an expression of type *t//e*, namely a common noun, say *dog* (translated *D*), this converts to $\lambda P\ [\forall x\ [D(x){\mapsto}P(x)]]$, which is of the type corresponding to the category *t/IV*, and which, when applied to an *IV*, namely *swims*, is converted back into the original translation under discussion (of the sentence *every dog swims*) $\forall x\ [D(x){\mapsto}S(x)]$, which is indeed of type *t*.

Why did we say in the first place that common nouns are of category *t//e*? The reason is that, by themselves, common nouns are neither names nor terms; **dog swims* is not a possible sentence. The reason *t//e* was picked is that the logic of common nouns is just that of predicates: *John is a waiter* is $W(j)$, just as *John swims* is $S(j)$; common nouns denote sets of individual entities.

We still have not united names and terms into a category of noun phrase, and while we know how to translate and indirectly interpret a sentence like *John swims*, we still do not see how to translate and interpret something like *every dog swims*. We have seen that a term must be of the category *t/IV*. This means that, when a term is combined with an *IV*, a *t* results. And it is true that combining *every dog* with *swims* yields the sentence *every dog swims*.

But this is hardly like combining *John*, of category *e*, with *swims*, of category *IV* (that is, *t/e*), to yield *John swims*, of category *t*. For *swims* denotes a function; applied to the argument *John*, it yields the value *t* (either T of F). But *every dog* does not supply a possible argument for *swims*. ⟨every dog, T⟩ is absolutely not a possible member of the function denoted by *swims*, for the simple reason that *every dog* is not of category *e*.

Rather, it is the set denoted by the predicate *swims* which is to be taken as argument by the referent function of the expression *every dog*! Remember that this is of category *t/IV*, and denotes a function from a set to a truth value. This particular function is expressed in *IL* by $\lambda P\ [\forall x\ [D(x){\mapsto}P(x)]]$ (the set of properties such that for all *x*, if *x* is a dog, *x* has the property in question). Applied to *swims*, this is $(\lambda P\ [\forall x\ [D(x){\mapsto}P(x)]])(S)$, which lambda-converts into the *IL* translation of *every dog swims*, namely $\forall x\ [D(x){\mapsto}S(x)]$, which is true iff for all *x*, if *x* is a dog, *x* swims.

We still have not united terms and names. Is there any way of doing so? The way Montague found to do so is to *treat a name as a kind of term*. Specifically, a name denotes not the individual directly, but *the set of properties which that individual has*. We have seen that the logical translation of *every dog* denotes a function from a property to a truth value—it is of type $\langle\langle s, \langle\ e/t\ \rangle\rangle, t\rangle$, since it combines with verb phrases to yield sentences. Now if *Napoleon* likewise denoted the set of properties which the individual so named has, then it would denote a function from a property to a truth value—it would also be of type

$\langle\langle s, \langle\ e/t\ \rangle\rangle, t\rangle$. There are a number of interesting philosophical questions raised by this treatment, but it does serve Montague's purpose of uniting the logical translations of terms and names in one type. Consequently, in Montague's system the type e is empty!

For each syntactic rule of English, there is a corresponding translation rule yielding the corresponding expression of *IL*, thus guaranteeing that there will always be corresponding NL and LTL expressions. Corresponding to syntactic rule **S1,** for example, is the translation rule **T1. T1** says:

> **T1.** If $\alpha \in P_T$ and $\delta \in P_{IV}$, and α,δ translate into α',δ' respectively, then $F(\alpha,\delta)$ translates into $\alpha'(^\wedge\delta')$.

Let α be *Napoleon*. Suppose that the translation of this in *IL* is $\lambda P[P\{n\}]$, that is, $\lambda P[^\vee P(n)]$. Further, let *swims* be translated $^\wedge swims'$. (Recall that swimming is a property, that is, an intension). In this case, the translation of *Napoleon swims* will be $(\lambda P[P\{n\}])(^\wedge swims')$.

This is very difficult to interpret, but there are some ways of transforming the expression into a simpler, but equivalent, expression which is easier to evaluate. (This process of simplification may be called a *derivation*.) First, by the definition of the brackets abbreviation, this expression is equivalent to $(\lambda P[^\vee P(n)])(^\wedge swims')$. By lambda-conversion, this becomes $^\vee swims'(n)$. This is true iff $n \in S$, where S is the set denoted by $[\![swims']\!]^{M,w,t,g}$.

We will assume a set R_S of syntactic rules for English and a corresponding set R_T of translation rules. To syntactically interpret the sentences of *IL*, we require a model. We start by defining the possible objects we require in our model. Let A be a set of individuals or entities; let W (Montague calls it I) be a set of possible worlds; and let T (Montague uses J) be a set of times.

If α is a type, then D_α is the set of possible denotations of that type. $D_e = A$. $D_t = \{0, 1\}$ (that is, either F or T). For any pair $\langle\alpha,\beta\rangle$, $D_{\langle\alpha,\beta\rangle}$ is the set of all functions from D_α to D_β. For example, $D_{\langle e,t\rangle}$ is the set of functions whose domain is the set of individuals and whose range is the truth values T and F. $D_{\langle s,\alpha\rangle}$ is the set of functions from world-time indexical pairs to the domain including D_α. $D_{\langle s,e\rangle}$ is the set of functions from pairs of worlds and times (that is, from sets of indices) to individuals, that is, the set of individual concepts. $[\![George\ Washington]\!]^{M,g}$ is of type $\langle s,e\rangle$, while $[\![George\ Washington]\!]^{M,g}(\langle w,t\rangle) = [\![George\ Washington]\!]^{M,w,t,g}$ is of type e.

An *interpretation* or *intensional model M* is an ordered quintuple consisting of $A, W, T,$ an ordering relation $\le$ on T (we will discuss $\le$ later in this chapter), and a function F which assigns an intension of type α to each constant of type α. Another function g will similarly assign corresponding values to all variables. If α is a meaningful expression, then $[\![\alpha]\!]^{M,g}$ is the semantic interpretation of α with respect to the model M and the function g, that is, its intension, while $[\![\alpha]\!]^{M,w,t,g}$, where w is some world and t some time, is the extension of α, the semantic interpretation of α with respect not only to M and g, but to a world w and a time t.

$[\![Miss\ Canada]\!]^{M,g}$ is then some intension; $[\![Miss\ Canada]\!]^{M,g}(\langle w,t\rangle) = [\![Miss\ Canada]\!]^{M,w,t,g} = c$, where c denotes the extension of *Miss Canada* relative to

$\langle M,w,t,g \rangle$, namely that individual who happens to be Miss Canada in w at t, given M and g.

Let *swims well* be translated into *IL* as *swims-well'*. Now, $[\![\textit{swims-well'}]\!]^{M,g}$ is an intension, a property—it denotes a function from world-and-time pairs to the characteristic function of the set of individuals who happen at that time and in that set of circumstances (say, in the world of someone's hopes) to swim well. $[\![\textit{swims-well'}]\!]^{M,w,t,g} = [\![\textit{swims-well'}]\!]^{M,g}(\langle w,t \rangle)$ denotes the extension of the expression in the world w at the time t, namely the characteristic function for the set of individuals who swim well at that time and in that world. If $[\![\textit{Harry}]\!]^{M,w,t,g}$, let us say Harry, is a member of the set of those who swim well (at time t and in world w), then $[\![\textit{swims-well'}]\!]^{M,w,t,g}([\![\textit{Harry}]\!]^{M,w,t,g}) = 1$. Notice that $[\![\textit{swims-well}]\!]^{M,g}(\langle w,t \rangle) = [\![\textit{swims-well'}]\!]^{M,w,t,g}$. In general, if β is of type $\langle s, \delta \rangle$, then $[\![\beta]\!]^{M,g}(\langle w,t \rangle) = [\![\beta]\!]^{M,w,t,g}$.

The nine semantic interpretation rules are as follows:

(1) If α is a constant, then $[\![\alpha]\!]^{M,g} = F(\alpha)$.

The value of α relative to $\langle M, g \rangle$ is whatever value the interpretation-assignment function F assigns to α.

(2) If u is a variable, then $[\![u]\!]^{M,g} = g(u)$.

The value of u relative to $\langle M, g \rangle$ is whatever value the assignment function g assigns to u.

(3) If α is in ME_α and u is a variable of type β, then $[\![\lambda u\, \alpha]\!]^{M,w,t,g}$ is that function h with domain D_β such that, whenever x is in that domain, $h(x)$ is $[\![\alpha]\!]^{M,w,t,g'}$, where g' is like g with the possible difference that $g'(u) = x$.

This tells us how to interpret expressions formed with the abstraction operator λ.

(4) If α is a member of $ME_{\langle \alpha, \beta \rangle}$ and β is a member of ME_α, then $[\![\alpha(\beta)]\!]^{M,w,t,g}$ is $[\![\alpha]\!]^{M,w,t,g}([\![\beta]\!]^{M,w,t,g})$.

This has to do with functional application. In this case, β serves as argument to α. Therefore the relative semantic value of the expression $\alpha(\beta)$ is whatever results when the relative semantic value of α (a function) is applied to the relative semantic value of β. For example, $[\![x^2(2)]\!]^{M,w,t,g} = [\![x^2]\!]^{M,w,t,g}([\![2]\!]^{M,w,t,g}) = 4$.

(5) If α, β are members of ME_α, then $[\![\alpha = \beta]\!]^{M,w,t,g} = 1$ iff $[\![\alpha]\!]^{M,w,t,g} = [\![\beta]\!]^{M,w,t,g}$.

The equation of two expressions p and q is true at an index $\langle w,t \rangle$, iff the extension of p (at $\langle w,t \rangle$) is the same as that of q. For example, the translation of *the morning star is the evening star* is true iff the morning star is indeed the same entity as the evening star.

(6) If v is a member of ME_t, then $[\![\sim v]\!]^{M,w,t,g} = 1$ iff $[\![v]\!]^{M,w,t,g} = 0$. (With interpretations of a similar kind for $\vee$, $\wedge$, $\rightarrow$, and $\leftrightarrow$.)

These interpretations follow from the meanings of the various operators. For example, if the translation ϕ in *IL* of *Napoleon has been exiled to Elba* is true (in w and at t), then $\sim\phi$, the translation of the negation of ϕ *(Napoleon has not been exiled to Elba)*, is false (in w at t).

(7) If v is a member of ME_α, and u is a variable of type α, then $[\![\exists uv]\!]^{M,w,t,g} = 1$, iff there exists an x in D_α such that $[\![v]\!]^{M,w,t,g'} = 1$, where g' is as in (3); similarly for $\forall u$, $[\![\forall uv]\!]^{M,w,t,g} = 1$ iff for all x in D_α, $[\![v]\!]^{M,w,t,g'} = 1$.

This follows from the meaning of the quantifiers *some*, $\exists$, and *all/every*, $\forall$. The translation of *everybody in Chicago loves bananas* will be true (in w at t) just in case it is true for each person p in the set denoted by *everybody in Chicago* (in w at t) that p belongs to the set designated (in w at t) by *loves bananas*. Similarly, *someone in Chicago loves bananas* will be true iff there exists at least one such person p.

(8) If α is in ME_α, then $[\![{}^\wedge\alpha]\!]^{M,w,t,g}$ is $[\![\alpha]\!]^{M,g}$.

(9) If α is in $ME_{\langle s,\alpha\rangle}$, then $[\![{}^\vee\alpha]\!]^{M,w,t,g}$ is $[\![\alpha]\!]^{M,w,t,g}(\langle w,t\rangle)$.

$^\vee$ and $^\wedge$ are operators which allow the formation of an infinite number of expressions of the type $^\circ\alpha$, $^{\circ\circ}\alpha$, $^{\circ\circ\circ}\alpha$, . . ., where $^\circ$ is one of these operators. (Montague actually utilizes only $^\vee\alpha$ and $^\wedge\alpha$.)

$^\wedge$ forms the intension of any expression; if a is an expression of type α, then $^\wedge a$ is the intension of a, of type $\langle s,\alpha\rangle$. $^\vee$ correspondingly forms the extension of any expression; if a is an expression of type $\langle s,\alpha\rangle$, then $^\vee a$ is the extension of a, of type α. For example, let P be some property (of type $\langle s,\langle e,t\rangle\rangle$). $^\vee P$ (at any index) is clearly just P (at any index) applied to $\langle w,t\rangle$. Similarly, if p is (at some index) some characteristic function for a set, an expression of type $\langle e,t\rangle$, $^\wedge p$ is just the intension of that predicate at that index, of type $\langle s,\langle e,t\rangle\rangle$. (We omit here the rules for L and M.)

As an example of how the system works, consider the sentence *John walks*. Its syntactic structure is diagrammed as an *analysis tree*:

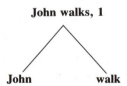

John walks, 1

John   **walk**

This tells us that *John walks* results from applying syntactic rule **S1** to *John* and *walk*. Structural ambiguities are resolved in certain cases by this device of marking the syntactic rule applied at each point.

An expression of category *IV* (i.e., *t/e*) translates into an *IL* constant expression of type $\langle e,t\rangle$. By convention, the translation of *walk* is *walk'*. But as we have seen, we want not the extension of the predicate *swims* but its intension—$^\wedge swims'$—of type $\langle s,\langle e/t\rangle\rangle$. *John*, being a term (= noun phrase), is an expression of category *t/IV* and therefore translates into one of type $\langle\langle s,\langle e,t\rangle\rangle,t\rangle$, that is, a function from a property to a truth value. We take it to denote the set of properties John has and translate it accordingly $\lambda P[P\{j\}]$.

This yields the translation in *IL* of *John walks*, namely, $(\lambda P[P\{j\}])\,(^\wedge walk')$, which says literally that the property of walking belongs to the set of properties which John has. We can derive from this the formula $walk'(j)$, a rather simple predicate-logic sort of formula which asserts that the predicate *walk'* holds of the entity called *j*, that is, j ∈ W, where W = {x:x walks}, and which is true just in case *j* (John) does walk.

The derivation goes like this:

(1) λ*P*[*P*{*j*}] (^*walk'*)
(2) ^*walk'*{*j*} from (1) by lambda-conversion
(3) ˅^*walk'*(*j*) from (2) by the brace convention (whereby α{β} = ˅α(β))
(4) *walk'*(*j*) from (3) by the ("down-up") principle that ˅^ cancel out (˅^α=α).

By semantic interpretation rule (4), given above, the value of *walk'*(*j*) is the result of applying the characteristic function of W = {x:x walks}, that is, the function denoted by *walk'*, to the entity denoted by *j* (John, let's say). If John ∈ W, $[\![walk'(j)]\!]^{M,w,t,g} = 1$, otherwise it = 0.

In other words, *John walks* is true iff John walks! This might seem a very complicated way of arriving at a truism, but Montague's semantics allows us to formulate a formal semantic theory which, given an adequate grammar for any NL and an accompanying set of translation rules, allows an automatic prediction for each expression of the language of its semantic value—in the case of sentences, the conditions under which they are true. This is precisely, however, what we demanded of a semantic theory in the beginning of our discussion above.

Thus while an adequate Montague grammar for any language has not yet been developed, there is nothing *in principle* which prevents the development of an adequate semantic theory for English (or any other natural language) within the Montague framework. To date, at least, Montague semantics remains by far the most thoroughly developed theory of semantics, and treatments of various languages (e.g., English, German, Kikuyu) of some considerable degree of coverage have been done within that paradigm. No other referential semantic theory has yet provided treatments of equal adequacy, and it is arguable that no semantic theory of any other (non-referential) type has provided treatments of natural languages of any degree of adequacy at all, in terms of what we have demanded of a semantic theory.

f. The Formal Semantics of the Priorian Tense Operators

Logicians were the first to encounter problems with tense and aspect. Since Aristotle tense logic, as the study of the logic of tensed expressions is known, has formed an integral part of logic. (Henceforth we will understand "tensed" as including aspect.) Tensed expressions enter into logic in two ways.

First, their logical properties follow from their meanings, but these depend on various temporal distinctions. For example, *John is running* implies *John has run* and *John will have run*, but *John is winning the race* implies neither *John has won the race* nor *John will have run the race*. This difference proceeds, we know, from the fact that running is an activity, whereas winning the race is an accomplishment.

Second, their logical evaluation is sensitive to temporal relations. *It will be 1990 next year* was true throughout 1989, but was false during 1988. *He is com-*

ing soon is true immediately before he comes, but false both after the event and at any relatively great distance in time before it.

The problem of tense at the outset is that of reconciling the dictum that only that exists which is *now*—the past and future do not exist—with the fact that what *was* now just now *is* now no longer now, and that which is now *about to be* now *is not* yet now. We have seen that Aristotle mentioned the paradox that, being a point in time, the present does not exist either, so that if we view time as a succession of present points in time, time can hardly be said to be real. On the other hand, if we view the present as an interval composed partly of the past and partly of the future, which the broad use of the present tense seems to support, then time still consists of a succession of intervals composed of nonexistent segments.

To deal with this paradox, Augustine proposes that events *are* always present, but that some events are yet to be present while others have been present.[20] Aquinas says similarly that "things are called past and future with respect to the present," adding, "for that is past which was present, and future what will be present."[21]

This result has not proven satisfactory to all, and in the twentieth century many scientists and philosophers have treated tensed language as a shorthand for a tenseless language. That is, *John was tall* is translated "at time t<s, John is tall" (where s is the speech-act time and t some moment in time prior to s). The early twentieth-century philosopher J. M. E. McTaggart rightly rejected such a translation, pointing out that "The battle of Waterloo is in the past" cannot be translated into "The battle of Waterloo is earlier than this judgment," because the former statement is something which is true but was once false, while its purported translation is either always true or always false.[22]

The philosopher P. T. Geach says:

> Such expressions as "at time *t*" are quite out of place in expounding scholastic views of time and motion. For a scholastic, "Socrates is sitting" is a complete proposition, *enuntiabile*, which is sometimes true, sometimes false; *not* an incomplete expression requiring a further phrase like "at time *t*" to make it into an assertion.[23]

Prior, quoting this passage, goes on to say that, though this has by now become a "commonplace," it was news in 1949; he himself had assumed it was both correct and traditional to regard propositions as "incomplete" and not amenable as such to "accurate logical treatment," so long as time references had not been filled in, rendering the proposition into something "either unalterably true or unalterably false."

Prior says that the example *Socrates is sitting* is found not only in the scholastics but in Aristotle, who says that " 'statements and opinions' vary in their truth and falsehood with the times at which they are made or held." This seemed to Prior to illuminate Aristotle's opinion that *there will be a sea-battle tomorrow* might be "not yet" definitely true or definitely false.

Prior was soon to be engaged in developing the first systems of formal tense logic, but the beginnings of a modern, formal logic of tensed statements had already appeared in J. N. Findlay's famous and oft-reprinted (1941) paper, written in response to McTaggart's famous argument against the reality of time.[24]

McTaggart argues that events have two kinds of temporal properties: in the "A-series" they are future, present, and past; in the "B-series" they are later than or earlier than. The latter set of relationships is unchanging—Queen Anne's death has always been, and always will be, later than William of Normandy's conquest of England. Therefore the B-series cannot, McTaggart argues, provide a basis for the understanding that time involves change. This comes from the A-series, in which events which were distantly future become progressively nearer until they are present, and then recede into the past, becoming progressively more distant from the present. But this requires that events at once be future, present, and past, which is paradoxical, as nothing can be at once more than one of the three.

If it be argued that events *were* future, *are* present, and *will be* past, so that no event is *at once* more than one of the three, he contends that this merely pushes back the paradox one step: "every moment, like every event, is both [*sic*] past, present, and future. And so a similar difficulty arises."[25] We are caught in an infinite regress. But if there can be no such thing as having been future, then there can be no change in the temporal properties of event and hence no such thing as time.

In the course of criticizing McTaggart's argument, Findlay says that

> it is hard to see, if we remain in any ordinary, unreflective state of mind, what is the problem that is being raised by those who say they can't see how what *is* the case at one time, is not the case at other times, or that they can't see how a happening that is future can ever come to be a happening that is past. . . . *Before* an event occurs we say, if we have evidence that it is not yet happening, that it hasn't yet happened, but that it will happen, while if it *is* happening we say that it is now happening, that it hasn't ceased happening and that it isn't about to happen, and *after* it has happened we say that it has happened, that it is no longer happening and that it is not going to happen. Stated in words these semantic rules might seem circular, but taught in connection with concrete situations they are wholly clear. And our conventions with regard to tenses are so well worked out that we have practically the materials in them for a formal calculus.[26]

He adds in his footnote 16:

> The calculus of tenses should have been included in the modern development of modal logics. It includes such obvious propositions as that x present = (x present) present; x future = (x future) present = (x present) future.

It is the working out of such a calculus which Prior and the other early tense logicians took as their task. When philosophers and linguists first set out to develop the formal semantics of tense, what they had to work with was the results of this research. Tense logicians were accustomed to utilize in their logical translation language the following type of operators—now usually called "Priorian":

$$F =_{def.} \text{`It will be the case that'}$$
$$G =_{def.} \text{`It will always be the case that'}$$
$$P =_{def.} \text{`It has been the case that'}$$
$$H =_{def.} \text{`It has always been the case that'}[27]$$

Thus if we symbolize "John leaves home" as p, then we can symbolize "John will leave home" as Fp (in the notation used by Prior). The tense-logical language is much richer than is needed for the translation of natural language sentences. It is possible, for example, to write FFp, 'it will be the case that it will be the case that John leaves home'; the closest we can come to this in reasonably ordinary language is "John is going to be going to leave home." But obviously this fails in many respects both as an ordinary expression and as a literal translation of FFp. On the other hand, there are a vast number of natural language tenses which this system does not cover: for example, if P is the perfect tense, how should we symbolize the preterite?

In the treatment of tenses in logic, it was assumed that the present tense made no essential contribution. If we interpret the present tense as "it is now the case that . . . ," then it is apparent that "it is now the case that p" *logically* means no more than p itself. The present tense is redundant from the point of view of a referential semantics, and for this reason many languages (e.g., Russian and colloquial Turkish) can get by without the present tense of the verb "be," that verb itself being (referentially) semantically void.

In tense logics within the tradition of modal logic, the present tense is left without explicit symbolization.[28] The past and future tenses are of course nonredundant in this sense, and the past and future are symbolized using the Priorian operators.

There are at least three potential reasons, however, for introducing into the logical translation language an operator to symbolize the present tense. First, as English distinguishes a present tense form from the other, nonsynonymous forms of verbs, it would seem necessary to distinguish in the logical translation language the translations of present tense sentences from those of other types to maintain the parallelism necessary for the induction of a semantic interpretation of English. And given that our translation should be both explicit and parallel to the semantic interpretation, it would seem that an implicit (unmarked) present tense operator is inadequate.

Second, the present is clearly not redundant in many of its uses—the futurate (*John leaves tomorrow*), frequentative (*John only dates redheads*), and gnomic (*water boils at 212 degrees Fahrenheit*)—and it is possible that the meanings underlying at least some of these uses will require a present tense operator in the translation.

Finally, at least in a compositional treatment of the complex tenses, there is a real contribution of the present to tenses such as the present perfect and present progressive (cf. the past perfect, the past progressive). If we were to introduce past tense and perfect aspect operators *Past* and *Perf*, so as to symbolize the past perfect of a sentence p as

$$Past(Perf(p))$$

then it would appear natural to introduce a present tense operator *Pres*, so as to symbolize the present perfect of a sentence p as, parallel to the above,

$$Pres(Perf(p))$$

in order to capture the constant contribution of the construct *Perf*(*p*) to the semantics of a sentence as a whole.

Insofar as *P* is understood as a past tense operator in systems such as Prior's, the past tense is taken as indefinite; that is, the Priorian past tense operator is taken to mark that the sentence *p* is true at *some* point in time prior to the present. That is, *Pp* means 'it has been the case that *p*' = '*p* is true at some time *t* earlier than now'. Likewise, the future is taken to be indefinite, so that *Fp* is 'it will be the case that *p*' = '*p* is true at some time *t* later than now'.

Following Prior, Montague includes in his translation language the Priorian operators *H* (Prior's *P*), translating the present perfect, and *W* (= Prior's *F*), translating the future.[29]

Partee points out in an oft-cited discussion that it is incorrect to treat the past and future tenses as indefinite.[30] A sentence like her example *I didn't turn off the stove* does not assert (existentially, indefinitely) that the speaker failed to turn off the stove *on a least one occasion in the past*, but rather (definitely) that the speaker did so *on some specific occasion in the past*.

If the past tense were indefinite, it would not differ in reading from the present perfect. But in standard English, at least, it does differ: the past tense is definite, and the truth conditions of past tense sentences depend not on there being some past time, or all past times, but rather on there being a specific past time, at which the (tenseless) sentence within the scope of the tense is true.

The same is not true of the perfect, which has at least some indefinite readings (and no clearly definite ones). In its "existential" reading, for example, the perfect clearly does not involve specific times. *I have forgotten to turn off the stove* (many times, on more than one occasion, at least once, etc.) does not require a specific time at which *I forget to turn off the stove* is true, but only that there be some time in the past at which I have done so.

It has been pointed out, however, that the past does seem to have at least some indefinite readings: *Brutus killed Caesar* does not seem to presuppose a definite occasion any more than *Trudeau has been to Moscow* does.[31]

The future, interestingly enough, functions as the mirror image of both the past tense and the perfect tense. *I will forget to turn off the stove* can be definite (*I fear that I will forget to turn off the stove when I make dinner tonight*) or indefinite (*sooner or later I will forget to turn off the stove*). The same is true of the conditional, which is what we would expect, as it is a kind of future-in-the-past: *I should have foreseen that when I made dinner that night I would forget to turn off the stove; it was inevitable that sooner or later I would forget to turn off the stove*.

If we accept that examples such as *Brutus killed Caesar* involve an indefinite reading for the past tense, then, *pace* Bennett and Partee, we can rescue the traditional notion of the future as the mirror image not of the (present) perfect, but of the past.[32] (Presumably it is the futurate which mirrors the perfect.)

We will in any case require tense operators in our logical translation language to capture the senses of the tenses of natural languages. The question is how many such operators are needed, and what they are.

There would seem to be needed at least a (definite) past tense operator (PAST or PAST$_{def}$), an (indefinite) operator translating the present perfect (PERF), and maybe two operators (FUT$_{def}$ and FUT$_{indef}$) translating the future, as well as possibly an indefinite PAST operator (PAST$_{indef}$). But what about complex tenses such as the present progressive, past perfect, and future perfect progressive? Do they each translate into a special operator?

The earliest works such as Bennett and Partee's 1972 paper (published in 1978), do not utilize a translation language, but provide semantic interpretation rules directly for sentence types of English. They state separate rules for each of the complex tenses, as for instance the past perfect progressive. However, their purpose is not to provide a compositional analysis of the complex tenses, and they do not argue for the necessity of such separate rules. We will return to the problem of the complex tenses below, but will consider here the question of multiple operators for the simple tenses.

Some have argued that we do indeed need separate definite and indefinite operators. Tichý utilizes two future operators, F (mirroring the definite past operator P) and Ff (mirroring the indefinite perfect operator Pf).[33] *Tom will be drunk throughout 1980* requires F for its logical translation, while (according to Tichý) *Tom will be drunk (ever) until 1980* requires Ff. Tichý recognizes that English makes no morphological distinction between the two tenses, and hence the future tense is ambiguous.

Presumably, then, if the past is likewise ambiguously definite and indefinite, two operators are required there too, although English fails to distinguish the two morphologically. An interesting question is whether the Priorian perfect operator P could serve for both the perfect and the indefinite past. Presumably it could not. The perfect, as has been pointed out since at least the days of Apollonius, occurs with the "present-tense" adverbials such as *just, today, now* which occur with the present tense:

John has just left.	John is just leaving.
John has walked today.	John is walking today.
John has eaten now.	John is eating now.[34]

But the perfect does not occur with the "past-tense" adverbials such as *two days ago, yesterday, last year* which freely occur with the past tense:

*John has left two days ago.	John left/*is leaving two days ago.
*John has walked yesterday.	John walked/*is walking yesterday.
*John has eaten the fish last year.	John ate/*is eating the fish last year.[35]

Thus the past, even when indefinite, differs from the perfect (*Brutus killed Caesar a long time ago: *Brutus has killed Caesar a long time ago*). Further support for this comes from the ambiguity, noted by Jespersen, of the past perfect. Tichý notes the ambiguity of the pluperfect form as a past-in-the-past and as a present-perfect-in-the-past.[36]

What Richards suggests, however, is that the definite/indefinite difference is not a difference in the meaning of the tenses per se—they are *not* ambiguous—and he offers unitary accounts of the definite/indefinite past and future. He discusses the possibility that the difference proceeds from an implicit adverbial (such as *once* or *ever*), or possibly from the lack of an explicit adverbial versus the presence of one.[37]

Supporting such a treatment, and casting doubt on the need for more than one operator each in the past and future, is precisely the fact that without an explicit adverbial, sentences out of context are assumed to have indefinite readings: *I went to Rome* can only mean 'I have at sometime gone to Rome'; *Tom was ill* can only mean 'Tom was once ill'. In most contexts, however, there will be only a definite reading: *Brutus killed Caesar* will mean only 'at that time, Brutus killed Caesar'. Compare these passages:

> There was nothing Brutus could do. Caesar was becoming a tyrant. Nothing could stop him now. When the Ides came, Brutus was ready. The moment had come. Brutus killed Caesar.
>
> There is considerable testimony that Brutus was there, that he had a motive, that he was prepared to commit the deed. There is no alibi. There is no testimony that he was absent or innocent. There is no doubt. Brutus killed Caesar.

In the first passage, "Brutus did *not* kill Caesar" could have meant only that he did not kill him *then*. It would have then been possible to say: "But he waited until later and killed him *then*." The second passage, however, does not set up any privileged moment. "Brutus did *not* kill Caesar" would be absurd in this context, even if we appended "but he waited until later and killed him *then*," as it denies what the passage implies, rendering it pointless.

But these facts do not depend on the meaning of the sentence itself, but rather on the context. Presumably, then, definiteness and indefiniteness are contextual— whatever the meaning of the past tense, it is neutral in this regard. It would seem that we need only one future (FUT) and one past (PAST) operator, along with a distinct perfect (PERF) operator.

g. The Present and the Future

What now of the present tense? Is a present tense operator necessary, and if so, is there just one? After all, the present might seem to be multiply ambiguous, given that we can distinguish at least these uses:

1.	futurate:	John arrives tomorrow.
2.	historical:	Napoleon crosses the Alps.
3.	stative:	John loves Mary.
		John believes in God.
4.	frequentative:	John dates redheads.
5.	reportative:	Mr. Blandings builds his dream house.
		They exit stage right.
		He shoots, he scores!
6.	indefinite:	He sings double bass.
		She drives trucks for a living.
7.	gnomic:	Two and two are four.
8.	descriptive:	The feline is a quadruped.
9.	performative:	I agree.
		I hereby declare you the winner.[38]

In other languages there are yet other uses of the corresponding simple present tense forms. For example, in German the present has a quasi-perfect sense in sentences such as *er ist schon zwei Stunden da*, literally 'he is already two hours there' = 'he's been there for two hours'.[39] It is possible that a use of the present with verbs of communication, as in *John tells me you're getting a new car,* constitutes a quasi-perfect in English.[40]

The futurate and historical present obviously are special uses, since the former refers to the future and the latter to the past. The pseudo-perfect use in German likewise refers at least partly to the past.

The other uses are distinguished by the time intervals they refer to; they therefore also differ in what combinations of Aristotelian aspects, aspectual verbs, and adverbials may occur. The stative use refers to the time of the speech act. If John loves Mary, he loves her right now; it is true at the present time that John loves Mary.

The frequentative/habitual use does not require this. If John dates redheads, it is not necessarily the case that he is dating a redhead at the present moment.[41] Further, while John may have loved Mary for some considerable time in the past and may continue to love her for some time in the future, this is at most implied, not stated. The gnomic and descriptive uses, on the other hand, refer to all time: two and two are always four, felines are always quadrupeds.

The reportative (''narrative'') use cannot literally refer to the speech-act time, or if it does, this is coincidental or represents a nonliteral sense. Mr. Blandings takes more time to build his house than it takes to talk about it; on the other hand, it probably takes more time to talk about scoring in hockey than it does to actually score. Certainly the scoring is over with before the announcer says, ''He scores!''

Although the reportative is used as if the event takes place at the speech-act time, it differs from more usual uses of the simple present, in that these implicitly refer to the speech-act time—if Mr. Blandings sees his wife, he sees her now—whereas the reportative uses the present tense for what is not essentially a tense referring to the speech-act time: if Mr. Blandings builds his dream house, he can hardly be said in the same way to build it *now*.

The reportative use is essentially one involving telic, that is performance, predicates, ones with definite ends. If an observer reports of a man under observation, ''He runs,'' the sense is implicitly an accomplishment—he runs a bit—and the addressee is entitled to infer that he has stopped running. If he fails to stop running, the accomplishment sense is inappropriate; from the point of view of the observer it is an activity, and a report in the progressive is more proper: *He is running*.

The reportative use has two subspecies that differ: the more ''narrative'' use actually involves the moment of the speech act, whereas the reportative does so only nominally. The latter is rarely if ever used of the actual present moment, for obvious reasons. It occurs in titles, in captions on photos and pictures, in stage directions, and the like. In this sense the usage is quite like the historical present.

The indefinite differs from the frequentative in two respects. First, the latter but not the former involves a series of events and hence allows adverbials of frequency:

He dates redheads every Monday.
He frequently dates redheads.
He dates redheads from time to time.
*She drives trucks for a living every Monday.
!She frequently drives trucks for a living.
?!She drives trucks for a living from time to time.

In these last examples the adverbials are permitted when there is a frequentative sense. If there are periods in her life when she drives trucks for a living, with periods in between when she does not, frequency adverbials are allowed. Here the adverbial refers not to the driving-of-trucks but to the driving-of-trucks-for-a-living.

A second difference is that frequentatives presuppose a series of occasions, whereas indefinites do not. Someone can drive trucks for a living before they have ever driven a truck. "When did she drive trucks for a living?" invites the time periods of her employment as a truck driver, not those of her actually driving trucks. "How often did she drive trucks for a living?" cannot mean "How often did she drive trucks?" For example, if she was a professional driver during two periods of time, and drove a truck five hundred times during each interval, "How often did she drive trucks for a living?" would normally elicit the answer twice, not one thousand times, whereas the reverse is true, in null context, of "How often did she drive trucks?"

The gnomic and descriptive differ in much the same way. The gnomic refers to something definite though eternal. It is true right now that two and two are four. But it is not true in the same way that the feline is a quadruped. It is odd to ask "When is the feline a quadruped?", but not "When are two and two four?"—even though the answer to the latter question is "always." The descriptive is a kind of gnomic indefinite.

The number of uses is not important, merely the fact that the present has different uses. However, the inferences which may be drawn from the present tense form are not independent of context. The simple present tense with a stative verb (*John loves Mary*) is understood (except when a frequentative—*John usually loves Mary*) to be true right now, but with a performance verb (*John sings*) it is understood to be not necessarily true right now.

We can assimilate the apparently anomalous historical present (which refers not to present time, but to the past) to the "genuinely" present uses, if we recognize that all that is in question here is the reference point. In both cases the time of the event (his shooting and scoring, Napoleon's crossing of the Alps) "coincides" with the reference time. (The quotation marks here reflect the fact that there is not a perfect coincidence between the two, for at least some uses of the present tense.) In the "genuine" uses of the present tense, the reference time furthermore coincides with the time of the speech act.

In the case of the historical present, however, the actual position of the reference time is treated not as prior to the time of the speech act, but as if it were at that time. Assuming some mechanism for this shift in reference time, the historical present requires no special treatment. The historical present seems to correspond to all the "genuine" uses of the present, and even the futurate.

Something similar to the historical narrative present occurs in the epistolary tenses of Latin. Whereas we write as if conversing, that is, from the point of view of the writer, the Romans took the view that letters should be written from the point of view of the reader. Thus instead of saying, "I am writing this letter to you," the Roman correspondent would write, "I was writing this letter to you," and so on for the other tenses.

In the case of the epistolary tenses there is again a shift of the reference time away from the moment of "speech" (the time of the actual writing) to the (presumedly) relatively future time of the reading of the letter. The writer's present is the reader's past, and so is put in the past tense. A similar shift of viewpoint is also involved in the famous case of the inscription of the Lacedaemonians: "Go tell the Spartans, thou who passest by, that here, obedient to their laws, we lie."[42] Even though this statement is written in the past of the presumed future reader, it is put in the present tense because it is in the future at the time of writing.

Clearly, in the case of the futurate use of the present, there is no coincidence of the event time and the moment of speech; the time of the speech act by definition cannot be part of tomorrow. But if we say *John arrives tomorrow*, the time of John's arrival must be included in tomorrow.

Since in many uses of the present there must be coincidence of the event time and the time of the speech act, there would seem to be prima facie evidence for ambiguity in the case of the present. But in fact there is more compelling reason to regard the present tense as actually a non-past tense, as it is in many languages (e.g., German, Russian, Japanese), in which case there is no ambiguity, no difference in meaning between the "genuinely present" and futurate uses of the tense. For those languages having such a non-past tense, we must define the present as the tense holding when the interval over which the event occurs or the situation obtains is not earlier than that of the moment of speech.

What licenses us to treat the present and futurate uses as aspects of one meaning rather than separate meanings attached to the present tense form? Nerbonne discusses arguments concerning the nonambiguity in German of the non-past tense as between present and future, but his arguments hold for English and other languages (e.g., Japanese) as well.[43]

The crux of the argument is that deletion under identity allows both readings: *I'm working on the first chapter now, and on the fourth tomorrow.* This would be impossible if the two senses of the present were different in meaning, since deletion under identity normally requires identity of reading as well as formal identity: *Tom loves cheese but can't stand butter* is ungrammatical where the deleted subject of the second clause is named Tom but is not coreferential with the subject of the first clause.

Moreover, in a sequence there is no requirement that the event times all coincide, or that all overlap with the moment of speech. In *John is arriving from Rome and Sue is coming in from Italy* there is no presupposition either that the two arrivals should coincide or even overlap in time, nor that either should necessarily overlap with the time of the speech act. The only requirement is that neither John nor Sue should already have arrived by the time of the speech act.

Accordingly there is no need to develop special mechanisms for any of the uses of the present, so long as we recognize certain facts about time, situations, events, and verbs. Having made allowances for nonliteral uses such as the historical present, the present can be treated as unambiguous. Additional meanings come from other elements of the sentence.

The question then is under what conditions *PRES (p)* would be true. There is an interesting asymmetry between speech-act times and other times in this regard. Consider the sentence *John loves Mary*. On any occasion of utterance, this sentence is true iff John loves Mary at that time. But utterances take time; therefore to say that John loves Mary now is to say that that is true as I speak (over a short but real interval of time). Yet we can ask whether it was true *at noon* (a point in time) that John loved Mary.

For the sake of convenience we can reduce points in time to a special case of intervals and say that sentences are always evaluated at an interval of time: it is true now that John loves Mary, it is true while I speak that John loves Mary, but ''John loves Mary'' was also true at noon. (We shall see below that there are more compelling reasons for arguing that sentences are true at intervals, not at points in time.)

One question which arises is how the future tense will differ from the futurate use of the present, given that the interpretation of the futurate allows the event time to be disjoint from, and later than, the present (properly defined). One answer is that English does not have a distinct future tense, and that *shall* and *will* simply function as modal auxiliaries like any other modal auxiliaries. One piece of evidence in support of this is the fact that the suppositional use of these verbs refers to present, not future, time: *that will be John coming up the stairs* presents a supposition about what is happening now, not in the future.

Backshifting also suggests that the future tense is not a true future. If it were, we would expect that, just as the past goes into a past perfect, and the present into a past, in past contexts, so the future would go into a future perfect or perhaps the present. But instead we find the special conditional tense:

> He said, ''John ate at noon.''
> He said that John had eaten at noon.
> He said, ''John eats (every day) at noon.''
> He said that John ate (every day) at noon.
> He said, ''John will eat at five.''
> *He said that John will have eaten at five.
> *He said that John eats at five.
> He said that John would eat at five.

Would seems to be *will* within the scope of a past tense. This is what we expect, if *will eat* is simply a modal within the scope of a present tense.

All modal auxiliaries have future implication, so that we need not attribute any specific futurative quality to the so-called future auxiliary verbs to account for their future reading. Furthermore, they retain in virtually all their occasions of use some specifically modal value, and it is apparently this modal value and not the future time itself which is asserted.

There has been much discussion of this issue, with some scholars arguing for the existence of a future tense in English and others against.[44] There are languages with a morphological future tense, Latin, Greek, and Lithuanian being examples. But in many other languages the future tense is, as in English, a periphrastic, analytic construction. In itself this is not an important difference. However, the English future involves a modal expression which often retains modal values.

Consequently, the question is whether the future meaning is *asserted* by such forms or merely *implied* by them. This is quite difficult to decide, and to a great extent depends on how we define the future tense. Prior to an adequate theory of modality, all one can say is that it does no great harm to assume a future tense. On the other hand, if it should turn out that, in an adequate account of modality, futurity follows from the use of the modal auxiliaries, it is very hard to see any justification for a special treatment of "shall" and "will." This is especially true if we wish to have a compositional treatment of expressions containing them.

The question then is how, given that the future can be indefinite in meaning, it is to be distinguished from the futurate use of the non-past. It is not clear that any differences between the two *are* semantic in nature. Even if they differ in definiteness—and Wekker has called this into question—such a distinction is, as we have noted, apparently contextual, hence seemingly pragmatic in nature, as Wekker suggests.[45]

It is clear that the future and the futurate will overlap, since the only requirement of the present tense is that event time not wholly precede the speech-act time. This is unexceptionable. *John arrives tomorrow* is equivalent to *John will arrive tomorrow*; if the one is true, so must the other be.

In a Reichenbachian system, future tenses will differ from present tense ones in terms of the relationship of a reference point, R, to the speech-act time, S. Future tenses have $S<R$, and present tense ones, $S=R$. From this point of view the future must differ from the futurate, as the latter is a kind of present tense.

In a compositional semantics, this does not, however, follow. In a Jespersenian treatment of the complex futurates, the auxiliary (*is, is going, is about*) receives a present tense interpretation, but the expression itself of the event is future (*to . . .*). The futurate use of the present tense (*he leaves on Tuesday*) is accounted for by the fact that the present is a non-past tense; the specific non-present reading is purely pragmatic in character, as shown by the fact that, in some contexts, *he leaves on Tuesday* can refer to present time—in the reportative or "narrative" use, for example (as in the captions of cartoons).

We should note that in some languages there occurs, as the mirror image of the non-past tense, what may be called a non-future tense—a tense opposed to the future, and covering what is in English both past and present.[46] Its only requirement is that the time of the event not wholly *follow* the speech-act time.

Thus, it would appear that at least three tense operators are needed for a compositional system of logical translation—PAST, PRES, and FUT. We do need a PRES operator, but only one operator for each of the three times. There seems to be no good reason to assert a need for a distinct futurate operator. However, PAST is disjoint from PERF. But even if we need a PERF operator in addition to PAST, the question is whether the present perfect will be translated into PERF. Before examining this issue, however, we must first look at how these operators are to be semantically interpreted.

h. Semantic Interpretation of the Tense Operators

To interpret the tense operators PRES, PAST, FUT, and PERF, we start by stating a model of time. Let T be the set of all instants of time t. Let $\leq$ be an ordering of T such that for any two members of T t_1 and t_2, $t_1 < t_2$ or $t_1 > t_2$ or $t_1 = t_2$. ($t_1 < t_2$ means "t_1 is earlier than t_2"; $t_2 > t_1$ means "t_2 is later than t_1"; $t_1 = t_2$ means "t_1 is identical to t_2"; $t_1 \leq t_2$ means "t_1 is earlier than, or identical to, t_2.") It is not certain whether T should be dense or not, that is, whether for any two members of T t_1 and t_2, there should always exist a point $t_3 \in T$ such that $t_1 < t_3$ and $t_3 < t_2$. Bennett and Partee, and Dowty, however, assume such a dense ordering.[47]

Now, I is an interval of T iff $I \subset T$ (that is, I is a proper subset of T) and for any t_1, $t_3 \in I$ such that $t_1 \leq t_3$, if t_2 is such that $t_1 \leq t_2 \leq t_3$, then $t_2 \in I$. That is, if there are three points t_1, t_2, and t_3, where t_2 is between t_1 and t_3 (if $t_1 = t_3$, necessarily $t_2 = t_1 = t_3$), then t_2 must also be a member of I. That is, an interval is a connected (proper) subset of T with no gaps.

An interval with only one member t is called a *moment* of time. We denote intervals by indicating their first and last moments. Let I be the interval between points t_1 and t_2 inclusive; now $I = \{t:t_1 \leq t \leq t_2\} = [t_1,t_2]$. Sometimes it is useful to define an interval by the last moment before and/or the first moment after it. Then we use () rather than []:

$$(t_1,t_2] = \{t:t_1 < t \leq t_2\}$$
$$[t_1,t_2) = \{t:t_1 \leq t < t_2\}$$
$$(t_1,t_2) = \{t:t_1 < t < t_2\}$$

An open-ended interval can be denoted using the infinity sign, ∞. Thus $(t_2,\infty) = \{t:t_2 < t\}$, that is, the set of times later than t_2.

Let $[t]$ be a moment of time and $[T]$ be the set of all intervals in T except for the empty interval. Let I'' be a member of $[T]$. Now, I is a *proper subinterval* of I'' iff $I \in [T]$ and $I \subset I''$. (That is, $I \subseteq I''$ and $I \neq I''$.)

I is an *initial subinterval of I''* iff there are no times t'' such that $t'' \in I'' - I$ (that is, I'' minus I) and $t \in I$ such that $t'' < t$. That is, if I is the initial subinterval of I'', then there are no times earlier than those in I which are also in I''. Similarly, I is a *final subinterval of I''* iff there are no times t'' such that $t'' \in I'' - I$ and $t \in I$ such that $t'' > t$. Since some I could $= [t]$, an initial or final subinterval can be an initial or final *point*. A point t is an *initial bound* for I iff t is not in I and t is the initial point in $\{t\} \cup I$. Similarly, a point t is a *final bound* for I iff t is not in I and t is the final point in $\{t\} \cup I$. When an interval I wholly precedes an interval I' (that is, the final point t of I and the initial point t' of I' are such that $t < t'$), we write $I[<]I'$.

Bennett and Partee assume that evaluation of an expression is relative in general not to a *point* or *moment* of time t but rather to an interval I. The notion of evaluation at an interval is intuitively satisfying for at least the following reason. While it is possible to say that *John is reading* was true *at noon*, we cannot say that *Mr. Blandings builds his dream house* is true *at noon*. If it is true at any time at all, it is obviously true "at" (over) an interval; we could say, for example, that it was true from April 1 of last year to June 1 of this one. We do not normally say that a sentence like *Mr. Blandings builds his dream house* is true over a given interval, for the obvious reason that the present cannot include the time of a completed event, but we can take *is* to refer to the evaluation time, whatever this may be.

As a first approximation to the interpretation of the tense operators PRES, PAST, FUT for the simple tenses, we present here the truth conditions stated in Bennett and Partee (1978). They do not use an LTL and semantically interpret natural language expressions directly. However, their truth conditions could easily be restated in a system using an LTL; those for a past tense sentence p could be restated as those for PAST (p'), where p' translates the tenseless sentence contained in p. (We shall see below what the translation rules would look like.)

Their system is non-compositional in that it provides different semantic interpretation rules for the present perfect, past perfect, present perfect progressive, and so on. We will consider the significance of this later, but will ignore the problem here, as it does not affect the operators for the simple tenses.

Their system is also non-compositional in interpreting as a whole expressions containing adverbials. They do this for two reasons. First, their truth conditions require that there be a *frame* time during which the event occurs. This frame time is normally specified by a time adverbial (unless given by the speech-act time, in the case of the present). The problem is with sentences not containing such an adverbial. These are treated as indefinite (*all people alive today will die; the ancient Romans were an aggressive bunch*), unless there is an understood frame given by the context or presupposed information (in the first example above, *sometime*, and in the second, *always during the time of the ancient Romans*). It was not easy to see how such assumed frames could be dealt with in a purely semantic treatment.

The second reason is more significant—the *scope paradox for adverbials*. Consider the Priorian operators P and F, and take the adverbs *yesterday* and *tomorrow*. How are we to represent in the LTL sentences like *yesterday Sue kissed Igor* and *tomorrow Sue will fix the plumbing*? If we write

> P[Y[*Sue kiss Igor'*]]
> F[T[*Sue repair the plumbing'*]]

we obtain the readings respectively of 'it was true in the past that yesterday Sue kissed Igor' and 'it will be true in the future that tomorrow Sue will repair the plumbing'. This is obviously not correct, since we are concerned with what is true *now*. But if we symbolize as follows

> Y[P[*Sue kiss Igor'*]]
> T[F[*Sue repair the plumbing'*]]

we obtain even worse readings: 'it was true yesterday that Sue kissed Igor in the past' and 'it will be true tomorrow that Sue will repair the plumbing in the future'. We need somehow to have no difference in scope between the tense operator and the adverbial. Since this is apparently impossible, Bennett and Partee seem to have thought it prudent to forgo the use of an LTL.

For our present purposes we can ignore these various problems. Their interpretations are a good first approximation to start our discussion with.

With most predicates, ongoing, present-time events are expressed not by the simple present tense (*Susan repairs the plumbing*) but by the progressive (*Susan is repairing the plumbing*). Bennett and Partee analyze the present progressive as follows, evaluating relative to a *moment* of time:

> *John is building a house* is true at I if and only if I is a moment of time, there exists an interval of time I′ such that I is in I′, I is not an endpoint for I′, and *John builds a house* is true at I′.[48]

That is,

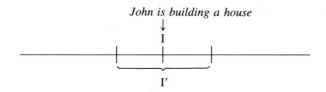

This is based on the notion that one is doing something at a moment *in* the time stretch over which that something *is done*.

The problem with evaluation at a moment is that we want sentences to be true or false (if they can be definitely true or false) at the time of the speech act. Speech-act time is, however, not a moment, but a larger interval—it takes time to utter a sentence. This introduces some obvious difficulties: under what conditions can *It is now precisely 12:08:45 p.m.* ever be said so as to be literally true? Yet we often say things of this sort which cannot literally be true—think of the sports announcer's *He shoots, he scores!* We must accordingly admit some vagueness (or to be more precise, a sort of *abus de langage*) in the use of present tense expressions. Alternatively we can omit the condition that *I* (the time of evaluation) be a moment.

There are some other problems with this analysis as well, principally the *imperfective paradox*: under the given analysis, the truth of *John is building a house* entails that of *John builds a house*, but John can certainly be said to be building a house even if he never actually builds one! (We will consider this problem below.)

Bennett and Partee analyze the past tense as follows:

> *John ate the fish* α is true at interval of time I if and only if I is a moment of time, α refers to an interval of time I′ and there exists a subinterval of I′, I″, such that I″[<] I and *John eats the fish* is true at I″.[49]

This captures the following situation (we have assumed α is *yesterday*):

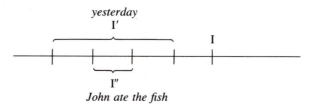

John ate the fish

This diagram is somewhat misleading, in that *I'* could include *I*, as in *John ate the fish today*. All that is required is that the time of his eating the fish wholly precede *I*. Here *I'* denotes a frame time during which the event occurred (the event time *I"* is a subinterval of the frame time *I'*). That the frame time in *at the precise moment when John opened the door, Sue was kissing Igor* is a moment follows from the meaning of the adverbial; consequently, for *I"* to be a subinterval of *I'* requires that *I"=I'*. It appears then that *I"* need not be a *proper* subinterval of *I'*. Further, that we can say *at the precise moment that John opened the door, Sue kissed Igor*, suggests that the same *abus de langage* as applied in the case of *it is now precisely 12:08:45* obtains in this case as well. The past tense here, like the Greek aorist in similar situations, has an ingressive meaning.

The truth conditions for the future are stated as follows:

> *John will eat the fish* α is true at interval of time I if and only if I is a moment of time, α refers to an interval of time I' and there exists a subinterval of I', I", such that either I is an initial point for I" or I[<]I" and *John eats the fish* is true at I".[50]

This presents the following situations, assuming the adverbials *right now* in (*i*) and *tomorrow* in (*ii*):

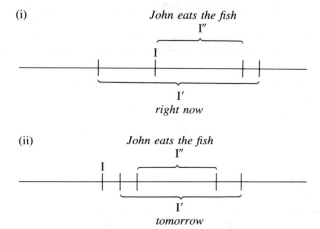

This allows two different situations—one in which the future event starts at present (i), and one in which it starts in the future (ii). It is obviously a weakness here to have two different interpretations for what is not perceived to be an ambiguity: *Susan will repair the plumbing* may be vague about whether she will start immediately, but it is not obvious that it is ambiguous. We can collapse the conditions by requiring that no points *t* in *I"* and *t'* in *I* be such that *t<t'*. The only reason for distinguishing conditions is that the future takes both "present tense" adverbials (*right now, today, this week*) and "future" ones (*tomorrow, soon, next week*).

Finally, Bennett and Partee treat the (present) perfect as a simple tense, representing the "extended now" of XN theory, and give the following set of truth conditions:

> *John has eaten the fish* α is true at interval of time I if and only if I is a moment of time, α refers to an interval of time I', I is a member of I', and there exists a

subinterval of I′, I″, such that either I is a final point for I″ or I″[<]I and *John eats the fish* is true at I″.[51]

Here *I* is the evaluation time, the adverbial denotes a frame time (e.g., *in the last week, since Tuesday, today, just now*), while *I″*, the event time, is in the frame time but not later than the evaluation time.

As in the case of the future, this presents the following situations (taking the adverbials respectively to be *just now* and *today*):

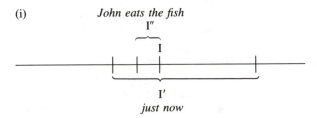

(i) *John eats the fish*

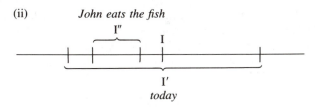

(ii) *John eats the fish*

Here the two subconditions represent a true ambiguity. In the one case something has just been done; in the other it was done a while ago. In the first case (with many verbs) the resultant state of affairs is normally inferred to still be the case: *he has just gone to the store* leads one to conclude *he is gone*, whereas *he has gone to the store today* does not; *he has just fallen ill* leads to the conclusion that *he is ill*, whereas *he has fallen ill today* does not.

There are a number of problems with this formulation, but the basic one is this. It is a completely non-compositional treatment, in which the analysis of the present perfect does not have any direct implications for those of the other perfect tenses. The question is, do we want and/or require a compositional treatment for the complex tenses (such as the present perfect)?

i. Complex Tenses and Compositionality

We have seen that some scholars have proposed systems in which the complex, analytic tense forms of English (and other languages) are treated as indivisible units for the purposes of semantic interpretation.[52] In such systems the present perfect, the past present, the present perfect progressive, and so on, are each given a special treatment.

Yet other scholars have argued that the progressive, the perfect, and each of the tenses require separate treatments, so that the analysis of the present perfect progressive, for example, follows from, or consists in, that of the present plus that of the perfect plus that of the progressive. This requires that the treatment of such complex forms be at least weakly compositional, in the sense that semantic interpretation of the expression as a whole consists in semantic interpretation of its constituent parts.

Intuitively a compositional approach makes sense. By Fregean compositionality, the meaning of an expression such as *has been running* depends on the meanings of the constituent expressions, whatever these may be, along with *their mode of composition*—how they are combined—assuming of course that such expressions are not idiomatic.

In the case of this example, we do intuit that the presentness of *has been running* (as opposed to, say, the pastness of *had been running*) comes from the present tense marking on *has*, that the perfectness comes from *have* (and/or the "perfect participial" ending *-en*), and that the progressiveness comes from *be* (and/or the "present participial" ending *-ing*).

However, there are many syntactically composite expressions in languages for which such a compositional semantic interpretation is not obviously appropriate. A classic case in point is the Catalan periphrastic past, a construction which is completely parallel in form with the periphrastic *future* tense of the other Romance languages. Catalan *jo vaig anar*, for example, is etymologically identical to French *je vais aller* and Spanish *(yo) voy ir*, both of which mean 'I am going to go' (literally, 'I go to-go'). But the Catalan form does *not* mean what it literally says—'I am going to go'. It is idiomatic.

The Catalan construction would seem to cry out for a non-compositional treatment, since the present tense is inherently non-past and non-perfect, and its other two components are often connected with non-past, non-perfect meaning. The auxiliary "go" is a future tense auxiliary in many languages, and the infinitive with "be" often conveys futurity (*he is to go soon*; the Russian periphrastic future) or perduration (*how was I to know that?*), so that it is hard to see how any one component could contribute pastness (or perfectness) to the meaning.

Yet a compositional treatment is not entirely precluded here. All that is necessary is to interpret "to go" (*anar*) as some kind of a past time auxiliary which serves to shift event time from the future time to the past. The auxiliary "go" in Romance marks futurate meaning, indicating the relationship R—E (R<E). In the case of the Catalan construction, it would indicate rather the relationship E—R (E<R).

This seems in fact to accord with the hypothesized origins of the idiomatic construction. Elcock says[53] that the Catalan "periphrastic perfect" probably did originally convey the same "aspect of time" as the French *je vais chanter*, but because in medieval narrative past meaning was frequently expressed by the "graphic" historic present ("a frequent example may be found in the recurring *il va ferir*[54] of Old French epic"), the periphrastic future came often to used of past events. Eventually, as a result, this periphrastic tense emerged in Catalan as what Elcock calls a "perfect" tense.

It is not certain that any universal principles of syntax or semantics are violated by such a treatment of the Catalan construction. But the approach does seem to be merely a trick for rendering the semantics of an idiom compositional. If we admit a compositional treatment of the Catalan periphrastic perfect, can we exclude a compositional treatment for any construction whatsoever?

Apparently not, for we can always assign some element *e* of the construction a semantic interpretation such that the interpretation of the construction as a whole follows from that of the other constituents plus that of *e*. There is no independent guide to whether such an assignment is appropriate, since we cannot assume that natural language expressions (such as the verb *anar*) have unambiguous, "natural" denotations. As Welsh points out (1986), "the principle [of compositionality], theory-independently, has little empirical content." It is only within the confines of a definite proposal as to what meanings are and how expressions are combined that it makes sense to talk of requiring compositionality.

In a sense we have been pursuing here a red herring. The reason why Bennett and Partee's treatment (1978) is not compositional is that it semantically interprets natural language expressions directly, and natural language expressions do not explicitly and unambiguously reveal logical structure. Fregean compositionality for natural language implicitly involves the kind of structural transformation which Montague builds into the special syntactic rules of the NL syntax.

It has been viewed in most theories as at least economical and as potentially insightful to translate surface NL expressions into equivalent LTL expressions before performing semantic interpretation on them. One reason for this is that the LTL can be designed so as quite literally to obey Fregean compositionality. Little syntactic mechanism is required to recursively specify the set of possible LTL expressions, and semantic interpretation rules can be precisely matched to the LTL syntax so as to allow the appropriate interpretation.

It is obviously required that we guarantee the appropriate translation of any given NL expression into the LTL, but no one has ever required that the LTL structures parallel those of the NL in any significant way. Hence it would be absurd to require a strongly compositional treatment of the complex tenses, one in which each constituent of the NL expression was assigned a distinct LTL translation for purposes of semantic interpretation.

In the various treatments by Dowty, for example, there is no LTL unit consisting of a tense operator and the perfect operator, yet in English the two combine into words such as *has* and *had*. In this case Dowty is not following Bach (1980) and others in treating tense as a modifier of the following verb (or verb phrase) rather than of the sentence as a whole.

Furthermore, Dowty treats endings such as *-en* and *-ing* as redundant, simply mapped morphologically onto verbs, based on the preceding verb. That is, a verb immediately within the scope of perfect *have* appears in the perfect participial form, while one immediately within that of progressive *be* appears in the present participial form. This is equivalent to the traditional treatment of auxiliaries in transformational generative grammar (as for example by Chomsky, 1957), in which *be . . . ing* and *have . . . en* are units, the endings being transformationally hopped (moved) over and adjoined to the following verb. That is, *have . . . en* marks the perfect, *be . . . ing* the progressive, and the units *been* and *running* in *has been running* are purely surface phenomena with no consequences in and of themselves for semantic interpretation.

In Dowty's treatments, *have* marks the perfect and translates into the PERF operator of *IL*,[55] as progressive *be* translates into PROG. The complement verb receives its own translation, but there is no LTL expression which combines perfect meaning with the meaning of the complement verb, thereby directly translating the perfect participle.

In a theory in which the perfect participle reflects perfect aspect, it might be argued that the *gone* of *has gone* is the same as that of *is gone*. In many Romance and Germanic languages *is . . . en* and *has . . . en* are variants which depend on the meaning of the verb and on the construction they occur in (e.g., reflexive verbs in French all take *être* 'be', but the corresponding nonreflexives may take *avoir* 'have'). In some languages (including English), however, the two constructions are different in meaning—"being eaten" is not the same as "having eaten"!

If both constructions are analyzed as incorporating a unit, the past or perfect participle, with the same interpretation in both cases, then obviously a compositional treatment of the perfect is called for in which not only is the perfect independent of the lexical verb, but the participial ending is not simply redundant. We could take the past participle as referring to *the state* denoted by the lexical base of the verb, and the auxiliaries *be* and *have* as respectively marking being in, and entering into, that state.

This is the kind of treatment which an event-based treatment (one in which *gone* refers to a state of gone-ness, and *have gone* to being in a state of gone-ness as a result of a previous event of going) might require. (See the last sections of this chapter on event-based analyses.) But it is not so clear if a treatment in which the notion of event were not basic would require it or even allow it.[56]

The difference between the two kinds of approach "compositional" and "non-compositional," is not really a semantic one. The semantic interpretation of the natural language induced by that of the LTL does not depend on the precise relationship of the LTL expressions to the natural language ones, since all that is essentially in question is whether the former correctly translate the latter. The only question then is if there is any reason to prefer a syntax for the LTL which is more or less like that of the NL it translates. Even if it always make sense to ask, for example, "what is the meaning of *been*?", it may or may not be useful (or necessary) to translate a syntactic atom like *been* into an expression of the LTL.

If it be argued that, after all, the LTL expression must be of the *type* which equates to the *category* of the NL expression, it must be pointed out in response that the category of a basic expression has nothing to do with that of an expression such as *been*, which results in Montague grammar from application of at least one specific syntactic rule. In transformational terms, the surface syntax (and morphology) of NL expressions is not necessarily relevant to their semantics.

The arguments which have been advanced for or against compositional treatments of NL semantics where interpretation is not direct, but induced by interpretation of the corresponding LTL expressions, are therefore in effect syntactic. Nerbonne, for example, argues *against* a compositional treatment of the German perfect.[57] Nerbonne criticizes just such a treatment of the perfect by Bäuerle.[58] Nerbonne, following Admoni, regards the perfect as consisting of "two context dependent variants," though not (semantically) ambiguous.[59]

For Nerbonne the perfect represents either an absolute tense or a relative tense. The absolute tense represents a situation in which event time precedes speech-act time. This meaning is equally captured by the preterite, and in this regard the preterite in modern spoken German is essentially a stylistic or pragmatic variant of the (non-futurate) present perfect. *Er hat den Brief geschrieben*, literally 'he has the letter written', means the same thing as *er schrieb den Brief* 'he wrote the letter'. Both the preterite and the absolute use of the present perfect are *definite* tenses.

But the (present) perfect is also a relative tense, holding of a situation in which the event time precedes the reference time. In this case, since the present of German is actually a non-future, it is possible to have a present perfect referring to the future (though the preterite generally cannot do so), as in *naechsten Freitag hat er den Brief geschrieben*, literally, 'next Friday has he the letter written', that is, 'he will have written the letter by next Friday'. In this use the present perfect is an *indefinite* tense.

The synonymy of a subcase of the present perfect with the preterite means that Bäuerle is forced by his compositional treatment of the perfect to regard the present perfect as ambiguous. The absolute reading presumably is translated by the PRET—preterite—operator, rather than by a combination of PRES and PERF.

Nerbonne sees the need for a "second, special, and non-compositional meaning" for the present perfect as a heavy cost which requires justification, although he admits that a compositional semantics is coherent and, in light of the paradigm of forms, attractive. Nerbonne does not provide an argument against the compositional proposal *as such* so much as an argument against the major positive argument *in favor* of the proposal. He points out that the kind of evidence which would positively establish a compositional translation is the existence of some element X with wider scope than the aspects (e.g., the perfect) but narrower scope than the tenses (e.g., the present), as would occur in this configuration:

PRES(X(PERF(p)))

Although Nerbonne reports a claim by Hendricks to have found such an element, he convincingly argues against the cited evidence.[60] Hendricks claims that durative adverbials have precisely the requisite scope in examples such as:

Erika hat diese Schlange schon   lange   getötet.
Erika has this   snake   already for-a-long-time killed.
'This snake has been dead *for quite some time now* and Erika killed it.'[61]

Nerbonne notes that "if the Perfect denotes the state resulting from Erika's killing the snake, then the temporal semantics [of this example] follows from the compositional view where *schon lange* has the scope of X." But he argues that in this type of example *schon lange* is *not* a durative, since "no clear example of duratives can replace *lange* here."

*Erika hat diese Schlange schon {tagelang / zwei Stunden} getötet.

"If [this] is at all interpretable, then [it is] only in the sense that the *act* of killing, not its results, lasted the specified length of time. Thus *lange* in [the earlier example] doesn't mean 'for a long time', but rather 'a long time ago'." And as such, it would not have the appropriate scope of X.

He is less successful, however, in arguing *positively* for non-compositionality. He points out that a few verbs allow the preterite to be used in a future sense: *warte, bis er hier war*, literally 'wait until he here was' = *warte, bis er hier gewesen ist*, literally 'wait until he here been is', 'wait until he's been here'. He argues from this fact that the preterite equates to neither tense nor aspect but to the perfect as a whole.

This argument makes a number of questionable assumptions. But even if it were true that this is a simple case of synonymy, it is not clear how it bears on the issue of compositionality. The truth conditions of the perfect are precisely equivalent, whether compositional or not. The issues choosing between them must be issues of the syntax of the translation language, not those of the NL, German.

Bach has, however, argued (1980) for a compositional treatment and against treating the complex tenses as non-compositional sentence operators on the grounds that, on this assumption, we cannot account for the fact that the NL morphosyntax of tenses is as it is. Nothing in such a theory would predict the parallelism of *has run, had run, have run,* or their nonparallelism with *is running*.

In such a theory it is entirely contingent how, and how many, NL tense forms equate to how many LTL expressions. The semantics should reflect the notion of *possible tense form*. That is, something like the Catalan periphrastic perfect would be considered idiomatic because it violates general principles of tense formation, whereas the English present perfect does not, given that *have* (and/or *-en*) marks the perfect aspect, and the present tense ending marks present (non-past) tense.

Such generalizations are at least language-internal, but potentially also language-independent. It seems appropriate to capture them in the form of a compositional interpretation in which something like *has been running* indeed is interpreted as the present tense of the perfect aspect of the progressive. For only such a treatment ultimately allows us an approach to the question of what a possible verb tense is.

The issue of compositionality actually comprises a number of independent issues. Johnson (1977) arrives at a fully compositional translation of the NL (Kikuyu) operators into LTL (*IL*) operators: each NL operator is matched by an LTL one in such a way that an iterative interpretation of the LTL expressions induces one for the NL ones. But the process of translation is not fully compositional, in that combinations of NL markers are translated into combinations of LTL operators. The reason for this is that Kikuyu marks aspect (as it does tense) by affixes, and status by the morphological pattern within the verb. Johnson sets out a paradigm of possible verb forms and then translates each member of the paradigm into the appropriate LTL translation.

Kikuyu (a Bantu language) has a verb with an "exceedingly complex" morphology;[62] the verb is marked for tense, aspect, status, negation, modality, and so on, as well as for agreement with the subject and sometimes the object as well. Kikuyu has six tenses, with metric distinctions[63] in the past and future: remote past, near past, immediate past, extended present, near future, and remote future tenses. It has three aspects—"progressive" (similar to the imperfective), "completive" (perfective), and perfect. (We discuss later in this chapter the relationship of the progressive to the imperfective.)

It also has two *statuses*—manifest and imminent. The manifest status is used, essentially, for events which are historical, and the imminent for those which are not, or are not yet, historical. The manifest paradigm is limited to the three past tenses and a "zero-tense," while the imminent is limited to the extended present and the futures, plus the simple present.[64] The difference between the two statuses is indicated by morphological structure: in the manifest the aspect markers are infixed within the stem, but in the imminent they are prefixed to it.

In the manifest there are all three aspects, but in the imminent only the completive occurs with the extended present and the futures, while the progressive and perfect occur only with the simple present. As we might expect, the progressive zero-tense manifest of "run" means 'is habitually running',[65] while the progressive simple present imminent means 'is running (right now)'.

A typical Kikuyu form is *a.ra.hanyūk.ir.e.*, 'he ran yesterday', based on *hanyūka* 'run'. The prefix *a-* marks subject concord; *-ra-* marks the near past tense; the infix *-ir-* (which turns the final *a* to *e*) marks the completive aspect.[66]

From the point of view of syntax, words ought to be unanalyzable atoms. Given the need to have translation match morpho-syntax, a fully compositional treatment of the process of translation for the Kikuyu verb is excluded. The fact that status is marked by the morphological structure of the word and not by an explicit morpheme would seem to exclude such a treatment.

What Johnson does is to set out a two-dimensional paradigm of the forms of the verb, indexing each form for its status-aspect-tense and for its concord class.[67] The root *hanyūka* 'run' is indexed $\langle 0,0 \rangle$ (it has no concord marking and no tense, aspect, or status). The "inflected" form *īhanyūka* is indexed $\langle 2,0 \rangle$. The form *yahanyūka* is indexed $\langle 3,0 \rangle$, indicating unmarked concord and its third place (present tense, perfect aspect, imminent status) in the paradigm.

A syntactic rule involving verbs is sensitive to these indices. For example, Johnson's rule S3 says, in part:

S3. If $\delta \in P_{IV}$ and the verb in δ has the index $\langle 2,0 \rangle$, then $F_2(\delta), \ldots F_6(\delta) \in P_{IV}$, where a) $F_2(\delta) = \delta'$ and δ' comes from δ by replacing the verb in δ with the corresponding form indexed $\langle 3,0 \rangle$.[68]

The corresponding translation rule T3 says in part:

T3. If $\delta \in P_{IV}$ and δ translates into δ', then
a) $F_2(\delta)$ translates into $\lambda x \mathrm{IMM}[\mathrm{PERF}[\delta'(x)]]$.[69]

Thus, the syntax does not directly concern itself with the morphology of the verb, and translation depends on the indices assigned verbs in the paradigm of forms, not on the morphology itself. Nonetheless, the result is an LTL translation in which each status, tense, and aspect receives a unique translation such that a compositional semantic interpretation is possible.

It is not always clear, when the issue of compositionality is debated, which of the issues is (are) in question. But there are no easy answers to any of these questions. As Cresswell has stressed, language must in some important sense be compositional,[70] but it remains unclear precisely what the sense is.

j. The Perfect

One area in which there has been particular controversy over the issue of compositionality is the perfect, especially where this represents a relative past tense (e.g., the pluperfect as a past-in-the-past). It is controversial whether the present perfect is a tense in its own right, different in important respects from both the past perfect and the future perfect, so that in a compositional treatment it should not receive an LTL translation parallel to these other complex tenses, or whether all three share significant properties which derive from their being perfect tenses, and hence should receive parallel translations (and interpretations).

The treatment of the perfects depends on their meanings. We saw in chapter 3, however, that there has been no agreement concerning this, especially where the present perfect is concerned, and that four major types of theory of the present perfect have arisen: ID: that the perfect is an *indefinite past* as opposed to the definite preterite; CR: that it has *current relevance* lacking in the case of the preterite; XN: that it represents the ''extended now'' (an interval of time to which the present belongs); and EB: that the perfect is a past tense embedded within the scope of another tense, a kind of relative tense.[71] (For a detailed account of EB theory, see the discussion in chapter 8 of syntactic theories of SOT.)

The EB treatment requires no distinctive PERFect (or PROGressive) operator. Semantic representations are abstract underlying (syntactic) representations. PRESent and PAST tense operators can both occur freely within the scope of another tense operator. The outermost tense of a sentence will be morphologically mapped on the surface by a tense morpheme. But an embedded tense is transformed into *have . . . en* (PAST) or *be . . . ing* (PRES). Accordingly, the semantic representation of *John has been running* will be something like this:

$$\text{PRES(PAST(PRES(John run)))}$$

Within the scope of PAST, the inner PRES will be transformed into the progressive *be . . . ing*; within the scope of the outer PRES, PAST will be transformed into the perfect *have . . . en*; and after application of the affix-hopping transformation and rules moving the tense into the verb phrase, we arrive at *John have-PRES be-EN run-ING*, which is transformed by the morphological and lexical rules of the language into *John has been running*.

The major difficulty with this treatment is that it allows indefinite iteration of tenses. There is nothing to disallow a structure such as

$$\text{PAST(PRES(PAST(PRES(John run))))}$$

This is presumably **John was having been running*, which happens not to be a possible English sentence. Longer and longer expectations become progressively less like English. Thus

$$\text{PRES(PAST(PRES(PAST(PRES(John run)))))}$$

would be **John is having had been running*. McCawley was forced to adopt a purely ad hoc solution to this problem, namely that all but one contiguous (underlying) PAST be deleted.[72]

Apart from the syntactic difficulties of EB theory (and no syntactician today would accept its underlying assumptions), it is unattractive in failing to account for many of the ways in which the perfect is used. These include Jespersen's resultative or permansive reading and the anterior or relative priority reading (*he had gone to the store*—and was still there—vs. *he had* [*once*] *gone to the store*); the four distinct readings McCawley and others have recognized (the existential, universal, stative, and "hot news"); futurate uses in such languages as English and German; and present-like uses in Greek, for example.

Further, in EB theory the meaning of the perfect would have to be the same as the past tense, the only difference being the presence or absence of an absolute reference time. It is hard to see how the relationship of the perfect to the preterite can be explicated in these terms, given the apparent meaning differences between the two.

In the CR and ID theories, the *meaning* of the perfect is precisely that of the preterite. Any difference is extrinsic to the semantics. In the case of CR theory, the perfect is simply a form used to express past time under certain pragmatic conditions. In ID theory the only difference lies whether the time being talked about is definite or indefinite. From the semantic point of view, there is again no real difference from the meaning of the preterite, since a *definite* time t_n in the past is simply one of the *indefinite* times t in the past.

One question which needs answering is whether the present perfect is ever truly ambiguous. Obviously, the Latin perfect is—it acts like both a primary tense and a secondary. But the question is whether the futurate perfect (*I'll leave when I've had my lunch*; [German] *in einem Jahr hat man das Haus gebaut* 'in one year the house will have been built')[73] and the preterite perfect of French and German (*je les ai vu hier* 'I saw [have seen] them yesterday'; *ich habe ihn gestern gesehen* 'I saw [have seen] him yesterday') represent different meanings or only contextual variants of the XN meaning. We will return to this question below.

As we have noted, the Priorian P operator merely requires that there exist *some* time in the past at which such and such was the case or took place. The weakest requirement that we can make of the perfect is indeed that the event occur at some time prior to the present.

This has been captured in a series of articles by Åqvist and Guenther[74] that define the operator HasBeen as follows: HasBeen A $=_{def}$ P$\diamondsuit$A ($\diamondsuit$ is the possibility operator, interpreted in a Diodorean way[75] as "there is a time t such that A is true at t"), that is, in the past, A was possibly the case. Relative to a model M and a pair of reference time r and speech-act time s, HasBeen A is true if e<r and r = s.

However, the solution for the perfect favored by McCoard (1978) and others following him is XN theory, treating the (present) perfect as a kind of present translated by an "extended now" operator XN, and assigning it truth conditions in terms of a period of time of which the present is the final subinterval.[76]

In other words, *John has gone* is true if *John goes* is true of some subinterval of an interval of which the present is the final subinterval. For example, for *John has gone today*:

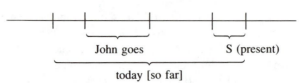

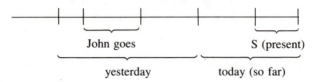

This will serve to distinguish it from the preterite, which allows events to occur on intervals excluding the present, as in *John went yesterday*:

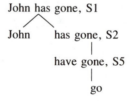

This explains why *John has gone to see Jane today* is acceptable, but not **John has gone to see Jane yesterday*.

k. Translation and Interpretation of the Perfect

Dowty presents an analysis of the English perfect based on XN theory which is nonetheless compositional.[77] Let us assume the following syntactic rules:

S2. If $\delta \in$ IV, $F_2(\delta) \in$ IV', where $F_2(\delta)$ is the present tense of δ.
S3. If $\delta \in$ IV, $F_3(\delta) \in$ IV', where $F_3(\delta)$ is the past tense of δ.[78]
S4. If $\delta \in$ IV, $F_4(\delta) \in$ IV', where $F_4(\delta) = will\ \delta$.[79]
S5. If $\delta \in$ IV, $F_5(\delta) \in$ IV, where $F_5(\delta) = have\ \delta'$ and δ' is the past participle of δ.

This allows structures as in the accompanying diagram.

                        John has gone, S1
                       ⟋   ⟍
                  John   has gone, S2
                                    |
                              have gone, S5
                                    |
                                   go

Notice that the syntax of English is not treated here as compositional in that *have gone* is not derived from *have* and *gone*. Nothing in principle precludes such a treatment, however.

Dowty recognizes that a tense may not be added to a structure already containing a tense. Accordingly he distinguishes types of intransitive verb phrases. The result of adding a tense is not simply IV, but rather IV'; it is only to IV, but not to IV', that the various elements may be added.

Is it not clear that distinguishing categories of syntactic expressions (and thereby complicating other portions of the syntax) is the appropriate way of handling this constraint. One possible alternative is to utilize Johnson's (1977) method of paradigms. As we have seen, this system likewise is non-compositional in the treatment of the verbs of the NL, but it has the advantage of not requiring a special type of phrase (though it may complicate the syntactic rules). A more "natural" set of rules might be captured by utilizing indices with separate places for each category (e.g., tense) of NL marker. For example, a third person singular, simple present tense indicative form such as *loves* might be indexed $\langle 3,1,1,1,1 \rangle$; a third person plural, simple past tense *were* would be $\langle 3,2,1,2,1 \rangle$; and so on. And the syntactic rules could be simplified through the use of rule schemata using variables ranging over members of these indices. For example, a certain function might convert a form having a certain index ι into a certain form $\phi\iota$.

The translation rules corresponding to the above syntactic rules of Dowty's are these:

T2. If $\delta \in$ IV, $F_2(\delta)$ translates as $\lambda\mathcal{P}$ [PRES $\mathcal{P}\{\delta'\}$].
T3. If $\delta \in$ IV, $F_3(\delta)$ translates as $\lambda\mathcal{P}$ [PAST $\mathcal{P}\{\delta'\}$].
T4. If $\delta \in$ IV, $F_4(\delta)$ translates as $\lambda\mathcal{P}$ [FUT $\mathcal{P}\{\delta'\}$].
T5. If $\delta \in$ IV, $F_5(\delta)$ translates as λx [HAVE $\delta'(x)$].

The truth conditions for the operators PRES, PAST, FUT, and HAVE may be stated as follows[80]:

$[\![$PRES $\phi]\!]^{r,s} = 1$ iff $[\![\phi]\!]^{r,s} = 1$ and r = s.
$[\![$PAST $\phi]\!]^{r,s} = 1$ iff $[\![\phi]\!]^{r,s} = 1$ and r < s.
$[\![$FUT $\phi]\!]^{r,s} = 1$ iff $[\![\phi]\!]^{r,s} = 1$ and r > s.
$[\![$HAVE $\phi]\!]^{r,s} = 1$ iff $[\![\phi]\!]^{r',s} = 1$ where r' is some interval of which r is a final subinterval.

The first three rules simply establish an ordering between the two points *r* and *s*. Otherwise, relative to these two points, the evaluation is the same.

The interpretation differs from those given by Bennett and Partee (1978) essentially only in that Dowty's rules evaluate expressions in terms of *two* times *r* and *s*, rather than just one, *s*. In fact, Dowty provides a mechanism for reducing these evaluations to evaluations in terms of just *s*; we shall see later why he introduces *r* into the index.

In the case of HAVE, we have already seen that there are *three* intervals involved—Bennett and Partee's *I* (the evaluation time), *I'* (the frame time), and *I"* (the event time). Dowty also has three times. Let *r* be some time, and *s* another time. HAVE ϕ is true at *r*, *s* just in case *r* is the last subinterval of an interval of time *r'* such that ϕ is true at *r'*, *s*. In effect, *s=I*, *r'=I"*, and *r=I'*.

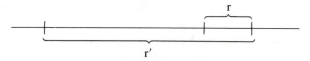

This system contains a compositional treatment of the perfect by dint of factoring out the relationships of R, E, and S. This involves separate operators for the tenses and for the perfect aspect, and interpretations of the appropriate sort. Instead of tying the "extended now" interval to the present, it is tied to the R point, whatever this may be.

1. The Compositionality of the Perfect

There is ample reason to believe that the appropriate treatment of the perfect *is* a compositional one. In English and other languages, the perfect occurs with all tenses, including the conditional (*would have gone*). Further, the perfect occurs in non-finite verb forms as well as finite (tensed) ones: gerunds, present/active participles, and nominalizations (*having gone*); the infinitive (*to have gone*); and past/ perfect participles and derived adjectives (*gone*).[81]

If a form such as *has forgotten* gains its tense from the tense marker (*-s*) and its aspect from the perfect marker *have* (and/or the past participial ending *-en*), then a fully compositional treatment of the present perfect is justified, assuming that all (nonidiomatic) uses of the (present) perfect can be accounted for in terms of one meaning, and that its meaning is treatable as a combination of tense and aspect.

There is good reason to believe that the perfect *is* an aspect, not merely a tense or part of a tense, namely that *has gone* may imply *is* (*still*) *gone*, and *has died, is dead*, while *is gone* entails *has gone* and *is dead, has died*. At least some readings of the perfect would seem therefore to require treatment as referring to a state resulting from a previous event. Having gone constitutes having entered into a state of goneness, while being gone constitutes being in a state of goneness.

However, XN theory in its classical form makes the meaning of the (present) perfect quite unlike a combination of tense and aspect, and thereby renders a compositional treatment impossible in any non-trivial sense. (It is always possible to arrive at a trivially compositional treatment, as we saw in the case of the Catalan periphrastic perfect tense.)

The perfects, like other tenses, all make essential reference to two times—the time of the event and a reference time. In XN theory, the present perfect requires not only that the reference time be the present, but further that the present be the final subinterval of an interval—the "extended now"—which includes the event time. This condition does not follow from the present as tense, which makes no reference to the (past) even time (but merely to the coincidence of reference and speech-act time), and it does not follow from the perfect as an aspect, which makes no essential reference to the present (but merely to the event preceding the reference time). That XN theory does not allow a compositional treatment of the perfect does not, however, disturb those scholars, like Nerbonne (1984), who are dubious of a compositional treatment.

One of the advantages of a neo-Reichenbachian approach, in which his analyses of the various tenses are factored out into separate tense (R, S) and aspect (E, R) relations (for example, that incorporated into Johnson's system), is that it allows simple definitions of possible tense and possible aspect (excluding such things as metric tenses which mark additional distinctions): the three possible tenses are $R<S$ (past), $R=S$ (present), and $R>S$ (future); the three possible aspects are $E<R$ (perfect or anterior), $E=R$ (imperfect), and $E>R$ (prospective or posterior). It also allows a fully compositional treatment of the verb tenses.

Where Johnson differs from Dowty is in not requiring that E occur on an interval of which R is the last subinterval. Her truth conditions for the PERF operator are as follows[82]:

[PERF ϕ]^{A,w,t,i,J,g} is that function h in H such that for all i_0 in I, $h(i_0) = 1$ if and only if for some j in J, $j < i$, and $\phi^{A,w,t,i,J,g}$ $(i_0) = 1$—otherwise, $h(i_0) = 0$.

Her *A* is Dowty's *M*; she uses in the same way as Dowty *w, t,* and *g*; *J* is the set *T* of intervals of time, and *j* some time in *J*; and *i* is the reference time (R). H is the set of functions from intervals to truth values.

What her semantic interpretation rule says is that *PERF* ϕ is true at some interval *i* of time, iff there is a time *j* prior to *i* such that ϕ is true of *j*. This is a weaker condition than Dowty imposes on the English perfect, since Johnson's condition would allow, for example, **I have seen her yesterday.*

Assuming some such compositional definition of the perfect, it can be seen how the various readings of the perfect follow. The perfect aspect is marked by the perfect auxiliary (and/or the participial ending), translated into the operator PERF. The tense, marked by the tense marker on the auxiliary (or if there is none, by that on the main verb), is translated by a tense operator such as FUT. At least within the context of a system like Johnson's, the classical Reichenbachian definitions of the various perfect tenses fall out from the definitions of the perfect and the various tenses. For example, the past perfect, E—R—S, falls out from the past tense being R—S and the perfect aspect E—R.

While things are not quite this uncomplicated, it is at least plausible that a simple, universal definition of possible aspect of some sort could be stated. But clearly, if the present tense is just R = S and the perfect aspect E<R, then the present perfect is E<R = S, but the XN theory imposes a stronger condition than this on the present perfect of English.

If the stronger conditions of the XN theory held throughout the perfect system of English, then it would be possible to argue that the perfect in English *is* compositional, though perfect aspect in English imposes stronger truth conditions than the perfect aspect of either German (which allows ''John has seen her yesterday'') of Kikuyu (according to Johnson) or apparently many other languages. For example, Inoue discusses pragmatic restrictions on two Japanese constructions which each correspond to one of the readings of the English perfect. In both, adverbials referring to entirely past intervals are possible.[83]

watashi wa,		
	wakai toki	'when (I) was young'
	kyonen	'last year'
	kyonen no 3-gatsu ni	'March last year'
	?sengetsu	'last month'

mushiba ni nayama.s.are.ta[84]   *koto ga ar.u.*
cavities by suffer-cause-passive past

'I've had the experience of suffering from cavities when I was young [etc.]' [cf. *?*I've suffered from cavities when I was young*].

Similarly,

John to ie ba,   kare wa,   kinoo   no asa
John speaking of he   TOPIC yesterday 's morning

eki   de tomodachi o   mat.te i.ru.
station at friend   OBJECT wait

'Speaking of John, he waited for his friend at the station yesterday morning.' [Cf.
*John has waited for his friend at the station yesterday morning.]

This would seem to suggest that one way languages can differ is whether they
impose on the perfect the weaker E<R or the stronger XN requirement. Given
the simplicity of the E<R requirement and the fact that we can more simply define
"possible aspect" with E<R, to retain compositionality we must apparently either
find some language-specific mechanism for imposing the stronger requirement or
abandon strong universals regarding aspect. It may be, for example, that the XN
requirement is a language-specific requirement independent of the universal truth
conditions for PERF.

English does *not* impose the XN requirement throughout its perfect system. The
past perfect and the future perfect seem to require only the weaker, neo-Reichenbachian condition and not the stronger, XN condition. The past perfect is indifferently a past anterior and a permansive past. This is true whether we are dealing
with indirect discourse, free indirect discourse, or even direct discourse:

(When Rome was founded), the Egyptians had already had over 2500 years of history. (permansive)
(In the preceding millennium) the Egyptians had briefly followed monotheism. (anterior)
(We can only hope that) by 2000 serious controls on air pollution will have long
been in place. (permansive)
(We can only hope that) by 2000 serious controls on air pollution will have long
since been put in place. (anterior)
(Herodotus suspected that) the Egyptians had already had over 2500 years of history.
(permansive)
(Herodotus never knew that) the Egyptians had briefly followed monotheism. (ante-
rior)
Herodotus was awed by the Egyptians. Had they not already had over 2500 years of
history? (permansive)
The priests of Amon-Ra were delighted by the downfall of the heretic pharaoh. The
Egyptians had briefly followed monotheism. But now it was back to business as
usual. (anterior)

Nor does English impose the XN requirement on non-finites, or in indirect
quotation. (In the latter, the difference between perfect and past is neutralized:
both *Sam believed that Sue had left* and *Sam believed Sue to have left* could refer
to either a belief of Sam's that "Sue left" or a belief of this that "Sue has left.")

There is a restriction on the main clause present perfect—but not on the past or
future perfects, nor on non-finites or indirectly quoted perfects—that adverbials
refer to the XN period. We can say that Egyptians had battled the Hyksos people
in the previous millennium or that the United States will possibly have elected a
black woman President by the end of the next century. But what we *cannot* say
is that Sue has kissed John yesterday or that the Union has defeated the Confed-
eracy in the nineteenth century.

Thus we can retain compositionality while not imposing the stronger XN requirement on all the perfects only if we accept that the perfect tenses are systematically ambiguous. All the three tenses and the non-finites *allow* an XN reading,

but only the present *requires* it; the other tenses and non-finites also allow a purely anterior (E<R) reading. The XN reading and the anterior reading in fact are different meanings, one compositional, deriving its semantics purely from those of the perfect aspect and the particular tenses, and the other not, its semantics requiring some special semantic treatment.

But simply to say that the present perfects with past tense adverbials are unacceptable is not explanatory. Clearly their unacceptability relates to the fact that they cannot be coherently interpreted, that they are "non-sensical." If so, it is doubtful that the XN requirement is the correct way of capturing this restriction. It seems unlikely that it is appropriate to build restrictions against non-reference-time adverbials into the semantics of the present perfect itself. The problem of why examples like *Sue has kissed Igor yesterday* are unacceptable would seem rather to concern the mismatch of reference by the tense to a period within the extended now, and adverbial reference outside of it.

In fact, it may be argued that precisely the same ambiguity applies to the present perfect as to the other tenses. The existential perfect is an anterior tense: this reading of *John has eaten ris-de-veau* does not require that his eating ris-de-veau occur in an interval containing the present: *John has eaten ris-de-veau only once— last year*. On the other hand, there is a reading of *John has eaten ris-de-veau* which does require reference to the present (as in *John has eaten ris-de-veau and is feeling ill as a result*).

In this reading, moreover, any gap between the period of the event and that of the reference time is excluded: *John has just eaten ris-de-veau—last year*. Accordingly we might argue that Johnson's weaker condition is appropriate for English, since it covers both the E<R and XN cases; even in the present perfect in main clauses, XN is only one of a pair of possible readings, and a contextually determined one at that.

But the present perfect still excludes past adverbials. Perhaps a more insightful way of looking at the problem is to say that it concerns not the present perfect but the adverbials. Leech points out that "with the Present Perfect as with Present Tenses in general, adverbials must have reference, in one way or another, to the present point of orientation 'now', while with the Past Tenses they must refer to some point or period of time in the past."[85]

The present perfect requires that R = S. The past tense adverbials which cause trouble with the perfect, we shall see below, are adverbials which make reference to R. Accordingly we can well understand how such an adverbial would be incompatible with the present perfect. The problem with *I have eaten ris-de-veau yesterday* is not that eating ris-de-veau must occur on a stretch of time including the present, the past adverbial indicating that it is not on such a stretch, but rather that *I have eaten ris-de-veau* has a present R point (R = S), while *yesterday* makes essential reference to the past (R<S).

But then, why does the XN requirement hold only of the present perfect, and not throughout the tense system? If the perfect tenses are in general ambiguous, and the problem is one of mismatch between adverbial and tense, we would expect similar problems with adverbials for all the tenses. The CR effects associated with the present perfect ought to appear in all tenses as well.

In fact, the reason the adverbial effects don't appear in the non-present tenses is that there is no possible mismatch of adverbials. Time anterior to the past is still past, and time anterior to the future may still be future. Both of the following examples are consequently acceptable:

The year before she had eaten ris-de-veau for the first time.
The day before she'll have eaten ris-de-veau for the first time.

However, because time anterior to the future may also be non-future, the latter example is acceptable only where reference is to a time posterior to the present. The future perfect reading of *she'll have eaten ris-de-veau for the first time in 1980* is at best very odd, when uttered after 1979.

As to current relevance, it applies no more and no less to the other tenses than to the present. The oddity of *Abe Lincoln has spoken at Gettysburg* is equally shared by *George Washington had lived in New York* (said of [*sic*] some time in the nineteenth century, say) and *George Bush has been president of the United States* (said of some time in the twenty-second century).

Accordingly there is no unique connection of the extended "now" with the *present* perfect. The perfect is ambiguous in all tenses, precisely between an anterior (E<R) and an XN reading. But are these different meanings or merely different "overtones," contextual meanings, or the like? Of course it is possible that the perfect is ambiguous. As we remarked in regard to Jespersen's theory, this leaves it an interesting problem why precisely *these* two meanings appear in language after language marked by the same category.

While an approach such as L. Anderson's (1981, 1986) is feasible, which would account for this concordance in terms of some overlap in a semantic space, alternately it might be that the perfect simply marks anteriority *in all cases*, in which case it is *not* ambiguous.

In both CR and ID theories, what is essential to the perfect is not its semantics but its pragmatics. CR theory is in fact a kind of XN theory, but one in which the strong XN requirement is a *pragmatic* condition on reference point choice, not a *semantic* condition on the temporal relationship of E to S.

There has been much investigation of the uses of the perfect,[86] especially regarding how to distinguish it from the preterite. If the two do have the same semantics, then the question is under what (presumably pragmatic) conditions the perfect or the preterite is chosen. In this case, there is no specific issue as to the relationship of the meaning of the perfect to its uses, since its meaning is the *same* as that of the preterite. If they do differ in their semantics, then of course there may be such an issue.

If a compositional, neo-Reichenbachian approach such as Johnson's proves adequate for English, the perfects will all make reference to a relatively past event time, that is, an event time that is past relative to some reference time. In the case of the present perfect, that reference time is given by the present tense: we are talking about the present.

We can see how in something like CR theory the semantics follows from the pragmatics in such a compositional treatment. Whatever we are talking about must have current relevance, since we are talking about the *present* time, even though the events are *past*. We can talk about criticisms of Abraham Lincoln because those criticisms persist into the present. Lincoln's own actions, however, do not. We could say (in 1988) *Ronald Reagan has been a popular president* because he was then still president (his presidency persisted in the then-present), but not *Jimmy Carter has been an unpopular president*, because he was not still the president. We can say *Jimmy Carter has been to Gettysburg* because he is (at this writing) in the present—but not *Abraham Lincoln has been to Gettysburg*, because he is not.

When the topic is something which *is* in the present, such sentences are acceptable. This will happen, for instance, when a past event is in a series of events which continue into the present. To the question "Has any U.S. president ever been to Gettysburg?" one might answer, "Well, Abraham Lincoln has been to Gettysburg, and every president since."

It is even possible to have such a series with only one member: *only President Carter has been attacked by a killer rabbit*. Although there is only one member here, and Carter is no longer president, this sentence is unexceptionable; the *only* shows that this is a series (albeit one with only one member). The elliptical *President Carter has been* (*attacked by a killer rabbit*) is far less acceptable (except perhaps for speakers who accord ex-presidents the title "president"), even in reply to the question, "has any U.S. president ever been attacked by a killer rabbit?"

Given that E<R, it is still possible for R = S or R<S (or R>S). If R<S, then R = E (assuming as we must that the ordering of times defines not absolute positions but relative "slots" in time), and the past tense falls out (E = R<S). But if R = S, then E<R, and the present perfect falls out. What is crucial is how R relates to S, and in CR theory this depends on pragmatic conditions determining the R point.

The very same situation could be expressed in the past tense (e.g., *Shakespeare did it*) or in the present perfect tense (*Shakespeare has done it*), depending on *what the temporal viewpoint (reference point) is*. This is dependent on many factors, as seen in the oddness of both ?*Shakespeare has lived in Stratford-on-Avon* and ?*Shakespeare recently set new records for the number of plays a playwright has running on Broadway at the same time*.

ID theory too allows the semantics to follow from the pragmatics in a neo-Reichenbachian analysis. The perfect requires that E precede R; the present, that R = S. In Reichenbach's system E precedes S, but this follows in Johnson's system from the fact that E<R and R = S. Nothing further is said about the relationship of E to S. Accordingly, the perfect is simply indefinite—*any* past interval *I* will serve as E. The preterite requires that *I* be some specific time, however. But this follows from the fact that the past tense is aspectually "neutral," E = R. We are talking about a specific time *I* which is our reference time, and saying that the event time corresponds to *that* R time.

The question then is how to build pragmatics into the theory. For the moment all we need say is that it is incorrect to say that *Abraham Lincoln has lived in*

Springfield is (in the real world and at the present time) *untrue*; rather, it is simply *inappropriate*, in the same way that any pragmatically deviant sentence (e.g., *Mars has a moon*) is inappropriate *in normal contexts*.[87]

There is nothing untrue about *Abraham Lincoln has lived in Springfield* (in the real world and at the present time), since it is perfectly acceptable in certain contexts (within a series, for example), and even out of context it does not describe a situation which (here and now) is unhistorical—it merely invites a false inference, namely that Abraham Lincoln is alive.

We can accept Johnson's E<R condition as a universal. The strong XN requirement is not *semantic* in nature, but has to do with the *pragmatic* conditions under which the R point is chosen. If we need only the weaker E<R condition on the perfects, then the perfect can at once be both unambiguous and fully compositional.

This leaves three problems, however: (1) that of the futurate perfect, considered below; (2) that of the neutralization of past and perfect in certain contexts, also considered below; and (3) that of the *passé antérieur*. We will take these up in reverse order (the futurate in the next section).

Before saying something about the *passé antérieur*, we should note that the present perfect of modern colloquial French (and certain German dialects) must be treated as ambiguous in the way the Latin perfect was. This is difficult to show for the *present perfect* in German, because German no longer obeys the classical sequence-of-tense rules. But the co-occurrence of the tense with both "present" and "past" adverbials is suggestive, and in any case nothing precludes such a treatment, which has the advantage of preserving a universal compositional treatment of the perfects.

All simple tenses in Romance can form perfects; hence the distinction of preterite and imperfect is mirrored in that of preterite perfect (*passé antérieur*) and imperfect perfect (pluperfect or past perfect).[88] A terminological excursus might be useful here, as the terms for these two tenses are among the most confused of all. Some grammarians simply distinguish the "second pluperfect" from the first (e.g., Prista, 1966). Others use the terms "pluperfect" and "past perfect" (or "preterit perfect").

In the case of Italian, it is traditional to distinguish the *trapassato remoto* 'remote trans-past' from the *trapassato prossimo* 'near trans-past'. Berinetto distinguishes the *piucheperfetto* 'pluperfect' (*trapassato prossimo*) from the *trapassato* (*trapassato remoto*).[89] Lo Cascio uses *past imperfect* (*trapassato prossimo*) and *past perfect* (*trapassato remoto*).[90]

It would seem, initially, that these two tenses cannot differ in meaning. Both imperfect and preterite have R<S and E=R; they differ only aspectually. The pluperfect has to do not with an event ongoing at R, but rather at some time E<R. The problem then is what it means to say that 'R was ongoing' or 'R was completed'. Of course, these tenses do not differ in this way.

In the standard language, the *passé antérieur* of French is first an anterior tense: it "expresses an isolated fact which took place in a determined and limited time, before another past fact: it is a 'past of the past,' " generally occurring in subordinate clauses following a temporal conjunction.[91] Thus:

Quand il les   eut reconnus, il leva   les bras en l'air.
when   he them had recognized he raised the arms in the air
'When he had recognized them, he raised his arms in the air.'[92]

The *passé antérieur* may also be used in main clauses with an adverbial to indicate an action which was rapidly completed.[93]

Ils   eurent rejoint la chasse en un instant.
they had   rejoined the hunt   in an instant
'They rejoined the hunt in an instant.'

The facts of usage in other Romance languages (e.g., Italian and Spanish) are not greatly dissimilar to the French.

In origin, the distinction of preterite perfect and imperfect may have been similar to that of any other pair of simple and perfect tenses, that is, the preterite perfect represented a preterite-in-the past and the imperfect perfect an imperfect-in-the-past, as in:

Souvent le   virent   et   le père et la
often   him regarded both the father and the

mère,   et la jeune fille qu'il   eut epousée.
mother, and the young girl that-he had married

'Often both his mother and father looked on him, and the young lady whom he had married.'[94]

The use of the *passé antérieur* is complicated and idiosyncratic, but it is clear that it is not compositional in any sense; in none of its uses does it represent perfect aspect combined with past tense. If it was originally a true preterite perfect, it was not compositional either, since the aspectual distinction, though marked in the auxiliary, actually pertained to the action of the main verb. The Romance *passé antérieur* is a counterexample to any important generalization regarding the perfect tenses and must be accorded a special treatment.

We turn now to neutralization. The perfect often reflects an underlying past (i.e., preterite). Both of the following sentences involve neutralization of the preterite-present perfect distinction:

   (i) Susan believed that Jane had studied electrical engineering for three years.
   (ii) Susan believed Jane to have studied electrical engineering for three years.

Susan's belief, as reported in both of these, could have been either of the following:

   (iii) Jane studied electrical engineering for three years.
   (iv) Jane has studied electrical engineering for three years.

In a Johnsonian neo-Reichenbachian analysis these facts are accounted for as follows. In (iii), the past tense reflects $R<S$ and the neutral aspect $E=R$. In (iv), the present tense reflects $R=S$ and the perfect aspect $E<R$. In (i), the tense of the embedded clause comes from the main (matrix) verb (by the principle of the maintenance of the R point), that is, $R<S$. The aspect does *not* change—$E<R$ is still true. But $E<R<S$ defines the pluperfect.

In the case of (iv), the embedded infinitive asserts that $E<R$. Once again, we

understand (iv) = (iii) because the R point is given by the matrix clause. But what sanctions transformation of (iii) into the embedded clause of (iv), given that the preterite assumes $R<S$ and $E=R$, but the perfect $E<R$? It would seem that a principled account of neutralization here is excluded by a compositional, neo-Reichenbachian treatment of the present perfect and the preterite.

Let us reexamine the problem in terms of the kind of analysis given by Allen (1986). Here a simple sentence like (iii) or (iv) refers to three times—E, R, S. Let us take S to be R_0. In the past, $R<R_0$ and $E=R$. Now, embed something like (iii) in a past context, as in (i). Let the R points of the two clauses be R_1 and R_2. Now, as a past, clause 1 of (i) has $R_1<R_0$. But clause 2 has $R_2<R_1$. Consequently, $R_2<R_0$, and the pluperfect falls out.

What now of (ii)? Here again clause 1 of (ii) has $R_1<R_0$. But clause 2 has no tense, only the infinitive, in which $E<R$. But since clause 2 has no tense of its own, R is still $R_1<R_0$. Consequently $E<R_1<R_0$, i.e., it is understood as a pluperfect.

Now what sanctions the move from the $E=R$ of (iii) to the $E<R$ of (ii) in the neo-Allenian approach? In this approach there is no constant R point across the sentence as a whole; rather, clauses relate pairwise. The situation described by (ii)—and by (i)—is presented in the accompanying diagram.

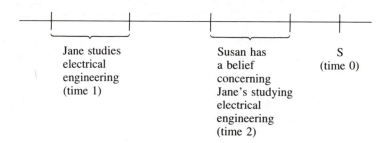

Jane studies	Susan has	S
electrical	a belief	(time 0)
engineering	concerning	
(time 1)	Jane's studying	
	electrical	
	engineering	
	(time 2)	

If we are talking from the perspective of time 1, then $E=R$ and $R<S$, and consequently $R_1<R_0$, and the past tense results. Now, if we embed an expression of this event at t_1 in the context of an expression of the event at time 2, assuming we are talking from the perspective of time 2, we have $R_1<R_0$, and $R_2<R_1$—which is the pluperfect.

Notice that from the perspective of t_2, $E_2<R_1$. It is because the event at t_1 is being related to the R point of t_2, and not directly to that of t_3 (namely R_0), that the leap from past to perfect is sanctioned. This would be impossible if the R of $E<R$ had to be R_0. In independent, main clauses with present tense verbs, R_1 just is R_0. Out of context, a past tense reflects $R_1<R_0$. But in context, given a next higher predicate with R point R_n, a relatively past tense simply reflects some R point $R_m<R_n$.

To explicate past tense neutralization within the context of a compositional neo-Reichenbachian theory of the perfect aspect, we must abandon Reichenbach's account of the reference point coherence of sentences and accept a neo-Allenian account. Dowty has presented something like that, albeit phrased in terms of independent sentences in discourse, rather than clauses in a sentence.[95]

A sequence of sentences $[\phi_0, \phi_1, \ldots, \phi_n]$ is true when uttered at j and construed as a connected narrative discourse iff for some $i_0, i_1, \ldots, i_n$, ϕ_0 is true at $\langle i_0, j \rangle$, ϕ_1 is true at $\langle i_1, j \rangle$, ... and ϕ_n is true at $\langle i_n, j \rangle$, and for each i_k ($0 < k < n$) $i_k + 1$ is equal to or relatively soon after i_k.

The effect of this is to require that pairs of sentences in sequences be either mutually coincidental or slightly in temporal sequence. ("Relatively soon" is highly dependent on the pragmatics, of course.) As it stands, this is too strong a requirement for some types of clauses within sentences, but it may be too strong a one for sequences of sentences in general as well. Compare:

> One morning he opened a matchbox. Inside it was a worm totally unknown to science. This sort of thing showed up in a Sherlock Holmes story once, of course. But it had never happened to him. Indeed, it never happens in real life.

> One morning he opened a matchbox and inside it was a worm totally unknown to science, and though this sort of thing showed up in a Sherlock Holmes story once, of course, it had never happened to him and indeed it never happens in real life at all.

We shall return to the issue of discourse coherence and sequence of tense rules in chapter 8 and need say no more concerning it here.

m. The Futurate Perfect

The futurate present perfect is a problem, because it clearly does not mean what the present perfect does. Nerbonne is forced to assign the futurate perfect (where the speech-act time s and the reference time r stand in the relation $s < r$) the following truth condition[96]:

$$A_{s,e,r} \vDash \text{PERF}(p) \text{ iff } e \leq r \text{ and } A_{s,e,r} \vDash p$$

That is, in the tense-logical notation adopted by Nerbonne (that type of notation, widely used in European semantic studies, we will describe below), PERF (p) is true (given that $s < r$ is the case, that is, the reference time is later than—in the future of—the speech-act time), iff there is an event time (e) not later than the reference time, and p is true with respect to s, e, r.

This differs from the truth conditions Nerbonne assigns the "normal" reading of the German perfect, namely, where it is not the case that $s < r$:

$$A_{s,e,r} \vDash \text{PERF}(p) \text{ iff } e = r < s \text{ and } A_{s,e,r} \vDash p$$

That is, PERF(p) is true (given that $s < r$ is not the case, that is, the reference time is *not* later than—in the future of—the speech-act time), iff the event time is coincident with the reference time and both precede the speech-act time, and p is true with respect to s, e, r. These are also essentially the truth conditions for the past tense in English.

Given that the present is often a non-past tense, we could consider relaxing the conditions on the present perfect so that, instead of requiring that the evaluation point I itself be that last subinterval of the "extended now," its last subinterval be some interval I' not earlier than I. This would combine the two readings into one.

This treatment has an advantage in solving a problem with the compositional treatment of the perfect. The present perfect requires only that $R = S$ and $E < R$. If the present can be indefinitely great, what precludes it from including a substantial chunk of the future as well as the past? In fact, we normally take the present in a broad, extended sense, as Aristotle said, to include an indefinitely great chunk of the future (consider *John comes home at noon every day, Susan repairs plumbing for a living, two and two are four*).

But this suggests that the present perfect should potentially include an indefinitely great chunk of the future as well. How do we account for the intuition that the present perfect refers *only* to situations in which $E < S$ is the case? The answer of course is that perfects require $E < R$, while the present requires $R < S$ and therefore $E < S$. But if R can include times later than S, then we would expect situations in which $S < E$ was the case. But this is precisely the futurate perfect.

In support of such a treatment is the fact that the futurates are semantically closely related not to the future but to the present. They take present adverbials as their R-point definers; for example: *John is now coming tomorrow, *John is tomorrow coming the next day*. Given the close ties of the perfect to the present, and of the futurate perfect to the futurate present, we would expect to treat the futurate perfect as a kind of present (non-past) tense, rather than a future one.

That the futurate perfect co-occurs with future tense adverbials (*when I have seen her later today*) is no argument against this, given that the futurate presents themselves allow future adverbials (*I see her/I'm seeing her later today*). As Jespersen says, "The use of the [English] perfect for before-future time in temporal and conditional clauses corresponds exactly with the use of the present tense for future time."[97]

There are, however, reasons to question such an approach. First, French has a futurate present perfect, but it also has a real future tense distinct from the present, so that treating the present as a "non-past" tense is more dubious in French than it is in English and German. (But French also allows a futurate use of the present.)

Second, English does not allow the futurate perfect in main clauses: !*Susan and John have married by the time you arrive* cannot be a futurate perfect (it is possible only as a historical present perfect), though in *if Susan and John have married by the time you arrive, just grin and bear it,* where it is a subordinate clause, it is possible as a futurate perfect. This suggests, given that the futurate present *is* allowed in main clauses (*Susan and John marry tomorrow*), that the two phenomena are *not* the same, and do not require—or allow—the same treatment.

Perhaps the strongest argument against treating the futurate perfect as involving the perfect, but with a non-past endpoint for the "extended now," is that it invites certain false inferences. If Nerbonne is correct that the perfect is to be interpreted in the same way as the preterite in German, then obviously the solution is foreclosed at least for German.

The "normal" present perfect has two principal readings. The event wholly precedes the reference time (*I've been to Rome a couple of times*), or the reference time is the final subinterval of the event time (*I've been in Rome up to now*). If we interpreted the futurate perfect as a variety of the "normal" perfect, it would require that the event wholly precede the reference time, now understood to include the future.

The problem is that the reference time also includes the present (S), but the event cannot precede the present. For example, *when/if/although Sue has married John* in the futurate (*when Sue has married John, she will learn what true tedium is*) cannot refer to a marriage in the past, but only to one in the future. This is similar to the case of the future perfect. There, although the relationships $E{<}R$ and $S{<}R$ are satisfied by the sentence *John will have married Susan*, the marriage must take place in the future. It has been argued that this restriction is a conversational implication in the sense of Grice (1975) and not part of the semantics.[98]

By "implicature" is meant something which invites an inference, but is not a logical implication. We saw earlier how saying that Mars has a moon in certain contexts invites the false inference that it has only one moon; its having but one moon is an implicature of the statement that Mars has a moon.

The implicature that the marriage is in the future is pragmatic: most of the time there is no point to using the future perfect, if the event is already past. But under certain conditions we can certainly use the future perfect of past events: *by the time he's fifty, John will have accomplished three great things: he will have married Susan, he will have bought an apartment in Tokyo, and he will have lost a million on the stock market and not even cried.*

In the same way, the facts about the futurate perfect seem pragmatic rather than semantic. When Sue has married John and moved into their apartment in downtown Tokyo and founded her firm of plumbers, she will be happy. Well, maybe she's already done the first, and has two to go. The problem with *when Sue has married John, she will learn the meaning of true boredom* is not with the present perfect; but with *when*; compare *since Sue has married John, she will learn the meaning of true boredom*. *When* turns the clause into an R point, but if the clause refers to a relatively past event, then that R point is a past R point; this renders the sentence incoherent when joined with the future R point of the main clause.

Accordingly, there does not seem to be a *semantic* problem as such with treating the reference time of the present perfect as non-past, and thereby collapsing the non-futurate and futurate present (or any other) perfects. (Is this universally valid? Are there not languages which lack the futurate present perfect?) How do we account for the fact that English does not allow the futurate present perfect in main clauses, though it allows the futurate simple present?

A further problem is that the present perfect does not seem to be vague in the way this account requires. In a given context, only one of the readings is possible, as shown by co-occurrence with adverbials:

> When Sue has married John tomorrow, you can kiss your inheritance goodbye.
> When Sue has married John in the past, you have always kissed the bride.
> *When Sue has married John tomorrow, you have always kissed the bride.
> !When Sue has married John in the past, you can kiss your inheritance goodbye.
>   (Acceptable perhaps in a science-fiction story about time travel.)

A related problem is that the perfect refers to, or leads one to infer, a current state (*John has gone, John is gone*), but the futurate perfect does not. Any resultant state is simply future. If John has left by the time you arrive, nothing will have happened which is relevant to the question of where John is *now*.

It seems then that the futurate perfect must translate into *FUT(PERF(p))* and not into the *PRES(PERF(p))* of the "normal" present perfect. This solution is in line both with traditional accounts of the futurate present perfect, and with contemporary treatments of the futurates in which they result from futures by transformational deletion of the future marker.

Jespersen points out that after subordinating conjunctions of time (*since, when,* . . .), "futurity need not (and therefore rarely is) indicated by the tense of the verb"; similarly he notes the "use of the perfect for before-future time in temporal and conditional clauses," as in *I shall be glad when her marriage has taken place,* and *we shall start at five if it has stopped raining by that time.*[99]

Proposals of this type were incorporated in early transformational syntax[100] in the form of a rule of *will*-deletion deriving futurate sentences such as *the Red Sox play the Yankees tomorrow* from structures underlying explicitly future sentences such as *the Red Sox will play the Yankees tomorrow*. The futurate present perfect and progressive would likewise be derived from structures underlying future perfects and progressive respectively (*the Red Sox will be playing the Yankees tomorrow* ⇒ *the Red Sox are playing the Yankees tomorrow; if the Red Sox will not have played the Yankees by tomorrow . . .* ⇒ *if the Red Sox have not played the Yankees by tomorrow . . .*).

Jenkins criticizes such attempts. The simple futurate present requires certainty, and it is this which rules out **the Red Sox do well tomorrow*.[101] The problem, Jenkins points out, is that the *will*-future does not require certainty, so *the Red Sox will do well tomorrow* is all right.[102] Lakoff would make the deletion sensitive to the pragmatics, but Jenkins points out that this still does not explain why *I know that the Red Sox will do well tomorrow* cannot be transformed into **I know that the Red Sox do well tomorrow*, where the pragmatics would seem to allow the deletion.

We have seen that there clearly are pragmatic differences between the future and the futurate. But are there *semantic* differences? That is difficult to say. On the one hand, there certainly are conditions under which one or the other construction is excluded. But are those conditions semantic? The dividing line between semantics and pragmatics has always been difficult to define ("the boundaries of this subject are not so clear as is sometimes supposed"[103]).

If we agree that the futurates *do not* differ from the future semantically, but only pragmatically, then we can collapse the future and futurate perfect in one, with one set of truth conditions. The question is how the pragmatics relates to the semantics. It would be wrong to ask, for example, how the futurate perfect could have peculiar pragmatic conditions on its use, if it has the same syntax and semantics as the present perfect.[104] Rather, the syntax and semantics *follow* the pragmatics. It is because some future event is viewed within the context of a certain set of pragmatic conditions that the futurate construction can be used to describe or assert it.[105]

One of the arguments in favor of the *will*-deletion solution is the co-occurrence of future adverbials with the futurates, but not with ordinary presents:

Susan arrives tomorrow. (only futurate)
Susan arrives at noon. (futurate or present)
Susan is arriving tomorrow. (only futurate)
Susan is arriving at noon. (futurate or present)
*Susan has arrived tomorrow.
Susan has arrived at noon. (present only)
If Susan has arrived by tomorrow afternoon . . . (futurate only)
?If Susan has arrived yesterday afternoon . . . (present only)[106]

Jenkins argues that co-occurrence with future adverbials is no argument for an underlying *will*: there can be no **if I will can hear your voice by tomorrow* underlying *if I can hear your voice by tomorrow*.[107] (**I can hear your voice by tomorrow* is impossible.) Therefore the adverbials provide no case for an underlying *will*.

In fact, while co-occurrence with future adverbials cannot necessarily be taken as an argument for the syntax, it may provide an argument for the semantics. The question is, do we translate the futurate perfect *PRES(PERF(x))* or *FUT(PERF(x))*? It would be tempting to collapse the presents and futurates by assuming a non-past reading of the present tense forms. But co-occurrence with future adverbials suggests that, whatever their source(s), the (surface) present tense forms *are* ambiguous, and that the proper translation of the futurates takes this into account. (We shall explore in the next section the relationship of adverbials to the tenses.)

What then of the German futurate perfect in main clauses? The Duden *Grammatik* gives examples such as this:

In einer halben Stunde habe   ich den
in a   half   hour   have (PRES INDIC 1SG) I   the
Brief geschrieben
letter write-PP

This it glosses as . . . *werde ich den Brief geschrieben haben* '(in a half hour) I shall (*werde*) have written the letter'.[108]

It would seem that for German a purely non-past, futurate treatment of the futurate present perfect is justified. Alternatively, we might adopt the same treatment as for English, translating the German into the LTL configuration *FUT(PERF(x))*. The only difference would be in the syntax of German, which allows the futurate perfect more freely than does English.

n. The Progressive

Parallel to the perfect, English has the progressive. The English progressive has proven intractable and its analysis controversial, as Allen (1966), Scheffer (1975), and the papers in Schopf (1974) attest. No one has ever specified in a complete and satisfactorily general way how it is used or how the progressive tenses differ in meaning from the corresponding simple tenses, though English speakers all agree that they do differ, often quite radically (*he eats lunch in the cafe, he is eating lunch in the cafe*), though sometimes in tantalizingly subtle ways (*it looks like rain out, it's looking like rain out*). No one has convincingly argued for any one basic meaning for it, but neither has anyone established that it lacks one.

A major puzzle is why it does not occur with certain predicates, and occurs only under certain conditions. Many authors have pointed out that, while it readily occurs with activity and accomplishment verbs, and with achievement verbs in series—

Sue is jogging. (activity)
Sue is repairing the plumbing. (accomplishment)
Sue is noticing a lot of drunks on the street these days. (achievement series)

—it cannot occur with achievement verbs otherwise (!*just at this moment I am noticing a stain on his shirt*), presumably because achievement expressions denote events occurring at instants of time, and therefore are incompatible with whatever the meaning of the progressive is. Generally it cannot occur with stative predicates either, presumably for similar reasons:

*Sue is noticing a drunk on the street. (achievement)
*Sue is being sick with scarlet fever. (state)

But there are certain cases in which even stative predicates allow the progressive:

Sue is believing in God more and more.
?Sue believes in God more and more.
Sue is living on cream cheese and lentil soup.
Sue lives on cream cheese and lentil soup.
Sue's inhabiting Max's apartment.
?Sue inhabits Max's apartment.
but:
The Turks inhabit Anatolia.
?!The Turks are inhabiting Anatolia.
I'm loving what you're telling me.
I love what you're telling me.
Just now I'm not feeling very well.
?Just now I don't feel very well.
Her slip is showing.
Her slip shows.
She's appearing to get off the horse and walk away.
?She appears to get off the horse and walk away.

Although the progressive is sometimes thought of as a peculiarity of English,[109] the category of progressive is apparently a universal, and a progressive has been identified in such languages as these, marked by the devices noted.[110]

Mandarin:	particle *zài*
Maltese:	construction with *qed*[111]
Irish Gaelic:	copula + *ag* 'at' + verbal noun
Romance:	'be' plus gerund[112]
French:	construction with *être en train de*
Swedish:	*hålla på att* 'keep on to' + infinitive
Icelandic:	with "be" plus "in" or "at"
Finnish:	*on* 'be' plus third infinitive in the inessive case
Mapuche	auxiliary verb *meken*

Marchand too assumes identity of the English progressive with the Romance "be" + present participle (gerund) constructions (e.g., Italian *stiamo preparando la tavola* 'we are laying the table'), though he claims there is a "functional" difference between English and Romance (in general) in regard to this usage.[113] The Romance periphrastic progressive is an optional variant of the simple tenses: *sto scrivendo* and *scrivo* both mean 'I am writing' and the latter is the more normal usage, whereas in English *I write* rarely can be used to mean 'I am writing'.[114]

Comrie however claims that languages do differ in their use of the progressive and that the English progressive is unusually wide in its range of uses.[115] In the absence of a common form (the cited "progressives" are marked in almost every conceivable way) or a common meaning (we return to this point below), the claim that the progressive is a universal is perhaps weakened to the sort of universal L. Anderson (1981, 1986) proposes for the perfect—a focal center of overlap of various categories.

In the absence of a generally agreed-upon meaning assignable to the progressive, equation of forms across languages could at best be only speculative, or serve as a shorthand way of asserting certain similarities of meaning or use between languages. The question is whether there is any commonality of meaning to progressives, or lacking such, what the similarities might be.

Some have proposed that the progressive (at least that of English) represents the imperfective aspect (just as the perfect tenses represent the perfect aspect). We assumed in chapter 2, in fact, that this is the case. Comrie, however, denies that the progressive is the same as the imperfective aspect, considering the progressive to be a subtype of the imperfective.[116]

A criticism of another sort is that of Zandvoort (1962), who argues that the progressive is *not* an aspect at all, since, unlike the imperfective of Slavic, it is not a formal, grammaticized category, and in any case it does not correspond to the (Slavic) imperfective—both *I write* and *I am writing* correspond to the imperfective.[117] Further, while the imperfective is the *unmarked* member of the imperfective-perfective opposition, the progressive is the *marked* member of the progressive-simple opposition.[118]

Hatcher seems to accept structuralist doctrine, while rejecting the usual analysis of the Slavic aspects, when she writes that the contrast between *to write* and *to be writing* is not comparable, say, to Russian *napisat'* versus *pisat'*, or French *il écrivit* versus *il écrivait*, "where each form has its own positive emphasis; instead, it is *a contrast between two constructions of which only one is inherently meaningful.*"[119]

Marchand writes that the difference in Romance between the simple and progressive tenses is purely stylistic. Since the Romance languages have distinct imperfective and perfective verb forms, a given tense may be inherently imperfective, as for instance the present, and no special marker of imperfectivity is required. English, however, "had never known the category aspect at all, so here it was the grammatical concept of imperfective single action that introduced the entirely new category of aspect into English."[120]

This seems to agree with Hatcher in making the progressive a positive marker, while retaining no positive value for the simple tenses. It is true that the present tense of English is as neutral as the past in regard to aspect: neither *he ate the cake* nor *he eats the cake* tells us if he ate/eats *up* the cake. (And even *eat up* may be incompletive in certain contexts.)

If the progressive does differ from the imperfective aspect in some way, what basic meaning, if any, does it have? Here there have been at least four major theories: [121]

1. durative aspect
2. action in process or progress
3. incompletion
4. progressive of the frame

The first theory involves durative aspect (or Aktionsart). Scheffer says that "of all the different basic meanings attributed to the progressive that of *duration* is found most often," and cites authors from Sweet (1891) to Lyons (1968). [122]

But there are many uses of the progressive that cannot be explained in terms of durativity (extension through time). [123] Scheffer cites examples having to do with "sporadic repetition" [124]: *she's always breaking things, the car's always breaking down*. The futurate progressive also is a problem, since at the time of the speech act, the action has not begun, much less endured: someone may refuse a drink in a pub by saying, "No thanks, I'm driving." This has nothing to do with durativity.

Perhaps a more serious problem is that of determining what "duration" means in this regard. Does it refer to continuance (endurance) or to mere extension (non-momentariness), or possibly to non-completion? [125] Under what conditions, precisely, can we say that an event has duration (durativity)? As soon as efforts are made to render explicit the notion of durativity, it becomes apparent that either the definition must be rendered so vague as to be virtually meaningless, or it cannot cover all the cases satisfactorily. Palmer notes: "much depends on the semantic content of the verb in the progressive. If it already expresses unlimited duration in itself it is rarely used in the progressive." [126] So it is no wonder that some authors see duration as a contextual meaning or an "overtone," rather than a basic meaning.

Some writers have seen the basic meaning of the progressive as "limited duration" or temporariness. In this regard, Leech notes the differences in meaning between the members of the following pairs of sentences:

My watch works perfectly. (permanent state)
My watch is working perfectly. (temporary state)

I live in Wimbledon. (permanent state)
I'm living in Wimbledon. (temporary state)

I enjoy the seaside. (state in general)
I'm enjoying the seaside. (state in particular, in actuality) [127]

In these (Portuguese) examples [128] the progressive is used where there is a temporal bound indicated by a time adverbial (explicit or implicit):

Ele estava   nadando   desde as 6 horas da   manhã.
he was (IMPF) swimming since the 6 hours of-the morning
'he had been swimming since 6 a.m.'

Estamos fazendo um bolo para mamãe.
we are   making a   cake for   mommy
'we are making a cake for mommy'

In this latter case Travaglia says that "the situation is felt as having a limited [*finita*] duration," presumably because the action must terminate with completion of the cake. This seems to confuse (effective) termination of a situation-in-the-world with (essential) termination of a situation type. Making-a-cake is naturally limited by the completion of the cake, but making a cake can go on indefinitely, and is no more temporally "limited" than any state or activity. After all, being ill or running in place must sooner or later terminate (at least for mortals), yet we would not say that states and activities have natural bounds.

In any case, limited duration can hardly be the basic meaning of the progressive; often there is no difference in limitation or permanence, as in these cases:

> he loves her more and more
> he's loving her more and more
>
> she proposes to run for Parliament
> she's proposing to run for Parliament
>
> your slip shows at the back
> your slip is showing at the back

In general, the progressive is no more limited or temporary than the corresponding non-progressive tense, even with explicit bounds. Compare:

> Since 1980 the oceans have risen every year.
> Since 1980 the oceans have been rising every year.
>
> Until he returns I remain just where I am.
> Until he returns I am remaining just where I am.
>
> From 1910 to 1920 they lived in Chelsea.
> From 1910 to 1920 they were living in Chelsea.

"Limited" and "temporary," if they are to be used in this context, must have such carefully restricted meanings as to render them trivial.

There *is* a sense in which the progressive (and the imperfective in general) is "limited," and this has to do with the phasic structure of events. We have seen in chapter 6 that the imperfective may be identified with a certain nuclear (medial) phase or set of phases. *John is reading* means that the medial phase of an act of John's reading coincides with the speech-act time. This identification, which in some form or other plays a role in the theories of Keniston, Coseriu, and Guillaume,[129] is exploited by ter Meulen in her theory of the progressive.[130] We will explore this idea further at the end of this chapter, in connection with the framework of Situation Semantics within which ter Meulen works.

The second theory on the meaning of the progressive involves action in process or progress, or a dynamic situation. We think of progress as change, and in the ordinary uses of the terms "progression," "progressive," and so on, change toward some definite end is a central concept. Thus progressivity is based on a process which is dynamic, and some authors have taken this facet as central.[131]

Ota says the progressive denotes the "process of action"; Allen mentions authors who see it as representing action which is "on-going."[132] Leech calls it the "progressive aspect," though he denies the label has any positive meaning as such.[133]

Travaglia[134] refers to "gradual development" of the action, citing

o   amor dos   tios   foi   transformando aquela criança
the love of-the uncle-and-aunt was (PRET) transforming   that   child
'the love of uncle and aunt was transforming that child'

It is certainly true that often enough the progressive *is* "progressive" or "dynamic":

> Tom is turning blue.
> Sue is getting rich.
> Igor is growing quiet.
> Max is running across the province.
> Cluny is repairing the plumbing.

The problem is that these are all accomplishments. Are other types of verbs "dynamic" in the progressive? Consider activities:

> Sue is swimming.
> There are no weeds growing in my yard.
> Max is running.
> Cluny is playing with the plumbing.

In what sense is any of these dynamic or progressive? There undoubtedly are readings which are dynamic, but is it not the case that these uses are accomplishments? For example, *the children are growing* might mean 'the children are *growing up*', in which case the achievement is to have grown up, that is, to have become "grown-up."

Vlach draws on the traditional notion that *is . . . ing* is true iff eventually . . . *ed* is true, that is, "if ϕ is a process sentence, then the process that goes on when the progressive of ϕ is true is the same one that goes on when ϕ is true. If ϕ is an accomplishment or achievement sentence, then the process that goes on when the progressive of ϕ is true is always one that will lead, if continued, to the truth of ϕ."[135] But this cannot be *the* basic meaning either, since *her slip is showing* leads to no definite goal or state.

Nor can "ongoingness" per se explicate the progressive. At a given moment, or over a given interval, a certain state may obtain or a certain event occur, but this is as true for the simple tense (*Tom read from noon to three; I hope you got the money*) as it is for the progressive (*Tom was reading from noon to three; I'm hoping you got the money*).

The third theory of the progressive involves incompletion, or lack of necessary completion. Scheffer sees this as a purely "subsidiary effect of the durative character of the progressive . . . its use to express incompletion. As the action is going on it is *ipso facto* incomplete."[136] On the other hand, Blansitt notes as an essential feature of the imperfective, and hence the progressive, that the "happening [is] not necessarily complete."[137] (This is a significant difference, as the imperfective marks incompletion, but not a lack of necessary completion.)

While it is true that the progressive generally does express incompletion and (nearly always) a lack of *necessary* completion, pseudo-performatives such as the following call into question whether incompletion can be an essential meaning: *I'm telling you that I love you, I'm warning you to stay away from me.* And the perfect progressive as well is difficult to account for from this point of view: *I've been playing cards all night with the boys* (*and now I just want to go home and sleep*). It is unclear that incompletion is any more essential a meaning of the progressive than is lack of permanence.

The fourth of the theories of the progressive involves the progressive of the frame. Jespersen does not see the progressive as expressing a characteristic of events such as duration, incompleteness, or progressivity (dynamicity).[138] Rather, he sees the progressive, as in *he was/is hunting,* as indicating a "frame" for another event or situation:

> hunting is felt to be a kind of frame round something else; it is represented as lasting some time before and possibly (or probably) also some time after something else, which may or may not be expressly indicated, but which is always in the mind of the speaker. In this way the hunting is thought of as being of *relatively longer duration in comparison with some other fact* (some happening or state, or simply some period or point of time).

He adds that "the essential thing is that the action or state denoted by the expanded [i.e., progressive] tense is thought of *as a temporal frame encompassing something else* which as often as not is to be understood from the whole situation."[139]

The progressive thus would seem to have much in common with the imperfect and like tenses, and the imperfective aspect, which likewise serve to encompass some other event or situation, though scholars of Romance and Slavic languages (see chapter 8) have emphasized not the temporal relationship as such, but the way in which the imperfective serves to establish a *background* against which the *foregrounded* information is asserted.

Consider for example *when Charles came in, Cluny was repairing the plumbing.* Jespersen is correct in saying that in this sort of case her repairing the plumbing serves as a frame to Charles's coming in—the latter event occurs *during* the former. But from a semantic point of view we can also say that the adverbial phrase *when Charles came in* is the frame, as it establishes a "frame time" for the *asserted* moment of Cluny's *being* engaged in repairing the plumbing, though an extended interval of her repair work is *implied.*

However, we may look at this in a third, *pragmatic* way. The clause *Cluny was repairing the plumbing* establishes a situation against which the event of Charles's entering is set, it gives a background, as if we were to say, "O.K., Cluny is repairing the plumbing, and Charles comes in." The progressive from this point of view does not so much mark a certain *meaning* as fulfill certain discourse-pragmatic *functions*. (We will explore this kind of analysis in chapter 8.) But we have wandered afield from the question of the basic meaning, if any, of the progressive.

The weakness of the frame analysis is that the progressive is meaningful even when no contained event is stated, so that Jespersen is forced to say that that event "as often as not is to be understood from the whole situation." But if we say that at noon yesterday Charles was watching Cluny repair some plumbing, *what* event is to be understood? Similarly, to say that nowadays governments are soaking the taxpapers seems not to point to any particular event contained by this frame. The problem with the frame analysis, indeed, is that the whole notion of a temporal frame is difficult in regard to the present progressive, which refers necessarily to an interval of time which must, in some sense, *coincide* with the "contained" event.

Apart from its "basic" meaning or meanings, the progressive has at least four subsidiary meanings which may be contextual or nonasserted, or pragmatic in nature. Some have been offered by various authors as *the* solution for recalcitrant examples not compatible with this or that theory of basic meaning.

The first of these subsidiary meanings is that of mere occurrence. Calver calls the present progressive the tense of "mere occurrence" and the "tense of pragmatism"; he says that "it is used in reporting events merely as such." The simple present, contrastingly, is the tense of "causality and natural law." "Notice how a law is empirically verified: *The sun rises at 7:10 today—Sure enough, it is rising on time.*" [140]

It is unclear what "mere occurrence" means, but it is not hard to find examples which call this distinction into question, where the simple and the progressive differ little in meaning—*John believes (is believing) more and more in the essential goodness of people.* Part of the problem is that both present and present progressive are ambiguous; what may be the criterial difference between them with a pair of given meanings, may not be such with regard to other meanings.

The second subsidiary meaning is overt activity. Hatcher similarly says that the progressive emphasizes "overt activity." She notes these contrasts:

She sees him now.
She is seeing him to the front door.
I hear him.
Be quiet, I'm hearing his lessons.
I taste something bitter.
I'm only tasting it. . . .
This tickles me.
You're tickling me!
I forget his name.
Oh, I'm forgetting my umbrella (i.e., walking away without it).
I tell you he's crazy.
He's telling them about the accident. [141]

The problem is not just with the notion of "activity" (is forgetting an activity, and in what sense is it "overt"?); the progressive does not require activity at all: *I'm feeling rather ill, I'm seeing stars.*

While neither Hatcher nor Calver state these conditions as absolutes, but as dependent on yet other conditions, the end result seems just a Ptolemaic system of fixes to make an inadequate generalization match the facts.

The third subsidiary meaning concerns intensity, emotional highlighting, or subjective involvement. Scheffer reports on various claims that the progressive is more intense or emotionally highlights the event.[142] Jespersen says that "the use of the expanded tenses often gives a certain emotional colouring to a sentence."[143] He offers as examples:

> She's always harping on that string.
> Now, that boy is again whistling his infernal melodies.
> What have you been doing to that picture?
> Someone has been tampering with this lock.

Hatcher emphasizes the subject's involvement—"the subject is busy or engrossed by his activity"—in examples such as these:

> I'm listening.
> I'm trying to keep my temper.
> I'm meditating.[144]

Apart from the problem of stating under precisely what conditions the progressive can be used with such overtones, the question again is what independence, if any, such notions have from the basic meaning assigned the progressive.

The fourth subsidiary meaning is that of habituality. Many writers[145] refer to cases in which the progressive has habitual meaning. Leech cites:

> I'm taking dancing lessons this winter.
> In those days, we were getting up at 7 o'clock.
> Mr. Robinson is cycling to work until his car is repaired.[146]

This usage would seem to contradict many of the meanings offered to explain the progressive (e.g., temporariness).

In all these cases these meanings are difficult to define in any satisfactory way and are limited to certain predicates and/or certain contexts. It is obvious that none is adequate as a basic meaning, and it is not clear to what extent they pertain to the progressive as such or to other elements in construction with it (e.g., the inherent Aristotelian classes of the predicates).

Complicating the problem of the progressives is their futurate use. The present (or past) tense can be used in a futurate sense of a relatively near future where there is a sense of a "fixed program," or of intention, as in *John leaves tomorrow; we dine at eight tonight; because John left the next day for Rome, we gave him a farewell dinner.*[147] The simple tense (*I start work tomorrow*) often conveys a *fixed* event, while the progressive (*I'm starting work tomorrow*) in contrast expresses *intent.*[148]

But it is hard to separate out the two notions in examples such as *I was coming to see you tomorrow, but I had a letter from my sister yesterday, and now I'm flying home instead.*[149] Vetter (1973) and Goodman (1973) have claimed that there is in fact no difference in meaning, though Vetter sees both as conveying planning, whereas Goodman finds predetermination.[150] Many writers have been puzzled by *the sun sets/is setting tomorrow at 8,* where the progressive clearly does not mean what the simple tense does, but it is not clear that any of the various theories account for the difference adequately.[151]

Finally, assuming we can assign some definite meanings to the perfect and the progressive, are the combinations of perfect and progressive compositional in relation to those meanings? If the progressive refers, for example, to ongoingness, and the perfect to completion, how can the two be reconciled?

It is obvious in any case that traditional approaches to the progressive have been less than satisfactory. Let us look at the progressive now from the point of view of the kind of truth-conditional, model-theoretic semantics we have been developing here.

o. Formal Semantics of the Progressive

Bennett and Partee give the following analysis of the present progressive (excluding its futurate and frequentative uses):

> *John is building a house* is true at I if and only if I is a moment of time, there exists an interval of time I' such that I is in I', I is not an endpoint for I', and *John builds a house* is true at I'.[152]

That is,

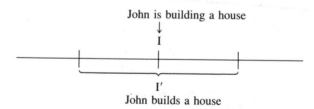

The problem with this is the imperfective paradox.[153] With activities, the past progressive implies the past, the past perfect, and the past perfect progressive: if John was pushing a cart, then it is automatically true that John pushed a cart, had pushed a cart, and had been pushing a cart. Similarly, the present progressive implies the present, the present perfect, and the present perfect progressive: if John is pushing a cart, then it is automatically true that (in one sense) John pushes a cart, has pushed a cart, and has been pushing a cart.

But with accomplishment verbs, this is not the case. Even if John never reached Rome, we could truthfully say that he was flying to Rome; if he gives up five minutes from now and never finishes his drawing, we can still truthfully say that right now he is drawing a unicorn. Dowty argues that the paradox (e.g., John was painting Susan's portrait, even though he never painted her portrait) cannot be resolved in terms of subject intention.[154] First, the subject might have no intention of, or no belief in, accomplishing the action—a man who is dying and does not believe he will live to finish it nonetheless can be said to be writing a symphony. Moreover, there are accomplishments with no agent: the rains are destroying the crops; the river was cutting a new channel.

Dowty assumes that the same progressive operator is in question with both activities and accomplishments, so the meaning of the progressive must be independent of the notion of successful completion.[155] The tack which Dowty takes is to treat the accomplishment as a possible outcome of the activity, and so he offers these truth conditions:

> [PROG ϕ] is true at I and w iff there is an interval I' such that $I{\subset}I'$ [and I is not a final subinterval for I'] and there is a world w' for which ϕ is true at I' and w', and w is exactly w' at all times preceding and [including] I.[156]

That is, at the point I (in world w) at which John is building a house (at which *John is building a house* is true), there is some possible world w' (which might or might not be w itself) such that w' is just like w up to the time I, and there is some time interval I' containing I such that *John builds [the] house* is true of I'. If John never completes his house in this world, there is some other (possible) one in which he does. Dowty has diagramed the situation:

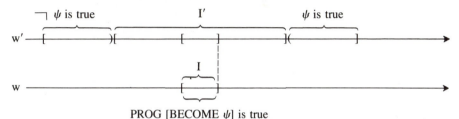

PROG [BECOME ψ] is true

(BECOME ψ designates the inchoation of the state denoted by ψ.) While Dowty discusses some problems with this and notes that "further refinements may be required," this treatment does seem to provide the sort of truth conditions appropriate to our intuitions of how the progressive is used.[157]

Dowty discusses the issue of whether this analysis is justified for non-accomplishments. Is it a necessary condition for John's being running that he continue running? It has been traditionally assumed that *John was reading at noon* entails that John continued reading after noon, that is, that his being reading was in a stretch of reading. Dowty cites *John was watching television when he fell asleep* to refute this. The only requirement is that John could have continued watching TV, not that he did.

The notion of "worlds like one another up to a point in time" is fraught with philosophical and technical difficulties, as Dowty points out.[158] For this reason other scholars[159] have proposed treatments in which the notion of possible future is utilized instead. This requires that time be branching, rather than linear, so that at any given moment there is not one, but an infinite number of possible futures.

Now the properties of time are these: let T be the set of times; then $<$ is a transitive "backward" ordering relation on T, namely such that for all t_1, t_2, $t_3 \in T$, if $t_1 < t_3$ and $t_2 < t_3$, then either $t_1 < t_2$ or $t_2 < t_1$, or $t_1 = t_2$.

A *history* on T is a subset h of T such that (1) for all t_1, $t_2 \in h$, if $t_1 \neq t_2$, then $t_1 < t_2$ or $t_2 < t_1$, and (2) if g is any subset of T such that for all t_1, $t_2 \in g$, if $t_1 \neq t_2$, then $t_1 < t_2$, or $t_2 < t_1$, then $g = h$ if $h \subseteq g$. This gives time the appropriate branching structure. Where t is a member of T, let H denote the set of histories containing *t*. In effect, each history in *H* is a connected path through an infinite number of points, and through each point *t* an infinite number of histories (paths) may be drawn.

Now we can say that, where *Inr(I)* denotes the set of histories just like that containing *I* up to and including *I*,[160]

> [PROG ϕ] is . . . true at *I* iff for each history *h* in *Inr(I)* there is an interval *I'* such that $I' \subset h$ and $I \subset I'$ and ϕ is true at *I'*.

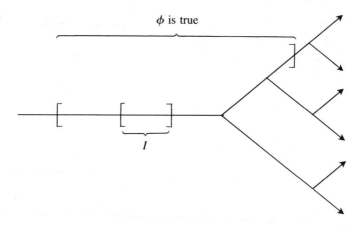

ϕ is true

I

Dowty has presented this in the accompanying diagram.

This treatment requires that the definitions of truth conditions for all other expressions be restated in terms of the notion "possible history." For example, those for the future operator are restated as follows[161]:

> [FUTURE ϕ]^{h,t} = 1 iff [ϕ]$^{h,t'}$ = 1 and $t' \epsilon h$ such that $t < t'$.

It is obvious that in general the notions possible world and possible history are equivalent, where by "possible history" we mean a sequence of times (or, alternatively, of events). To say that there is a possible world in which John will (finish) paint(ing) a unicorn is to say no more than that there is a possible sequence containing the present in which, at some time posterior to the present, John does (finish) paint(ing) a unicorn. There is one important difference, however. It makes perfectly good sense to say that an event takes place at the same time in two different worlds. For example, imagine the possible world *w'* which would have resulted from Montcalm defeating Wolfe on the Plains of Abraham. Now, imagine that in this world *w'* World War I also ended, as it did in the real world w_0, by an armistice at 11:00 a.m. on November 11, 1918. It makes perfectly good sense to say that World War I ended at the same time in both worlds.

But what does it mean to say that two future events are simultaneous in two different possible futures? In a branching time model, times on different branches (and hence in different histories) are not ordered relative to one another. One solution, offered by Thomason, is to utilize metric (clock) time, counting from the moment of branching.[162] For example, let the moment at which *w'* diverges from *w* be called *t*. Then, assuming time runs at the same rate in all histories, any point *t'* in history *h* which is *n* units of time from *t* will be said to be simultaneous with a time *t''* in some history *h'* which is likewise *n* units from *t*. In this way we get the simultaneity across histories that we need, so as to handle sentences like *If I were in New York right now, I would do such and such*.

The problem with this approach is that it cannot handle cases like the following: *if time had speeded up, it might have been the year 2001 already*. This asks us to match up "simultaneous" times in two worlds with different metrics of time. It is not clear whether this sentence "makes sense," but it does not seem to be meaningless. Given that we will need the notion of possible worlds in any case for intensions and world-creating predicates like *dream*,[163] it is not clear what advantages branching time offers us; it certainly complicates our semantics.[164]

Dowty discusses a unitary treatment of the ordinary progressive and the futurate progressive, suggested to him by Lauri Kartunnen.[165] What Kartunnen suggested was that [PROG ϕ] be true at an interval *I* iff ϕ is true at some interval *I'* which includes *I* or else is later than *I* (in some appropriate possible history containing *I*). Dowty rejects this proposal on the grounds that the progressive is ambiguous, citing Prince's (1973) example *Lee was going to Radcliffe until she was accepted by Parsons*.[166] He says:

> The imperfective reading, which Prince paraphrases as "Lee's going to Radcliffe was in progress until she was accepted by Parsons", entails that Lee did go to Radcliffe (since *go to Radcliffe* . . . is naturally interpreted as an activity). The futurate progressive reading, paraphrased as "Lee's going to Radcliffe (at some future date) was the plan until she was accepted by Parsons", does not have the same entailment, but on the contrary conversationally implicates that Lee did not go to Radcliffe.

That is, the futurate progressive reading leads us to infer that Lee did not go to Radcliffe (though it neither entails nor implies this).

Dowty accepts the notion that planning and predetermination are involved in the futurate progressive.[167] If so, then, he claims, the facts of the futurate progressive follow from the analysis of the "imperfective" ("normal") progressive. That is, he treats the futurate progressive as a combination of the progressive with a "tenseless" future, and interprets the latter in a similar way to what follows (in a model with branching time):

> [*tomorrow* ϕ] is true at *I* iff (1) ϕ is true (in all histories containing *I*) at some interval *I'* such that *I'* is included within the day following the day that includes *I*, and (2) the truth of ϕ at *I'* is planned or pre-determined by facts or events true at some time $t \leq I$.[168]

He has presented the situation in which *tomorrow* ϕ is true in the accompanying diagram.

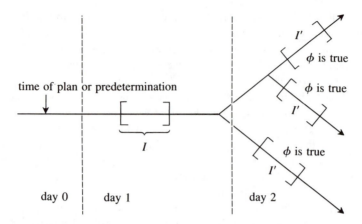

He says further:

A futurate progressive will thus have the logical form [PROG[*tomorrow* ϕ]], and such a sentence would be true at an interval I_0 if there is an interval $I_1 \supset I_0$ such that [*tomorrow* ϕ] is true at I_1 in all inertia histories containing I_0. And . . . [*tomorrow* ϕ] would . . . be true at I_1 if ϕ is true at a future interval I_2 in all histories containing I_1, and ϕ is planned or predetermined at some time at or preceding the lower bound of I_1.

He has diagramed this situation in the accompanying illustration.

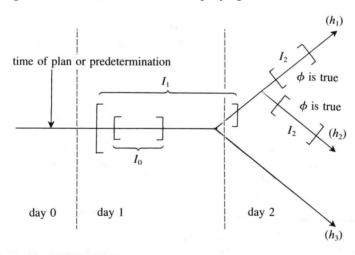

It is unclear how truth conditions which are so dependent on pragmatics could be fully formalized. In effect, this treatment of the futurates amounts to an admission that the difference in meaning between the futurates and either the corresponding simple tenses or the future tenses is pragmatic, not semantic, in nature.

p. Imperfective and Perfective

We have developed mechanisms for the perfect and progressive in English. Presumably the perfect aspect in other languages having explicit perfect marking (e.g., the Romance and Germanic languages) would be similarly treated, with a PERF operator and truth conditions similar to those given for PERF in the indirect interpretation of English, though even in German and French there will be important differences in the treatment of the perfect from that in English.

But what about the perfective and the imperfective? We have seen that the perfective is not the same as the perfect aspect. Slavic explicitly marks the perfective and the imperfective, but Russian for example has no explicit marker of the perfect. Greek and many other languages seem to have sets of perfect tenses distinct from their perfective ones.

The truth conditions for the perfective, whatever these may be, seem to be quite different from those for the perfect. We have treated the perfect as referring to an action prior to the reference time. But the perfective does not necessarily refer to a prior action (*samolët iščez* 'the plane disappeared' clearly does not[169]), though it may, as in *zriteli uselis' na svoi mesta* 'the spectators had taken their seats'.[170]

If the perfective remains to be accounted for, what about the imperfective? Can we perhaps identify it with the progressive? It is true that the present progressive of English often translates the Russian present imperfective (*ždem teb'a* 'we're waiting for you'[171]), as well as the simple present tense of Romance, Germanic, and Greek. From a structuralist point of view, the difficulty with this is that the Slavic imperfective is unmarked, while the English progressive is marked.

This is less of a problem, perhaps, than the fact that the truth conditions for the progressive will not work for the imperfective. As we have seen, some scholars view the progressive as a restricted subtype of the imperfective. The difference between the two is clearer in the past tense than in the present. The English progressive is true iff the event or situation includes the reference time, and possibly concludes in the relative future.

But the Slavic imperfective can be used in situations in which the action stands completed, so that

> out of context or situation, the sentence *Turisty podnimalis' na goru* can be understood in two ways: (1) as conveying action in progress; i.e., not yet having attained its boundary and, consequently, non-integral [The hikers *were* climbing the mountain]; (2) as conveying the fact of an action which has taken place and, consequently, [is] implicitly integral [The hikers *had climbed* the mountain].[172]

Similarly, the imperfect tenses (present, imperfect, future) of Greek, Latin, and the Romance languages—plus the corresponding simple tenses of Germanic, even of English—are ambiguous in this regard. First, they can denote a series of completed actions (though the series itself is not necessarily complete): *lúō* 'I free (in general), (Spanish) *canto cada día* 'I sing every day'.

More important, "they sang," "they sing," "they will sing" can all refer to complete as well as incomplete action. Whether the action is complete (*Garbo laughs!*, *Mr. Blandings builds his dream house*), or incomplete (caption on news-paper photo: *demonstrators gather in front of embassy*), or unclearly one or the other, depends on the lexical content and on the context.

In itself, as Marchand (1955) pointed out, English (and Germanic in general) has no distinction of imperfective and perfective—its simple tenses are ambiguous in this regard, and its complex tenses mark other distinctions (perfect and/or pro-gressive). What about the Romance and classical languages? The imperfect seems to be a marked imperfective form in contrast with the preterite, which is perfective (or possibly a neutral form). The facts of these languages, as we have seen, are complicated, but we may assume that they all do mark an aspectual distinction which we may term that of perfective and imperfective.

The problem is that they do not mark it explicitly. Arguably, Greek sometimes marks perfective tenses with a sigmatic stem, as it marks perfect ones by redupli-cated (kappatic) ones, and imperfective ones by a nonconsonantal stem. But there is no systematic use of stems to mark this distinction in Latin or Romance.

The question is whether in analyzing these languages operators such as PFVE and IMPVE would be required, so that the imperfect tense form, for example, would translate into something like PAST (IMPVE) in the LTL. Is such a com-positional treatment not once again merely a convenience? One difference a com-positional treatment will make, however, has to do with adverbials—as we shall see in the next section of this chapter—for adverbials have co-occurrence restric-tions relative to tenses and aspects. The problem is that such restrictions are de-fined on the NL expressions, not directly on those of the LTL.

Therefore, from the point of view of a formal semantic theory such as Mon-tague semantics, it may merely be a convenience to translate compositionally, rather than, for example, translating the imperfect tense of French by an IMPERF operator. It is true that, in a system of direct interpretation, it would be less than general to interpret each tense form separately. But this may simply argue against indirect interpretation.

We saw earlier that Johnson's neo-Reichenbachian theory[173] defines three as-pects in terms of the relations of E and R: thus the perfect is defined by E<R. To translate the three aspectual categories formally marked by Kikuyu, Johnson uses the operators PERF (for the perfect aspect), COMP (for the completive aspect), and PROG (for the progressive aspect). In her 1981 article she calls the latter the imperfect (IMPF) aspect, noting that "imperfect" is just (Comrie's) "imperfec-tive" and "completive" (his) "perfective."[174] We will see that the truth condi-tions for COMP are in fact what we want for the perfective, and those of the "imperfect" (PROG) close to those we want for the imperfective.

The perfect, we may assume, is universally defined by the relationship E<R. The relationship E = R defines for Johnson the "completive" aspect, as follows: it "is used to mean that there is a single interval of time (in episode-time), that this interval coincides with reference-time, and the episode named by the verb is true at that interval."[175] The formal definition (truth conditions) are:

COMP ϕ is true relative to $\langle w,i,J \rangle$ if and only if $J = \{i\}$ and ϕ is true relative to $\langle w,i \rangle$.

"This definition says that reference-time is the same as episode-time, and the embedded sentence is true at that particular time." Here i is the event time interval and w the evaluation world (ϕ is true at $\langle w,i \rangle$); J is the reference time (treated here as a sequence of intervals); "J = {i}" says that R = E.

We would expect then that E>R would define a third aspect. This looks like the prospective, however, not the imperfective. Moreover, neither Dowty's treatment of the progressive in English nor Johnson's treatment of the imperfect (PROG) is E>R. However, Johnson's treatment of the imperfective comes close to E>R.

Johnson identifies "completive," "imperfect," and "perfect" aspect as "three principal categories of verb aspect form," found in various languages and explicitly marked in Kikuyu:

> in relation to the time of an event, it is possible to distinguish three temporal phases which are significant in terms of the evolution of the event through time: (a) the actual time of the whole event itself, including its completion; (b) the range of times leading up to the completion of the event, during which various developments take place which bring the event into being; and (c) the range of times that follow the end of the event, and contain its results. The three aspect-form categories each allow for reference to one of these phases: [completive to (a), imperfect to (b), and perfect to (c)].[176]

Johnson's view here serves as a kind of link between Guillaumist thought and event-based semantics such as we will discuss below in this chapter. An event moves through development into being, it endures a certain time, and then it leaves behind effects. Another way of viewing the same process is to say that it moves through successive phases from pre-inception to the post-terminal perfect (transcendental) phase. She diagrams the three stages as follows:

$R = E$ for completive aspect

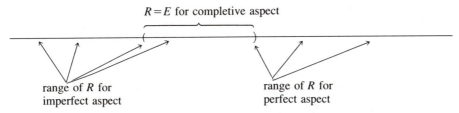

range of *R* for
imperfect aspect

range of *R* for
perfect aspect

Johnson defines the imperfect thus: for some t. in E, $R[\langle]\{t\}$.[177] That is, there is some time in the event time such that the reference time precedes it—E and R overlap, with some portion of E later than R. This guarantees that the event continues after the reference time. The truth conditions given in Johnson (1977) are much more complicated than this; they are similar to Dowty's treatment of the English progressive.[178]

The Kikuyu "progressive" overlaps with the English progressive, and even has very similar alternative meanings to the latter. Johnson says that

> a partially completed episode is only one of the possible situations described by a progressive sentence in Kikuyu. In fact, what we need is a progressive operator which works roughly as follows. PROG ϕ is true for interval i (in a world w) if and only if i is contained within a longer interval, for which latter interval one of three

things is true: (1) ϕ is repeatedly true (for the interative/habitual and continuous action interpretations), or (ii) ϕ is going to become true (for the futurate interpretation), or (iii) ϕ is not yet true for any interval in w, but various sub-episodes of the complete episode ϕ have already come to be true (for the imperfective interpretation with an accomplishment verb).[179]

She diagrams these as shown below:

(i) iterative/habitual meaning (if there were no gaps, this would be the continuous action meaning)

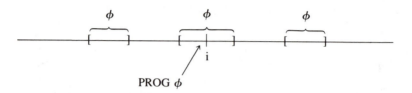

(ii) futurate meaning

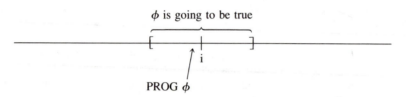

(iii) imperfective meaning (ψ, ψ', ψ'' describe characteristic subparts of the episode ϕ)

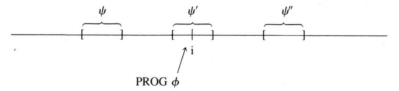

She can then develop the formal condition for the PROG operator as follows:

PROG ϕ is true in a model relative to an index $\langle w,i,J \rangle$ if and only if J is an interval sequence, there is more than one member of J, i is a sub-set of the union of all intervals in J, and for all j in J, there is some $J' \subset I$ and some ψ such that $[\phi \underline{\Delta} \psi]$ and $[\text{COMP}\psi \vee \text{FUT}\psi]$ is true at the index (w,j,J').[180]

This definition involves three important notions—*interval sequence, the subepisode relation*, and *the epistemic future*.[181] By an interval sequence, Johnson means a set of consecutive nonoverlapping intervals such as {j,j',j''}:

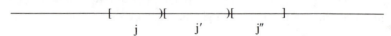

The subepisode relation identifies conditions under which one episode (e.g., *John began to run*) may be considered a characteristic subpart of another (e.g., *John ran*). The definition below "says that a sentence y describes a (characteristic) sub-episode described by f if and only if y is always true at some sub-interval of a time at which f is true." In other words, *John began to run* is a characteristic subpart of *John ran* iff *John began to run* is always true of some time t $\subseteq$ i, where i is the time over which *John ran* is true. Johnson adds the condition that ϕ can entail ψ only if ϕ just is ψ[182]; otherwise, trivial episodes (*John did something*) and irrelevant ones (*John was either tall or not tall*) would be allowed by the definition. Using *true$_e$* because reference time plays no role in the definition, Johnson defines:

> [$\phi \underline{\Delta} \psi$] is true$_e$ in a model relative to an index $\langle w,j \rangle$ if and only if (1) if ϕ is true$_e$ at $\langle w',j' \rangle$, then there is some j" $\underline{\Delta}$ j' such that ψ is true at $\langle w',j'' \rangle$, and (2) if $\phi \rightarrow \psi$, then $\phi = \psi$.[183]

Finally, a function E selects for each index $\langle w,j \rangle$ "the set of worlds whose subsequent development is consistent with reasonable expectations (at j in w) concerning the future."[184] She then utilizes this notion in defining the "epistemic" operator FUT as follows:

> FUTϕ is true relative to an index $\langle w,i,J \rangle$ if and only if for all w' such that w' is a member of $E(\langle w,i \rangle)$, there is some j' such that j' ϵ J, i $<$ j' and ϕ is true$_e$ at $\langle w',j' \rangle$.[185]

"What this definition says is the FUTϕ is true in a world w for a reference-time i if and only if every world which is consistent with reasonable expectations at i in w is a world in which ϕ comes to be true at a later time."

Johnson argues that *this* definition of FUT captures what is usually meant by "prospective" aspect.[186] It is true, as Allen for example points out, that it would be a mistake to assert that the prospective (e.g., certain readings of *John was to leave the next day, John was leaving the next day, John left the next day*, and the like in other tenses) merely require R $<$ E, since these are all acceptable even in case John *did not* leave the next day: *Susan gave John a farewell party because he was leaving* (*was to leave, ?would leave, ?left*) *the next day for the army, but fortunately they discovered his thanatophobia and he wasn't drafted.*

Johnson then defines the PROG operator thus:

> PROGϕ is true in a model relative to an index $\langle w,i,J \rangle$ if and only if J is an interval sequence, there is more than one member of J, i is a sub-set of the union of all intervals in J, and for all j in J, there is some J'$\subset$I and some ψ such that [$\phi \underline{\Delta} \psi$] and [COMP$\psi$ $\vee$ FUTψ] is true at the index $\langle w,j,J' \rangle$.[187]

"What this amounts to is saying that a sentence PROGϕ is true if and only if *its* reference-time falls within a succession of intervals, and in reference to each of *these* intervals, it is true to say that a particular sub-episode of ϕ takes place, or that this sub-episode may be reasonably expected to take place later." As we said above, the effect of this is essentially that of Dowty's treatment of the English progressive.

We can simplify the treatment of the imperfective by saying that R $<$ E in the sense that the *termination* of the event must follow the reference time. (We could further generalize by saying that all the aspects are defined by the relationship to R not of E itself but the termination of E.) But to make complete sense of this proposal we need to consider, as we do below in this chapter, the theory of events and their phases.

A successful universal set of truth conditions for the operators PERF, IMPF, and COMP (alias PERF, IMPVE, and PFVE) along the lines of Johnson's (1981) proposals or the kind of simplification envisaged here seems feasible.[188] The specification of such conditions would serve to confirm the intuitive identification of aspects in Slavic, Kikuyu, Greek, and other languages.

It would further have two satisfying consequences. First, it would resolve debates about the meaning, markedness, and equation of the various aspects. Second, it would demarcate the fundamental *meaning* of each of the aspects as opposed to the *uses* they are put to. A formal definition of this kind does seem to fulfill the task we initially assigned to a formal semantics—to provide an objective analysis of the aspects (and tenses). As Hoepelman says, the writing of (fragments of) formal grammars "has the advantage of creating clearness in the discussion, which is moved to a formal level."[189]

q. Temporal Adverbials

The formal semantics of tense and aspect is considerably complicated by the fact that time specification involves not only verbs and verb phrases but other types of expressions as well, such as noun phrases (*ex-mayor, husband-to-be,* etc.) adjectival phrases (*former, future, most recent, . . .*), and, most important, temporal (time) adverbials.

Either a deep or an extensive survey of the formal semantics of adverbials here would take us too far afield, though they have so much to contribute to the semantic interpretation of the expressions they occur in and have such important interrelationships with tense, aspect, and other types of temporal markings, that their study has in recent years become largely inseparable from that of tense and aspect (and vice versa). Consequently, we must have a fair amount to say about them here.

Time adverbials have just begun to be studied. Too much remains to be learned concerning them to allow more than the general outlines of an ultimate understanding of their formal semantics in this chapter and the next. All this despite a very large literature which includes numerous studies even of individual adverbs— for example Hoepelman and Rohrer (1981) on the German adverbs *noch* 'still, yet' and *schon* 'already', and Åqvist and others (1977) on *soon* and *recently.*

Some remarks on the range of the morphology and internal syntax of time adverbials might be useful to start with. Some time adverbials are lexical adverbials, that is, adverbs:

> already, always, earlier, eventually, forever, formerly, frequently, henceforth, hereafter, heretofore, immediately, lately, later, Mondays, mornings, never, now, nowadays, occasionally, often, once, presently, recently, sometimes, soon, then, thenceforth, thereafter, thereupon, today, tomorrow, yesterday, yet, . . .

Aside from time adverbs, of which every language has a very large, but finite, number, there are an infinite number of nonlexical (phrasal) temporal adverbial expressions:

after the party; after all the guests had left; all next week; at night; at noon; at 8:00 a.m. on June 11, 1945; at 12:00 p.m. today; before now; every day; every once in a while; for a day; from now on; from time to time; in an hour; in June; last Tuesday; never on Sunday; next week; now and forever; now and then; once in a great while; since Tuesday; twice last week; until we meet again; within the twinkling of an eye; . . .

Many adverbial expressions are in form nouns:

June, Monday, today, yesterday, . . .

or noun phrases in general:

last week, next year, the day before yesterday, this coming Tuesday, tomorrow morning, every day, some time ago, . . .

(*Now* can act as a noun, too.) Such noun phrases have the external syntax of adverbials, that is, they can occur anywhere that other adverbials occur:

$$
\text{he did it} \left\{ \begin{array}{l} \text{regularly} \\ \text{just now} \\ \text{today} \\ \text{every day} \end{array} \right.
$$

$$
\left. \begin{array}{l} \text{often} \\ \text{Mondays} \\ \text{every day} \end{array} \right\} \text{he skips lunch}
$$

only today   he skipped lunch

$$
\text{I'll do it} \left\{ \begin{array}{l} \text{soon} \\ \text{right now} \\ \text{some time in the near future} \end{array} \right.
$$

$$
\text{I did it} \left\{ \begin{array}{l} \text{quite recently} \\ \text{some time ago} \\ \text{some time during 1985} \end{array} \right.
$$

In terms of their internal syntax, other than the temporal noun phrases, nonlexical (phrasal) abverbials generally have one of the following three forms:

1. adverbial phrases, with adverbs as their core constituents ("heads"): a few minutes later, all too soon, just now, long ago, not long after that, not often, not too soon, not very quickly, often enough, only now, quite often, very quickly, very soon, . . .
   or with temporal noun phrases as cores: just this moment, nearly noon, not next week, only today, . . .
   or with other adverbials as cores: not just now, not until June, not while I'm in charge here, only so long as you are quiet, . . .
2. prepositional phrases: after June, after the party, after the sofa (*move the table after the sofa*), after the termination of our contract, after your medicine (*you'll feel better after your medicine*), before now, before Tuesday, during most of 1848, since last June, until tomorrow afternoon, up to now, . . .
3. adverbial subordinate clauses: after our contract terminated, after our contract terminates, as Tom was leaving, before you can say anything, since you went away, until we meet again, while the band played on, so long as we both shall live, . . .

There are, however, some idiomatic expressions which do not obviously fall into any of these categories:

for good, for once and for all, from now on, hour after hour, now and forever, right
away, right off, right off the bat, . . .

Furthermore, time adverbials can combine with one another (or be conjoined)
to form expressions of ever greater, and indefinitely great, complexity:

as often as you like but for no more than an hour, evenings at eight, every Monday
morning at 11:00 a.m., for a few minutes before dinner this evening, not more than
three times per month in the winter and four times a month otherwise, sometimes
when the wind comes from the north, . . .

As with other adverbials, there are two syntactic positions time adverbials can
have. They may occur outside (and preceding) the sentence proper, possibly set
off with a comma or other punctuation (in spoken language, by comma intonation,
etc.), that is, as sentential adverbials:

At present we live in London.
By next weekend I'll be sick of exams.
Day by day we are getting nearer to death.
Five minutes later the rescue party was leaving.
For generations, Nepal has produced the world's greatest soldiers.
In those days, we were getting up at 7 o'clock.
Next they're playing the Schubert Octet.
Next year we're going to have a holiday.
One day I shall die.
Suddenly I remembered the letter.
This time last year I was travelling around the world.
Twenty years later, Dick Whittington would be the richest man in London.
When the spring comes, the swallows return.
When we arrived she made some fresh coffee.[190]

They may also, like any other type of adverbial, appear within the predicate
phrase (verb phrase) of the sentence, before the verb:

He *rarely* lets us know what he's doing.
I *always* said he would end up in jail.
I *sometimes* buy shirts at Harrods.
I *still* haven't seen him.
War *no longer* solves any problems.

Or they may follow the verb (in English, if this is a copula or auxiliary):

I've *always* walked to work.
I was *recently* reading about an invention. . . .
They're *still* eating their dinner.
This strange individual was *later* to be defendant in one of the most notorious murder
trials of all time.

Or they can come at the end of the verb phrase:

Brahms completed his first symphony *in 1876.*
Crime is the best policy *these days.*
He cycles to work *most days.*
I shall remember that moment *until I die.*
I start work *next week.*
Tonight the competitors will have been driving their cars *continuously for twenty-
four hours.*
You will feel better *after this medicine.*

It is possible in theory for an adverbial to occur elsewhere in the verb phrase, but in English at least this is quite uncommon. *He will leave work* soon *for an unpaid holiday* is less favored than the following paraphrases:

> *Soon* he will leave work for an unpaid holiday.
> He will leave work for an unpaid holiday *soon*.
> He *soon* will leave work for an unpaid holiday.
> He will *soon* leave work for an unpaid holiday.

(Any other word order is impossible; while *soon* may interrupt the collocation *will leave*, it may not interrupt the phrase *for an unpaid holiday*: **he will leave work for* soon *an unpaid holiday*, etc. Nor may it separate verb and object, though it may separate object and adverbial: **he will leave* soon *work for an unpaid holiday*.)

Dowty (1979) treats natural language time adverbials as syntactically of different kinds, including both sentential adverbials of category (t/t), forming sentences from sentences (e.g., *today* in *today I saw a finch*); and verb (predicate)-phrase adverbials of category (IV/IV), forming verb phrases from verb phrases, like *for an hour* in *John slept for an hour*.

This categorization seems supported by such syntactic tests as the one provided by *do-so* "pronominalization." Given that *do so* (or its absence) must replace a constituent of the sentence, the sentences below—

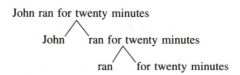

—suggest that *ran* and its collocation with *for twenty minutes* are both constituents, and moreover of the same syntactic category. In other words, the structure of the sentence *John ran for twenty minutes* is:

```
        John ran for twenty minutes
           /\
       John    ran for twenty minutes
                  /\
               ran    for twenty minutes
```

For twenty minutes, like most time adverbials, can appear either as a sentence adverbial (often in sentence-initial position, with or without a comma to set it off), as in *for twenty minutes, it looked like peace was about to break out*; or as a verb-phrase adverbial (possible in a number of positions, but not sentence-initially), as in *yesterday she twice ran for twenty minutes*.

Do sentence adverbials and verb-phrase adverbials form one syntactic class? Arguing against different syntactic categories is the fact that there are no differences of internal syntax between the two groups; membership cannot be predicted by form only: sentential adverbials look just like VP ones. They obviously differ in external syntax, however; as regards co-occurrence, they do fall into two different syntactic categories—(t/t) and (IV/IV).

As in the case of the categories of subordinating conjunctions and prepositions, which often share members (e.g., English *after, before, since* and German *während* 'during, while', *seit* 'since'), we must accept (near-)systematic ambiguity.[191]

Given that the internal syntax of each category is not unified, can we establish one category of sentence-adverbial and another of VP adverbial? Neither their translation into the LTL nor their semantic interpretation depends, in general, on adverbials' belonging to either such category. The connection between the internal and external syntax of a complex (phrasal) adverbial is not mediated in the Montague framework by category labels or rules such as "sentential adverbials may be prepositional phrases."

The internal syntax of something like *by now* depends solely on the syntactic categories of *by* and *now*. That *by now* can combine with something like *she had given up hope* to form *she had given up hope by now* depends only on the syntactic category of *by now* (which falls out from those of *by* and *now*), and on that of the sentence *she had given up hope*.

That adverbials can co-occur and have different scopes relative to one another—and even produce scope ambiguities—falls out from these facts. In the case of the example *in her youth she jumped rope over and over again for twenty minutes*, there is no doubt that *in her youth* has widest scope. But there are two possible readings, depending on which of *over and over again* and *for twenty minutes* has wider scope.

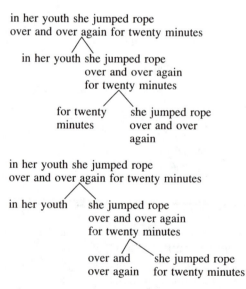

It is for this reason that we tend to use word order to mark scope. If we want the reading where *over and over again* has wider scope, we say *in her youth, she over and over again jumped rope for twenty minutes*, thereby indicating the scope relationship between the two adverbials within the scope of the sentential adverb.

The interpretation of an adverbial in a given sentence depends on many syntactic, semantic, and pragmatic conditions; in general one is *not* free to use any possible word order with a given meaning in a given context. The syntactic conditions on the placement of adverbials in any NL are still not fully known, though there is an extensive literature on this question.[192]

In general, the interpretation of expressions containing time adverbials depends most centrally on the semantic nature of the adverbials themselves. As we have seen, at least as early as Apollonius Dyscolus, grammarians noted that adverbial expressions of time differ as to their co-occurrence with tenses. This seems to follow from the association of adverbials with different time sectors—past, present, and future. There is something natural in expressions such as

> *As I speak to you*, I *am lunching* with my boss.
> *Yesterday* I *lunched* with my boss.
> *Tomorrow* I *shall lunch* with my boss.

that is missing in expressions like the following, in which "natural" links of time and adverbial are disregarded:

> **As I speak to you*, I *was lunching* with my boss.
> **Yesterday* I *shall lunch* with my boss.
> **Tomorrow* I *lunched* with my boss.

But not all adverbial expressions are inherently "past," "present," or "future." Many are neutral in this regard:

> *Monday* I *am lunching* with my boss.
> *Monday* I *lunched* with my boss.
> *Monday* I *shall lunch* with my boss.
>
> I *often lunch* with my boss.
> I *often lunched* with my boss.
> I *shall often lunch* with my boss.

The interpretation of such neutral adverbials depends on their context. With a past tense verb, a neutral adverbial is normally interpreted as past, with a future as future, and so on: *John left Monday* = 'John left last Monday'; *John will leave Monday* = 'John will leave next Monday'.

The interpretation also depends on aspect, since the futurate *John is leaving Monday* = 'John will leave next Monday', but *John leaves Monday* does not necessarily = 'John leaves next Monday', and can mean 'John leaves *every* Monday (in general)'. The interaction of aspect with Aristotelian aspect means that the interpretation of neutral adverbials also depends indirectly on Aristotelian aspect. (Contrast !*Monday John is ill*, which can be a present—albeit not one literally referring to the present time—but not a futurate, with *Monday John runs a marathon*, which can be either.)

In some cases in which a tense is not used in a literal sense, adverbials co-occur on a semantic, not a syntactic basis. Past time adverbials (or neutral adverbials used with past time reference) often can be used with the historical present, at least in colloquial speech:

> And then *last night* Nixon *gets* up there. . . .
> So *meantime*, I'm *tying* up the sail.
> *When we drove up*, I *see* all these kids. . . .[193]

But future time adverbials can be used freely with the futurate present:

> *This following year* Sue *turns* 40.
> *Tuesday next* we *leave* for Rome.
> *Next year* we're *vacationing* in France.

As in the case of the example with *meantime* above, the interpretation of adverbials in such cases is independent of the literal tense of the verb.

Another way in which time adverbials differ from one another is that some are *indexical* or *deictic* and refer to times relative to the moment of evaluation (generally the moment of speech):

> just now, last week, next Monday, now, nowadays, this morning, at this moment, today, tomorrow, the day before yesterday, at present, . . .

But others are purely referential, and refer to times independent of the moment of speech:

> at noon on July 4, 1957; in 1848

Here we may distinguish *anaphoric* and *chronological* adverbials. The former refer back to some time already referred to in the context:

> Sue was happiest *when they lived in Europe*.
> *Then* she was as happy as she ever was.

(Here *then* means 'when they lived in Europe'.) Chronological adverbials, while not deictic, fix times directly and do not refer back to anything in the context, though they may depend on background information in the universe of discourse. Dates depend, for example, on a presupposed chronological framework. Thus:

> He was born *on the third of June, 1848*.
> *In the third year of the Ch'ien Lung emperor*, something very odd occurred.
> *In the year 1 of the Revolution*, a decree was signed.

Adverbials need not refer to definite times like *now* or *1848*. They may be indefinite:

> all day long, an hour a day, for an hour, frequently, often, sometimes, thereupon, . . .

Some of these are anaphoric pro-terms, dependent on some understood time reference: *thereupon* means 'right after *that* time'. But expressions such as *all day long* and *sometimes* may be similarly understood. In *you can eat celery all day long and not gain an ounce*, the adverbial has no definite time reference, but in *the day after her husband left her, Susan felt ill all day long*, it is understood to refer to the complete interval of the day following the day on which her husband left her.

The interpretation of adverbials depends on more than their syntactic category and their referential semantics, that is, how they locate events. Adverbials also differ as regards discourse pragmatics, and this depends partly, but not exclusively, on their inherent aspectual meanings.

It has been recognized since at least Bennett and Partee ([1972] 1978) that most time adverbials fall into one of the three following groups:

1. The *frame adverbial* refers to "an interval of time within which the described action is asserted to have taken place."[194] They most often denote intervals of time. Indexical examples include *last week, next month, the day before yesterday, this morning, three days ago, today, yesterday;* non-indexical ones include *in 1848* and *on June 7, 1848*. Frame adverbials may also refer to moments of time: *now; precisely at noon on June 7, 1848*.

A special subcategory of frame adverbials refer to intervals anchored at one end, possibly at the present time—*since last Tuesday, before Tuesday next*—or possibly at some other time: *since the preceding Tuesday, before the following Tuesday*.

2. Adverbials of *number* and *frequency* refer either to the number of times a type of event occurred[195]—*at least once, on a few occasions, several times, twice, two times*—or to the frequency: *annually, hourly, once a month, several times a year, twice a year*.[196] These tell us how many times per unit of time something occurred (*hourly* = 'once per hour').

Expressions such as *every hour* are to be taken as equivalent to '(at least) once per hour', and so on. And those like *at regular intervals, regularly, repeatedly* mean 'once per [unspecified] unit of time'. There are an infinite number of vague, indefinite expressions of this type:

> every once in a while, every so often, from time to time, hardly ever, on occasion, now and then, scarcely ever, very often, . . .

There are also an infinite number of precisely quantified expressions of the type *biannually, every other hour, hourly, twice every three years*.

Adverbials of frequency and number are disjoint from frame adverbials in their discourse functions, as we shall see in the next chapter.

3. *Durative* adverbial phrases "indicate the duration of the described event by specifying the length of time that it is asserted to take."[197] Typical examples are prepositional phrases headed by *for*, like *for an hour*.

Nerbonne refers to a class of adverbials he calls *Frist* adverbials, using the German word for "period."[198] These are also called *containers* in the literature. Typical examples are prepositional phrases headed by *(with)in* or *inside of*, like *(with)in an hour*. These adverbials are used to specify the duration of telic processes. Like durative adverbials, which specify the duration of an atelic process (*she swam for an hour*), these adverbials refer to an interval (*in a hour*).

But they are unlike duratives and like frame adverbials in that they do not say anything about the nature of the event, but merely situate it within a certain interval. To say that "she spotted the hidden letter within minutes" is not to say how long the spotting took, which is instantaneous (though it does tell us how long it *took* for her to spot the letter, which requires an interval of time); rather, it says within what interval of time the event occurred.

Are frame adverbials and *Frist* adverbials in fact different categories? There are two reasons for differentiating them. First, frame adverbials freely occur with all the various Aristotelian aspects:

> Susan was ill all day yesterday. (state)
> Susan was running all day yesterday. (activity)

Susan repaired the plumbing yesterday. (accomplishment)
Susan repaired faucets all day yesterday. (series of accomplishments)
Susan noticed a worn-out washer yesterday. (achievement)
Susan noticed more and more leaky faucets yesterday. (series of achievements)

Frist adverbials do not so occur, however, being limited to performances (nonserial accomplishments and achievements):

!Susan was ill within an hour. (This can only have an inchoative reading.)
!Susan was running within an hour. (This too can only have an inchoative reading; the simple tense too has a marginal, inchoative reading: ?!*Susan ran within an hour.*)
Susan repaired the faucet within the hour.
!Susan repaired faucets within the hour. (But note: *Susan repaired several faucets within the hour.*)
*Susan noticed more and more leaky faucets within the hour.

There is a second reason for differentiating frame adverbials and *Frist* adverbials. Frame adverbials serve to indicate the reference time. They are Dowty's "main tense" adverbials and as such have greater scope than the *Aktionsarten* and aspects, and are closely related to tense.[199] *I went home Monday* forces *Monday* to refer to a past Monday, in certain contexts last Monday, while *I'm going home Monday* forces it to refer to a future Monday, often next Monday.

But *Frist* adverbials simply locate event time (*John had left home within a month of graduating*). They freely occur within the scope of both aspect and *Aktionsarten*, and this is why Dowty refers to both durative and *Frist* adverbials as "aspectual adverbials."[200]

We can say that there is a two-dimensional categorization of temporal adverbials. Frame adverbials and *Frist* adverbials denote time intervals within which certain time intervals fall. Durative adverbials denote time intervals with which a certain time interval coincides. Number and frequency adverbials state how often and/or with what frequency a series of events occur.

What have been called "frame" adverbials are just those containers which tell us, as durative and other adverbials may, where the reference time falls. All of these function then as sentential, "main tense" adverbials. On the other hand, all these may function as predicate phrase (VP) adverbials. We may summarize the types of adverbials as follows:

  I. affect R—sentential (main tense) adverbials
    A. how often?—number and frequency adverbials (1)
    B. when?
      i. within when?—frame adverbials (3)
      ii. for how long?—durative adverbials (5)
  II. affect E—verb phrase adverbials
    A. how often?—number and frequency adverbials (2)
    B. when?
      i. within when?—*Frist* adverbials (4)
      ii. for how long?—durative adverbials (6)

Here are some examples, keyed to the preceding table:

1. *Once in a while,* I wish I were a prince.
2. I often wish I were lucky *once in a while.*

3. I read a great book *yesterday*.
4. With speed-reading, I could read a great book *within a minute*.
5. *For a couple of weeks* Lady Jane was Queen of England.
6. They kept Lady Jane in the Tower *for a long time*.

Verb phrase adverbials are inside the scope of, and independent of, sentential adverbials. As it happens, not all combinations are felicitous. The time period of the event must be shorter than the frame containing it. Thus *yesterday I swam for an hour* is fine, but *yesterday I swam for thirty hours* is not felicitous in contexts with normal presuppositions. (It is unexceptionable, however, on planets having longer days or shorter hours than ours, or at indices in which either the astronomy of the solar system or the system of chronology is altered.) For similar reasons, *for an hour I swam all day* is very odd, while *yesterday I swam for an hour* is fine.

Multiple adverbials of the same type obey similar pragmatics. You can swim every Tuesday at five o'clock, but cannot so easily swim every five o'clock on Tuesday; you can swim every week for a month, but not easily every month for a week. You can come home at noon on July 4, 1967, but not in 1967 on July 4 at noon. (Though you can, of course, return home in 1967, on July 4, and at noon.)

These are pragmatic constraints, not semantic, so there is no reason to prevent our syntax from generating and translating such monstrosities. Whether the semantics interprets things like *John loved Sue for an hour for a week* as (necessarily) false (contradictory) or as meaningless depends on one's theory of semantics and how one feels about the baldness of the present king of France, the sentence *the present king of France is bald* having been argued either to be meaningless or to be false.[201]

Bennett and Partee[202] assert that some adverbials (seem to) serve at once as frame *and* durative (or *Frist*) adverbials:

Susan ate bananas for a week.
Susan fell ill within a week.

If so, this would account for the fact that no durative adverbial can co-occur with *for a week* in the first example (**Susan ate bananas for a week for a month*), and no *Frist* adverbial with *within a week* in the second (**Susan fell ill within a week inside of a month*). But the frame in both cases is not asserted—it must be presupposed or inferred. Out of context, there is no frame. Duratives and *Frist* adverbials alike do not serve as both sentential adverbials and VP adverbials *at once*.

As was observed in Binnick (1969), there is an interesting ambiguity with accomplishments. Durative adverbials can refer either to the period of the activity or to that of its resultant state: thus *the sheriff of Nottingham jailed Robin Hood for four years* can mean either the sheriff took four years to jail, or spent four years in jailing, Robin Hood, or that the term of sentence was four years. Similarly, *he subscribed to the magazine for four years* could mean either that on one occasion he ordered four years' worth of the publication, or that on four annual occasions he ordered one year's worth of it.

What we can say is that durative adverbials generally occur with atelic expressions and containers with telic ones. This is why duratives can occur with achievements or accomplishments in series:

> He spotted the same peculiar automobile near his house every day for four years.
> He swam across the university pool all week (but the next Monday he returned to using the pool at the Y).

It is also why containers can occur with activities and states where these are understood as telic, that is, as having natural terminal bounds, as in:

> Within the week, he swam in the university pool.
> Within a week, he was ill.

In these examples, it is a special *Aktionsart* reading—inchoactive or terminative—which allows the container adverbial. *The car was running like new within a week of going into the repair shop* is read "the car *began to* be running like new within a week of going into the repair shop"; *she was ill with malaria within a week* means she began to be ill.

It should be noted that containers may have implicit starting bounds as well as explicit ones. An end-point may be stated, as in *within the last week,* or an initial point may be, as in *within the next hour.* However, the sentence *within a week, Sue was down with malaria* presupposes, but does not assert, some initial bound (e.g., that of her flying to Asia). Generally the initial bound with future tenses is presupposed to be S (*within a week, you'll be begging to come home*).

We need not say more here concerning time adverbials; we will return to them below. The question of how they are to be translated into the LTL and semantically interpreted in a model such as the Montague one is important, but consideration of it would take us too far afield.[203]

Such a discussion as we have had here of temporal adverbials would seem already to have provided a long enough excursus on a tangent. But it is impossible to consider tense and aspect in isolation from adverbials. One area in which this is evident is that of scope, for at least with Priorian tense operators, the co-occurrence of tenses with time adverbials generates a problem known as the Adverbial Scope Paradox, which we consider in the next section.

r. Time Adverbials and the Adverbial Scope Paradox

The interpretation of expressions containing time adverbials depends on the semantic scope of the adverbial. Sentential adverbials may have verb-phrase adverbials within their scope: *yesterday I went home in the morning* means that "I went home in the morning" is true of yesterday. It seems clear that the scope of an adverbial relative to the tense makes for a difference in interpretation. In this last example, the tense is within the scope of the adverbial *yesterday* and outside that of *in the morning.* Compare *yesterday I was going to go home* (possibly I was going to go home today) with tense inside the scope of the adverbial, and *I was going* (possibly a week ago) *to go home yesterday* with tense outside its scope. (Differences in scope account for the possibility of seemingly contradictory examples such as *yesterday I was leaving tomorrow* 'it was true yesterday that I was to leave tomorrow'.)

In general, tense is *within* the scope of a semantically sentential adverbial (such as the *yesterday* in *yesterday I went home in the morning*), and *without* that of a semantically verb-phrase adverbial (such as the phrase *in the morning*). Adverbials which are syntactically verb-phrase adverbials may be semantically sentential. *Yesterday John went home in the morning* and *John went home in the morning yesterday* do not appear to differ as regards the semantic interpretation of the adverbial *yesterday*.

The relationship of tense and time adverbials has posed a great challenge to formal semantics, since, as has often been pointed out, there is (with Priorian operators, at least) a paradox in regard to the relative scope of tense and adverbial.[204]

Consider the sentence *John slept yesterday*. If it were translated into the LTL as

$$\text{yesterday}'(\text{PAST}(\text{sleep}'(\text{John}')))$$

it would mean that it was the case at some time yesterday that "John sleeps" is true in the (relative) past. This is, however, not the meaning of *John slept yesterday*, since this interpretation excludes the case where John's sleeping takes place in the present relative to yesterday, which is precisely what the sentence does assert.

If it were translated as

$$(\text{PAST}(\text{yesterday}'(\text{sleep}'(\text{John}'))))$$

however, this would mean that it was the case at some time in the past that "John sleeps" is true of yesterday. But this renders the coincidence of the past reference time and the past event time accidental, whereas in fact the sentence asserts their coincidence. Moreover, for those speakers for whom *yesterday* can mean 'the day before that' (and for those logicians for whom *yesterday* can mean that only in this context), this is an incorrect interpretation, in that it excludes the case where John slept on some given day in the past (as opposed to the day before that day), which of course is what the sentence actually means, *yesterday* denoting a certain day in the past and not the day before that day.

The question then is how to capture the meaning of sentences such as *John slept yesterday*, in which a definite tense combines with a definite adverbial expression of time. One solution to the scope paradox, which has sometimes been adopted, is the "syntactic solution."[205] Rather than treating the tense and the adverbial as independent elements which can be introduced separately into a sentence, they are syntactically linked and introduced together.

In this proposal a sentence like *John slept yesterday*, which contains a temporal adverbial, is generated syntactically by combining a tenseless sentence like *John sleep* with the temporal adverbial, in this case *yesterday*. The tense of the verb is a concomitant result of the combination of the adverbial with the (tenseless) sentence. There is therefore no scope of the adverbial relative to the tense and hence no scope paradox.

Dowty's (1979) system[206] works like this. Dowty assumes sentence-final adverbials adjoin to tenseless sentences at the same time as tense. For the three simple tenses, he presents these syntactic rules[207]:

S36. If $\alpha \in$ TmAv, $\phi \in$ t, then $F_{36}(\alpha, \phi) \in$ t, where $F_{36}(\alpha, \phi) = \phi'\ \alpha$, ϕ' is [the result of changing the main verb in ϕ to past tense].

S37. If $\alpha \in$ TmAv, $\phi \in$ t, then $F_{37}(\alpha, \phi) \in$ t, where $F_{37}(\alpha, \phi) = \phi'\alpha$.

ϕ' in S37 is the result of changing the main verb in ϕ to present tense. In Dowty (1979) he assumed adverbials are added to sentences marked with the present tense; thus S37 need make no mention of this. But in Dowty (1982) he assumed tenseless sentences, but did not change S37 to reflect this change.

S38. If $\alpha \in$ TmAv, $\phi \in$ t, then $F_{38}(\alpha, \phi) \in$ t, where $F_{38}(\alpha, \phi) = \phi'\alpha$, ϕ' is [the result of changing the main verb in ϕ to future tense].

This yields analysis trees such as:

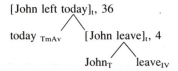

$[\text{John left today}]_t$, 36

today $_{\text{TmAv}}$ $[\text{John leave}]_t$, 4

John$_T$ leave$_{IV}$

"Yesterday" or "Monday" must be thought of as denoting in any given context a set of intervals, rather than a single interval, which might seem more intuitive. This is because we want *John slept yesterday* to be true where the interval over which he slept is *in* yesterday, but is not *equal to* yesterday (he didn't necessarily sleep all day and all night).

Since there are many possible yesterdays or Mondays—we can say *every Monday* or *some Monday(s)*—time adverbials must be treated as denoting sets of sets of intervals of time. That is, *(on) Thursday* denotes the set of all sets of intervals within a Thursday, that is, $\lambda T \exists t[t \subseteq \text{Thursday} \wedge T(t)]$.[208]

Now, *John left on Thursday* will be true if John's leaving took place on Thursday. That is, if *on Thursday* denotes a set T of sets of intervals, and *John leaves* denotes some interval j, then *John leaves on Thursday* is true iff $\{j\} \in$ T. The problem is that *John leave* does *not* denote an interval of time. This is puzzling. After all, a sentential time adverbial like *on Thursday* ought to denote a function from propositions (functions from indices to truth values) to truth values, and given that *John leave* denotes a proposition and *John leaves on Thursday* (in, say, the present-tense interpretation) denotes a truth value, why is there a problem?

To handle this, Dowty proposes the following. He translates the non-adverbial part of the sentence not into a simple expression of the subject-predicate form, but into an expression which asserts that that predication takes place *at* a time, and the tense is captured by the relationship of that time to the evaluation time. The translation rules matched to S36–38 are, where $[\![t^*]\!]^i = i$:

T36. $\alpha'(\lambda t[t < t^* \wedge AT(t, \phi')])$
T37. $\alpha'(\lambda t[t = t^* \wedge AT(t, \phi')])$
T38. $\alpha'(\lambda t[t > t^* \wedge AT(t, \phi')])$[209]

T36, for example, says that the adverbial α' takes as argument the set t of times such that t is earlier than t^* (i.e., which are in the past) and ϕ' is true at t. Given that the adverbial is a function from sets of intervals to truth values, it is clear that this is equivalent to saying that the time of the event belongs to the time denoted by the adverbial, that is, that the event takes place during the time denoted by the adverbial.

One question is how to guarantee that the tense matches the time of the adverbial (so we don't get, e.g., *John slept tomorrow*). One way of doing this is to assure that when the tenseless sentence is combined with the adverbial, the verb automatically changes into the appropriate tense. This will require adverbials to be categorized for time. Such a system would work well for adverbials such as *yesterday*, *nowadays*, and *tomorrow*, which are each associated with one of the time sectors, but would seem to be impossible for neutral adverbials such as *now*, *this afternoon*, *Fridays*:

> Now he was in great danger.
> Now he is in great danger.
> ?!Now he will be in great danger.

> This afternoon she worked very hard.
> This afternoon she is working very hard.
> This afternoon she will work very hard.

> Fridays she always visited her aunt.
> Fridays she always visits her aunt.
> ?!Fridays she will always visit her aunt.

Under the syntactic solution, in effect, the tense becomes redundant.[210] (Kiparsky, 1968, argues precisely this, that tenses are essentially redundant, serving as agreement markers.)

The disadvantage of the syntactic solution, as Dowty points out, is that a completely different set of syntactic rules generates the tenses of sentences without adverbials from those that generate the tenses of sentences with them.[211] *John slept* gets its past tense in a different way than does *John slept yesterday*.

Furthermore, Dowty notes that the syntactic solution accounts for sentences with multiple time adverbials (e.g., *I first met John Smith at two o'clock in the afternoon on Thursday in the first week of June in 1942*) no more than it does for those without any.[212] From this point of view the syntactic solution is less than satisfying.

But Dowty points out a more fundamental problem with it. In truth-conditional, model-theoretic theories such as Montague semantics, the "logical form" of the sentence which is semantically interpreted is the syntactic analysis tree of the sentence. But then the syntactic solution is equivalent to treating the combination of tense and adverbial as a constituent unit of the sentence—something like *yesterday PAST* applied to the timeless *John leave*—whereas the two are really syntactically independent, with *yesterday* applying to the tensed *John left*. Any "solution" along the lines of the syntactic one is a "kludge," an artificial fix which ignores the fundamental problem(s). Let us turn then to a "semantic" solution.

s. Multidimensional Indexing

Following Johnson (1977), Dowty (1982) proposes a "semantic" solution to the problem of adverbial scope, based on an idea of Hans Kamp's (1971). Kamp was interested in the problem of embedded futures. The following two sentences are not synonymous:

> A child was born who would be king.
> A child was born who will be king.

The first merely requires that the child be a king at some point relatively future to its birth; this could be some point in the past. But the second sentence makes it explicit that the kingship is not in the past. The first sentence is easily translated, using standard logical notation plus Priorian operators as in (a) below; but the second cannot be so translated, since, although the future tense of *will be* is within the scope of the past tense, it is also future relative not to the past, but to the present.

To solve this, what Kamp does is introduce a non-Priorian operator, N, which shifts the reference time from the (past) time of the event (here, of birth) to the (present) time of the speech act; the second sentence can now be translated as in (b) below.

> (a) $P\exists x$ [child$'$(x) $\wedge$ born$'$(x) $\wedge$ F king$'$(x)]
> (b) $P\exists x$ [child$'$(x) $\wedge$ born$'$(x) $\wedge$ NF king$'$(x)]

In effect, the interpretation of a sentence may involve not just one indexical (evaluation) time, but two—the speech-act time, and a reference time which may differ from it. In the case of the sentence *a child was born who will be king*, the past tense *was born* takes as its reference time some $t<S$, but *will be* takes S itself. This two-index system allows a *semantic* solution to the scope problem. The reference time is independent of the evaluation time, so the interpretation of the adverbial is independent of that of the tense.

As already discussed, such a dual-indexed system was adopted by Johnson for her work on Kikuyu. In accord with her neo-Reichenbachian system, Johnson stated truth conditions for the tense operators in terms of reference and speech-act times, and for aspect operators in terms of event and reference times.[213] Dowty's adaptation likewise utilizes two time indices i (=r) and j (=s).[214] Truth at an evaluation time j is defined indirectly—a sentence p is true at j iff there is some time (reference) i such that p is true relative to i and j.

All the truth condition rules are stated in terms of these two index times. For example, PRES(ϕ) will be true relative to i and j iff ϕ is true relative to $\langle i, j \rangle$ and $i=j$. There is no explicit reference to the event time e, because in simple tenses e just is r (i) (that is, E=R). It is in the interpretation of the aspects that E must be explicitly introduced into truth conditions, but in Dowty and Johnson there is no evaluation relative to e, and indices simply contain two times.

There are a number of problems other than the scope paradox solved by a two-dimensional index.[215] Obviously Kamp's solution requires something like a two-dimensional index. He argues that the indexical (definite) character of the preterite cited by Partee (1973) can be accounted for in terms of two index times: " 'ϕ is true$_z$ at $\langle i,j \rangle$' is interpreted as 'ϕ is true when uttered at j and used to talk about the time i.' "[216]

Another use he finds for the 2-D system is in accounting for conditional *would* and for *used to*. He proposes to treat *would* ϕ as true at $\langle i,j \rangle$ iff ϕ is true at $\langle i',j \rangle$ for some $i' > i$.[217] He proposes further that *used to* differs from the past tense in the way *would* differs from *will*. *Used to* ϕ is true at $\langle i,j \rangle$ iff ϕ is true at $\langle i',j \rangle$ for some $i' < i$. That is, *would* is an indefinite future and *used to* an indefinite past, but these are tenses in which reference time is shifted away from evaluation time.

The reader who goes to Nerbonne (1984) or the various works in the tense-logical tradition (such as those of Åqvist and Guenther) will find there what is apparently a *three*-dimensional system in which indices contain e, r, and s. In fact, Nerbonne's system is 2-D just like Dowty's and Johnson's, and is in effect a notational variant of the neo-Montagovian system. In Nerbonne's system,

$$X_{x,y,z} \models a$$

means "a is true in model X relative to x, y, z." For example, in

$$A_{s,e,r} \models p \text{ iff } F(p,e) = 1$$

s is the speech act time, e is the event time, r is the reference time, p is some sentence, and F is a function assigning denotations to expressions (here, truth values to sentences); the "turnstile" sign, $\models$, means "satisfies." "$A_{s,e,r} \models p$"— read "$A_{s,e,r}$ satisfies p"—means 'p is true in the model A at the index $\langle s,e,r \rangle$'. ("Satisfies" can be thought of, roughly and informally, as "renders true.")[218]

For example, Nerbonne's rule for the PRETerite operator used in translating German is this:

$$\text{for all } A,s,e,r: A_{s,e,r} \models \text{PRET}(p) \text{ iff } e = r < s \text{ and } A_{s,e,r} \models p.[219]$$

A very similar notation is widely used in studies within the tense-logical tradition, especially in Europe. There a model is taken to include not only an assignment of values to variables and constants, a set of times T, and a linear ordering on those times, but also a valuation on propositions and, most significant, a speech-act time s and a reference time r. Evaluation is relative to a time *t*. Hence the following (several slightly different notations appear in the literature):

This is read "A is true at e in the model $M^{s,r}$." This is essentially equivalent, however, to Nerbonne's notation, because the model $M^{s,r}$ includes s and r. (These examples are not quite in the spirit of the tense-logical literature, however.)[220]

These notations are essentially equivalent to the notation used here. Here, for example, is Dowty's PAST tense interpretation rule[221]:

$$[\![\text{PAST } \phi]\!]^{i,j} = 1 \text{ iff } [\![\phi]\!]^{i,j} = 1 \text{ and } i < j$$

In this instance, Nerbonne's use of three index times is merely a simple way of stating the truth conditions. But Nerbonne argues that such a 3-D system is necessary in other cases, and generalizes the usage.[222] There are other suggestions in the literature that two indices are inadequate, and that a third is necessary. We know that Reichenbach's three-time (E, R, S) system can be captured with only two index times, but can Bull's, with its fourth axis of orientation (for the conditional perfect)?

There are a number of reasons a priori why we might suspect a need for three index times. One has to do with the problem which I will call Cavett's Problem. Dick Cavett once had a television program which he regularly began with a monologue of topical humor. This program was taped in the early evening for showing later the same night. One particular night for some reason the broadcast was purposefully delayed, so that when the show was taped it was understood that it would be shown not later that night, as usual, but rather three days later. Knowing that events in the interm could render his opening monologue not only not timely, but possibly outdated or even absurd, Cavett wished to make his audience aware of this. But either deliberately or accidentally he got himself humorously tied up in words, unable to properly explain the situation.

The reason was that he could not assume a unique speech-act time. He said something like this: "Because the humor in the opening monologue is rather topical, I wanted you to know that we're not taping this show right now, I mean we aren't taping it earlier this evening. I mean we aren't . . . weren't taping it tonight, but three nights ago." The problem is that there was a time t at which the program was being taped, a time t' when it would be shown, and two shadowy times t'' and t''' at which, respectively, it would normally be shown relative to t and normally be taped relative to t''.

Choosing t (his actual S) as the moment of speech (evaluation time) led him to utter the infelicitous *we're not taping this show right now, I mean we aren't taping it earler this evening.* But to choose t' as moment of speech leads to the equally infelicitous *we weren't taping it tonight, but three nights ago.*

The difficulty here comes from the fact that a videotaped program *looks* as live as a conversation but in fact *functions* like a written communication. In trying to explain the relationships between the sets of times t, t', t'', and t''', Cavett had to step outside the framework of the apparent reality of the tape and required in effect two different moment-of-speech times, which is impossible; but neither alone was adequate to his task, for one was the *real*, psychological moment of speech and the other the *apparent* one.

It is the perennial problem of the time traveler reporting events; are they to be relativized to psychological time (*I left home tomorrow*) or to chronological time (*I will leave home tomorrow*)? Neither one seems very satisfactory. (Cf. the amusing description, in chapter 15 of Douglas Adams's novel *Restaurant at the End of the Universe*, of Dr. Dan Streetmentioner's *Time Traveller's Handbook of 1001 Tense Formations.*)

We need not consider oddities such as the linguistic peculiarities of time travel to see that there is a problem here, for epistolary tenses and the historical tenses serve as well to demonstrate the relativizability of the moment of speech.

We might point to the famous epitaph of the Lacedaemonians in Simonides (fragment 92), which we have already quoted: "Go tell the Spartans, thou who passest by, that here, obedient to their laws, we lie." Although the Lacedaemonians are dead, the time of evaluation for this auto-epitaph (whether real or pseudo-) can only be subsequent to the (presumed) speech-act time.

Whether a statement takes the language user's speech-act time as the evaluation time, or the audience's (recipient's) speech-act time (the time at which the message is "decoded") as evaluative, as in the case of the epistolary tenses, hardly matters. If the evaluation time V is just S, then the sentence can never be necessarily true for both speaker (writer, signer) and listener (reader, viewer), since there is always a gap between utterance and uptake, however slight.

For speech and manual signing we can usually pretend there is no gap, because it is so trivial, but writing, videotaping, sound recording, and so on continually raise versions of Cavett's Problem. When we read in a letter, "I'm sitting here on my rocking chair," we don't think it false because no longer true, any more than a Roman who wrote "I was sitting here on my rocking chair" was not (yet) telling the truth. We need to evaluate in regard to independent R and S, and we require *both* of them to be fixed by context, not absolutely. (Once again, S seems to be simply the *first* reference point.)

But this seems to involve a shift in V away from S, that is, it seems to refocus the deictic center from the ego to the other (or to some other). This is true with other indexical terms as well. It is a joke even on the children's television program *Sesame Street* when statements such as "I'm here" are found puzzling, because after all, no one can ever literally be *here* so long as they are actually *there* (away from the individual who is the ego). Cavett's Problem then is in the realm of pragmatics rather than semantics, and does *not* demonstrate a need for more than two index times.

As we suggested above, one system which seems to require three index times is Bull's, with its four axes of orientation. The conditional perfect (*would have*) is analyzed by Bull as involving the $-V$ (minus vector) position on the RAP (retrospective anticipated point) axis, which is accessed from the RP (retrospective point) axis, which in turn is accessed from the PP (present point) axis.[223] In familiar terms, PP $= S$; the link of PP to RP, $R<S$; the link of RP to RAP, $R<R'$; and the minus vector, $E<R'$.

In a compositional neo-Reichenbachian treatment, however, we translate the conditional perfect as PAST(FUT(PERF(x))), with a future operator relative to the past reference point. The interpretation of PERF involves only E and R, that of the relative FUT operator only two R's (we can Allenize the absolute neo-Reichenbachian system so as to generalize; S is then simply R_0), and that of PAST only R and S (i.e., R_0).[224]

Another proposal which claims to require two distinct reference points is Mondadori's treatment (1978) of *might have*, which he claims is a "perfect future" indexed to three different times. *Might have* is modal in character and so perhaps outside of the scope of the present work, but arguably no more so than the conditional perfect (*would have*).

Mondadori argues as follows:

> "might have" is not a past (perfect) tense of "might". It is the dual of the future perfect "will have". Just as the latter is a past in the future, so the former is a future

in the past—the future of a past.[225] Just as the future perfect is (temporally) indexed to an event which is past to a given future time, so "might have" is indexed to an event which is future to a given past time. (Actually, as we shall see. . . , "might have" is *also* indexed to the event to which "might" is itself indexed.)[226]

At some point in the past, let us say, "φ might be true" (in future) was true. What sanctions us saying at the present time "φ might have been true" is not just that "φ might be true" was true at the time, but that at some relatively future time "φ is not true" came to be true. We evaluate a statement such as Mondadori's example *Ljubojevic might have been the world champion of chess in 1978* relative to two past times.

Even if Mondadori's claims are correct, the question is whether a compositional treatment along the lines of PAST(PERF(POSS(x))) might not render a 3-D system of indexing unnecessary here, just as in the case of the conditional perfect. This formula would be true if it was true in the past that it had been the case that *x* was possible. That *x* was not in fact to be realized is not clearly an assertion of *might have*, but is possibly a Gricean implicature.[227] After all, what is the point in most contexts of saying that something had been possible, if in fact it came true?

But I see nothing contradictory in saying that *Ljubojevic might have been the world champion of chess in 1978 and in fact was.* Compare *not only might Ljubojevic have been the world champion of chess in 1978—he in fact was.* This latter might result where two individuals were arguing about Ljubojevic's chess-playing ability (say, in relation to whoever was in fact the chess champion in 1978), but were unaware of whether he became champion or not that year. The party arguing for his ability might have looked up the chess records and clinched their argument for Ljubojevic's ability by this example sentence given above.

We do not want to introduce a major new theoretical construct without ample exploration of the already available devices. Given that such a proposal depends on the treatment of the modal operator POSSible (and how the semantics and pragmatics of *may* are related to those of *might*), we can say no more about this issue here, however.

Nerbonne argues for a need for three index times.[228] His argument is similar to one of McCawley's (1971). Nerbonne argues that in a past perfect used definitely, there is reference to two past times. In the case of his example *Ed had lost (and was in a bad mood)*, understood to mean that here was a definite time of his losing, and his being in a bad mood at a subsequent time is due to his having lost at that time, there is reference not only to the time of his being in a bad mood, but also to that of his losing (a past R point is embedded within the scope of another past R point).

The problem once again is that we have been defining tenses solely in terms of *r* and *s*, and aspect in terms of *e* and *r*. Thus in defining tenses, *e* plays no role. Nerbonne and the tense-logical tradition must utilize the full, three-time index in defining even the simple tenses, because they do not have a compositional treatment of tense and aspect. Especially when we relativize the R point of one clause not to S directly, but to that of another clause, Nerbonne's argument does not force the adoption of a 3-D system.

One further suggestion of the need for a 3-D system comes oddly enough from Dowty.[229] He is concerned with the semantics of examples such as *John will meet a man who will find a unicorn tomorrow*. The translation of this seems to require a FUT operator within the scope of another FUT operator, but that is not in fact appropriate here, since the time of his finding a unicorn is not relatively post-future, but absolutely future. Dowty finds this perplexing and proposes evaluation ("true$_3$") relative to a triple $\langle i,j,k \rangle$ representing reference time, a "quasi-speech act" time and actual speech-act time respectively; truth ("true$_1$") is defined indirectly via this "true$_3$."

We need not concern ourselves with the mechanics of this proposal. A priori, one might suggest a solution along the lines of Kamp's solution, utilizing a NOW operator, for the embedded future is relativized to the present, not to the higher future operator (of greater scope). But a consideration of this problem belongs to that of the general issue of sequence of tense rules and embedded (relative) tenses in chapter 8.

While there have been many purported arguments for relativizing evaluations to a triple of times, all depend on controversial assumptions and none is so convincing that such a system need be introduced into a theory with compositionality; such a system in a non-compositional theory is in effect equivalent to a compositional system utilizing a pair of times.[230] This is not to say that we might *not* for various other reasons require such a three-dimensional system, but it seems that for the analysis of the tenses, at least, the necessity for such a system is questionable.

t. Events and *Aktionsarten*

In the kinds of systems we have been considering up to now, the central notion has been that of a certain proposition being true relative to a certain index, as for instance a pair consisting of a time interval and a possible world. *John loves Jane* is glossed in such a system as something like "the proposition that 'John love Jane' is true at the present time in the (speaker's) real world." We saw something like this in Dowty's use of the operator AT, necessitated by the fact that, while adverbials such as *yesterday* referred to one kind of thing—(sets of sets of) temporal entities—the sentences they combined with referred to quite another, and nontemporal, sort of thing.

The gloss "the proposition that 'John love Jane' is true at the present time in the (speaker's) real world" does not strike one as very intuitively satisfying. We have a sense that what sentences like this one really mean is something like "an event of John's loving Jane (in some way) coincides with the present time in the (speaker's) real world." That is, a sentence like *John loves Jane* is not "about" a proposition, but rather an *event*.

Similarly, the usual systems force one to interpret the various *Aktionsarten* in the following way. *John is beginning to love Jane*, for example, is glossed as something like "the proposition that 'John begin to love Jane' is true at the present time in the (speaker's) real world." But intuitively, this sentence says that at the present time, an event of John's loving Jane is in its initial phase, that is, "the initial phase of an event of John's loving Jane (in some way) coincides with the present time in the (speaker's) real world."

Many scholars have attempted to incorporate this insight into a formal semantics for tense and aspect, taking as central not the *truth of propositions* but the *occurence of events*. Event-based systems have been proposed at least by Åqvist and Guenther (1978), Cresswell (1974–1985), Saurer (1984), and Woisetschlaeger (1976). (This last contribution to the subject we have already discussed in section g of chapter 6.) For the most part these proposals (none of which has been completely successful) are simply elaborations of the familiar systems. A radical alternative offered in recent years, however, is that of Situation Semantics. First we will look at event-based systems close to the familiar Montague tradition, then we will say something about this departure from it.

Intuitively, the notion of "event" is clear enough: the dictionary defines *event* as "anything that happens or is regarded as happening; an occurrence; something that occurs in a certain place during a particular interval of time." But this definition is problematical in at least two ways. First, it allows too many things to count as events. For example, it may happen that Susan is ill from noon till three in the afternoon. This certainly is something which occurs over an interval of time. But is Susan's being ill from noon till three in the afternoon an event? Many have argued that states are *not* events.[231] Moreover, suppose that John stands in a corner for an hour while not thinking of a white bear. This might well be considered an activity, but is it an event? It occurs in a time interval, to be sure. But it is like a state in that nothing happened, at least nothing *changed*.

Some scholars argue that the event requires that there be change, that there be a time interval *I* over which neither of a state *s* nor a state *s'* holds, such that *I* forms the terminal bound for *s* and the initial bound for *s'*. As we have seen, Woisetschlaeger sees events as "characterized by the fact that they progress from an initial state to a terminal state."[232] Thus the event of Tom's returning home is bounded by his not being home and his being home. From this point of view, states—possibly excepting permanent states—could also be regarded as events, since an illness, for example, is bounded by states of good health.

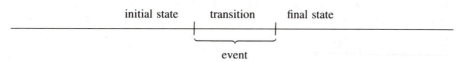

It is arguable whether activities any more than states fulfill the requirement for eventhood of transition. It is not clear if mere activity constitutes an event in that sense. It is true that things are not the same after John has stood in a corner for an hour, not thinking of a white bear. For one thing, John is now more of an experienced stander-in-the-corner-while-not-thinking-of-a-white-bear than he was before. But this seems to render the notion of change trivial. After Sue has been ill for three hours, she is a more experienced patient than she was before.

An event token is an instantiation of an ideal type of structure consisting of phases. Not every interval or sequence of intervals containing an occurrence is an event in this sense. For example, if Sue falls ill on June 1 and recovers on June 9 after a number of treatments, this constitutes an event, with a set of phases. But if Sue happens to be ill from June 2 to June 8 in the course of these events (or rather this event), it is not correct to say that this interval contains an event as such, even though it contains a number of subevents.

A second and more important problem concerns the ontological status of events. Events are slippery objects ontologically speaking, and many scholars simply assume an intuitive notion of event without further explication. Events are often taken to be spatial as well as temporal, but they are essentially purely temporal, for though they may have spatial extension, they need not. (Where did the Renaissance take place, exactly?) If it be argued that events must have spatial extension, then there are clearly many things which are intuitively events, but have no spatial extension. The Big Bang that began the universe is a radical case in point.

Cresswell reports that "[E. J.] Lemmon commenting . . . on Davidson's analysis of action sentences suggested that events be identified with the space-time points they occupy."[233] But to say that an event of John's kissing Sue took place over a certain interval of time is not to say that that event *was* that interval, since many other events may also have taken place over that interval. In what sense can an event and an interval of time coincide, or an event occur *within* an interval?

Cresswell notes two further difficulties with the identification of events with sets of space-time points. One is the problem, raised by R. L. Clark, of "saying just which sets of space-time points constitute 'genuine' events." Cresswell notes that this is not really a problem: saying that events are the space-time points they occupy does not commit us to saying *which* such sets of points they are. And in fact, Åqvist and Guenther make no distinction between states of affairs and events, and allow *any* interval of time as an event, thus dealing with Clark's problem in another way.[234]

The second problem Cresswell discusses is more serious.[235] To say that an event is a set of space-time points assumes that they are space-time points of *some* world. But the *same* event can occur in different worlds, though the same space-time points cannot. The death of Scott is the same event in a world in which he wrote *Waverly* as in one in which he did not. If events can be identified across worlds, and events are simply sets of space-time loci, then why can space-time loci not be identified across worlds? This problem serves to cast further doubt on the ontological status of events, at least as chunks of space-time.

Events do seem intuitively to be, or have a close relationship to, mere collections of times, but insofar as an event *is* a connected set of times, events seem merely to be a shorthand way of talking about propositions, given that the set of times (moments) occupied by a given event e is the set of moments t such that the propositional content of a statement concerning the event is true at t. "An event of John's loving Jane (in some way) coincides with the present time in the (speaker's) real world" turns out to be effectively equivalent to "the proposition that 'John love Jane' is true at the present time in the (speaker's) real world."

But let us return to our main discussion and, for purposes of it, ignore such ontological doubts. At the worst, it may turn out that the "proposition language" (ways of discussing statements that involve the notion of "propositions being true at indices'') and the "event language" (ways of discussing statements that involve the notion of "events occurring at points") are simply different ways of talking about the same thing.

Events play a central role in some theories of the *Aktionsarten*, as we have seen. Woisetschlaeger (1976) is an early attempt at such an event-based theory. He uses only a simple predicate logic to "analyze" English sentences. He introduces the notions of event, subevent, and type of event. All are intuitively clear. To say that Sue kissed Bill yesterday is to say that an event of the type SUE KISS BILL (i.e., of the type of Sue kissing Bill) occurred yesterday.

Every event contains subevents. An event may incorporate intermediate states. Thus if Susan is getting well, then between her being ill and her being well there are an infinite number of states of her being better than before. Woisetschlaeger defines a subevent as what happens between two states, at least one of which is an intermediate state.[236]

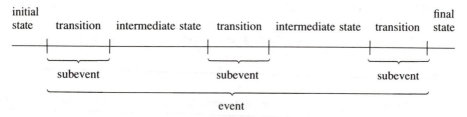

He lets $S_p(x)$ mean "x is a subevent of an event of type P," where P refers to the propositional content of a statement of the event.

A pause (what we have called a "gap") is an interval which does not contain a (certain) occurrence or state, but which is bounded by intervals which do.[237] Woisetschlaeger uses $P(x)$ to mean "x is a pause." Thus if Walter paused in filing the day's mail, it must be the case that he had just been engaged in filing the day's mail, and would in the next time interval be so engaged again.

Walter's filing the mail from noon to 2:00 p.m. is in some important sense the same activity as his filing the mail from 3:00 to 5:00 p.m., though it is not literally the *same* activity (since it took place at a different time).[238]

Woisetschlaeger uses an operator DUR similar to Dowty's AT or Cresswell's (1985) *occ*. DUR(x,y) means "x occurs during y." *Walter was filing the day's mail* is analyzed as follows:

$$(\exists x) \, (S_p(x) \, \& \, DUR \, (x, t_1))$$

Here t_1 is some time interval wholly prior to the speech-act time. This analysis says that there is a subevent of an event of type P which occurs during some past time. This accounts for the implication of incompletion, because it does not guarantee that *all* subevents occurred in the past. Similarly, *Walter filed the day's mail* is analyzed as:

$$(x) \; (S_p(x) \supset DUR(x,t_1))$$

This says that if something is a subevent of an event of type P, then it occurred at a certain time wholly in the past. This accounts for the implication of completion: *all* subevents of Walter's filing the day's mail occurred at t_1.

In this way, Woisetschlaeger captures the notion that "aspect quantifies over subevents."[239] His view is that the imperfective expresses that *some* subevent of the event token in question took place during the given interval, while the perfective expresses that *all* of its subevents took place in that interval. This may seem a somewhat indirect way of capturing the traditional notion of the perfective as complexive or punctative (the event is viewed as complete within a point locus), while the imperfective "extends" the event or views it from within (the event is seen as encompassing the vantage point). But it is necessitated by the need to treat the *Aktionsarten* as essentially different ways of referring to the subevents of event tokens (some, like the initial phase, are privileged, but others, such as the final subevent preceding a pause, have no special status).

There are a number of problems with Woisetschlaeger's approach (as noted in chapter 6), not the least of which is the failure to individuate events. To say that something is a subevent of *an* event token of type P is not to say that it is a subevent of *the* event token of type P in question. His analysis of *Walter filed the day's mail* says that every portion of Walter's filing the day's mail took place during a certain interval; as it stands, this precludes Walter's having done any filing of the mail on any other day. What is meant, of course, is the event of filing on one day, on one occasion. (*Walter often files the day's mail* refers to a series of events, in which case *the day* is variable; in *Walter filed the day's mail*, *the day* is undefined, but constant.)

This problem is not resolved by utilizing the time period t_1 to individuate the event token, even if this is understood to refer to a definite time period. The reason for this is that not all subevents are tied to t_1; for example, in the analysis of the cessative, *Walter stopped filing the day's mail*, $(\exists x) \; (\exists y)(S_p(x) \; \& \; P(y) \; \& \; x<y \; \& \; DUR(x,t_1))$, there is no requirement that y be limited to t_1, and in fact it precedes it. But we are not concerned with cases where Walter had once been filing the day's mail, but rather with those where he had just been doing so. Reference to t_1 thus fails to resolve the problem.

There is much that is interesting in Woisetschlaeger's analyses of the *Aktionsarten*. As we saw in chapter 6, he taxonomizes the various *Aktionsarten* in terms of six parameters.[240]

1. existential vs. universal quantification over subevents
2. independence from vs. dependence on sequential information (required by 'precede')
3. reference to pauses vs. no reference to pauses
4. first vs. last subevent
5. subevent before pause vs. subevent after pause
6. pause asserted vs. pause negated

In fact, as Woisetschlaeger notes, "What is not brought out very clearly [by the taxonomy and the accompanying list of criteria] is that this entire structure is built out of only three non-logical concepts: that of a subevent, that of pause, and that of temporal precedence."[241]

We can see how Woisetschlaeger's taxonomic criteria are built out of these notions. In describing an occurrence, we can choose to refer to *all* phases of an occurrence, as in *Walter filed the day's mail*, or only *some*, as in *Walter began filing the day's mail*. If we refer to all, we can refer to pauses or not (*Walter filed the day's mail*). If we refer to some, we can describe occurrences either without regard to information about sequencing, as in *Walter was filing the day's mail*, or with regard to it, as in *Walter resumed filing the day's mail*. In the latter case we can either refer to pauses, as in *Walter resumed filing the day's mail*, or not, as in *Walter began filing the day's mail*.

Criterion #1, as we have seen, serves to distinguish imperfective from perfective (which are both treated by Woisetschlaeger as *Aktionsarten*).

Criterion #2 distinguishes those *Aktionsarten* referring to sequences of subevents (e.g., the continuative) from those which do not (e.g., the imperfective). The analysis of *Walter kept filing the day's mail* is:

$$(\exists x)\sim(\exists y)(S_p(x) \ \& \ P(y) \ \& \ x<y \ \& \ DUR(x,t_1))$$

This says that there is an x and there is no y such that x is a subevent of an event of type P, y is a pause, x is earlier than y, and x occurred at a point wholly past. The sequence of x and y is what differentiates the continuative from the imperfective—he was not merely filing the mail (x), but he was continuing to do so (there is no sequential pause y).

Actually, there is a problem here, since what is really wanted is not that there is no pause y following x, but rather that the interval y following x not be a pause. As regards the interval t_1 the above simply says that Walter was filing the mail, not that he had just been or would immediately still be doing so, which is what the continuative requires.

#3 distinguishes not only "determinative" from perfective, but "interruptive" from imperfective, as well as inceptive/completive from cessative/continuative/resumptive. The analysis of an interruptive is this:

$$(\exists x)(\exists y)(S_p(x) \ \& \ P(y) \ \& \ DUR(x, t_1) \ \& \ DUR(y, t_1))$$

This says that x and y (as above) both occurred at a certain time wholly past. The closest English rendering of such a case in the spirit of Woisetschlaeger's examples might be *Walter was interrupted in filing the day's mail*. The explicit reference to a pause is distinctive here.

#4 distinguishes inceptive from completive. The inceptive is analyzed:

$$(\exists x) \ (S_p(x) \ \& \ (y) \ ((S_p(y) \ \& \ x\neq y) \supset x<y) \ \& \ DUR \ (x, t_1))$$

This says that there is an x such that x is a subevent of an event of type P and that for all y, if y is a subevent of an event of type P and is distinct from x, then x is earlier than y, and x occurred at a point in time wholly past. (As stated earlier, this is not quite correct, since it fails to distinguish the phases of *this* event token of type P from those of other events of type P.) Roughly, *Walter began to file the day's mail*. The completive—*Walter finished filing the day's mail*—is analyzed:

$$(\exists x) \; (S_p(x) \; \& \; (y) \; ((S_p(y) \; \& \; x \neq y) \supset y < x) \; \& \; DUR(x, t_1))$$

The distinction is whether we are talking about the first interval (it precedes all other subevents of the event token) or the last (it follows all other subevents of that token).

#5 distinguishes cessative/continuative from resumptive. *Walter resumed filing the day's mail* is analyzed:

$$(\exists x) \; (\exists y) \; (S_p(x) \; \& \; P(y) \; \& \; y < x \; \& \; DUR(x, t_1))$$

Walter ceased filing the day's mail is analyzed:

$$(\exists x) \; (\exists y) \; (S_p(x) \; \& \; P(y) \; \& \; x < y \; \& \; DUR(x, t_1))$$

Here what is crucial is whether the subevent occurred before or after a pause. As we have noted before, there is more to this than the analyses themselves show. For example, it is not enough to be doing something after not doing it, to say that one has *resumed* doing it; rather, one must have been doing it in the time interval immediately preceding the pause. Meaning postulates are required to fill the need of capturing such facts.

Finally, #6 distinguishes cessative (where a pause is asserted) from continuative (where the lack of a pause is asserted). Thus the fundamentals for a theory of *Aktionsarten* are provided. What is most valuable in Woisetschlaeger's work is the explicit treatment of *Aktionsarten* as involving subevents of event tokens. However, it is unclear whether mere reference to unprivileged subevents will suffice, and to what extent reference to phases will be required. Phases are not simply subevents, however these are defined. Phases are regular and necessary subevents of ideal event types. They are typical, in the sense that we recognize them as part of a type of event, even if a particular token of an event type happens to be lacking in one or more of its phases.

Accomplishments typically include a culmination, even if the actual termination is not the culmination. If Sue was running across Canada and ran from Vancouver to Winnipeg and then stopped, we do not say either that she did not run across the country at all or that she was merely running, but rather that she tried and failed to run across the country—she stopped running across the country before she had (in fact) run across the country.

In our account so far, it is a mystery how we can ever truthfully say that anyone has failed at any task which is still possibly fulfillable, since any pause, no matter how long, might later turn out to be merely a temporary (and hence "trivial"!) gap. (In a sense, for example, H. H. was always continuing on the Journey to the East in the novel of that name by Hermann Hesse, even though he believed that he no longer was participating in it and indeed that the journey no long was going on, since it was eventually revealed that his "nonparticipation" was in fact a stage in the journey.)

Presumably there is some kind of pragmatic presuppositions having to do with appropriate time periods or intentions or the like, which serves to delineate event boundaries. However, although these points raise some interesting questions concerning the individuation of events, a discussion of them here would take us much too far afield.

u. A Formal Semantic Theory with Events

Woisetschlaeger fails to provide a formal semantic theory. A well-developed attempt at elaborating an event-based system within the Montague tradition is that of Saurer (1984). Saurer introduces a new type of entity, the event e, and asserts that what tenseless sentence nuclei denote at an index is a set of events. The verb *walk*, for example, will translate into IL as $\lambda x\ \hat{e}\ walk'$ (e,x), that is, the (characteristic function of a) set of walkings (event tokens of the type *walk*). Applied to John (j), this yields by lambda-conversion $\lambda e\ walk'$ (e,j), namely the (characteristic function of the) set of walkings by John (event tokens of the type *John walk*). Applied further to some event e', this yields $walk'$ (e',j), namely (roughly) "e' is a walking by John."

The major divergences in Saurer's system from proposition-based Montague systems are these[242]:

1. e is the type of (individual) events.
2. If $\phi \in ME_{\langle e,t\rangle}$ then PAST (ϕ), PRES(ϕ), and FUT(ϕ) $\in ME_t$.
3. If $\phi \in ME_{\langle e,t\rangle}$ then PERF(ϕ), PROG(ϕ) $\in ME_t$.
4. Saurer utilizes a branching-futures (backward-linear, forward-branching) system of time with a set of possible alternative futures defined on a set of times.
5. Possible histories replace possible worlds in indices.[243]
6. He introduces a function, *time*, from the set E of events to the set T of times, which assigns each event in E a member of T (the time of occurrence of the event).
7. Tenseless sentences of NL translate into LTL expressions of type $\langle e,t\rangle$.

Saurer offers the following example to show how this works.[244] *A man walk* translates into the LTL as:

$$\lambda P\hat{e}Vx[man'(x) \wedge P\{e,x\}]([^{\wedge}walk'])$$

This applies the function denoted by the subject phrase *a man* to the intension of *walk*. The former is translated as referring to the (characteristic function of the) set of properties such that for all events there is an x which is a man and x has that property in one of the events. (The analysis of *a man* is simply a variant of the familiar one, as dictated by the introduction of events.)

By lambda-conversion, this converts to:

$$\hat{e}Vx[man'(x) \wedge [^{\wedge}walk']\{e,x\}]$$

By the convention on curved brackets, this yields

$$\hat{e}Vx[man'(x) \wedge [^{\vee}[^{\wedge}walk']](e,x)]$$

which reduces by the down-up principle to

$$\hat{e}Vx[man'(x) \wedge walk'(e,x)]$$

This reduces by various meaning postulates stated by Saurer[245] to the following (in slightly simplified form):

$$\hat{e}Vu[man'(u) \wedge walk'(e,u)]$$

Let us suppose a deep structure like this:

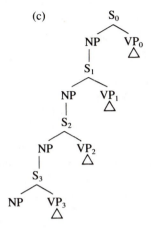

On the second cycle (the first involving two separate S's, namely S_3 and S_2), the VP of S_3 is raised and adjoined to that of S_2, and the now superfluous S_3 and NP nodes are pruned from the tree:

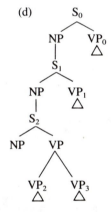

The same procedure on the next cycle raises the VP of S_2 and adjoins it to that of S_1, while at the same time pruning out the superfluous S_2 and NP nodes. Following the same predicate-raising on the last (highest) cycle, the structure looks like this:

In support of this analysis, Ross points out that auxiliaries are treated as verbs by at least the transformational rule of *gapping*. Gapping optionally deletes all but the first in a series of identical verbs:

> John ate cake, Sue (ate) cookies, and Igor (ate) candy.

Auxiliary verbs can gap as well:

> John can sing, Sue (can) dance, and Igor (can) tell jokes.
> John has sung, Sue (has) danced, and Igor (has) told jokes.
> John is singing, Sue (is) dancing, and Igor (is) telling jokes.
> John was insulted, Sue (was) laughed at, and Igor (was) told to leave.

If auxiliaries are just verbs, these facts fall out automatically.

Further, Ross argues that a number of rules, including verb-phrase-deletion, treat as constituents the following sequences, which according to his analysis are integral constituents of the sentence, but according to Chomsky's are not (presumably only constituent units can be explicitly affected by transformations, e.g., moved or deleted) [76]:

> Tns—mood
> Tns—have
> Tns—be
> Tns—Mod—have
> Tns—Mod—be
> Tns—have—be
> Tns—Mod—have—be

VP-deletion seems to act to delete a constituent (presumedly a VP) under identity [77]:

Mike
- *built a house*
- is *building a house*
- may *build a house*
- must *have been building a house*
- has *a house*
- is *sick*

and Tom
- did
- is
- may
- must (have (been))
- has
- is

too.

This would argue for a derived structure in which each of these sequences is a constituent; once again, according to Ross's analysis these are constituents, but according to Chomsky's they are not.

Two transformational rules, rather than deleting such constituents, pronominalize them. *So* may replace a constituent under identity [78]:

They said that Tom
- likes ice cream
- may be here
- is working hard
- had left
- might have been singing

and so he
- does.
- may.
- is.
- had.
- might.
- might have.
- might have been.

Similarly, *which* or *that* . . . [79]:

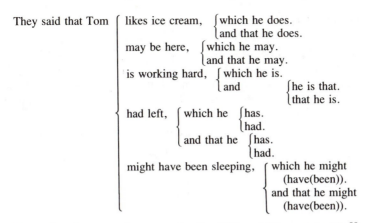

Normally, these words pronominalize NP's which contain S's[80]:

I hope *that we win in Vietnam*, but no sane man hopes so.
It may seem *that we will win*, to our glorious president, but it doesn't seem so to me.

If auxiliaries are verbs, and combinations of them with non-finite verb forms (*will sing, will have, will be, has sung, has been, is singing*) constitute syntactic constituents, they must, Ross argues on the basis of the semantics, be main verbs taking clausal complements; the non-finite forms accompanying them on the surface are the remnants of those clauses following radical transformation.

Not all syntacticians accepted Ross's arguments at the time, and today many of the assumptions he makes would be unacceptable to the vast majority of scholars of *syntax*. But the issue here involves the *semantic* implications of the treatment.

McCawley's (1971) analysis is similar to Ross's but extends it by treating tense itself as a ''higher verb,'' at least in the case of the past. That is, in the deep structure of *Susan would have been singing*, the highest ''verb'' will be neither *have* nor *be* but an abstract tense called ''Past''.

In support of this apparently strange and counterintuitive proposal, McCawley draws on the neutralization facts educed by Hoffman.[81] Recall that Hoffman observes that in certain environments the distinction of the past, present perfect, and past perfect is neutralized, and for all three there simply appears *have*.

In similar contexts the abstract tense Present is realized as zero.[82] Just as the non-finite in *John is believed to have admired Spiro Agnew* reflects an underlying past tense (cf. *it is believed that John admired Spiro Agnew*), so that of *John is believed to admire Spiro Agnew* reflects an underlying present (cf. *it is believed that John admires Spiro Agnew*).

The key to the syntactic solution is that *all* tenses are relative. For Huddleston (following Bull and Allen, but much in the spirit of the *Grammaire générale*), most but not all tenses are in effect relative.[83] A tense does not ''situate'' a process in time, but rather ''orders'' it relative to a point of reference,[84] which he calls the ''axis of orientation.'' Past means before, present means simultaneous with, and future means after the axis, respectively. In some cases ''the axis is the situation of utterance; in these cases tense is obviously a deictic category." The axis of orientation may be established by reference to "the process expressed in the next higher sentence"[85]; in such cases the tense will not be deictic.

Embedded tenses and matrix ones alike are oriented to an orientation time (OT); for all but the topmost tense this is the reference time of the matrix, but for the topmost one it is the speech-act time. This is the Prior/Allen concept and differs little from Smith's concept of the OT.

The various surface forms may nearly all be analyzed as relative tenses:

tense	*is analyzed as*
past	past
present	present
futurate present	future
present (progressive)	present-in-present
futurate present (progressive)	future-in-present
past progressive	present-in-past
futurate past progressive	future-in-past
present perfect	past-in-present
futurate present perfect	future-in-present-in-past
past perfect	past-in-past

Of course it is open to us to reinterpret as follows, in the spirit of Prior and the tradition of totally relative tense systems:

past	present-in-past
present	present-in-present
futurate present	future-in-present

McCawley and Ross make explicit that each deep structure tense represents an RT and that RT's correspond to deep structure tenses. This does not, however, mean that each surface tense represents an RT or that RT's correspond to surface tenses. Both the number and morphological marking of surface tenses depend on the transformation of underlying tenses.

Given that in theory any tense might be embedded below an auxiliary verb, the question is how the various possible combinations relate to the surface structures observed. There can be, and must be, only one finite verb form per surface clause. Thus the highest tense surfaces as a morphological tense marker on the highest verb. Other verbs appear as the appropriate non-finite forms, as governed by the matrix verb: modals take infinitival complements; *have*, the perfect participle; and *be*, the progressive participle.

In non-finites, Past appears as *have*, and the Present as zero. Thus *John has eaten* (past-in-present) represents the underlying combination Present ($\Rightarrow$ -*s*) Past ($\Rightarrow$ *have*), while *John had eaten* (past-in-past) represents Past ($\Rightarrow$ -*ed*) Past ($\Rightarrow$ *have*). Past ($\Rightarrow$ -*ed*) Present ($\Rightarrow$ zero) (present-in-past) is represented by *John ate* and Present ($\Rightarrow$ -*s*) Present ($\Rightarrow$ zero) (present-in-present) by *John eats*. In this way, the relative nature of surface tenses is captured by treating them as transformed relative to underlying matrix tenses indicating the OT. This leaves the question of tenses interpreted relative to a tense in another surface clause; we shall return to this question below.

In Hoffman neutralizations past, present perfect, and past perfect all result in simple perfects in non-finites. McCawley proposes a rule to handle this[86]:

$$have \text{ }_{AUX} \rightarrow 0 \text{ in env. } have \text{\_\_\_\_}$$

That is, all but the first in a sequence of *have*s is deleted.

Given this, a surface sentence may have an infinite number of underlying sources, since we cannot tell from the surface structure how many *have*s have been deleted; a surface *have* could in theory represent all that is left of an indefinitely large number of underlying tenses. In practice, however, it is unusual to find as many as *three* such underlying sources of *have* in one clause; McCawley claims that in *when John had married Sue, he had known Cynthia for five years* we have the past ("the unmentioned reference point") of the past (John's marrying Sue) of a present perfect (*John has known Cynthia for five years*).[87] The situation reported is one in which there are four times $t<E_1<R_1<S$ such that (1) R_1 is past relative to S; (2) E_1, the time at which John marries Sue, is past relative to R_1; and (3) t, the time at which John knows Cynthia, is five years prior to, and present perfect relative to, E_1.

Evidence for the number of embedded tenses comes from the number of possible adverbials, McCawley says, there being one adverbial per underlying tense. *John had already eaten at three*, for example, is ambiguous, depending on whether *at three* modifies the event time or the reference time (and there probably are some other marginally acceptable readings as well). In the case of the reading in which the eating occurred at three, we could have an additional adverb: *John had at six already eaten at three*. In the other reading, only point in time (E = R) is in question and hence only one adverbial is possible.

Given that tenses are freely inserted into deep structures, it is possible to have an indefinitely large number of tenses per surface clause. But clearly there cannot be many more than three points incorporated into a clause (cf. *she will have been about to go*), which makes it seem odd to have an indefinite number of different derivations for sentences, involving an indefinitely large number of underlying tenses. The deletion of all but one *have* seems a purely ad hoc device for handling this problem.

Notwithstanding these problems, McCawley argues that his account provides a principled explanation for Chomsky's formula.[88] Tense can appear only once, because in any other position it becomes null (zero) or *have*; modals can be preceded by tense only because of their defective morphology (they lack infinitive and participial forms and hence could not incorporate affixes other than tense—though how in practice this lack of appropriate forms forces the positioning of modals is not spelled out by McCawley); progressive *be* must be last because of a(n ad hoc?) constraint to the effect that stative predicates cannot occur first in a complement; and there cannot be more than one *have*, because all others in a string are deleted.

Unlike McCawley, Hoffman assumes that the abstract tenses Past and Non-past are features on verbs, and that both HAVE and BE appear in deep structure as aspectual markers. As in McCawley and Ross, however, auxiliary verbs take sentential complements. An adverbial is associated with a verb, but adverbials do not have entire sentences within their scope. Accordingly, the deep structure of *yesterday you were coming tomorrow* is illustrated in the accompanying diagram[89]:

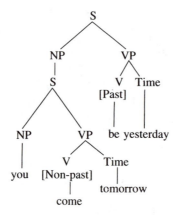

The affixes of tense and both *-en* and *-ing* are surface manifestations of the features on verbs. The highest verb is realized as a finite verb; Past becomes *-ed* and Non-past zero or *-s* as appropriate. Other verbs appear as non-finite forms. In the case above, the higher verb, *be*, is marked as past, and so the past tense *were* appears on the surface. The lower verb, *come*, is marked as Non-past. Since, in the scope of *be*, this is realized as a non-finite (there being only one finite form per surface clause), zero appears for the non-past tense, and *coming* results.

In Huddleston's system, tense relativization is governed by the relative scope of markers. Thus the present perfect, meaning a past-*in*-present, is captured by a higher verb HAVE marked Present (Non-past), with*in* the scope of which is a lower verb, the lexical verb, marked Past (which Past appears on the surface as the past participial ending we call *-en*, e.g., *gone, swum,* etc.).

The futurate present perfect thus requires an additional tense; this could be on the modal auxiliary (*will* say), or could be supplied by another verb in the context, either in another clause (*I'll leave when I've had my say*) or another sentence (*I'll leave when I'm good and ready and not before; when I've had my say; when I've been made to feel appreciated*). (As in the case of Smith's theory, it is an interesting question how we know when one tense is within the scope of another, if they are not *syntactically* related within one sentence.)

None of the theories based on syntactic solutions contains a full, explicit statement of how SOT works. Ross treats SOT as a feature-changing rule.[90] Where the higher verb is Past and the lower Present, the tense feature of the lower verb is changed to accord with that of the higher: *John said, "I am happy"* becomes *John* said *that he* was *happy*. But Ross never fully formulates such a rule, nor does he discuss its implications for morphology. For some reason Costa treats SOT rather as some kind of (unspecified) copying rule.[91]

Either approach seems at best a purely descriptive device. The question is *why* tense features change in the way they do, in the contexts in which they do. If it were a simple matter of feature change, we would still seek to know why the feature changes, and changes as it does.

Huddleston does not present a rule as such, but he does develop a theory, based on Bull's axes of orientation, of why tenses change as they do. He points out that in the context of a past tense matrix verb, as in *he finished it after/before/while John washed up*, the *-ed* of the complement verb does not reflect the underlying tense (which is past in only one of these cases), but rather "is due to the past axis."[92] Similarly, the non-past tense in the embedded clause of *he will finish it after/while/before John washes up* is attributed to the future axis of the matrix verb tense.

In the case of indirect discourse, too, "surface tense reflects the axis."[93] Here Huddleston makes explicit that the embedded surface past in *John said that he was unwell* is a present-in-past, and is to be interpreted as the statement "I am unwell." In cases such as *he said it would rain*, verbs like *will*, which "can never have past tense associated with them may nonetheless combine with the *-ed* morpheme." He proposes to handle free indirect discourse by postulating an underlying verb (of saying, etc.), which is deleted and does not appear on the surface.[94]

In the case of dependent tenses which are deictic, that is, oriented not toward the next highest matrix verb but toward S, Huddleston speaks of "reorientation."[95] It is open to us to interpret both this reorientation and the orientation of dependent tenses as involving some kind of syntactic or morphological transformation. Huddleston never spells out any such rule. The other possibility is to interpret these as constraints on the co-occurrence of tenses. This is not an unnatural interpretation, given the non-transformational treatments of Bull and Allen, which involve the notion of axis of orientation, and Huddleston's treatment of adverbials and matrix verbs governing the underlying tense of clauses and complements respectively. Huddleston's theory is remarkably similar in some respects to Smith's later R-point theory.

Though Huddleston's theory for all its informality is superior in its detailed coverage to McCawley's, none of the syntactic solutions addresses the real problems or offers a comprehensive explanation for the observed phenomena, any more than the R-point theories do. While syntactic or semantic principles may be adduced for this or that temporal relationship, only a set of special cases is presented. There is reason to believe that consideration of pragmatic principles will lead to a unified explanation.

d. Semantic Problems for the Syntactic Solution

Whatever one can say about the syntactic solution from a syntactic point of view (and the syntax assumed in the theories of Huddleston, McCawley, and Ross would be regarded today by almost all syntacticians as obsolete), there are many problems from other points of view. We will discuss six of them here.

1. *The futurate and future perfect.* Costa notes that certain "putative" sequences of tenses "fail to turn up."[96] Some may be "idiosyncratic gaps": the simple *will*-less future cannot undergo SOT,[97] while the *will*-less *-ing* future, very close to it in meaning, does allow SOT:

John said that Vann $\left\{ \begin{array}{l} was\ leaving \\ *left \end{array} \right\}$ for Rome later that day.

Riddle offers an example in which the simple past standing for an underlying future does occur, however:

> Jane leaves next Thursday.
> But you told me that she left tomorrow.[98]

Whatever the problems with the simple past in such cases, they clearly are not as simple as an idiosyncratic gap involving the future. Riddle offers the following example, in which both the simple past and the past progressive are possible, although clearly, pragmatic constraints apply to both[99]:

> I thought that Jane $\left\{ \begin{array}{l} *leaves \\ *is\ leaving \\ left \\ was\ leaving \end{array} \right\}$ next Saturday,
>
> but she just told me she $\left\{ \begin{array}{l} leaves \\ is\ leaving \\ ?left \\ ?was\ leaving \end{array} \right\}$ tomorrow.

Riddle attributes the failure of the non-pasts to appear embedded in the first conjunct clause (*I thought that . . . Saturday*) to the contradiction between the implication by the embedding verb *thought* that the embedded clause in the first conjunct (*Jane . . . next Saturday*) is false, and the presupposition of the embedded verb (*leaves, is leaving*) that it is true. The pasts are acceptable because they have no such presupposition.

In the second conjunct (*she just . . . tomorrow*), however, the non-pasts are preferable because the embedded clause (*she leaves tomorrow*) may be true, and because *just* "gives such a sense of immediacy that the past tense forms sound very awkward."[100]

In any case, it is very difficult if not impossible to account for these phenomena in terms of any purely syntactic constraints (and perhaps even in terms of semantics). Pragmatic factors—the speaker's beliefs, for example—seem to play a crucial role in determining choice of tenses.

2. *The problem of superfluous* have*s (overrichness).* The embedded past theory requires, as we have seen, that all but the first of a string of *have*s should be deleted. That is, the theory overgenerates *have*s and then must introduce an ad hoc device for deleting them. There is no syntactic evidence for such a superfluity of underlying tenses, despite the arguments presented by McCawley for multiple tenses.[101] Furthermore, we would expect that all tensed languages would have the same superfluity of tenses, though they might differ in how they handle it. However, no languages allow anything like *John had had gone*. This suggests that the entire problem is pure artefact.

3. *Non-finites.* Costa observes that SOT doesn't apply in non-finites[102]:

> Marmaduke believed $\left\{ \begin{array}{l} that\ he\ was \\ *himself\ to\ have\ been \\ himself\ to\ be \end{array} \right\}$ of royal blood.

The CIA $\left\{\begin{array}{l}\text{didn't bother to}\\ \text{tried to}\\ \text{were quick to}\end{array}\right\}$ $\left\{\begin{array}{l}\textit{deny}\\ \textit{*have denied}\end{array}\right.$

that they *had transformed* South Korea into an austere police state.

She accounts for these in purely syntactic terms which we need not detail here.

Riddle argues that infinitives do not incorporate underlying tenses; that *have* in infinitives is not a relative past tense marker but rather, as in Smith's theory, a relational marker of anteriority; and that *have* appears in infinitives "only when it is impossible to infer on pragmatic grounds that the lower verb has time reference, prior to that of the higher verbs." [103]

Since infinitives do not present assertions, but merely propositions, Riddle argues, they do not have underlying tenses associated with them. [104] They require an explicit marking of time relative to the matrix only when this is not inferable from that verb. *Decide* and *expect*, for example, take relatively future complements, since you can decide (or expect) things only about the future: in *Peter decided to go* and *Peter expected to go*, the infinitive is understood as relatively future. Similarly, *like* and *tend* take relatively present complements: in *Peter liked to go* and *Peter tended to go*, the infinitive cannot be understood as relatively future.

It is only where the governing verb gives no indication of the temporal reference of the infinitive that *have* is required to indicate anteriority. Verbs of belief or knowing require *have* as a marker of anteriority, since both past and non-past complements are possible, but do not otherwise require it. Thus the question for Riddle is not why *Marmaduke believed that he* was *of royal blood* cannot be paraphrased by *!Marmaduke believed himself* to have been *of royal blood*, but rather why we would expect it to be.

Riddle avoids any special syntactic devices or complications by treating the facts about the perfect in infinitival complements as falling out from general pragmatic principles of interpretation.

4. *Had left* is not = *left*. Costa argues that *have* may be simply omitted in certain complements which contain a punctual simple past tense verb [105]:

Sue suspected that Bill $\left\{\begin{array}{l}\textit{left}\\ =\\ \textit{had left}\end{array}\right\}$ shortly

before the police arrived.

The same goes for generic complements:

She mentioned that men $\left\{\begin{array}{l}\textit{were wont}\\ =\\ \textit{had been wont}\end{array}\right\}$ to

fight battles on the slightest provocation in the middle ages.

Riddle points out that the two tenses are not synonymous here. [106] *Bill left before the police arrived* is ambiguous, one reading being that Bill intentionally left so as to avoid the police (in fact they might never have arrived); but *Bill had left before the police arrived* lacks this reading. Costa's generic example throws this point into question; it seems to depend on the well-known idiosyncratic properties of *before*.[107] We shall see evidence below, however, that the tenses are pragmatically different—evidence in favor of a treatment in which different tenses are selected to begin with, over a treatment in which one shifts to the other.

5. *Oriented and reoriented dependent tenses.* Costa assumes that in examples such as *Marmaduke was convinced that he* was *of royal blood*, in which SOT rules are obeyed, the underlying present tense undergoes some kind of transformation.[108] Riddle argues against the need for any syntactic solution.[109] As with infinitives, she treats this problem by setting out a number of pragmatic criteria for the use of the past tense in complements.[110] Given such pragmatic constraints, any need for an otherwise unmotivated syntactic solution is avoided.

We have seen that Lakoff (1970) presents many examples in which SOT seems to be violated. We have seen above that Huddleston, somewhat in the spirit of R-point solutions, argues that in some such cases the lower verb is treated as having deictic tense, and there is a reorientation to the present ("we can assign an additional feature to the verb, marking it as having deictic tense").[111]

It is common in both R-point and syntactic solutions to regard interpretation of embedded tenses independently of that of their matrix as exceptional and requiring explanation; for instance, under what conditions is tense "reoriented"? Riddle proposes rather that independent interpretation of embedded tenses is the general case, and that it is dependence on the matrix which is the special case requiring explanation. Further, the explanation is not a *semantic* one couched in terms of the relationships of S and various R and E points. Rather, dependence (that is, concord) of tenses occurs under certain *pragmatic* conditions.

She states that "SOT rules are in fact themselves pragmatic rules which select underlying tenses in the first place, and that a unified treatment of SOT phenomena and tense selection in general is much more explanatory" than accounts involving specific SOT mechanisms with accidental or principled gaps in the predicted patterns.[112]

We leave discussion of pragmatic conditions on tense choice for the next section, but clearly a unified account which would deal with the examples hitherto considered exceptional without postulating special devices is preferable to one which does. It remains to be seen if such a theory is possible.

6. *Futures.* So far we have had little if anything to say concerning matrix verbs in the future tense. The future does not work like the past or the present. Richards points out that *Max was aware that he was ill* is ambiguous as to whether the time of his being ill was contemporaneous with, or independent of, the time of his being aware.[113] But *Max will be aware that he will be ill* is not ambiguous in this way; if the time of his being ill will be contemporaneous with the time of his being aware, we must say *Max will be aware that he is ill*.

We have seen above that some have dealt with the futurate ("will-less future") in embedded clauses by assuming a deletion of the *will*. Here this would be problematic: where does the *will* in *Max will be aware that he will be ill* come from? Richards further considers the pair:

> Max was aware that he would be ill.
> ?Max was aware that he will be ill.[114]

He argues that the *would* is a shifted *will*. The nonoccurrence of the second example is simply an idiosyncratic gap in English; presumably English has a number of idiosyncratic gaps where *will* is concerned.

Dowty reports on another discussion of the problems of the future by Ladusaw (1977).[115] Ladusaw is interested in sentences like these:

John will find a unicorn that has walked.
John will find a unicorn that {is walking.
                                                 {walks.
John will find a unicorn that will walk.

Here there is an ambiguity as to whether the reference time of the embedded clause is the same as that of the embedding verb or is deictic: will John find a unicorn that has already walked (now) or which will have walked at the time he finds it? This ambiguity is predicted by the existence of different scopes for the two verbs. In one reading, the future has wider scope than the present: it will be the case that John finds a unicorn, and that that unicorn is walking; in the other, the reverse is true: there is a unicorn which is walking, and it will be the case that John finds it.

But in the following examples, there is no such ambiguity:

Mary has found a unicorn that has walked.
Mary has found a unicorn that {is walking.
                                                 {walks.
Mary has found a unicorn that will walk.

The solution Ladusaw adopts[116] is a syntactic solution similar to the one proposed by Costa[117] to handle non-finites, although couched in terms of Montague grammar rather than Generative Semantics.

What he suggests is that, at the point where the SOT transformation applies, the tense of the embedded relative clause is *outside* the scope of the tense of the main clause, and only afterward is it inside.[118] This is accomplished by a transformation *lowering* the noun phrase containing the relative clause into the main clause. The deep structure of *Mary has found a unicorn that is walking* is approximated in the accompanying illustration.

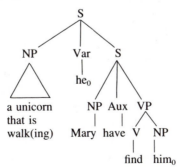

In DS, the relative clause is outside the scope of the auxiliary *have*. But *after* SOT applies, a rule of NP-lowering lowers the NP containing it into its surface position, in which it is apparently within the scope of *have*. This correctly predicts that *Mary has found a unicorn that is walking* is unambiguous, with the present only being deictic. The missing "narrow scope" deep structures will surface differently, for instance as *Mary has found a unicorn that has walked*.

Despite the apparent success of Ladusaw's proposal in handling his problematic examples, he himself notes cases where his solution fails:

> John said that someone will be in his apartment.
> John said that someone would be in his apartment.
> Bill sought a man who will be leaving.
> Bill sought a man who would be leaving.[119]

Precisely the same problems arise here, but Ladusaw's solution is excluded for syntactic reasons. Further, in the case of the second pair, Dowty points out that Ladusaw's solution predicts that the first should allow only a *de re* reading (as regards a man who will be leaving, Bill sought him), and the second only a *de dicto* one (Bill sought a man such that that man will be leaving); but this prediction is not borne out. Both sentences are ambiguously *de re* or *de dicto*.

What Dowty proposes is that FUT be a "substitution operator" which substitutes "the reference time of the main clause for the speech time of the subordinate clause. Thus tense operators embedded within FUT will relate their reference time to the reference time of the main clause, instead of relating their reference time to the actual speech time."[120]

Consider *John will find a unicorn that is walking*. We want two readings—one in which the unicorn is walking now, and one in which it will be walking then. We can capture this with two different syntactic analyses, roughly:

> [a unicorn which is walking]$_i$ John will find it$_i$
> John will find [a unicorn which is walking]$_i$

In the former case, the NP is lowered as in Ladusaw's proposal. Slightly modified to omit irrelevant detail, the translation is:

$$\exists x \, [\text{unicorn}'(x) \land \text{PRES}[\text{walk}'(x)] \land \text{FUT}[\text{find}'(j,x)]]$$

In the latter case, the translation is:

$$\text{FUT}[\exists x \, [\text{unicorn}'(x) \land \text{PRES}[\text{walk}'(x)] \land \text{find}'(j,x)]]$$

But interpreting FUT as a substitution operator means that in the latter case PRES is interpreted relative to the future, not to the present.

Dowty points out that if *that*-clauses, unlike relative clauses, do not allow lowering-in of the NP, then parallel examples with *that*-clauses should be unambiguous.[121] He claims that this prediction is supported by such examples as *John will say that a unicorn is walking*, which can mean only that the unicorn is walking at the time John speaks. However, Dowty admits that there are apparent exceptions, as for instance Terence Parsons's example *one day John will regret that he is treating me like this*, in which the lower present tense can (and in my speech at least, must) refer to the present (S), not to the future time, of John's regretting.

Here Dowty points to pragmatic, discourse-structural conditions on tense choice.[122]

He contrasts Parsons's example with *but Smith will claim on the witness stand that he is in Mexico*, where the embedded present cannot refer to S, and the intended reading can be achieved only with *was* (cf. the example from *Henry V: and gentlemen in England, now a bed, Shall think themselves accurst they were not here*).[123]

Dowty says that "the time of the general topic of discourse in which a sentence occurs affects the possibilities for sequence of tense interpretations," thereby rendering inadequate the analysis he gives, but in the absence of a "discourse analysis" he must "leave it to future research to develop an extension of this approach which also gives the proper interpretation for [Parsons's example]."

What should be noted here in regard to both the R-point and syntactic treatments of tense is the range of complex devices required to handle what seem to be relatively straightforward phenomena. No great generalizations appear, and English, for one, is made to seem a language rife with idiosyncracies.

Perhaps the greatest problem with any kind of syntactic or, indeed, semantic solution (such as in the R-point theories) is that they cannot apply to independent sentences in discourses, even though the very same rules would seem to be required to handle the apparently identical phenomena within and without sentences. It would appear that neither the R-point solution nor the syntactic solution is adequate in either descriptive or explanatory terms. If pragmatic factors enter into tense choice, as Riddle argues is the general case, and many others accept at least for special cases, then perhaps a purely pragmatic theory—not only of SOT, but of tense use in general—will prove both preferable and necessary, and this is what an increasingly large number of scholars have been seeking.

e. Pragmatic Theories of Tense and Aspect: Use and Meaning

Meaning-based theories of tense and aspect fail to account not only for SOT phenomena, but for many ways in which tenses and aspects are used. While such theories are not designed to account directly for usage, especially in text or discourse as opposed to within sentences, it has been assumed by many scholars that the uses a form can be put to depend crucially on the meaning(s) associated with that form.

In recent years a number of students of tense and aspect in Romance and Slavic languages have challenged that assumption and attempted to provide more adequate accounts of the uses of verbs in discourse, based not on semantic concepts but rather on pragmatic ones.

The central problem is that there are competing forms such as the Romance preterite and imperfect, which have essentially the same *meaning*, but which do not seem to be *used* in the same way. And even where the meanings differ in some way, that difference seems inadequate to explain, in and of itself, differences of use. That such differences are not accidental, and require systematic explanation, is shown by the occurrence in many languages of similar phenomena. For example, where a language has a form marking perfective aspect and another marking imperfective, the former is more likely to be used in narrative, the latter in description. The question then is, what has aspect to do with such discourse functions?

Often too, tenses and aspects are used in apparently nonliteral ways. We have already seen a number of such uses, in which use is plainly at odds with "literal" meaning. Below, four typical phenomena of this type are discussed.

The Imperfect(ive) and the Perfect(ive)

The imperfect and preterite (Greek aorist, Latin perfect) tenses differ in aspect, but not in tense. Yet they are quite different in usage. As noted above, the preterite is more likely to be used in narrating events, and the imperfect in description, though this difference is not obviously explicable in terms of aspect. The Slavic imperfective and perfective differ likewise solely in aspect, and show a similar difference in use to the Romance imperfect and preterite.

Sometimes the English progressive tenses contrast with the simple, nonprogressive tenses in the same way; the progressives are consequently subsumed by some scholars under the category of imperfective. Insofar as the simple tenses contrast with the progressive, they are like the perfective, though as regards meaning we have seen that the English past and future are ambiguously perfective or imperfective.

Traditionally, the difference of preterite (aorist, perfective, etc.) and imperfect (imperfective) forms in these various languages has been presented as one of narrative tense versus a description of circumstance [124]; as a definite recounting of a single event versus a description of something [125] (Portuguese: *nós liamos* quando ele *chegou* 'we were reading when he arrived'); as providing the thread of the story versus describing the scenes the personae occur in. [126] This last point may be illustrated by examples in Spanish:

> Mientras *estuvieron* [preterite] solos, Bringas y su mujer apenas *hablaron* [preterite].
>
> While they *remained* alone, Bringas and his wife scarcely *spoke*.
>
> Mientas *duró* [preterite] la cena, las graciosas espectadoras *no cesaban* [imperfect] en su charla picotera.
>
> So long as the dinner *lasted*, the gracious spectators *did not stop* their prattling talk.
>
> Mientas *llegaban* [imperfect], el joven Bernal *asistía* [imperfect] todas las tardes al te.
>
> While they *were coming*, young Bernal *attended* the tea every afternoon.

Or the preterite and imperfect are seen as rendering principal action versus secondary circumstances. [127] Thus in French:

> (Charles XII), sans s'étonner, *fit* faire des retranchements réguliers par ses trois cents Suédois: il y *travailla* lui-même; son chancelier, son trésorier, ses secrétaires, les valets de chambre, tous ses domestiques *aidaient* à l'ouvrage. Les uns *barricadaient* les fenêtres, les autres *enfonçaient* les solives derrière les portes . . . , etc. etc.
>
> [Charles XII], without being surprised, *had* (simple past, lit., 'made') his three hundred Swedes make regular entrenchments: he *worked* (simple past) on it himself; his chancellor, his treasurer, his secretaries, his valets, all his domestic servants *helped*

(imperfect) with the work. Some *barricaded* (imperfect) the windows, others *drove in* (imperfect) the beams behind the doors. . . .

Further, the preterite and imperfect are seen as presenting sequenced versus non-sequenced actions,[128] and narrative versus the frame of that narrative.[129]

The simple past tense of English is ambiguous in these regards, and consequently sequences of past tenses may be sequential or simultaneous:

> He enjoyed and admired the sonnets of Petrarch. (simultaneous)
> He addressed and sealed the envelope. (sequential)[130]

This is not to say that any particular case is ambiguous; there are conditions in which one or the other interpretation is applicable. The first example above cannot be understood sequentially nor the second simultaneously, because the verbs in the first are stative and so non-telic, whereas those in the second are performances and therefore telic.

The imperfect is often said also to present an action as if it were present, or ongoing, or dynamic:

> Modern French writers tend more and more to use the Imperfect, where one might . . . expect the Past Definite; . . . the Imperfect often becomes a stylistic device for presenting a past action more graphically, as something actually going on before the mind's eye. This development is part of a wider change in outlook: the modern tendency is to envisage the past as a scene or a picture, whereas to the medieval mind it appeared above all as action. . . . broadly speaking, [Modern French] prefers the static tense (Imperfect), while [Old French] preferred the dynamic (Past Definite). Modern French employs the Past Definite only to denote an action or series of actions presented as having happened at a given time in the past, the Imperfect to describe an action or series of actions in progress at a given time in the past.[131]

We saw above that the use of the preterite (perfective) to express sequences of events and to present the events in a narrative is ascribed to its representing events as completed wholes, whereas the imperfect(ive) is used rather to describe or present circumstances because it represents action as ongoing and hence incomplete; consequently the Greek aorist is more common in narration per se, the imperfect in description.[132]

An alternative theory is that the imperfect is a kind of present-in-the-past and hence represents events not in their own right but inherently as simultaneous with another event: "[The imperfect] marks, normally, *an action contemporaneous with another past action.*"[133]

Oddly enough, the ambiguity of the past tense in German apparently has led Curme to conclude that it is the incompleteness, the imperfectness, associated with the past tense which allows its use in narrative.[134] He associates incompleteness with temporal coincidence: "hence the past tense has for its leading idea that of the simultaneity of two or more related past acts or conditions," and so can "represent single acts or facts as links in a chain of facts," and is therefore the common narrative tense. It is unclear precisely what Curme means by all this (but cf. the characterization by Brunot and Bruneau below).

While the distinguishing features of the use of the two aspects are intuitively clear, there are a number of problems. First, the imperfect can be used in narrative for a foregrounded event, if it serves to demarcate divisions in the text—traditional grammarians write of the "imperfect of 'rupture.' " Brunot and Bruneau explain:

> In modern French, since around 1850, one can read sentences of this type:
>
>> Lorsque le notaire arriva avec M. Geoffrin . . . elle les *reçut* elle-même et les invita à tout visiter en détail. Un mois plus tard, elle *signait* le contrat de vente et *achetait* en même temps une petite maison bourgeoise. (Maupassant, *Une vie*, p. 292)
>>
>> When the notary arrived with M. Geoffrin . . . she received (simple past) them herself and invited (simple past) them to examine everything in detail. A month later she *signed* (imperfect) the contract of sale and *bought* (imperfect) a little bourgeois house.
>
> The imperfect has here a great expressive value. It's that this tense normally indicates *an action contemporary with another past action*. Here, a month passes between the visit and the signing. In general, the imperfect of "rupture" occurs after a simple past; it is *always* accompanied by a *precise indication of time*.[135]

A very similar use of the past progressive is found in English, especially after indications of temporal transitions such as *soon after* or *next moment*:

> the next moment she was tapping at her husband's dressing room
> In another minute they were standing in the glare of the Circus
> Where's Mr. Luttrell? he heard her say. In another moment she was greeting him
> Three days later he was having tea with her at Claridge's
> Manning shook off his early Evangelical considerations, started an active correspondence with Newman, and was soon working for the new cause.[136]

The imperfect has also increasingly come to mark the beginnings and endings of texts—the so-called "imperfect of opening and closing."[137]

Moreover, the imperfect has other uses in narrative, at least in French, where it has been encroaching for at least a century on the ground of the old narrative tense, the preterite or simple past: "the Imperfect Indicative in Modern French is increasingly adopting a preterite role, loose but none the less real."[138]

In Russian, likewise, the imperfective can be used under certain conditions for narration. Forsyth presents an entire narrative in the imperfective.[139] We have already seen examples he presents in which the imperfective is used for a completed event in the past: 'have you read *Anna Karenina*?—I have': *vy čitali ⟨⟨Annu Kareninu⟩⟩?—Čitali*.[140]

No doubt the imperfective past in Russian, French, or English differs in numerous respects from the corresponding perfectives, and does not overlap with them in usage as stylistic variants. But the question is how to explain partial functional overlap in terms of total semantic disjunction.

Another problem is the use of the imperfect tense in many languages for non-past events or states. In the Romance languages the imperfect has many such uses, and in the Germanic languages the preterite likewise can be used in many non-past contexts. We shall see that in many languages the preterite or imperfect may be used for present or future conditionals (*if I were rich, if I were to win the lottery*). Thus in French:

> Si tu *étais* blessé, passe la consigne à un autre.
> 'If by any chance you'*re* wounded, give the orders to someone else.'[141]

In Spanish the imperfect subjunctive may express a non-past condition:

Si tuviese/tuviera dinero lo compraría/comprara. 'If I had [imperfect subjunctive] money, I would buy [conditional indicative or imperfect subjunctive] it.' [142]

The imperfect is often substituted for the perfect for a variety of purposes; thus the "hypocoristic" imperfect, the imperfect of endearment:

Ah! qu'il *était* joli, joli mon petit Maurice. 'Oh, how cute, cute my little Maurice is.' [143]

Many writers observe the use of the imperfect for politeness:

Je *voulais* vous demander quelque chose. 'I wanted to ask you something.' [144]

Compare *I would like to ask you something; what was your name again?*

Future and Futurate

There is a wide range of devices for referring to future time, including the future tense itself: *they will go (tomorrow)*; futurate tenses of various kinds, including the present tense: *they go (tomorrow)*; the present progressive tense: *they are going (tomorrow)*; the present perfect: *if they have gone (by the time you return . . .)*; in some languages, the imperfect (e.g., in French): *si le petit avait quelque chose cette nuit, n'aie pas peur* 'if the little one should get sick (lit., 'had something' [imperfect]) tonight, don't be afraid' [145]; and periphrastic (often idiomatic) futures with various auxiliary verbs: *they are going to go (tomorrow)*; (French) *qu'est-ce que vous allez faire?* 'what are you going to do?'.

Although all these sundry devices presumably have the same temporal meaning of futurity, they clearly differ in their use. The following differ in several ways:

> If you will leave tomorrow . . .
> If you are leaving tomorrow . . .
> If you are to leave tomorrow . . .
> If you are going to leave tomorrow . . .
> If you leave tomorrow . . .

All but the last presuppose the addressee's leaving, but the middle three assume some sort of plan, intention, or arrangement. It is odd to say *if the sun is setting (is to set, is going to set) at 5:00 p.m. tomorrow . . .* except in a context where this is reportative—someone has claimed that the sun will set at 5:00 tomorrow: *if the sun is setting at 5:00 p.m. tomorrow, then how come it set at almost 6:00 today?*. The last example presupposes nothing about their leaving. Transposed into the past, these become hypothetical future conditions:

> If you would leave tomorrow . . .
> If you were leaving tomorrow . . .
> If you were to leave tomorrow . . .
> If you were going to leave tomorrow . . .
> If you left tomorrow . . .

In German the future is a highly marked tense, the simple perfect being more usual, especially in the colloquial language. For Curme the present "by reason of its pithy terseness is felt as more forceful than the longer and more accurate but weaker future," and so is "used to express something confidently expected: Kommt er? Er kommt. Will he come? He surely will." [146] In contrast, the future "is often, especially in colloquial speech, used to express a probability or supposition . . . usually with the force of a present tense: Karl wird [wohl] krank sein = Karl ist wohl krank. ['Karl is (certainly) sick', lit. 'Karl will (certainly) sick be']." [147] Compare *Er wird der Morder sein* '(I guess) he is the murderer' [lit., 'he will the murderer be'].[148]

A very similar usage is found in French:

> Pourquoi donc a-t-on sonné la cloche des morts. Ah! Mon Dieu, ce sera pour Mme Rousseau.
> 'Why did they sound the death-bell? Oh, my God, it's probably for Mme Rousseau.'
> (lit., 'Why then has-one sounded the bell of-the dead [pl.]. Oh! My God, it will-be for Mme Rousseau.)[149]

Compare *Cet homme-là, il sera l'inspecteur?* 'That man over there, (I suppose) he would be the inspector?' (lit., 'that man-there, he will-be the inspector?').[150]

The anterior future (future perfect) may similarly express a supposition concerning the past:

> Il n'est pas là, *il aura manqué* son train.
> 'He isn't there, he probably missed his train.' [151]

Compare in German *sie wird wohl in der Stadt zu Mittag gegessen haben* 'she will (*wird*) undoubtedly have (*haben*) eaten (*gegessen*) lunch ('at noon'—*zu Mittag*) in the city'.[152]

In Spanish a similar usage occurs:

> Qué hora es?—Son las tres.
> 'What time is it?—It is three o'clock.'
>
> Qué hora es?—Serán las tres.
> 'What time is it?—It is *probably* (lit., 'it will be') three o'clock.'
>
> Resolví cinco años ha retirarme de los negocios.
> 'Five years ago (lit., 'it has five years') I decided to retire from business.'
>
> Resolví, hará cinco años, retirarme de los negocios.
> 'I decided *some* five years ago (lit., 'it will have five years') to retire from business.' [153]

Note the future perfect in:

> Pero ¿que interés habrá tenido Mendoza en ello?
> 'But what interest can Mendoza have had in it?'

The conditional is similarly used for conjectural pasts:

> Su madre tendría entonces treinta años.
> 'His mother *was* then *probably* thirty years old.'

Similar usages occur in English as well:

> He is waiting for us downstairs. He will be wondering where we are. I expect he'll have had his tea.[154]

The imperfect in French and other Romance languages may be used, like the present and present perfect in the Germanic languages, to express a future condition; in this use it partly accords with the English futurate progressive:

s'il *pleuvait* (maintenant; ce soir) je resterais.
'if it was raining (now; this evening) I would remain'[155]

In several languages in Ultan's sample—Central Sierra Miwok, Hausa, Japanese, and Sanskrit—the future may mark probability; it may mark possibility or potentiality in Sanskrit, Old Irish, Korean, Lithuanian, Russian, Tsimshian, Modern Greek, and Guarani. It may mark supposition in Dutch, Lithuanian, Rotuman, Dakota, and Japanese.[156]

Perfect and Past

We have seen that the present perfect and the past tenses overlap to a great extent. One major theory concerning the differences between the two has been that the perfect represents something as currently relevant, whereas the preterite or imperfect divorces the situation from current relevance.

It is to this difference that many writers ascribe an important difference in use of the two forms in many languages. It is true that the preterite is more likely to be a narrative tense than is the perfect, but in both French and (some varieties of) German, the perfect has replaced the old simple past as the regular narrative past tense, whereas in American English the simple past and even the past progressive are often used where a Britisher would use the perfect.

But in a wide range of languages the two forms have special modal uses. In German the perfect may be reportative, and the past, evidential.[157] The present perfect has been said to represent a past event as an "independent fact, not as a link in a chain of related events," while emphasizing the "bearing" of this past event on the present.

Accordingly an eyewitness naturally uses the past tense in narrating events "as he has seen them take place in their relations to each other . . . : *Gestern ertrank ein Kind* ['yesterday a child drowned']." On the other hand, a party who has only heard of these events naturally uses the present perfect to recount them, because "they are to the speaker only independent facts: *Gestern ist ein Kind ertrunken* [lit., 'yesterday is a child drowned']."

In Scandinavian the perfect may be inferential (as we shall see below).[158] The Turkish inferential form seems to have originated in an inferential perfect, while the evidential originated in a past tense.[159]

Historical Tenses

The present, present perfect, and future all may be used as "historical" tenses representing past events. The historical present is traditionally regarded as rendering a narrative "more vivid,"[160] as putting us into the action ("the author makes us in some way assist in the action"),[161] "to present past events as if they were occurring at the moment of speaking."[162]

Not only is it possible in a great many languages to utilize the present to refer to past time, but a perfect past or pluperfect may be replaced by the present perfect, and the conditional by the future:

> Napoléon arrive à Ste-Hélène où il mourra en 1821.
> 'Napoleon arrived in St. Helena, where he would die in 1821.' (lit., 'Napoleon arrives in St. Helena, where he will die in 1821')[163]

Traditionally the historical tenses have been seen essentially as shifting the point of view—in our terms, the reference point—to the time of the speech act, purely as a stylistic device. It is not even as well motivated as the epistolary tenses of Latin, and is purely optional. Some have claimed that it is an artless, natural device of the oral storyteller imported into literature. Curme, for example, says it has always been "characteristic of popular and colloquial speech," but "in both English and German came into the literary language late along with a freer and wider sway of imagination and feeling which made it possible."[164] Yet others have seen it as an artificial device which has gone the other way! While most writers have explained that the use lends "vividness" to narrations, until recently there has been little effort to study in detail the conditions under which, and the purposes for which, the "historic" tenses are actually used.

Semantic theories of many kinds have sought to account for these differences in tense and aspect use in terms of differences in meaning. For example, differences in usage between the preterite (simple past) and imperfect have been ascribed to various semantic differences between the two:

the preterite is	the imperfect is
complexive	non-complexive
perfective	imperfective
punctative	extended
definitive	indefinite
conclusive	non-conclusive
simply past	present-in-the-past

All these various theories fail because the criterial difference(s) they posit prove to be neither sufficient nor necessary conditions for the uses they purpose to explicate.[165] The same sorts of arguments presented earlier against semantic solutions to the SOT problem can be adduced in the case of tense selection itself.

We have seen that Riddle (1978) seeks to define pragmatic conditions for sequence-of-tense tense "shift" in English. Similarly, Inoue (1975) seeks to define pragmatic conditions on the use of the perfect in English and Japanese. Both argue for pragmatic accounts of tense selection, and this seems essentially correct, if not as a full account then certainly an essential component of one. As of yet, however, no real pragmatic theory can be said to have emerged.[166] However, a number of observations have been made which are highly suggestive.

f. Aspect, Foregrounding, and Backgrounding

In the case of the different uses in texts of the aspectually distinct perfective and imperfective, preterite and imperfect, a useful distinction has been made, as for

example by Hopper, between "the parts of the narrative which relate events belonging to the skeletal structure of the discourse," which he calls the "foreground," and "supportive material which does not itself narrate the main events,"
the "background." [167]

He notes that in Swahili there are explicit markers of foregrounded and backgrounded events—respectively *ka-* and *ki-*:

Tu-ka-enda kambi-ni, hata usiku tu-ka-toroka, tu-ka-safiri   siku kadha,
we   went camp to and night we   ran off we   traveled days several

tu-ki-pitia   miji   fulani, na humo mwote hamna mahongo.
we   passed villages several and then all   was-not tribute

'We returned to the camp, and ran away during the night, and we traveled for several
days, we passed through several villages, and in all of them we did not have to pay
tribute.' [168]

Here the last two statements are subsidiary and provide additional information,
but are not in the main sequence of events. The foregrounded events are presented
in sequence, in the same order in which the events occurred; but the background
events are essentially simultaneous, in any event not sequential.

Hopper hypothesizes that only foregrounded clauses are actually narrated.
Backgrounded clauses are not themselves part of the narration, but instead support, amplify, or comment on it. In a narration, the author asserts the occurrence
of events. In backgrounding one may find even irreal forms—like subjunctives,
optatives, "modal" verb forms, and negation. [169]

Perfective and imperfective are associated with foreground and background respectively, particularly in narration, the perfective forming the story line, the imperfective supplying "supportive or subsidiary background information, such as
description, characterization, and commentary." For this reason the perfective is
associated with "punctual," "dynamic," or "kinetic" verbs, and the imperfective with "stative" or "durative" ones. [170]

Foreground and background are concepts from discourse studies: Wallace lists
several analysts of the structure of discourse who divide discoursal information
into foreground and background. He characterizes the former as constituting

the more important events of a narrative, the more important steps of a procedure,
the central points of an exposition, the main characters or entities involved in an
episode. The background includes events of lesser importance, subsidiary proce-
dures, secondary points, descriptions, elaborations, digressions, and minor characters
or things. [171]

There has been some effort made to connect textual foregrounding and backgrounding with the Gestalt psychological distinction of figure and ground, but the
ultimate significance of this for our present purpose is quite unclear. [172]

There is no question that the choice of tense and aspect functions so as to
foreground or background material. Wallace observes that the present makes an
account more "vivid," "bringing it into the immediate foreground." Using the
"past" tense to refer to the present (as in conditions) has the effect of downplay-
ing the "certainty, immediacy, or reality of the assertion, that is, backgrounding
it." The future tense is also seen as belonging to the background, since it functions

to "give predictions, intentions, and desires rather than the narration of actual events." [173]

In particular, tense is closely linked to aspects of discourse such as focus, topic, and salience. The question is, if perfective is foregrounded and imperfective backgrounded, then under what conditions does something get fore- or backgrounded? What do we mean by "major," "important," and the like?

Hopper presents a set of properties differentiating foreground and background (simplified here, with the contrasts numbered for reference) [174]:

FOREGROUND [His PERFECTIVE]	BACKGROUND [His IMPERFECTIVE]
1. Chronological sequencing.	Simultaneity or chronological overlapping.
2. View of an event as a whole.	View of a situation or happening not necessarily completed.
3. Identity of subject maintained.	Frequent change of subject.
4. Unmarked distribution of focus in clause (with presupposed subject and asserted verb).	Marked distribution of focus (subject focus, instrument focus, or focus on sentence adverbial).
5. Human topics.	Non-human topics.
6. Dynamic events.	Descriptive situations.
7. Events indispensable to narrative.	Situation necessary for understanding motives, attitudes, etc.
8. Realis.	Irrealis.

Hopper [175] illustrates this opposition with data from a study by Reid. [176] Reid observes that the *passé simple* is favored in the environments:

1. Actions as opposed to states [cf. Hopper's #6].
2. Affirmative as opposed to negative verbs [cf. #8].
3. Human subjects as opposed to non-human subjects [cf. #5].
4. First person subjects as opposed to third person subjects.
5. Singular as opposed to plural subjects.
6. Main character of discourse as subject as opposed to secondary character as subject [cf. #3].
7. Main clause as opposed to subordinate clause [cf. #7].
8. Proper name subject as opposed to pronominal subject.

The more salient something is, the more likely it is to be foregrounded, although this depends strongly on the specific context. That the list of salient features is not entirely ad hoc but reflects some set of deep principles is shown by the fact that the same sort of factors that enter into aspect choice enter into transitivity; compare to Hopper's and Reid's lists above the well-known "Transitivity Scale" of Hopper and Thompson. [177]

By why does salience underlie foregrounding? This is a very complex issue and no good answer can as yet be given; it is too facile to say that the things which are most important to speakers are most likely to form part of the main structure of discourse. Ultimately, a better understanding of discourse structure and the flow of information in discourses and texts must form part of the foundations of an explanation of tense and aspect choice. But for present purposes it perhaps suffices to point out that the choice of tense and aspect is at least in part contextually determined and affected by pragmatic factors such as the speaker's presupposi-tions.

g. Salience and Relevance

In this regard, a number of scholars have attempted to organize hierarchies of more or less salient categories. Based on their work, Wallace presents a division of categories into those which are relatively "more salient" (and tend to be fore-grounded) and those which are "less salient" (backgrounded).[178] He claims that these differences in salience enter, in various languages, into aspects of noun-verb agreement; into the marking of subjects and objects; into the use of noun phrases or agents, subjects, or topics; and, in diachronic grammar, into certain types of morphological and syntactic change.

It is probable, however, that a binary opposition of "relatively more salient" and "relatively less salient" is less appropriate than a non-discrete scale of rela-tive salience along the lines of Chvany's (1985) work, which presents a parame-terized hierarchy of saliency.[179]

Hopper observes that in foregrounded clauses the subject of the verb is "topical and highly presupposed," because it tends to be animate and definite, and because of the relative continuity of topic-subject in ongoing narration.[180] Actions predi-cated of animate, definite subjects are expected to be expressed in the main verb and its complements. He notes that, according to Forsyth's *A Grammar of Aspect*, the choice of perfective or imperfective verb forms is conditioned not only by the discourse functions of foreground and background but also by focus (i.e., the marking of new and old information) in the sentence.

In Russian, aspectual choice is highly sensitive to focus structure. The imper-fective is used when the verb and its complements do not represent the new infor-mation (i.e., when the subject is in focus):

—Kto pisal [imperfective] "Voynu i mir"?
'Who wrote "War and Peace"?'

—Tolstoi pisal [imperfective] "Voynu i mir."
'Tolstoy wrote "War and Peace".'

Ya ubiral [imperfective] komnatu včera, a kto ubiral [imperfective] segodn'a ne znayu.
'I cleaned the room yesterday, but who cleaned it today I don't know.'[181]

But when the verb is in focus, the perfective is used:

V etoy porternoy ya obdumyval svoyu dissertatsiyu i napisal [perfective] pervoe l'ubovnoe pis'mo k Vere. Pisal [perfective] karandašom.
'In this tavern I pondered my thesis and wrote my first love letter to Vera. I wrote it in pencil.'[182]

Such aspects of discourse structure as topic, focus, and the like interact with salience to determine aspect choice, but function crucially on their own in tense choice. Salience is closely linked to two notions prevalent in the literature: relevance, and currency or inclusivity of time. We have seen how these concepts entered into the debate over the present perfect tense.

The present perfect is said by Fleischman to be used of either a situation or an event begun in the past but still going on, including one "whose reference period satisfies this criterion (e.g., *today, in the past ten years*, . . .)"; or one completed, but regarded as still relevant at the present moment.[183] The first two of these essentially correspond to the "extended now" of XN theory, but the third is straight out of current relevance (CR) theory.

Since it is possible to use the past tense of a time period which potentially includes the present (*he went home early today, I went to school several times this week*), the question arises how to decide whether it does so. In effect, with neutral adverbial expressions, there is a question of deciding the reference point—a past which excludes S, or a present which includes it. The adverbial in and of itself cannot decide tense selection in these cases.

In CR theory, "relevance" does not have its ordinary sense, but a special technical one. Furthermore, its many "concrete realizations" are highly dependent on "the particulars of word-choice and context." CR theorists assert an abstract principle of relevance; according to McCoard, "some state resulting from a prior event continues to hold." To McCoard this "state" appears in some cases, however, "to be an ineffable construct of the speaker's mind having no other demonstrable property than that it calls forth the perfect." He consequently concludes that CR theory "fails ultimately to have any explanatory power as a theory."[184]

Current relevance is indeed highly subjective, as Fleischman observes. Although the temporal location of an event may be fixed relative to R (and ultimately, S), the speaker may choose devices (tense, aspect, modals, time adverbs) so as to represent the event in various ways, for example, in a logical or causal relation to some other event or situation. This is subjective and not necessarily shared with other speakers. She relates "the *subjectivity* of current relevance" to aspect, and specifically to what J. M. Anderson (1973) and Comrie (1976) have labeled *prospective* and *retrospective* aspects, namely, "ways of viewing an event in which a (non-chronological or not primarily chronological) connection is established between the event and the reference point, in the case of 'present' relevance, between the event and 'now'."[185]

Similarly, Haugen notes that in the choice of past or perfect, "an objective event occurring in a certain time sphere is not so important as the view of the event in the speaker's mind and the standpoint he adopts in referring to the event."[186] Li and his coauthors make essentially the same point.[187] Waugh too sees tense in French as not objectively characterizing the "narrated situation with reference to the speech situation," but rather from the subjective viewpoint of the speaker.[188]

Fleischman notes that present relevance tends to be interpreted differently from one language to another, even between dialects of the same language.[189]

The inference of continuance from use of the perfect Leech relates to

> a general tendency of self-centredness in human speech, whereby . . . we understand a word or phrase to refer to something close at hand rather than distant. . . .
> if we recognize that the indefinite past meaning always involves a period leading up to the present, it is easy to see how this period can become reduced, by subjective

assumption, from 'always' to 'within the last few days', or even 'within the last few minutes'.[190]

Consider the difference between these pairs of sentences:

> Have you visited the Gauguin exhibition? (i.e., 'while it has been on')
> Did you visit the Gauguin exhibition?
> The dustman hasn't called at our house. (i.e., today)
> The dustman didn't call at our house.

The first example leads us to infer that the Gauguin exhibit is still continuing, whereas the simple past makes it clear that it is not. The third sentence, Leech says, is definite and presupposes a "special time period (probably a day)"; "it does not mean that the dustman has not called at least once in the past; it means rather that the dustman has not called during a period in which his regular visit is expected."

We can see then that both sides in the perfect debate were correct. The perfect requires a reference period which is, or includes, the present, but it does so because only thus is it currently relevant. Indeed, it is because it is currently relevant that a completed past event such as *even Shakespeare has written some awful plays* is possible.

Waugh agrees with many scholars when she characterizes the present tense as the unmarked tense in the system: it has the greatest range of reference, its information is the least specific, and its possibilities for variation of interpretation in context are greatest. None of these interpretations, however, is inherent; she sees them as consequences of the present's unmarked nature.[191]

The past, by contrast, is "restricted from the speech situation," in that what happened in the past is no longer true at S, since the action terminates in the past. Another way in which it may be so "restricted" is that it is hypothetical or contrary to fact (irreal) and therefore "non-observable": "It is pushed out of the direct and perceivable reality of the speech situation, it denies the coordination of observation of the narrated event and observation of the speech situation."[192]

The future is not restricted in the same way the past is, but neither is it unrestricted. According to Waugh, the future, though not yet realized at S, is marked for, presupposes, some kind of "objectivity": the speaker vouches for the existence of the narrated event but at the same time "confirms that its existence is projected into a more objective realm, that its objective existence is independently ascertainable outside of the speech situation."[193]

The futurate "presupposes a degree of participation, interest or personal involvement in the situation that is generally not conveyed, or must be conveyed by other means, when a more neutral, psychologically detached future is chosen."[194] Similarly, as we shall see, the perfect often conveys personal involvement, as opposed to the more "objective" past.

h. Shift of Past to Present: The Perfect

What kinds of situations require the use of the present reference point, and hence the present perfect tense? These would seem to be those in which a past event, or an event with a past component, is not "restricted" from the speech situation.

Current relevance has been discussed by Li and his coauthors (1982) in connection with the Mandarin Chinese particle *le*. They conclude that the basic function of *le* is to indicate a "Currently Relevant State." [195] They note in regard to currency that the unmarked "current" time is S; however, if another reference time besides the speech situation is being referred to in the conversation, then by extension the sentence with *le* may be claimed to be relevant to that particular R point. [196] The time may even be hypothetical, as in this example:

wǒ yào shi Zhōngguo-rén jiu   bu huì   shuō zèmma
I   if   China-person then not likely speak such
zāo-de   Zhōngguo-huà le
bad-NOM China-speech C[urrent] R[elevant] S[tate]
'If I were Chinese, then I wouldn't be speaking such bad Chinese.'

Further requirements for the use of *le* are (1) relevance: *le* is used when some state of affairs is " 'relevant' for the speaker and the hearer, and the speaker assumes that the hearer can figure out from the context in just what ways it is relevant" [197]; and (2) a state: *le* always concerns a state of affairs, one that is claimed to be currently relevant to some given time. [198]

Li and his colleagues further note that the specific ways in which *le* signals current relevancy can be grouped into five broad categories: *le* can convey a CRS if the state of affairs

is a changed state of affairs
corrects a wrong impression
reports "progress so far"
determines what will happen next
is the speaker's total contribution to the conversation at that point. [199]

We will discuss these five categories in turn.

If a state continues or is generally true, *le* cannot appropriately be used. However, it may be used if there has been a change. [200]

tā   zhīdao nèi-ge   xiāoxi
s/he know that-CL[assifier] piece of news
'S/he knows about that piece of news.'
tā   zhīdao nèi-ge   xiāoxi   le
s/he know that-CL[assifier] piece of news CRS
'S/he knows about that piece of news.' (S/he hadn't before.)

Leech points out that the English present perfect may represent a result of a past action which is still operative at the present time, observing that "this meaning is clearest with 'transitional event verbs' denoting the switch from one state to another":

The taxi has arrived. (i.e., 'The taxi is now here.')
He has been given a camera. ('He now has the camera.')
I've recovered from my illness. ('I'm now well again.')
Someone has broken her doll. ('The doll is now broken.') [201]

By comparison, the simple past "permits us (and in fact encourages us) to conclude that the result [of the action] has disappeared." [202]

Change includes sudden discovery of a fact:

xià yǔ *le*
fall rain CRS
'It's raining.'

"A sentence like [the preceding] can be used not only when it has just begun to rain, but also when the speaker has just discovered that it is raining." [203]

James reports on a somewhat similar usage in Latin, in which "the past indicative can be used when the speaker wishes to express surprise at discovering that something unexpected is the case":

ehem, tun   hic eras,   mi Phaedria?
what   you-question here be-past my Phaedria
'What! Are you here, Phaedria?' [204]

Similarly, in Greek the imperfect of 'be' "may express a *fact* which is just recognized as such by the speaker or writer, having previously been denied, overlooked, or not understood":

Ouk ára moûnon éēn erídōn génos, all' epì gaîan eisì dúō
'there is not after all merely one race of discords, but there are two on earth'

Ou sù mónos ár' êsth' épops?
'are you not then the only epops (as I thought)?' [205]

The Turkish inferential, as in *Kemal gelmiş* 'Kemal came', has among its various uses that of expressing surprise. [206] In this example, one possible reading is that "the speaker hears someone approach, opens the door, and sees Kemal—a totally unexpected visitor."

A similar usage occurs in another Altaic language, Mongolian. The Modern Mongolian verb ending -*jee*, traditionally labeled a "past imperfect," [207] can express sudden awareness or knowledge [208]; in the Mongolian translation of Stevenson's *Treasure Island*, when the pirate finds Billy Bones dead, he rushes out and exclaims, "Bill uxčixjee!" ('Bill's dead'). However, later on in the book, when Jim Hawkins tells Ben Gunn that Flint is dead, he says, "Flint uxčixsen," using a pragmatically neutral form. The first one conveys a sense of "hot news"; the latter is a mere report of a fact.

In Japanese this use of the perfect is subsumed in the past tense, which then "has a present perfective [*sic*] function." [209] As Nakau points out, the simple past tense (-*ta*) form has a "modal" meaning, indicating

> the speaker's present awareness, with some degree of surprise, that his past desired or anticipated event has been realized. It is characteristically associated with interjective expressions such as *hora* 'look!', *nanda* 'what/why!', and *yappari/yahari*, translatable as 'as I expected/anticipated'. [210]

For example:

Hora, asoko ni itaban-bosi ga mie-ta!
'Look! There's the first evening star over there!'

In this example, "the speaker becomes aware at the moment of speech that the event of his seeing the first evening star, which he has expected to take place over a period lasting up to the present moment, has actually come true."

What has been called in the literature, following McCawley (1971), the "hot news" sense of the perfect, is precisely this usage we have outlined in various languages. Although the event is past, it has present relevance to the extent that only in the present time is it known, realized, or appreciated. It should be pointed out, however, that surprise, or a realization contrary to one's beliefs, can be expressed in English by the past tense, with a rising (exclamatory) intonation, as Riddle shows.[211] Compare:

> I didn't know that people *rode* (?*ride*) cable cars in San Francisco.
> I didn't realize that Gdansk was (?*is*) on the Baltic.

As regards the second usage of *le*, to correct a wrong impression, consider this sentence first:

wǒ hē   qìshuǐ
I   drink 7-Up
'I (want to) drink 7-Up'

This is simply a way of expressing a preference. But the same sentence with *le* ('[but] I have been drinking 7-Up') might be appropriate as a response by "someone responding to the hostess' claim that s/he is not taking any of the food offered to her/him." The usage is related to the previous one, in that the speaker is "correcting a wrong impression."[212]

"Progress so far" is the third usage.

Sometimes a state of affairs is relevant to the current situation in that it brings the hearer 'up to date' on the progress made so far. . . . So if the hearer knows, for example, that the speaker is working on Tang dynasty poetry, the speaker can say

Táng shī   sān- bǎi-   shǒu wǒ bèi-   chu- lài- le   yi- bàn *le*
Tang poem three- hundred-CL I   memorize- exit- come- PFV one-half CRS
'I've memorized half of the Three Hundred Tang Poems now (so far).'[213]

Of the fourth usage of *le*, Li and his colleagues state: "Another class of contexts in which a state of affairs is relevant are those in which that state *determines* what happens next. For example, [the sentence below] could be currently relevant as a signal to the hearer that something else can happen now":

wǒ xǐ- hǎo- le   yīfu   *le*
I   wash-finish-PFV clothes CRS
135'I've finished washing the clothes (so:
 i. now we can go to the movies
 ii. you can do your yoga in the laundry room
 iii. I'm free to play chess with you, (etc.))'[214]

Fifth and last, *le* often functions "as though [it were] a sentence-final punctuation marker," telling the "hearer that the proposition is relevant to the speech situation by being 'newsworthy' in and of itself; it brings a statement into the current situation by tagging it as the speaker's total contribution as of that moment."[215]

i. Modal Functions of the Perfect

A major function of the present perfect in many languages is to distinguish evidential, inferential, and reportative utterances. When a language contrasts the perfect with a simple preterite (past tense), if the latter has an evidential function, the perfect is likely to be inferential or reportative.

Slobin and Aksu (1982) and Waugh and Monville-Burston (1986) ascribe this to the "distancing," the objectivity, associated with the past.[216] For Slobin and Aksu, "an important cognitive factor of the speaker's experiential participation in the referred to event accounts for the seemingly heterogeneous range of semantic and pragmatic functions of the two basic tense forms in Turkish."[217] They contrast the "contents at the center" with that at "the periphery of the speaker's immediate consciousness."

Haugen (1972) discusses an inferential use of the perfect in Scandinavian. He illustrates the usage with an example from Ibsen's *Hedda Gabler*:

> In Act 3 . . . the heroine is awaiting the triumphant return of her beloved genius Ejlert Løvberg from the Dionysian revel to which she has sent him. She fully expects him to have worn "vineleaves in his hair," her symbol for the *joie de vivre*. The report by Judge Brack, however, is thoroughly disillusioning, and in an aside she says,
>
> > Således *er* det altså *gåt* for sig.
> > Da *har* han ikke *havt* vinløv i håret.
>
> This passage is quite correctly translated by William Archer as: "So that is what *happened*. Then he *had* no vine-leaves in his hair." . . . The information conveyed is an inference on Hedda's part, since Judge Brack has never heard about the "vineleaves" and could not have told her this.[218]

Haugen further presents a contrastive example from Swedish.

> Under hela 1930-talet *har* partiet oavbrutet *gått* framåt ända till dess att det erövrade majoritaten vid 1940 års val till andra kammeren.
> 'During the 1930's the party constantly *advanced* until it won the majority at the 1940 election to the second chamber.'[219]

"Here the victory of 1940 is presented as a historical fact, while the advance during the 1930's is a supposition derived from this fact." Haugen speculates that "the inferential perfect represents a projection of the 'current relevance' of the perfect into a specific time in the past, by means of which its timelessness is reduced in favour of a special kind of timeliness."[220]

One area in which speaker involvement enters into choice of forms is in the distinction between witnessed/evidential and non-evidential, whether reportative, hearsay, or inferential. We have seen that Curme claims that the past tense is naturally used in German by an eyewitness for events which someone who knows about them only from hearsay would recount in the perfect.[221]

Whatever the value of Curme's explanations, it is true that tense choice involves the evidential-reportative distinction in many languages, and that such choice is probably historically at the root of the evidential-inferential dichotomy in Turkish, which has separate past tenses differing in this regard.[222]

Inoue contrasts two constructions in Japanese. She observes that the construction *-te iru* is reportative; the speaker is "making an objective and evidential statement." In contrast with the past in *-ta*, this form conveys a strongly evidential sense; at the very least the speaker has good reason for the statement.[223] Inoue asks us to consider the sentence

> John wa, 1960-nen ni General Motors o yame-sase-rare- ⎰a. te i-ru.
>   year in   leave-cause ⎱b. ?ta.
> 'John was laid off by General Motors in 1960.'

She comments that here

> the speaker is reviewing John's employment record. It shows that John was laid off by General Motors in 1960. The *-te ire* phrase is appropriately used, and it conveys exactly that feeling, that the speaker is looking at a record and he is making an objective statement. The *-ta* phrase in this case sounds somewhat inappropriate because it is a straightforward past tense expression.

A contrasting example is this one:

> watashi wa, onaji-toshi ni Chrysler o yame-sase-rare- ⎰a. ?*te i-ru.
> I   same year in   leave-cause ⎱b. ta.
> 'I was laid off by Chrysler in the same year.'

Here she comments:

> The speaker is now talking about himself—he has learned that, in 1960, John was laid off by General Motors and he is saying that *he* was laid off by Chrysler that same year. The sentence ending with *-te iru* sounds awkward because the reportative sense of *-te iru* makes it sound as if the speaker has forgotten about it, and has had to talk about it by looking at his own record. . . . The native speaker reacting to this sentence and trying to make sense of it might think that this person is senile.

j. Shift of Past to Present: The Historical Tenses

In many languages, past events may be narrated using present tenses which are then termed "historical." Although the historical present is best known, the future can serve for the conditional, the present perfect for the past perfect, and the present futurates for the past futurates. Compare:

> Napoleon was exiled to Elba, but he would not stay there long. Soon he had escaped and was attempting a comeback. But the French had had enough of his adventures. It was to end only in his going into island exile again.
> Napoleon is exiled to Elba, but he will not stay there long. Soon he has escaped and is attempting a comeback. But the French have had enough of his adventures. It is to end only in his going into island exile again.

Historical tenses are recorded and discussed in the literature in, among others, Latin, Greek, Romance (French, Spanish), Germanic (English, German), and Japanese.[224]

Traditionally this usage is considered to render the narrative "vivid," to involve the audience, to put the events "before their eyes." It is attributed to a desire to render the narrative dramatic, as if it were a play or movie being observed as the action unfolds.[225]

The shift from the detached, objective past into the present, which is set in the context of the speech-act situation, and hence is subjective, precisely serves to render the account subjective. Another difference is that events in the present are highlighted, foregrounded. Therefore the historic tenses may have discourse functions, for example demarcative ones. Wolfson (1979) argues that it is the shift into or out of the historic present, and not the historic present itself, which marks the demarcation, but Schiffrin (1981) argues the reverse.

k. Shift of Future to Present: The Futurates

In such languages as English, German, and Japanese, the present tense is actually a non-past and does not inherently refer to present, as opposed to future, time. In these languages future constructions are marked, and have additional, modal meanings associated with them.

However, the present used for future time is not neutral either. Such futurate tenses have attached to them various meanings which proceed from the fact that the present has "current relevance," brings the narrated event or described state into the speech-act situation. Furthermore, there are in many languages special constructions used for future time, as we have seen. Some writers have spoken of the "prospective," as a mirror image of the "retrospective" perfect.[226]

Fleischman reviews a number of the theories which have been offered to account for the differences between the future and the futurates.[227] She criticizes them all as "either erroneous readings of the contrast, or, alternatively, as valid but limited readings (i.e. overtones), too narrow to account for a significant portion of the data."

She rejects the "near" or "proximate" future theory of certain writers because of examples like these:

> If Winterbottom's calculations are correct, this planet *is going to burn itself out* 200,000,000 years from now.
>
> Un jour vous *allez vous faire écraser* par une voiture!
> 'Someday you're *going to get yourself run over* by a car!'[228]

She also rejects solutions which stress epistemic notions (Joos, 1964) or contingency (Binnick, 1972), illocutionary force (Boyd and Thorne, 1969), intentionality (Jespersen, 1931), and the like.[229] Instead Fleischman, like Lakoff, sees the crucial factor in the use of the futurates to be "present" (or "current") relevance.[230]

Thus the futurate is used when "the future situation . . . *is viewed by the speaker* as growing out of, or somehow in relation to, the present world-state."[231] Specifically, "what the go-future conveys . . . is essentially pragmatic information: it expresses *the speaker's subjective view* of the situation at the moment of utterance. His perspective on the situation may change, though the situation itself remains fixed in time."

Dès qu'il *viendra*—car il *va venir* . . .
'as soon as he comes—for he is going to come . . .'

Nous *allons jouer*; tu *joueras* d'abord, et moi, je *jouerai* ensuite.
'we're going to play (now); you'll play first, then I'll play.'

Fleischman further connects the 'go-future' with subjectivity, and specifically with "speaker involvement":

> The go-construction presupposes a degree of participation, interest, or personal involvement in the situation that generally is not conveyed, or must be conveyed by other means, when a more neutral, psychologically detached future is chosen. Admittedly, these nuances are often extremely subtle and highly context-sensitive, in addition to varying from one language to another.

Waugh (1986; Waugh and Monville, 1986) stresses the use of the simple past in French to mark causal links. The same is true of the use of the futurates. Writers have brought forth such notions here as control, intention, scheduling, and contingency, which, while insufficient to account for all uses, certainly characterize many of them.

Where conditions are concerned, there is a great difference between the future and the futurate. English does not allow the future in an *if*-clause; the use of *will* there is purely modal:

> When I am married, and have gone away for some weeks, I shall be easier at heart if you will come home here.
> What you got to say to me?—A great many things, if you will come away somewhere, where we can talk comfortably.
> I shan't be happy unless he'll come.[232]

While examples of *shall* do occur—see the one below—Jespersen characterizes the use as "rare" and implies that it is unnecessary:

> I shall be much surprised if the right honourable Baronet shall be able to point out any distinction between the cases.[233]

1. Shift of Present and Future to Past

We have seen that it is possible to shift present events into the past tense (and future into conditional). If the shift of past to present serves to render objective subjective, to foreground the background, and to mark current relevance, then it would seem that the reverse is true where the opposite shift is concerned—the subjective is rendered objective,[234] the foreground is backgrounded, and a lack of current relevance is marked.[235]

One effect of a shift from non-past to past is to render objective what would otherwise be subjective; there is no speaker involvement.[236] Because of its ability to distance, to detach the event from the speech-act situation, the past may be used for irrealities: the hypothetical is expressed in many languages through use of the past tense. In contrary-to-fact situations, it is used in English: *If I knew*

John said that Vann $\begin{Bmatrix} was\ leaving \\ *left \end{Bmatrix}$ for Rome later that day.

> I thought that Jane $\begin{Bmatrix} *leaves \\ *is\ leaving \\ left \\ was\ leaving \end{Bmatrix}$ next Saturday,
>
> but she just told me she $\begin{Bmatrix} leaves \\ is\ leaving \\ ?left \\ ?was\ leaving \end{Bmatrix}$ tomorrow.

> Marmaduke believed $\begin{Bmatrix} that\ he\ was \\ *himself\ to\ have\ been \\ himself\ to\ be \end{Bmatrix}$ of royal blood.

The CIA $\begin{Bmatrix} \text{didn't bother to} \\ \text{tried to} \\ \text{were quick to} \end{Bmatrix}$ $\begin{Bmatrix} deny \\ *have\ denied \end{Bmatrix}$

Sue suspected that Bill $\begin{Bmatrix} left \\ = \\ had\ left \end{Bmatrix}$ shortly

She mentioned that men $\begin{Bmatrix} were\ wont \\ = \\ had\ been\ wont \end{Bmatrix}$ to

more than I do, I wouldn't be here.[237] Similarly the imperfect can be so used in French:

> si j'étais   plus vieille, je serais   plus contente
> if I be-past more old   I will-be-past more happy
> 'If I were older, I would be happier'[238]

Here are examples of present and future hypotheses in the imperfect:

> Si j'*avais* de l'argent, j'irais au théâtre (aujourd'hui, demain).
> 'If I *had* the money, I'd go to the theater (today, tomorrow).'
>
> Si le petit *avait* quelque chose cette nuit, n'aie pas peur.
> 'If the little one *should get* sick tonight, don't be afraid.'[239]

There are numerous modal functions associated with the shift to the past. Since the past is objective where the present is subjective, it is not surprising that the Turkish evidential is etymologically a past tense, or that, when an event grows distant in the past, it is likely to shift from inferential to evidential. As Slobin and Aksu point out, "all history is reported in this form."[240]

Even hearsay, normally reported in the inferential, may be given in the evidential, if it comes as no surprise. Slobin and Aksu report, for example:

> in 1974, our minds were being increasingly prepared for Richard Nixon's resignation. When the event finally took place, it was quite natural to report it—although it was certainly a matter of hearsay—in the past of direct experience, *-di*:
>
> *Nixon istifa   et-ti.*
> Nixon resignation make
> 'Nixon resigned.'[241]

James points out the use of the conditional in French for the reportative.[242] A future tense verb may be used to make a "strong prediction that something is the case in the present." Combining the past tense with this (in the form of the conditional) distances the statement—the speaker "is reporting what others have said and therefore cannot personally vouch for the accuracy of the statement," as in the example

> le roi serait   à Paris
> the king will-be-past in Paris
> 'It appears that the king is in Paris.'

The conditional in French may be used for what a newspaper cannot or will not vouch for:

> Selon les dernières informations, le tremblement de terre aurait fait des centaines de victimes.
> 'According to the latest information, the earthquake has caused hundreds of victims.'[243]
>
> Il l'aurait   tué
> he him-have [COND 3SG] killed
> 'He is alleged to have killed him.'[244]

A very similar usage is found in English:

> —From whom did you receive the letter?
> —From Bill.
> —That *would be* your cousin in Australia?
>
> —When did you last see the deceased alive?
> —At the party.
> —That *would have been* late Tuesday evening?

What is in question in these uses of the conditional and the conditional perfect is not merely the surmise or supposition marked by the future and the future perfect, but, as indicated by the backshifting into conditional and conditional perfect respectively, a distancing indicative of a reportative quality: the speaker is using a fact reported by someone else, probably the addressee. Had the speaker said, "That will be your cousin in Australia?" or "That will have been late Tuesday night?", there would be no such implication; the speaker would simply be making a supposition.

The past can express other indirections as well. Prominent among these is the expression of politeness by distancing the act referred to from the speech-act situation. Whereas the future can express an impolite command (*You will leave now!*), the conditional, especially in an interrogative form, distances the imperative from the present situation and renders it thereby polite:

> Would you/could you hand me that cup?
> I was wondering if you could tell me what time it is?[245]

Something similar is reported for German modal verbs put in the past.[246]

Similarly, a number of scholars have seen the past tenses of the modal verbs as expressing tentativeness.[247] *She may improve* expresses greater likelihood than *she might improve*. Similarly, the past subjunctives of the modals in German express greater tentativeness than the present of *mögen* ('may')[248]:

Er mag   krank sein
he mögen [PRES INDIC 3SG]   ill   be
'He may be ill'

Man möchte   meinen, dass . . .
one   mögen [IMPF SUBJ 3SG] think   that
'One might think that . . .'

Er könnte   krank sein
he können [IMPF SUBJ 3SG] ill   be
'He might be ill'

Er dürfte   krank gewesen sein
he dürfen [IMPF SUBJ 3SG] ill   been   be
'He might well have been ill'

In the same way, conditions have traditionally been held to be "more" or "less vivid." Consider these examples:

> If John comes tomorrow, I will give him the money.
> If John came tomorrow, I would give him the money.

James comments:

> The difference between these two is subtle, but [the latter] seems to indicate slightly
> more doubt as to whether John will come tomorrow than does [the former], and in
> addition, in [the latter] the speaker seems to be in some way distancing himself more
> from what he is talking about. The formal distinction often involves, but does not
> necessarily involve, past tense marking (e.g., in Classical Greek, future less vivid
> conditionals are marked by optative mood rather than by past tense, and in Nitinaht,
> by a special particle).[249]

She notes that English, French, Old Irish, Russian, Tonga, Haya, Cree, and Garo
in her sample do use past tense for this purpose.

m. Toward a Formal Theory of Discourse Tense: Events and Discourses

Model theoreticians have assumed that the truth conditions of sentences can be
articulated in abstraction from verbal contexts—in other words, in isolation. For
Kamp and Rohrer this is the wrong way to tackle the problems of tense and
aspect, since they see tenses primarily as establishing temporal relations between
sentences in discourse.[250] For many recent students of tense, tense is a phenomenon of text, not of isolated sentences—it is text within which the R point is established.[251] Kamp argues that certain temporal phenomena can be understood only
in terms of how discourse participants (e.g., speaker and hearer in conversation)
process the information which a discourse provides.[252]

One important facet of language which truth-conditional, model-theoretic theories of meaning have tended to ignore is precisely the stringing of sentences together over time (or, as in writing, in a sequence which can be recovered over
time), and the consequences this has for the interpretation of each of the individual
sentences in particular discourses or texts. But for Nerbonne the problem of time
in narration is precisely to understand sequentiality; he emphasizes that a narration
is a sequence of sentences whose tenses refer to a temporally ordered sequence of
events.[253]

Thus far, the thinking of such scholars as Kamp, Rohrer, Nerbonne, and Dowty
on discourse is not distant from that of the informal pragmaticists whose work we
have been drawing on and discussing. But a major difference between the two
groups is that the former are against informal approaches. Nerbonne says, ''I take
it that . . . a formal view of things always results in tighter hypotheses and more
exact predictions than accounts of what I would like to call 'an informal pragmatic
sort'.''[254] Accordingly there has been an effort by the scholars mentioned above,
among others, to develop a formal theory which nonetheless captures the facts of
tense and aspect use in discourse while avoiding the problems attendant on truth-
conditional, model-theoretic approaches which ignore it.

In a series of papers (1979, 1981; Kamp and Rohrer, 1983), Kamp was critical
of sentence-bound approaches and developed an alternative theory. The starting
point was his observation that a sequence of sentences is not to be judged true,
simply because each and every sentence in it is separately judged true; the dis-

course imposes a structure, and it is iff this structure models some real-world sequence of events that the truth of the discourse as a whole can be determined.[255]

Consider for example the following sequence:

> Napoleon died. Napoleon addressed his troops under the pyramids. Napoleon was born in Corsica.

In this case each of the sentences is true, but the events took place in the reverse of the order presented. Taken as a "story," there is clearly something untrue about this discourse.

In Kamp's theory, it is the discourse representation structure (DRS), not the individual sentence as such, which is semantically interpreted.[256] As Kamp and Rohrer put it:

> A discourse D with DRS K is true iff it is possible to embed K homomorphically into the real world, i.e. to associate with (in particular) the discourse events of K real events that meet all conditions, including those pertaining to temporal order, which K specifies of the corresponding discourse events.[257]

The DRS is constructed via a set of discourse rules applying pairwise to the sentences of the discourse.[258] Starting with a text containing n sentences in sequence $(S_1, \ldots S_n)$, the first sentence is parsed and its syntactic representation is fed into the discourse representation rules, which yield a discourse representation K_1 for S_1. Then the procedure is repeated for S_2, except that a new representation K_2 is obtained from K_1 and the syntactic parse of S_2. This procedure in turn is repeated, until the discourse representation structure K_n for the text as a whole has been obtained from K_{n-1} and the syntactic parse of S_n.

The point of the DRS is precisely to provide a model of (i.e., information concerning) the temporal relationships holding between the various events (or states of affairs) mentioned in a discourse. Although the procedure is couched in terms of intersentential relations, the DRS essentially concerns events, not the sentences used to express them.

Thus in the case of complex sentences (*when Tom entered the room, Max left it*) or those constructed by conjunction (*Tom entered the room and Max left it*), the construction of the DRS proceeds in the same way, but clausewise,[259] there being no essential difference between the information supplied by each of the individual sentences above and the sequence *Tom entered the room. Max left it*, or between the three-sentenced discourse above about Napoleon and the three-claused sentence *Napoleon died, addressed his troops under the pyramids, and was born in Corsica.*[260]

In the theories of DRS construction of Kamp, Rohrer, and Hinrichs, a special role is assigned to the event.[261] We have seen theories which take intervals of time as basic, and define events as intervals or sets of subintervals; semantic interpretation is relative to an index which includes at least one interval or point of time. We have also seen theories in which events are treated as primitives, that is, as entities in the ontology (i.e., the theory makes mention of events as things), and in which possible histories (sequences of events) may replace possible worlds as indexical elements.

For Kamp there are problems with treating events as constructed from intervals or instants of time rather than the reverse (constructing intervals from events), and he proposes ways in which, following the ideas of Bertrand Russell, Norbert Wiener, and others, this construction of intervals can be done.[262] We are not concerned here with precisely how this is to be done, but for purposes of discussing Kamp's theory, assume that it can be.[263]

Kamp has two arguments that events must be more primitive than times. First, events are vague.[264] We do not know in most cases over what precise intervals of time events occur, nor do we care. We can interpret a statement such as "someone invented the wheel" without knowing precisely when this event occurred. Furthermore, we do not know in principle, even in those cases where some time is specified, where the end points of the event occur, that is, we can specify an event without knowing over precisely what interval it occurs; but the reverse is not true. If events are defined in terms of sets of intervals, then clearly each such interval must be definitely and fully specified.

For example, John's dying may have taken some considerable time, and perhaps he literally expired at, say, 10:28:04 on June 3, 1958. But when did he *begin* dying? Impossible to say. Even if we define the beginning of his dying as the point of onset of whatever caused his death, it is not always possible even in principle to state a definite initial interval, and in practice it is nearly always impossible. Suppose he died of pneumonia. To say that he had terminal pneumonia in June of 1958 does not require that we know precisely when the pneumonia began, only that it began no earlier than the first day of June.

Or again, let us suppose that there was a definite period of time, the Renaissance, and that this period of time came to an end. When did it do so? Again, impossible to say. Even if we suppose that there is a definite period of time reasonably identified as the Renaissance, which began in, say, the thirteenth century and ended in the seventeenth, we cannot say precisely when it started or ended. In general, when we talk of a certain event or a state of affairs which held true over a period of time, or we name a period of time (the Renaissance, the Great Depression, World War II, Sam's fiftieth anniversary party, John's last illness, etc.), we are not aware of, or concerned with, precise initial and final intervals.

The notion of truth at an interval seems doubly misplaced, not only because we cannot specify the interval over which an event takes place or a state of affairs holds true, but also because the time of evaluation must itself be vague.[265] If I say that something is true right now (or at a certain other time), it is vague in regard to what interval of time the claim is made. This is because such times are themselves vaguely defined by events (the speech act, say) or states of affairs (as things are now, as they were then, etc.).

Hinrichs sees the ability to handle vagueness as a great advantage of event-based systems over "traditional," interval-based ones.[266] In an event-based system vagueness creates no problems; events are simply vague. If we need precise intervals, they are constructed out of events. One way of doing this is to consider instants which serve as minimal overlaps (intersections) between events.

Hinrichs notes that Kamp's approach allows one to account for pseudo-instantaneous events such as the sportcaster's "He shoots! He scores!" If an instant is definable naturally as the intersection of a set of pairwise overlapping events (e.g., the last instant of E_1 is the first instant of E_2), and we extend the notion to "the set of events in which all members temporally overlap all the other members," then the instant of which "he shoots!" is true contains only one event and hence fits the extended definition of an instant, since all members of that set of events overlap all the other members.[267]

Kamp's second argument for the primitiveness of events has to do with gaps.[268] We have seen that activities are gappy. If Susan works from 9:00 to 5:00, that does not mean that she literally works every instant in that interval. It might literally be true at, say, 10:15 that she is not working, but on a break. There is some question then as to whether it is true that she worked from 9:00 to 5:00. Clearly it is true in some important sense, but it is not literally true, and thus in an interval-based semantics there is some question as to whether the particular event token of her working can be defined in terms of a definite interval of time.

As Kamp points out, it is difficult, if not impossible, to specify what it means to be doing something "in the strict sense," and equally hard to define an interval *during* which an activity goes on in terms of instants of time during which one is doing something in the "strict" sense. If we take events as primitives and couch our semantics in terms of them, we need not concern ourselves with well-defined intervals.

It may be that both situations (events) *and* intervals will be required. Kamp's theory has been criticized by Vet and Molendijk, who, while agreeing that events are primitives and are not to be constructed from intervals, suggest that it would be much more insightful to "dissociate the event/state and the interval at which it is the case" along the lines of the theory of Bartsch. Consider this example:

> Dis quelque chose! cria-t-elle   à son mari.   Celui-ci
> say some   thing shouted (PRET)-she to her husband this
>
> avait   systématiquement refusé   d'ouvrir   la bouche.
> had (IMPARF) systematically   refuse (PP) of-open (INFIN) the mouth
>
> ' "Say something!" she shouted at her husband, who had systematically refused to open his mouth.'

Vet and Molendijk argue:

> If events are regarded as primitives, it is impossible to determine where [the event expressed by *avait . . . refusé*] might begin or stop, since it is possible . . . that the husband . . . is not speaking yet at the reference point and perhaps this will continue afterwards. The indignation of [the wife] has to be understood as . . . caused by her husband's behaviour . . . during a certain interval which lies before the reference point and which ends before this point. This means we have to take into account the interval here and not the behaviour . . . which may continue beyond the interval (or not).[269]

We saw that Kamp argues that certain temporal phenomena can be understood only in terms of how discourse participants process the information which a discourse provides. The role of tenses Kamp sees as precisely that of serving to indicate how information should be incorporated into representations of text or discourse.[270]

For example, the French *imparfait* and *passé simple* (or, in the colloquial language, the *passé composé*) cannot be distinguished in terms of truth conditions in isolation. *Marie chanta* and *Marie chantait* (both meaning 'Mary sang') are true under precisely the same conditions. For Kamp, as for the informal pragmaticists, the choice of tense depends on the function of the sentence in text.[271]

As we have seen, traditional theories of the difference between the two tenses revolve around contrasts such as these:

passé	*imparfait*
punctual	durative
as if event occurs in an instant	event takes place over time
closed	open
event is a completed whole	event is partial and incomplete
narrative movement	no narrative movement
the story line is advanced	the event is not part of the main story line
exterior	interior
the event is viewed from outside	the event is viewed from within [272]

As we know, each of these theories captures part of the truth, but none is fully adequate in itself to explain the differences between, and account for each of the uses of, the two tenses.

A simple succession of sentences in the *passé*, as in the English simple past tense, serves to indicate a sequence of events whose order is isomorphic to the order of the sentences.[273] That is, ordinarily we interpret a sequence such as

> John got in his car. He drove to town. He ran into an old friend. They had tea together.

as representing a sequence of events in which (1) John got in his car, (2) he drove to town, (3) he ran into an old friend, and (4) they had tea together.

In general, the *imparfait* does not work this way. A sequence in which one of a pair of sentences is in the *imparfait* is generally not thus interpreted; rather, the *imparfait* sentence is seen as overlapping (if not perfectly coinciding) with the other.[274]

In an ordinary narrative a series of events recounted in the simple past (*passé simple* or *composé*), present, or future is understood as representing an ordering of events isomorphic to the series of events.[275] That is, given a sequence of past tense sentences $S_1, S_2, S_3, \ldots, S_n$, the events $e_1, e_2, e_n, \ldots, e_3$ which they respectively recount are understood to be temporarily ordered relative to one another as follows:

Pierre entra.   Marie téléphonait.
Pierre entered (PASSÉ) Marie teleponed (IMPARF)
'Pierre entered. Marie was telephoning'[276]

Here the events depicted are not sequential; it is understood that when Pierre entered (when the event of Pierre's entering occurred), Marie was telephoning (was in a state of telephoning).

In a situation such as this one, the event in the imperfect temporally encompasses that in the simple past, as shown in this diagram:

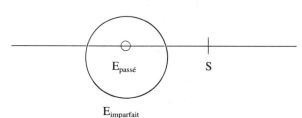

$E_{passé}$ S

$E_{imparfait}$

Here the event in the imperfect constitutes a state which holds at the time of the event reported in the past tense. (Both events precede the time of the speech act, S.)

Similarly to Allen and Smith, Kamp interprets each event as providing the reference point for the next event. For example, in the sequence

> (S1) Napoleon was born in Corsica.
> (S2) Napoleon came to be ruler of the French.
> (S3) Napoleon was defeated by the Allies.
> (S4) Napoleon died in exile.

the event time e_1 of Napoleon's birth (S1) is at some time $R_1 < S$. The past tense of *came* in S_2 represents co-occurrence with some time R which precedes S. But this R cannot be R_1, since R_1 precedes R. (Note that e_2 recounted in S_2 takes place later than e_1, which coincides with R_1.) Thus the past tense of S_2 serves not only to indicate that the event e_2 (Napoleon's coming to be ruler of the French) precedes S (t_0) and corresponds to some R_2, but also that R_2 is later than $R_1(=e_1)$. The same is true with the other sentences in the discourse.

According to Kamp and Rohrer, at each stage in the discourse a particular time or event in the DRS is marked as the reference point. Most often this reference point is transferred to the next event introduced into the discourse representation by a sentence in the *passé simple*.[277] (Recall that the past tense is defined in part by the relationship E = R.)

Accordingly, the successive stages of the representation for the past tense part of a sample narrative text can be schematized as follows, where $e_1, e_2, \ldots$ are the successive events which the successive past tense sentences $S_1, S_2, \ldots$ of the narration refer to; where $R, R_2, \ldots$ are the successive R points for the sentences in the representation; and where S is the speech-act time[278]:

$R_1 = e_1 \qquad R_2 = e_2 \qquad R_3 = e_3 \qquad R_4 = e_4 \qquad\qquad\qquad S$

The *imparfait* works differently, however. The *imparfait* (or the English past progressive, say) does not advance narrative time. Rather than an event being understood as sequential, it is understood as coincidental with a preceding event. With an *imparfait*, the interval of the event or state of affairs *includes* the reference point; further, it does not advance the R point.[279] Thus the representation of a sequence such as *Pierre entra. Marie téléphonait* would be this[280]:

$$R_2 = R_1 = e_1$$

S

e_2

Other tenses which do not advance the R point include the pluperfect and the conditional (future-in-the-past); they differ, however, from the *imparfait* in that they place the new event in (respectively) the past or the future of the R point.[281] Moreover, they can create subsidiary R points. Consider the following text:

Le téléphone sonna.₁   C'était   Madame Dupont à l'appareil.₂ Son
the telephone rang (PASSÉ) it-was (IMPARF) Madame Dupont on the-phone her

mari   avait pris   deux cachets d'aspirine,₃ il avait
husband had taken (PLUPF) two tablets of-aspirin   he had

avalé   sa lotion contre les aigreurs d'estomac,₄ il s'était
swallowed (PLUPF) his syrup against the acidity of-stomach he himself-was

mis   un suppositoire contre la grippe,₅ il avait pris   un
put (PLUPF) a suppository against the flu,   he had taken (PLUPF) a

comprimé à cause de son asthme,₆ il s'était   mis   des gouttes dans
tablet   because of his asthma, he himself-was put (PLUPF) some drops in

le nez,₇ et puis il avait allumé   une cigarette.₈ Et alors il y   avait
the nose, and then he had lit (PLUPF) a cigarette and then it there had

eu   une enorme   explosion.₉ Le docteur réfléchit   un moment;₁₀
had (PLUPF) an enormous explosion the doctor reflected (PASSÉ) a moment;

puis il lui conseilla   d'appeler   les pompiers.₁₁
then he her advised (PASSÉ) of-calling (INFIN) the firemen

'The telephone rang. It was Madame Dupont on the phone. Her husband had taken two aspirin tablets, he had swallowed his stomach ache syrup, he had given himself a suppository for the flu, he had taken a tablet because of his asthma, he had put some drops in his nose, and then he had lit a cigarette. And then there had been an enormous explosion. The doctor reflected a moment; then he suggested that she call the fire department.'

The structure is diagramed in the accompanying illustration.[282]

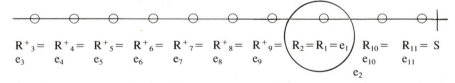

$R^+_3 =$ $R^+_4 =$ $R^+_5 =$ $R^+_6 =$ $R^+_7 =$ $R^+_8 =$ $R^+_9 =$ $R_2 = R_1 = e_1$ $R_{10} =$ $R_{11} = S$
e_3 e_4 e_5 e_6 e_7 e_8 e_9 e_{10} e_{11}
                                                                              e_2

Here the subsidiary R point (R^+) of the pluperfect does advance, within the sequence of events in the pluperfect, but does not advance the R point of the main line of the narrative.

The fact is, however, that the simple tenses do not always transfer the reference point. Compare these texts:

> Tom sat up and got out of bed. He looked for his glasses but couldn't find them.
> Tom sat up because he felt woozy. He didn't feel well at all. He wished he'd stayed asleep.

The first of these recounts four sequential events, whereas the second talks only of one point in time.

The difference between these texts is not due simply to the fact that all but the first of the past tense verbs in the second text recount states of affairs, whereas all the verbs in the first recount actions. Compare:

> Tom jumped up and down. He waggled his arms. He shouted loudly. No one noticed him.

Here we have a series of actions, yet this passage is entirely intelligible (and grammatically correct) under the assumption that all the sentences refer to the same time. Clearly the problem has to do with the Aristotelian classification of verbs. States (*was, felt,* etc.) and activities (*jumped, waggled,* etc.) do not advance narrative time, do not transfer the R point, but accomplishments and achievements do. The last sentences in the two texts below are sequential to the rest of their texts:

> The plane was in a stall; it descended slowly. Everyone on board was worried. It *touched down,* however, with barely a shudder.
> The patient breathed with difficulty. His face was blue, almost gray. The onlookers felt sad. He *died* suddenly but not unexpectedly.

It is well recognized by now and emphasized by recent authors [283] that there is an interaction of aspect, which Smith calls *viewpoint aspect* (and which we might also term "perspective aspect"), [284] with the Aristotelian classification, which Smith calls *situation aspect.* (Recall that the *passé* is perfective and the *imparfait* imperfective in aspect.)

Smith and some others see the Aristotelian classification as a categorization of situation types. [285] Others see them as classifying syntactic categories such as verbs and sentences, [286] though the class of a sentence (clause) or other structure containing a verb does not necessarily bear the same category label as the lexical verb it is built around. Here we have already adopted the policy of indifferently using these terms to refer to either situations or the linguistic structures which model them, and there seems to be no great difficulty with calling both the verb phrase "cross the street" and the event (type or token) of crossing the street "accomplishments."

There occurs in some recent literature an unfortunate terminological innovation, namely the use of the term *Aktionsarten* to refer to the Aristotelian classes. [287] The term *Aktionsarten* is already burdened with myriad uses; it can only be confusing to regard, say, stativity as an *Aktionsart*. In this case, at least, it is also rather odd to see stativity regarded as a "kind of action" (*mode d'action*), given that states are not actions, and statives do not refer to actions.

This use of the term is a complete break with the tradition, which reserves the term *Aktionsart* for either the "viewpoint" aspects (e.g., perfective and imperfective) or such modifications of action as inceptivity, intensity, or durativity. In recent years, as we have seen, there has indeed been a tendency to limit the term to those categories relating to aspectual auxiliary verbs and equivalent morphological markers (e.g., inchoative verbs in Greek and Latin, *begin* in English). *Aktionsart* has always been a term at once vague and ambiguous; it would be unfortunate if it were to follow the fate of *aspect* and become a mere trash-bin category for everything temporal which is neither status, tense, nor mood.

Returning to the Aristotelian classes in narrative, we noted above that a performance (i.e., accomplishment or achievement) moves narrative time forward, but a state or activity does not.[288] If both events are performances, then the events are understood as sequential:

> John entered the president's office (accomplishment).
> The president walked over to him (accomplishment).
>
> John entered the president's office (accomplishment).
> The president woke up (achievement).[289]

If, however, either event is not a performance (i.e., is a state or activity), then the events are understood as cotemporal:

> John entered the president's office (accomplishment).
> The president sat behind a huge desk (state).
>
> John entered the president's office (accomplishment).
> The clock on the wall ticked loudly (activity).

As we have seen, some scholars add further categories (Freed, series with subtypes of this; Smith, habituals and generics)[290]; these too fail to advance the narrative.[291] Generally, these latter types—states, activities, series—overlap with previous events or situations. The texts

> John entered the president's office. John often visited the president.
> John enters the president's office. John generally visits the president about this time every day.

would not be understood to involve a temporal sequence.

As we saw earlier, in our discussion of the progressive, the progressive has the effect of rendering performance quasi-stative, and hence nonsequential.[292] Thus the sequential examples above could be rendered nonsequential by changing simple tenses to the progressive:

> John entered the president's office (accomplishment).
> The president was walking over to him (accomplishment).
>
> John entered the president's office (accomplishment).
> The president was waking up (achievement).

Here the president's walking over to him (or his waking up) coincides with John's entrance (to be more precise, overlaps with it). Generally, nonperformances—states, activities, series, and the like, and non-performances in the progressive—overlap with previous events or situations.

The "constructions rules" for DRS's are designed to capture facts like these. We understand a DRS for some discourse D with n clauses to be an event structure ε_n constructed in part as follows. Hinrichs defines an event structure ε_i as an 8-tuple[293]:

$$\varepsilon_i = \langle E_i, <_i^+, <_i^-, O_i^+, O_i^-, V_i^+, V_i^-, D \rangle.$$

Here

E_i is a set of events.
$<_i^+$ and $<_i^-$ are precedence relations.
O_i^+ and O_i^- are overlap relations.
V_i^+ and V_i^- are interpretation functions.
D is a discourse.

Kamp explains that the relations and functions are paired (with $+$ and $-$ members), because the "information about temporal order that can be derived either from ongoing discourse or from the (limited) accuracy with which our concepts mark the boundaries of the events they determine" is only partial.[294] He goes on to say that we may have only partial information, that e_1 is not completely before e_2: $e_1 O e_2$ may be the case, or $e_2 << e_1$. Similarly, we may know that two events are not simultaneous, without knowing which came first. The way Kamp handles this is to assign each of the relations $<<$ and O both a *negative* and a *positive* extension. For example, the positive extension of $<<$ will contain those pairs $\langle e_1, e_2 \rangle$ such that e_1 definitely precedes e_2; the negative extension will contain the pairs $\langle e_1, e_2 \rangle$ such that e_1 definitely does *not* precede e_2. ("$<<$" is used here instead of Kamp's symbol for complete precedence.)

Returning to our event structure, if some e_j is an event captured in the event structure (e.g., John's reading the newspaper one morning), then $e_j \in E_i$ (it is one of the members of the set of events E_i). If e_j temporally precedes the speech-act time e_s, then $e_j <_i^+ e_s$ is a member of $<_i^+$. (The relation "temporally precedes" includes the pairing $\langle e_j, e_s \rangle$, that is, "e_j temporally precedes e_s".) If e_j and some e_k overlap, then $e_j O_i^+ e_k$ is a member of O_i^+. If an expression ϕ refers to an event e_j, then the interpretation function V_i^+ returns e_j as the value of ϕ, that is, $V_i^+(\phi) = e_j$ (i.e., the expression *John read the newspaper one morning* has the interpretation, refers to, e_j, which is John's reading the newspaper one morning).

Hinrichs offers, following Kamp (1979), an example of a "construction rule" used to fit an event described in the past tense in some sentence S_i into an event structure by constructing, from an event structure into which the events represented by sentences $S_1, \ldots, S_{i-1}$ have been entered, a new one including that one represented in S_i[295]:

If sentence $S_n = \langle \phi, k \rangle$ contains a subexpression $\langle \psi, n \rangle$ with $\psi \in S_p$, and $\langle \psi, n \rangle$ has maximal scope in discourse D, then modify the event structure $\varepsilon_i = \langle E_i, e_s, e_{r'}, <_i^+, <_i^-, O_i^+, O_i^-, \subseteq_i^+, \subseteq_i^+, V_i^+, V_i^-, D \rangle$ in the following way:

(1) add $e_{i+1} \in E_i$,
(2) add $e_{i+1} <_i^+ e_s$,
(3.1) if $\psi \in S_{P \ (ACC \cup ACH)}$, then add $e_{i+1} \subseteq_i^+ e_r$ and $e_{i+2} \in E_i$. Replace e_r by e_{i+2} and add $e_{i+1} <_i^+ e_{i+2}$,
(3.2) if $\psi \in S_{P \ (ACT \cup ST \cup PROG)}$, then add $e_r \subseteq_i^+ e_{i+1}$,
(4) add $e_{i+1} \in V^+(\psi)$,
(5) erase the index n of $\langle \psi, n \rangle$ in D.

Notice that Hinrichs has expanded the event structure by including parameters for the speech-act time e_s and the reference time e_r respectively, and further by including two relations for temporal inclusion, once again in positive and negative versions. (If $e_j \subseteq_i^+ e_k$, then either e_j takes place at the same time as e_k, or the time at which e_j takes place is included in the time at which e_k takes place.)

A nontechnical way of looking at an event structure is to view it as a set of events with temporal relations defined pairwise between them, reflecting the view, stated above, that tenses serve precisely to indicate how information should be incorporated into representations of text or discourse.[296]

The above rule presented by Hinrichs can be understood as follows.[297] Hinrichs explains that clause (1) of the rule introduces a new event e_{i+1} into the set of events E_i of the event structure. Clause (4) defines this e_{i+1} as the value of the positive interpretation function V^+ applied to the syntactic expression y. Clause (2) places e_{i+1} before e_s (the time of the speech act). Clause (3) distinguishes the treatment of the various *Aktionsarten*[298] and the progressive. Hinrichs notes that regardless of which *Aktionsart* is involved, the event e_{i+1} is always linked to the reference point of the discourse. It is this linkage which marks the anaphoric function of the past tense.

Precisely how the past tense event is related to the reference point depends on the Aristotelian class of the event. If it is a performance (accomplishment or achievement), the time of the event is included in the reference point; but nonperformances—activities, states and events in the progressive—act the other way round: the reference point is contained in the time of the event.

Furthermore, performances introduce a new reference point replacing the old one and ordered after it. Clause (3) of the construction rule assures that two consecutive performances in a discourse are always in a temporal sequence, because the two events will be included in two reference points which are themselves sequential. Because nonperformances contain their reference points, they can overlap any other event in the discourse.

Let us see how this rather intimidating rule works by examining an example in detail. Consider the discourse D = *Tom entered the room₁ and sat down₂.*[1] *He was breathing hard₃.*[2] The superscript numbers here index the sentences in D, and the subscript numbers index the clauses. The *if*-clause of the construction rule bids us find a past tense clause ($\psi \in S_P$) of an indexed sentence, which clause has the "maximal scope" in D, that is, is the clause which "takes in" as much of D as possible (is earliest in D); this is clause₁: here, *Tom entered the room*. Then S_n is *Tom entered the room and sat down*, and n = 1 (this is S^1). Here k = 1 and $\phi =$ *Tom entered the room and sat down*. The subexpression ψ is *Tom entered the room* with index n = 1.

Clause (1) of the construction rule tells us to add e_{i+1} to the event structure ε_{i+1}. Since i up to now is 0, i + 1 = 1. We add e_1 to E_1. This adds Tom's entering the room to the structure. Clause (2) states the ordering of e_1 relative to e_s; since we are dealing here with a rule for past tense sentences, e_1 precedes e_s, therefore $e_1 <^+ e_s$ is added to the positive relation $<_1$, that is $<_i^+$, where i = 1. (Below we will write $_i^+$ and $_i^-$, where i is to be understood as whatever value i has at that point.)

Since entering a room is an accomplishment, we look at clause (3.1) of the rule. Here ψ, *Tom entered the room*, is indeed a clause in the past and a performance, that is, $\psi \in S_{P \, (ACC \, \cup \, ACH)}$. Clause (3.1) tells us to add $e_1 \subseteq_i^+ e_r$ to the relation $\subseteq_i^+$ (thereby building into our structure that e_1 is included temporally in the reference time e_r), to add e_2 to E_1 (to build in that there is an event e_2), to replace e_r by e_2 (thereby building in that e_2 has the reference point transferred to it—it is the new reference point, since performances in the past advance the reference time); and to add $e_1<_i^+e_2$ to $<_i^+$ (thereby building in that e_1 precedes e_2).

Clause (4) of the rule tells us that the interpretation of *Tom entered the room* is e_1; that is, $\langle$*Tom entered the room,* $e_1\rangle$ is in V_i^+. Clause (5) tells us to erase the index $n=1$ of *Tom entered the room*$_1$, so that when the next pass of the rule's application occurs, the maximal scope will be that of clause$_2$. We have completed the construction of an event structure ε_i for the position of D up to and including clause$_1$ of the sentence, namely $\varepsilon_{i=1}$, ε_1.

At this point, assuming an initial past r_0, the event structure includes this:

$$e_1 = \text{Tom enter the room}$$
$$r_0<^+s$$
$$e_1<^+s$$
$$e_1<^+r_1$$
$$e_1\subseteq^+r_0$$

We are still operating within sentence $S_{n=1}$, but now we are concerned with the subexpression $\psi = $ *(Tom) sat down*, with index $n=2$, which again is in the past tense (belongs to S_p). Since the index of clause$_1$ of this sentence has been erased, $n=2$ has maximal scope in D. We are bid by clause (1) of the rule to add to the structure $e_{i+1=2}$. By clause (2) we add to $<_i^+$ the pair of $\langle e_2,e_s\rangle$. Now we are once again dealing with a performance, therefore we again apply clause (3.1). We add $e_2\subseteq_i^+e_r$ to $\subseteq_i^+$; e_2 is included in the reference time e_r. Furthermore, we add an e_3 to E_i, and replace e_r by e_3. $e_2<_i^+e_3$ is added to $<_i^+$.

By clause (4) of the construction rule, *(Tom) sat down* is the value of e_2. We now erase the index $n=2$ of *sat down*. At this point, our structure includes this:

$$e_1 = \text{Tom enter the room}$$
$$e_2 = \text{Tom sit down}$$
$$r_0<^+s$$
$$e_1<^+s$$
$$e_2<^+s$$
$$e_1<^+e_2$$
$$e_2<^+r_2$$
$$e_1\subseteq^+r_0$$
$$e_2\subseteq^+r_1$$

On the next pass, we will examine clause$_3$ of the sentence. This time clause (3.2) of the rule comes into play, since we are dealing with a sentential clause in the progressive. No new e_r is introduced; the reference point is not advanced. All that happens is that $e_r\subseteq_i^+e_3$ is introduced into $\subseteq_i^+$; for progressives, the reference time is included in the event time. The event structure ε_3 then includes:

$$e_1 = \text{Tom enter the room}$$
$$e_2 = \text{Tom sit down}$$
$$e_3 = \text{Tom be breathing hard}$$
$$r_0<^+s$$
$$e_1<^+s$$
$$e_2<^+s$$

$$e_3 <^+ s$$
$$e_1 <^+ e_2$$
$$e_1 \subseteq^+ r_0$$
$$e_2 \subseteq^+ r_1$$
$$r_2 \subseteq^+ e_3$$

The event structure ε_3 adequately models what we understand the temporal relations to be within the discourse D. We will not further discuss these technicalities here.

A complete DRS, as regards tense and aspect, is a representation containing a set of situations with temporal relations defined between them. (A generally complete DRS would obviously be far more complex than this, having to refer to every entity referred to in the discourse and every one of their properties or relations.)

n. The Pragmatics of Discourse Tense

So far we have seen that the imperfect never, but the simple past generally (depending on the Aristotelian classes), advances narrative time.

As it happens, there are exceptional cases in which the *imparfait* does indeed serve to "advance the action" or in which the *passé* fails to do so. Based on observations in Hinrichs's unpublished (1981) thesis, Kamp discusses cases such as these:

> Pedro éteignit   la lumière. Maintenant il faisait
> Pedro extinguished (PASSÉ) the light   now   it made (IMPARF)
> absolument noir; les volets étaient   fermés.
> absolutely black the shutters were (IMPARF) shut

> 'Pedro extinguished the light. Now it was completely black; the shutters were closed.'

> Cette année-là vit   plusieurs changements dans la vie de nos héros.
> that year-there saw (PASSÉ) several changes   in the life of our heroes
> Paul épousa   Francine. Jean-Luc partit   pour l'Afrique et
> Paul married (PASSÉ) Francine Jean-Luc left (PASSÉ) for Africa   and
> Pedro s'acheta   un âne.
> Pedro bought (PASSÉ) himself a donkey

> 'That year saw several changes in the lives of our heroes. Paul married Francine. Jean-Luc left for Africa, and Pedro bought himself a donkey.'[299]

Here, in the first example the second verb, although imperfective, *does* serve to advance time (it was dark after Pedro extinguished the light). In the second example the sequence of *passés* does *not* advance time: for all we know, these three events were simultaneous, and if not, we do not know their order.

Such exceptional uses have been commented on by Dry (1978, 1983) and Smith (1983, 1986) as well. The following example, drawn by Smith from Ducrot (1979), is another in which the *imparfait* clearly moves narrative time:

> Idiot que je suis! L'année dernière j'achetais   un appareil de photo
> idiot that I am the-year last   I-bought (IMPARF) a device of photograph

dont   je n'avais   besoin et, cette année, je n'ai   même pas
of which I not-had (IMPARF) need   and this year   I not-have even   nothing
de quoi de me   payer   le cinéma.
of what of myself to pay for the cinema

'What an idiot I am! Last year I bought a camera which I didn't need and this year,
I don't have even enough to pay for a movie.' [300]

The second imperfect here is cotemporal with the first; but both precede the present time indicated by *je n'ai* 'I don't have'. Even if this last were in the past (*passé*), however, narrative movement would occur.

Here are further examples of the *passé* exceptionally being used not to advance the narrative [301]:

Le président a   parlé   à la télévision   hier   soir;
the president has spoken (PASSÉ COMPOSÉ) on the television yesterday evening
et ce matin, il parle toujours.
and this morning, he speaks still

'The president spoke on TV last night and this morning he is still speaking.'

J'ai   embrassée   l'aube   d'été.   Rien   ne
I have kissed (PASSÉ COMPOSÉ) the-dawn of-summer. nothing not
bougeait   encore au   front des   palais. L'eau   était
stirred (IMPARF) yet   at-the front of-the palaces the-water was (IMPARF)
morte. Les camps   d'ombres   ne quittaient   pas la route du   bois. J'ai
dead   the camps of-shadows not left (IMPARF) not the way of-the wood I-have
marché,   reveillant les haleines vives et tièdes, et les
walked (PASSÉ COMPOSÉ) awakening the breaths alive and warm and the
pierreries   regardèrent,   et les ailes se
precious stones looked on (PASSÉ SIMPLE)   and the wings themselves
levèrent   sans   bruit.
lifted (PASSÉ SIMPLE) without sound

'I embraced the summer dawn. Nothing was stirring yet on the façades of the palaces. The water was dead. The camps of shadows in the woodland road had not been struck. I walked, awakening vivid warm breaths, and the precious stones looked up, and wings rose without a sound.' (Rimbaud, ''Aube'') [302]

In the Rimbaud example, there is no reason to believe that the stones looking up or the wings rising take place at any other time than the time when the narrator is walking. Smith regards the use here of ''walked'' as inceptive, as she does the use of ''spoke'' in the first example immediately above, since neither serves to create a temporal sequence of events when conjoined with another past tense or the present, as we would expect. In the first example the activity, which is still continuing, only began in the past, and the normal sense that the *passé* provides of a completed whole is canceled.

Such examples as the ones just cited do not differ in principle from examples in which the Slavic imperfective is used to narrate events or the perfective to describe ongoing situations or states. Given that the English simple past and past progressive tenses resemble the French *passé* and *imparfait* respectively, we are not surprised that parallel exceptional examples can be cited for these English tenses as well.

The question is how to account for such examples. Obviously the best theory would be an explanatory one which did not treat such uses as exceptional, but in which they proceeded from known facts and were predictable in given contexts, as they indeed seem to be.

As we have seen, the central point for Kamp and Hinrichs concerns the role of the reference point. The *passé* serves to shift the reference point, while the *imparfait* does not, but rather indicates a time interval which includes the reference point already established by the discourse.[303] This is why a sequence of sentences in the *passé* models a temporal sequence of events: each event is later than the preceding one, and so the reference point of each sentence is later than the preceding one.

When no reference point is established by context, the *passé* requires an adverbial to establish one (*aujourd'hui maman est morte* 'today Mother died', as in Camus's *L'étranger*), but if one is already established, then it is assumed that the event in the *passé* may serve in itself to establish a new, slightly posterior reference point. The *imparfait*, however, may establish a reference point only through an adverbial. In the Ducrot example above, "last year" (*l'année dernière*) suffices to establish a reference point. (The example is repeated below.)

> Idiot que je suis! L'année dernière j'achetais un appareil de photo dont je n'avais besoin et, cette année, je n'ai même pas de quoi de me payer le cinéma.
>
> 'What an idiot I am! Last year I bought a camera which I didn't need and this year, I don't have even enough to pay for a movie.'

In Kamp's light-extinguishing example, "now" (*maintenant*) serves the same purpose.[304]

How precisely do adverbials enter into temporal determination? As we have seen, based on the classification by Smith (1980), Hinrichs (1986) distinguishes between three types of adverbials, adding a fourth of his own:

1. *Deictic*—may not be bound ("captured") by some discourse-specified time. Defined in terms of speech-act time only (for some speakers, also reference time). Examples: *last week, a week ago, yesterday, now, this moment, in three days, tomorrow.*
2. *Dependent*—must be bound by some discourse-specified time. Defined in terms of that time. Examples: *previously, earlier, (at) the same time, afterwards, later.*
3. *Flexible Anchoring*—may be bounded by some discourse-specified time. Defined in terms of either such a time or speech-act (reference) time. Examples: *on Tuesday, before John left.*
4. *Complete (Independent) Dates*—may not be bound by some discourse-specified time. Defined absolutely, without reference either to discourse context or to the speech act (or reference time). Examples: *in the nineteenth century; in 1875; in January 1965; on March 2nd, 1980.*[305]

Hinrichs observes that any type of temporal expression may be bound and any type may bind, as opposed to the treatment in Partee (1973), which deals only with tenses bound by adverbials (*Sheila had a party last Friday and Sam got drunk*—Sam got drunk *last Friday*) or by conjunctions (*When Susan walked in, Peter left*—Peter left *when* Susan walked in).[306] He offers examples:

tense bound by tense: He took off$_1$ his clothes, went into the bathroom$_2$, took a shower$_3$ and went to bed$_4$. (Here $e_1 < e_2 < e_3 < e_4$ by narrative sequence. Each tense represents an R point sequential to the previous R point.)

temporal adverbial bound by tense: They wheeled me into the operating room$_1$ and put me under sedation$_2$. Three hours later$_3$ I woke up$_4$. (Here $e_1 < e_2$ by narrative sequence. $e_2 < t_3$. e_4 is at t_3. *Three hours later* depends on the time they wheeled the speaker into the operating room.)

temporal adverbial bound by temporal adverbial: This week$_1$ I toured London$_2$. On Thursday$_3$ I saw the Tower$_4$. (e_2 is at t_1. t_3 is in t_1. e_4 is in t_3. *On Thursday* depends on *this week*.)

temporal conjunction bound by temporal adverbial: Last Saturday$_1$ when the State Fair ended$_2$, all hotels in town were booked$_3$. (t_2 included in t_1. e_3 is at t_2. *When the State Fair ended* depends on *last Saturday*.)

temporal conjunction bound by tense: They ordered two Italian salads and a bottle of Frascati$_1$. When the waiter brought the wine$_2$, they noticed$_3$ that they had forgotten their checkbook$_4$. ($e_1 < t_2$ by narrative sequence. e_3 is at t_2. $t_4 < t_3$. *When the waiter brought the wine* is sequential to the time at which the subjects ordered the food and wine.)

temporal conjunction bound by temporal conjunction. When all the cars poured out of the parking lot$_1$ after the concert was over$_2$, a big traffic jam developed$_3$. ($t_1 > t_2$. $t_2 < e_3$. The *when* clause depends on the time of the *after* clause.)

temporal adverbial bound by temporal conjunction: When Melissa left the party$_1$, Bill left$_2$ five minutes later$_3$. ($t_1 < t_3$. e_2 is at t_3. t_3 depends on t_1.)

Hinrichs argues that adverbials as well as tenses enter into the system of event structures, though deictic adverbials and independent dates do not shift the R point. In both

> Tom was in love with Sue. Yesterday he fell in love with Tammy.

and

> Tom was in love with Sue. In June of 1987 he fell in love with Tammy,

the shift of R point between the pairs of sentences is entirely due to narrative sequence. But the other types of frame adverbials do shift the R point. In

> Tom was in love with Sue. Previously he fell in love with Tammy.

and

> Tom was in love with Sue. Before meeting Sue at the mall, he fell in love with Tammy.

the adverbials serve to shift the R point away from (and these cases to a point earlier than) the R point established by the first sentence in each text.

This is why imperfects seem to shift the R point, creating narrative movement, with an accompanying adverbial, but not without such an adverbial: the adverbial shifts the R point. In (i) below, there is no adverbial and hence no narrative movement; in (ii), a deictic adverbial and again no narrative movement; and in (iii), a non-deictic and narrative movement:

> i. John ate dinner. He was unhappy.
> ii. John ate dinner. Yesterday he was unhappy.
> iii. John ate dinner. Soon he was unhappy.

Presumably, non-deictic frame adverbials shift the R point; rules for them must be written into the construction rules for DRS's. One type of adverbial which has generated much controversy is the adverbial subordinate clause. Hinrichs disputes the analysis of *when*-clauses given by Heinämäki (1978) and proposes that *when*-clauses provide a temporal frame, a reference point, which acts as an antecedent for the event in the main clause.[307] If both clauses are performances, they can have any temporal order relative to one another: $e_1 < e_2$, as in *when John wrecked the car, Bill fixed it*; $e_2 < e_1$, as in *when the Smiths threw a party, they invited all their friends;* or $e_1 O e_2$, as in *John built a sailboat when Bill wrote a detective story.* If no more than one is a performance, $e_1 O e_2$: *everybody was away when John destroyed the documents.* *When*-clauses typically move the narrative along, introducing a new R point ordered after the last one in the context.

The construction rule for *when*-clauses which Hinrichs introduces is this[308]:

If $S_n = \langle \psi, k \rangle$ contains a subexpression (*when* ϕ, n) with $\phi \in S_p$, and $\langle when\ \phi, n \rangle$ has maximal scope in discourse D, then modify the event structure ε_i as follows:

(1)   add $e_{i+1} \in E_i$, $e_{i+2} \in E_i$,

(2)   add $e_{i+1} <_i^+ e_s$, $e_{i+2} <_i^+ e_s$, $e_r <_i^+ e_{i+2}$, and replace e_r by e_{i+2},

(3.1) if $\phi \in S_{p(\text{ACC} \cup \text{ACH})}$, add $e_{i+1} \subseteq_i^+ e_{i+2}$,

(3.2) if $\phi \in S_{p\ (\text{ACT} \cup \text{ST} \cup \text{PROG})}$, add $e_{i+2} \subseteq_i e_{i+1}$,

(4) $e_{i+1} \in V^+(\phi)$,

(5)   erase the index n of $\langle when\ \phi,\ n \rangle$ in D.

This operates just like the construction rule we considered above.

We saw that imperfectives typically establish a new R point only with the assistance of an adverbial. But many scholars, including Kemp and Rohrer, have pointed out that imperfectives may establish new R points even in the absence of a (relevant) adverbial, when there is a change of state.[309] By a change of state is meant a transition from one state of affairs to another: from being sick to being well, from not noticing something to noticing it, from it being day to it being night. Consider Hinrichs's (1981) example:

Jean tourna   l'interrupteur. La lumière éclatante l'éblouissait.
Jean flipped (PASSÉ) the-switch   the light   brilliant him-dazzled (IMPARF)
'John flipped the switch. The brilliant light dazzled him.'

Here the imperfect creates a changed state—he was not dazzled (there was not yet any brilliant light), now he is (now that there is a brilliant light). Exceptional cases of sequential imperfects all arguably involve changes of state.

If changes of state allow imperfects to advance the narration, they also allow states and activities to do so. Under similar conditions, Hinrichs finds that even the progressive, whcih normally may not advance the action, may do so, as this example:

Mr. Darby slapped his forehead, then collected himself and opened the door again. The brush man was smiling at him hesitantly.[310]

Here the ''change of state'' is provided by psychological progress; Mr. Darby became aware of the brush man smiling at him after opening the door.

Dry (1978, 1983) offers numerous examples in which stative expressions advance narrative time, when there is an understood change of state. This may be marked, as in the examples below from Dry, by an adverbial:

> She could feel . . . the pressure of Calvin's hand about hers. Without warning . . . she felt a pressure she had never imagined.
>
> Alleyn received a curious impression of dimly lit faces that peered. . . . Suddenly, he felt intolerably oppressed. . . .[311]

Without the indicated adverbials, the stative *felt*s in the second sentence of each example would not be understood as advancing narrative time.

But a change of state need not be explicitly marked. A contrast may be implicit in the context, as in these examples:

> This time she was pushed out of the frightening fifth dimension with a sudden jerk. There she was, herself again, standing with Calvin beside her.
>
> Away in front, the engine whistled. Trees, hills and road, slid sideways and were gone.[312]

In the first example, her "being there" is understood as later than her being pushed out. The adverbs *there* and *again* serve to contrast respectively with an implicit "elsewhere" and a state in which she was not "herself." In conjunction with being pushed out, the picture is one of a resultant state—being there, being herself—consequent on an event, being pushed out. Similarly, in the second case, their being gone is indicated as consequent on their sliding sideways.

Causal relations, often implicit in context, constitute a change of state and allow narrative advance with stative expressions, as in these further examples cited by Dry:

> Then she was enfolded in the great wings of Mrs. Whatsit, and she felt comfort and strength.
>
> . . . though she had looked up [the principal products of Nicaragua] dutifully the night before, now she could remember none of them. The teacher was sarcastic. The rest of the class laughed.[313]

She felt comfort because (and consequently *after*) she was enfolded in the arms of Mrs. Whatsit; the teacher was sarcastic because of (and consequently following) her not being able to remember the products.

We can see the implicit causality in these examples, if we compare them with ones where causality is unlikely, given normal presuppositions about the world:

> Then she was enfolded in the arms of Mrs. Jones, and she felt wet.
>
> . . . though she had looked up the information the night before, now she could remember none of it. The teacher was very tall. The members of the class were even taller.

There are two things to be observed about these two texts. First, the adverbs "then" and "now" serve to establish that these are pseudo-narratives or parts thereof. Though these (partial) discourses strike one as disconnected, since the conjunction of statements within each of them seems pointless—for example, what has her not remembering the information to do with the height of her teacher and the members of the class?—the fact that they are presented as narrative structures invites an interpretation in which causality is read in.

Insofar as we can interpret these at all, the statives are interpreted as advancing narrative time. She felt wet because, not merely when (at the same time), she was enfolded in the arms of Mrs. Jones (perhaps Mrs. Jones is a mermaid fresh from the water); somehow the tallness of the class is consequent on her failure of memory (perhaps her embarrassing failure of memory has induced an abnormal mental state in which she perceives everyone else as physically taller than she is).

Without the *then*, the first example may be interpreted as a non-narrative discourse, a set of disconnected facts. Similarly, without the cues that tell us to interpret the second example as a narrative, we would have to interpret the statives as cotemporal, not sequential. Compare:

> Rocket Roger had a great game. He played very well.
> Rocket Roger had too many lobsters at lunch. He had terrible indigestion.

In the first example, playing very well is plausible grounds for saying that someone had a great game, but having a great game is not reason for playing well. Thus the activity of playing well is not interpreted as sequential to having a great game. But in the second example, having too many lobsters is a plausible cause for indigestion, so that this passage would normally be read with the state of having indigestion sequential to the activity of having too many lobsters. There are other readings, of course, but the point is that this is a possible and normal reading.

While change of state is an intuitively satisfying way of characterizing the exceptional cases of narrative movement, Dry came later to question whether "change of state" was either a sufficient or a necessary condition for exceptional narrative movement. For example, in *At twelve the sky was threatening and at one there was no change* there is an explicit indication that there has been no change of state, yet there is a narrative movement with a sequence of statives (marked by the contrastive adverbial *at one*).[314] This suggests that change of state is not a necessary condition.

Dry came to see change of state as a special case of a more general phenomenon: "those constructions that move time refer to sequenced points, not changes of state."[315] It may be recalled from the discussion above of the Aristotelian aspects that they represent events with different inherent structures—what Dry calls "temporal schemata."[316]

Accomplishments and achievements have culminative, not merely terminal, phases. They make essential reference, that is, to final intervals of time. Since achievements are punctual, they also make essential reference to initial intervals (points) of time. This contrasts with activities and states, which make no essential reference to either initial or final intervals.

Dry characterizes the essential feature of imperfective aspect as being that it makes no reference to the boundary points of a situation, but only its "inside portion" or its extension or repetition (e.g., *John used to build chairs, John builds chairs, every weekend John builds a chair*).[317] The perfective, on the other hand, views a situation as a whole and hence makes reference to its boundary points.

We can see why perfectives such as the simple past normally advance narrative time while imperfectives such as the *imparfait* do not. The past refers implicitly to initial and final intervals. In *John saw Jane and said hello*, there is a last moment of John's seeing Jane and a first moment of his saying hello. They act as boundaries disallowing overlap of the two events. But in *John was looking at Jane and was saying hello*, there is no reference to any initial or final intervals and hence nothing to block overlap.

In the case of the perfective, the Aristotelian classes matter because achievements and accomplishments presuppose boundaries, while states and activities do not. What then of the past tenses of various languages with nonperformances? In fact, such uses are understood to make reference to boundaries. They may be inchoative or terminative or merely complexive. The first two constitute changes of state, while the last implies two changes of state. Consider: *Within a few minutes, the irate geni transported Max all over the world—Max stood in a dusty Afghani bazaar, swam in an Amazonian tributary, clung to a rock atop Mt. McKinley*. Here the series of states are understood as sequential, because the perfectives are complexive and establish boundaries between them.

Dry concludes ''that it is reference to sequenced temporal points which triggers the illusion of time movement; and that the points most often referred to are the initial and final points of situations.''[318] She captures in a single statement the various criteria for both normal and exceptional narrative movement that we have seen—perfective aspect with performances; imperfective aspect with temporal adverbials; or, with a change of state, either imperfective aspect or perfective aspect (with nonperformances). (It remains to account in a general way for nonmovement with performances and the simple past.)

Dry then goes on to identify foreground with the string of sentences in a text or discourse which refer to sequenced points and thereby create a narrative line.[319] The set of foregrounded sentences—the ones which are ''important,'' ''essential,'' and ''propelling''—is identified with that of those sentences which trigger ''the illusion of temporal movement,'' and the identification of what is ''important'' or ''essential'' is seen as determined not by inherent prominence, but by ''quasi-grammatical features such as aspect, temporal schema, and the semantics of temporal connectives.'' If this proved correct, the way would apparently be open to a unified theory of the semantic categorizations aspect, *Aktionsarten,* and Aristotelian aspect, along with pragmatic ones such as that of foreground and background.

A somewhat different view of the pragmatics of narrative movement is that of Dowty (1986).[320] Dowty points out that with performances—accomplishments and achievements—the truth of a sentence at an interval I entails its falsity at any subinterval I' of I; but this requires that it also be false at any superinterval I' containing I, for if it be true at I', then it cannot be true of any subinterval of I', as for instance I itself.

This serves to explain why a sequence of performances must be sequential. For two events e and e' (expressed respectively by a sequence of sentences S and S') to overlap would require that there be a nonempty set of times T during which both S and S' hold. But T is a subinterval not only of the time I during which e occurs, but of the I' during e'. Therefore there can be no T over which both S and S' are true, and hence e and e' cannot overlap.

Now, this clearly is not true with nonperformances, which *can* overlap. But Dowty argues that coincidence is neither asserted nor entailed in such cases, but merely *implicated*. Thus in

> Mary entered the president's office. There was a bound copy of the president's budget on his desk.

nothing indicates that the budget had been there; we infer this. We further infer that it continued to be there for some time after her entrance.

Dowty argues that *all* the Aristotelian classes advance narrative time, but that it is only with certain ones like the statives that it is (Griceanly) *implicated* that the situation held at a time contemporaneous with the reference point already indicated by the context.[321] Consider for example, *John turned off the light. It was completely dark.* For some of the scholars we are considering, it is a change of state which exceptionally allows the stative in the second sentence to indicate a new reference time, that is, to advance narrative time.

But for Dowty, there is nothing exceptional about this. Dowty argues that Aristotelian categories play no direct role in determining sequentiality, and states a *Temporal Discourse Interpretation Principle (TDIP)* as follows:

> Given a sequence of sentences S_1, S_2, . . . , S_n to be interpreted as a narrative discourse, the reference time of each sentence S_i (for i such that $1 < i < n$) is interpreted to be: (a) at a time consistent with the definite time adverbials in S_i, if there are any; (b) otherwise, a time which immediately follows the reference time of the previous sentence S_{i-1}.[322]

That is, no distinction is made between the aspects or the Aristotelian aspects; the TDIP makes no mention of the various classes and locates the reference times of states in the same way as those of performances.[323] Their interpretation, however, is heavily dependent on pragmatics, he says: the inferences we draw about which events or states in a narrative overlap with which others in that narrative do not depend on the times sentences are *asserted* to be true, but rather (in part) on the times at which we *assume* that states actually obtain or events actually occur, intervals of time which in some cases may be greater than the intervals over which they are explicitly asserted.

Hinrichs agrees that pragmatic conditions determine whether states and activities will be interpreted as overlapping or sequential, at least in the case where one of the sentences contains a performance and the other a nonperformance.[324] Hinrichs views this as a case of "vague" ordering. But for Dowty there is no problem: narrative sequences of sentences *always* define a sequential ordering, even with pairs of nonperformances. In the case of the following example:

> Jameson entered the room, shut the door carefully and switched off the light. It was pitch-dark around him because the Venetian blinds were closed.

Hinrichs says that, "due to the nature of the preceding accomplishment, the state of the room's being dark cannot overlap this preceding event but has to follow it." The same kinds of pragmatic conditions would constrain *any* pair of sentences.

Dowty treats even descriptive statives (*the man was tall*) as temporally ordered.

In the case of adverbs, he suggests that these interact with pragmatic conditions. Consider this example:

> John went over the day's perplexing events once more in his mind. Suddenly he was fast asleep.[325]

Here the *suddenly* cancels the pragmatic inference that the state obtained earlier.

The temporal interpretation of sequences of sentences is seen by Dowty as not involving explicit "normal" and exceptional conditions, but rather the simple principle of sequence itself, with the precise relationships implicated rather than asserted. What is literally said in a discourse does not in and of itself suffice to determine the meaning of the discourse as a whole, much less its truth. Therefore the construction of a DRS as a model of a discourse does not suffice, and given adequate pragmatic conditions, it is not necessary, for the interpretation of discourses.[326]

Dowty reads Kamp as requiring that the construction of the DRS be prior to semantic interpretation, but argues that this is impossible, first, because construction of the DRS depends on disambiguation in context of temporal relationships. This depends in part on real-world knowledge and on general pragmatic principles. But Dowty assumes that this is a semantic process of interpretation which must be prior to DRS construction.[327] However, it is not clear that this is semantic in the required sense. Certainly there are various ways Kamp could avoid the paradoxical conclusion.

More important is Dowty's claim that the determination of aspectual classes depends on semantic interpretation.[328] The Aristotelian class relevant to DRS construction cannot be read off from the syntax, since such classification takes place not on the level of the verb or even necessarily on that of the verbal (verb and associated complement) or that of the verb phrase as a whole. *Run* is an activity, *run a mile* is an accomplishment, *is running a mile* is a quasi-stative, *begin running a mile* is an achievement, and *often begin running a mile* is a series; *Tom and Bill ran the mile* could be a (joint) accomplishment or a series of accomplishments.

Nerbonne (1986) presents essentially the same treatment as Dowty with his "Reichenbach's Pragmatics" (RP), similar to Dowty's TDIP,[329] and utilizing pragmatic principles to cancel temporal sequence, as seen in the following clause of the RP principle:

> It is . . . conversationally implicated that, for all S_i, if S_i is atelic (a state or activity), then there is no t such that $t_r(S_{i-1}) < t < t_r(S_i)$.[330]

That is, there is no sequence of R points in such a case. But Nerbonne admits that, as a formal view of narration (we can treat the TDIP or Nerbonne's RP as a definition of narration rather than a characterization of something independent and predefined),[331] the TDIP or RP leaves open too many possibilities for exception.

He concludes by saying that it would be more useful to regard the RP as a "scheme of conversational implicature—i.e. a principle which holds in the absence of contrary indication."[332] To make this work would require, as Nerbonne notes, some account of the differential treatment of atelic and telic expressions.[333]

We turn now to a closer look at some areas which we have not yet discussed, but which play a significant role in a more general understanding of discourse tense and aspect, and hence tense and aspect in general.

o. Perspective

The work we have been discussing only lays the foundations of a general and explanatory theory of discourse tense and aspect, and hence of tense and aspect in general. The theories of Smith, Hinrichs, and Kamp and Rohrer enable us to say a fair amount concerning the establishment and maintenance of R points by events and adverbials, and how events relate to those R points. But they leave a number of questions unanswered.

While we have been considering narratives as single lines, it is clear that actual texts are complex hierarchical structures containing subtexts, and that tense in these subtexts can differ in important ways from tense in the main lines. Partee (1984) sees "simple linear progression" as "just one mode of discourse organization," as a possible value of a "higher-order parameter" which can vary for "different subparts of a discourse." [334]

Although the various scholars discussed above—Kamp and Rohrer, Hinrichs, Dowty, Nerbonne—concerned themselves with discourse and text, they have been criticized for taking structures larger than the sentence insufficiently seriously, as not distinguishing tense in main narrative lines from subsidiary lines,[335] as not recognizing that such notions as that of the R point pertain to the text, *not* to the sentence.[336]

One problem which the work of Kamp and Rohrer fails adequately to address is that of subsidiary R points, as in the case of a sequence in the pluperfect. We have seen that the pluperfect fails to advance the R point, so that in a sequence such as

> Tom felt frustrated. He had forgotten to warn Max of his coming. He decided to call.

we understand the last event to depend on the time of the first one, not on that of the second. But in some sense the pluperfect clearly does affect the R point, as in a long sequence of pluperfects:

> He had gotten up on time that morning, had gotten dressed and had his usual breakfast, had gone to work as usual, had sat down at his desk as he did every day, and would have set right to work, had he not found waiting for him an unexpected summons to the boss's office.

Each event after the first is dependent on the previous one, just like a sequence of simple pasts. This is precisely the situation in which we have seen Kamp and Rohrer refer to "subsidiary R points." [337]

The problem is a much more general one, however, than this suggests. A sequence in a tense such as the pluperfect indicates a shift of *perspective* away from the one that is general in the narrative. Phenomena such as *discours indirect libre* (free indirect discourse) pose a great problem for understanding tense, since in such cases there also is a shift out of the narrative's general perspective.[338] In free indirect discourse and "flashbacks" we find an independent tense acting like a dependent one, as if there were an implicit matrix verb:

> Frédéric eut   envie d'accepter.   Mais comment
> Frederic had (PASSÉ) desire of-accept (INFIN) but   how
>
> expliquerait-il   son séjour définitif   à Nogent? Il n'avait
> would explain (COND)-he his stay   permanent at Nogent   he not-had (IMPARF)
>
> pas un costume convenable; enfin   que   dirait   sa mère? Il
> not a   suit   proper   finally what would say (COND) his mother He
>
> refusa.
> refused (PASSÉ)

'Frederic wished to accept. But how would he explain his staying at Nogent? He didn't have a proper suit; finally what would his mother say? He refused.'

> Marie était   malheureuse. Deux ans   auparavant, lorsqu'elle
> Marie was (IMPARF) unhappy.   two   years before   at the time that-she
>
> avait divorcé   et   vendu sa maison, elle avait cru   que tout
> had   divorced (PLUPF) and sold her house she had   believed (PLUPF) that all
>
> allait   changer.
> was going (IMPARF) to change

'Marie was unhappy. Two years before, at the time when she had gotten divorced and sold her house, she had believed that all was going to change.'

Rohrer points out that while normally *lorsque* would be followed by the *passé antérieur*, not the pluperfect, the latter can occur in flashbacks and free indirect discourse.

Parentheticals and relative clauses are other cases in which there is a shifting of perspective.[339] Historical tenses, and a number of other phenomena we have seen brought out by informal pragmaticists, seem likewise to involve a shift in perspective.

Kamp and Rohrer, in their discussion of the phenomenon of temporal perspective, note that we have a choice as a basic perspective of either speech-act time or some contextually determined time.[340] Consider this passage:

> Kissinger arriva au Caire le 6 juillet. Deux jours après, il partit pour Jérusalem.
> 'Kissinger arrived in Cairo on July 6; two days after, he left for Jerusalem.'

The *passé simple* forms *arriva* and *partit* present each of these events as "a separate unit seen from a later vantage point," that of the present (ST). Now consider these examples:

> Kissinger arriva au Caire le 6 juillet. Il
> {partait   } pour Jérusalem deux jours après.
> {allait partir}
>
> 'Kissinger arrived in Cairo on July 6; he
> {was leaving   } for Jerusalem two days after.'
> {was going to leave}

Here "the perspective shifts towards the reference point of the last sentence in the [*passé simple*]."

Kamp and Rohrer contrast these passages:

à ce moment il n'y avait plus que 25 personnes dans la salle
'at this moment there were no more than 25 people in the room'

maintenant il n'y avait plus que 25 personnes dans la salle
'now there were no more than 25 people in the room'

The first of these takes the speech-act time as perspective; the second takes as perspective a past time established in context.

What flashbacks and free indirect discourse generally involve is a shift from the perspective of the speaker to that of the subject or other protagonist.[341] Kamp and Rohrer point out the shift in perspective in the last sentences of this example from Flaubert's *Education sentimentale*:

Jamais Frédéric n'avait été plus loin du mariage. D'ailleurs,
never Frederic not-had been (PLUPF) more far from-the marriage besides,

Mlle Roque lui semblait une petite personne assez ridicule.
Mlle. Roque to-him seemed (IMPARF) a little person enough ridiculous

Quelle différence avec une femme comme Mme Dambreuse! Un bien autre avenir
what difference with a woman like Mme. Dambreuse a well other future

lui était réservé! Il en avait la certitude aujourd'hui.
to-him was (IMPARF) reserved he of-it had (IMPARF) the certainty today

'Frederic had never been further from marriage. Moreover, Mlle. Roque seemed to him a sufficiently ridiculous little person. What a difference with a woman like Mme. Dambreuse! Quite another future was reserved for him! He was certain of it today.'

In such cases Kamp and Rohrer refer to the *personal perspective*. They admit that there are a number of unanswered problems in connection with the notion, though, such as how we know who the relevant protagonist is in each case, or what the perspective is at any given point.

We have already commented on the shifting perspectives in the present work. Treating one of the cited sources as a document extant here and now, we say, for example, "Aristotle *says* . . ."; but looking at it in a historical perspective, we may say, "Aristotle *said* . . . or, from the perspective of a later work, "Aristotle *had said* . . ."

What all these sundry phenomena have in common is that the reference point is not where it "normally" is. Consider the case of the historical tenses: *Napoleon stands beneath the pyramids.* We have gone from the R<S of the narrative past to the R = S of the historical present. In the case of the "presumptive future" (*you will be Max's friend*), we have gone from the present (R = S) to the future (R>S).

SOT phenomena were treated by Jespersen, Reichenbach, and others as involving a shift in the R point. The independent *the earth is round* is present (R = S); embedded under a past tense, it becomes past: (Aristotle knew that) *the earth was round* (R<S). Such phenomena as free indirect discourse involve a similar shift of R, although to a contextually determined time rather than to a matrix time.

The problem of subsidiary and shifted R points is just a special aspect of the general problem of the R point. Much recent work on temporal reference—notably that of Lo Cascio and his coworkers[342]—may be seen as attempts to elaborate, and to extend to suprasentential units, the principles enunciated by Smith, in light of the theory of discourse representation of Kamp and Rohrer and/or the binding by antecedents of temporal anaphora as explored by Partee (1973, 1984).

The results to date have not provided a general and explanatory theory. The principles stated in these various works[343] are complex, partial, exception-ridden, and far from explanatory, but they do introduce a number of useful concepts.

What this research makes clear is that the issue of the R point really comprises three separate issues. First, how are R points established? In particular, how is the initial R point in a text determined? Second, what determines whether and how the R point is maintained (or changed) in the course of a narrative? Rigter (1986) contrasts "horizontal" and "vertical" relations in the text. The R point depends in part on the "horizontal" movement of the narrative, as the R point advances or fails to advance. It also depends on the "vertical" movement into and out of subdomains which may share the matrix R point, or depend on points elsewhere in the text, or establish R points of their own. Third, for any given tense marker (or adverbial), how is it determined to what time its R point is oriented or anchored?

For the most part we have been concerned here with cases where evaluation is to S and there is a contextually given R point. But evaluation is not always at S, as Smith's Orientation Principle shows. In fact, a tense marker may potentially refer back to a great number of different points. Consider this example:

> Paolo ha detto alle 5.05 che alle 2 in punto l'ingegnere è uscito di casa. Un'ora dopo è stato ritrovato morto nella sua macchina.
>
> 'Paolo said at 5:05 p.m. that at two o'clock sharp the engineer went out. An hour later (*un hora dopo*) he was found dead in his car.'[344]

If "he" in the second sentence is the engineer, there are two possible times that he could have been found dead—at 3:00 or at 6:05, though the former is the preferred reading, because the coherence of the sequence seems to come from Paolo's reporting both facts. If it comes from the engineer's death being in some way connected with, or even caused by, Paolo's statement, the preferred reading would be the latter one. It all depends on which R point—the one established by the *passato* form *ha detto* or that established by *è uscito*—serves as the R point for *è stato ritrovato*.

If the adverbial had been "an hour earlier," it would be obvious that it was the engineer who was found dead, and that he was found an hour before 5:05 p.m., not at 3:00. Without any adverbial (*he was found dead in his car*), the sequence seems of dubious coherence; it is not clear when the person was found, or who he was. It is even possible that some third person is intended, whereas with the adverbial such a reading, while possible, is highly unlikely. (We would need a much wider chunk of text to tell.) Which R point the adverbial *an hour later* and the *passato prossimo* tense of the second sentence both depend on can only be determined in context and in light of our real-world knowledge. The question is how this is done.

Even with this possibility of multiple R points, there would be only a relatively simple problem if any tense at all or just any adverbial could serve as an antecedent, if not necessarily *the* antecedent, of another tense or adverbial. But only certain tenses or adverbials establish R points, and among those which do, only some can serve as antecedents for some other given indicator in the text. So we can speak of the problems of the establishment and maintenance of R points on the one hand, and the binding or orientation of R points on the other.

Rigter has objected to the term "R point" and prefers the term "focal episode" or *focus*.[345] He speaks of "focal *episode*" rather than "reference *point*," because the reference "point" is in fact an "episode" (event or situation) over an interval. The term *focus* is drawn from the observation by Kamp and Rohrer[346] that in cases such as Hinrich's (1981) example

> Jean tourna l'interrupteur. La lumière éclatante l'éblouissait.
> 'Jean turned the switch. The brilliant light dazzled him.'

the second sentence can be interpreted as referring to a time period immediately following that referred to by the first, because the first is understood to imply a change of state, a new situation temporally following that event.

In such cases it seems possible to focus, without any further explicit indication, on the subsequent period, that is, to understand that period, and not the event which initiates it, as the new reference point. Kamp and Rohrer view this as an inchoative use of the *passé,* in which it brings about a state. But such a "focal period" is *in* neither the text nor the context, but is merely inferred; it would accordingly be odd to say that it is "referred to" in the text.

The initial R point of a text depends on the speech-act situation, but is not automatically given by it. The speaker may choose various perspectives. Bull says that relative to a point of observation, events can be experienced, recalled, anticipated, or contemplated only "on a high level of abstraction."[347] The experience, recall, and anticipation of events roughly correspond, respectively, to a reference time simultaneous with, previous to, or posterior to ST. The abstraction contemplation corresponds to a "timeless" truth such as *two and two are four*.

Coseriu similarly distinguishes the " 'perspectives' that correspond to the position of the speaker with respect to the verbal action." The action talked of can "proceed parallel to [the speaker] and include the time point of the speech act, or as well, from the point of view of the speaker, can be anterior ('retrospective perspective') or posterior ('prospective perspective')."[348]

This should not suggest, however, that such differentiation is an objective given, supplied by ST. In discourse a particular event can be reported in virtually any tense. It is up to the speaker to choose the perspective. In recent work, as we have seen, pragmatic conditions (as yet poorly delineated) have been seen as central to the choice of perspective, whether global to the text (thereby establishing the initial RT) or pertaining to a subdomain (subtext).

Most scholars have wrongly assumed that tense has to do with a unique S point given by the speech-act situation. Phenomena such as the Latin epistolary tenses and "Cavett's Problem," discussed earlier, call this assumption into question. In ordinary verbal (or manual) discourse the time of the speech act (the time of the "enunciation"), the time of the reception of the message by the hearer, and the time of evaluation (or orientation) generally coincide. But it is questionable whether this is true of either writing or mechanically recorded speech (or manual signing), in which the time of reception or decoding (t_{decod}) differs from the time of enunciation (t_{enun}).

Further, the evaluation or orientation time (t_{eval}) may not necessarily coincide with either t_{decod} or t_{enun}. Often enough the t_{enun} is irrelevant to evaluation; when we read a sign saying "No Smoking," we don't care when it was written or printed or posted. Nor is t_{decod} always relevant either. The historical present, for example, is not *false* for the event's not coinciding with t_{decod} (nor with t_{enun}). To understand Cavett's Problem, certainly, we need at least the three points in time, t_{decod}, t_{enun}, and t_{eval}.[349]

Nor is S always appropriate as an evaluation time when, as the discourse is spoken or the text is written, the t_{enun} advances: it takes time to write or say something.[350] But this does not necessarily imply any corresponding movement in the time of evaluation, and most written texts are interpreted without regard to the fact that t_{enun} is not constant throughout. (Nor is t_{decod} either constant or necessarily relevant, of course. The interpretation of speech in a tape recording does not depend on when, or in what order, parts of the tape are listened to.)

In texts, the initial R point is generally established by S, but not always. Let us use Lo Cascio's term *GPT = Given Primary Time* for the orientation of the text as a whole.[351] This time has the greatest scope in a text; it is to it that all other tenses in the text or discourse ultimately relate.

There is, unfortunately, a certain ambiguity in the way "text" and "discourse" have been used. Clearly if we mean by "text" (or "discourse") a single document (or stretch of speech), then it is not true that such a text *always* has a single GPT with greater scope than all of its tenses and temporal adverbials. But "text" ("discourse") has also been used precisely for a document (unit of speech) of which this is indeed true, and a constant GPT would seem to be the defining characteristic of at least certain types of text.[352]

It is not precisely correct to say that the GPT is automatically given by S. Lo Cascio in fact distinguishes four kinds of GPT.[353] GPT may coincide with t_{enun}, in which case he calls it GPTE. A text beginning without any adverbial (e.g., Rider Haggard's *it is a curious thing that at my age . . . . I should find myself taking up a pen to try to write a history. I wonder what sort of history it will be when I have finished it. . . .*) can have only such a GPTE. In the absence of any specific localization in time, the GPT (and hence the initial R) is simply t_{enun}.

Another possibility is a GPTD based on the t_{decod}. A text beginning *You have already read a good thirty pages and you begin to take to the story* can have only such a GPTD. Here it is the reference to the reader and the act of reading that requires that the GPT and the initial R equal t_{decod}. The choice of GPT is thus sensitive to pragmatics, though nothing very general can as yet be said concerning this point.

If there is a chronological indicator, the initial R is fixed relative to GPT (whether this be t_{decod} or t_{enun}) but is localized by the indicator. *He arrived in Paris in 1914* establishes the initial reference time ("GPTC") as that of the indicator (*in 1914*). Without a chronological indicator we must assume a "neutral," unlocalized GPTN:

when he arrived in Paris he was twenty establishes R as the time of his arrival in Paris.

In the absence of an explicit indicator of any kind, as in the well-known beginning of Wolfgang Borchert's story *Die drei dunklen Könige*, we must simply infer some point in time as GPTN[354]:

Er tappte durch die dunkle Vorstadt. Die Häuser standen abgebrochen gegen den Himmel. Der Mond fehlte und das Pflaster war erschrocken über den späten Schritt.

'He tottered through the dark suburb. The houses stood broken up against the sky. There was no moon and the pavement was shocked at the late step.'

The nature of the GPT depends on the tense used, on any localizer (expression locating E) present, and on the pragmatics of the text. The present perfects of colloquial French, German, and Italian require such pragmatics, since they are polysemous. If the first main clause in an account is in the present perfect, and there is no further time indicator, we need to draw on real-world knowledge to infer whether the GPT is a GPTE or a GPTN, and sometimes the further context is required to disambiguate. The same is true in those American English dialects in which the past tense may equate to the British present perfect. (Cf. *I went to Europe. I don't need to go there again.*)

In subsidiary "domains" such as a sequence in the pluperfect, the GPT plays only an indirect role. Each such subdomain has its own secondary GST. The events directly bound by the GPT form part of the main sequence in the narrative, Lo Cascio's "Main Set" (MS). Those dependent on a GST form a "minor set" (mS). A minor set may have further subsidiary minor sets.[355] (We will delineate below the text grammar which is central to Lo Cascio's theory.)

GPT and GST correspond to Rigter's notion of the "present of the discourse domain," which in turn is to some extent a generalization of Smith's Orientation Time and Rohrer's Temporal Perspective Point.[356]

The principles of R-point maintenance and change in subsidiary domains seem not to differ, in general, depending on whether syntactic dependence is involved or not. The pair of sequences below are for the most part semantically equivalent:

Sam thought that Martha drove well and he would have wanted her to operate his tractor-trailer for him, but he didn't think her working for him would be a good idea.

Sam thought that Martha drove well. He would have wanted her to operate his tractor-trailer for him. But he didn't think her working for him would be a good idea.

We have seen that, for sentences with complements, Smith (1978, 1981) proposed two principles. By the Sharing Principle, the complement could *share* the R point of the matrix verb, having no R of its own; any adverbial in the complement locates E but does not establish R[357]:

They told us	that Tom had arrived
yesterday	three days earlier.
E⊂yesterday = R<S	E⊂three days earlier<R

By the Orientation Principle, the complement does establish its own RT, and the adverbial serves to establish it; but the RT of the matrix clause, not ST, is the anchor for the adverbial and the orientation of the tense[358]:

The investigator will insist next month	that he talked to the suspects three weeks earlier.
E$\subset$next month $= R_1 > S$	E$\subset$three weeks earlier $= R_2 < R$

In certain cases both these prinicples can apply.

Smith also discusses cases in which the complement has a different tense from that of the matrix; these require the Extended Sharing Principle.[359] In cases such as *the prosecuting attorney claims that the nurse was tired now*, the complement requires some contextually given RT other than the matrix.

Smith argues that a reference time is established by a combination of tense and adverbial, not by tense alone.[360] The complement may or may not have its own RT. In the case of complements and matrix clauses, what matters is not the order of the clauses but the relation of c-command. A tense-adverbial pair (temporal expression, TE) x can only anchor another, y, if x c-commands y.[361] This is because of scope relations; the antecedent must not be in a lower domain than the anaphor. In (a) and (b) below the italicized, c-commanding TE anchors the other; in (c) and (d) the italicized, c-commanded TE does not.

a. The secretary *will announce on Tuesday* that he resigns in three days.
b. That the secretary resigns in three days *will be announced on Tuesday*.
c. That the secretary *resigns on Tuesday* is being announced in three days.
d. The secretary announces in three days that he *will resign on Tuesday*.

Smith points out that these relationships hold between sentences as well as within them, but she does not discuss this in detail. It is precisely the goal of Lo Cascio and his associates to apply Smith's insights to suprasentential structures, in line with their view that RT is a notion belonging to text, not to the sentence alone. For a number of reasons, their work is not conducted within a model utilizing discourse representation structures. In fact, they give no explicit formal rules of semantic interpretation, and it is not clear how they intend the informal rules they do give.

Smith argued that not every combination of tense and adverbial can establish an RT, and shows that the following combinations do:

> Present tense + Present adverbial = Present RT
> Present tense + Future adverbial = Future RT
> Present tense + Past adverbial = Past RT [Historical Present]
> Past tense + Past adverbial = Past RT[362]

A rather different view is held by Lo Cascio, who distinguishes the discourse role of tenses from that of adverbs. It is events alone which serve as RT's for later events.[363] The role of tense is to indicate relations to the evaluation time (which may be ST or some other time), and to structure the discourse: "Tenses express a temporal relation only with respect to temporal entities, functioning as evaluation times, which belong to a higher position in the (syntactic and semantic) hierarchy."[364] Adverbials function principally to localize events absolutely and relatively in time.[365]

We must restrict both tenses and adverbials further. To understand either the establishment of R points (or the anchoring of discourse elements), it is necessary to make a fundamental distinction between those tenses (and those adverbials) which can establish an RT and those which cannot. This distinction, albeit in another context, was possibly already noted in ancient times and, as we saw in part I, played an important part in certain traditional grammatical theories under the rubric of *definite* and *indefinite tenses,* though what was meant by this changed over time.

While there is some disagreement about how to classify the various tenses, we may say at least that the modern European tenses generally fall into two groups, the simple tenses in one, and the complex tenses in the other. Most of the simple tenses are "absolute," with E equal to R, while most of the complex ones are "relational," with E equal to some other time (in the perfects, E precedes R). The *passé composé* is in the first group when it is a past tense (like the Latin aoristic perfect), and in the second when it is a true present perfect (like the Latin primary perfect).

The imperfect to a limited extent (i.e., under certain conditions) acts like a group I tense (as classified below), but is generally in group II. The *passé antérieur* is difficult to place, since it has properties in common with both groups. It apparently advances the R point in narrative, for example. But it occurs in main clauses only under special circumstances. Leaving it (and the conditionals) aside, the tenses may be classified as follows:

I	II
present	present perfect, *passé composé*
simple past, *passé composé*	pluperfect
future	future perfect
(imperfect)	imperfect

The group I tenses are "definite," and the group II "indefinite," though it is hard to say precisely what we mean by this. Intuitively, a definite tense may (or may not) pick out a time, whereas an indefinite one cannot. As Partee (1973) pointed out, *I didn't turn the stove off* means the speaker didn't turn the stove off at a certain time, not never at all, whereas something like *I haven't been to Europe* means 'I have never been to Europe'.

But we have seen that the past has indefinite uses (*Julius Caesar didn't get to taste ice cream*). And Lo Cascio (1986) groups the present perfect with the definite group because, in one reading at least, it can denominate a definite point. Thus *I haven't been to Europe* can mean 'right now', as opposed to 'ever'. A more precise characterization is required.

The classification presented by Lo Cascio is as follows:

I	II
present	
present perfect	pluperfect
past	*passé antérieur*
future	future perfect
imperfect	imperfect
conditional	conditional perfect[366]

Houweling (who omits the conditionals from his list, and places the imperfect only in II) distinguishes tenses as "autonomous" (I) and "non-autonomous" (II),[367] identifying the former as perfective—tenses which generally move the R point—and the latter as imperfective—tenses which do so only under certain special conditions.[368] Autonomous tenses are those, he says, which can "realize a complete communication" in their own right, and have to do with the ability of the tense to stand on its own out of context.

This distinction, like that of definiteness, is difficult to define precisely, and is highly conditioned. Houweling finds the Italian present progressive (*mi sto facendo la barba* 'I am shaving') odd in an "autonomous" sentence, but notes that the same tense in a question (*che cosa stai facendo?* 'what are you doing?') is fully acceptable.

The distinction of the groups has also been viewed (by Lo Cascio, for example) as one of *deictic* tenses (I), which refer to the GPT and so maintain the narrative line, as opposed to *anaphoric* tenses (II), which do not.[369] (This is not a very felicitous terminology, as "deictic" tenses may be used anaphorically, though the "anaphoric" tenses may not be used deictically.)

Rigter speaks of *domain* tenses, which create a focus relative to the "present" (GPT or GST) of the same domain, and *domain-shift* tenses, which do not relate to chronological ordering *within* a subdomain, and create a focus outside it.[370] In the sequence

> Tom predicted that they would start the car, would get in, but would not go anywhere.

the conditionals are conditionals in relation to the past tense of *predicted*, and not because a conditional is required *within* the scope of *predict*. The conditional perfect relates to the conditional much as the other perfects relate to their corresponding simple tenses. But the conditional is not a *deictic* tense.

This distinction of deictic and anaphoric applied to tenses may be applied as well to adverbials. We may speak of "deictic" adverbials linked to ST (I) and "anaphoric" ones linked to some other time (II):

I	II
today	earlier
tomorrow	before that
yesterday	then
now	the following Tuesday

Again, the terminology is unfortunate, since "deictic" adverbials may be used anaphorically (as in *he was now a famous man, today he was going to return home—or so he intended*), though the reverse is not possible.

Chronological adverbials are a special case, in that they take their reference neither from the GPT or GST nor from some earlier R point, but absolutely, limited only by the framework defining them. Compare:

> She left the next day.
> She left yesterday.
> She left at noon on June 3, 1848.

In the first case, *the next day* is anaphoric and linked to the time of her leaving. *Yesterday*, however, is understood in relation to the present—it denotes the day before the ST. Finally, *at noon on June 3, 1848* is relative neither to the time of her leaving nor to the ST, but only to a certain system of clock and calendar time.

Adverbs of frequency and duration[371] do not as such situate events or states at all, and so they can serve as frame adverbials only when there is an implicit time reference. Consider the following examples:

> For a week $\left.\right\}$ she inspected plants.
> All during June $\left.\right\}$
> Every few weeks $\left.\right\}$ she would inspect a plant.
> Once a month $\left.\right\}$

They seem out of context. To interpret them requires an implicit, presupposed time reference, such as "for a week *during that time*."

In Lo Cascio's theory, binding of one temporal element by another depends strongly on text structure; the text grammar he develops is the most sophisticated one used to date in a theory of tense. He constructs a strongly hierarchical grammar for texts as follows.[372] While a single narrative line is possible in a "text," it is not necessary. Hence the global text is a set $\overline{T}$ (read "T-bar") of texts. Each such text $\overline{T}$ is a *main set* (MS) of events, with its own GPT; coherence of the text is indicated by maintenance of this GPT.

The main set consists of one or more *main units* (Mu). Each of these has an initial time of its own, established by a clause with a deictic tense marker (T_d). A main unit consists of such a T_d plus one or more *minor sets* (mS).[373] Each minor set in turn consists of one or more *minor units* (mu); each such minor unit has a clause with an anaphoric tense indicator (T_a) plus one or more minor sets. There is no limit thus to the complexity of a text. These rules are presented in the form of a context-free phrase-structure grammar[374]:

$$\overline{T} \rightarrow T_1 \pm T_2 \pm T_n$$
$$T \rightarrow GPT + MS$$
$$MS \rightarrow Mu_1 \pm Mu_2 \pm Mu_3 \pm Mu_n$$
$$Mu \rightarrow T_d \pm mS_1 \pm mS_2 \pm mS_n$$
$$MS \rightarrow mu_1 \pm mu_2 \pm mu_n$$
$$mu \rightarrow T_a \pm mS_1 \pm mS_2 \pm mS_n$$

Real texts and discourses are considerably more complex than these rules suggest. Conjunction, subordination, and sequencing may provide neatly hierarchical structures, but relative clauses and parentheticals demand a third dimension, as they are not strictly within the domain they appear to be in. Neither Lo Cascio nor anyone else has had anything very systematic to say about the functioning in discourse of the tenses of such structures.

The relationship of a tense marker to the GPT and GST depends not only on the nature of the tense itself but on its place in this hierarchy of textual structures. That is, it is in principle impossible to properly understand the use of a tense marker without knowing its place in the discourse or text, and no theory which does not take this into account will be adequate.[375]

A shift of temporal perspective marks a shift into a minor set. Among the grammatical devices which govern such a shift are world-creating verbs.[376] We have seen how SOT rules may fail under certain pragmatic conditions. Both versions of the following example are possible, depending on pragmatic conditions:

$$\text{Aristotle knew that the earth} \begin{Bmatrix} \text{was} \\ \text{is} \end{Bmatrix} \text{flat.}$$

With a past tense *was*, the complement is situated in the world of Aristotle's beliefs and since he is in the past, a belief about the contemporary state of his world must likewise be in the past: the perspective is a past one; we are concerned with the past GST (R for *was* is the event time of the matrix clause, in accord with Smith's Sharing Principle). But with the present *is*, the complement clause is situated in the world of the speaker's beliefs; the perspective is a present one, the orientation is directly to ST (t_{enun}). (Recall that the R point may be ST or some other time. In *you have read here that Aristotle already knew that verbs belong to different aspectual classes*, reference must be to t_{decod}, not $_{enun}$.)

Similarly, the difference between

$$\text{John} \begin{Bmatrix} \text{had left} \\ \text{left} \end{Bmatrix} \text{before midday.}$$

depends on whether his leaving is being related to the current narrative line, or shifted to the speaker's perspective.

The question of how a perspective is maintained or changed during the course of a text or discourse is not different in principle from that of how the initial GPT is chosen. R points can be established or changed only in relation to a given point of orientation, be it GST or GPT.

Perspectives and changes in perspective are closely linked to discourse structure. The main set is marked by deictic relations, that is, by states of affairs directly tied to the GPT.[377] Those which are directly tied to a GST and form subsidiary lines (minor sets) bear an anaphoric relation to some other point—the GST. One function of tenses is to distinguish the main line from those of subsidiary domains, and hence to structure the text.[378]

p. Orientation

In the main set a tense is deictic and forms part of the main textual line; it is bound by an immediately adjacent deictic tense. Lo Cascio states:

Binding Rules for the Main set
   In order to belong to the Main set a clause marked by a deictic tense (T_d) is time-bound by the immediately preceding (or, albeit rarely, following) deictic tense controlled by the same [GPT] and generally provided that the antecedent is not in a (syntactically) subordinate clause.[379]

He restates this later in purely configurational terms:

Temporal relation at the Main set level
   If y is a Main unit *Mu* and thus a unit marked by a deictic tense, then x can be the antecedent of y if x is a Main unit *Mu*, thus a unit also marked by a deictic tense, and x governs y and there is no other governing category between x and y.[380]

Government is essentially immediate c-command: the governing element is one level up from the governed element. The condition that there be no other intervening governing category is the *adjacency* condition, which says that it is the adjacent deictic tense which matters for a particular deictic tense.

The main set consists of a set of main units each with a deictic tense. So long as we do not enter into a subdomain, the (deictic) tense serves as part of the skeleton of the narrative, like a bead on a string. Each deictic is bound by the previous one. If there is a shift from past to future, say, reflecting a shift from RT<ST to RT>ST, then we are in a different subtext of the global text.

This is what Adelaar and Lo Cascio mean by saying that the main set rule seems to be appropriate only for those narrative texts in which the deictic tenses form a sequence of the same type (e.g., are all past tenses, or all future tenses— tenses which place all the events in the same "sector"),[381] texts in which the temporal relations of states of affairs all belong to the same temporal sector.[382]

But they question whether tenses advance the R point at all, noting that a deictic tense should not express any temporal relation relative to a preceding state of affairs, but only to the GPT.[383] If so, the movement in a narrative text can be given only by connective temporal adverbs or our knowledge of the world.

They offer this example:

Paolo *è venuto* a trovarci e ci *ha raccontato* dell'incendio. *È andato* a trovare anche Maria.
'Paolo *came* to see us and *told* us about the fire. He *went* to see Mary.'

(The italicized verbs are all in the *passato prossimo*.) Here the second sentence does not depend on the first, but only on the GPT. Only if an adverbial makes explicit a sequence (*and then he went to see Mary*), or our real-world knowledge combined with pragmatic principles leads us to infer an ordering (*because of what we said, he went to see Mary*), is a sequence established.

They insist that we distinguish the *relation* of the reference point to the point of orientation or evaluation (e.g., R<S, R = S, R>S) from the *location* of the R point: only an adverbial can explicitly establish the location, otherwise the location is only inferable, and tenses do not in themselves locate them at all.[384] (This is presumably why, not separating the two notions, Smith sees R as generally established by the combination of tense and adverbial.) If they are correct, then movement (what they call "direction")[385] of the R point is entirely pragmatic. The reason bounded situations advance the R point and unbounded ones do not is purely pragmatic, and narrative movement is not part of the semantics of the tenses.

Anaphoric tenses do not form part of the main set, but an anaphoric tense (T_a) is part of a minor unit of a minor set. Furthermore, unlike independent (true) deictics, they may take their reference from another anaphoric tense. Deictic tenses can of course appear in subordinate clauses, but Lo Cascio and his colleagues deny that such tenses are truly in a subsidiary domain, and speak of "false deictics", as in:

Domani Maria *andrà* al cinema con Paolo, ma non *vuole*. Dopodomani lei *dirà* a sua madre che (il giorno prima) *è andata* al cinema da sola.

'Tomorrow Mary *will go* to the movie with Paul, but she [her mother] *does* not *agree*. The day after tomorrow Mary *will tell* her mother that (the day before) she *went* [*passato prossimo*] to the movie alone.' [386]

But they state that it would be too strong to say that deictic tenses in subordinate structures are all really anaphoric, since the future at least retains its deictic value in examples such as *Paolo* ha detto *che Gianni* verrà a trovarlo. '*Paul* said (*passato prossimo*) *that John* will come *to see him*'. These cases are similar to those handled by Smith's Orientation Principle.

Lo Cascio accounts for cases of dependent deictics in what are apparently independent clauses by saying that "the surface structure of an independent sentence" hides "the true nature of a clause which should also function as a dependent clause." [387] The case in question is this:

Paolo *ha detto* a me (due giorni fa) che Gianni gli *aveva*/*ha telefonato* (la mattina alle 5). Un'ora dopo si *è sentito* male.

'Paul *said* [*passato prossimo*] to me (two days ago) that John *had called* [PLUFP]/ *called* [*passato prossimo*] (that morning at 5). An hour later *he felt ill* [*passato prossimo*].'

Here the clause *an hour later he felt ill* could be dependent on the preceding clause.

Lo Cascio establishes the following rules for the minor set tenses: [388]

Binding rules for the minor set
 In order to belong to the minor set a clause marked by an anaphoric tense (T_a) finds its antecedent:

  1. In a clause marked by a deictic tense immediately preceding or immediately following, or
  2. In a clause marked by an anaphoric tense immediately preceding; particularly when that clause carries a lexicalized reference time through a temporal adverb. If the reference time is not explicitly indicated, the binding function of that clause is weakened.

Lo Cascio later restates these binding rules in terms of c-command in a way similar to Smith's statement:

Temporal relations at the Main unit level
 If y is an anaphoric tense then x is the antecedent of y if x c-commands y and is in the higher domain, so that it functions as head, or if between x and y there is no other category which c-commands y. Node *Mu* is an absolute barrier for a c-command relation and binding. [389]

The last part of this defines the scope of the unit within which coherence of tense is maintained.

The clause "If y is . . . head" concerns cases such as *he said to him that he had decided to leave*, in which an anaphoric tense depends on a preceding matrix deictic tense. This is essentially equivalent to Smith's Sharing Principle; the higher clause establishes the RT for the lower clause. The anaphoric tense may be syntactically independent (*He reported his decision to him. He had decided to leave*). The clause "or if between . . . c-commands y" concerns cases such as *they had said that he had already left three days before*, in which one anaphoric tense depends on another. This is essentially the Extended Sharing Principle. The two clauses share RT, but RT is oriented to other than ST. Again, the anaphoric tense may be in another sentence: *They had spoken as follows. He had already left three days before.* In the case of coordinate anaphorics, Adelaar and Lo Cascio once again claim that sequencing is pragmatic, not semantic.[390] In the absence of contextually given information, it is impossible to define sequentiality for examples such as this:

> Paolo disse che Gianni *aveva mangiato* una mela e che *aveva cantato* gioia.
> 'Paul said that John had eaten an apple and had sung with joy.'

(Both the tenses in italics are pluperfects.) It is unclear how his singing for joy relates to his eating the apple; it follows it if it is because of the eating of the apple, but out of context we cannot say how the conjoined clauses relate. The same is true of syntactically independent anaphorics, of course:

> Paul told us what had happened. John had eaten an apple. He had sung with joy.

Lo Cascio and Rohrer observe that situations are possible in which anaphoric tenses are not evaluated with respect to times which belong to the same Mu, but rather with respect to a time indicated by a sentence or temporal adverb in another major unit. "At first sight this seems to contradict the rules proposed by Lo Cascio."[391] They offer an example:

> Paolo *ha detto* che Gianni *avrebbe giurato* che *aveva ascoltato* i nastri il giorno precedente.
> 'Paolo *said* [*passato prossimo*] that Gianni *would have sworn* [i.e., would swear] that he *had listened* [PLUPF] to the tapes the day before.'

Here the time of listening to the tapes ("the day before") is evaluated with respect neither to the time of Paolo's speech act nor to that of Gianni's. They ascribe this possibility to the greater referential freedom of adverbials over tenses.[392] But the same possibilities seem to occur in the absence of such an adverbial:

> Paolo *said* that Gianni *would swear* that he *had listened* to the tapes.

With complements other than those under a verb of saying, the complement tense may be evaluated with respect to a higher tense, though one not outside the Mu:

> Paolo *è* certo che non *sarà* contento che tu *sarai* alla stazione ad aspettarlo.
> 'Paolo *is* sure that *he will be* glad that *you will be* at the station waiting for him.'[393]

Here the third E depends not on the second, but on the first.

Relative clauses, as Smith noted (1981), work differently from other subordinate structures. It is hard to state hard-and-fast rules for relative clauses, and they seem to be evaluated with respect to an arbitrarily chosen time.[394] Where the matrix does provide the reference, there are limitations, however. The matrix tense and the relative clause tense must belong to the same sector:

> He wrote to the girl whom he had met in Rome.
> He invited the girl whom he would hire as a secretary.

He invited the girl whom he had hired as a secretary.
He will invite the girl whom he had hired as a secretary.[395]

In this last sentence, the relative clause is not evaluated relative to the matrix.
Lo Cascio and Rohrer state the following rule:

> The anaphoric verbal tense of a relative clause can be evaluated with respect to a
> time denoted by an arbitrary clause and is therefore free of the restrictions imposed
> by subordination. In some cases the antecedent can be given by the matrix if the
> verbal tense of the relative clause and of the matrix express the same type of tem-
> poral relation.[396]

Smith states that both precedence and c-command matter for relative clauses.[397]
Here temporal anaphora works just like nominal anaphora, in that the antecedent
cannot both precede and c-command its anaphor. Where both clauses can establish
RT, the first anchors to ST and the second to the first: *Sally married last April a
man who won a fellowship in May.* Where one is intrinsically dependent, it can
anchor on the other only if the other is not both preceded and c-commanded by
it. Consider *John was marrying in three days a woman he met on Thursday;* here
met on Thursday cannot provide an anchor, Smith says.[398]

The theory needs to take into account the difference between restrictive and
nonrestrictive relative clauses. As has often been commented on, nonrestrictive
relative clauses are not really subordinate,[399] and generally represent a commitment on the part of the speaker. A deictic tense in such a relative clause may be
purely deictic, while an anaphoric tense takes its reference outside the matrix:

Sheila will read all about those islanders,
who $\begin{Bmatrix} \text{had} \\ \text{have} \\ \text{will have} \\ \text{have had} \\ \text{had had} \\ \text{would have had} \end{Bmatrix}$ a weird cargo cult.

These embedded anaphoric tenses cannot depend on a future matrix tense.
Sometimes a deictic tense may, however, depend on the matrix:

Sheila read all about those islanders, who had a weird cargo cult.
Sheila read all about those islanders who had a weird cargo cult.

The second of these excludes a deictic reading—it is only the islanders with a
cargo cult at the time of Sheila's reading that she read about. But surprisingly,
the nonrestrictive, while allowing a *de re* reading (e.g., the islanders may have
had this weird cult in the eighteenth century), also allows a *de dicto* reading. And
the following examples exhibit the same ambiguity, though it is necessarily subtle
in the case of the present:

Sheila reads all about those islanders, who have a weird cargo cult.
Sheila will read all about those islanders, who will have a weird cargo cult.

In the present, it is possible that (deictically) Sheila reads about the islanders and
they have (*in general*) a cargo cult, but also that (anaphorically) she is reading
about them and they have (*at the time she is reading*) a cargo cult. It is only the

relative permanence of having a cult that makes this a distinction with little if any difference. With the future, the readings are respectively that she will read about them and they will (at some future time) have a cargo cult, and that she will read about them and *at that time* they will have such a cult.

What we can say, in the cases in which a deictic in a nonrestrictive relative clause is acting anaphorically, is that it is really like a flashback or free indirect discourse. Compare:

> Sheila read about those islanders, who had a weird cargo cult.
> She read about those islanders. They had a weird cargo cult.

These share precisely the same ambiguity.

What, if anything, of any generality can we say, given all this? Contemporary research has not provided us with a simple overall picture, and though some generalities seem to be emerging, we are left with a bewildering array of principles which are either exception-ridden and far from totally general, or difficult to state formally, or both, and in any case not very explanatory.

The difficulty is that the various authors we have been citing look at the problem of tense as one of the *interpretation* of markers. Given a certain tense form with or without an accompanying adverbial, how are we to interpret it (in context)? Given that a large number of factors determine the use of markers such as tenses and adverbials, this leads to the complexity and fragmentation we have seen. A better way to look at the problem, and one more conducive to generalization, is to view it as a *generative* problem, namely, from the point of view of what factors enter into tense choice in the first place.

q. Localization

So far we have considered at length the evaluation or orientation time and the reference time, but have had little to say about the times of situations (events and states) themselves. In recent years an important distinction has been made between "focus" (reference) and *localization*, that is, temporal location, both relative and absolute.[400] A narrative in the past tense tells us the sequential order of the events, but other than the fact that all the events recounted are past, nothing is said concerning *when* they took place. This is why early modern grammarians considered the simple past "indefinite": it doesn't *in itself* tell us when the state of affairs described took place.

To fully interpret a text, it is necessary to locate each of its situations in relation to the other situations in the text (which ones does each one precede? follow? coincide with?), but also absolutely. "Absolutely" here does not mean "in the real world of time." In many texts an alternate universe is in question, and its situations cannot be directly related to the speaker's speech-act situation. In many science-fiction stories, systems of chronology are employed which have no connection to the real world, yet precise localizations in time are fully interpretable and not meaningless (e.g., *in the third year of the Denebian Empire*). Absolute time within the text involves the GPT, established within some universe of discourse, and not necessarily the ST.

Nor must it be assumed that interpretation requires total precision. Most adverbials are inherently vague and imprecise. *He went home today* tells us only within what period he went, not precisely when. Even *he went home today at noon* need not be precise. We can of course be more and more precise:

—When did John break his arm?
—Last Monday.
—When exactly?
—In the afternoon.
—O.K., but WHEN?
—Around 5 o'clock, I think.[401]

But we can stop at any point without thereby rendering the text uninterpretable, and indefinitely increased precision does not necessarily fully specify absolute time. If we say that John broke his arm last Monday, the lack of precision of this statement does not render it uninterpretable. In general we don't *need* to be totally precise about situations, and it is likely that we could not be even if we wanted to.[402]

Tenses in themselves can perform the task of localizing situations neither relatively nor absolutely. They indicate only which sector of time a situation falls in, and what ordering the situation has relative to others in the text—depending, as we have seen, on numerous pragmatic factors.

For these tasks what are required are adverbials. Not all adverbials localize, however. Frequency adverbials (*every week, once a week, twice*) and duration adverbials (*for a week*) cannot localize. All other types do localize.

Chronological adverbials always fix events absolutely, but provide no information concerning relative order, except implicitly. If we know that one event took place at a time earlier than that at which a second event took place, we know that the two events are ordered. But there is no direct link between the two. The sequence

Tom left. Susan left later.

asserts a relative ordering, but we don't know precisely when Susan left, only that her leaving was later than Tom's. On the other hand, the sequence

Tom left on June 3, 1967. Susan left on June 10, 1967.

asserts no ordering, though it implies one. The sequence

Tom left on June 3, 1967. Susan left five minutes later.

both asserts an order and localizes Susan's leaving.

Chronological adverbials are rarely absolute in themselves, but in context they act as if absolute. *In June* could refer to any June, but in context it may be quite as definite as *in June of 1967*. There is not as much difference between chronological adverbials and deictic ones as some writers have professed. Out of context, *in June* is as variable as *today*, and in context *today* can be as precise as *October 14, 1066*.

Deictic adverbials do not serve to order situations either, except implicitly:

Tom left yesterday. Susan left today.

Such adverbials are always oriented toward the GPT. Consider these sentences:

> He ate today.
> He has eaten twice today.
> Tom denied that he ate today.
> Tom denied that he has eaten twice today.
> Tom will deny that he ate today.
> Tom will deny that he has eaten twice today.

In all the above, *today* refers to the global GPT, regardless of whether or not it is embedded or accompanies a deictic or anaphoric tense.

Anaphoric adverbials assert relative orderings. They may be oriented toward the local OT or some other, as we have seen. Other adverbials fix them relative either to the local OT or to the global one, depending on various factors. For many speakers, *he said that he would paint the house today* is ambiguous, depending on whether *today* relates to the subject's perspective (the relevant OT is the time of the subject's speech act) or the speaker's (OT = ST). Anaphoric adverbials can choose only the local OT: *he said that he would paint the house within a week* does not share this type of ambiguity. Adverbials of frequency and duration do not localize events at all: *he said he would paint the house for an hour* and *he said that he would paint the house often* tell us nothing about *when* the painting took place, other than at some time subsequent to the subject's speech act.

Adelaar and Lo Cascio deny that what they call "direction"—narrative movement—has to do with the shift in the R point, seeing this rather as the result of localization.[403] We have seen that pragmatic conditions govern whether a sequence of past tenses is interpreted as a narrative with movement through time. The sequence

> He ate cake. He ate cookies. He ate ice cream.

may be a catalogue of events with no defined order, or a narrative sequence, depending on the context, real-world knowledge, and various discourse pragmatic principles as yet poorly understood.

Adelaar and Lo Cascio are correct in saying that deictic tenses "are not able to impress movement to the story as they do not give any information whether the state of affairs lies before or after other [ones] belonging to the same text," but are not entirely correct in adding "unless they are accompanied by anaphoric temporal adverbs." Such adverbials are neither sufficient nor necessary for movement. Narrative movement may well be implicated in context even in their absence:

> One by one the cities flashed by. Their train passed Rome. They thundered through Paris. The boat train took them via Calais and Dover to London.

Here the initial sentence, combined with our knowledge of geography, tells us this is a narrative sequence.

The presence of adverbials cannot guarantee sequentiality. If events are localized, as by adverbs, then their sequence is inferable. But the reverse is not true, of course, and the relationship of localization to sequentiality is not automatic, but depends on pragmatic factors again. This is because adverbials may take different perspectives.

Now that the problem of tenses in discourse has been analyzed as constituting a set of problems—those of perspective, orientation, localization, and perhaps yet others—we can begin to move from overly simplistic solutions for "the problem of tense" toward a more adequate understanding. But these issues are not, in a sense, problems of *tense* at all, for many languages are perfectly capable of marking distinctions of the relevant kinds and maintaining temporal functions in discourse without marking tense as such. A theory of *tense* is not what is wanted, then, but a more general theory of *time* indication. This requires a look at so-called tenseless languages.

r. Tenseless Languages: The Problem of the Semitic Verb

Biblical Hebrew is often cited as a classic example of a tenseless language. Yet a survey of the history of the analysis of the verb system of Hebrew and that of the closely similar Quranic Arabic reveals how little really lies behind such a claim.

The classical Semitic languages, Biblical Hebrew and Quranic Arabic, each possess just two finite "tense" forms—an unprefixed form (*qtl, qatal-*, etc.) and a prefixed form (*yqtl, yaqtul-*, etc.)[404] In traditional Hebrew and Arabic grammar, possibly under the influence of Western grammar,[405] these forms were considered to represent the past and future[406] tenses respectively,[407] the absence of a distinctive present tense being accounted for by the fact that the present time does not exist per se. To the medieval grammarian Ibn Janah, the present is "merely an assumption; it has no reality." It is "merely a line of demarcation between the past and the future and may be compared to a point in geometry which is indivisible. An act has temporal reality only in terms of past and future."[408] This is, of course, a reflection of the Aristotelian doctrine of the present.

Although Western scholars at first accepted these traditions, by the early nineteenth century it was realized that this theory meets with numerous counterexamples in which the "tenses" are not used in accord with their supposed values.[409] For example, consider the "prophetic perfect"—the *qtl* form used with future meaning, as in *hēn gāza'nū 'ābadnū kullānū 'ābadnū* 'See, we have perished! We are done for, we are all done for!'" (Numbers 17:27); and the "past imperfect," a *yqtl* used with past meaning: *kō h-yittēn šᵊlomoh lᵊ-hiram šānah bᵊ-šānah* 'Solomon would give this to Hiram year by year' (1 Kings 5:25).[410] In fact, as Kustár points out, either of the forms can be used with any of the meanings of past, present, or future.[411]

In McFall's survey of the translations of Hebrew "tense" forms in the RSV (Revised Standard Version) Bible, of 13,874 *qtl* forms, 10,830 are indeed translated with the past tense, but 2,454 with the present and 255 with the future.[412] Of 14,299 *yiqtol* forms 5,451 are translated with the future and 3,376 with the present, but 774 with the past. (The remaining forms have various modal functions.) He also presents a list of identical forms translated now with the past, now with the future.[413] The same *yiqtol* form is 'was called' in 1 Samuel 9:9, but 'shall be called' in Genesis 17:5; the same *qtl* form is 'I have given' in Genesis 1:29, but 'I will give' in Genesis 17:16.

Similar facts obtain in Arabic. Golian stresses the "non-tense"[414] character of the opposition of *kataba* and *yaktubu*, pointing out that "the perfective *kataba* can be translated in French by the past, present, or future, and the same is true for the imperfective *yaktubu*."[415] In Aartun's survey of forms found on randomly selected pages of a certain Arabic text,[416] 98.7% of the *qatal* forms are past in meaning, but 1.93% are future (though none are present), while 72.34% of *yaqtul* forms are present and 14.89% future, but 12.77% are past. Since the work of Ewald (*Critical Grammar of the Arabic Language*, 1831–33, and *Critical Grammar of the Hebrew Language*, 1835), it has generally been held that the "tense" forms actually represent perfective and imperfective aspect (that is, complete and incomplete action) respectively.[417]

Complicating the picture where Hebrew is concerned is the role of the proclitic conjunction *w-* 'and'. It was stated in the grammatical tradition that this (word spelled with the letter) "waw" is "conversive"; that is, it serves to convert past to future tense, and future to past.[418] As early as the tenth century, the grammarian Japheth ha-Levi was calling this the "future waw" (*waw 'atīdī*) from the fact that the *qtl* form prefixed with it often has future meaning.[419]

Certainly it seemed generally to be the case that with this conjunction the finite verb forms of Biblical Hebrew—if they represent tenses—have the opposite tense value from their usual one; the waw + *qtl* is (generally) a future, not a past, whereas the waw + *yqtl* is a past, not a future.[420] The aspect theory of Ewald and his followers raised significant questions in regard to the waw conversive theory, which was based on absolute tense, and every theory of the Hebrew "tenses" since has had to address itself to the role of the waw.

It has generally—but not universally—been assumed that the "tense" systems of the two languages, Quranic Arabic and Biblical Hebrew, are essentially identical, so that the correct theory for one language should also be that for the other. In the case of Arabic, four types of theory have been propounded regarding the value of the "tenses"—aspect, relative tense (Kurołowicz, 1973), absolute tense (Aartun, 1963), and modality (O'Leary, 1923).[421]

In the case of Hebrew, the waw has been explained in various ways, but the most successful theories entail treatments of the "tense" forms either as expressing relative tense or explaining them in terms of discourse pragmatics.[422]

In general we can say that the theories of classical Semitic "tense" group themselves as follows: theories which explain the facts in purely semantic terms versus those involving pragmatics, and, within the former group, those involving aspect, relative tense, absolute tense, or something else (as in the work of Turner[423]; O'Leary, 1923; and Kustár, 1972). Mixed theories also occur, such as that presented by Comrie (1976).

It is striking how positively the various theories are presented, as if no controversy existed.

Aspect

> . . . biblical Hebrew, as well as other Semitic languages, makes no time-distinction (that is, past, present, and future) in the verb-forms. . . . The difference in tense is determined by whether the action, in the mind of the speaker, is completed or uncompleted.[424]

> The difference between *kataba* and *yaktubu* is essentially other than one of tense [*temporelle*]. It is aspectual. . . . We designate the first form by the term "perfective," the second by that of "imperfective."[425]

Mixed Aspect/Tense

> Summarising the uses of the [Arabic] Imperfective and Perfective, we may say that the Perfective indicates both perfective meaning and relative past time reference, while the Imperfective indicates everything else (i.e. either imperfective meaning or relative non-past tense). The Arabic opposition Imperfective/Perfective incorporates both aspect and (relative) tense.[426]

Relative Tense(?)

> The primary meaning of *iaqtulu* is action simultaneous with the moment of speaking; the primary meaning of *qatala* is action prior to the moment of speaking.[427]

Absolute Tense

> . . . the opposition found in the Arabic verbal system between *qatal-* on the one hand and *yaqtul-* on the other, is an opposition with a temporal character. That is: the opposition between the two verb forms must be put together with the temporal oppositions in languages in which such oppositions are generally recognized.[428]

It seems puzzling, given the huge amount of study applied to the Bible and the Quran, that there can be such divergent opinion as to the analysis of the verb systems. In fact there is no *real* controversy in regard to the interpretation of *particular* verbs; the problem arises only in regard to the two types of verbs *in general*.

We have seen that the tense theory may have resulted from an uncritical acceptance of Western grammatical models on the part of Semitic scholars, and that after Ewald it has met with little acceptance (despite Aartun, 1963), because of the large number of counterexamples. Ewald's work was done at a time when the concept of aspect was just beginning to have an impact on Western grammatical thought. However, although most scholars still adhere to some version of the perfective-imperfective theory, there is ample reason to criticize any simple identification of the classical Semitic system with the Slavic or Graeco-Roman one.

The main criticism which has been made of the aspect theory is that there are counterexamples to it similar to those in the case of the tense theory. McFall cites, for example, 2 Samuel 14:5, "And she answered, Of a truth I am a widow woman, and mine husband is dead." Here "is dead" represents a *yqtl* form. McFall says: "It is hardly likely that [the *yqtl* form in question] has a present tense significance here, i.e. 'and my husband is dying'. She is obviously referring to a past completed event.'' [429] McFall also points out the stative use of the perfective. [430] An example such as 'I am old and grey' (1 Samuel 12:2) [431] clearly cannot refer to completed action.

Another criticism of the aspect theory is that it falsely predicts that, out of context, the verb forms should have no tense value. Yet in Arabic at least, perfective forms are normally interpreted, out of context, as past and never as present or future, while the reverse is very nearly true of the imperfective. [432] We have seen above the figures Aartun presents for the uses of the forms: 98.07% of the *qatal* forms are past in meaning (1.93% are future, but none are present), while 72.34% of *yaqtul* forms are present and 14.89% future, and only 12.77% past. [433]

Consider modern Arabic, for example Maltese. The Maltese sentence *Ġanni mexa mid-dar sa l'iskola* Borg translates as 'John walked (*mexa*) from home (*mid-dar*) to school (*sa l'iskola*)', while translating *Ġanni jimxi mid-dar sa l'iskola* 'John walks from home to school.' [434] He accounts for the tense difference by noting that, since a completed action can occur only in the past, and not in the present, *mexa* must be past ("prior to the moment of speaking"). Since *jimxi* refers to a recurrent action (it is not a true present tense in Maltese), it can be only present in tense.

Neither of these points follows, however, from the aspectual theory itself. An action can be completed in the future. An action can be recurrent in the past or the future. And it is odd to say that an action cannot be complete in the present, while claiming that actions can recur in the present.

The wide range of meanings of the imperfective in Hebrew can be read as characteristic of the unmarked member of an opposition (though formally it is the perfective which is unmarked, i.e., prefixless). The imperfective can represent incomplete actions in any tense, or a habitual, or a wide range of modal meanings—potential, permissive, desiderative, obligative, injunctive, and conditional. [435] By contrast, the perfective has no modal uses.

Supporting this claim is the use of the imperfective for complete events in the future, as in Comrie's example *Fa 'llāhu taḥkumu* (imperfective) *bayna-hum yawma 'l-qiyāmit* 'But (*fa*) God (*'llahu*) will judge (*tahkumu*) between them (*bayna-hum*) on the Day (*yawma*) of Resurrection (*'l-qiyamit*).' [436]

Comrie argues, from the fact that the perfective is never present in tense, that it combines perfective aspect with (relative) past tense. Supporting this claim are examples such as *ʾajīʾu* (imperfective)-*ka ʾīdā 'ḥmarra* (perfective) *'l-busru* 'I shall come (*ʾajīʾu*) to you (-*ka*) when (*ʾīdā*) the unripe date (*'l-busru*) ripens (shall ripen, *'ḥmarra*)'. [437] Here the perfective is past, but past relative to the future event designated by the imperfective verb *ʾajīʾu*.

Borg however suggests [438] a connection of the perfective with absolute (rather than relative) past time, citing the impossibility of *Niġik* (imperfective) *meta jkun* (imperfective) *sar* (perfective) *it-tamar* 'I [will] come to you (*niġik*) when (*meta*) the dates (*it-tamar*) will have (*jkun*, '[will] be') ripened (*sar*, 'became')', corresponding to Comrie's Classical Arabic example. [439]

Returning to the issue of aspect, the counterexamples cited above raise questions concerning the theory. But if the opposition is not fundamentally one of aspect (i.e., completeness vs. incompleteness), what does it involve? One solution is to accept that the fundamental opposition is rather one of tense, either absolute tense (Aartun), or relative tense (Kuroɫowicz, 1973), or a mix of relative tense and aspect (Comrie, 1976), with secondary or contextual meanings (such as aspect or absolute tense) subordinate to these.

Kuroɫowicz argues that the distinction is essentially one of relative past tense versus relative present tense. What he actually says is that "the primary meaning of *iaqtulu* is action simultaneous with the moment of speaking; the primary meaning of *qatala* is action prior to the moment of speaking."[440]

He then states that imperfectivity and futurity are secondary meanings of the *iaqtulu* form, while pluperfectness and future perfectness are those of the *qatala* form. Each also has "tertiary" functions: in the case of the imperfect, imperfective preterite and future; in the case of the perfective, perfective preterite and future.[441]

Kuroɫowicz's argument proceeds from the fact that there is no crosscategorizing of tense and aspect such as we find in Slavic (where, except in the present, perfect and imperfect forms contrast, e.g., *ya pisal: ya napisal* 'I wrote'). Nor is there any combination of tense and aspect in one form such as we find in Romance, where, for example, the perfect past (*passé simple* or *preterite*) contrasts with the imperfect past (*imparfait*), the *passé anterieur* with the pluperfect, and so on.

While Kuroɫowicz is undoubtedly correct when he states that European scholars simply assumed that if the opposition in Semitic was not one of tense, it must be one of aspect,[442] he himself with equally little justification assumes two crucial points. The first is that a binary system of the Semitic type, with no crosscutting category of tense, cannot be an opposition of aspect. His reason seems irrelevant—that aspect has to do with stems marking types of action. The second assumption is that the primary meaning of the forms has to do with tense. It is true that out of context the perfective seems to refer to past time almost exclusively, but so does it refer to completion. No clear reason is offered, however, for deciding on the primary meaning.

Kuroɫowicz actually treats the "aspects" as primarily representing relations to the time of the speech act, hence something like absolute time. But he phrases the definitions in terms of S alone, not R, thereby ignoring the work of both Reichenbach and Bull. The fact is, as Comrie's example cited above demonstrates, in many contexts the Semitic verb represents relative time. If the perfective, for example, sometimes represents an event preceding R, and S is just the first R point, then why not conflate the two into relative pastness, but defined relative to R, not S?

It is open to us to claim that relative past uses of the perfective are purely contextual, but that in and of itself does not account for that meaning in context. If the basic meaning is relative tense, then neither the "normal" use of the perfective nor that in Comrie's example require any special explanation. As it is, Kuroɫowicz provides no explanatory account of the secondary or tertiary uses of the Arabic "tense" forms; in this theory they are essentially contingent. Yet it is clear that they follow from universal facts of language use. Assigning relative tense as the fundamental opposition would avoid Comrie's awkward dual meaning of the perfective while accounting for the facts.

In fact, there are ample hints of a relative tense theory in Kurołowicz's treatment, as when he writes: "The only non-modal opposition of personal verb forms is *i̯aqtulu:qatala* equal to simultaneity (or non-anteriority):anteriority, tense being context-conditioned."[443]

s. The Problem of Waw and the Pragmatics of the Semitic Verb

The main difficulty that all semantic theories of the Biblical Hebrew "tenses" run into is the treatment of the Hebrew conjunction written with waw; no theory of the Hebrew "tenses" which cannot account for their behavior when linked to waw can be adequate.

The "waw conversive" theory was already current among Hebrew grammarians in the tenth century; waw could seemingly convert past into future and future into past.[444] Even disregarding the replacement of tense by aspect as the meaning of the "tense" forms, this theory is untenable. McFall points out, however, that any of the four forms (*qtl* and *yqtl* with or without waw) can bear either of the aspectual meanings,[445] as does Kustár, who rejects the idea that the forms with waw constitute "a grammatical extension by which forms with a new meaning may be generated."[446] Kustár suggests that the difference between forms with or without waw lies rather purely in the realm of syntax.

An early attempt to deal with the problem raised by the conjunction is the "waw inductive" theory. The central idea here is that the waw causes the force of one clause to be induced into another. Thus tense (or aspect) in subordinate structures is, not surprisingly, subordinate. Gell states the classical waw-inductivist position:

> It is evident that when the Sacred Writers intend any order to be observed in their narrations or speeches, using the particle [waw] before the words to maintain it, each circumstance is related in the order in which it occurs; and subordinate present or future tenses are only ever wanted for such a purpose. There is no occasion for a tense to express, after a forementioned event, another which occurred antecedently, or was past in relation to it; that is, there is no occasion for any temporal power in subordinate preter[ite]s, corresponding with that of subordinates in other tenses. Subordinate preter[ite]s, therefore, seem never to have any proper temporal power of their own, as subordinate presents and futures have; and they are made a generally disposable force; by which any narration or speech may be expressed, without implying the order of the acts involved in it. They have only the inducted power of the Governing [*sic*] verb.[447]

In criticism of this theory, McFall observes that future actions, whether on a relative or absolute time scale, are by definition non-past events; consequently, future tenses can refer only to future events.[448] McFall also notes that Gell is wrong when he says, "there is no occasion for a tense to express, after a forementioned event, another which occurred antecedently, or was past in relation to

Aspect

it," since the twelfth-century grammarian David Kimḥi cites just such examples "where the 'future' refers to a past time antecedent to the time referred to by another verb preceding it":

> And there is a [waw] which points to a time that is past before [the past action of] the verb that is before it [in the text], 'Behold, Thou wast angry, and we sinned' . . . , meaning, For we had previously sinned, therefore Thou wast angry with us. [Also] 'A man will die when he has been ill', meaning 'when he had previously been ill, for before he dies he will be taken ill and be sick.'[449]

Kustár argues persuasively that waw indicates simply a close logical connection between sentences and has no temporal value at all.[450] If so, then what do we make of the flawed but nonetheless valid observation that in the waw construction what is generally a perfective seems to have imperfective and/or non-past meaning, while the imperfective has perfective and/or past meaning?

The key here is the observation that there are strong constraints on the sentences conjoined by waw. Kustár quotes Köhler's important observation that when an independent, explicit subject is combined with the imperfect and waw in a "narrative" clause—some 773 cases in Genesis, for example—then the predicate always precedes the subject. The reverse order, subject–verb, never occurs.[451]

Although Köhler drew no further conclusions from this, Kustár sees it as central to the puzzle of waw. Verb–subject is the normal, unmarked order in Hebrew[452]; other orders reflect some special emphasis, as in 'it was the serpent that deluded me' (Genesis 3:13), with subject-first order.

Kustár observes that Hebrew uses waw only when stressing the "close connection of sentences."[453] Where the close connection of two sentences is already understood, waw is not found. Waw is used to construct "series of thoughts and actions." This series exhibits a distinct word order. The verb is always initial, and can appear equally in the *qtl-* or *jqtl-* forms. The verb-initial clause connected to the preceding one with waw he calls a "waw-consecutive clause." The prevalence of such clauses he takes to indicate that Hebrew emphasizes series of actions. The waw-consecutive clause has a special function.

Kustár's theory follows too from the observation of Michel that

> in the construction perfect-imperfect [consecutive clause], the two tenses do not have the same meaning. The perfect appeared to present a fact which stands absolutely at the beginning of a series of actions or remains explanatory disengaged from the flow of action; the imperfect [consecutive clause] on the contrary appeared following the perfect to indicate an action resulting from the fact, following an imperfect [consecutive clause], a resultant member in the course of a continuous chain of actions developing out of and following one another.[454]

Kustár argues that there is no objective difference in meaning or use between the two forms, that the only difference is that the *qtl* forms represent "determining," and the *jqtl* forms "determined," sentences. He cites minimal pairs of discourses differing only in the one verb form. For example:

> [Isaiah] 36.20–21: "Where is there one of all the gods of these countries, who his own country has saved (*hṣjlw*) from my hand, that your God should save (*jṣjl*)

Jerusalem from my hand? They were silent (*wjḥrjšw*), and replied (*wl'-'nw*) to him nothing. . . .''

[2 Kings] 18:35–36: ''Where is there one of all the gods of these countries, who his own country has saved (*hṣjlw*) from my hand, that your God should save (*jṣjl*) Jerusalem from my hand? The people were silent (*whḥrjšw*), and replied (*wl'-'nw*) to him nothing. . . .''[455]

Here the only difference, according to Kustár, is that in Isaiah the speaker wishes to emphasize the cause of the silence, but in Kings, the silence as a consequence.[456]

Again:

[Isaiah] 39.1–2: ''At that time sent (*šlḥ*) Merodach-Baladan, the son of Baladan, the kind of Babylon, messengers with letters and gifts to Hezekiah: for he had heard (*wjšm'*), that he had been sick (*ḥlh*) and was again well (*wjḥzq*). And Hezekiah was pleased (*wjśmh*) with them and showed (*wjr'm*) them his treasury-house. . . .''

[2 Kings] 20.12–13: ''At that time sent (*šlḥ*) Merodach-Baladan, the son of Baladan, the king of Babylon, messengers with letters and gifts to Hezekiah: for he had heard (*šm'*), that he had been sick (*ḥlh*) and was again well (*wjḥzq*). And Hezekiah harkened to them (*wjšm'*) and showed (*wjr'm*) them his treasury-house. . . .''[457]

If the waw adds no temporal (tense or aspect) meaning, then the difference between verbs with waw and verbs without waw cannot be a semantic one. But apparently it is, for the forms with waw are generally seen as ''reversing'' the values the ''tenses'' normally have. To reconcile the two, we must assume that the forms without waw and those with it do *not* in fact differ in semantics, but the only way this is possible is if the ''tense'' forms do not differ from one another in meaning to begin with. But since it is unlikely, on the evidence, that any semantic distinction is in question, there must be some pragmatic difference.

Consequently Kustár proposes that the essential difference between the two forms is that of ''determining'' (*determinierend*) and ''determined'' (*determiniert*):

Through the use of the *qtl*- and *jqtl*-aspect categories the speaker distinguishes those actions in the immediate relationship of the actions to one another which are to be considered by him as determining and which as determined, that is, which actions are to be considered as starting point, reason-determining motive, purpose, consequence, or outcome of another action, to which reason, purpose or determining motive the speaker wishes to refer. The determining action is indicated by the *qtl*-form and the determined one by the *yqtl*-form. It depends exclusively on the view and the judgment of the speaker, which actions he views as determining and which as determined.[458]

Kustár is not entirely clear on what he means by ''determining'' and ''determined.'' It is possible to read the difference as the foreground-background distinction discussed here earlier. The *yqtl* with past meaning, for example, would then be precisely equivalent to the complexive (but backgrounding) use of the French imperfect (*imparfait*).

Close to this interpretation of this theory of Kustár's is the pragmatic, background/foreground interpretation of O'Leary (1923). O'Leary's theory is, however, even less clear than Kustár's, and other interpretations of his intentions are possible. O'Leary writes:

> The "perfect" of West Semitic . . . expresses a state or action which is definitely asserted and regarded as certain as contrasted with the imperfect expressing what may be, what is possible, or can be treated as an accessory, causal, conditional, etc. The perfect is declaratory, with emphasis on the assurance, regardless of whether the time is present, part, or future, although, of course, the past is usually regarded as known and settled more than could possibly be the case with the present or future, but in promises or bargains the perfect is used even though it must refer to future time because the emphasis is on the assurance and certainty of the promise made, and so in prayers, blessings, curses, and in prophecy.[459]

He cites a number of examples from the Quran, noting:

> The angels refer in the imperfect to events which they regard as probable, but of which they have no certain knowledge, but the events described as actually having taken place are in the perfect. Even in conditional clauses the perfect is used if the condition is assumed to have taken place, as "if you are in doubt as to that which we have revealed" (Qur'an, ii, 23).

O'Leary also says that "as the perfect describes a certain and assured act or state, so the imperfect describes the incomplete, or dubious, or possible, as well as the subordinate statement which is not emphasized as the object of assertion."[460]

It is possible to read this as a pragmatic theory of discourse value—that is, the imperfective represents backgrounded information, and the perfective, foregrounded. Alternatively, however, it may also be read as a semantic theory, assigning modal or status value to the forms. Modal value would be supported by the fact that it is only the imperfective which serves as the base for modal forms. In this case it would be the distinction of certainty versus possibility which is central. Emphasis on actuality suggests, however, a distinction of status—real versus irreal, that is, between events which have transpired versus those which as yet have not, and may never do so.

Another theory which is difficult to interpret but which seems to lie in roughly the same area as those of O'Leary and Kustár is that of Turner, reported by McFall. Turner proposes, according to McFall, that

> *qtl* expresses the action or state as the attribute of the person or thing spoken of; the *yqtl* form expresses or represents the verbal action as in or of the subject, the produce of the subject's energy, the manifestation of its power and life, like a stream evolving itself from its source. Whereas the first represents the act or state as an independent thing: the Factual; the second expresses the same act or state as a process, and one that is passing before our very eyes: the Descriptive.[461]

McFall is quite right to characterize these rather arcane ideas as "difficult [for the Western mind] to grasp."[462] But when McFall notes that, in Turner's view, "while in the *qtl* form the verb is the defined and leading element, to which the subject is subordinated, in the *yqtl* form the subject takes the leading place,"[463] we can see elements of Kustár's theory, or something not dissimilar. Moreover, at times McFall represents Turner's theory as something similar to discourse pragmatic theories of foregrounding/backgrounding:

> Because [the] two forms have such divergent functions the speaker is free to employ them at any moment to advance the story or event in the most telling way. When the Hebrew prophet wishes to relate events lying in the future, the fact that he uses the *qtl* form indicates that he is more interested in the results—the facts of the new situation—than in the manner they were arrived at. On the other hand, the Hebrew historian, who already knows all the facts of his story, shows by his choice of *yqtl* forms that he is interested in the actual forging or shaping of the facts of history: history is presented as it is actually happening.[464]

Explicitly based on discourse-pragmatic distinctions is the theory of Givón (1977, 1982). He says the imperfect represents in Early Biblical Hebrew "the *in-sequence, realis, punctual* aspect responsible for carrying the main-line ('back-bone') of the story," and normally "involves *continuation of the same subject/topic*."[465] On the other hand, the perfect "marks out-of-sequence clauses which in real time had preceded the preceding clause(s) in the narrative. It is also the main avenue for introducing a new subject/topic in narrative." It is typically found in "subordinate-presupposed" clauses and may be found in relative clauses.

Clearly the forms have distinct discourse-pragmatic functions, though there are competing ideas as to precisely what those functions are. The question remains whether pragmatics or semantics is primary, and if the latter, what the primary opposition in *meaning* of the two classical Semitic "tense" forms is. Do the roles of the forms follow from their (aspectual?) meanings, or do their (implied?) values come as contextual consequences of their uses?

The problem of the Semitic "tenses" is a difficult one to resolve, foremost because we are here dealing with dead languages. Although Biblical Hebrew and Quranic Arabic have never ceased to be used as literary languages and have continuous traditions, it would be wrong to assume that their users in the period of self-conscious grammatical study have had any reliable *Sprachgefühl* for them. For example, McFall concludes that "the pronouncements of medieval Jewish grammarians do not inspire us with confidence in the light of our present knowledge of the Hebrew language and comparative Semitic philology."[466]

On the other hand, Borg among others[467] stresses the continuity in development of the tense systems of modern Arabic (e.g., Maltese) from that of Quranic Arabic, and many writers note the similar development of tenses in modern Hebrew, based on elaborating the system of Biblical Hebrew.[468] Aartun, on the other hand, lays great store on the statements of the Arabic grammatical tradition.

Furthermore, it is obvious from our preceding discussion of pragmatic theories of tense and aspect that virtually any of the various theories could be correct as regards the "basic" or "general" *meaning* (*Gesamt*, or *Grundbedeutung*) of the forms while accounting for *interpretations* in ways consistent with any of the other theories, especially in context—as "contextual," "secondary," implicative meanings, "overtones," and so forth.

The question then is the purely theoretical one of how to distinguish what is primary (or essential or asserted) from what is secondary (or context-bound or conveyed). This is difficult to do in the case of artificial languages such as literary

Aspect

ones, especially those which have long been fossilized. To gain a better perspective on these issues, we need to look at living, colloquial "tenseless" languages.

t. "Tenseless" Languages

The general importance of the preceding discussion of the Semitic verb is that the very same issues arise in regard to a great many languages which lack absolute tense systems. Examples that are familiar from the literature include the creole languages, Chinese, and the sign language of the deaf.[469] Gonda concludes a discussion of many languages lacking tense markers as such by underlining that "it is often the context or situation, linguistic or non-linguistic, which makes clear what the time of the predication is and what are the other implications of the forms used."[470]

The American Sign Language of the deaf (ASL) has often been described as a tenseless language, having "only the type of time locutions in which time of the speech act is NOT maintained."[471] There are no past or future tense markers as such.[472]

Other sign languages of the deaf are likewise tenseless. Thus in British Sign Language (BSL) "aspectual marking . . . is more fully grammaticalised . . . than deictic time reference."[473] The "modulations" (Bergman expressly avoids the term "inflections") of the Swedish Sign Language verb mark aspectual distinctions such as iterativity, but not ones of tense.[474]

What we find in these various sign languages are either sign variations marking various kinds of aspectual distinctions,[475] or aspectual markers such as the completive marker *FINISH* of ASL and BSL.[476] It is typical too to have a "time line," signing toward the back or behind the shoulder of the signer referring to (relatively) past time, signing forward or in front of the shoulder referring (relatively) future time.[477]

Muysken characterizes at least one of the preverbal particles typically found in creoles as a past tense marker (e.g., Haitian *te*), as opposed to clearly aspectual markers such as that for durativity (or progessivity, e.g., Sranan *e*) and modal particles such as that for potentiality (e.g., Seychellois *pu*).[478] The claim is that the tense particle precedes mood and aspect particles in the preverbal string of words. Past tense particles listed include Jamaican/Sranan *ben*, Krio *bin*, Papiamentu *taba*, and Philippine Creole *ya*.[479]

In each case, however, Muysken presents considerable evidence to question the identification of these "past tense" (and other "future tense") particles. In the case of Papiamentu, he notes:

> *Tabata* marks non-punctual past, *a* simple past. *Te* marks indicative mood in the present tense, and non-punctual aspect when combined with *lo* and *taba-*. It is possible that *tabata* is only historically composed of the separate elements *taba* and *ta*. In that case, we would have *ta* and *tabata* alternating with each other.[480]

He then presents these examples:

> bo lo ta kanta
> you   sing
> 'you will be singing'

bo lo a kanta
'you will have sung'

Given these facts, it is not too hard to construct a model for the language lacking (absolute) tense, at least in regard to the supposed past tense. Whatever *ta* and *taba* may be, they do not seem to be simply past tense markers; *a* functions like a perfective or a relative past tense marker, and *lo* may or may not be a true future tense (given the absence of a clear past tense marker and the lack of any present tense marker at all).

In Negerhollands, *lo:* is a definite future marker as opposed to *sa*, which is an indefinite future marker.[481] There is a supposed past tense marker *ha*, but once again no present tense marker. Muysken himself refers to the "past tense (anterior?) marker."[482]

As to São Tomense, he says:

> the major distinction is between completive and non-completive aspect. . . . The past is marked with *(s)tava*, non-punctual with *sa* (only in the present), and the future tense is marked with *te* in the completive, and with *bi* in the non-completive.[483]

Once again there is no present tense marker.

Given the close interlacing of tense and aspect, it is difficult to be convinced that the cited "tense" particles do indeed mark tense, given the lack of a present tense marker. It would be interesting to know more about what happens to these tense particles in subordination, but Muysken, for example, presents little data on this.

Interesting in this regard is the study by Mufwene (1984) of Jamaican and Guyanese creoles. Mufwene uses the term "tense" in an unusual sense—he categorizes tense markers as realis and irrealis, categories properly speaking divorced from tense and belonging to either mood or status.[484] The realis is further divided into an "anterior" category and an unnamed (presumably non-past or non-anterior) one; the irrealis is simply the category "subsequent."[485]

Something like this is in fact not an uncommon system. Eilfort (1986) argues that Tak Pisin, for example, has non-finite complement clauses and that the simple distinction of "realized" and "non-realized" action (realis:irrealis) is basic in that language.

Mufwene's categorization proceeds from "the working assumption that any main verb . . . is time-inflected in terms of . . . 'tense', which marks the chronological relation of the described state of affairs to the speech event time (ST) and/or a reference time (RT . . .)." That is, Mufwene is *assuming* that either absolute, deictic tense, or relative tense is being marked in addition to aspect, though it is not being claimed that (absolute) tense is marked. We might compare the situation in American Black English, where L. Anderson (1971), for example, states that *been* "conveys some relative or absolute past meaning."

In the course of Mufwene's study it is made amply plain that it is indeed relative tense—anteriority and subsequence—that are in question. First, in context, tense is not an obligatory category, as in *las mont im go a Trinidad* 'last month he went [literally, 'go'] to Trinidad'.[486] This is more typical of relative tense systems than of absolute ones. Further, the so-called tense markers readily occur in contexts in which they have relative meaning: *Di mont bifoo im* (*ben*) *go a Inglan* 'the month before he had gone/went to England'[487]; *Jien veks bikaa Tam ben go a baa* 'Jane is/was angry because Tom went/had gone to the tavern'.[488]

There is ample reason then to doubt that what are often called tense markers actually mark absolute, as opposed to relative, tense, if they mark tense (as opposed to aspect) at all. The situation in these various languages is apparently not very different from a classical "tenseless" language such as Chinese.

To conclude: while current theory insists that, regarding the various languages we have been discussing, *one* of the approaches is correct—there *is* a basic meaning (or use) for each of the verb forms in opposition—there is as yet no general agreement on whether it is meaning or use which is primary. Further, if meaning is primary, there is no agreement as to what kind of meaning that meaning is—deictic or absolute tense, relative tense, or aspect (if not something else, such as status or mood).

It is most widely agreed that absolute tense is not generally in question in these various cases, and most scholars do not accept status or modality. But whether relative tense or aspect is involved, and what aspect *means* in this context (completive vs. non-completive, complexive vs. non-complexive, etc.), remain as yet controversial points, just beginning to be explored in a profound way in the literature on "tenseless" languages.

From the point of view of the language learner or user, this controversy is perhaps of little significance. While there is no question that much detailed research (and much defining of as yet rather vague concepts) remains to be done, before we can say that we really understand how the various temporal marking devices are used in these languages (and in languages in general), the outlines seem clear; it is now possible to offer on principled bases alternative but largely equivalent accounts for the vast majority of examples.

What emerges is that tense and aspect are neither gratuitous and largely pointless distinctions, nor distinctions which simply and naturally follow from the nature of time itself. After all, spatial relations are not obligatory categories of the verb in a great many languages (though they are in some), even though spatial relations are just as "natural" as temporal ones. It has so long been assumed that temporal specification is "natural," that the *role* of tense (and aspect) in the *use* of language has remained largely taken for granted and left unexamined.

Clearly, tenses and aspects have distinctive pragmatic functions. Whether these functions are primary in themselves or derivative of meanings is less significant for teacher, student, or the everyday speaker (at least), than the observation that generally there is some point to the specification of temporal relations *beyond the mere indication of temporal relations themselves*. It is significant, too, that the uses of forms are not automatically given: verb forms serve to *do* things, and what they can do is obviously linked to what they can mean.

There seems to be a wide range of things they do. They serve to structure discourses by foregrounding or backgrounding information, by providing the logical structure of narrative, or indeed by indicating the very nature of the discourse

as narrative or something else. They serve to indicate logical relationships between statements or reported events, even if this is mere temporal sequence. They
serve to glue events together into sequences of events or to indicate their independence from one another. They serve to indicate perspective and distinguish that of
the speaker from those of subjects and other participants. They interrelate crucially
with the systems of marking indicating the information flow through the discourse
or text. They invite inferences and provide overtones.

As yet little is understood of the pragmatics of tense and aspect. The central
question for future scholarly research must undoubtedly be not "what does it
mean?" but rather "how is it used?" We have seen that in the late 1980s even
the school of formal semantics is turning to the consideration of such questions.
In the search for understanding, the "informal" researches of literary scholars
may play an important role, reflecting as they do centuries of careful observation
of particular uses of the various verb forms.

u. Beyond Tense and Aspect

The extensive discussion of tense and aspect here hardly exhausts the questions
raised by the expression of temporal relationships in natural language. One area
we have had almost nothing to say about is that of *metric* tense systems. We saw
in the case of Kikuyu that the kind of tense system some of the Greeks erro-
neously saw in their own language *does* exist in Kikuyu: there are near and distant
pasts and futures. Comrie (1985) devotes his entire chapter 4 to this type of system. Some languages have up to five distinct past tenses and, correspondingly,
five different futures, differing in degree of remoteness from the present. Whether
any significant generalizations can be drawn concerning this type of system remains to be seen.

We have also had very little to say here concerning the third great verbal category, mood. While mood interacts with tense and aspect in various ways, as we
have seen, it is not principally concerned with temporal relationships per se, and
thus falls outside the scope of the present work. A recent survey of the topic is
by Palmer (1986).

But tense, aspect, and mood do not exhaust the verbal categories concerned
with time. We have seen that there is in addition what Johnson (1977, 1981) calls
existential status, based on the terminology (*status*) attributed by Jakobson (1971:134)
to Whorf (though Whorf, at least in the 1956 work, uses the term "assertion" for
this type of category).[489]

Johnson treats status as a semantic category within the terms of Reichenbach's
theory: it represents the relationship of E to S. But status is seemingly understood
by Whorf as a pragmatic category. In any case, how many statuses there are in
fact (Reichenbach theory predicts no more than three: E<S, S>E, and S = E) has
not been investigated. At the moment status remains a largely unexplored area
with no general theory.

Nor is it easy at this stage of our knowledge to draw any general conclusions
even where tense and aspect are concerned. Despite Dahl's (1985) survey of tense

systems in a wide range of languages, and the various papers which came out of the Stanford University Language Universals project (e.g., Ultan, 1978), few languages have been surveyed, and very few investigated in depth. The reader of the present work should not be misled into thinking that the lengthy consideration here of Latin, Greek, English, German, Russian, Romance languages, Kikuyu, and others constitutes a wide sampling, or that the extensive literature surveyed produces either width or depth of knowledge. A comparison of Nakau (1976) and Soga (1983) on Japanese, for example, suggests that we are far from convergence on an adequate theory of tense and aspect in Japanese, which is one of the most investigated of languages.

This is not a criticism of these valuable works or of the large number of scholars who are conducting the primary research, but simply a reflection of the primitiveness of our tools and the relatively short time span during which intensive work utilizing modern semantic and pragmatic theories has been conducted. The semantic tools date back no further than 1970 or so, and both pragmatics and discourse studies to this day have relatively little by way of anything useful to offer the student of tense and aspect.

With the exception of adverbials, we have been concerned here exclusively with verbs, as the title of this book emphasizes. But other parts of speech also contribute greatly to time reference and interact in interesting ways with the semantics of verbs and adverbials. Jespersen cites such time-related nominal expressions in English as

> ex-king
> the late Lord Mayor
> a future Prime Minister
> the present owner of the house
> what was once his home
> the life to come
> the expectant mother of his child
> prospective governors[490]

He further notes time affixes in many languages which may be added to nouns with effects similar to *ex-, late, former, future* in English.[491] Since participles have substantive uses, it is possible in Greek and Latin, for example, to distinguish *scribens* 'someone writing now, present-time writer' from *scripturus* 'someone who will write, future writer'; the past or passive participle in English often has past or perfect active meaning: a *well-read* man is one who *has read* much and well.[492]

It is obvious that many types of substantives, and in particular those which are deverbal in nature—infinitives and participles—bear temporal meaning or interact in interesting ways with other expressions which do the same. Often such expressions mark aspect or *Aktionsart* and denote situations or phases thereof, as we have seen. Much more could be said concerning these than we have done here. But even "ordinary" nominals relate to time in two ways. First, many nominals which are not obviously deverbal in nature denote situations or portions thereof in much the same way deverbal substantives do. There is not much to choose between *during the fighting, during the fight,* and *during the combat.* In some work within the GS paradigm such superficially non-deverbal substantives were viewed as reflecting abstract verbs which had always to be nominalized.[493]

But even quite ordinary nominals are time-bound in the sense that they carry with them various presuppositions. *Pompeii was a bustling city* invites an imperfective reading ranging over the totality of Pompeii's (past) existence, because it belongs to the past; the sentence seems in no way incomplete. (Yet other readings are possible if we are talking of Pompeii at some definite point in time, say, when Vesuvius erupted, or if we are talking of Pompeii as the ruins extant today.) Replace *Pompeii* with the name of a contemporary city and all this changes: *Toronto was a bustling city* (apart from a reading for some speakers of "Toronto *used to be* a bustling city") seems incomplete out of context, because only a definite reading is possible. To date no investigation has been conducted of the interaction of such temporal presuppositions with the sorts of issues discussed in the present work.

Dowty (1972) discusses what he calls "temporally restrictive" adjectives. His model examples are these:

The girl married $\begin{cases} \text{young.} \\ \text{on the streetcorner.} \\ \text{wearing a white dress.} \end{cases}$

I saw John $\begin{cases} \text{asleep.} \\ \text{studying in the library.}^{494} \end{cases}$

The sense of each of these modifiers is '*when* she was young', '*when* he was asleep', and so on. Dowty relates a number of syntactic properties of adjectival modifiers to their temporal properties; all the above refer to temporary states.

The difference between temporary and essential (and hence more or less permanent) qualities is directly marked in many languages. In Russian the adjective has two different paradigms, the "long" form and the "short."[495] The former refer, roughly, to essential, permanent characteristics, while the latter are generally nonessential and temporary. Thus *bol'noy* means 'sickly, poor of health', while *bolen* means 'ill (at the moment)'; *zanyatoy* is 'generally busy', while *zanyat* is 'busy (at the moment)'.

A similar distinction is marked in some Romance languages—for example Spanish[496]—by using different auxiliary verbs. *Estar* is used with expressions of location (*está alta* 'it's high up') or temporary state (*está borracho* 'he's drunk'), while *ser* is used for essential or enduring states (*es borracho* 'he's a drunkard'). The difference can be quite subtle, if not entirely subjective, as illustrated by this pair of examples:

Ahora que está   rico no se   acuerda   de cuando empezaba
now   that (s/he) is rich not oneself (s/he) reminds of when   (s/he) began (IMPF)
a ganarlo.
to to earn-it

'Now that she (he) is rich she (he) doesn't remember when she (he) was beginning to earn it.'

Ahora que es   pobre abomina   de la riqueza.
now   that (s/he) is poor (s/he) abominates of the wealth

'Now that she (he) is poor, she (he) abominates wealth.'[497]

Bolinger (1971) cites a number of syntactic facts suggesting a covert distinction of the same kind in English. An essential and an "accidental" quality do not readily conjoin:

> He's sick and afflicted.
> It's safe and reliable.
> *He's wicked and afflicted.

A modifier equivalent to a *ser*-taking expression may be preposed, but not one equivalent to an *estar*-taking expression:

> From what city is he?
> ?In what city is he?

A parenthetical is more readily inserted between a noun and a "permanent" modifier than a "temporary" one:

> The squadron is, admittedly, from England.
> ?The squadron is, admittedly, in England.

Think and *hold* take only permanent complements:

> I thought/hold him (to be) { clever. / *ready. / *singing.

On the other hand, *get* takes only temporary ones:

> The { coffee / *climate } got cold.
> Mary got { sick. / *intelligent.

It is not clear that the essential difference in each of these cases is one of time—permanent or relatively permanent versus temporary or relatively temporary—or not. But certainly this distinction interacts with other expressions of temporal relations. To say that someone is (*está*) drunk (right now) is to say that they have drunk (too much alcohol); to say that someone is (*es*) (a) drunk (right now) is to say that they *habitually* drink too much alcohol.

There are also various other categories of the verb having primarily to do with nontemporal relations or properties which interact closely with tense and aspect. Mood is one such category. Another example of this concerns the verbs of motion (verbs in the semantic field of 'go') in Russian.

In Russian, "verbs of motion" have, alongside the distinction of perfective and imperfective, another (and obligatory) distinction of *determinate* action (e.g., *bežat'* 'to run') and *indeterminate* action (*begat'* 'to run').[498] (Both the determinate and indeterminate occur only in the imperfective.) There has been much controversy over the essential difference between the two categories of verb, though it is generally agreed that the determinate is the marked (positively defined) member of the opposition.[499]

Some of the definitions of the determinate which have been offered include:

actions taking place in one direction, continuously, at a given moment[500]
motion in a definite direction, actually taking place at a given time[501]
[motion taking place in a] precise direction with an underlying sense of purpose[502]

The distinction of unidirectionality is illustrated by this pair of examples:

(indeterminate *xodil*)
ya poter'al perčatki, kogda xodil v teatr.
I   lost   gloves   when   went to theatre
'I lost my gloves when I went to the theatre'

(determinate *šёl*)
ya poter'al perčatki, kogda šёl v teatr.
'I lost my gloves while I was on my way to the theatre.'[503]

Obviously, whatever the central meaning of this distinction, which in fact seems not to be essentially a temporal one, there is a clear relationship to aspect at least (and it is often treated in conjunction with it), since the perfective lacks this distinction. But the study of the Russian verbs of motion goes beyond the scope of the present work.

In what other directions might the study of tense and aspect be extended? Doubtless there are numerous phenomena not yet discussed in the literature remaining to be investigated. A character in one of Len Deighton's novels says, "When I get all my questions answered fully, I know I'm asking the wrong questions." In the study of tense and aspect we have probably been asking the right questions, then, for few if any have as yet been completely answered; but we have probably not been asking *all* the right questions. In recent times we have learned a very great deal about temporal expression in language, and we understand it far better than we did even a dozen years ago, but as yet we can hardly claim to understand it fully.

Summary

a. Tense

Grammatical tense. Among the grammatical categories marked by the verb is that of tense (chapter 1, section a). Tense may be marked morphologically, by a variation in the form of the verb itself (*walk* vs. *walked*), or syntactically, by an auxiliary word (*will walk*), or by both (*walk, has walked*) (1.a–c). Tense is the category most closely reflecting distinctions of time (1.a) There are, however, other categories concerned in some way with time—aspect (5.a), mood (3.a; 8.i,l), and status (3.f, 2.g). Moreover, verb forms rarely mark tense without at the same time indicating some of these other distinctions as well (1.b,c).

Times and tenses. To the European mind, at least, time seems to be a line divided into the three sectors of past, present, and future (1.a). Aristotle considered the present merely the boundary between past and future, though the present tense is used for past and future events near that boundary (1.a; cf. 3.h).

According to naive theories of meaning, grammatical tense directly reflects the threefold division of time, each tense referring to the appropriate sector of time (1.a). However, few if any languages exhibit precisely the three tenses that this predicts (1.a).

Consequently the original goal of the theory of tenses was simply to reconcile the three times with the tenses actually found (1.a,b). The solution was to find some kind of meaning distinctions by which to label the various tenses (1.d,e). Only later was it recognized that finding such labels was inadequate to account for either the meanings or uses of the tenses.

The 'four pasts' theory of tense. At first the Greeks attempted to account for tenses in terms of an a priori theory, based on meaning distinctions (1.b). The Attic Greek verb had seven tenses; apart from present, future, and future perfect, there were four past tenses which were seen to differ from one another in three ways: definiteness (whether a tense indicates a specific time), metric tense (degree of distance from the present), and aspect (completion of action) (1.b,c).

According to this theory, the (present) perfect tense represents the recent, and the pluperfect the distant, past; the perfect and pluperfect mark completion, and the imperfect, incompletion; the perfect is definite, marking events which have just happened, while the others are indefinite; and the aorist simply indicates pastness with no further distinctions (1.b). Similarly, the Greek future perfect is a near future (1.b).

Stoic-Varronian aspectual theory. A closer examination of the Greek language itself led the Stoics to some kind of aspectual theory: the tenses mark not only distinctions of time but also whether the action is perfect (complete) or imperfect (incomplete) (1.e, 2.d). Varro adapted this theory to Latin (2.d).

Greek and Latin distinguish perfect tenses ([present] perfect, past perfect [pluperfect], future perfect) from imperfect ones (present, [past] imperfect, future), the Greek aorist being neutral as to aspect (1.b–c,e). The Stoics apparently considered the future neutral as well (1.e).

Simple and complex tenses. The modern European languages developed tense systems richer in some respects than those of the classical languages (2.b). The perfect and imperfect tenses of the modern languages employ complex (periphrastic, analytic) forms (e.g., *has gone, is going*), the simple forms (*goes*) generally being neutral as to aspect (2.d).

The ambiguous Latin perfect has been superseded by two unambiguous tenses, the simple preterite (past) and the complex present perfect; moreover, each simple tense now has a corresponding perfect tense (2.b). Further, parallel to the future tenses, there has developed the future-in-the-past (conditional, *they would leave [later that day]*), with its own perfect (the conditional perfect or past conditional, *they would have left [by then]*) (2.b).

Universality. Simple application of classical grammar to the tenses of the modern languages proved difficult and led to a new type of theory, relative tense (6.a–c). While radical empiricists have doubted the possibility of a universal grammatical system for tenses (2.d, 3.g), and the application of (traditional) theories of tense to non-Indo-European languages has proved problematical (2.e), it has usually been assumed that a general, universal, and explanatory account is both possible and desirable.

In the ancient period this was based on presumably universal notions of time (1.a). In the medieval and rationalist periods the "logic" of tense was appealed to (2.a), which in practice often meant Latin grammar. In the modern period there has been a real effort at developing scientific approaches (2.f).

Definite and indefinite. While metric tense has played no role in the theory of European tenses, definiteness has; early grammarians of the modern European languages distinguished the present perfect (definite) from the (indefinite) preterite (2.a,c). To this day many see this distinction as the fundamental difference between the two (3.f). Since Pickbourn in the eighteenth century, however, it is the perfect which is considered indefinite, since it does not presuppose a specific time (2.c,d; 3.f).

Relative tense theory. Relative tense theories (2.a–c) first arose in connection

with the tense systems of modern European languages (2.a–b). Although distinct
from aspectual theories, the boundary between the two has always been somewhat
unclear (2.d).

In relative tense theories (which spring from the work of Scaliger in the fifteenth century via the seventeenth-century *Grammaire générale*), a distinction is
made between absolute (simple) tenses—past, present, and future—which relate
directly to one of the sectors of time, and relative (compound) ones, which relate
to another time (2.c). The imperfect, pluperfect, and the (Latin) periphrasis meaning 'was going to' are respectively the present, past, and future in the past; the
future, future perfect, and the periphrasis 'shall be about to' are the corresponding
present, past, and future in the future (2.b,c).

Modern theories treat all tenses as relative, the "absolute" tenses being simply
the present, past, and future tenses of the present (2.g). For Jespersen (early twentieth century), the past, present, and future were the main divisions of time; past
and future also contained subordinate prospective (posterior) tenses—*be going to,
be about to*—and retrospective (anterior) tenses (in form the perfects) (2.g). He
distinguished anteriority from the perfect aspect (2.g). The present had no subsidiary times because it was just an indivisible point (3.h; cf. 1.a). Nor did Jespersen
consider the conditional to be a posterior past (2.g).

The theories of Reichenbach (1947) and Bull (1960) are relative tense theories
(3.h). Reichenbach introduced the notion of reference point. He factored tenses
into the twin relationships, first, between an abstract reference point and the time
of the speech act, corresponding to tense proper, and second, between the event
time and the reference point (aspect); the pluperfect represents an event prior to a
reference point itself prior to the present (i.e., a past-in-the-past or anterior past)
(3.h). Reichenbach was the first to adequately treat the conditional (though not
the conditional perfect); it involves an event following a past reference point (3.h).

Bull's theory is based on the relation of "axes" of orientation (present and
past, and anticipatory and retrospective versions of each) to one other, and of
times (vectors) within those axes; the pluperfect is the minus vector on the retrospective point axis. Bull could treat the conditional perfect (unanalyzable by others) as the zero vector of an axis of anticipation seen from a point viewed retrospectively from the present (3.h).

Meaning and use. Finding labels for tenses (e.g., "past in the past," "complete action in the past," etc.) proved inadequate to account for either meanings
or uses of the tenses in a number of respects, and the a priori categories of the
traditional theories failed to match the realities of languages; for example, no
theory of Latin grammar handled the perfect well (2.f, 3.g).

Jespersen was able to reconcile theoretical categories with grammatical distinctions through a structuralist approach which distinguished form, function (grammatical category), and "notion" (meaning or use) as independent systems (2.f,
3.g).

The (present) perfect illustrates the difficulties of relating meaning and use;
while it presumably has one meaning, it has numerous uses (3.f,g). Monoseman-
ticists such as Jespersen assume a grammatical category has but one basic mean-

ing, while polysemanticists allow for a number of meanings, possibly clustered around a prototypical set of concepts (3.g).

But the question is how in either case the various uses of a category reflect its meaning(s); while the use of a tense often follows from its meaning, it is not always easy to account for all uses in terms of meaning(s) (3.g). The reconciliation (and distinction) of use and meaning has become a central goal of tense theory (3.f,g).

Early theorists failed to take into account the role of context in determining tense use. For autonomists, basic meanings are vague and contexts add specifying meanings to them, while for contextualists, meanings are ambiguous and contexts select from among them (3.g).

Tenses in context. Tenses often show values unlike their "normal" ones in certain contexts, especially when within the scope of another tense, and in such contexts there are restrictions on the occurrence of tenses (3.a–e). Some theories hold that tenses have basic meanings which may, however, be shifted (3.c–e, 8.b) or transformed (8.c) under the influence of other tenses.

The theories of Bull and Reichenbach (3.h) and their followers involve no shifting but assign meanings once and for all in context (3.h,i; 8.b), and define constraints on sequences of tenses similar to the traditional rules (3.d,e). Reichenbach's system allows statement of such rules in terms of the reference point (3.h; 8.b,c).

b. Topical Summary

Present. The present has various uses (7.f,g), including that of future (futurate, 7.g,m) and (historical) past (8.j). Basically it refers to an interval of time including the literal present point in time (7.f–h; 8.m,n). The present denotes events coinciding with both the reference time and the time of the speech act (3.h, 7.h). There is some reason to regard the present tense of some languages as a non-past tense (1.d–e) encompassing the future. It is aspectually imperfective (1.e, 2.d) or neutral (2.c,d).

Future. There is some question in many languages as to whether there is a future tense as such (1.a). The future refers to an interval of time following the literal present point in time (2.f,g; 7.f–h). The future denotes events coinciding with the reference time, which follows the time of the speech act (3.h, 7.h). It is aspectually imperfective or neutral (1.e; 2.c,d). The future perfect represents an event prior to, or completed by, some time in the future (7.j–l). The futurate present differs from the future in conditions of use (pragmatics), not in meaning (7.g,m). The future and the futurates alike have special modal functions (3.a, 8.k).

Preterite (past). The simple past tense refers to an interval of time preceding the literal present point in time (2.f,g; 7.f,h). The past denotes events coinciding with the reference time, which precedes the time of the speech act (3.h, 7.h). The simple past tense (preterite) is aspectually imperfective or neutral (1.e; 2.c,d). In

Latin the perfect acted for the preterite (1.e). In modern European languages—colloquial French and German—the complex perfect does so as well (6.f; 7.i,l).

Preterite versus present perfect. The perfect form apparently marks either anterior time or perfect aspect (2.g). In non-finites, perfect forms ambiguously represent the past as well as the perfect (3.e). The present perfect does not presuppose a definite time, while the preterite does (2.c,d; 3.f). One major theory holds that the present perfect represents events occurring on a stretch of time which includes the present (7.h–l). Another sees it as an embedded past tense (7.j, 8.c). Recently it has been viewed as simply the present tense of the perfect aspect, but with a special set of pragmatic conditions on its use (7.l). The past and present perfect have special, but distinct, modal functions (8.h,i,l).

Preterite versus imperfect. The preterite differs from the imperfect tense in aspect—complete or neutral preterite versus non-complete imperfect (1, 2.d, 5.d). The imperfect may represent a backshifted present in a past context (2.c,f–g; 3.d,h; 8.a–d). The preterite is used to foreground information, and forms the skeleton of narrative while the imperfect backgrounds information (8.e–g). The preterite generally advances narrative time, while the imperfect does so only under special conditions (8.m–p).

Pluperfect. The pluperfect represents an event prior to or completed by a reference point itself in the past (1; 2.c,d,f,g; 3.h; 7.h–l). It may represent a backshifted past or present perfect in a past context (2.e,f–g; 3.d,h; 8.a–d).

Conditional tenses. The conditional, formerly considered a mood (2), properly represents an event which follows a reference point in the past (3.h). The conditional perfect represents an event anterior to an event following a past reference point (3.h). The conditionals may represent backshifted embedded futures in a past context (2.f–g; 3.d,e,h; 8.a–d).

Progressive tenses. The many theories of the distinctive meanings of the progressive tenses are not very satisfactory (7.n). The progressive seems to indicate that the reference time or frame overlaps with the event (7.n–p). This identifies the progressive with the imperfective aspect (7.n,p). Not every use can be accounted for in this way, however (7.n). The progressive puts stronger pragmatic requirements on events than does the imperfective in general; it must allow for a possible world or future in which an accomplishment is achieved (7.n–p, t–v). Alternatively it represents an internal phase of a completed occurrence (5.e,g,h; 7.v).

c. Aspect

The concept of Aspect. Tense is so closely interwoven with aspect that no account of tense alone can hope to adequately account for the uses of verb forms (4). Aspect is overtly marked in Slavic languages but not in Western European ones, and so the concept came into the grammatical tradition from Slavic studies; the term itself translates Russian *vid* 'view' (5.a). In Slavic, all verbs in all tenses are obligatorily marked for imperfective or perfective aspect; both *ona pročitala* and *ona čitala* mean 'she read', but they are not synonymous. The difference intuitively has to do with completion versus non-completion (5.a). Aspectual distinctions, though not overtly marked, do play an important role in the Western European languages (1; 2.d,g; 5.a).

Aspect, Aktionsarten, *and Aristotelian aspect.* There have been at least three independent phenomena termed aspect, with much confusion of them, especially as regards non-Slavic languages such as the Germanic ones (5.b; 6.a,g). Since Streitberg (nineteenth century), the term *Aktionsarten* 'kinds of action' has been a rough synonym of *aspects* (5.b, 6.g). However, the *Aktionsarten* are properly lexical categories such as the distinction between German *jagen* 'hunt' and *erjagen* 'catch', while the aspects are properly grammatical categories applicable to the same verb (5.b, 6.g). Both aspect and *Aktionsart* have been confused with a third, unmarked category, Aristotelian aspect (usually called the Vendlerian categories) (5.b, 6.a).

Perfective and imperfective. Each of these Slavic aspects has a range of meanings; structuralists assume that these are contextual meanings and that between the aspects there is one basic opposition of meaning (5.c). For structuralists, following Saussure and Jakobson (early twentieth century), there is a "marked" member of this pair of opposed forms which is positively defined and an "unmarked" member defined as meaning anything else (5.c). The imperfective is the unmarked member of the Slavic opposition (5.c). The positive meaning of the perfective is complexive, referring to the total act from beginning to end (5.c).

Application of structuralist thought to the analysis of the Greek verb has led to no great consensus on either what the relevant aspectual categories are (though seemingly the perfect tenses represent a perfect aspect, the imperfect ones equate to the imperfective, and the aorist to the perfective); what the unmarked members of the oppositions are; or what each marked member means. This calls into question structuralist methodology. That structuralism says nothing directly about the content of expressions, but only taxonomizes them, calls into question the value of the enterprise itself (5.d).

Aristotelian aspect. Aristotle is credited with distinguishing being (state) from doing (activity); later scholars (Ryle, Kenny, Vendler in the mid-twentieth century) developed a classification of verbs into states, activities, accomplishments, and achievements (5.b, 6.a); a fifth category, series, may be needed as well (6.b). Verkuyl (1972) showed that this is not a classification of verbs but of expressions as large as the sentence (6.d). Various criterial tests for membership have been developed (6.a,b).

Underlying the classification is an ontology, an account of what kinds of situations or occurrences there are. Various classificatory taxonomies of situations have been offered to account for the categories found (6.b).

The linguistic properties of expressions reflected in the criterial tests are explicable in terms of the properties of the corresponding situations (6.b–e). States are non-dynamic, persistent, usually non-agentive, and lack non-trivial gaps (6.c). Performances (accomplishments and achievements), as opposed to activities, are telic, inherently involving a culminative phase (6.d). Achievements differ from accomplishments in being instantaneous, lacking the activity phase preceding the accomplishment of the goal itself (6.e).

Phase. The Aristotelian types are defined in terms of their ideal phasic structures; by phase is meant a stage in the development of a situation (6.b–e). Phase was first studied by Guillaume (early twentieth century) in the context of an eccentric ideationalist theory of tense and aspect (6.f). Others further developed the concept in theories of the *Aktionsarten* (6.f,g). Noreen (early twentieth century) taxonomized *Aktionsarten* partly in terms of phase, though he did not utilize the term (6.g). Woisetschlaeger (1976) developed a logical theory of possible phasic structures of the *Aktionsarten* based on the notions of pause, change of state, and so on (6.g).

Defining aspect. It is now possible to distinguish the three kinds of "aspect": Aristotelian aspect is a classification of situations and expressions for them in terms of phasic structural types; the *Aktionsarten* constitute a classification of expressions for subsituations, phases, and subphases of situations; and true aspect concerns the temporal relationship of a situation to the reference frame against which it is set (6.h).

Aspect has to do with the relationship of the event time E to the reference frame R; complexive (perfective) aspect has E within R, imperfective has E and R overlapping, and perfect has E preceding R (6.h, 7.p).

Aspectual theories have included some—Harris's, for example—which also took into account the beginnings or other phases of actions. Harris proposed an inceptive aspect (*I was beginning to write*) alongside the completive (*I had finished writing*) and "extended" (*I was writing*); the simple, aspectually neutral tenses (*I ate*) he called "aorist" (6.c,d). This is to confuse aspect and *Aktionsart*.

d. The Formal Semantics of Tense and Aspect

Formal semantics. Without an objective theory of semantics, disputes about tense and aspect are futile; resolutions to issues can best be accomplished within a formal semantic theory (4, 7.a). There have been three types of theories of meaning: referential (expressions have meaning by virtue of referring to things in the world), ideational (expressions have meaning by virtue of referring to ideas), and functional (expressions have meaning by virtue of being usable); but only within the referential framework has a theory of tense and aspect been developed (7.a). In this framework, all linguistic expressions refer either to things in the world or to abstract objects—truth values and sets (7.b).

Truth-conditional, model-theoretic semantics defines meaning in terms of truth conditions for expressions, utilizing models of reality to state such conditions (7.c). The most developed such theory is Montague's (1970s), in which the central method is that of translating natural language expressions into those of a logical translation language (LTL) and then semantically interpreting the expressions of that language (7.c–e). Tenses and aspects are captured in the form of operators: thus the simple past tense is translated in one LTL by PAST.

The operators for the simple tenses. Tense operators were first employed in the 1950s in Prior's tense logic, following ideas of Findlay's (7.f). A present tense operator may be needed as well (7.f); the present has many uses, but only one meaning (7.g). The future requires a future operator (7.g), but the apparent ambiguity of definiteness in past and future tenses does not require extra operators (7.f). Semantic interpretation of these operators requires a model of time and a definition of the notion of "interval of time" (7.h).

Compositionality and the perfect. Early work in formal semantics (early 1970s) for the Priorian operators eschewed a compositional treatment of the complex tenses (in which the present perfect, representing the present tense of the perfect aspect, is translated as *PRES(PERF)*) because of the adverbial scope paradox: there is no way of translating, for instance, *came yesterday* into an LTL using Priorian operators (7.h).

Although most scholars came to adopt some form of compositional treatment for the complex tenses (7.j–o), Nerbonne (1984) argued against such for the perfect (7.i). Johnson's (1977) paradigmatic approach to Kikuyu points to the possibility of a semicompositional approach (7.i,k). There is a confusing array of issues regarding compositionality which has never been satisfactorily resolved, but it seems that a compositional treatment is required only in a limited sense (7.i).

The perfect. The difficulty of the English present perfect in regard to compositionality is that it does not only act as the present of the perfect, and its meaning has been controversial (3.f, 8.j–l). The theory of the perfect as an embedded past requires a compositional treatment, but no special perfect operator (8.c). In the theories of the perfect as an indefinite past (1.b; 2.a,c,d; 3.f; 7.j) and a past with current relevance (7.j, 8.e–g,i), the (present) perfect differs only pragmatically, but not in meaning, from the past.

In extended now (XN) theory it has a distinct and possibly non-compositional treatment (7.j). Dowty (late 1970s) developed a compositional XN treatment using the operator HAVE (7.k). The problem is that XN theory, whether compositional or not, renders the present perfect unlike the other perfects; Johnson however defines the perfect universally in a way unlike XN (7.l,p). The solution is that the perfect does require a distinct compositional perfect operator and the special XN "meaning" in English is pragmatic (7.l).

The progressive. Much the same issues of compositionality arise in regard to the progressive (7.n). Various meanings for the progressive have been proposed—continued action, dynamic action, durative action, interior of an event, incompletion, unlimitedness—but none is satisfactory. Jespersen proposed treating it as the frame for another event (7.n).

Early formal treatments such as that of Bennett and Partee ran into the imperfective paradox: *Mr. Blandings was building his dream house* does not entail *Mr. Blandings built his dream house* (7.h,o). Dowty proposed dealing with this problem by using possible worlds, branching time, and the notion of inertia world; this treatment encompasses the futurate progressive (7.o). Problems with the notion of branching time led to later approaches, especially within the situation semantics framework (1980s), based on such notions as possible history (7.t,u), partial event (7.u), and open region (7.v).

Progressive and imperfective. Although the progressive has generally been identified with the imperfective aspect, there are important differences between the two (7.n,p). Johnson defined in Reichenbachian terms (in terms of the E-R

relation) three aspects using the operators COMP (perfective), PROG (imperfective), and PERF (perfect) (7.l,p). The progressive is a type of imperfective (7.o,p).

The adverbial scope paradox. Adverbials play an important role in temporal
reference (8.q), not least in creating the scope paradox (7.r). There are many types
of temporal adverbial in languages (7.q). At first a syntactic solution for the paradox was adopted, in which tenses are not independent of adverbials, but this
solution fails (7.r). There seems to be good reason to adopt a two- or even three-
dimensional indexing approach, based on the work of Kamp (1970s–1980s) and
Johnson, which allows adverbials to have scopes relative to the tense operators
(7.s).

Event-based systems. The notion of branching time brings with it problems
which prompted some to develop theories replacing the notion of possible world
with that of possible history, inertia world with possible future, and interval with
event (7.t); a formal theory is presented in 7.u. In the 1980s events have also
played a central role in formal pragmatic theories (8.m).

A more radical break with the Montague tradition is that of Situation Semantics
(1981 on), which bases meaning not on truth conditions but direct reference to
situations (7.v). While relatively little work on tense and aspect has as yet been
done within this paradigm, new treatments of the progressive especially have been
offered by various scholars (7.v).

e. Pragmatics

Informal pragmatics. Conditions on use loom large in the theory of tense and
aspect (3.d,f,g,i; 7.j,n; 8.a,d–l). Pragmatic solutions couched in terms of such
conditions have been offered for the difference of perfect and preterite (7.j; 8.e–
g,i), for sequence of tenses (8.a,d,e), for the difference in use of the preterite and
imperfect tenses (8.f,g,n), and for the futurate uses of tenses (7.m,k). Such (informal) pragmatic accounts presumably obviate any need for a specifically (formal) semantic account.

Formal pragmatics. Informal pragmatic accounts have been held to be as inadequate in their own way as formal but purely semantic accounts. In recent years
an effort has been made to develop a formal pragmatic theory using the methods
of formal semantics and the results of informal pragmatics. In particular, interest
has been focused on the structure of discourse (text) and its role in tense selection
(8.m–q).

The major method here is the construction of a model, the discourse representation structure, for discourses as a whole, taking as primitives events rather than
intervals (8.m). In narrative, the preterite and other "deictic" tenses advance the
reference point, but the imperfect and other "anaphoric" tenses do not (8.m,o).
The Aristotelian classes affect this as well (8.m,n). Ultimately, however, it is
pragmatic conditions which determine this advancement with any tense and Aristotelian class (8.n).

This approach, essentially an extension of the methods of formal semantics to
larger units than the sentence, has been criticized as overly simplistic in its ap-

proach to text structure and the treatment of the advancement of subsidiary R points in texts (8.o–q).

The problems of sequence of tenses (3.d,e; 8.a,d,e), and subsidiary R points are seen, along with various other phenomena (8.h–l), as just special cases of the general problem of shifting of perspective (8.o). This involves not only establishment of the R point at each point in a narrative, but also its relationship to a hierarchy of orientation times (8.o). An approach has recently been developed in which pairwise tense relations as found in the work of Allen (1966, 3.i) and Smith (1970s–1980s, 8.c) is married to a grammar of text, and constraints on tenses are defined in terms of structural configurations such as c-command and the scopes of general orientation times (8.o,p).

While perspective and orientation account for the relations of tenses, they do not account for localization in time; adverbials more than tenses serve for this (8.q).

The problem of tenseless languages. Many languages lack markers of tense; the question is how they capture temporal distinctions. The classical Semitic languages lack markers of absolute tense, but there has been a debate over what their verbs do mark—aspect, relative tense, and so on (8.r,s). An increasingly prevalent view is that they mark a pragmatic distinction of foregrounded and backgrounded information, rather than a semantic distinction at all (8.s). There has been a similar debate over whether creoles have tense or merely aspect (8.t).

Ultimately, what is required is an account of how tenseless languages indicate temporal distinctions. This will require a better understanding of tense and aspect in discourse and text than we possess at present (8.t).

Beyond tense and aspect. Tense and aspect do not exhaust linguistic categories relating to temporal distinctions; there are also mood (3.a,b; 8.i,l) and status (3.f, 2.g). The Russian verb distinguishes determinate from indeterminate motion (6.d,e; 8.u); many languages distinguish temporary states from permanent ones by markings in verb or adjective (6.c, 8.u). Nouns, adjectives, and other parts of speech may also mark or presuppose temporal distinctions (8.u).

Envoi

We are like dwarfs seated on the shoulders of giants; we see things more clearly than the ancients and more distant, but this is due neither to the sharpness of our own sight nor the greatness of our own status but because we are raised and borne aloft on that great mass.—Bernard of Chartres, in McFall (1982:xiii)

Among the virtues of the grammarian is this one, *to be ignorant of some things.*—Bernard of Chartres, quoted by John of Salisbury, in Peck (1911:231)

It does not wrap things up; it is a prelude, but a time comes for preludes, after a long series of deafening finales.—Dwight Bolinger (1975:554), in Hopper (1982:16)

I have not the vanity to think that I have discussed the subject so fully as it deserves: but, I hope, I shall be allowed to have made some progress in it. . . . And should this little attempt be the means of exciting some person of better abilities, and more leisure, to pursue the inquiry further, and do full justice to the subject, I shall think the pains I have taken in it amply rewarded.—James Pickbourn (1789:xvii–xviii)

Notes

Chapter 1

1. In the *Sophist* 262a (1961:1009) the Stranger says, "By 'verb' we mean an expression which is applied to actions."
2. *Poetics* XX.9 (1932:77). Cf. *On Interpretation* III (1938:119): "A verb is a sound which not only conveys a particular meaning but has a time-reference also."
3. Bråroe (1974:v).
4. Tedeschi and Zaenen (1981:xvi).
5. Barwise and Perry (1983:288). Aspect is discussed at length in part II of the present book. It is a regular feature in the grammars of many languages, for example Russian and the other Slavic languages, where it is overtly marked in the verb, just as tense is. In English and many other European languages aspectual distinctions are indicated by the use of auxiliary verbs—e.g., *have* and *be*. The phrases *I was eating* and *I had eaten* differ primarily in aspect, the first indicating ongoing, incomplete action, and the second, completed action. However, we shall see that things are not quite this simple, and completeness is not the only aspectual category.
6. Lakoff (1970:838). Similar statements are to be found in the works of many authors, for example in Diver (1963:141):

   It is a curious feature of modern linguistic analysis that the English language, widely and intensively studied though it has been, should contain within it a number of areas about which there remains widespread disagreement. Nowhere is this more apparent than in the domain of the English verb. To the question "What are the meanings of the English verb forms?" such American descriptivists as Francis, Hill, Hockett, Joos, and Twadell have, in recent years, given answers that are to a considerable extent mutually contradictory.

7. Harris (1751:97).
8. Nearly all the modern languages of Europe, of Iran, and of northern India are descended from an ancient language we call Proto-Indo-European, which was spoken probably somewhere in east central Europe some five thousand years ago. Consequently these languages have a number of properties in common which they do not necessarily share with non-Indo-European languages. The cultures of the ancient peoples speaking these languages—the Romans, Greeks, Persians, and Indians, for example—also reflect to some extent a shared cultural heritage from their Indo-European forebears.
9. For example, in Buddhist texts cited by Schumann (1974:111): "the Three Times

(past, present, and future)''; and Guenther (1971:65, 67): "the three divisions of time."
Similarly in Rudolph (1983:295ff.): "the three periods."

In the *Sophist* 262d (1961:1009), the Stranger refers to "facts or events in the present or past or future." (Plato here is using these terms of the times, not the tenses.)
In the *Parmenides* 151e–152a (943f.), Plato does write that "to 'be' means precisely
having existence in conjunction with time present, as 'was' or 'will be' means having
existence in conjunction with past or future time." (Cf. 141d–e, 935.) But he has no
theory of the three times, simply accepting the naive, "intuitive" notion.

10. *Iliad* 1.70 (1951:61).
11. In Latin, *Parcae*; in Greek, *Moîrai*. Shakespeare's "three weird sisters" in *Macbeth*
    are probably a distant echo of the three Fates. On the names and character of the Fates,
    see Plato, *Republic* X.617b ff. (1961:841). Unlike those of the Scandinavian *Norns*
    mentioned below, the names of the Graeco-Roman Fates have no etymological con-
    nection with time. (The information here and in the text is largely drawn from Grimm,
    1883:405ff.)
12. *Physics* VI.233f. (1934:117).
13. Diogenes Laertius VII.141 (1925:245).
14. Ibid., IV.217a–218a (1929:373); cf. Harris (1751:106), Gale (1968:9). This problem
    is essentially one of how a finite amount of time can consist entirely of a sum of
    durationless instants.
15. *Physics* IV.217b (1929:373).
16. Ibid., VI.234a (1934:119).
17. Ibid., IV.222a (1929:411).
18. Jespersen (1924:258) says that, although the present is theoretically an instant without
    duration, "in practice 'now' means a time with appreciable duration, the length of
    which varies greatly according to circumstances." Even if it is argued that strictly
    speaking the present tense only *states* what is true at this instant in time, though it
    implies a greater duration for a state of affairs, series of events, situation, etc., the
    problem remains of how something can be true *at an instant*. In chapter 7 we discuss
    the role of instants and intervals of time in the semantics of tense and aspect. (For
    discussion of instants and intervals, see Hamblin, 1971.)
19. Harris (1751:118f.).
20. Comrie (1976:98–105) discusses the use of locative or spatial expressions for time
    distinctions. He discusses (129f.) the localist theory, which holds that tense and/or
    aspect are inherently locational. See Traugott (1978) for examples from numerous lan-
    guages of locational expressions, and Ultan (1978) for the use of such expressions in
    marking futurity.
21. Comrie (1976:99); Bartsch (1986:7). A similar construction is proposed by the gram-
    marian Jespersen (among others) as the origin of the English present progressive tense,
    e.g., *he is gardening*. For discussion of this controversial proposal (which is assumed
    by Bartsch), see Jespersen (1931), chs. 12 and 14; Scheffer (1975); and the papers by
    van der Gaaf (1930) and Mossé (1925, 1957) collected in Schopf (1974).
22. *Parmenides* 152a (1961:944).
23. But as the philosopher McTaggart (1968) points out, the relationships between events
    on the line do not change. That particular noon will forever follow the first of these
    moments and precede the third.
24. *Praesens* is the present active participle of *praesum* 'be before'. Its synonym, *instans*
    (English *instant*), is that of *insto* 'stand within', translating the Greek *enestós*, which
    in turn is the perfect active participle of *enístēmi*, 'be within'.
    Praeteritum is the perfect participle of *praetereo* 'go by, pass'; this translates Greek
    pareléluthos, the perfect active participle of *parérkhomai* and *paroikhoménos*, the per-
    fect medio-passive participle of *paroíkhomai*, both meaning 'go by, pass'.
    Futurus is the future active participle of *sum* 'be', translating Greek *méllōn*, the
    present active participle of *méllō* 'be about to be, be likely to be'.
25. The philosopher Richard Gale has written (1968:vii), apropos of some famous philo-

sophical arguments against the reality of time, "Time, of course, is real: ask any woman [or man?—R. B.] who has just seen the first wrinkle on her face in the mirror." It hardly matters if time is real; at the very least we talk as if it is. One of the functions of language is to say things about the world, hence language must be able to say things about time—as Harris, quoted above, insists. The question is, what precisely are the properties of language (and languages) that allow it (and them) to do so?

26. Dionysius Thrax (1867:53, 1874:12). See too Steinthal (1890:I, 310), who cites Diogenes Laertius VII.141.

27. *On Interpretation* I.16a (1938:115).

28. Ibid., 117. "Nouns" here may be taken to mean "linguistic expressions."

29. Pinborg (1975:79, 94).

30. Russian, like English and German, has only two tense forms marked as modifications of the verb (i.e., morphological tenses), a past and a nonpast: *solntse sadits'a* 'the sun is setting'; *solntse sadilos'* 'the sun was setting'. The "present" tense of Russian is used under certain circumstances for a future, but Russian has a periphrastic future as well: *utrom* ('in the morning') *bud'em* ('we are', i.e. 'we will') *gul'at'* ('[to] go for a walk'). Greek, Latin, and the Romance languages have future tense forms distinct from the present, e.g., Latin *amavi* 'I loved', *amo* 'I love', *amabo* 'I shall love'.

31. However, an anonymous reviewer of the present work has correctly pointed out that we intuit "a closer link between *will* and future time reference than in the case of the other constructions"—out of context we consider *John will be there* to be future, but we do not so consider *John must be there*. Nonetheless, the use of *will* (or *shall*) is neither a sufficient nor a necessary condition for a future time interpretation, since many sentences with *will* are not in the future tense, and many sentences in—or at least "conveying"—the future tense do not mark it with *will*. Of course the same is true of any other modal.

    Will differs from other modals in that its use to mark futurity is "grammaticized," i.e., within the grammar of the language it is a systematic marker or indicator of futurity; the other modals simply convey futurity without literally marking it. The applicability of the notion of grammaticization to cases such as this one is dependent, however, on a number of theoretical considerations.

32. It is an interesting question in what other senses, if any, this might be true. If we took tense to be a semantic category rather than a category having to do with the formal markers of members of that semantic category, then such languages might well "have tense," even though they lacked formal tense markers. Many such members of semantic categories are unmarked in languages. Thus the present tense of English is usually just the bare verb, e.g., *love* (except for the third person singular, e.g., *loves*).

    Overt marking is not necessarily required for a language to have a semantic category. English clearly distinguishes count nouns (*boy*) from mass nouns (*water*)—count nouns can be pluralized, can take the article *a*, etc., while mass nouns cannot—but has no overt marker(s) of the distinction. This grammatical distinction reflects a semantic one, since assigning a meaning to a nonsense word such as *grib* suffices to tell us which of the two grammatical classes it falls into.

33. See chapter 8 for discussion of precisely what the "tense" markers of these languages mark.

34. As far as time is concerned, Friedman, in an article concerning the American Sign Language (ASL) of the deaf (1975:941), includes it among the concepts which "any language must provide for." Friedman writes (p. 951) that "speakers have a tripartite distinction in the conceptualization of time." In ASL, time is treated metaphorically as a line passing through the body, and events in the future are signed in front of and away from the "speaker" (signer), while those in the past often are indicated by gestural reference behind the signer, such as throwing the hand back over the shoulder.

    Discussing the communicative capacities of "tenseless" languages specifically in the context of sign languages of the deaf, Brennan (1983:10f.) comments that "recent work in linguistics has attempted to demonstrate that all natural languages have the same temporal expressive power no matter what the grammatical tense system. Thus, although there are tense-less languages [their] verbs do have aspectual markings and the languages do have other ways of marking time reference—e.g., temporal adverbs.''

35. Here vowel length is represented by the macron or "long mark," thus: "ā," so that omicron ("small" or short *o*) would be *o*, but omega ("big" or long *o*), *ō*. The accents are those of written Greek. In ancient Greek the acute (´), grave (`), and circumflex (ˆ) accents represented a rise, fall, and rise-fall of pitch respectively.

36. See chapter 3 for a discussion of mood. The "passive" and "active" voices may briefly be characterized by the active sentence *John loves Jane*, which (roughly) focuses on the performer of an action, and its passive counterpart *Jane is loved by John*, which focuses on the affected party. Greek also had a "middle" voice, chiefly used (roughly) when the action was performed on, or for, the subject: *phaínomai* 'I appear' (lit., 'I show myself'); *títhētai* 'one makes (for oneself)'. On the middle voice, see Goodwin (1894:267ff.).

37. Modern Lithuanian is highly unusual in actually having precisely the three tenses of past, present, and future, as Chung and Timberlake (1985:204) point out.

38. Michael notes (1970:9) in his study of early English grammars: "The categories used by the early writers of English grammars . . . were, and have remained, [those not only] of the renaissance grammarians but to a very large extent those of the [Greek] grammarians of the first and second centuries B.C.''

39. Diogenes Laertius IX.52 (1925:465).

40. Peck (1911:70). Plato never offered an explicitly formulated account. See, however, n. 9 above.

41. An anonymous reviewer has pointed out that in most recent literature German uses Latin *Tempus* rather than *Zeit*. As we note here, *tempus* is itself ambiguous.

42. By Michael (1970:403).

43. *On Interpretation* III.16b (1938:119). Aristotle has in mind here the logic of statements. For the kind of considerations which were in question, see Kneale and Kneale (1962:49ff.).

44. *Poetics* (1932:77).

45. See Robins (1979:23f.).

46. Robins (1979:27).

47. Apollonius Dyscolus (1981:37).

48. Dionysius Thrax (1867:53, 1874:12). Similarly, Priscian says, "There are three tenses [*tempora*], present, past, and future. But the past is divided in three, into the imperfect past, perfect past, and pluperfect past.'' (Latin had no aorist tense.) See Michael (1970:117), Robins (1979:59). (The quotations from Priscian here and below are, unless noted, from VIII.38, 1857:405f.)

49. Cf. Priscian VIII.54 (1857:415f.). See Pinborg (1975:92), Steinthal (1890:II, 302f.). *Parakeímenos* is the present medio-passive participle of *parakeísthai*. *Hupersuntélikos* is 'over' plus 'complete, finished', the perfect passive participle of *suntéleō* 'finish'. *Perfectus* is the perfect passive participle of *perficio* 'complete, finish'.

50. Priscian VIII.38 (1857:405f.). The eighth-century Latin grammarian Alcuin (Michael 1970:118), following Priscian, calls the perfect *praeteritum paulo ante* 'past [passed] a little before', as opposed to the pluperfect, which he calls *praeteritum multo ante* 'past [passed] much before'. Apollonius Dyscolus (second century A.D.) likewise characterizes the pluperfect as what was "done long ago" (1981:161).

51. Priscian VIII.54f. (1857:415f.). From *aóristos* come the terms *infinitus* 'infinite, undefined' (Priscian VIII.54f., 1857:415ff.) and *indeterminatus* 'indeterminate, unlimited' (in the thirteenth-century grammarian Roger Bacon, 1902:168). Priscian is here simply repeating observations to be found in the marginal commentaries on Dionysius (1857:249ff.), though he adds the observation that the Latin perfect, like the aorist, is indifferent to distance in time.

52. Apollonius (1981:161).

53. The perfect active participle of *parateínō* 'lie along'.

54. The Greeks generally neglected the future perfect (*tethnḗksō* 'I shall have died'), re-garding it "as a feature largely peculiar to the Attic dialect and not much used in that" (Robins, 1979:30).
55. Stephanos in Dionysius Thrax (1867:251).
56. Priscian VIII.38 (1857:405).
57. *Paulo post futurum* precisely translates *met' olígon méllon* 'what is to be after a little while'.
58. Michael (1970:118) and Robins (1979:59) observe that Priscian discusses, and rejects, this division. Michael's discussion is somewhat misleading in the terms he uses

    Future simple (*futurum infinitum*)
    Future perfect (*future exactum*—Varro; *paulo post futurum*; *futurum Atticum*)

    when he says "this has been suggested by Varro."

    In Varro (IX.96, 1951:516f.), none of these terms is to be found. Moreover, the term *futurum exactum* as later used suggests the distinction of near and far future as reported by Priscian: the "exact future" is so called for the same reason that Renais-sance grammarians were to call the present perfect "definite"—because, as a time near to the present, it requires no additional time reference to make sense, as do, however, the future and the simple past tenses.

    But here Varro is instead distinguishing the future as representing incomplete action ('I shall learn') from complete action, expressed by the future perfect ('I shall have learned').
59. Robins (1979:59) points out that, oddly enough, the form cited by Priscian, *scripsero* 'I shall have written', "is precisely the form which differentiates its paradigm from the perfect subjunctive paradigm (*scripserim*, I wrote)."
60. Dionysius (1867:53, 1874:12).
61. In a marginal note in Dionysius (1867:249f.). By "sound" what is meant is essentially morphology. Where we would say that two forms of a verb have different endings or affixes, the Greeks would have said that the one verb "changes" a sound or group of sounds for another "at the end." The ancients never developed a distinct theory of morphology, or word structure, as such, and insofar as they did, they tended to confuse it with etymology, using "change" indifferently in a literal, diachronic sense or a more metaphorical, synchronic one. (See Matthews, 1974, on traditional treatments of word structure.)
62. That is, the paired tenses share a *stem*: the present and the imperfect share the "pre-sent" stem, and the perfect and pluperfect the "perfect" stem, while the aorist and future both have "sigmatic" stems. The notion of stem, especially as regards the Greek verb, is discussed in section c below. A stem is the form to which an ending is added; thus adding *-ō* 'I' to the present (active indicative) stem yields *lúō* 'I am freeing', but adding it to the future (active indicative) yields *lúsō* 'I shall be freeing'. The "future" stem, for example, is an abstraction from the specific stems actually found, such as the future active indicative.
63. Each of these forms has a name in traditional grammar, but these names are not very felicitous, since each form in fact performs several functions. For most verbs of mod-ern English, the "past tense" (*loved*) is identical in form with the past ("perfect" or "passive") participle (as in *she is loved*), which also serves as a gerund or verbal adverb (*loved by Bill, she nonetheless felt unloved*).

    The plain or bare form is an "unmarked" infinitive (*they can go now*) but also an imperative (*go now!*), and (except in the third person singular) a present tense form (*they go now wherever they want*). The *-ing* form is not only the present ("progres-sive" or "active") participle (*he is running*), but also a gerund (*running for the bus, he broke his leg*), a verbal adjective (*running dogs*), and even a verbal noun (*running is good for you*).

    On the other hand, labels such as the "*-en*" form are equally misleading, as the "*-(e)d*" form includes *was, were, went, ran, saw, flew, gave, brought*, while the "*-en*" form includes *had, gone, run, flown, brought*.

64. It is not always easy to tell, however, precisely what the function of each component is. Because of fusion of morphemes over time, Greek exhibits a great many "portmanteau" morphs bearing more than one meaning. Thus the verb *lú.ō* contrasts in tense, voice, and mood, as well as in person and number, with other verb forms.

Some linguists have therefore treated the ending *-ō* as marking not only the first person singular ('I'), but also the active voice, indicative mood, and present tense. Others, however, see the ending as marking only the first person singular, with the other distinctions indicated by the absence of any explicit marking. This is similar to a problem which arises in the case of English present tense verbs, where the present tense seems to be marked, except in the third person singular, only by the *absence* of any marker.

It is due to the problems caused by such analytical indeterminacies that S. Anderson (1985:150, 161) prefers the term "formative" to "morpheme," and concludes in regard to the ending *-o* 'I' (of Latin) that the "association between form [*sic*] and the categories it expresses is not a simple, one-to-one relation, and the choice of either 'person/number' or 'tense/mood' as the 'meaning' of the ending 'morpheme' is a distortion of the facts."

Anderson here comes close to adopting the type of work-and-paradigm model implicit in the ancients, saying that in languages like Latin "the entire (possibly highly complex) form is related to the entire cluster of grammatical categories it marks." In Anderson (1988), he explicitly adopts what he calls an "extended" word-and-paradigm model.

65. *On Interpretation* I.16a (1932:117).
66. See chapter 3 for discussion of mood.
67. *Lúō* means 'I free, am freeing'; *lúomai* means 'I am being freed'. The active verb marks its subject as the agent, the participant performing an action; the passive marks it as the patient, the recipient of the action.

This distinction of active and passive voice English marks by use of the auxiliary verb *be* accompanied by a passive ("past" or "perfect") participle, which in the case of most verbs is the *-(e)d* form (*was loved*). But the synthetic Greek language marks it in the form of the verb itself (and secondarily in the form of the personal ending, since *-ō* 'I', for example, is used only in the active voice, and *-mai* 'I' only in the middle and passive). (On voice, see n. 36.)

68. Dionysius Thrax (1867:46ff., 1874:11f.).
69. The dual, already a moribund form, was limited in use.
70. As Robins (1979:36) points out, there is no necessary connection between the future and aorist sigmatic stems, and they are probably not etymologically related (see Buck, 1933:279, Chantraine, 1945:290). In any case, in terms of Greek grammar it is only coincidence that both are sigmatic. But this could not have been known to the ancients.
71. As Robins (1979:36) suggests.
72. Since the terms *present* and *past* have already been used in other ways here, we will use the terms "primary" and "secondary" to avoid confusion.
73. Apollonius (1981:181).
74. The primary tenses use the secondary endings in the optative mood, however.
75. Goodwin (1889:258f.). The indicative is however also possible (261), being "a more vivid form of expression than the optative, with no difference in meaning."
76. Goodwin (1894:281f., 290f.). See section a of chapter 3.
77. The analyses in these examples are partial and are mainly limited to the most salient points. See the table of abbreviations and symbols for the abbreviations used.
78. Goodwin (1889:107f.).
79. Apollonius (1981:161). The passage has been somewhat edited. On *án* see Goodwin (1889:64ff., 1894:277f.). On the use of "***" see note 87 below.
80. Apollonius (1981:160, 164).
81. Ibid., 160.
82. In Dionysius Thrax (1867:261).
83. As suggested by Pinborg (1975:92).

84. Varro IX.96 (1951:517).
85. Varro X.47f. (1951:569f.).
86. Greenough et al. (1903:301).
87. However, only the tense shifts, while the perspective as a whole does not: *scribebam hodie* 'I was writing today' is possible, but not **scribebam heri* 'I was writing yesterday'. (Robin Lakoff, personal communication.)

    The asterisk (*) indicates an ''ungrammatical'' example, one not accepted by speakers as part of the language. Below we will also use ''?*'' for not quite as unacceptable examples, and ''?'' to mark an even lesser degree of unacceptability. We will also use ''!'' to mark a grammatical sentence which is, however, unacceptable relative to some given meaning. For example, !*Tom is being stupid* is grammatical, but not with the meaning 'Tom is stupid', only with the meaning 'Tom is acting stupidly'.
88. Greenough et al. (1903:371).
89. Ibid., 302ff. Some desinences are, however, restricted to primary or secondary tenses: for example, -*ō* 'I' occurs only in the primary tenses.
90. Pinborg, however, comments (1975:92) that such a use of the term by the Stoics would be unprecedented.
91. Robins (1979:36, 59).
92. Pinborg (1975:92).
93. Priscian VIII.53 (1857:415).
94. Holt (1943:3).
95. I translate here the Greek terms he uses. A somewhat more complicated interpretation along the same lines by Karl Barwick is reported in Pinborg (1975:93).
96. Pinborg (1975:94).
97. Goodwin (1894:209, 1889:7).
98. This does not apply, however, to the progressive present perfect, e.g., *I have been looking forward to meeting you*, *I have been waiting here for two hours*. (Robin Lakoff, personal communication.)
99. Steinthal (1890:II,302).
100. *temps*.
101. See Pinborg (1975:93) for some interpretations of the Stoic system that either treat it as purely a tense system, or relegate aspect to a secondary role in it not equal to tense, and for bibliographic indications of sources on the Stoic theory.
102. *suntelikos* 'perfect, complete'.
103. ''Time'' here and just below translates *temps*, which, like Greek *khrónos*, is ambiguously 'time' or 'tense'.
104. Holt (1943:3f.).
105. *Arten*.
106. Steinthal (1890:I,309–11).
107. Ibid., 313.
108. Ibid., 310.
109. Apollonius (1981:161).
110. Greenough et al. (1903:293, 298). Of course, relative to the time of the speech act, any future act is incomplete. But the distinction between the ''future imperfect'' and the ''future perfect'' (as one of incompletion vs. completion) has to do not with completion at the present time—the time of the speech act—but rather with some *future* point in time. *I shall be going* reports incomplete action *at some future time*, as *I shall have gone* reports action completed at some future time.
111. Andrews and Stoddard (1850:86).
112. See Salus (1969:97).
113. Robins (1979:75f.).

Chapter 2

1. Bursill-Hall (1975:181ff.). On the medieval period, see also Michael (1970), Padley (1976), and Robins (1979).

2. Bacon (1902), Bursill-Hall (1975:201), Robins (1979:96).
3. Bursill-Hall (1975:205), Robins (1979:76f.).
4. Medieval grammar developed with logic (Bursill-Hall, 1975:199). Bursill-Hall speaks (1963:44) of the "logicization" of grammar: "grammar became associated with the formulation of concepts of reality and their expression by language. This led to the belief that the universality of reality, as conceived and understood by the universality of human reason, could be expressed by the universal language, Latin" (1975:201). See too Bursill-Hall (1963:46), Michael (1970:165).
5. Bursill-Hall (1963:47ff., 1975:201).
6. Robins (1979:20): "as . . . Dionysius Thrax pointed out, the morphological component of grammar largely consists of 'the working out of analogy.' " This is somewhat misleading, but, making allowances for the differences between modern and ancient grammatical theory, is probably correct. Certainly both modern and ancient linguistic thought depends greatly on analogy.
7. Michael (1970:165).
8. Nebrija seems, however, to have been aware of the *futurum exactum* in Latin, which he recognizes in his *Introductiones in Latinam linguam* of 1508—see Jellinek (1913–14:II,327). The forms here are Nebrija's, which differ only slightly from those of modern Spanish.
9. By a periphrastic tense is meant here a complex form representing a tense, e.g., the English present perfect (*I have loved*). In traditional grammar there is a presupposition that the periphrastic form is in lieu of some simple, synthetic form. While it is true that many of the periphrastics here have simple counterparts, either logically or etymologically speaking, this is not true of all (for example the conditional perfect), nor is it presupposed by the use of the term "periphrastic": here this term means no more than "analytic construction" or "complex form," though it is used indifferently for forms and the categories they mark.

   It is possible to have "supercomplex" (*surcomposé*) periphrastic forms, as in French and in some German dialects, in which the simple past tense has been lost in the colloquial (mainly the spoken) language and replaced by complex tenses, e.g., *j'ai eu chanté* 'I had sung' (*j'ai eu* for *j'avais*).
10. Claius (1578:96).
11. Michael (1970:163), Robins (1979:127).
12. Robins (1979:123).
13. Translated as *General and Rational Grammar* (1753).
14. Ellegård (1973:667b).
15. Robins (1979:125).
16. Michael (1970:168).
17. Harris (1751:131).
18. *Grammaire générale* (1660:104), *General and Rational Grammar* (1753:103).
19. Ibid., 1660:103f.; 1753:102f.
20. The subject of an active sentence such as *I read the book* is said to perform an action; that of a passive sentence such as *the book was read by me*, to undergo a "passion."
21. Estienne (1557:35). *I'aimoye* is modern *j'aimais* 'I was loving, used to love, would love'.
22. *non amare più.*
23. Castelvetro, *Giunta fatta al Ragiomento degli Articoli et de'Verbi de messer Pietro Bembo* (Modena, 1563), p. 51. Cited by Kukenheim (1932:164f.). The translation is mine.
24. Ramsey (1956:382). Note that this construction, although etymologically equivalent to, and identical in form with, the Latin periphrastic perfect, differs in tense: Spanish *soy amado* 'I am loved' is a present, whereas Latin *amatus sum* is a perfect.
25. Ramsey (1956:385).
26. Ewert (1966:176).
27. Lewis (1967:122).

28. Ibid., 128. See Slobin and Asku (1982). The aspectual values of the Turkish endings are discussed in Johanson (1971).
29. On English and evidentials in general, see L. Anderson (1981, 1986), Chafe (1986).
30. Goodwin (1889:14).
31. Ibid., 15.
32. Houweling (1986:163), Lo Cascio (1986:202). Bertinetto (1986:19) distinguishes the *piucheperfetto* (pluperfect) proper from the *trapassato* or *"piucheperfetto II."* (The *trapassato prossimo* and *remoto* are matched by the *passato prossimo*—present perfect—and *remoto*—simple past.)
33. Ramsey (1956:362).
34. Marchand (1955), Blansitt (1975).
35. There are idiomatic pseudo-performatives, viz. *take* in *I take my hat off to whoever chose the musical selections for the evening* (heard on C.T.V. television, February 26, 1987).
36. English has also developed a periphrastic construction with the auxiliary verb *do* for purposes of negation, interrogation, and emphasis. This last use is optional, but in modern English only the auxiliary verbs and *be* (and, optionally, *have* as well) can be directly negated or preposed: *I am not eating, I am not rich, I will not leave, I haven't a cent to my name; am I eating?, am I rich?, will I leave?, have I a cent to my name?*, but *I do not eat, I do not have money, do I eat?*
37. Jespersen (1924:254).
38. In American English it is possible to use the past tense indefinitely as if it were a perfect: "Were you (ever) to Europe?" (or "Did you [ever] go to Europe?"). (See Jespersen, 1924:271.) The American usage may well reflect German, as so often is the case when American differs from British usage. Cf. *Warst Du schon (ein)mal in Europa?*
39. Kukenheim (1932:165).
40. *duplex*.
41. Kukenheim (1932:165): 'I have read the gospel today'; modern *j'ai* 'I have', *aujour-d'hui* 'today'; *lu* means 'read' (past participle).
42. 'I saw the king when he was crowned'; modern *je* 'I', *vis* 'saw'; *fut* means 'was'.
43. 'To have'.
44. Estienne (1557:35): modern *j'ai* 'I have', *vu* 'seen'.
45. The present perfect is known in Italian as the *passato prossimo* "recent past', and the preterite as the *passato remoto* 'remote past' (Lo Cascio, 1986:202). The *Grammaire générale* (1660:104) quantifies the distance in time, stating that the preterite represents an event more than a day past: *j'écris hier* 'I wrote yesterday' is all right, but not *j'écris ce matin* 'I wrote this morning'.
46. Nebrija (1926:98). 'I had loved you, when you loved me'.
47. Scaliger (1540:293f.). *Perfect* = "complete."
48. Lily and Colet (1549), Lily (1567); R. Johnson (1706:287ff.).
49. Lily (1945, fol. C.v), Michael (1970:542).
50. R. Johnson (1706:290).
51. Scaliger (1540:295), Holt (1943:5).
52. *absoluta*.
53. Scaliger (1540:293f.).
54. *Grammaire générale* (1660:104ff.), *General and Rational Grammar* (1753:104f.).
55. Harris (1751:119ff.).
56. Aichinger (1754:290). 'Tenses' here translates *Zeiten*.
57. "Future mixed with the imperfect."
58. "Simple future."
59. "Imperfect of the subjunctive," i.e., the conditional.
60. Aichinger (1754:295):

Ich	wuerde		gehen,	wenn	mir	der Gang	bezahlet
I	become (PAST SUBJ 1SG)	go (INF)	if		to me	the fare	pay (PP MASC NOM)

wuerde.
become (PAST SUBJ 1SG)
'I would go, if my fare were paid.'

Wir hofften,   er wuerde   Israel erloesen.
we hope (PAST 1PL) he become (PAST SUBJ 1SG) Israel redeem (INF)
'We hoped that he would redeem Israel.'

61. Madvig (1887:288).
62. Ibid. It is somewhat misleading then for Jespersen (1924:254) to number Madvig's lines, since it implies that there is no principled difference between the status of the labelless line 1 and that of the labelled lines 2 and 3.
63. Baebler (1885:61). The examples are 'I shall read' and 'I shall have read' respectively. The peculiarity of the terminology, and the fact that this passage occurs in only one manuscript, suggests a possible error. A useful companion to Baebler's work is the collection of texts found in Thurot (1869).
64. Linacre (1523, fol. 11; cf. 1524), Scaliger (1540:296f.), Michael (1970:118, 408).
65. According to Jellinek (1913–4:II,328n.).
66. *Operis perfectionem praescribit*. Scaliger (1540:297).
67. Linacre (1523, fol. 11; cf. 1524), Jellinek (1913–14:I,328).
68. Linacre (1523, fol. 10 verso; cf. 1524).
69. Jellinek (1913–14:I,328).
70. Ibid., 327f., 329, 331.
71. Aichinger (1754:296).
72. Harris (1751:128f.).
73. McFall (1982), Friedman (1975:942f., 951f.).
74. Comrie (1985:63).
75. Harris (1751:119f.).
76. Ibid., 121f. Cf. Michael (1970:412f.). Harris's Greek examples have been transliterated.
77. Michael (1970:462).
78. Lowth (1762:56), Michael (1970:413).
79. Lowth (1762:54).
80. Michael (1970:402).
81. Sweet (1898:85).
82. Sweet (1898:100ff.).
83. Michael (1970:416).
84. Pickbourn (1789:121ff.). This system is in some respects a precursor of the "architectonic of time" of Gustave Guillaume. (See Guillaume, 1929, 1965.) While Guillaume has many followers in France (see Le Goffic, 1986) and Quebec (see Hirtle, 1967, 1975), his ideas are generally unknown elsewhere and have not influenced the course of later studies to any extent. His idiosyncratic and metaphysical-sounding terminology, along with a reliance on intuitions of meaning, are barriers to anglophone scholars in the North American tradition. His was, however, perhaps the first systematic study of the phases of actions. Both Guillaume and the phases of actions are discussed in chapter 6 of the present book.
85. Pickbourn (1789:4f.).
86. Ibid., 40.
87. Michael (1970:417).
88. Ibid., 405f.
89. Lewis (1967:136).
90. Vaughan (1709:33f.).
91. Ibid., 37ff.
92. Norman (1965), Haenisch (1961).
93. Norman (1965:23ff.).

94. Ibid., 37.
95. Norman (1965:22).
96. Von Möllendorff (1892:8f.).
97. Marsack (1975:30).
98. Neffgen (1902:21ff.).
99. Ibid., 25.
100. *Wohlklang.*
101. Neffgen (1902:19).
102. Minguella (1878:41).
103. Ibid., 45ff.
104. Von Möllendorff (1892:9f.).
105. Jespersen (1924:56f.).
106. Cf. Jespersen's critique (1924:255).
107. Kufner (1962:89).
108. Saussure (1966:81).
109. Jespersen (1924:277).
110. Wilson (1950:108).
111. *I see people moving over there* leaves open the possibility that what is seen is an illusion or that the speaker is in some way in error; *can see* excludes such doubts.
112. Like performative verbs (*estimate, agree*), these verbs do not report actions when used (as they normally are) in the present tense first person, but rather "perform" actions. But unlike true performatives, quasi-performatives do not name the action they perform. Saying *I agree* constitutes an act of agreeing, whereas saying *I suppose*, a speech act, is not an act of supposing.
113. See Bolinger (1971) and Fraser (1976) on the semantics of these "phrasal" verbs in English. There has been much discussion of the corresponding use of the verbal prefixes of German under the general rubric of *Aktionsarten*—"kinds of action". See part II for discussion.
114. Goodwin (1894:269).
115. Greenough et al. (1903:295ff.).
116. Goodwin (1894:270).
117. Ibid., 269.
118. Jespersen (1924:257, 1931:1f., 1933:230f.).
119. Ibid., 254–56.
120. Ibid., 256.
121. Ibid., 258. We saw in chapter 1 that Aristotle had made the same observation.
122. Ibid., 269.
123. Allen (1966:141).
124. Reichenbach (1947:290).
125. Diver (1963:143), cited in Hackman (1976:83). A typo in Hackman's example (i) from Diver vitiates Hackman's discussion.
126. While these facts do indeed support his conclusion, the former example is not very apt, given the possibility of sentences such as *now he had eaten enough*; Jespersen fails here to distinguish different uses of the adverb *now*. Cf.:
    (1) Now he has eaten enough. Now he ate enough.
    (2) Now, he has eaten enough. Now, he ate enough.
    In (2) *now* has no real temporal value and can be used with any statement whatever, while in (1) it is ambiguous. In one reading *now* means "next" or "at that time" and can be replaced by *then* in many cases; the first example in (1) could occur in historical narration. It has, however, a second reading where it means "consequently" or "at long last;" in this case it is closer to *finally* or *consequently*. (Cf. *finally he has eaten enough*.) In yet a third reading it does indeed mean "at the present time." With this reading of *now*, !*now he became ill* makes no sense, whereas *now he has become rich* is fine. Cf.: *then he was poor, but now he has become rich*,

then he was poor but now he became rich. Not all of these three readings are available, however, when *now* occurs in other positions: ?**he ate enough now,* ?*he has eaten enough now.*

127. Jespersen (1924:271).
128. Ibid., 286–89.
129. Comrie (1976:52).
130. Ibid., 56.
131. Jespersen (1924:284).
132. Ibid., 285.
133. Jespersen (1931:94). See too Jespersen (1924:262, 1931:90).
134. This example is ambiguous. The reading in question here—in which Jill believed Jack would leave the day after that of her act of belief—is in fact unacceptable, though the other reading (or readings?), involving his having left at some time prior to the time of her believing, is acceptable.
135. McCoard (1978:206f.). The examples are from Sobin (1974:129).
136. The examples are from Emonds (1975).
137. Jespersen (1933:239). Examples from Allen (1966:143).

Chapter 3

1. Greenough et al. (1903:341).
2. Ibid., 280.
3. Goodwin (1889:5).
4. Dionysius (1867:47, 1874:12).
5. E. g., Priscian (1857:421).
6. Charisius (1857:338).
7. Donatus (1864:155f., 503).
8. Apollonius III.24 (1981:163).
9. For the recent history of the discussion, which is too complicated to review here, see Gonda (1980:1ff.) and Palmer (1986), chapter 1.
10. Apollonius III.55 (1981:176), Priscian VIII.65 (1857:423), Lyons (1977:2), Jespersen (1924:313).
11. Apollonius III.88 (1981:186f.).
12. Ibid., 187f.
13. Ibid., 200.
14. Householder notes (Apollonius 1981:200) that Apollonius "has already excluded the main use of the independent subjunctive, the first person hortatory uses which he called ["suggestive"] back in Ch. 109, and has never mentioned the prohibitive uses of the aorist subjunctive with *me*." Apollonius's argument in 109 doesn't seem to support his conclusion, even granted that the first persons are not "imperative."
15. *Odyssey* XXIV.491, in Goodwin (1889:4).
16. Goodwin (1889:3), Woodcock (1959:96f.).
17. Ramsey (1956:440f.).
18. Lockwood (1968:129).
19. E. g. Priscian (1857:407), Donatus (1864:155, 359, 381, 411, 503).
20. Greenough et al. (1903:280, 282).
21. Donatus (1864:414), Charisius (1857:340).
22. Greenough et al. (1903:280).
23. Woodcock (1959:87f.).
24. Pinborg (1975:91).
25. Lyons (1968:307).
26. Apollonius III.62 (1981:178f.), (1981:178, 204).
27. Harris (1751:143)—despite Lyons's claim (1968:307) that the interrogatives are not traditionally considered modal.
28. It is interesting to observe the distinction Fr. Minguella makes in his Tagalog grammar

(1878:45) between the etymological (i.e., syntactic) and the "natural" (notional) definitions of the subjunctive:

According to the first, every utterance composed of two or more verbs, with dependence of one on another, is *subjunctive*, because the etymology of the *subjunctive* is *a verb joined to another, on which it depends*. . . . The subjunctive, according to its nature, is *the expression, vague in regard to time, of the acts of the will, or of the relation to things*. In the first case, it takes the denomination of *optative = desire*, or *dubitative*; and in the second, of *conditional* or *unconditional*; but always the *subjunctive* requires two verbs, expressed or tacit.

29. Lyons (1977:739), Gonda (1980:2).
30. E. g., by Palmer (1986).
31. Jespersen (1924:316).
32. Palmer (1986:4).
33. Ibid., 6.
34. Ibid., 33ff.
35. Ewert (1966:257).
36. Wilson (1950:113).
37. Jespersen (1931:161ff.). Many of these usages are impossible in British English.
38. Example is U.S., used by Jespersen to exemplify a verbal report. Jespersen has British examples.
39. Example is U.S., used to exemplify the construction with no verbal report; Jespersen characterizes this as primarily an American usage.
40. Jespersen notes the usage with *lest* is American.
41. Jespersen notes the usage with *that* is rare.
42. Goodwin (1889:256).
43. Ibid., 258.
44. Ibid., 259.
45. Ibid., 263.
46. Ibid., 38f., 41.
47. Ibid., 22f.
48. Ibid., 170. Cf. pp. 23f., 204.
49. Ibid., 25f., 28.
50. And in Esperanto, under Slavic influence—Jespersen (1924:294).
51. Cole (1974).
52. Greenough et al. (1903:325).
53. Ibid., 328.
54. Goodwin (1879:300f.).
55. Greenough et al. (1903:369), Goodwin (1879:316).
56. Robin Lakoff points out (personal communication) examples such as *I guess Sue is sweet*, in which the dependent clause does seem to be asserted. However, *guess* is a pseudo-performative, so that this case is really like that of *I agree that Sue is sweet*; it is not the dependent clause, but the higher verb, which is functioning assertively. As a denial of some criticism of Sue, the sentence *I think Sue is sweet* does assert her sweetness: but with emphatic *I*, as a statement of *who* holds this opinion, it does not (though it presupposes it). In the first case, *think* is functioning as a pseudo-performative like *guess*, *suppose*. Cf. the use of the pseudo-performatives (*I suppose*, *I guess*) for grudging agreement.
57. Greenough et al. (1903:374). *Polliceri* and *arbitror* are "deponent" verbs, combining passive form with active meaning.
58. Ibid., 244. *Rex* is nominative because the verb is passive and what ordinarily is an object—here understood, 'he'—is the subject.
59. Ibid., 375. Greenough et al. supply the lacuna.
60. Ibid., 205.
61. Goodwin (1879:315).
62. Price (1971:242). His glosses.
63. In Charisius (1857:263f., 388f.). On the "optatives" see Diomedes in Charisius (1857:391).

64. 'I speak, however much you may understand'.
65. 'I speak, however much you may have understood'.
66. 'I speak so that you may understand'. The "future optative" is present subjunctive in form.
67. 'I spoke, however much you may have understood'.
68. 'I spoke, however much you might have understood'.
69. *finitivus*.
70. 'I spoke, however much you may have understood'—perfect with imperfect.
71. 'I spoke, however much you might have understood'—perfect with pluperfect.
72. 'I had spoken, however much you may have understood'—pluperfect with imperfect.
73. 'I had spoken, however much you might have understood'—pluperfect with pluperfect.
74. 'I shall speak, however much you may understand'.
75. 'I shall speak, however much you may have understood'.
76. 'I shall speak, if you will have understood'. *Intellexis* is the future perfect indicative, but in Roman grammar this was treated as a future subjunctive. The perfect active subjunctive differs from the future perfect active indicative only in the first person singular—*intellexerim* '(that) I may have understood' versus *intellexero* 'I shall have understood'.
77. 'I shall speak so that you may understand'.
78. 'I spoke so that you may do'.
79. 'I spoke so that you might do'.
80. *in futuro suspendit*.
81. '(that) I may have said (it) even if you knew (it)'.
82. '(that) I might have said (it) even if you had known (it)'.
83. '(that) I may have written (it) even if you had known (it)'.
84. '(that) I might have written (it) even if you knew (it)'.
85. Though some restrict the term "rule of 'sequence of tenses' " to the subjunctive: Greenough et al. (1903:302), Ernout and Thomas (1953:406). The quotation below is from Charisius (1857:388f.).
86. However (*autem*), Catiline, while (*cum*) they are quiet (*quiescunt*), they try you (*te . . . probant*); while they suffer (*patiuntur*), they judge you (*decernunt*); while they are silent (*tacent*), they shout (*clamant*) about (*de*) you.
87. He came (*venit*) also (*et*) to (*ad*) the shores (*ripas*) where (*ubi*) he used (*solebat*) often (*saepe*) to play (*ludere*).
88. He (*ille*) had spoken (*dixerat*) and (*et*) already (*iam*) a brighter (*clarior*) flame (*ignis*) is heard (*auditur*) throughout (*per*) the town (*moena*).
89. Although (*quamquam*) the mind is horrified (*horret*) to remember (*meminisse*) and in grief (*luctuque*) hides away (*refugit*), I shall begin (*incipiam*).
90. Greenough et al. (1903:302f.).
91. Andrews and Stoddard (1850:223f.).
92. Lakoff (1968:181).
93. Ronconi (1959:170).
94. Ernout and Thomas (1953:419).
95. Ibid., 408.
96. Ibid., 414, 418f.
97. Greenough et al. (1903:305), Ernout and Thomas (1953:409).
98. Ernout and Thomas (1953:409).
99. Greenough et al. (1903:304), Ernout and Thomas (1953:409f).
100. Ernout and Thomas (1953:410ff.).
101. Greenough et al. (1903:323ff.), Woodcock (1959:234ff.).
102. Spaulding (1967:55f.) notes that the conditional sometimes is followed by a present subjunctive when it refers to a present or future event, as in:
    Pensé sería lo mejor que le de [present] a Almudena la esmeralda.
    I thought the best thing would be that he give the emerald to Almudena.

103. Ewert (1966:256f.). The subjunctives are difficult to gloss. Roughly, the examples below translate, '(that) I have sung, (that) I sang, (that) I had sung'.
104. Curme (1922:239f.). Glosses: 'he says (PRES INDIC) he is (PRES SUBJ) ill, he has (PRES SUBJ) already done it, he will (PRES SUBJ) come tomorrow, he will have done it within a week; he said (PAST INDIC) he was (PAST SUBJ) ill', etc.
105. Cf. Latin *dicet se esse felicem* with present infinitive after future indicative (example from Robin Lakoff).
106. Ewert (1966:257).
107. Price (1971:215), from which the example comes; Brunot and Bruneau (1949:385).
108. Brunot and Bruneau (1949:387).
109. Grebe (1966:601f.).
110. Curme (1922:240f.). Literal glosses:

I am ill   He says/said he is ill

I { did / have done / had done } it   He says/said he has done it

After I had read, I wrote   He says after he has read, he has written a letter
  a letter

I will come   He says/said he will come

I will have done it within   He says/said he will have done it within a week
  a week

111. Jespersen (1924:296f.).
112. Lockwood (1968:133). On the other hand, the subjunctive has spread at the expense of the indicative as a marker of indirect discourse: Lockwood (1968:137) cites *er sagt, dass er krank sei* and notes that it differs in no way from the indicative *er sagt, dass er krank ist* 'he says he's ill'.
113. Grebe (1966:601f.).
114. Greenough et al. (1903:375), Ernout and Thomas (1953:434f.), Woodcock (1959:238f.). Examples from Greenough and Woodcock.
115. Jespersen (1931:112ff.).
116. Respectively the imperfect indicative ('if I had the money') and preterite subjunctive.
117. Goodwin (1889:28ff.).
118. Ibid., 30.
119. Ibid., 31f.
120. Ibid., 34. Plato, *Crito* 46A (1961:31).
121. Passive form, medio-passive meaning.
122. Goodwin (1889:36).
123. Ibid., 47.
124. Ibid., 48. The next example is also drawn from p. 48.
125. Ibid., 49, 51.
126. Ibid., 53.
127. Greenough et al. (1903:307, 309).
128. Ibid., 378f. The representations of the future perfect have been omitted here. They are rare and formed differently from these constructions with simple infinitives.
129. Ibid., 312–14.
130. Comrie (1976:58ff.).
131. Ibid., 60.
132. McCawley (1971:104).
133. Ibid., Comrie (1976:58).
134. McCawley (1971:104), Comrie (1976:57).
135. Comrie (1976:59).
136. And Palmer (1971:101).
137. Slobin and Aksu (1982:187). Haarman (1971:94).
138. L. Anderson (1982a).
139. Pickbourn (1789:40f.).

140. Ibid., 36.
141. Ibid., 28. Pickbourn comes very close here to a version of the XN theory.
142. Ibid., 18.
143. Ibid., 3. Once again, it is noticeable to what extent he is moving toward what Mc-Coard calls XN theory.
144. McCoard (1978:76).
145. Hall Partee (1973:602f.). It has been quoted, for example, by Bäuerle (1979:228), Dowty (1979:330f.), Nerbonne (1984:11), and Saurer (1984:41).
146. Barwise and Perry (1983:35).
147. I.e., the preterite. The "Second Past Tense" below is the present perfect.
148. White (1761:83f.).
149. Bryan (1936:369), McCoard (1978:65).
150. McCoard (1978:64f.). Quotation slightly edited.
151. Bryan (1936:363, 367), McCoard (1978:126).
152. Pickbourn (1789:31), McCoard (1978:124). Cf. Harris (1751:115ff.), who points out the indefinitely great extent of periods of time which are "Now." It is interesting that Theodore of Gaza says (Harris, p. 129n.) of the perfect that it is "the completion of the present." This may relate to a version of the XN theory, though Harris views the statement in the light of his own theory of (completive) aspect.
153. McCoard (1978:19).
154. Dowty (1982:27).
155. For further discussion, see chapter 7.
156. Hermerén (1978:18).
157. Comrie (1976:38).
158. Allen (1966:91).
159. Chatterjee (1982:336).
160. Hopper (1982:4), Allen (1966:91).
161. Winograd (1974:75), quoted in McCoard (1978:19).
162. Allen (1966:94).
163. Jespersen (1931:47).
164. Perkins (1983:26).
165. These positions may or may not be antithetical, depending on how they are couched. The debate has often assumed much simpler and much clearer positions than actually obtain.
166. Antal (1963:48, Hermerén 1978:68f.).
167. Quoted by Hermerén (1978:70f.).
168. Ehrman (1966:10).
169. Allen (1966:142).
170. Reichenbach (1947:290).
171. Jespersen (1924:286–89).
172. Ibid, 257.
173. Reichenbach (1947:290).
174. Ibid., 290.
175. Ibid., 297.
176. Ibid., 295f.
177. That is, complex.
178. Reichenbach (1947:293).
179. Ibid., 294f.
180. Ibid., 295.
181. Comrie (1981:26).
182. E.g., by Comrie (1981:26f.) and Dinsmore (1982:237).
183. E.g., Johnson (1981:149), the source of this diagram.
184. The term "status" is due to Whorf but first received wide attention thanks to Jakobson. See Jakobson (1971:134). See too Johnson (1981:148f.).
185. Bull (1960). See Allen (1966:145ff.), McCoard (1978:92ff.).

186. Bull (1960:17).
187. Ibid., 15. Given the psychological (subjective or ideational) foundations of Bull's theory, this observation is bound to remind one of Guillaume's (1965) focus on temporal motion as a mental, rather than an objective, phenomenon. For Guillaume the past tense, for example, reflects the motion of the mind back to an event, rather than the motion of that event past the mind.
188. Ibid., 17.
189. The eight are *v-d, would v, v-0, will v, had v-n, would have v-n, have v-n, will have v-n*, where *v-d* is the past tense form, *v* the unmarked infinitive, *v-0* the present tense form, and *v-n* the perfect participial form.
190. Allen (1966:145).
191. Bull (1960:4ff.).
192. McCoard (1978:94f.).
193. 'Wait, I'm coming out in a moment'.
194. 'Tomorrow I'm reading you a lecture'.
195. Donatus (1864:414).
196. Miege (1688:70).
197. De la Touche (1696:240). Glosses: 'I leave tomorrow'; 'they are going away next week'; 'Monday she's having her friends to tea'.
198. Ibid., 244. Glosses: 'I doubt that my brother *will come* today'; 'God grant that you *win* your case'; 'before he *dies*'; 'so that *they don't perish*'.
199. Pickbourn (1789:22ff.).
200. Ibid., 49f.
201. See for example Binnick (1971, 1972) and Palmer (1971:51ff.).
202. Reichenbach (1947:296).
203. Jespersen (1924:260).
204. Jespersen (1931:75).
205. *Will* can be used, but not as a future tense marker: *If you'll (just) bring the mustard, I'll supply the rest of our dinner.* (Example from Robin Lakoff.)
206. Allen (1966:170f.).
207. *The man who was to leave the next morning* would be far more acceptable in this sense, however, than *the man who left the next morning.*
208. *He never guessed that he would become President one day* is ambiguous. One reading = 'it was never the case that he guessed that . . .' This is acceptable with the tag *and he never did (become President).* The intended reading (where *never guess* is being used similarly to its use in *you'll never guess who's here*) does not felicitously co-occur with the tag.
209. Allen (1966:167ff.).
210. Ibid., 166f.
211. Prior (1967:13).
212. Allen (1966:150).
213. McCoard (1978:99f.).
214. Allen (1966:168).
215. Ibid., 101.
216. McCoard (1978:101f.).

Chapter 4

1. Lyons (1968:304f.).
2. Gonda (1980:10).
3. Jespersen (1924:277).
4. The question is whether or not such grammatical tenselessness reflects the absence of temporal distinctions such as are marked by tense forms in tensed languages, and if not, then how such tenseless languages make up for the lack of grammatical tense.
5. Waugh (1975:444).

6. Whorf (1956:58, Gale 1968:378).
7. Whorf (1956:57f., Gale 1968:377f.).
8. N. W. Schroeder, *Institutiones ad Fundamenta Linguae Hebraeae*, 3rd ed. (Groningen: Bolt, 1810), cited in McFall (1982).
9. Wallace (1982:202).
10. Comrie (1976:72).
11. Traugott (1978:372).

Chapter 5

1. Macaulay (1978:416ff.).
2. Rassudova (1984:14).
3. Goedsche (1940:189).
4. According to Fontaine's history of Slavic aspect (1983:17ff.). The brief history of Slavic aspectology presented here is based on Fontaine, pp. 17–25, from which the extracts, in my translations, are drawn.
5. Fontaine (1983:25).
6. Georg Curtius, *Die Bildung der Tempora und Modi im Griechischen und Lateinischen sprachvergleichend dargestellt* (Berlin: Wilhelm Besser, 1846), cited by Friedrich (1974:S9).
7. Streitberg (1891:77).
8. E.g., Verkuyl (1972:3).
9. Streitberg (1891, 1920).
10. Streitberg (1891:70ff.).
11. Aristotle (1952:574). Cf. Kenny (1963:173), Dowty (1979:52f.), Mourelatos (1981:193ff.).
12. Plato (1961:216), Mourelatos (1981:195).
13. Motions: *kínēseis*; actualizations: *enérgeiai*.
14. *Metaphysics* 1048b.18–36 (Aristotle 1933:446ff.). The quotation here is taken from p. 449.
15. Ryle (1949:149ff.); Kenny (1963), cited in Dowty 1979:53f.; Vendler (1957).
16. Kenny (1963:173).
17. Aristotle (1957:96ff.).
18. Aristotle (1934:334ff.).
19. Streitberg (1891:72).
20. Grebe (1966:71).
21. Forsyth (1970:20ff.).
22. Cited in Golian (1979:64f.).
23. Ibid., 74.
24. The notion of *phase* or *stage* plays a central role in certain theories of tense and aspect, for example those of Guillaume (1929, 1965) and Joos (1964), but is especially important in a number of recent theories, as we shall see.
25. Jespersen (1924:286ff.).
26. Verkuyl (1972:6f.).
27. Friedrich (1974:S6), Garey (1957:92).
28. McCoard (1978:8).
29. Holt (1943:12f.).
30. Robins (1979:201).
31. Holt (1943:31).
32. Ruipérez (1954:34).
33. Holt (1943:23).
34. Waugh (1975:440).
35. The problem of which features to use and how to define the positive member of each pair raises a number of complicated and controversial questions which are not relevant here. The examples are meant simply for purposes of illustration.

36. Ruipérez (1954:14ff.).
37. Jakobson (1956, 1971:136). Cf. (1932, 1971:15). See too Jakobson (1941).
38. Holt (1943:27).
39. Greenberg (1966:14–20) discusses frequency; his data seem to show that in phonology at least unmarked members of oppositions are indeed of higher frequency. For example, in a sample from Chiricahua Apache, the ratio of oral vowels to nasal was 12.8:1.
40. This points up a number of indeterminancies in this approach to markedness. In those cases where the verb serving as base to the affixation is already a perfective formed with an affix, the imperfective will of course be morphologically more, not less, complex than the perfective. In terms of statistics, there is some question as to what it means to say that most verbs perform in a certain way, since it is unclear whether this has to do with verb types or verb tokens. There may well be more imperfectives formed from perfectives, if only because most prefixally derived verbs are perfective, and most primary verbs have several such derivatives. But it is not clear what the relative frequencies of forms of such imperfectives are relative to those which are primary.
41. For references to the literature see Forsyth (1970).
42. Examples from Forsyth (1970:2,5).
43. Rassudova (1984:15).
44. Forsyth (1970:14).
45. Comrie (1976:16–20).
46. Rassudova (1984:16f.).
47. Forsyth (1970:3).
48. See Johnson (1977:33f.) and McCoard (1978:1ff.).
49. Allen (1966:91), Hopper (1982:4).
50. Waugh (1975:439).
51. Forsyth (1970:5).
52. Ibid., 2. However, Friedrich (1974:S30) is critical of the view that the imperfective is unmarked.
53. Ibid., 7.
54. Ibid., 347.
55. Comrie (1976:4).
56. Forsyth (1970:5).
57. Ibid., 349.
58. Rassudova (1984:14).
59. Holt (1943:16). In both diagrams, Holt's Greek terms have been translated.
60. The future perfect has been omitted here because of the dual (reduplicated, perfect/sigmatic, future) nature of the stem.
61. Holt (1943:3).
62. Ibid., 7, Friedrich (1974:S6).
63. Only a few exceptional verbs have active future perfect forms.
64. Holt (1943:25f., 44). Holt uses a "division" sign with dots over and under the more familiar plain negative sign ($-$).
65. Jakobson (1932, 1971:4).
66. Jakobson (1971:136). E.g., *woman* in the narrow sense of 'adult human female' stands in opposition to *girl* (non-young vs. young), but in the broad sense of 'human female' it does not, but includes the sense of "girl." (A girl is, roughly, a "young woman.")
67. Waugh (1975:440f.).
68. Ruipérez (1954:17ff.).
69. Uses of the future which are apparently present in tense (*that will be Bill now*) are actually modal uses of the "future" auxiliaries. The periphrastic futures in Germanic retain their etymological modal values to a great extent, and to a certain extent even when primarily used as markers of futurity.
70. Holt (1943:25f.).

71. Ruipérez (1954:23ff.).
72. Including Golian (1979:51ff.), Kahane (1956), and Lyons (1968:314f.).
73. Holt (1943:44).
74. Comrie (1976:62).
75. Friedrich (1974:S26f.).
76. The Neogrammarians or Junggrammatiker were linguistic scholars in the last quarter of the nineteenth century who sought to supersede the atomism of earlier scholarship. As a group, they are today chiefly remembered for their dictum that sound change is without exception. See Robins (1979:182ff.). On Delbrück, see n. 100.
77. Lyons (1968:314ff.).
78. Goodwin (1889:13f.).
79. Ruipérez (1954:45).
80. Ibid., 47.
81. Holt (1943:28ff.). See too Lyons (1968:314). Cf. Plato (1961:31.).
82. Ruipérez (1954:49).
83. Ibid., 51f.
84. Ibid., 59.
85. Ibid., 62.
86. Ibid., 53.
87. Ibid., 65.
88. Ibid., 63f.
89. Ibid., 46.
90. Cf. Goodwin (1889:9; 1894:269).
91. Goodwin (1889:11, 8f.).
92. Ibid., 12.
93. Ibid., 16. Goodwin's examples have been transliterated. Imperfect and aorist respectively: 'he was breaking the peace' vs. 'he broke the peace'.
94. Ruipérez (1954:70ff.).
95. Ibid., 77.
96. Ibid., 79.
97. Ibid., 89.
98. Goodwin (1889:16). Citations below from p. 12f.
99. Ruipérez (1954:68ff.).
100. E.g., Berthold Delbrück, *Vergleichende Syntax der Indogermanischen Sprachen*, Part 2 (Strassburg: Karl J. Trubner, 1897), pp. 230ff. Cited by Friedrich (1974) and Ruipérez (1954).
101. Ruipérez (1954:80f.).
102. Ibid., 84.
103. Ibid., 89.
104. Ibid., 108, 111.
105. Ibid., 164.
106. Holt (1943:28, 33). Citation from p. 45.
107. Friedrich (1974:S13).
108. Golian (1979:51).
109. Friedrich (1974:S19).
110. His footnote: "Just as the Latin perfect blends the Indo-European perfect and aorist."
111. Friedrich (1974:S21).
112. That is, perfectness.
113. Kahane (1956:328f.).
114. Kahane (1956:328).
115. Ruipérez is criticized by Kahane (1956) on methodological grounds.
116. Townsend (1985:286f.).

Chapter 6

1. Mourelatos (1981:194).
2. See section d.
3. Thus he is using "aspect" to include *Aktionsarten*.
4. Dowty (1979:52).
5. Freed (1979:16).
6. For example, *start, resume, stop, continue.*
7. For example, *running, to run.*
8. That is, the progressive or expanded "tense" form.
9. For example, *running.*
10. Benerjee (1983:32f.).
11. Vendler (1957, 1967:97ff.). Cf. Mourelatos (1981:191f.), Dowty (1979:54).
12. Aristotle (1933:446ff.).
13. Aristotle (1957:96ff.).
14. Aristotle (1934:334ff.).
15. Ryle (1949:149ff.).
16. Ibid., 150.
17. Dowty (1979:55ff.), Freed (1979:49ff.).
18. Kenny (1963:175).
19. Freed (1979:49ff.).
20. Ibid., 63.
21. Dowty (1979:56).
22. Binnick (1970).
23. Dahl (1981:84).
24. Kenny (1963:175).
25. Dowty (1979:61).
26. Freed (1979:49f.).
27. See Dowty (1979:58, 241f., 252.).
28. Freed (1979:51ff.).
29. Ibid., 59.
30. Ibid., 59ff.
31. To use the terminology of Gabbay and Moravcsik (1980).
32. Barwise and Perry (1983:7).
33. Dowty (1979:76). Bennett and Partee (1978:11ff.), however, assume time is dense—there must always be such a t'.
34. Rescher and Urquhart (1971:169).
35. Both these approaches will be discussed in chapter 7.
36. Mourelatos (1978:423, 1981:201).
37. Gabbay and Moravcsik (1980:62ff., 70).
38. Ibid., 70.
39. Freed (1979:18f.).
40. Ibid., 53.
41. Ibid., 18f.
42. Soga (1983:201).
43. A somewhat similar set of distinctions had been made in regard to the *Aktionsarten*, as reported by Pollak (1920:385ff.).
44. Bergman (1983:5), following Lyons (1977).
45. Pinkster (1984:274ff.).
46. Activities do not so obviously involve a change of state. Dowty (1979:184) calls them "indefinite change of state predicates."
47. This view is that of Gabbay and Moravcsik (1980:62ff.).
48. Siegel (1976), Bolinger(1973). See the last section of chapter 8.
49. Gabbay and Moravcsik (1980:62ff.).

50. A *process* is defined by Rescher and Urquhart (1971:155), as "a programmed sequence (temporal sequence) of repeatable state-types."
51. Rescher and Urquhart (1971:160).
52. Ibid., 161.
53. Freed (1979:55ff.).
54. Ibid., 158.
55. Woisetschlaeger (1976:18).
56. Von Wright (1963), Davidson (1969:225ff.), Dowty (1977:58).
57. This is the usual analysis, though as an anonymous reviewer of my manuscript correctly pointed out, many such "changes of state" seem trivial.
58. Woisetschlaeger (1976:19).
59. Dowty (1979:52).
60. Garey (1957:106ff.).
61. Jespersen (1924:272f., 1931:92). Cf. Allen (1966:196).
62. Dahl (1981:80).
63. Pinkster (1984:277), Gabbay and Moravcsik (1980:62ff.), Bergman (1983:5). Various other definitions are listed by Declerck (1979:762f.).
64. McCoard (1978:9) reports the identification of perfectivity with telicness. Declerck (1979:762) notes at least one definition in the literature which explicitly states that telic verbs "imply" that the action *reaches* a goal. Most of the definitions she reports, however, simply assert that the action *tends toward* a goal. Dahl (1981:81) reports that some (unnamed) "Western" scholars recognize only a distinction of telicness ("the T property") and not one of perfectivity ("the P property").
65. Garey (1957:106). Glosses: 'Pierre arrived' (imperfect also: 'Pierre was arriving'); 'Pierre played' (imperfect also: 'Pierre was playing'). A similar chart is found in Dahl (1981:82).
66. Declerck (1979: 768f.) draws the conclusion from this that these expressions are "ambiguous" or neutral in regard to the bounded/unbounded distinction. If the ambiguity derives, as suggested below, from the aspectual neutrality of the English past tense, then her conclusion that there is a three-way categorization of bounded, unbounded, and unmarked for boundedness is unwarranted.
67. E.g., as noted by McCoard (1978:141) and by Garey (1957); Macaulay (1971); Dowty (1972); R. Kittredge, "Tense, Aspect and Conjunction: Some Inter-relations for English" (Ph.D. diss., University of Pennsylvania, 1969), cited by McCoard (1978); King (1969); and H. Klein, "Das Verhalten der telischen Verben in den romanischen Sprachen erortert an der Interferens von Aspekt und Aktionsart" (Ph.D. diss., Johann Wolfgang Goethe-Universität, Frankfurt a. Main, 1969), cited by McCoard (1971).
68. Comrie (1976:45).
69. The point is emphasized by Declerck (1979:764).
70. Declerck (1979:767) says that she agrees with W. Zydatiss that the use of the progressive form renders bounded processes unbounded, and that "this is the only position that is consistent with the results of the (generally accepted) tests." Sentences like *John was knitting a sweater* are compatible with adverbials like *for hours* and incompatible with adverbials like *in an hour*.
71. Dahl (1981:83).
72. Ibid., 84, 86.
73. For discussion and references, see Foote (1967), from which the above examples have been taken.
74. Freed (1979), following Dillon (1977:33ff.).
75. Freed (1979:52f.).
76. Dowty (1979:184).
77. Freed (1979:33f., 38ff.). The discussion below is based on pp. 31, 35, 38f.
78. Soga (1983:29).
79. Pinkster (1984:277).
80. Mourelatos (1978:423, 1981:202).
81. Gabbay and Moravcsik (1980:62ff.).

82. Joos (1964:138) is wrong in suggesting that the term *phase* itself dates back only to Trager and Smith (1951:78); as we have seen, it was already in use by Keniston by 1936. But Trager and Smith and Joos use it in a special way. "Phase" has traditionally meant a stage of the action—beginning, continuation, end, etc. They, however, refer to the *perfect* as a phase. We shall see that it can be treated as the post-terminative phase of a situation, but it also can be viewed as an aspect, which seems closer to the intentions of Trager and Smith, and Joos.
83. As evidenced by the papers in Le Goffic (1986).
84. Valin (1975:145).
85. See Hirtle (1975:17, 1967:20).
86. Diagram from Guillaume (1965:9). *Temps in posse* 'time in possibility'; *temps in fieri* 'time in being-done'; *temps in esse* 'time in being'; *temps chronogénétique* 'chronogenetic time'.
87. Valin (1975:131). The most important study of the *surcomposé* tenses of French is probably Cornu (1953), which is Guillaumist.
88. See Hirtle (1975:33), Valin (1975:141).
89. Dietrich (1983:201ff.) gives a brief overview.
90. Coseriu's "planes" accord not with the "statuses" (as that term is used in contemporary aspectology—see chapter 7), but rather with Bull's axes of orientation (discussed in chapter 3).
91. Coseriu (1976:94), Dietrich (1983:203).
92. The simplex pluperfect is found also in Rumanian (*facusem*) and some Spanish dialects (*hiciera*) (Bourciez, 1910:301, 564; Elcock, 1975:155f.).
93. Coseriu (1976:96), Dietrich (1983:204).
94. Trager and Smith (1951:78).
95. Joos (1964:139f.).
96. Ibid., 141.
97. For history and references, see Pollak (1920) and Verkuyl (1972:2ff.).
98. A. Noreen, *Vart språk* (Lund, 1911–12), cited by Pollak (1920:384ff.).
99. Lewis (1975:148).
100. The diagrams in Dietrich (1983:122f.) and Coseriu (1976:88f.) do not completely capture Keniston's intentions. A scheme not dissimilar to that of Keniston is presented by Travaglia (1981:47). Keniston's scheme influences that of Coseriu (1976; cf. Dietrich, 1983:201).
101. Coseriu (1976) uses the term "view." Many writers differentiate *view* from *aspect*, but it is just as ambiguous a term, with many uses in the literature.
102. Woisetschlaeger (1976:20, 24ff.).
103. *Keep, keep on*, and *continue* are not entirely synonymous. For me the example *Walter kept filing the day's mail* is not entirely acceptable; at least it has special nuances (as do both *Walter kept on filing the day's mail* and *Walter continued filing the day's mail*). If there is a single pile of letters which he files over a period time, *keep on* would be better; *keep* is better if there is a series of letters or groups of letters which come in at different times during the day. *Continue* is indifferent to gaps: *after a long lunch break, Walter continued filing the day's mail*. (Perhaps *continue* is ambiguous, one reading being 'resume'.) But *keep* and *keep on* are not indifferent to gaps: !*after a long lunch break, Walter kept (on) filing the day's mail* cannot mean that he resumed filing after the break which had begun before the break. Notice too that *Walter continued to file the day's mail* differs from *Walter continued filing the day's mail* in regard both to the possibility of iteration and that of resumption. The semantics of the aspectual auxiliaries is more complex than Woisetschlaeger's discussion suggests.
104. Woisetschlaeger (1976:25).
105. There is an interesting question as to whether in this sort of situation we can properly say, e.g., that Walter filed mail from noon to 5:00 or not. Can you be said to have worked all day, if you break for lunch?
106. Woisetschlaeger (1976:20).

107. The triviality of a gap is not an objective matter of length of time. If Walter pauses for an instant to stretch, it is still possible to say that he resumed working after pausing to stretch. On the other hand, gaps of that length are usually trivial; it would be odd to say that the average worker resumes working (say) 112 times during the course of the average workday. The conditions under which one can be said to *stop* doing something or *resume* doing it are clearly dependent on those under which one can be said to be doing something while not literally doing it, and these are not based on objective measures.
108. The discussion here is based on Freed (1979:38f.).
109. Comrie (1976:3), Holt (1943:6), Friedrich (1974:S2).
110. Lyons (1977:705).
111. Freed (1979:29).
112. Bybee (1985:21).
113. Ibid., 28.
114. Ibid., 32 (and elsewhere).
115. Freed (1979:29).
116. Lyons (1977:705f.).
117. Johnson (1977:19ff., 1981:152ff.).
118. Jakobson (1957:130).
119. Event time, in Reichenbachian terms.
120. Johnson (1977:20f.).
121. Ibid., 20.
122. Chung and Timberlake (1985:213f.).
123. Ibid., 203.
124. As an anonymous reviewer of my manuscript pointed out, the Russian example is not quite comparable to the others, since Russian has no pluperfect in contrast with the preterite.

Chapter 7

1. König (1980:269).
2. On the various types of theories of meaning, see Alston (1964, 1967, 1967a), Kalish (1967), Kretzmann (1967).
3. There are a number of well-known paradoxes which depend on assuming that negative expressions such as *no one* refer to entities. A couple of oft-quoted ones are:
   Nothing is better than a long and happy life.
   A peanut-butter-and-jelly sandwich is better than nothing.
   Therefore, a peanut-butter-and-jelly sandwich is better than a long and happy life.

   No cat has two tails.
   A cat has one more tail than no cat.
   Therefore, a cat has three tails.
4. Aristotle (1938:115).
5. Montague (1974), Partee (1975, 1976), Dowty et al. (1981).
6. Frege (1892, 1949, 1952), Gorovitz et al. (1979:101), Dowty et al. (1981:142).
7. In a referential semantic theory in the Fregean tradition, the referent of a sentence is its truth value. But this does *not* mean that all sentences sharing a truth value are synonymous with one another, merely that they are coreferential. Even in referential theories, reference does not exhaust meaning.
8. Among them Van Emde Boas and Janssen (1979:111) and Welsh (1986).
9. Kalish (1967:350f.).
10. Semantics should be formal in a second sense as well, though this is less important for present purposes. It should be statable in an unambiguous language, such as a logical calculus. See Kalish (1967).
11. Kretzmann (1967:397). The terms *sense, intension,* and *connotation* are often used interchangeably, as are *reference, extension,* and *denotation,* though some theoreticians have defined technical distinctions between the members of each group.

12. Carnap (1956).
13. The question of whether yet other parameters are necessary is discussed by Lewis (1969).
14. For references, see Partee (1975, 1976) and Dowty et al. (1981). The following simplified presentation of Montague semantics, given here to offer some idea of how Montague's program can be carried out, is based on these works plus Johnson (1977), McCawley (1981), and Allwood et al. (1977).
15. Ajdukiewicz (1935), Bar-Hillel (1967:59), Cresswell (1973:70ff.), Allwood et al. (1977:132ff.), McCawley (1981:409f.). The discussion below assumes that constituent branching is binary, i.e., an expression can have at most two immediate constituent expressions. This is not required by the theory of categorial grammar but is widely assumed in Montague grammar to be generally, if not exclusively, the case.
16. Lyons (1968:227ff.).
17. For substantial fragments of the Montague grammar of English, see Montague (1973), given also in Dowty et al. (1981, ch. 7), Partee (1975), and Dowty (1979:250ff.).
18. Montague uses the latter of these notations; the former is due to McCawley (1981).
19. We will discuss below how these expressions are utilized.
20. St. Augustine, *Confessions* XI, ch. xvii.f.
21. Cited in Prior (1967:9). Aquinas (1955) provides a commentary on *De Interpretatione* 16b. 17–19.
22. In Gale (1968:93). See Prior (1967:3).
23. Prior (1967:15f.).
24. Ibid., 1ff., McTaggart (1968). For discussion and bibliography on replies to McTaggart, see Gale (1968).
25. Gale (1968:95f.).
26. Ibid., 159.
27. Prior (1957, 1967), Rescher and Urquhart (1971).
28. Thus, the sources in n. 27. Logically, Pres(p) = p, where "Pres" represents the present tense.
29. Montague (1973, 1974a:105, 1974b:262).
30. Partee (1973:602f.). See Bäuerle (1979:228), Dowty (1979:330f.), Nerbonne (1984:11), Saurer (1984:41).
31. Richards/Heny (1982:75, 133).
32. Bennett and Partee (1978:6).
33. Tichý (1980:360f.).
34. Cf. Bennett and Partee (1978:8f.).
35. It would seem that the force of this point is somewhat weakened by the fact that in many languages, e.g., German, there is no incompatibility of past tense adverbials and the present perfect: *ich habe ihn gestern gesehen* 'I saw [literally 'have seen'] him yesterday' (Wilson, 1950:108). However, in modern German the "present perfect," like the French *passé compose*, serves as a past tense; we may hypothesize that only when the "present perfect" is in fact a past tense can it co-occur with past tense adverbials. If so, the German examples present no problem.
36. Tichý (1980:361).
37. Richards (1982:76–80).
38. There are very interesting discussions of the various uses of the simple present in Calver (1946) and Leech (1971), from which I have drawn some of the ideas here.
39. Nerbonne (1984:44). Cf. Kufner (1962:89). The "quasi-perfect" quality comes from its referring to an action begun in the past.
40. Pointed out by Leech (1971:7f.). Here the meaning of the present is equivalent to a present perfect: e.g., "John tells me" = "John *has told* me."
41. Thus we can say that John dates redheads, but he is not dating one right now (whether we mean by this that he literally is not engaged in dating a redhead at this moment, or that, although he generally dates redheads, he is currently going through a period in which he does not do so). But it would be at best odd to say that John loves Mary,

but does not love her right now (unless we are taking *love* to ambiguously refer to more and less serious—or general—feelings).

42. Translation by W. L. Bowes of Simonides, fragment 92, in Bartlett (1968:70b).
43. Nerbonne (1984:45ff.).
44. The three main positions found in the literature are as follows:
    1. The Germanic modals "shall" and "will" are ambiguously modal or futuric. Thus Leech, (1971:52): "*Will* and *shall* have the double function of modal auxiliaries and auxiliaries of the future." But is *function* the same thing as *meaning*?
    2. The future auxiliaries *are* future tense markers, with other meanings being contextual. Thus Wekker (1976:67): "*will* is essentially a marker of future time, and . . . all the various nuances of meanings by which it may be coloured are overtones of the idea of futurity."
    3. English and Dutch at least do not *really* have a future tense, and the futuric value of the modals is simply the future meaning all modals have. Thus Joos (1964:159): "it's about time to dispose of the notion that *will* is a 'future tense' auxiliary. Like *every* modal . . . it has a connotation *of futurity*"; Ebeling (1962:90): "All [the] possibilities [of interpretation of expressions with Dutch *zullen*, such as a promise, assurance, etc.] do not impair the unity of the meaning ZULLEN"; and Perkins (1983:42): "the use of WILL and SHALL to refer to future time is secondary to a more modal function." Cf. Hermerén (1978:34); and Barwise and Perry (1983:289): "the English auxiliary system treats the future WILL as a modal."

    Because we are not treating mood in this book, this issue cannot be discussed. Obviously it can be resolved only if mood is properly distinguished from tense, and if the dividing line between semantics and pragmatics is clearly delineated. The question of whether the future auxiliaries "will" and "shall" of English and Dutch (and German dialects) are ambiguous depends on what lies on the semantics side of that line.
45. Wekker (1976:7f.).
46. Ultan (1978).
47. Bennett and Partee (1978:11), Dowty (1979:139).
48. Bennett and Partee (1978:13).
49. Ibid., 35.
50. Ibid., 37.
51. Ibid., 39.
52. Bennett (1977), Bennett and Partee (1978).
53. Elcock (1975:458f.).
54. 'he's going to strike', lit. 'he goes to strike'.
55. Or to HAVE (Dowty, 1982:35).
56. The issue is essentially that of the compositionality of the perfect. See section 1.
57. Nerbonne (1982:394ff., 1984:156ff.).
58. In Bäuerle (1979).
59. Vladimir Admoni, *Die deutsche Sprachbau* (Munich: Beck, 1970). Cited by Nerbonne (1984).
60. In Ronald Hendricks, "Aspect and Adverbs in German" (Ph.D. diss., Cornell University, 1981). See Nerbonne (1982:396ff.).
61. Hendricks, op. cit. (n. 60), p. 34. Cited by Nerbonne (1982, 1984).
62. Johnson (1977:25).
63. On metric tense systems, see Comrie (1985, ch. 4).
64. Johnson (1977:27, 30).
65. Johnson's gloss.
66. The order of morphemes in the manifest paradigm is (1) subject concord marker, (2) tense prefix, (3) stem with aspect infix. In the imminent paradigm there is a prefix but no infix. See Johnson (1977:26–30).
67. Johnson (1977:171).
68. Ibid., 176. This rule and the next are truncated here.
69. Ibid., 177.
70. Cresswell (1985b:10).
71. See Huddleston (1970), McCawley (1971).
72. McCawley (1971:101f.)

73. Wilson (1950:109), lit. 'in one year has one the house built'.
74. Åqvist (1976), Guenther (1978), Åqvist and Guenther (1978), etc.
75. See Prior (1957, 1967).
76. Bennett and Partee [1972] (1978:39), Johnson (1977:67), Bäuerle (1979:79), Dowty (1979:342, 1982:32), Richards (1982:91ff.), and Saurer (1984:79).
77. Dowty (1982:35).
78. "F_{36}" in S37' (Dowty 1982:35) is a typographical error for "F_{37}."
79. "F_{36}" in S38' (Dowty 1982:35) is a typographical error for "F_{38}."
80. Dowty (1982:32), replacing Dowty's i, j with r, s for reasons which will become clear below.
81. Richards (1982:91ff.).
82. Johnson (1977:159).
83. Inoue (1975:81f., 97).
84. Morphological analysis given by Inoue.
85. Leech (1971:39f.).
86. E.g. by Inoue (1975, 1978, 1979).
87. In many contexts, this sentence would invite the false inference that Mars has but one moon. It thus violates the Gricean principle that the speaker is as helpful to the addressee as possible (e.g., statements should not invite false inferences).
88. E.g., Grandgent and Wilkins (1915:64), Ramsey (1956:332).
89. Bertinetto (1986a:18f.).
90. Lo Cascio (1986:202).
91. Grevisse (1949:557).
92. Price (1971:228).
93. Grevisse (1949:557), Brunot and Bruneau (1949:382); example from Price (1971:229).
94. Brunot and Bruneau (1949:381).
95. Dowty (1982:38).
96. Nerbonne (1984:151).
97. Jespersen (1931:75).
98. James McGilvray, personal communication, 1975.
99. Jespersen (1931:24, 75).
100. Jenkins (1972).
101. Cf. the title of Vetter (1973): *someone solves this problem tomorrow*.
102. Jenkins (1972:175).
103. Stalnaker (1972:380).
104. This is a point of view adopted by syntax-centered theories such as those of Noam Chomsky, or semantic-centered theories such as Generative Semantics.
105. This point of view has much in common with some of the theories in chapter 8.
106. There is a marginal futurate reading of this last: "if it turns out that Susan has arrived yesterday afternoon . . ."
107. Jenkins (1972:178).
108. Grebe (1966:98).
109. The obligatory use of the present progressive for situations coinciding with the speech act is uncommon even among languages which have "progressive" tenses. The language whose use most closely approximates that of English in this regard is, as far as I can tell, Mongolian. (See Poppe, 1970.)
110. Blansitt (1975), Comrie (1976:32), Dahl (1985:90ff.)
111. Dahl (1985:90) gives *qieghed*, but Borg (1981:3) gives *qed*, which he says "is assumed to be an abbreviation of the present participle *qieghed* 'he is located' of the verb of location 'qaghad' 'he was located'."
112. Except in French. Spanish and Portuguese use *estar*, the locative-'temporary' copula (rather than the 'essential-permanent' *ser*); Italian uses the cognate *stare* 'be' (as opposed to *essere*), but forms a progressive only in the present and imperfect tenses (Marchand, 1955:50). Portuguese of Portugal and many dialects of other languages prefer a construction with 'at' + infinitive (Dietrich, 1973:13, 16f.).

113. Marchand (1955:50).
114. For non-stative non-performatives, the simple present is rarely used for situations coincident with the speech act, though examples do occur in formal English:
Sirs, I write this letter to you today to bring to your attention the following facts.
I run for public office knowing full well how slight my chances are of success.
An anonymous reviewer of my manuscript argues that the Romance progressives are not synonymous with the simple tenses, as Marchand suggests, for they cannot substitute for the latter in their serial readings (*canta* can mean 'is singing', but *está cantando* cannot mean 'sings').
115. Comrie (1976:35).
116. Ibid., 12. He sees the imperfective as having to do with continuousness, to which the progressive adds nonstativity.
117. Zandvoort (1962; 1970:124), Scheffer (1975:17).
118. What Zandvoort says (1970:123), basing himself purely on form, is that *either* the perfective or imperfective may be the marked member of an oppositional pair, whereas the English progressive is *always* the marked member. We saw in chapter 6 that arguments from markedness run up against, first, the ambiguity of the term "marked," and second, the contentious question of how forms in different systems are to be compared. It is not clear in precisely what way a difference in "markedness" across languages matters in categorizing semantically similar forms.
119. Hatcher (1951:187). The emphasis is mine.
120. Marchand (1955:50ff.). As an anonymous reviewer has pointed out, the simple tenses are not always substitutable for the "progressive" tenses, even if the reverse is true.
121. The literature is too vast, and views too divergent, to more than sample here. There is no general source for the progressive as a whole. For the English progressive, extensive bibliography and discussion are found in Allen (1966), Scheffer (1975), and Schopf (1974). No comparable work on Romance exists, though surveys of views on the Romance tense/aspect systems, with some discussion of the progressives, are found, e.g., in Coseriu (1976), Dietrich (1973), and Travaglia (1981).
122. Scheffer (1975:21), Sweet (1891:101), Lyons (1968:316). We saw above that duration has also been linked with the imperfective, and some of the authors cited below do either identify the progressive with the imperfective or treat it as a subtype of it.
123. Scheffer (1975:23).
124. Examples from Palmer (1965).
125. See Palmer (1965:60) for some differing interpretations.
126. Ibid., 60.
127. Leech (1971:16).
128. From Travaglia (1981:36f.).
129. Keniston (1936), discussed by Coseriu (1976:88f.) and Dietrich (1983:121ff.); Coseriu (1976), discussed by Dietrich (1983:201ff.); Guillaume (1929, 1965).
130. Ter Meulen (1985).
131. Dahl (1985:93): the progressive "is normally used of dynamic situations." For Marchand (1955:47), "the basic function of the Progressive Form is to denote one single action observed in the dynamic process of happening."
132. Ota (1963:2), Scheffer (1975:18), Allen (1966:32).
133. Leech (1971:14).
134. Travaglia (1981:48).
135. Vlach (1981:291). Cf. the treatment of the progressive by Dowty (1977, 1979), and the critique in ter Meulen (1985).
136. Scheffer (1975:85).
137. Blansitt (1975:4).
138. Jespersen (1931:178ff.).
139. Ibid., 180.
140. Calver (1946:173).
141. Hatcher (1951:201).

142. Scheffer (1975:86, 91).
143. Jespersen (1931:180).
144. Hatcher (1951:203).
145. E.g., Blansitt (1975:3ff.).
146. Leech (1971:27).
147. Scheffer (1975:92f.).
148. Palmer (1965:89); see Scheffer (1975:94).
149. Scheffer (1975:94).
150. Prince (1982:453).
151. See Dowty (1977:68, 1979:156).
152. Bennett and Partee (1978:13).
153. Dowty (1977, 1979).
154. Dowty (1977:46).
155. Ibid., 47.
156. Ibid., 57, Dowty (1979:146).
157. We shall discuss below whether these conditions are also the appropriate ones for the imperfective aspect.
158. Dowty (1977:61f., 1979:150ff.). Likewise, the concept of "worlds which are the natural continuations of a given world at a point in time" is fraught with difficulties. We discuss below in connection with Situation Semantics the attempts by Hinrichs (1983) and ter Meulen (1985) to deal with the progressive while avoiding such difficulties.
159. Thomason (1970), Tedeschi (1981).
160. Dowty (1977:63, 1979:151). Cf. Tedeschi (1981:254), attempting to resolve certain difficulties with Dowty's formulation perceived by him.
161. Dowty (1977:64).
162. Ibid., 65, Dowty (1979:153).
163. See McCawley (1981:326ff.).
164. Though Tedeschi (1981) argues that it has advantages in the treatment of conditionals, this falls within the realm of modals and therefore outside the scope of the present work.
165. In a personal communication.
166. Dowty (1977:69, 1979:157).
167. Vetter (1973), Goodman (1973).
168. Dowty (1977:70); the passage below is from (1979:158).
169. Rassudova (1984:13).
170. Ibid., 28.
171. Ibid., 93.
172. Ibid., 14.
173. Johnson (1977, 1981).
174. Johnson (1981:153, n. 4).
175. Johnson (1977:60).
176. Johnson (1981:153f.).
177. Ibid., 154.
178. Johnson (1977:159).
179. Ibid., 86ff.
180. Ibid., 95.
181. Ibid., 86ff., 91f.
182. Ibid., 91.
183. Ibid., 90f.
184. Ibid., 91f.
185. Ibid., 93.
186. Ibid., 94.
187. Ibid., 95.
188. Despite the doubts expressed by Hoepelman (1978:58).

189. Hoepelman (1978:59).
190. These examples and the next two sets of examples are from Leech (1971).
191. This sort of thing in categorical grammar has disturbed linguists used to theories in which the syntactic category of an expression is not so dependent on its external syntax.
192. E.g., Greenbaum (1969), Bartsch [1972] 1976.
193. These and the following examples are from Wolfson (1979:174–77).
194. Bennett and Partee (1978:22).
195. Saurer (1984:61ff.) calls these *count* adverbials.
196. Bennett and Partee (1978:22f.).
197. Bennett and Partee (1978:29).
198. Nerbonne (1984:61).
199. Dowty (1979:325).
200. Ibid., 332.
201. Allwood et al. (1977:153), McCawley (1981:240f.), Levinson (1983:170ff.). On presupposition, see Allwood et al., ch. 9; McCawley, ch. 9; Levinson, ch. 4.
202. Bennett and Partee (1978:30).
203. See, e.g., Dowty (1979, 1982), Heny/Richards (1982), and Saurer (1984) on English; and Nerbonne (1984) on German. Cresswell has conducted an extensive program of research into time adverbials, reported in Cresswell (1973, 1974, 1978, 1985, 1985a), etc. On adverbial subordinate clauses, see Heinämäki (1974).
204. Bennett (1977:503), Cresswell (1973:195f.), Dowty (1979:323ff., 1982:23f.), Richards (1982:63ff.), etc.
205. Cresswell (1973:196), Dowty (1979:323ff., 1982:24ff.).
206. Reported in Dowty (1982).
207. Dowty (1982:26). Cf. (1979:327f.).
208. Dowty (1982:25).
209. Dowty (1982:26). Cf. (1979:327f.).
210. Cresswell (1973:196).
211. Dowty (1982:28).
212. Ibid., 38.
213. Cf. Comrie (1971), Dinsmore (1972).
214. Dowty (1982:31ff.).
215. Ibid., 36ff.
216. Ibid., 37. The sequence-of-tense phenomena cited in support we will discuss in chapter 8.
217. Ibid., 46.
218. On the notion of satisfaction, see McCawley (1981:69–73, 167–70).
219. Nerbonne (1984:21).
220. Rightly or wrongly, the present work largely ignores the tense-logical tradition, e.g., the kind of work predominantly found in the various anthologies edited by Rohrer (1977, 1978), Guenther and Rohrer (1978), Guenther and Schmidt (1978), etc. Often using brilliant insight, such work deals precisely with the issues we are dealing with here, but within such a different context, often so divorced from the "natural" syntax and semantics of natural languages, that it has had little if any impact on the study of the semantics (not to mention the pragmatics) of tense and aspect within such paradigms as Montague semantics, which most scholars today would see as more contributory to progress on the issues considered here.
221. Dowty (1982:32).
222. Nerbonne (1984:26ff.).
223. Bull (1960:31).
224. We will need to generalize the neo-Reichenbachian system in any case to handle subordinate clause tenses, though this issue we leave for chapter 8.
225. This is just what Mondadori means by saying, "it is the dual of the future perfect."
226. Mondadori (1976:223).

227. Grice (1975). For discussions, see McCawley (1981:sect. 8.3), Levinson (1983, ch. 3). That is, in context and given certain pragmatic principles, it is inferable from, though not implied by, what is asserted.
228. Nerbonne (1984:27).
229. Dowty (1982:51f.).
230. Nerbonne discusses (1984:28ff.) the possible need for more than three index times.
231. E.g., Woisetschlaeger (1976:18).
232. Ibid.
233. Cresswell (1974 = 1985:24).
234. Åqvist and Guenther (1978:185).
235. Cresswell (1985:25).
236. Woisetschlaeger (1976:19).
237. This is too strong, owing to Woisetschlaeger's failure to individuate event tokens. We discuss this problem below.
238. There is an interesting question, which we raise here several times, as to whether in this sort of situation we an properly say, e.g., that Walter filed mail from noon to five or not. Can you be said to have worked all day if you break for lunch?
239. Woisetschlaeger (1976:20).
240. Ibid., 24f.
241. Ibid., 25.
242. Saurer (1984:20ff.).
243. His system thus resembles that discussed by Tedeschi (1981) and Dowty (1982).
244. Saurer (1984:27).
245. Ibid., 26f.
246. McCawley (1981:46). McCawley says: "Meaning postulates are supposed to supply steps in inferences that follow from the meaning of the 'nonlogical element' in question. . . . The distinction between meaning postulate and rule of inference is only as good as the difference between 'nonlogical element' and 'logical element', which is to say that it is far from clear that the difference has any substance."
247. See Dowty et al. (1981:236).
248. Saurer (1984:40).
249. Ibid., 41.
250. Ibid., 42f.
251. Ibid., 44.
252. Ibid., 48.
253. Ibid., 49f.
254. Ibid., 51.
255. Ibid., 79.
256. Ibid., 109.
257. Guenther (1978:208). A typographical error there omits the "∼".
258. Åqvist and Guenther (1978:15f.).
259. Ibid., 175.
260. Ibid., 185, 192ff.
261. Barwise and Perry (1983:7).
262. The brief characterization of the theory below is based on Barwise and Perry (1983), Hinrichs (1983), and Cooper (1985a, 1986). The minor inconsistencies in symbolism mirrored below should not prove confusing. In Barwise and Perry (1983) situation types are unlocated. A state of affairs is a situation type which is located, consisting of an ordered pair comprising a location *l* and a situation type *s*. Here we follow the system of Cooper (1985a).
263. Cooper (1985a:5). Cooper (1986:21) prefers the term *history* to "course of events," because it does not seem so exclusively tied to events alone (as opposed, say, to states); a similar terminology is employed by Bartsch (1986).
264. From Hinrichs (1983:177), using his notation.
265. Barwise and Perry (1983:19).

266. In Cooper (1985:116).
267. Cooper (1985).
268. Partee in Cooper (1985:53); Cooper (1985a:50).
269. Van Bentham (1985:33ff.).
270. The picture in his chapters 6–8 is that of a rich, inchoate, incoherent field, so it is too soon to say that Barwise and Perry are wrong, and it is impossible usefully to summarize his treatment here. Van Bentham is optimistic (p. 75): "The various analogies and cross-connections presented in this chapter [7] may be signs that a condensation could take place to one simple, stable, formal framework, which still leaves open quite diverse ideological uses."
271. Barwise and Perry (1983:288).
272. Cooper (1985a:5, 1986:21).
273. Cooper (1985a:9f., 1986:24f.).
274. Cooper (1986:26).
275. The discussion here is based on Cooper (1985a:11ff.).
276. Cooper (1985a:25, 1986:27). Same source (1986:27) for the temporal ill-formedness constraint below. In (1985a:27) he states it somewhat differently.
277. Cooper (1986:29). In Cooper (1985a:30) he states this constraint somewhat differently.
278. Cooper (1985a:30).
279. Ibid., 33.
280. Ibid., 36. On p. 29 of the same work Cooper defines for activities the constraint:
    Spatial extendability
    If r is a non-stative relation then any realized history which contains the fact
    $$\langle 1,r,x_1, \ldots, x_n,1 \rangle$$
    does NOT also contain the fact
    $$\langle 1',r,x_1, \ldots, x_n,0 \rangle$$
    for any $1'$ properly temporally including 1.
    This is due to the fact that, if an activity, say, occurs in a space s, it also occurs in any cotemporal space s' containing s. If Jim is eating sushi in Chicago then it must be the case that he is eating sushi in Illinois, given that Illinois includes Chicago.
281. Robin Cooper's unpublished manuscript (1982), "Situation Semantics, Stages, and the Present Tense" (Hinrichs, 1983:181, fn. 17; see also Cooper, 1985a) was apparently the first effort within *SS* to deal with progressives.
282. Hinrichs (1983:173) notes similar examples had been pointed out by Vlach (1981:285) and Cooper, op. cit. sup. (n. 281), p. 22.
283. Terence Parsons, "Modifiers and Quantifiers in Natural Language." Unpublished ms., 1983.
284. Hinrichs (1983:180).
285. Ibid., 176, Barwise and Perry (1983:94ff.). But see Cooper (1986:26).
286. Ter Meulen (1985:413).
287. Ibid., 414, Cooper (1985a:17f.).
288. Bartsch (1986:23).
289. Ibid., 24.
290. Ibid., 25.
291. Ibid., 26.
292. Ibid., 29.

Chapter 8

1. Examples from McGilvray (1974:5).
2. Reichenbach (1947:293).
3. Ibid., 294f.
4. Ibid., 295.
5. From Dinsmore (1982:219).
6. McGilvray (1974:5).

7. Ibid., 6.
8. Prior (1967:13). Cf. Dowty's observation (1982:45) that "subordinate clause times
   . . . don't intuitively 'feel' indexical to me—in particular, I don't think they come
   out to be systematically ordered in a past tense narrative discourse in the same way as
   the main clause reference times do." We shall discuss below theories such as Smith's
   (1978, 1981) of the anchoring of R points.
9. Similar to examples commented upon by Jespersen (1924) and others.
10. Reichenbach (1947:295f.).
11. Lakoff (1970:842).
12. Costa (1972:44f.).
13. McGilvray (1974), Hornstein (1977, 1981), Smith (1978, 1981).
14. Reichenbach (1947:296).
15. Hackman (1976:76f.). See McGilvray (1974:5).
16. McGilvray (1974:10f.).
17. Hackman (1976:77).
18. Hornstein (1977:523ff., 1981:134ff.).
19. Hornstein (1977:527).
20. Ibid., 534.
21. Smith (1978:43, 72; 1981:214f., 217).
22. This term is used as a technical term by Adelaar and Lo Cascio (1986:257) with
    roughly the meaning of temporal "sector." The sectors are the past, present, and
    future, into which time is divided.
23. Cf. Smith (1978:46, 1981:216). Smith does not consider the future tense in English to
    have a relational value other than that of the present.
24. Reichenbach (1947:294).
25. Smith (1981:217). Smith uses RT for Reichenbach's R, ST for S, and ET for E.
26. Adverbials are not necessary defined relative to ST. *Now*, for example, may refer to
    ST or may not (*he said that he was now rather ill*).
27. Smith (1978:45f., 1981:216).
28. Hinrichs (1986:78).
29. Smith (1981:218f.). The slightly different categorization followed by Hinrichs (1986:78)
    is given in Smith (1980).
30. Smith (1981:219f.).
31. Smith (1980).
32. Smith (1981:220f.).
33. Smith (1978:47, 1981:216f.).
34. Smith (1978:49).
35. Adelaar and Lo Cascio (1986:259) point out, however, that present or neutral adver-
    bials with the future tense must refer to times in the future: *he leaves today, but she
    on Tuesday* can refer to times only in the future. But there is nothing inherently futur-
    ate about either type of adverbial. Smith's account is unexplanatory.
36. Smith (1981:217).
37. Smith (1978:55).
38. Smith (1981:217).
39. Smith (1978:53).
40. Ibid., 50.
41. Smith (1978:50ff., 1981:222).
42. Smith (1978:46, 53ff.; 1981:216).
43. It is not clear if McCawley's objection (1971:103f.) to the treatment of the present
    perfect as a relative past is relevant here.
44. Smith (1978:69ff., 1981:222).
45. She in fact treats subordinating conjunctions (1981:215) as prepositions followed by
    sentences, and considers such subordinate clauses time adverbials like any other, but
    distinct from separate clauses such as complement and relative clauses. See for ex-
    ample Smith (1978:53).

46. Smith (1978:56ff., 1981:221ff.).
47. Smith (1978:72), Smith (1978:58, 1981:222).
48. Smith (1981:215).
49. Smith (1978:60, 1981:222).
50. Smith (1978:61). Cf. (1981:221f.).
51. Insertions in square brackets are mine.
52. Smith (1978:59).
53. Smith (1978:46, 1981:215).
54. Smith (1978:61ff., 1981:223ff.).
55. Smith (1981:224).
56. Smith (1978:62f.).
57. Ibid., 64ff.
58. Ibid., 65.
59. Ibid., 66.
60. Cf. the treatment by Costa, which we will discuss in the next section below.
61. Smith (1978:67).
62. Smith (1981:228ff.).
63. Ibid., 229. A similar treatment of tense as involving reference, and specifically the binding conditions stated within the theory of Government and Binding, is to be found in Shin's treatment (1988) of Korean, following Murvet Enç, "Anchoring Conditions for Tense," *Linguistic Inquiry* 18.643–57 (1987). In Government-and-Binding theory, tenses are treated in the same way as any other referential expressions, and are subject to syntactic binding conditions.

   The relevance to tense and aspect theory of a syntactic approach to binding is questionable, for the same kind of referential phenomena occur across sentences in discourse as within sentences. Since the completion of my manuscript, Anne Zribi-Hertz has published an article ("Anaphor Binding and Narrative Point of View: English Reflexive Pronouns in Sentence and Discourse," *Language* 65, 695–727, 1989) in which she argues that while the binding conditions of the Government-and-Binding theory may be adequate for intrasentential binding of reflexive pronouns, they are inadequate for transsentential phenomena dependent on discourse-pragmatic conditions. As explained in chapter 8, such conditions enter crucially into the use of tense and aspect.

   Zribi-Hertz suggests (p. 724) that "structural constraints such as the binding conditions might actually draw their motivation from discourse" and that "any structural theory of anaphora must be completed by discourse principles." My supposition is that she is correct and, further, that *all* reference (including temporal reference) is ultimately dependent on discourse-pragmatic conditions, from which syntactic binding conditions are derivable as special cases. If this supposition is correct, current referential theory within syntax will not have proven significant in the long term for tense research. At present this supposition, like all attempts to derive syntactic consequences from pragmatic theories, remains highly speculative.
64. Smith (1981:232).
65. Ibid., 233.
66. Hackman (1976:77).
67. Jespersen (1931:163).
68. Cf. her example (1981:223) *Bill will admit that Mary had been spirited away.*
69. See too Bråroe (1974).
70. For a history and critique of the GS movement, see Newmeyer (1980), chapters 4 and 5.
71. Hofmann (1966:VII-7ff.). Example numbers and letters omitted.
72. Ibid., VII-9ff.
73. Some dialects allow combinations of two modals: *might could*, etc., as was once pointed out to me by Charles Pasley, a speaker of such a dialect.
74. This analysis assumes that *will* is not an actualization of the future tense. Moreover, it

treats *will* as incorporating the present tense, and *would* the past tense. That *will* shifts to *would* in past tense (indirect-quotation) contexts supports this analysis: cf. *John will swim tomorrow* and *John said he* would *swim the next day*.

75. Ross (1969:83). Cf. Huddleston (1970:781f.), McCawley (1971:97f.).
76. Ross (1969:77).
77. Ibid. The indexed brackets indicate that the sentences summarized here are to be read horizontally. The italicized portions at the left—minus the tense in the case of *built a house*—are what have presumably been deleted in the clauses at the right.
78. Ibid., 82.
79. Ibid., 84.
80. Ibid., 81. The italicized portions are presumably what *so* replaces in each case.
81. McCawley (1971:100ff.).
82. Ibid., 101.
83. Huddleston (1970:790).
84. Smith (1981) would say orientation time.
85. That is, in Smithian terms, the matrix ET determines RT_2.
86. McCawley (1971:101).
87. Ibid., 103.
88. Ibid., 101f.
89. Somewhat simplified from the tree diagram given by Huddleston (1970:782).
90. Ross (1967:333).
91. Costa (1972:41, 48).
92. Huddleston (1970:791).
93. Ibid., 792.
94. Ibid., 793.
95. Ibid., 793ff.
96. Costa (1972:42).
97. The tense-shift transformation.
98. Riddle (1975:2).
99. Ibid., 3.
100. One possible interpretation is that in American English the perfect and the past are optionally neutralized on the surface, but the tense may still act in many ways like a perfect rather than a past; here the adverb *just* reveals the underlying perfect tense.
101. McCawley (1971:102f.).
102. Costa (1972:49).
103. Riddle (1978:105ff., 117ff.).
104. Ibid., 107.
105. Costa (1972:43).
106. Riddle (1975:3).
107. Cf. Heinämäki (1974).
108. Costa (1972:42).
109. Riddle (1975:1f.).
110. Riddle (1975, 1978).
111. Huddleston (1970:794).
112. Riddle (1975:1).
113. Richards (1982:89).
114. Ibid., 90.
115. Dowty (1982:39ff.).
116. Based on a proposal of Robin Cooper's (Dowty, 1982:41).
117. Costa (1972:49).
118. Dowty (1982:41).
119. Ibid., 42.
120. Ibid., 49f.
121. Ibid., 50.
122. Ibid., 51.

123. Example in Jespersen (1931:163).
124. Speight (1962:35, 40).
125. Prista (1966:57).
126. Ramsey (1956:325f.).
127. Brunot and Bruneau (1949:376).
128. Forsyth (1970:9), cf. ibid., 65; Comrie (1985:27).
129. Jespersen (1931:182f.).
130. Examples from Leech (1971:9).
131. Ewert (1933:253f.). Cf. Saunders (1969:154f.) and, on the English progressive, Scheffer (1975:29).
132. Goodwin (1889:16f.).
133. Brunot and Bruneau (1949:377).
134. Curme (1922:212).
135. Brunot and Bruneau (1949:377).
136. Jespersen (1931:183f), sources omitted.
137. *Ouverture* and *clôture*. Saunders (1969:155), Waugh (1975:457), Waugh and Monville (1986:857).
138. Saunders (1969:154f., 161).
139. Forsyth (1970:4).
140. Ibid., 5.
141. Waugh (1975:459).
142. Ramsey (1956:453).
143. Saunders (1969:155). Example from Waugh (1975:464).
144. Waugh (1975:464).
145. Ibid., 460.
146. Curme (1922:211f.).
147. Ibid., 214.
148. Ultan (1978:104).
149. Example from Waugh (1975:468).
150. Ultan (1978:104).
151. Example from Brunot and Bruneau (1949:383).
152. Lockwood (1968:125).
153. Ramsey (1956:339f.).
154. Jespersen (1931:263ff.).
155. Brunot and Bruneau (1949:377).
156. Ultan (1978:103f.).
157. Curme (1922:213).
158. Haugen (1972).
159. Slobin and Aksu (1982:188), Johanson (1971).
160. Curme (1922:211).
161. Brunot and Bruneau (1949:374).
162. Silva-Corvalán (1983:761). See Schiffrin (1981:46) and Wolfson (1979:169) for other statements of this sort.
163. Waugh (1975:466).
164. Curme (1922:211).
165. The same may be said of theories regarding the other tenses discussed above.
166. It is noteworthy that Brown and Yule's *Discourse Analysis* (1983) fails to discuss tense, while Levinson's *Pragmatics* of the same year barely mention it.
167. Hopper (1979:213).
168. Ibid., 213f. Example drawn from Lyndon Harries, ed., *Swahili Prose Texts* (London: Oxford University Press, 1965).
169. Hopper (1979:215f.).
170. Waugh and Monville-Burston (1986:847).
171. Wallace (1982:208). He mentions Joseph E. Grimes, *The Thread of Discourse* (The Hague: Mouton, 1975); Hopper and Thompson (1980); Larry B. and Linda K. Jones,

"Multiple Levels of Information in Discourse," in Linda K. Jones, ed., *Discourse Studies in Meso-American Languages* (Dallas: Summer Institute of Linguistics, 1979); and Longacre and Levinson (1978).

172. For discussion, see Wallace (1982), Chvany (1985).
173. Wallace (1982:210).
174. Hopper (1979:216).
175. Ibid., 217.
176. Wallis Reid, "The Quantitative Validation of a Grammatical Hypothesis: The *passé simple* and the *imparfait*" (*Papers of the Northeastern Linguistic Society* 7, 1976), cited by Hopper (1979).
177. Hopper and Thompson (1980:252).
178. Wallace (1982:211f.).
179. Chvany (1985:255).
180. Hopper (1979:217f.).
181. Ibid., 218.
182. Ibid., 219.
183. Fleischman (1983:194).
184. McCoard (1978:31f.).
185. Fleischman (1983:191f.). Reference is to J. M. Anderson, *An Essay Concerning Aspect* (The Hague: Mouton, 1973).
186. Haugen (1972:135), quoting Maja Dubravić.
187. Li et al. (1982:40).
188. Waugh (1975:456).
189. Fleischman (1983:200).
190. Leech (1971:33).
191. Waugh (1975:445f.).
192. Ibid., 461.
193. Ibid., 465. The same may be said of the conditional, relative to some point in the past.
194. Fleischman (1983:190).
195. Li et al. (1982:22).
196. Ibid., 23.
197. Ibid., 24.
198. Ibid., 25.
199. Ibid., 28.
200. Ibid.
201. Leech (1971:34).
202. Ibid., 36.
203. Ibid., 31.
204. James (1982:386f.). Her length marks are omitted here.
205. Goodwin (1889:13).
206. Slobin and Aksu (1982:187).
207. Poppe (1970:131).
208. Discussion here based on Binnick (1979:1).
209. Nakau (1976:470).
210. Ibid., 470f.
211. Riddle (1978:70).
212. Li et al. (1982:33).
213. Ibid., 34f.
214. Ibid., 36.
215. Ibid., 37.
216. Cf. Waugh (1975:472f.).
217. Slobin and Aksu (1982:186, 188).
218. Haugen (1972:133f.).
219. Ibid., 137.

220. Ibid., 139.
221. Curme (1922:213).
222. See Slobin and Aksu (1982) and Johanson (1971).
223. Inoue (1975:107ff.).
224. Latin: Greenough et al. (1903:295); Greek: Goodwin (1889:11); French: Brunot and Bruneau (1949:374), Saunders (1969), Waugh (1975); Spanish: Ramsey (1956:336); English: Jespersen (1931:19f.); German: Curme (1922:211); and Japanese: Soga (1983:15f., 217ff.).
225. Saunders (1969), Waugh (1975:450f.), Wolfson (1979:169), Schiffrin (1981:46), Wallace (1982:210).
226. Fleischman (1983:192), Comrie (1976:65).
227. Fleischman (1983:189f.).
228. Ibid., 188.
229. Jespersen (1931:218).
230. Fleischman (1983:189), Lakoff (1970:846).
231. Fleischman (1983:190).
232. Examples from Jespersen (1931:252).
233. Ibid., 280.
234. Waugh (1975:465, 472f.), Waugh and Monville (1986:849).
235. Fleischman (1982:191, 194, 200).
236. James (1982:396), Palmer (1986:210ff.).
237. James (1982:377).
238. Ibid., 379.
239. Waugh (1975:459f.).
240. Slobin and Aksu (1982:197).
241. Ibid., 196.
242. James (1982:386).
243. Waugh (1976:478).
244. Palmer (1986:73).
245. James (1982:391).
246. Palmer (1986:63).
247. James (1982:387).
248. Palmer (1986:63).
249. James (1982:388).
250. Kamp and Rohrer (1983:250), Dowty (1986:39). Although earlier writers such as Smith (1978, 1981)—and even Reichenbach, implicitly (1947:288f.)—had indicated that the same principles in general apply to independent sentences as clauses within sentences, this was seen as an extension of intrasentential principles to the extrasentential realm, and not as intrinsically intersentential in nature. Principles of discourse structure and pragmatics played only an incidental, and not very explanatory, role.
251. Houweling (1986:170), Vet and Molendijk (1986:136).
252. Kamp (1979:381).
253. Nerbonne (1986:83f.). Cf. Kamp (1979:402f.), Dowty (1986:19).
254. Nerbonne (1986:92).
255. Kamp and Rohrer (1983:252).
256. Kamp (1979:403), Dowty (1986:38).
257. Kamp and Rohrer (1983:252).
258. Kamp and Rohrer (1983:251).
259. Kamp (1979:381), Kamp and Rohrer (1983:253), Dowty (1986:57f.).
260. There *are* some differences, though. See, e.g., Partee (1984:261) for some conditions associated with adverbial subordinate clauses that do not pertain to simple sequences.
261. They don't claim that events are essential to the construction of DRS's; a theory with DRS's in which events apparently play no direct role is that of Rigter (1986).
262. Kamp (1979:passim, 1981:52), Dowty (1986:45), Hinrichs (1986:65f.).

263. Dowty (1986:45) denies, in any case, that this is a crucial difference between Kamp's theory and his own interval-based theory.
264. Kamp (1981:44).
265. Ibid., 43.
266. Hinrichs (1986:65f.).
267. Ibid., 66.
268. Kamp (1979:394f., 1981:44).
269. Vet and Molendijk (1986:144). Cf. Bartsch (1986).
270. Kamp (1979:400f.), Kamp and Rohrer (1983:280), Dowty (1986:39).
271. Kamp (1979:400, 1981:42, 45), Kamp and Rohrer (1983:253). Below we shall see alternative ways of understanding the difference between the *imparfait* and the *passé*.
272. See Kamp (1979:400f., 1981:4).
273. Kamp (1979:402f.), Kamp and Rohrer (1983:251f.).
274. Dowty (1986:39).
275. Kamp and Rohrer (1983:252).
276. Ibid., 253.
277. Or the past in English.
278. See Kamp and Rohrer (1983:253f.).
279. Ibid., 253. This follows from the nature of the perfective and the imperfective aspects (cf. Johnson, 1977:20, 1981:154, 173). In the perfective (and the *passé* is perfective) R = E, but in the imperfective (the *imparfait* is imperfective), R is in E.
280. Kamp and Rohrer (1983:254f.).
281. Ibid., 256, 264.
282. Ibid., 256f.
283. E.g., Dowty (1986:37), Hinrichs (1986:68), Dry (1981:233, 1983:23f.), Bach (1986:6), Smith (1986:97).
284. Smith (1983:480).
285. Smith (1983:481, 1986:97), Dry (1983:24), Bach (1986:6). Cf. Hinrichs (1986:71).
286. E.g., Dowty (1986:43f.).
287. E.g., Dowty (1986:37), Hinrichs (1986:68ff.), Nerbonne (1986:91). Cf. Smith (1986:100).
288. Dowty (1986:37), Hinrichs (1986:68).
289. Dowty (1986:37f.).
290. Smith (1986:104).
291. Dowty (1986:57).
292. Hinrichs (1986:68f.)
293. Ibid., 65, though he extends it on p. 70 to an 11-tuple.
294. Kamp (1979:384f.).
295. Hinrichs (1986:70).
296. Kamp (1979:400f., 1981:46), Kamp and Rohrer (1983:250). Cf. Dowty (1986:39).
297. Hinrichs (1986:71). The statement has been modified slightly to increase readability.
298. That is, Aristotelian classes.
299. Erhard Hinrichs, ''Temporale Anaphora im Englischen'' (Master's thesis, Universität Tübingen, 1981), cited by Kamp (1981:50).
300. Smith (1986:107).
301. Ibid., 109, 114, from David Birdsong.
302. Rimbaud (1962:268).
303. Kamp and Rohrer (1983:254), Dowty (1986:39).
304. Kamp and Rohrer (1983:258f.).
305. Hinrichs (1986:78f.).
306. Ibid., 63.
307. Hinrichs (1986:75). Examples below from this and Heinämäki (1978).
308. Hinrichs (1986:77).
309. Kamp and Rohrer (1983:259).

310. Hinrichs (1986:70).
311. Dry (1981:236).
312. Ibid., 238.
313. Ibid.
314. Dry (1983:23).
315. Ibid.
316. Ibid., 23f.
317. Ibid., 24f.
318. Ibid., 47.
319. Ibid., 47ff.
320. Dowty (1986), sections 5 and 6. Adelaar and Lo Cascio (1986:287ff.) argue that *none* of the Aristotelian types advances narrative time.
321. Dowty (1986:48).
322. Ibid., 45.
323. Ibid., 48.
324. Hinrichs (1986:68ff.).
325. Dowty (1986:50).
326. Even those who operate with DRS's recognize that DRS construction is partly inference-driven (Rigter, 1986:100). Also, it is widely accepted that pragmatic knowledge is required to situate events (Adelaar and Lo Cascio, 1986:287ff.).
327. Dowty (1986:40).
328. Ibid.
329. Nerbonne (1986:86).
330. Ibid., 91.
331. Cf. Partee (1984:260f.) and Rigter (1986:104) on linear narrative being but one type of text. We discuss this point further below.
332. Nerbonne (1986:94).
333. Ibid., 95n.
334. Partee (1984:260f.). See too Rigter (1986:104).
335. Adelaar and Lo Cascio (1986:252) criticize Kamp and Rohrer (1983) for failing to distinguish "domains" from "subdomains."
336. Houweling (1986:170).
337. Kamp and Rohrer (1983:256). Comrie (1986) has a number of interesting observations to make in regard to the pluperfect and the conditional.
338. In such cases Rohrer (1986:81) speaks of a "transposition" (shift) of tenses. The following two examples are his.
339. See Lo Cascio (1986:233, 239ff.) and Rohrer (1986:86, 91f.).
340. Kamp and Rohrer (1983:263ff.).
341. Ibid., 266ff.
342. Rohrer (1986), Lo Cascio (1986), Lo Cascio and Rohrer (1986), Adelaar and Lo Cascio (1986).
343. Plus those of Rigter (1980), Vet and Molendijk (1986), and Bertinetto (1986).
344. Lo Cascio (1986:207f.). All the tenses are the *passato prossimo*, i.e., present perfect: 'said' *ha detto*, 'went out' *è uscito*, 'was found' *è stato ritrovato*—lit. 'is been found'.
345. Rigter (1986:102).
346. Kamp and Rohrer (1983:259).
347. Bull (1960:17). Cf. p. 22ff.
348. Lo Cascio (1986:197) suggests that there is possibly a "universal GPTU" for "eternal truths." Cf. Houweling (1986:173).
349. Rigter (1986:101), making a similar point, distinguishes S, which is given *outside* the text, from what he calls P (essentially Lo Cascio's GPT; see below), which is *inside* the text.
350. Ibid., 104.
351. Lo Cascio (1986:193).
352. See Lo Cascio (1986:224, n. 5) for some discussion.

353. Ibid., 194ff. The examples immediately below, except that for GPTE, are translations of his Italian ones.
354. Borchert (1959:185). Kamp and Rohrer (1983:259n.) comment on the "stylistic device" of opening a story in the *passé* or *imparfait* without an explicit adverbial, thereby forcing an inference, a pseudo-presupposition, of a GPT. This device reduces the distance between audience and storyteller.
355. Lo Cascio (1986:198f.).
356. Rigter (1986:101), Smith (1981:223), Rohrer (1986:85).
357. Smith (1978:57). Cf. Smith (1981:221).
358. Ibid., 61. Cf. Smith (1981:223).
359. Smith (1978:64).
360. Smith (1981:216f.).
361. Ibid., 229f.
362. Ibid., 216f. The adverbial must belong to the same sector (past or non-past) as the tense, except in the case of the historical present. But this is a general requirement for the co-occurrence of tense and adverbial: e.g., *they left tomorrow, they are leaving yesterday*.
363. Lo Cascio (1986:200, 204f.). Adelaar and Lo Cascio (1986:285) discuss apparent counterexamples, such as the one below, and argue that there is an implicit tensed clause (*yesterday* (*when* . . .) . . .) which actually gives the reference point:
Ieri *avevo* già *parlato* con Maria.
'Yesterday I *had* already *spoken* to Mary.'
364. Adelaar and Lo Cascio (1986:269).
365. Ibid., 270.
366. Lo Cascio (1986:202). His terms (and Houweling's, below) have been translated here.
367. Houweling (1986:163).
368. Ibid.
369. Lo Cascio (1986:201f.). Lo Cascio sees the classification into perfective and imperfective as a separate classification from that of deictic and anaphoric.
370. Rigter (1986:107).
371. Adelaar and Lo Cascio (1986:270) call these "neutral" adverbials because they "localize without referring to any given time, so that they do not quantify a temporal distance" of the event from that given time, as deictic and anaphoric adverbials do.
372. Lo Cascio (1986:209ff.).
373. Ibid., 210, 215.
374. Ibid.
375. Ibid., 199.
376. That is, verbs, like *believe, dream, want*, which create intension contexts. For discussion, see McCawley (1981:326–40). Rigter (19861:101) and Lo Cascio (1986) point out the role of such verbs in establishing subdomains.
377. Lo Cascio (1986:209ff.).
378. Of course, this is not the only function of tenses, nor is the structure of texts given only by tenses. Further, it must be borne in mind that few if any texts, much less discourses, have a simple, linear structure with only one main line. This type of text grammar represents an idealization and perhaps an oversimplification, for all the concern with details of text structure.
379. Lo Cascio (1986:210f.). Lo Cascio and Rohrer (1986:233) point out, however, that a preceding deictic in a relative clause (which is hence lower in the structure) may bind a deictic:
Ho dato il libro a Maria che lo *ha portato* alla biblioteca. Un'ora dopo è andata dal medico ed
è *ritornata* alle 3.
'*I gave* the book to Mary who *took* it to the library. An hour later *she went* to the doctor and *returned* at 3.' (All verbs in italics are in the *passato prossimo*.)
Here E_3 (*è andata*) may have E_2 (*ha portato*) as its antecedent.
380. Ibid., 223.

381. The *sectors* are the three times: past, present, and future. Others call these "relations" (from the fact that they are defined by the relationship of E to S), "planes" (Coseriu, 1976:92), "time-spheres" (Hirtle, 1967:19), etc., and may restrict them to just two—past and present, or past and non-past, or actual and inactual—on various grounds. (Cf. the use of the term "relations" in Lo Cascio and Rohrer, 1986:241, 245.) The sectors are in general relative to an evaluation time, which may be other than ST (Adelaar and Lo Cascio, 1986:257); in this latter case they are like Bull's vectors, not his axes.

382. Adelaar and Lo Cascio (1986:254).

383. Ibid., 59f.

384. Ibid., 257, 270, 287. Similarly, Bertinetto (1986).

385. Ibid., 287.

386. Adelaar and Lo Cascio (1986:267f.).

387. Lo Cascio (1986:214f.).

388. Ibid., 211. (1) below is exemplified by Comrie's example (1986:18):
Old James' boat approached the pier. He had docked before I began fishing.
where the anaphoric tense (pluperfect) of the first clause of the second sentence takes as its reference point the deictic tense (simple past) of the following clause, not the preceding one.

389. Lo Cascio (1986:223).

390. Adelaar and Lo Cascio (1986:266, 289).

391. Lo Cascio and Rohrer (1986:235).

392. Ibid., 245.

393. Ibid., 238.

394. Lo Cascio and Rohrer (1986:239). They say that the reference point must be given *in* the text; that is incorrect for the *de re* relatives.

395. Ibid., 240.

396. Ibid., 241.

397. Smith (1981:231).

398. I have no clear intuitions for sentences like this one, nor do other speakers I have asked about them. My experience with other speakers suggests that when sentences achieve a certain level of temporal complexity, the number of possible relationships out of context is so large that they cannot readily be processed by speakers. Or it may be that sentences of this type, with multiple time references, are so unusual that speakers cannot imagine suitable contexts.

399. See Lo Cascio and Rohrer (1986:240, 248n.). Despite what they say, restrictive relative clauses are at least much more subordinate in nature than nonrestrictive ones.

400. E.g., by Bertinetto (1986) and Adelaar and Lo Cascio (1986:270ff.).

401. Bertinetto (1986:57). The precise degree of vagueness of, e.g., *around 5 o'clock*, depends on the scale. Which scale we choose is pragmatically determined; we usually know how precise to be.

402. Bertinetto (1986:58) cites McCoard's observation (1987:83f.) on the vagueness of *growing old, getting to know someone*, etc.

403. Adelaar and Lo Cascio (1986:287).

404. Aartun (1963:17), Comrie (1976:78, 95), Rabin (1970:311f.), Waldman (1975:1285).

405. Kukenheim (1951:91f.), Kustár (1972:4f.), McFall (1982:7). But Blanc (1975:1267) is skeptical regarding Greek influence on early Arabic grammarians.

406. Or present-future: cf. Rabin (1970:311); or non-past: Aartun (1963:17).

407. E.g., O'Leary (1923:234).

408. W. Chomsky (1957:163).

409. Aartun (1963:17f.), McFall (1982:11ff.).

410. Williams (1976:30f.).

411. Kustár (1972:5f.).

412. McFall (1982:186f.).

413. Ibid., 215f., 18f.

414. *Non-temporel.*
415. Golian (1979:27).
416. Aartun (1963:25).
417. G. H. A. von Ewald, *Grammatica critica linguae Arabicae* (Leipzig: Hahn, 1831–33) and *Kritische Grammatik der hebraischen Sprache*, 2nd ed. (Leipzig, 1835; Trans., London, 1836), cited by McFall (1982). See Aartun (1963:18ff.), Borg (1981:141), W. Chomsky (1957:162f.), Fleisch (1957:170f.), Golian (1979:26), McFall (1982:43f., 56f.), Rabin (1970:311), Williams (1976:29f.).
418. Kustár (1972:26f.), McFall (1982:17ff.).
419. McFall (1982:3).
420. Ibid., 17.
421. We shall see that this last can also be read as based on "status."
422. Kustár (1972), Rabin (1970), Waldman (1975).
423. McFall (1982:77ff.).
424. W. Chomsky (1957:162).
425. Golian (1979:20f.).
426. Comrie (1976:80).
427. Kurołowicz (1973:115).
428. Aartun (1963:111).
429. McFall (1982:35).
430. Ibid., 56.
431. Williams (1976:30ff.).
432. Comrie (1976:78).
433. Aartun (1963:25).
434. Borg (1981:97).
435. Williams (1976:30ff.).
436. Comrie (1976:79).
437. Ibid.
438. Borg (1981: section 6.0).
439. Borg (1981:180).
440. Kurołowicz (1973:115).
441. Ibid., 118.
442. Ibid., 116.
443. Ibid.
444. McFall (1982:4).
445. Ibid., 18–21.
446. Kustár (1972:32).
447. Philip Gell, *Observations on the Idiom of the Hebrew Language* (London, 1818), p. 14f., in McFall (1982:25f.).
448. McFall (1982:26).
449. Ibid., 9.
450. Kustár (1972:29f.).
451. L. Köhler, *Syntactica* IV (*Vetus Testamentum* III, 1953), p. 303, cited by Kustár (1972:35). The translation is mine.
452. Williams (1976:96ff.).
453. Kustár (1972:40).
454. D. Michel, *Tempora und Satzbestellung in den Psalmen* (Bonn, 1960), cited by Kustár (1972:41).
455. Kustár (1972:46).
456. Ibid., 47.
457. Ibid.
458. Ibid., 45f.
459. O'Leary (1923:235f.).
460. Ibid., 236.
461. McFall (1982:77ff.).

462. Ibid., 182.
463. Ibid., 79.
464. Ibid., 83.
465. Givón (1982:129).
466. McFall (1982:16).
467. E.g., Aartun (1963:113).
468. W. Chomsky (1957:163).
469. Givón (1977, 1982) explicitly offers analyses of the creole languages and Biblical Hebrew which make them out to have the same system.
470. Gonda (1980:15).
471. Friedman (1975:942f.).
472. Frishberg and Gough (n.d.:6).
473. Brennan (1981:11).
474. Bergman (1981:6).
475. Fischer (1973).
476. Brennan (1981:11).
477. Friedman (1975:951f.), Brennan (1981:12ff.).
478. Muysken (1981:182).
479. Ibid., 184.
480. Ibid., 193.
481. Ibid., 193f.
482. Ibid., 194.
483. Ibid.
484. Mufwene (1984:201).
485. Ibid., 222.
486. Ibid., 200.
487. Ibid.
488. Ibid., 220. Eilfort (1986) argues that Tak Pisin has non-finite complement clauses and that the simple distinction of "realized" and "non-realized" action (realis:irrealis) is basic in that language.
489. Whorf (1956:113, 144; cf. 59f.).
490. Jespersen (1924:282).
491. Ibid., 283f.
492. Jespersen may be incorrect, however, in treating *mounted soldiers* and *possessed of landed property* as structurally parallel to this example: it is not clear that *mounted* in the former is not an adjectival rather than a verbal form, and *possessed* can hardly mean 'having possessed'.
493. G. Lakoff (1965), for example, derives *aggression* from an underlying verb *aggress* which happens not (except secondarily, in the speech of some speakers only, as a back-formation) to occur as such in English.
494. Dowty (1972:51).
495. Borras and Christian (1971:80ff.), Pulkina (n.d.:184ff.), Siegel (1976).
496. Ramsey (1956:307ff.).
497. Ibid., 312. Ramsey had 'you', not 'he', in the first example (and 'he' in the second). The forms are the same in either case.
498. Borras and Christian (1971:184ff.), Foote (1967).
499. Foote (1967:6).
500. V. V. Vinogradov, ed., *Grammatika russkogo iazyka*, 2 vols. (Moscow: Izd. Akad. nauk, 1952–54), vol. 1, p. 460, cited by Foote (1967).
501. Leon Stilman, *Russian Verbs of Motion*, 2nd ed. (New York: Columbia University Press, 1951), p. 3, cited by Foote (1967).
502. Borras and Christian (1959:163).
503. Borras and Christian (1971:185).

References

N.B.: "(tr)" following entry indicates in-text translation(s) by R. B.

Aarsleff, Hans, Robert Austerlitz, Dell Hymes, and Edward Stankiewicz, eds. 1975. *Historiography of Linguistics. Current Trends in Linguistics*, vol. 13, ed. T. A. Sebeok. The Hague: Mouton.

Aartun, Kjell. 1963. *Zur Frage altarabischer Tempora*. Oslo: Universitetsforlaget.

Adelaar, Mascia, and Vincenzo Lo Cascio. 1986. "Temporal Relation, Localization, and Direction in Discourse." Lo Cascio and Vet (1986), 251–97.

Aichinger, Carl Friedrich. 1754. *Versuch einer teutschen Sprachlehre*. Vienna. Repr. Hildesheim: Georg Olms, 1972. (tr)

Ajdukiewicz, Kazimierz. 1935. "Die syntaktische Konnexität." *Studia Philosophica* 1.1–27. Trans., 1967, "Syntactic Connexion," *Polish Logic*, ed. S. McCall, 207–31. Oxford: Clarendon Press.

Aksu-Koç, Ayhan A., and Dan I. Slobin. 1986. "A Psychological Account of the Development and Use of Evidentials in Turkish." Chafe and Nichols (1986), 159–67. Based on Slobin and Aksu (1982).

Allen, Robert L. 1966. *The Verb System of Present-Day American English*. The Hague: Mouton.

Allwood, Jens, Lars-Gunnar Andersson, and Östen Dahl. 1977. *Logic in Linguistics*. Cambridge: Cambridge University Press.

Alston, William P. 1964. *Philosophy of Language*. Englewood Cliffs, N.J.: Prentice-Hall.

———. 1967. "Language, Philosophy of." Edwards (1967), vol. 4, 386–91.

———. 1967a. "Meaning." Edwards (1967), vol. 5, 233–41.

Anderson, Lloyd B. 1971. "The Black English System of Tense and Aspect: Its Origin in Natural Language Change." Ms., rev. of talk given at SECOL VI.

———. 1981. "Evidential Universals and Mental Maps: Experience, Aspect, and Mood." Unpublished, Washington, D.C.

———. 1986. "Evidentials, Paths of Change, and Mental Maps: Typologically Regular Asymmetries." Chafe and Nichols (1986), 273–312. Later version of Anderson (1981).

Anderson, Stephen R. 1985. "Inflectional Morphology." Shopen (1985), 150–201.

———. 1988. "Morphological Theory." Frederick J. Newmeyer, ed., *Linguistics: The Cambridge Survey*. Vol. 1: *Linguistic Theory: The Foundations*, 146–91. Cambridge: Cambridge University Press.

Andersson, S.-G. 1972. *Aktionalität im Deutschen: Eine Untersuchung unter Vergleich mit dem Russischen Aspektsystem*. 2 vols. Uppsala: Acta Universitatis Upsaliensis.

Andrews, E. A., and S. Stoddard. 1850. *A Grammar of the Latin Language; For the Use of Schools and Colleges*. 18th ed. Boston: Crocker and Brewster.

Antal, L. 1963. *Questions of Meaning*. Janua Linguarum, series minor, 27. The Hague: Mouton.

Apollonius Dyscolus. 1981. *The Syntax of Apollonius Dyscolus*. Trans. and ed. Fred W. Householder. Amsterdam: Benjamins.

Aquinas, Thomas. 1955. *In Aristotelis Libros Peri Hermeneias et Posteriorum Analyticorum Expositio*. Turin: Marietti.

Åqvist, Lennart. 1976. "Formal Semantics for Verb Tenses as Analyzed by Reichenbach." Teun A. van Dijk, ed., *Pragmatics of Language and Literature*, 229–36. Amsterdam: North-Holland.

Åqvist, Lennart, and Franz Guenther. 1978. "Fundamentals of a Theory of Verb Aspect and Events within the Setting of an Improved Tense-Logic." Guenther and Rohrer (1978), 167–99.

Åqvist, Lennart, Franz Guenther, and Christian Rohrer. 1977. " 'Soon' and 'Recently.' " Rohrer (1977), 67–81.

Aristar, Anthony, and Helen Dry. 1982. "The Origin of Backgrounding Tenses in English." *PCLS* 18.1–13.

Aristotle. 1929–34. *The Physics*. Trans. Philip H. Wicksteed and Francis M. Cornford. London: Heinemann, and Cambridge, Mass.: Harvard University Press (Loeb Classical Library). Vol. 1 revised, 1957.

———. 1932. *The Poetics*, with Longinus, *On the Sublime*, and Demetrius, *On Style*. Trans. W. Hamilton Fyfe. London: Heinemann, and Cambridge, Mass.: Harvard University Press (Loeb Classical Library).

———. 1933. *The Metaphysics*, I–IX. Trans. Hugh Treddenick. London: Heinemann, and Cambridge, Mass.: Harvard University Press (Loeb Classical Library).

———. 1934. *Nicomachean Ethics*. Trans. H. Rackham. London: Heinemann, and Cambridge, Mass.: Harvard University Press (Loeb Classical Library).

———. 1938. *Organon I: The Categories. On Interpretation*. Trans. Harold P. Cooke. *Prior Analytics*. Trans. Hugh Tredennick. London: Heinemann, and Cambridge, Mass.: Harvard University Press (Loeb Classical Library).

———. 1957. *On the Soul, Parva Naturalia, On Breath*. Trans. W. S. Hett. London: Heinemann, and Cambridge, Mass.: Harvard University Press (Loeb Classical Library).

Arnauld, Antoine. 1964. *The Art of Thinking: Port Royal Logic*. Trans. James Dickoff and Patricia James. Indianapolis, Ind.: Bobbs-Merrill. Trans. of *La logique, ou l'art de penser* (Paris, 1662).

Bach, Emmon. 1980. "Tenses and Aspects as Functions on Verb-Phrases." Rohrer (1980), 19–37.

———. 1986. "The Algebra of Events." *Linguistics and Philosophy* 9.5–16.

Bacon, Roger. 1902. *The Greek Grammar of Roger Bacon and a Fragment of His Hebrew Grammar*. Ed. Edmond Nolan and S. A. Hirsch. Cambridge: Cambridge University Press. (tr)

Baebler, J. J. 1885. *Beitraege zu einer Geschichte der lateinischen Grammatik im Mittelalter*. Halle. Repr. Hildesheim: Verlag Dr. H. A. Gerstenberg, 1971. (tr)

Banerjee, Dr. Satya Ranjan. 1983. *Indo-European Tense and Aspect in Greek and Sanskrit*. Calcutta: Sanskrit Book Depot.

Bar-Hillel, Yehoshua. 1967. "Syntactical and Semantic Categories." Edwards (1967), vol. 8, 57–61.

Bartlett, John. 1968. *Familiar Quotations*. 14th ed. Boston: Little, Brown.

Bartsch, Renate. 1976. *The Grammar of Adverbials*. Amsterdam: North-Holland. Trans. Ferenc Kiefer, of Bartsch, *Adverbialsemantik*, Frankfurt am Main: Athenaeum (1972).

———. 1986. "On Aspectual Properties of Dutch and German Nominalizations." Lo Cascio and Vet (1986), 7–40.

Barwise, Jon. 1989. *The Situation in Logic*. Stanford: Center for the Study of Language and Information.

Barwise, Jon, and John Perry. 1983. *Situations and Attitudes*. Cambridge, Mass.: MIT Press.

———. 1985. "Shifting Situations and Shaken Attitudes: An Interview with Barwise and Perry." Cooper (1985), 105–61.

Bäuerle, Rainier. 1979. "Tense Logics and Natural Language." *Synthese* 40.

———. 1979a. *Temporale Deixis, temporale Frage: zum propositionalen Gehalt deklarativer und interrogativer Saetze*. Tuebingen: Narr.

Bäuerle, Rainier, U. Egli, and A. von Stechow, eds. 1979. *Semantics from Different Points of View*. Berlin: Springer-Verlag.

Bäuerle, Rainier, Christoph Schwarze, and Arnim von Stechow, eds. 1983. *Meaning, Use, and Interpretation of Language*. Berlin: Walter de Gruyter.

Bennett, Michael. 1977. "A Guide to the Logic of Tense and Aspect in English." *Logique et Analyse*, n.s., 80.491–517.

———. 1981. "Of Tense and Aspect: One Analysis." Tedeschi and Zaenen (1981), 13–29.

Bennett, Michael, and Barbara Partee. 1978. *Toward the Logic of Tense and Aspect in English*. Bloomington: Indiana University Linguistics Club. Revision of 1972 ms.

Bergman, Brita. 1983. "Verbs and Adjectives: Some Morphological Processes in [Swedish] Sign Language." Kyle and Woll (1983), 3–9.

Bertinetto, Pier Marco. 1986. "Intrinsic and Extrinsic Temporal References: On Restricting the Notion of 'Reference Time.' " Lo Cascio and Vet (1986), 41–78.

———. 1986a. *Tempo, Aspetto e Azione nel Verbo Italiano: il Sistema dell'Indicativo*. Florence: Presso l'Accademia Della Crusca.

Bickerton, Derek. 1975. *Dynamics of a Creole System*. New York: Cambridge University Press.

Binnick, Robert I. 1970. "Studies in the Derivation of Predicative Structures." *Papers in Linguistics* 3.237–340, 519–602.

———. 1971. "*Will* and *be going to*." *Papers from the 7th Regional Meeting, Chicago Linguistic Society*, 40–52. Chicago: Chicago Linguistic Society.

———. 1972. "*Will* and *be going to* II." *PCLS* 8.3–9. Binnick (1971) and (1972) appear in Werner Bauer et al., eds., 1974, *Studien zur generativen Grammatik*, 118–37, Frankfurt am Main: Athenaion.

———. 1979. "Past and Perfect in Modern Mongolian." Henry G. Schwarz, ed. *Studies on Mongolia—Proceedings of the First North American Conference on Mongolian Studies*, 1–13. Bellingham: Western Washington University.

Blanc, Haim. 1975. "Linguistics among the Arabs." Aarsleff et al. (1975), 1265–84.

Blansitt, Edward L., Jr. 1975. "Progressive Aspect." [*Stanford University*] *Working Papers on Language Universals* 18.1–34.

Bolinger, Dwight. 1971. *The Phrasal Verb in English*. Cambridge, Mass.: Harvard University Press.

———. 1973. "Essence and Accident: English Analogs of Hispanic *Ser-Estar*." *Issues in Linguistic Theory: Papers in Honor of Henry and Renee Kahane*, ed. Braj Kachru et. al., 58–69. Urbana: University of Illinois Press.

———. 1975. *Aspects of Language*. 2nd ed. New York: Harcourt, Brace, Jovanovich.

Borchert, Wolfgang. 1959. *Das Gesamtwerk*. Hamburg: Rohwohlt Verlag.

Borg, Albert J. 1981. *A Study of Aspect in Maltese*. Ann Arbor: Karoma.

Borras, F. M., and R. F. Christian. 1971. *Russian Syntax*. 2nd ed. Oxford: Clarendon Press. 1st ed., 1956.

Bourciez, E. 1910. *Éléments de linguistique romane*. Paris: Klincksieck. (tr)

Boyd, Julian, and James P. Thorne. 1969. "The Semantics of Modal Verbs." *Journal of Linguistics* 5.57–74.

Bråroe, Eva Ejerhed. 1974. *The Syntax and Semantics of English Tense Markers*. Stockholm: Stockholm University Institute of Linguistics.

Brennan, Mary. 1983. "Marking Time in British Sign Language." Kyle and Woll (1983), 10–31.

Brown, Gillian, and George Yule. 1983. *Discourse Analysis*. Cambridge: Cambridge University Press.

Brunot, Ferdinand, and Charles Bruneau. 1949. *Précis de grammaire historique de la langue française*. Paris: Masson. (tr)

Bryan, W. 1936. "The Preterite and the Perfect Tenses in Present-Day English." *Journal of English and Germanic Philology* 35.363–82.

Buck, Carl Darling. 1933. *Comparative Grammar of Greek and Latin*. Chicago: University of Chicago Press.

Bull, William E. 1960. *Time, Tense, and the Verb*. Berkeley: University of California Press.

Bursill-Hall, G. L. 1963. "Mediaeval Grammatical Theories." *Canadian Journal of Linguistics* 9.40–54.

———. 1975. "The Middle Ages." Aarsleff et al. (1975), 179–230.

Bybee, Joan L. 1985. *Morphology: A Study of the Relation between Meaning and Form*. Amsterdam: Benjamins.

Calver, Edward. 1946. "The Uses of the Present Tense Forms in English." *Language* 22.317–25. Reprinted in English in Schopf (1974), 377–97.

Camus, Albert. 1948. *The Plague*. Trans. Stuart Gilbert. New York: Knopf.

Carnap, Rudolf. 1956. *Meaning and Necessity: A Study in Semantics and Modal Logic*. Chicago: University of Chicago Press. Enlarged ed.

Chafe, Wallace L. 1970. *Meaning and the Structure of Language*. Chicago: University of Chicago Press.

———. 1986. "Evidentiality in English Conversation and Academic Writing." Chafe and Nichols (1986), 261–72.

Chafe, Wallace L., and Joanna Nichols, eds. 1986. *Evidentiality: The Linguistic Coding of Epistemology*. Advances in Discourse Processes, 20. Norwood, N.J.: Ablex Publishing.

Chantraine, Pierre. 1945. *Morphologie historique du grec*. Paris: Klincksieck. (tr)

Charisius (Flavius Sosipatrus Charisius). 1857. *Artis grammaticae libri V* with Diomedes, *Artis grammaticae libri III*, etc. Ed. Heinrich Keil. *Grammatici Latini*, vol. 1. Leipzig: Teubner. Repr. Hildesheim: Georg Olms Verlagsbuchhandlung, 1961. (tr)

Chatterjee, Ranjit. 1982. "On Cross-Linguistic Categories and Related Problems: A Discussant's Notes on the Tense/Aspect Symposium." Hopper (1982), 335–45.

Chomsky, Noam. 1957. *Syntactic Structures*. Janua Linguarum, 4. The Hague: Mouton.

———. 1965. *Aspects of the Theory of Syntax*. Cambridge, Mass.: MIT Press.

Chomsky, William. 1957. *Hebrew: The Eternal Language*. Philadelphia: The Jewish Publication Society of America.

Chung, Sandra, and Alan Timberlake. 1985. "Tense, Aspect and Mood." Shopen (1985), 202–58.

Church, Alonzo. 1940. "A Formulation of a Simple Theory of Types." *Journal of Symbolic Logic* 5.56–68.

Chvany, Catherine V. 1985. "Backgrounded Perfectives and Plot-Line Imperfectives: Towards a Theory of Grounding in Text." Flier and Timberlake (1985), 247–73.

Claius (M. Iohannis Claius Hirtzbergensis). 1578. *Grammatica Germanicae Lingvae*. Leipzig. Repr. Hildesheim: Georg Olms, 1973. (tr)

Cogen, Cathy. 1977. "On Three Aspects of Time Expression in American Sign Language." Lynn Friedman, ed., *On the Other Hand: New Perspectives of American Sign Language*, 197–214. New York: Academic Press.

Cole, Peter. 1974. "Hebrew Tense and the Performative Analysis." *Papers from the Tenth Regional Meeting, Chicago Linguistic Society*, 41–51. Chicago: Chicago Linguistic Society.

Comrie, Bernard. 1976. *Aspect*. Cambridge: Cambridge University Press.

——. 1981. "On Reichenbach's Approach to Tense." *Papers from the 17th Regional Meeting, Chicago Linguistic Society*, 24–30. Chicago: Chicago Linguistic Society.

——. 1985. *Tense*. Cambridge: Cambridge University Press.

——. 1986. "Tense and Time Reference: From Meaning to Interpretation in the Chronological Structure of a Text." *Journal of Literary Semantics* 15.12–22.

Cooper, Robin, ed. 1985. *Situations and Attitudes*. (*Linguistic and Philosophy* 8.1.)

——. 1985a. "Aspectual Classes in Situation Semantics." Center for the Study of Language and Information, Stanford University, report no. CSLI-85-14-C.

——. 1986. "Tense and Discourse Location in Situation Semantics." David Dowty, ed. *Tense and Aspect in Discourse*. (= *Linguistics and Philosophy* 9.1, 17–36.) Revised version of unpublished ms., 1983.

Cornu, Maurice. 1953. *Les formes surcomposées en français*. Bern: A. Francke.

Coseriu, Eugenio. 1976. *Das romanische Verbalsystem*. Ed. Hansbert Bertsch. Tuebingen: Verlag Gunter Narr.

Costa, Rachel. 1972. "Sequence of Tenses in That-Clauses." *Papers from the 8th Regional Meeting, Chicago Linguistic Society*, 41–51. Chicago: Chicago Linguistic Society.

Cresswell, M. J. 1973. *Logics and Languages*. London: Methuen.

——. 1974. "Adverbs and Events." *Synthese* 28.455–81. Reprinted in Cresswell (1985), 1–39.

——. 1978. "Adverbs of Space and Time." Guenther and Schmidt (1978), 171–99. Reprinted in Cresswell (1985), 41–66.

——. 1979. "Interval Semantics for Some Event Expressions." R. Bäuerle, U. Egli, and A. von Stechow (1979), 90–116. Reprinted in Cresswell (1985), 143–71.

——. 1985. *Adverbial Modification: Interval Semantics and Its Rivals*. Dordrecht: Reidel.

——. 1985a. "Adverbial Modification in Situation Semantics." Cresswell (1985), 193–220.

——. 1985b. *Structured Meanings*. Cambridge, Mass.: MIT Press.

Cunha, Celso, and Lindley Cintra. 1985. *Nova Gramática do Português Contemporâneo*. 2nd ed. Rio de Janeiro: Editora Nova Fronteira. (tr)

Curme, George O. 1922. *A Grammar of the German Language*. 2nd, rev. ed. New York: Frederick Ungar.

Dahl, Östen. 1981. "On the Definition of the Telic-Atelic (Bounded-Unbounded) Distinction." Tedeschi and Zaenen (1981), 79–90.

——. 1985. *Tense and Aspect Systems*. Oxford: Basil Blackwell.

Davidson, Donald. 1969. "The Individuation of Events." Nicholas Rescher, ed. *Essays in Honor of Carl G. Hempel*, 216–34. Dordrecht: Reidel. Reprinted in Donald Davidson, *Essays on Actions and Events*, 163–80. Oxford: Clarendon Press, 1980.

Davidson, Donald, and Gilbert Harman, eds. 1972. *Semantics of Natural Language*. Dordrecht: Reidel.

Declerck, Renaat. 1979. "Aspect and the Bounded/Unbounded (Telic/Atelic) Distinction." *Linguistics* 17.761–94.

DeLancey, Scott. 1982. "Aspect, Transitivity, and Viewpoint." Hopper (1982), 167–83.

De la Touche, Pierre. 1696. *L'art de bien parler françois*. Amsterdam. Repr. Geneva: Slatkine, 1973. (tr)

De Vuyst, Jan. 1983. "Situation-descriptions: Temporal and Aspectual Semantics." Alice ter Meulen, ed., *Studies in Modeltheoretic Semantics*, 161–76. Dordrecht: Foris.

Dietrich, Wolf. 1973. *Der periphrastische Verbalaspekt in den romanischen Sprachen*. Tuebingen: Max Niemeyer. Spanish trans. 1983: *El aspecto verbal perifrástico en las lenguas románicas*. Trans. Marcos Martínez Hernández. Madrid: Editorial Gredos (Biblioteca Románica Hispánica). (tr)

Dillon, George L. 1973. "Perfect and Other Aspects in a Case Grammar of English." *Journal of Linguistics* 9.271–79.

————. 1977. *Introduction to Contemporary Linguistic Semantics*. Englewood Cliffs, N.J.: Prentice-Hall.

Dinsmore, John. 1982. "The Semantic Nature of Reichenbach's Tense System." *Glossa* 16.216–39.

Diogenes Laertius. 1925. *Lives of Eminent Philosophers*. 2 vols., trans. R. D. Hicks. London: Heinemann, and Cambridge, Mass.: Harvard University Press (Loeb Classical Library).

Dionysius Thrax. 1867. *Dionysii Thracis Ars Grammatica et Scholia in Dionysii Thracis Artem Grammaticam*. *Grammatici Graeci*, part 1, vol. 1, 3. Leipzig: Teubner. Repr. Hildesheim: Georg Olms, 1951. (tr)

————. 1874. *The Grammar of Dionysios Thrax*. Trans. Thomas Davidson. St. Louis: R. P. Studley. Reprinted from the *Journal of Speculative Philosophy*.

Diver, William. 1963. "The Chronological System of the English Verb." *Word* 19.141–81.

Donatus (Probus Donatus Servius). 1864. *De arte grammatica libri* with *Notae laterculi*. Ed. H. Keil and T. Mommsen (*Notae*). Heinrich Keil, *Grammatici Latini*, vol. 4. Leipzig: Teubner. Repr. Hildesheim: Georg Olms Verlagsbuchhandlung, 1961. (tr)

Dowty, David R. 1972. *Studies in the Logic of Verb Aspect and Time Reference in English*. Austin: Department of Linguistics, University of Texas.

————. 1977. "Toward a Semantic Analysis of Verb Aspect and the English 'Imperfective' Progressive." *Linguistics and Philosophy* 1.45–78.

————. 1979. *Word Meaning and Montague Grammar*. Dordrecht: D. Reidel.

————. 1982. "Tenses, Time Adverbs, and Compositional Semantic Theory." *Linguistics and Philosophy* 5.23–55.

————. 1986. "The Effects of Aspectual Class on the Temporal Structure of Discourse: Semantics or Pragmatics?" *Linguistic and Philosophy* 9.37–61.

Dowty, David R., Robert E. Wall, Stanley Peters. 1981. *Introduction to Montague Semantics*. Dordrecht: D. Reidel.

Dry, Helen. 1981. "Sentence Aspect and the Movement of Narrative Time." *Text* 1.233–40.

————. 1983. "The Movement of Narrative Time." *Journal of Literary Semantics* 12.19–53.

Ducrot, Oswald. 1979. "L'imparfait en français." *Linguistische Berichte* 60.1–23.

Ebeling, C. L. 1962. "A Semantic Analysis of the Dutch Tenses." *Lingua* 11.86–99.

Edwards, Paul, ed. 1967. *The Encyclopedia of Philosophy*. New York: Macmillan and the Free Press; London: Collier Macmillan. Repr. 1972.

Ehrman, Madeleine. 1966. *The Meanings of the Modals in Present-Day American English*. The Hague: Mouton.

Eilfort, William H. 1986. "Non-Finite Clauses in Creoles." *Proceedings of the Twelfth Annual Meeting of the Berkeley Linguistics Society*, 84–94.

Elcock, W. D. 1975. *The Romance Languages*. Rev. ed. London: Faber and Faber.

Ellegård, Alvar. 1973. "Study of Language." *Dictionary of the History of Ideas*, ed. Philip P. Wiener, vol. 2, 659–73. New York: Charles Scribner's Sons.

Emonds, Joseph. 1975. "Arguments for Assigning Tense Meanings after Certain Transformations Apply." E. Keenan, ed., *Formal Semantics of Natural Language*, 351–70. Cambridge: Cambridge University Press.

Ernout, Alfred, and François Thomas. 1953. *Syntaxe latine*. 2nd ed. Paris: Klincksieck. (tr)

Estienne, Robert. 1557. *Traicté de la grammaire françoise*. Paris. Reprinted in *Traités de grammaire*. Geneva: Slatkine Reprints, 1972. (tr)

Ewert, Alfred. 1966. *The French Language*. Rev. ed. London: Faber and Faber.

Findlay, J. N. 1941. "Time: A Treatment of Some Puzzles." *Australasian Journal of Philosophy* 19. Often reprinted, e.g., in Gale (1968), 143–62.

Fischer, Susan D. 1973. "Two Processes of Reduplication in the American Sign Language." *Foundations of Language* 9.460–80.

Fischer, Susan, and Bonnie Gough. 1978. "Verbs in American Sign Language." *Sign Language Studies*, 17–48. Reprinted in William C. Stokoe, ed., *Sign and Culture*, 149–79. Silver Spring, Md.: Linstok Press, 1980.

Fleisch, Henri. 1957. *Études sur le verbe arabe*. Paris: Adrien-Maisonneuve. (tr)

Fleischman, Suzanne. 1983. "From Pragmatics to Grammar: Diachronic Reflections on Complex Pasts and Futures in Romance." *Lingua* 60.183–214.

Flier, Michael S., and Alan Timberlake, eds. 1985. *The Scope of Slavic Aspect*. Columbus, Ohio: Slavica Publishers.

Fontaine, Jacqueline. 1983. *Grammaire du texte et aspecte du verbe en russe contemporain*. Paris: Institut d'études slaves. (tr)

Foote, I. P. 1967. "Verbs of Motion." *Studies in the Modern Russian Language*, no. 1. Cambridge: Cambridge University Press.

Forsyth, John. 1970. *A Grammar of Aspect*. Cambridge: Cambridge University Press.

Fraser, Bruce. 1976. *The Verb-Particle Combination in English*. New York: Academic Press.

Freed, Alice. 1976. "An Event Analysis of Aspectual Complement Structures." Unpublished ms., Montclair State College and Univ. of Pennsylvania.

———. 1979. *The Semantics of English Aspectual Complementation*. Dordrecht: Reidel. (Ph.D. diss., University of Pennsylvania, 1976.)

Frege, Gottlob. 1892. "Über Sinn und Bedeutung." *Zeitschrift für Philosophie und philosophische Kritik*, n.s., 100.25–50. Translated as "On Sense and Nominatum," Herbert Feigl and W. S. Sellars, eds., *Readings in Philosophical Analysis*. New York: Appleton-Century-Crofts. Translated as "On Sense and Reference" in Frege (1952), 56–78. Often reprinted, e.g., Moravcsik (1974), 13–32.

———. 1952. *Translations from the Philosophical Writings of Gottlob Frege*, ed. P. T. Geach and M. Black. Oxford: Basil Blackwell.

Friedman, Lynn A. 1975. "Space, Time, and Person Reference in American Sign Language." *Language* 51.940–61.

Friedrich, Paul. 1974. "On Aspect Theory and Homeric Aspect." *International Journal of American Linguistics*, Memoir 28, S1–S44.

Frishberg, Nancy, and Bonnie Gough. n.d. "Time on Our Hands." Unpublished ms.

Gabbay, Dov, and J. Moravcsik. 1980. "Verbs, Events, and the Flow of Time." Rohrer (1980), 59–84.

Gale, Richard M. ed. 1968. *The Philosophy of Time*. London: Macmillan.

Garey, Howard B. 1957. "Verbal Aspect in French." *Language* 33.91–110.

General and Rational Grammar. 1753. London: J. Nourse. Trans. of *Grammaire générale et raisonée* (1660), attributed to Thomas Nugent. Repr. Menston, England: Scolar Press, 1968.

Givón, Talmy. 1977. "The Drift from VSO to SVO in Biblical Hebrew: The Pragmatics of Tense-Aspect." Charles Li, ed., *Mechanisms for Syntactic Change*, Austin: University of Texas Press.

———. 1982. "Tense-Aspect-Modality: The Creole Proto-Type and Beyond." Hopper (1982), 115–63.

Goedsche, C. R. 1940. "Aspect versus Aktionsart." *Journal of English and Germanic Philology* 39.189–97.

Golian, Milan. 1979. *L'aspect verbal en français?* Hamburg: Helmut Buske Verlag. (tr)

Gonda, Jan. 1980. *The Character of the Indo-European Moods, with Special Regard to Greek and Sanskrit*. 2nd ed. Wiesbaden: Otto Harrassowitz.

Goodman, Fred. 1973. "On the Semantics of Futurate Sentences." *Ohio State Working Papers in Linguistics* 16.

Goodwin, W. W. 1889. *Syntax of the Moods and Tenses of the Greek Verb*. Rev. ed. London: Macmillan.

———. 1894. *Greek Grammar*. New ed. London: Macmillan.

Gorovitz, Samuel, Merrill Hintikka, Donald Provence, and R. G. Williams. 1979. *Philo-*

sophical Analysis: An Introduction to Its Language and Techniques. 3rd ed. New York: Random House.

Grammaire générale et raisonée. 1660. Paris: Pierre le Petit. Ascribed to Claude Lancelot and Antoine Arnauld. Repr. Menston, England: Scholar Press, 1967.

Grandgent, C. H., and E. H. Wilkins. 1915. *Italian Grammar*. Rev. ed. Boston: D. C. Heath.

Grebe, Paul, ed. 1966. *Grammatik der deutschen Gegenwartssprache. Der Grosse Duden*, vol. 4. 2nd ed. Mannheim: Bibliographisches Institut. (tr)

Greenbaum, Sidney. 1969. *Studies in English Adverbial Usage*. London: Longman.

Greenberg, Joseph H. 1966. *Language Universals: With Special Reference to Feature Hierarchies*. Janua Linguarum, series minor, 59. The Hague: Mouton. Revised from version in *Current Trends in Linguistics*, vol. 3. The Hague: Mouton, 1964.

Greenberg, Joseph H., et al., eds. 1978. *Universals of Human Language*, vol. 3: *Word Structure*. Stanford: Stanford University Press.

Greenough, J. B., et al., eds. 1903. *Allen and Greenough's New Latin Grammar for Schools and Colleges*. Rev. ed. Boston: Ginn and Company.

Grevisse, Maurice. 1949. *Le bon usage, cours de grammaire française et de langage français*. 4th ed. Gembloux, Belgium: Duculot. (tr) Golian (1979) cites from 8th ed., 1964.

Grice, H. P. 1975. "Logic and Conversation." D. Davidson and G. Harman, eds., *The Logic of Grammar*, 64–74. Encino, Calif.: Dickenson. Also in P. Cole and J. Morgan, eds., *Speech Acts* (Syntax and Semantics 3), 41–58. New York: Academic Press.

Grimm, Jacob. 1883. *Teutonic Mythology*. Vol. 1. London: George Bell. Repr. New York: Dover, 1966.

Guenther, Franz. 1977. "Remarks on the Present Perfect in English." Rohrer (1977), 83–98.

———. 1978. "Time Schemes, Tense Logic and the Analysis of English Tenses." Guenther and Schmidt (1978), 201–22.

Guenther, Franz, and Christian Rohrer, eds. 1978. *Studies in Formal Semantics*. Amsterdam: North-Holland.

Guenther, Franz, and S. J. Schmidt, eds. 1978. *Formal Semantics and Pragmatics for Natural Languages*. Dordrecht: Reidel.

Guenther, Herbert V. 1976. *Buddhist Philosophy: In Theory and Practice*. Boulder: Shambala.

Guillaume, Gustave. 1929. *Temps et verbe: théorie des aspects, des modes et des temps*. Paris: Champion. (tr)

———. 1965. *Temps et verbe: théorie des aspects, des modes et des temps* suivi de *L'architectonique du temps dans les langues classiques*. Paris: Champion. Includes reprint of Guillaume (1929). (tr)

Haarman, Harald. 1970. *Die Indirekte Erlebnisform als grammatische Kategorie. Eine eurasische Isoglosse*. Veröffentlichungen der Societas Uralo-Altaica 2. Wiesbaden: Otto Harrassowitz.

Hackman, Geoffrey James. 1976. "An Integrated Analysis of the Hindi Tense and Aspect System." Ph.D. diss., University of Illinois.

Haenisch, Erich. 1961. *Mandschu Grammatik*. Leipzig: VEB Verlag Enzyklopaedie. (tr)

Hall Partee, Barbara. 1973. "Some Structural Analogies between Tenses and Pronouns." *The Journal of Philosophy* 70.601–9.

Hamblin, C. L. 1971. "Instants and Intervals." *Studium Generale* 24.127–34.

Harris, James. 1751. *Hermes*. London: H. Woodfall. Repr. Menston, England: Scholar Press, 1968.

Hatcher, Anna G. 1951. "The Use of the Progressive Form in English." *Language* 27.254–80. Reprinted in Schopf (1974), 177–216.

Haugen, Einar. 1972. "The Inferential Perfect in Scandinavian, a Problem of Contrastive Linguistics." *Canadian Journal of Linguistics* 17.132–39.

Heinämäki, O. T. 1974. "Semantics of English Temporal Connectives." Ph.D. diss., University of Texas.

Heny, Frank. 1982. "Tense, Aspect and Time Adverbials. Part II." *Language and Philosophy* 5.109–54. This article is the continuation of Richards (1982).

Hermerén, Lars. 1978. *On Modality in English. A Study in the Semantics of the Modals.* Lund Studies in English 53. Lund: CWK Gleerup.

Hinrichs, Erhard. 1983. "The Semantics of the English Progressive—A Study in Situation Semantics." *Papers from the 19th Regional Meeting, Chicago Linguistics Society*, 171–82. Chicago: Chicago Linguistic Society.

―――. 1986. "Temporal Anaphora in Discourses of English." *Linguistics and Philosophy* 9.63–82.

Hirtle, Walter H. 1967. *The Simple and Progressive Forms: An Analytical Approach.* Quebec: Les presses de l'Université Laval.

―――. 1975. *Time, Aspect, and the Verb.* Quebec: Les presses de l'Université Laval.

Hoepelman, Jaap. 1978. "A Note on the Treatment of the Russian Aspects in a Montague-Grammar." Rohrer (1978), 49–98.

Hoepelman, Jaap, and Christian Rohrer. 1981. "Remarks on *Noch* and *Schon* in German." Tedeschi and Zaenen (1981), 103–26.

Hofmann, T. Ronald. 1966. "Past Tense Replacement and the Modal System." Anthony G. Oettinger, ed., *Mathematical Linguistics and Automatic Translation* (*NSF* 17), VII-1–VII-21. Cambridge, Mass.: The Computation Laboratory, Harvard University. Reprinted in James McCawley, ed., *Notes from the Linguistic Underground* (Syntax and Semantics 7), 85–100. New York: Academic Press, 1976.

Holisky, Dee Ann. 1978. "Stative Verbs in Georgian, and Elsewhere." *International Review of Slavic Linguistics* 3.139–62.

―――. 1980. "A Contribution to the Semantics of Aspect: Georgian Medial Verbs." Ph.D. diss., University of Chicago.

―――. 1981. "Aspect Theory and Georgian Aspect." Tedeschi and Zaenen (1981), 127–44.

Holt, Jens. 1943. "Études d'aspect." *Acta Jutlandica* 15, part 2. (tr)

Homer. 1951. *The Iliad of Homer.* Trans. Richmond Lattimore. Chicago: University of Chicago Press.

Hopper, Paul J. 1979. "Aspect and Foregrounding in Discourse." *Discourse and Syntax* (Syntax and Semantics 12), ed. Talmy Givón, 213–41. New York: Academic Press.

―――, ed. 1982. *Tense-Aspect: Between Semantics and Pragmatics.* Amsterdam: John Benjamins.

Hopper, Paul J., and Sandra A. Thompson. 1980. "Transivity in Grammar and Discourse." *Language* 56.251–300.

Hornstein, Norbert. 1977. "Towards a Theory of Tense." *Linguistic Inquiry* 8.521–57.

―――. 1981. "The Study of Meaning in Natural Language: Three Approaches to Tense." *Explanation in Linguistics*, ed. N. H. Hornstein and David Lightfoot, 116–51. London: Longmans.

Houweling, Frans. 1986. "Deictic and Anaphoric Tense Morphemes." Lo Cascio and Vet (1986), 161–90.

Huddleston, Rodney. 1970. "Some Observations on Tense and Deixis in English." *Language* 45.777–806.

Imbs, Paul. 1960. *L'emploi des temps verbaux en français moderne.* Paris: Klincksieck.

Inoue, Kyoko. 1975. "Studies in the Perfect." Ph.D. diss., University of Michigan.

―――. 1978. "How Many Senses Does the Present Perfect Have?" *Papers from the 14th Regional Meeting, Chicago Linguistic Society*, 167–78. Chicago: Chicago Linguistic Society.

―――. 1979. "An Analysis of the English Present Perfect." *Linguistics* 17.561–89.

Jakobson, Roman. 1932. "Zur Struktur des Russischen Verbums." In *Charisteria Gvilelmo Mathesio qvinqvagenario a discipulis et Circuli Lingvistici Pragensis sodalibus oblata*, Prague. Reprinted in Jakobson (1971), 3–15. (tr)

————. 1941. *Kindersprache, Aphasie und allgemeine Lautgesetze*. Uppsala: Lundquist.

————. 1956. "Shifters, Verbal Categories, and the Russian Verb." Cambridge, Mass.: Dept. Slavic Languages and Literatures, Harvard University. Reprinted in Jakobson (1971), 130–47.

————. 1971. *Selected Writings*, vol. 2: *Word and Language*. The Hague: Mouton.

James, Deborah. 1982. "Past Tense and the Hypothetical: A Cross Linguistic Study." *Studies in Language* 6:375–403.

Jellinek, Max Hermann. 1913–14. *Geschichte der neuhochdeutschen Grammatik von den Anfangen bis auf Adelung*. 2 vols. Heidelberg: Carl Winter. (tr)

Jenkins, Lyle. 1972. "*Will*-Deletion." *Papers from the 8th Regional Meeting, Chicago Linguistic Society*, 173–82. Chicago: Chicago Linguistic Society.

Jespersen, Otto. 1924. *The Philosophy of Grammar*. New York: Norton. Repr. 1965.

————. 1931. *A Modern English Grammar on Historical Principles*. Part IV: Syntax, vol. 3. London: George Allen & Unwin, and Copenhagen: Ejnar Munksgaard. Repr. 1961.

————. 1933. *Essentials of English Grammar*. London. Repr. University, Ala.: University of Alabama Press, 1964.

Johanson, Lars. 1971. *Aspekt im Türkischen: Vorstudien zu einer Beschreibung des Türkeitürkischen Aspektsystems*. Acta Universitatis Upsaliensis—Studia Turcica Upsaliensia 1. Uppsala: University of Uppsala.

Johnson, Marion R. 1977. "A Semantic Analysis of Kikuyu Tense and Aspect." Ph.D. diss., Ohio State University.

————. 1981. "A Unified Temporal Theory of Tense and Aspect." Tedeschi and Zaenen (1981), 145–75.

Johnson, Richard. 1706. *Grammatical Commentaries*. London. Repr. Menston, England: Scholar Press, 1969.

Joos, Martin. 1964. *The English Verb: Form and Meanings*. Madison: University of Wisconsin Press.

Kahane, Henry R. 1956. Review, Ruipérez (1954). *Language* 32.324–29.

Kalish, Donald. 1967. "Semantics." Edwards (1967), vol. 4, 348–58.

Kamp, Hans. 1971. "Formal Properties of "Now.' " *Theoria* 37.227–73.

————. 1979. "Events, Instants and Temporal Reference." Bäuerle et al. (1979), 376–417.

————. 1981. "Évènements, représentations discursives et référence temporelle." Martin and Nef (1981), 39–64.

Kamp, Hans, and C. Rohrer. 1983. "Tense in Texts." Bäuerle, Schwarze, and Stechow (1983), 250–69.

Keniston, Hayward. 1936. "Verbal Aspect in Spanish." *Hispania* 19.163–76.

Kenny, Anthony. 1963. *Action, Emotion, and Will*. London: Routledge and Kegan Paul.

King, Harold V. 1969. "Punctual versus Durative as Covert Categories." *Language Learning* 19.183–90.

Kiparsky, Paul. 1968. "Tense and Mood in Indo-European Syntax." *Foundations of Language* 4.30–57.

Kneale, William and Martha. 1962. *The Development of Logic*. Oxford: Clarendon Press. Repr. with corrections, 1975.

König, Ekkehard. 1980. "On the Context-Dependence of the Progressive in English." Rohrer (1980), 269–91.

Kretzmann, Norman. 1967. "Semantics, History of." Edwards (1967), vol. 4, 358–406.

Kufner, Herbert L. 1962. *Grammatical Structures of English and German*. Chicago: University of Chicago Press.

Kukenheim, Louis. 1932. *Contributions à l'histoire de la grammaire italienne, espagnole et française à l'époque de la Renaissance*. Amsterdam: N. V. Noord-Hollandsche Uitgevers-Maatschappij. (tr)

————. 1951. *Contributions à l'histoire de la grammaire grecque, latine, & hébraïque à l'époque de la Renaissance*. Leiden: Brill. (tr)

Kurołowicz, Jerzy. 1949. "Le système verbal du sémitique." *Bulletin de la société linguistique de Paris* 45.47–56.

———. 1973. "Verbal Aspect in Semitic." *Orientalia*, n.s., 42.114–20.

Kustár, Peter. 1972. *Aspekt in Hebräischen.* Basel: Friedrich Reinhardt Kommissionsverlag. (tr)

Kyle, Jim, and Bencie Woll. 1983. *Language in Sign: An International Perspective on Sign Language.* London: Croom Helm.

Ladusaw, William. 1977. "Some Problems with Tense in PTQ." *Texas Linguistic Forum* 6.89–102.

Lakoff, George. 1965. "On the Nature of Syntactic Irregularity." Ph.D. diss., Indiana University. Published as *Irregularity in Syntax.* New York: Holt, Rinehart, and Winston, 1970.

Lakoff, Robin T. 1968. *Abstract Syntax and Latin Complementation.* Cambridge, Mass.: MIT Press.

———. 1970. "Tense and Its Relation to Participants." *Language* 46.838–49.

Leech, Geoffrey N. 1971. *Meaning and the English Verb.* London: Longmans.

Le Goffic, Pierre. 1986. *Points de vue sur l'imparfait.* Caen: Centre d'études linguistiques de l'université de Caen.

Levinson, Stephen C. 1983. *Pragmatics.* Cambridge: Cambridge University Press.

Lewis, David. 1969. "General Semantics." Davidson and Harman (1972), 169–218. Also in Partee (1976), 1–50.

Lewis, G. L. 1967. *Turkish Grammar.* Oxford: Oxford University Press. Corrected printing, 1975.

Li, Charles N., Sandra A. Thompson, and R. M. Thompson, 1982. "The Discourse Motivation for the Perfect Aspect: The Mandarin Particle *LE.*" Hopper (1982), 19–44.

Lily, William. 1567. *A Shorte Introduction of Grammar* with *Brevissima Institutio sev Ratio Grammatices.* London. Repr. New York: Scholars' Facsimiles and Reprints, 1945.

Lily, William, and John Colet. 1549. *A Short Introduction of Grammar.* London. Repr. Menston, England: Scolar Press, 1970.

Linacre, Thomas. [1523?]. *Rudimenta Grammatices.* London. Repr. Menston, England: Scolar Press, 1971. (tr)

———. 1524. *De Emendata Structura Latini Sermonis Libri Sex.* London. Repr. Menston, England: Scolar Press, 1968.

Lo Cascio, Vincenzo. 1986. "Temporal Deixis and Anaphor in Sentence and Text: Finding a Reference Time." Lo Cascio and Vet (1986), 191–228.

Lo Cascio, Vincenzo, and Christian Rohrer. 1986. "Interaction between Verbal Tenses and Temporal Adverbs in Complex Sentences." Lo Cascio and Vet (1986), 229–50.

Lo Cascio, Vincenzo, and Co Vet, eds. 1986. *Temporal Structure in Sentence and Discourse.* Dordrecht: Foris.

Lockwood, W. B. 1968. *Historical German Syntax.* Oxford: Oxford University Press.

Longacre, Robert E., and Stephen Levinson. 1978. "Field Analysis of Discourse." Wolfgang Dressler, ed., *Current Trends in Textlinguistics*, 103–22. Berlin: de Gruyter.

Lowth, Robert. 1762. *A Short Introduction to English Grammar.* Repr. Menston, England: Scolar Press, 1967.

Lyons, John. 1968. *Introduction to Theoretical Linguistics.* Cambridge: Cambridge University Press.

———. 1977. *Semantics.* Cambridge: Cambridge University Press.

Macaulay, R. K. S. 1971. "Aspect in English." Ph.D. diss., UCLA.

———. 1978. Review, Comrie (1976) and Friedrich (1974). *Language* 54.416–20.

Madvig, J. N. 1887. *A Latin Grammar.* London: Parker and Co.

Marchand, Hans. 1955. "On a Question of Aspect: A Comparison between the Progressive Form in English and That in Italian and Spanish." *Studia Linguistica* 9.45–52.

Marsack, C. C. 1975. *Samoan*. London: English Universities Press. Teach Yourself Books. 4th, corrected impression.

Martin, Robert. 1981. "Le futur linguistique: temps linéaire ou temps ramifié?" Martin and Nef (1981), 81–92.

Martin, Robert, and Frederic Nef, eds. 1981. *Langages* 64. Special issue on grammatical tense.

Matthews, P. H. 1974. *Morphology: An Introduction to the Theory of Word-structure*. Cambridge: Cambridge University Press.

McCawley James D. 1971. "Tense and Time Reference in English." *Studies in Linguistic Semantics*, ed. Charles Fillmore and D. T. Langendoen, 97–113. New York: Holt Rinehart. Reprinted in James D. McCawley, *Grammar and Meaning*, 257–72. New York: Academic Press, 1976. Some of the material also appears, with some revision, on pp. 215ff. of James McCawley, *The Syntactic Phenomena of English*, vol. 1. Chicago: University of Chicago Press, 1988.

———. 1981. *Everything That Linguists Have Always Wanted to Know about Logic*. Chicago: University of Chicago Press.

McCoard, Robert W. 1978. *The English Perfect: Tense-Choice and Pragmatic Inferences*. Amsterdam: North-Holland.

McFall, Leslie. 1982. *The Enigma of the Hebrew Verbal System*. Sheffield: The Almond Press.

McGilvray, James. 1974. "Tenses and Beliefs." Unpublished ms., McGill University.

McTaggart, J. M. E. 1968. "Time." Gale (1968), 86–97. Reprinted from J. M. E. McTaggart, *The Nature of Existence*, vol. 2, book 5, ch. 33. Cambridge: Cambridge University Press, 1927.

Michael, Ian. 1970. *English Grammatical Categories and the Tradition to 1800*. Cambridge: Cambridge University Press.

Miege, Guy. 1688. *The English Grammar*. Repr. Menston, England: Scolar Press, 1969.

Minguella, Fr. Toribio. 1878. *Ensayo de Gramática Hispano-Tagala*. Manila: Plana y Ca. (tr)

Mondadori, Fabrizio. 1978. "Remarks on Tense and Mood: The Perfect Future." Guenther and Rohrer (1978), 223–48.

Montague, Richard. 1973. "The Proper Treatment of Quantification in Ordinary English." J. Hintikka et al., eds., *Approaches to Natural Language: Proceedings of the 1970 Stanford Workshop on Grammar and Semantics*, 221–42. Dordrecht: Reidel. Reprinted in Montague (1974), 247–70. Generally referred to as "PTQ."

———. 1974. *Formal Philosophy*. Ed. Richmond H. Thomason. New Haven, Conn.: Yale University Press.

———. 1974a. "English as a Formal Language." Montague (1974), 188–221. Originally in Bruno Visenteni et al., eds., *Linguaggi nella Società e nella Tecnica*, 189–224. Milan: Edizioni di Comunità, 1970.

———. 1974b. "Universal Grammar." Montague (1974), 222–46. Originally in *Theoria* 36.373–98 (1970).

Moravcsik, J. M. E., ed. 1974. *Logic and Philosophy for Linguists: A Book of Readings*. The Hague: Mouton.

Morgan, Jerry L. 1969. "On Arguing about Semantics." *Papers in Linguistics* 1.49–70.

Mossé, Fernand. 1925. "Le renouvellement de l'aspect dans germanique." *Mélanges linguistiques offerts à N. J. Vendryes*, 287–99. Reprinted in Schopf (1974), 309–19.

———. 1957. "Réflexions sur la genèse de la 'forme progressive.' " *Wiener Beitraege zur englischen Philologie* 65.155–54. Reprinted in Schopf (1974), 377–97.

Mourelatos, Alexander P. D. 1978. "Events, Processes, and States." *Linguistics and Philosophy* 2.415–34.

———. 1981. "Events, Processes, and States." Tedeschi and Zaenen (1981), 191–212.

Mufwene, Salikoko S. 1984. "Observations on Time Reference in Jamaican and Guyanese Creoles." *English World-Wide* 4.199–229.

Muysken, Pieter. 1981. "Creole Tense/Mood/Aspect Systems: The Unmarked Case?" Pieter Muysken, ed., *Generative Studies on Creole Languages*, 181–99. Dordrecht: Foris.

Nakau, Minoru. 1976. "Tense, Aspect and Modality." *Japanese Generative Grammar* (Syntax and Semantics 5), ed. Masyoshi Shibatani, 421–82. New York: Academic Press.

Nebrija. 1926. *Gramática de la Lengua Castellana*. Ed. I. González-Llubera. London: Oxford University Press. Based on edition of 1492. (tr)

Neffgen, H. [1902]. *Grammatik der Samoanischen Sprache*. Vienna: A. Hartleben.

Nerbonne. John. 1982. "The German Perfect." *Papers from the 18th Regional Meeting, Chicago Linguistic Society*, 390–99. Chicago: Chicago Linguistic Society.

———. 1984. *German Temporal Semantics: Three-Dimensional Tense Logic and a GPSG Fragment*. Ohio State Working Papers in Linguistics 30.

———. 1986. "Reference Time and Time in Narration." *Linguistics and Philosophy* 9.83–95.

Newmeyer, Frederick J. 1980. *Linguistic Theory in America: The First Quarter-Century of Transformational Generative Grammar*. New York: Academic Press.

Norman, Jerry L. 1965. "A Grammatical Sketch of Manchu." Berkeley: Department of Oriental Languages, University of California.

O'Leary, Delacy. 1923. *Comparative Grammar of the Semitic Languages*. London: Kegan Paul.

Ota, Akira. 1963. *Tense and Aspect of Present-Day American English*. Tokyo: Kenkyusha.

Padley, G. A. 1976. *Grammatical Theory in Western Europe, 1500–1700: The Latin Tradition*. Cambridge: Cambridge University Press.

Palmer, F. R. 1965. *A Linguistic Study of the English Verb*. London: Longmans.

———. 1986. *Mood and Modality*. Cambridge: Cambridge University Press.

———. 1987. *The English Verb*. 2nd ed. London: Longmans. Revision of Palmer (1965).

Palmer, L. R. 1961. *The Latin Language*. London: Faber and Faber. 3rd, corrected impression.

Partee, Barbara Hall. 1973. "Some Structural Analogies between Tenses and Pronouns in English." *The Journal of Philosophy* 70.601–9.

———. 1975. "Montague Grammar and Transformational Grammar." *Linguistic Inquiry* 6.203–300.

———, ed. 1976. *Montague Grammar*. New York: Academic Press.

———. 1984. "Nominal and Temporal Anaphora." *Linguistics and Philosophy* 7.243–86.

Peck, Harry Thurston. 1911. *History of Classical Philology*. New York: Macmillan.

Perkins, Michael. 1983. *Modal Expressions in English*. London: Frances Pinter.

Pickbourn, James. 1789. *A Dissertation on the English Verb*. London. Repr. Menston, England: Scolar Press, 1968.

Pinborg, Jan. 1975. "Classical Antiquity: Greece." Aarsleff et al. (1975), 69–126.

Pinkster, Harm. 1984. *Latijnse Syntaxis en Semantiek*. Amsterdam: B. R. Gruner. (tr) Translated as *Lateinische Syntax und Semantik*. Tuebingen: Narr, 1987.

Plato. 1961. *The Collected Dialogues of Plato, Including the Letters*. Ed. Edith Hamilton and Huntington Cairns. Princeton: Princeton University Press. *Crito*, trans., Hugh Tredennick, 27–39; *Ion*, trans., Lane Cooper, 215–28; *Parmenides*, trans., F. M. Cornford, 920–56; *Republic*, trans., Paul Shorey, 575–844; *Sophist*, trans., F. M. Cornford, 957–1017.

Pollak, H. 1920. "Studien zum germanischen Verbum. Über Actionsarten." *Beiträge zur Geschichte der deutschen Sprache* 44.353–425. (tr)

Poppe, N. N. 1970. *Mongolian Language Handbook*. Washington, D.C.: Center for Applied Linguistics.

Price, Granville. 1971. *The French Language: Present and Past*. London: Edward Arnold. Corrected ed., 1975.

Priebsch, R., and W. E. Collinson. 1962. *The German Language*. 5th, rev. ed. London: Faber and Faber.

Priestley, Joseph. 1762. *A Course of Lectures on the Theory of Languages and Universal Grammar*. Warrington, England. Repr. Menston, England: Scolar Press, 1970.

Prior, Arthur. 1957. *Time and Modality*. Oxford: Clarendon Press.

————. 1967. *Past Present and Future*. Oxford: Clarendon Press.

Priscian (Priscianus Caesariensis). 1857. *Prisciani Grammatici Caesariensis Institutionum Grammaticarum Libri XVIII*. Vol. 1. *Libros I–XII Continens*. Ed. Martin Hertz. *Grammatici Latini* Ed. Heinrich Keil, vol. 2. Repr. Hildesheim: Georg Olms, 1961. (tr)

Prista, Alexander da R. 1966. *Essential Portuguese Grammar*. New York: Dover.

Pulkina, I. M. n.d. *A Short Russian Reference Grammar*. 3rd ed. Moscow: Progress Publishers.

Rabin, Chaim. 1970. "Hebrew." Charles Ferguson et al., eds., *Linguistics in South West Africa and North Africa* (Current Trends in Linguistics 6), 304–46. The Hague: Mouton.

Ramsey, M. M. 1956. *A Textbook of Modern Spanish As Now Written and Spoken in Castile and the Spanish American Republics*. Rev. Robert K. Spaulding. New York: Holt Rinehart and Winston.

Rassudova, O. P. 1984. *Aspectual Usage in Modern Russian*. Trans. Gregory M. Eramian. Moscow: Russky Yazyk.

Reichenbach, Hans. 1947. *Elements of Symbolic Logic*. New York: Collier-Macmillan, and London: Macmillan. Repr. New York: The Free Press, 1966. Pp. 287–310 reprinted in Moravcsik (1974), 122–41.

Rescher, Nicholas, and Alasdair Urquhart. 1971. *Temporal Logic*. Vienna: Springer-Verlag.

Richards, Barry. 1982. "Tense, Aspect, and Time Adverbials, Part I." *Linguistics and Philosophy* 5.59–107. Heny (1982) is the continuation of this article.

Riddle, Elizabeth. 1975. "A New Look at Sequence of Tenses." Paper read at annual winter meeting, Linguistic Society of America.

————. 1978. "Sequence of Tenses in English." Ph.D. diss., University of Illinois.

Rigter, Bob. 1986. "Focus Matters." Lo Cascio and Vet (1986), 99–132.

Rimbaud, Arthur. 1962. *Rimbaud*. Penguin Poets. Trans. Oliver Bernard. Harmondsworth: Penguin.

Robins, R. H. 1979. *A Short History of Linguistics*. Rev. ed. London: Longmans.

Rohrer, Christian, ed. 1977. *On the Logical Analysis of Tense and Aspect*. Tuebingen: Gunter Narr.

————, ed. 1978. *Papers on Tense, Aspect and Verb Classification*. Tuebingen: Gunter Narr.

————, ed. 1980. *Time, Tense, and Quantifiers. Proceedings of the Stuttgart Conference on the Logic of Tense and Quantification*. Tuebingen: Max Niemeyer Verlag.

————. 1986. "Indirect Discourse and 'Consecutio Temporum.' " Lo Cascio and Vet (1986), 79–98.

Ronconi, Alessandro. 1959. *Il Verbo Latino: Problemi di Sintassi Storica*. Rev. ed. Florence: Felice le Monnier. (tr)

Ross, John R. 1967. "Constraints on Variables in Syntax." Ph.D., diss., MIT. Revised version published as *Infinite Syntax*. Norwood, N.J.: Ablex, 1986.

————. 1969. "Auxiliaries as Main Verbs." *Studies in Philosophical Linguistics, Series One*, ed. William Todd, 77–102. Evanston, Ill.: Great Expectations.

Rudolph, Kurt. 1983. *Gnosis*. Trans. R. M. Wilson. San Francisco: Harper and Row.

Ruipérez, Martin Sanchez. 1954. *Estructura del Sistema de Aspectos y Tiempos del Verbo Griego Antiguo: Análisis Funcional Sincrónico*. Theses et Studia Philologica Salmanticensia, 7. Salamanca: Colegio Trilingüe de la Universidad. Trans., M. Plenat and P. Serca, *Structures du système, des aspects et des temps du verbe en grec ancien*. Paris: Les Belles Lettres, 1982. (tr)

Ryle, Gilbert. 1949. *The Concept of Mind*. London: Hutchinson.

Salus, Peter H., ed. 1969. *On Language: Plato to von Humboldt*. New York: Holt Rinehart and Winston.

Saunders, H. 1969. "The Evolution of the French Narrative Tenses." *Forum for Modern Language Studies* 5.141–61.

Saurer, Werner. 1984. *A Formal Semantics of Tense, Aspect and Aktionsarten*. Bloomington: Indiana University Linguistics Club.

Saussure, Ferdinand de. 1966. *Course in General Linguistics*. Ed. Charles Bally and Albert Sechehaye in collaboration with Albert Riedlinger. Trans., Wade Baskin. New York: McGraw-Hill. Repr. of 1959 ed., Philosophical Library.

Scaliger, Julius Caesar. 1540. *De causis linguae Latinae libri tredecim*. Pagination cited here is from 1609 edition (Paris: Commelin). (tr)

Scheffer, J. 1975. *The Progressive in English*. Amsterdam: North-Holland.

Schiffrin, Deborah. 1981. "Tense Variations in Narration." *Language* 57.45–62.

Schogt, Henry. 1968. *Le système verbal du français contemporain*. The Hague: Mouton.

Schopf, Alfred, ed. 1974. *Der Englische Aspekt*. Darmstadt: Wissenschaftliche Buchgesellschaft.

Schumann, Hans Wolfgang. 1974. *Buddhism: An Outline of Its Teachings and Schools*. Wheaton, Ill.: The Theosophical Publishing House (Quest Books).

Shin, Sung-Ock. 1988. "Tense Indexing and Binding." *Papers from the Sixth International Conference on Korean Linguistics*, ed. Eung-Jin Baek, 640–54. Seoul: Hanshin Publishing Company.

Shopen, Timothy, ed. 1985. *Language Typology and Syntactic Description*, vol. 3: *Grammatical Categories and the Lexicon*. Cambridge: Cambridge University Press.

Siegel, Muffy. 1976. "Capturing the Russian Adjective." Partee (1976), 293–309.

Silva-Corvalán, Carmen. 1983. "Tense and Aspect in Spanish Oral Narrative." *Language* 59.760–80.

Slobin, Dan I., and Ayhan A. Aksu. 1982. "Tense, Aspect and Modality in the Use of the Turkish Evidential." Hopper (1982), 185–200. Basis for Aksu and Slobin (1986).

Smith, Carlota. 1978. "The Syntax and Interpretation of Temporal Expressions in English." *Linguistics and Philosophy* 2.43–99.

———. 1981. "Semantic and Syntactic Constraints on Temporal Interpretation." Tedeschi and Zaenen (1981), 213–37.

———. 1983. "A Theory of Aspectual Choice." *Language* 59.479–501.

———. 1986. "A Speaker-Based Approach to Aspect." *Linguistics and Philosophy* 9.97–115.

Sobin, N. 1974. "Aspects of the Temporal Interpretation of English Sentences." Ph.D. diss., University of Texas at Austin.

Soga, Matsuo. 1983. *Tense and Aspect in Modern Colloquial Japanese*. Vancouver: University of British Columbia Press.

Spaulding, Robert K. 1967. *Syntax of the Spanish Verb*. Liverpool: Liverpool University Press. Repr. of earlier ed.: New York: Holt, 1952.

Speight, Kathleen. 1962. *Italian*. New ed. London: Teach Yourself Books.

Sperber, Dan, and Deirdre Wilson. 1986. *Relevance: Communication and Cognition*. Oxford: Blackwell.

Stalnaker, Robert C. 1972. *Pragmatics*. Davidson and Harman (1972), 380–98.

Steinthal, Heymann. 1890. *Geschichte der Sprachwissenschaft bei den Griechen und Römern mit besonderer Rücksicht auf die Logik*. 2nd ed. 2 vols. Repr. Hildesheim: Georg Olm, 1961. (tr)

Streitberg, Wilhelm. 1891. "Perfective und imperfective Actionsart im Germanischen." *Beitraege zur Geschichte der deutschen Sprache* 15.70–177. (tr)

———. 1920. *Gotisches Elementarbuch*. 5th ed., rev. Heidelberg: Carl Winters Universitätsbuchhandlung.

Sweet, Henry. 1898. *New English Grammar. Logical and Historical: Part II—Syntax*. Oxford: Clarendon Press. (Part I, 1891.)

Tedeschi, Philip J. 1981. "Some Evidence for a Branching-Futures Semantic Model."
     Tedeschi and Zaenen (1981), 239–69.
Tedeschi, Philip J., and Annie Zaehnen, eds. 1981. *Tense and Aspect*. Syntax and Seman-
     tics 14. New York: Academic Press.
Ter Meulen, Alice G. B. 1983. "The Representation of Time in Natural Language." Ter
     Meulen (1983a), 177–92.
————, ed. 1983a. *Studies in Modeltheoretic Semantics*. Dordrecht: Foris.
————. 1985. "Progressives without Possible Worlds." *Papers from the 21st Regional
     Meeting, Chicago Linguistic Society*, 408–23. Chicago: Chicago Linguistic Society.
Thurot, Charles. 1869. *Extraits de divers manuscrits latins pour servir à l'histoire des
     doctrines grammaticales au Moyen Age*. Paris. Repr. Frankfurt/Main: Minerva, 1964.
Tichý, Pavel. 1980. "The Logic of Temporal Discourse." *Linguistics and Philosophy* 3.343–
     69.
Townsend, Charles E. 1985. "Can Aspect Stand Prosperity?" Flier and Timberlake (1985),
     286–95.
Trager, George L., and Henry Lee Smith, Jr. 1951. *An Outline of English Structure*. Wash-
     ington: American Council of Learned Societies. Pagination cited here is from 5th
     printing, 1957.
Traugott, Elizabeth Closs. 1978. *On the Expression of Spatio-Temporal Relations in Lan-
     guage*. Greenberg et al. (1978), 369–400.
Travaglia, Luiz Carlos. 1981. *O Aspecto Verbal no Português. A Categoria e Sua Expres-
     são*. Uberlândia: Universidade Federal de Uberlândia. (tr)
Ultan, Russell. 1978. "The Nature of Future Tenses." Greenberg et al. (1978), 83–123.
Valin, Roch. 1975. "The Aspects of the French Verb." Hirtle (1975), 131–45.
Van Bentham, Johan. 1985. *A Manual of Intensional Logic*. Stanford: Center for the Study
     of Language and Information. 2nd ed., rev. 1988.
Van der Gaaf, W. 1930. "Some Notes on the History of the Progressive Form." *Neophil-
     ologus* 15. Reprinted in Schopf (1974), 356–70.
Van Emde Boas, P., and T. M. V. Janssen. 1979. "The Impact of Frege's Principle of
     Compositionality for the Semantics of Programming and Natural Languages." *Be-
     griffsschrift Jenaer Frege-Konferenz 1979*, 110–29. Jena: Universtät Jena.
Varro. 1938. *On the Latin Language*. 2 vols. Trans. and ed. Roland G. Kent. London:
     Heinemann, and Cambridge, Mass.: Harvard University Press (Loeb Classical Li-
     brary).
Vaughan, Thomas. 1709. *A Grammar of the Turkish Language*. London. Repr. Menston,
     England: Scolar Press, 1966.
Vendler, Zeno. 1957. "Verbs and Times." *Philosophical Review* 66.143–60. Revised in
     Vendler (1967), 97–121; reprinted in Schopf (1974), 213–34.
————. 1967. *Linguistics in Philosophy*. Cornell: Cornell University Press.
Verkuyl, H. J. 1972. *On the Compositional Nature of the Aspects*. Dordrecht: Reidel.
Vet, Co. 1980. *Temps, aspects, et adverbes de temps en français contemporain: essai de
     sémantique formelle*. Geneva: Librairie Droz.
————. 1981. "La notion de 'monde possible' et le système temporel et aspectuel du
     français." Martin and Nef (1981), 109ff.
————. 1983. "From Tense to Modality." Ter Meulen (1983a), 193–206.
Vet, Co, and Arie Molendijk. 1986. "The Discourse Functions of the Past Tenses in French."
     Lo Cascio and Vet (1986), 133–60.
Vetter, D. C. 1973. "Someone Solves This Problem Tomorrow." *Linguistic Inquiry* 4.104–
     8.
Vlach, Frank. 1981. "The Semantics of the Progressive." Tedeschi and Zaenen (1981),
     271–92.
Von Möllendorff, P. G. 1892. *A Manchu Grammar with Analysed Texts*. Shanghai: The
     American Presbyterian Mission Press.
Von Wright, Georg Henrik. 1963. *Norm and Action*. New York: Humanities Press.

————. 1968. *An Essay in Deontic Logic and the General Theory of Action.* Acta Philosophica Fennica 21. Amsterdam: North-Holland.

Vroman, William Vieira. 1976. "Predicate Raising and the Syntax-Morphology-Semantics Cycle: Latin and Portuguese." Ph.D. diss., University of Michigan.

Waldman, Nahum M. 1975. "The Hebrew Tradition." Aarsleff et al. (1975), 1285–1330.

Wall, Robert. 1972. *Introduction to Mathematical Linguistics.* Englewood Cliffs, N.J.: Prentice-Hall.

Wallace, Stephen. 1982. "Figure and Ground: The Interrelationships of Linguistic Categories." Hopper (1982), 201–23.

Waugh, Linda, R. 1975. "A Semantic Analysis of the French Tense System." *Orbis* 24.436–85.

Waugh, Linda R., and Monique Monville-Burston. 1986. "Aspect and Discourse Function: The French Simple Past in Newspaper Usage." *Language* 62.846–77.

Wekker, H. Charles. 1976. *The Expression of Future Time in Contemporary British English.* Amsterdam: North-Holland.

Welsh, Cynthia. 1986. "Is the Compositionality Principle a Semantic Universal?" *Proceedings of the Twelfth Annual Meeting of the Berkeley Linguistics Society,* 551–63.

White, James. 1761. *The English Verb.* Repr. Menston, England: Scolar, 1969.

Whitney, A. H. 1956. *Finnish.* London: English Universities Press (Teach Yourself Books).

Whorf, Benjamin Lee. 1945. "Grammatical Categories." *Language* 21.1–11. Reprinted in Whorf (1956), 87–101.

————. 1950. "An American Indian Model of the Universe." *International Journal of American Linguistics* 16.67–72. Reprinted in Whorf (1956), 57–64; Gale (1968), 377–85.

————. 1956. *Language Thought and Reality: Selected Writings of Benjamin Lee Whorf.* Ed. John B. Carroll. Cambridge: Mass.: MIT Press.

Williams, Ronald J. 1976. *Hebrew Syntax: An Outline.* Toronto: University of Toronto Press. 2nd ed.

Wilson, P. G. 1950. *German Grammar.* Sevenoaks, Kent: Houghton and Stoddard (Teach Yourself Books).

Winograd, Terry. 1974. "When Will Computers Understand People?" *Psychology Today* 7 (May).

Woisetschlaeger, Erich F. 1976. *A Semantic Theory of the English Auxiliary System.* Bloomington: Indiana University Linguistics Club.

Wolfson, Nessa. 1979. "Conversational Historical Present Alternation." *Language* 55.168–82.

Woodcock, E. C. 1959. *A New Latin Syntax.* London: Methuen.

Wunderlich, Dieter. 1970. *Tempus und Zeitreferenz im Deutschen.* Munich: Max Hueber Verlag.

Zandvoort, R. 1962. "Is 'Aspect' an English Verbal Category?" *Studies in English* (Gothenburg) 14. Reprinted in R. W. Zandvoort, *Collected Papers,* vol. 2, 109–25. Groningen: Wolters-Noordhoff, 1970.

INDEX

The *Aktionsarten* with separate entries are: complexive, continuative, durative, frequentative, habitual, iterative, momentaneous, punctual.

The individual Aristotelian aspect entries are: accomplishment, achievement, activity, performance, series, state.

The individual aspect entries are: aorist, bitranscendent, completive, immanent, imperfect, imperfective, perfect, perfective, progressive tenses and aspect, prospective, retrospective, Semitic imperfective, Semitic perfective, transcendent.

The individual mood entries are: imperative, indicative, infinitive, non-finite moods, optative, participle, perfect infinitive, perfect participle, subjunctive.

The general tense entries are: anterior tenses, composite tenses, definite tenses, futurate tenses, historical tenses, indefinite tenses, metric tense, past tenses, perfect tenses, posterior tenses, primary tenses, progressive tenses and aspect, prospective tenses, relative tense, retrospective tenses, secondary tenses, Semitic tenses, supercomplex tenses, tense, tenses.

The individual tense entries are: aorist (Greek), conditional, conditional perfect, future, future perfect, future pluperfect, imperfect, imperfect perfect, non-past, *passé antérieur, passé composé*, past, past progressive, perfect (Latin), perfect future, pluperfect, present, present perfect, present progressive, present-future, preterite.

A (Papiamentu), 444
A-series, 243
Aartun, K., 435–38, 443
Absolute tense in Semitic, 435–36
Absolutum. See *Futurum exactum*
"Accidents," 15–16, 68, 158
Accomplishment. *See also* Performance
  achievement phase of. *See* Culmination
  achievement versus, 177–78, 180, 194–97
  activity phase of, 187, 194, 291
  activity versus, 175–76
  advances narration, 400
  counter-subinterval property, 194
  culmination, 325
  defined, 143–44, 172–73
  durative, 194, 196
  dynamic, 286
  gappy, 185
  gradual achievements, 194

and the imperfective paradox, 290
in progressive, 282
series, 182
telic, 193–97
temporal ill-foundedness, 335
tests for, 175–78
Achievement. *See also* Performance
  accomplishment versus, 177–78, 194–97
  advances narration, 400
  conative, 174–75, 185
  culmination. *See* Culmination
  defined, 143–44, 172–73
  gaps in, 185
  gradual, 194
  momentaneous or punctual, 181, 194, 196–97, 411
  non-phasic, 185, 194–97
  phase. *See* Culmination
  in progressive, 194, 282
  punctuality constraint, 335
  quasi-accomplishments, 174
  "real" present tense, 188
  series, 182
Actio. See Action; Aspect
Action. *See also* Activity; *Aktionsarten*; Aspect
  complete. *See* Perfect aspect; Perfective aspect
  determinate, 193, 450–51
  ékhein (state), 144, 172
  enérgeia (activity, state), 143–44, 172
  energeîn (activity), 144, 172
  in process, 284–86
  incomplete. *See* Imperfect aspect; Imperfective aspect
  indeterminate, 193, 450–51
  kinds of. *See Aktionsarten*
  kínēsis (performance), 143–44, 172
  poíēsis (performance), 144, 172
  prâksis (activity), 144, 172
  word, 3
Activity
  accomplishment, versus, 175–76
  atelic, 189, 193
  defined, 143–44, 171–73, 181
  does not advance narration, 400
  and events, 188–94
  exceptional narrative advance, 409
  gappy, 185–86
  and the imperfective paradox, 290
  indefinite change of state, 483 *n.* 46
  performance versus, 189
  phase of accomplishment, 187, 194, 291
  in progressive, 282
  quasi-accomplishments, 176
  series, 182